D0872610

My Impossible Life

Liza Cheuk May Chan

陳綽薇

On the front cover: The author at about age 7 months (photograph by author's Dad); Victoria Harbour and skyline of Central, Hong Kong, on January 1, 2007 (photograph by the author and author's youngest sister, Vivian).

On the back cover: Framed photographs of author and her three younger sisters given by the author to Mom on Mother's Day, 2002 (photograph by Vivian); Victoria Harbour and skyline of Central, Hong Kong, on January 1, 2007 (photograph by the author and Vivian).

ISBN: 978-1-54390-982-1 (print)
ISBN: 978-1-54390-983-8 (ebook)

Dedication

This Book is Dedicated to
My Mom and Dad
Whom I have Missed more Profoundly than
I Will Ever Dare Acknowledge.

Dedication

This Book is Dedicated to
My Mom and Dad
Whom I have Missed more Profoundly than
I Will Ever Dare Acknowledge.

CONTENTS

Acknowledgements

Traversing life's bumpy, long and winding road, we cross paths with many, karmic fellow travelers one and all. Each enriched our life and enlivened our life story, especially those we seemed to have known through the millennia within the first nanoseconds of the encounter. My list of heroes, heroines, teachers, cheerleaders and comrades may be more extensive than many, but even this list is not exhaustive. In all likelihood, I might have inadvertently overlooked a saint or two who had illuminated my way along the way, and to those "unnamed saints," I offer my sincere apologies. By the same token, it seems hardly fair that someone who has been a lodestar all of my life gets just a mention below, much as someone who happened to intersect my path in a chance meeting. Likewise, I have made no distinction between one who had been a steadfast supporter over the decades from another who had graced my life but for a brief shining moment. It is not for me to judge; I am here only to express my deepest gratitude:

Carol-Ann Allen; Rita Au-Yeung Tung Yee; Mathew J. Baltz, P.T.; Dr. K. E. Barker; bee berman and Nigel Fogg; Maureen H. Burke, Esq.; Dr. Sara E. Byer, Ph.D.; Annie Chan Mei Ying; Katherine Ma Chau; Anita Liu Chow; Susan Fung Chow; Judy L. Clay-Phifer, R.N.; Jill Danbert; (the late) Dr. Zira DeFries, M.D.; Laura DiGregorio; Connie Eiland; (the late) Isabella Chong

Gosiengfiao; (the late) LaVerne and Mike Gruskiewich; Henry M. Grix, Esq. and Howard Israel; Dr. Nirmala Nancy Hanke, M.D.; Kathryn Hannan, LMT, NCTMB; May Chien Ho; Daniel J. Hoekenga, Esq.; Annemargret Hofstetter; Diana Cheung Hom; Tara Hummingbird; Victor and Vicki Iagnemma; Hazel C. Karbel, LMSW; Cherry Fung Kwan; Dr. Kim Man Lai and Janet Lu; Sheldon G. Larky, Esq.; Lau Ko Chung ("Susie Wong," "Ah So"); Elise S. Levasseur, Esq.; Dr. Sabine Lucas, Ph.D.; Dr. Lui Chiu Yu and Dr. Cheung Wai Man; Jennifer ("Ah Fook") Luk; Ann H. Mark and Linda J. McArtney; Rosalind Stephenson Melis; Dr. Nancy K. Merbitz, Ph.D.; Grace Ho Ng; (the late) Poon Chor Ying; Betty Jo Price; Amara Surakomol (Amy) Prior, LMT; Dr. Jacqueline Pullinger; Eric C. Pylkas and Remedios Tillman; Edna Reese, C.N.A.; The Hon. Rosalyn H. Richter and Janet Weinberg; Mary L. Ricks and (the late) Cathy Tonn; Dr. Leslie L. Rocher, M.D.; Sylvia Wong Seid; Patricia Shaw; James W. Shimoura, Esq.; Raina Tsung So; Dianne L. Sortzi; Larry J. Stringer, Esq.; Flora Sun and Bob Weiler; Marc M. Susselman, Esq.; Vivian Fung Tewksbury; Dr. Tong Han Cheung; Elaine Tsui Yee Lin; Selina Wang Sou Chien; Julia Wong Yee Lin; Pearl Wong Po Chu and "Ellen;" Sandra Lau Wong; Fatima Wu; Rebecca Chin Yeung; Winnie Yu Tsang; Mona Chin Wells; Helen Y. Zia and Lia Shigemura; and (the late) Prof. Hannah J. Zawadzka.

Above all, my most heartfelt gratitude is reserved forever for my dear, dear family: my late Dad, But Yue Chan (陳不愚), my late Mom, Eva Ho Chan (何懿華), my sisters Lina Cheuk Ling Chan (陳綽玲), the late Lilian Cheuk Lin Chan (陳綽蓮), and Vivian Cheuk Wai Chan (陳綽瑋), and my niece (Lina's daughter)

Juliana Ka Yan Li (李嘉姻), each of whom in his or her unique way made my life possible, so that I may pursue the impossible.

Preface

The unexamined life is not worth living. - Socrates

Reflecting on my life, let alone *examining* it, was not what I had ever set out to do. Socrates' entreaty notwithstanding, examining my life was not my *modus operandi;* I was too busy "doing." All of us are too busy "doing" one thing or another. Our "to do" list seems never-ending.

Yet, I did spend more than twenty years of my adult life, more or less continuously, in psychotherapy. I was not consciously trying to examine my life. I was clueless about a lot of things in my life, and thought those therapists, counselors, psychologists and psychiatrists would have the answers for me. There were "issues" to be analyzed and resolved, as they would frame the situation at hand, and those unresolved issues would invariably lead to further and other issues. Many thousands of dollars and years later, I remained as lost as ever, but at least I kept "working on it."

Then, one day the proverbial life-altering event happened. I was left with no option but to hop off the treadmill, drop out of the rat race, halt my automaton existence, and take stock *mindfully*. Introspection did not come easily or naturally to me, nor did any discernible answers manifest readily as if on cue. It took more than ten years for me to begin to connect the dots. This book is the result of those years of what at first seemed to be involuntary contemplation, followed by unexpected revelations, and ultimately, inspiration. Perhaps in another ten years, or even ten months, my understanding and interpretation might be quite different, but for now, this is the snapshot—if ever there is an oxymoron—of my life.

As Mark Twain wisely observed: "Truth is stranger than fiction, but it is because fiction is obliged to stick to possibilities; Truth isn't." Indeed, in my case, life has truly been full of "impossibilities."

Prologue

Friday, November 18, 2005. I was listening to WUOM, my local National Public Radio station. Terry Gross was interviewing author Joan Didion on "Fresh Air."

Earlier that week, Didion's memoir, *The Year of Magical Thinking*, won the National Book Award for nonfiction. "Life changes fast," Didion deadpanned. "Life changes in the instant. You sit down to dinner and life as you know it ends." On December 30, 2003, Didion and her late husband, John Gregory Dunne, sat down to dinner. They never did finish that fateful dinner because his life, as they knew it, ended in an instant.

In the evening of December 31, 2003, fifteen days into my half-century mark, I was allowed more than an instant—a relatively generous fifteen or so minutes, in fact—to gather whatever I could to get out of my home of seventeen years, to walk away from my 26-year life partnership. Little did I realize then that life, as I had lived it for fifty years, would soon end, and that I would be embarking on my journey of the proverbial rebirth.

It was about 9 p.m. on that frigid New Year's Eve. There I was, driving aimlessly on the streets of suburban Detroit, with not much more than my briefcase, a pillow and a blanket, and a trunkful of what passed for my prized possessions: my cameras. Imee Ooi's *Chant of Metta* was swirling in my BMW's CD player. It was not quite a month earlier when that alluring and haunting music first wafted in the air and into my ears, sparked a revolution in my subconscious, and life, as I knew it, changed in an instant.

By the time I found a hotel for the night, none of the restaurants seemed to be open on this oddly desolate night. My mind could not even focus on whether I was really in need of food. There was a pantry in the hotel lobby; I picked up a chocolate chip cookie. "No charge—on the house," the clerk at the front desk smiled as he waved me by. This "act of random kindness," dispensed with impeccable timing, transformed the unpretentious cookie into a scrumptious New Year's Eve feast for me.

2003 had started on a high note. My parents had just celebrated their 50th wedding anniversary and my father's 80th birthday in December of 2002. My youngest sister, Vivian and her husband, Ted, and my other younger sister, Lina, flew in from Hong Kong, and Lina's daughter, Juliana, traveled from Toronto, to join in the festivities which included lavish Chinese banquets in two cities (Windsor and Toronto), formal family portraits by a professional photographer, and of course, gifts galore and many memorable home-cooked meals by Mom, our very own chef nonpareil. Then everyone dispersed, and I was back to my 12-hour workdays as an immigration attorney in a large corporate law firm, and to facing the grim reality that Mom was losing her 3-year battle with colon cancer.

Mom passed away at 3:59 p.m. on Sunday, July 27, 2003. Even though I had more than three years to prepare for that eventuality, I was hardly ready for the life-transforming metamorphosis triggered by her departure. My relationship with Mom had been complex, even contentious, oftentimes agonizing. In life, Mom bestowed her approval frightfully sparingly. Now, years after her passing, I have finally learned that another's approval is irrelevant, even superfluous, in my soul's search for life's truths and inner peace.

Six years hence, my life bears little resemblance to the supercharged, high-flying, fast-tracking, über-pressure, left-brain-dominant life as an attorney in a so-called silk stocking law firm. Memories of life, love and dreams are exhorting me to commit remembrances to print. No more self-sabotage; I goaded myself to crystallize disparate thoughts, distill the vast reservoir of recollections, and weave my tapestry to fill however many blank pages to come.

Liza Cheuk May Chan (陳綽薇)
Friday, August 28, 2009
Ann Arbor, Michigan

I.

Vigil

The frantic telephone call from Dad came mid-morning on Thursday, July 17, 2003; I was, but of course, at the office. He sounded distraught, mumbling incoherently about Mom's being in the bathroom and his not being able to help her back to the bedroom. "Call Jacques, the hospice nurse," I urged, and assured him that I would be coming over right away. They lived in Windsor, Ontario, Canada, across the river from Detroit, and about an hour's drive from my office in Bloomfield Hills, a northern suburb of Detroit.

Instead of dropping everything and dashing out to my car, I found myself dazed, mindlessly mulling over some files. It was as if by delaying my departure my mother's life would be prolonged, and the inevitable would be postponed or even reversed. A special Practice Group luncheon was scheduled to begin at 11:30 a.m. I even took time to go downstairs to the Multi-Purpose Room to excuse myself to the Group Leader from the luncheon before heading out to the parking lot. Survival by denial came so instinctively for me.

I do not recall the hour-long drive to Windsor or clearing customs and immigration at the border, but when I arrived at my parents' house, reality didn't sink in but struck hard. An ambulance, with the back loading doors open and engine running, was parked in the driveway. I hurried into the house, just in time to find two medics in the process of carrying Mom, strapped on a gurney, from the upstairs bedroom down through the hallway and out the front door. The medics paused briefly in the hallway; the woman medic asked if I had seen Mom recently. "Of course," I replied, "just this past weekend, as a matter of fact." She shook her head, muttering under her breath that Mom was in rather dire shape, words that I did not want to hear and wished I did not hear.

Dad, clearly quite in shock, rode with me as I followed the ambulance to the Windsor Regional Hospital where Mom's oncologist, Dr. Sam Yoshida, was standing by. I was allowed to stand watch over Mom in one of the corridors in the Emergency Room. I gently put my hands on her belly, which by then was protruding with the liver tumor that seemed to have grown to gigantic proportions overnight. I whispered comforting words to her. She seemed to be semi-conscious, and appeared to sense my presence or heard my voice, and even managed a smile. I could hardly accept the fact that Mom, the matriarch, the pillar of our family, the center of gravity for our universe, seemed to have run out of time for "living with" cancer.

No sooner had Mom been transferred to the Oncology Clinic floor when Dr. Yoshida "flew" down the hallway to her examination room. Barely a couple of minutes later, he emerged from the room, and in as calm a voice as he could manage, he informed us that Mom had indeed taken a turn for the worse, much worse, since he last saw her a couple of weeks prior. He was admitting her to the special hospice room in the hospital, and advised that close family members should gather as soon as possible. I swallowed hard and fought back tears; it was clearly not the time to be maudlin. Mom had told us that she wanted to stay at home as long as possible, but she did not want to die at home. Jacques had told me about the special hospice room at the hospital. So, there we were—the end game. Mom had admonished in the past: "Don't ever say 'Game Over' unless you really mean it." How I really did not want it to be "Game Over" there and then.

I had had many months to prepare for this contingency, yet somehow—denial at work again?—I did not have with me Lina's telephone number in Hong Kong. By the time Dad came up with the number, I could not get the international call through with my calling card (this was before the smart phones, Skype, FaceTime, etc.). Reluctantly, I had to rely on my capable secretary, Dianne, to relay the message; I felt awful that Lina had to get the sad news from a stranger at 3 o'clock in the middle of the night. Lina's return call came almost instantaneously; she had already talked with our youngest sister, Vivian, and they were booking the next flight to Detroit.

Growing up in Hong Kong, Lina and I were not particularly close as sisters, even though we were fewer than two years apart in age. Our temperament, interests, personality diverged diametrically. Mom assigned her to attend a Catholic school, and me to an Anglican school. We were Brownies and joined the Girl Guides but in different Companies. Hence, none could have anticipated the convergence of our paths as we trudged through our midlife years.

Lina interrupted her university studies in Regina, Saskatchewan, got married and gave birth to her daughter, Juliana, when she was not quite 22 years of age. A decade later, she emigrated to Windsor with Juliana, resumed her studies, earning her Bachelor's and MBA degrees in one swell swoop. When our parents, then in their 60's and who had resided in Hong Kong all their lives, expressed an urgent interest in emigrating to Canada—bearing in mind that the sovereignty of Hong Kong was to revert to China in 1997, barely 8 years after the Tiananmen Square massacre—Lina promptly sponsored their exodus from the British Crown Colony. By the time our parents arrived in Windsor in early 1993 as Canadian Landed Immigrants, well in advance of Hong Kong's handover to China, it was Lina's turn to exit the scene. With her usual element of surprise and dispatch, she repatriated to Hong Kong, leaving Juliana in our parents' care. Rising through the ranks in the emerging e-commerce sector, she was climbing the proverbial corporate ladder, making a very decent living and enjoying the good life in Hong Kong. Just as surprising, though, for this consummate "Material Girl," she started talking about crystal healing soon after she returned to Hong Kong. Since 2001, she had even returned several times to attend weekend workshops in Southfield, a Detroit suburb, to learn Reiki, which at that time was a total alien concept to me. By early 2003, she had apparently joined a Shingon (Japanese Esoteric) Buddhist temple in Hong Kong. In relative short order in the ensuing years, she gained certification as a Karuna Reiki Master. Even more astonishing, in January of 2007, after several years of intense studies and practice in the Shingon Buddhist tradition, she attained the rank of Acharya (Master Teacher) in an elaborate and solemn ceremony on Mount Koya, Japan. With the blessings of her Buddhist Master Edward Li Kui Ming, since early 2008, Lina has been practicing full-time as an "Enlightenment Reiki" healer in Hong Kong. Lina the "Material Girl" had completed her transformation to Lina the "Monk." Life is indeed full of surprises if not outright mysterious.

Lilian was just shy of two years younger than Lina. She was born with Down syndrome with fairly severe mental retardation.

She could not speak either—her speech came out as unintelligible sound bites, yet over the years, we had somehow learned to understand and communicate with each other. As I was not quite four years old when she was born, early memories of Lilian were spotty and incoherent. Disability wasn't a word I understood well then, and her life did not make sense to the very young me; yet, I had always felt a special kinship with her and it was reciprocal. In the 1950's, despite its allure as the Pearl of the Orient, treatment options, rehabilitation opportunities, social support and services for Down syndrome children in Hong Kong were next to nonexistent; families were left to their own devices. My parents were admirably ingenuous in providing for Lilian the best they knew how and within the constraints of their resources. Unfortunately, that meant Lilian was removed from our family at a very young age, a separation that left an indelible shadow on each of us. At the time the call was made for the family to gather around Mom, Lilian was convalescing from her bout with breast cancer. It was not, in any case, feasible for Lilian to travel to Canada, and she would just have to bid Mom farewell from a distance.

Vivian, our baby sister, joined our growing family a little over two years on the heels of Lilian's debut. I remember vividly the morning she was born. We had a live-in amah then. Those were the days when domestic help was still easy to come by and relatively affordable. She was an elderly lady, and quite new on the job. I woke up that morning to discover, to my horror, the unusual disappearance of Mom and Dad. Amah fixed breakfast for Lina and me: it was salted fish mixed with rice, with a *coup de grace* dab of butter. No, that was not our usual breakfast fare. In fact, I could not stomach amah's "self-styled cuisine" at all; that was also why I remember that morning so well. Mercifully, Dad came to my rescue shortly thereafter; he had come home to fetch Lina and me. He asked us with discernible excitement and elation, "Do you want to go see a little red apple?!" It was a rhetorical question, to which Lina and I enthusiastically responded in the affirmative all the same, if only to get away from the salted fish breakfast.

I knew as soon as we arrived at our destination that this "little red apple" was someone special. It was a private hospital quite far away from our little flat in Kennedy Town, a rather humble neighborhood on the west side of the Hong Kong Island. The hospital room was quiet, spacious, elegant, white, bright and airy, a deluxe-class welcome for this "little red apple." For me, it was love at first sight for my new baby sister. I did not know what prompted me to walk up to Vivian and pinch her nose, but the next thing I knew was my Grandmother's flying across the room to take my hand off Vivian's nose. My expression of love for my baby sister was apparently mistaken for attempt to suffocate her. From that serene and tender setting, one can readily see how Vivian and Mom had bonded from Vivian's very first breath. Little did I know then that Vivian and I would share a life connection, literally, decades later.

Fast forward to the early morning of July 18, 2003, which also happened to be the last day of Vivian's 8-year employment as an internal audit manager with a joint venture subsidiary of British Petroleum in Shekou, China. Vivian had planned on taking a few weeks to pack and move her belongings into storage in Hong Kong before returning to Windsor in early August to, as she put it, spend the rest of her life taking care of Mom. Obviously, Mom had other plans and a vastly different timetable.

By late afternoon, July 17th, Mom had been moved to a very spacious, private room in the hospice section of the hospital. She was drifting in and out of consciousness. Concerned that she had not eaten since breakfast, if she had breakfast, I asked the nurse on duty to ensure that dinner be served promptly. She stared at me as if I were insane, as she thrust a booklet into my hand. The title of the booklet, I believe, was "When a Loved One is Dying." I reiterated my request which by then had escalated to the order of a demand: "Mom needs to eat; please bring her dinner tray now!" She obliged, and a tray appeared moments later. I would peruse the booklet later in the wee hours of the night. It explained the dying process, how someone in the active process of dying would not need food nor be able to eat. That was another reality check that unceremoniously pierced my shield of denial; one way or another, it seemed, I was compelled to grapple with my Mom's imminent demise.

I had by then called Bev, my life partner of almost 26 years, to bring me a change of clothing. I needed to get out of my "lawyer uniform;" casual clothes and shoes would give me a small measure of relief, I was hoping. By the time Bev arrived at the hospital in the early evening, Mom was awake and quite conscious. She was excited to see Bev, stretching her frail hand to meet Bev's. Bev did not visit for long; that turned out to be the last time they would see each other. Since Mom seemed to have stabilized somewhat, we decided to take a break and have dinner at a nearby Chinese restaurant. At dinner, Bev whispered to me that I had better spend the night with Mom as she did not think Mom would make it through the night. I was startled by her suggestion; denial with a capital "D" was again blinding me. That was the exasperating dichotomy about Bev: she could be downright mean and cruel as far as my family was concerned, but then again, she could also be the heroine of the moment, as she was at that juncture and on a handful of other occasions. Some years later, I would gain insight into that seeming contradiction. In the meantime, after dinner, I drove Dad home; he was visibly exhausted from the day's ordeal. There, I picked up Mom's pillow and told Dad that I would take it to Mom at the hospital on my way home. Without telling Dad so as not to alarm him, I decided to spend the night at the hospital with Mom.

There was a recliner in Mom's room, next to her bed, and I spent the night there, standing watch, standing guard, sitting, thinking, weeping, and dozing on and off. I finished reading the "When A Loved One is Dying" booklet. Most miserable reading, I thought to myself. There was a tiny library on the floor, next to the kitchenette where I would brew one cup of tea after another. There I found more books on death and dying. I went through the motion of flipping through several, as if that would better prepare me for what was to come or to help me cope with what was happening. There was a compact stereo in the room. I tuned to a station playing classical music, and as each note floated quietly in the stillness of the room, I was recalling that fateful day in late April, 2000 when this entire unpleasant affair first unfolded. . . .

It was also on a Thursday, in late April of 2000, when I received a call from Dad in the evening; I was still at the office. He calmly informed me that he took Mom to see Dr. Wallace Liang, the family doctor, earlier that day, and the doctor had promptly admitted her to the hospital, he said, as a "precautionary measure" as she appeared dehydrated.

I was shocked, but I should not have been. I had visited my parents a couple of weeks prior. While Mom did complain that she was not feeling well, she was not specific about what was ailing her, and she did not appear to be in particular distress. So, I thought she was simply vying for my attention, or that it was a ploy so that Dad and I would give up our planned outing for the day to stay home and keep her company. Hence, I told her that since she was not feeling well, she should stay home and rest, while Dad and I would go and attend a camera show. She stayed home that day, and Dad and I attended the show. At the time, I congratulated myself for being able to—after decades of psychotherapy—finally assert my independence vis-à-vis Mom. Sadly, that quixotic decision of mine would turn out to haunt me and saddle me with overwhelming guilt; she was indeed very unwell.

Dad's tone of voice on the phone was not urgent; he indicated that Mom was resting comfortably at the hospital, and she was scheduled for some diagnostic tests in the coming days. With that reassurance, I was not unduly concerned, and planned to visit Mom at the hospital that Saturday. Perhaps there was another pinch of denial at work with my reasoning that went something as follows: if I did not (have to) rush over and visit her in the hospital, then Mom must not be very ill.

Mom had always been healthy and stout; to me, she embodied invincibility and infallibility. She was the original feminist by necessity. She was tireless and industrious, raising four children while working full-time as a secretary to the managing director of a shipping company in Hong Kong. She was a meticulous homemaker, tending to every detail, whether it be cooking, cleaning, provisioning for our clothes and school supplies, or planning a family outing. She was also a stern disciplinarian, bringing us up according to the strictest moral and ethical code. Mom expected us to attain academic excellence as well as to excel in all approved extracurricular activities that filled our after-school hours and weekends. I had always perceived my mission in life as one of relentlessly pursuing accomplishments, shooting for the stars, and never letting Mom down.

I walked into Windsor Regional Hospital that April Saturday morning, and would walk out hours later a changed person. If only I could stop the clock, freeze action, I would then not have to acknowledge the grim reality confronting me.

Dad was already at the hospital in Mom's semi-private room when I arrived mid-morning. They were both absolutely elated to see me, especially Mom—she practically leapt out of the hospital bed. She smiled broadly, almost jubilantly. I remembered that smile distinctly; it signified a sense of relief and joy, and . . . her pride and trust in me. In that same instant, my heart dropped to the floor while it leapt out of my throat all at once—Mom's countenance had changed completely from just two weeks ago. In that split second, I knew instinctively that Mom was gravely ill. "But how could it be!?" I screamed inside myself. Why didn't her family doctor detect this insidious disease sooner, much sooner? After all, she had regular checkups. I would come to realize, in the ensuing weeks and months, that the Ontario nationalized health care system, known as "OHIP," could only be regarded with utmost disdain.

Mustering every resolve in me to steady my voice and temper my gaze so as not to betray my true emotions, Mom and Dad and I engaged in the usual banter, as if it was just any other visit on a sunny April Saturday. As soon as I could leave the room for a brief break, I went to the visitor's lounge and broke down. I reached for my cell phone and called Bev. My speech was too agitated and I was too upset to make any sense, but I simply had to share with someone the fact that I was in a state of total shock. I did not believe Bev said anything reassuring or calming, or perhaps I was beyond consoling. Or perhaps, more to the point, I was conditioned not to expect any understanding or support from Bev, especially when the crisis in question concerned a member of my family, particularly my Mom.

I spent most of that day with Mom in her hospital room; she was in good spirits and did not appear to be in acute distress or pain. My drive home that evening was surreal, and yet harsh reality was simply too oppressive and left no room for denial in that instance. Whatever was ailing Mom, the knot in my stomach told me that it was very deadly, and I genuinely feared that I might lose Mom soon. The proverbial infantile fear of losing one's parent was overpowered only by my overwhelming sense of guilt stemming from not having tended to her complaint of discomfort two Saturdays earlier. Granted, two weeks would not have made any difference, given the gravity of her malady which had to have been incubating for months if not years. Logic, however, was decidedly irrelevant at those moments of profound remorse and grief.

Throughout the drive home, I sobbed to the rhythmic wails of Carlos Santana's guitar in his then brand new bestselling album, "Supernatural;" I needed music with enough decibels to drown out my sorrow. Little did I know then that "supernatural" would be a recurring theme in the months and years to come.

As it was Easter weekend, there was only a skeletal staff on the hospital floor, and no diagnostic test could be performed. Dad and I fretted and Mom languished in the hospital for another two weeks before we finally had a diagnosis, one with the dreaded "C" word: colorectal cancer, Stage III-IV. Mom took the news with dignity and composure, while Dad looked glum and forlorn. I took the news in—what else?—total denial, convinced that surgery and the wonders of modern medical science would restore Mom to perfect health in short order.

Surgery was set for May 9, 2000. Vivian had flown in from Hong Kong, and Lina would follow the next day. I had the first glimpse of the severity of Mom's condition only in the morning of the surgery when the lead surgeon calmly informed us that, while he would try his best to remove the tumor, he could not promise that the tumor was excisable. "How could her tumor be inoperable?! That is simply unacceptable," I mumbled to myself and left it at that, as Mom was being wheeled into the operating room with us doing our best as her cheerleading team.

Dad, Vivian, Bev and I left the hospital to while away a few hours. We distracted ourselves with having lunch and accompanying Vivian to her appointment with the optician. It was a beautiful, warm, sunny Spring day, but it was a surreal day all the same. We returned to the hospital mid-afternoon, and were told that Mom was still in surgery. It would be almost 6 p.m. before we were paged to meet the surgeon. He looked exhausted, but smiled as he greeted us. Without going into the technical details of the operation, the surgeon happily reported that he indeed was able to remove the tumor. Because of the extent of the surgery, Mom was fitted with a colostomy which, according to the surgeon, was reversible when Mom recovered sufficiently. All of us (with the exception of Bev) literally jumped for joy at the excellent news. I naively interpreted—or I deliberately chose to interpret—the surgeon's comments as indicating complete surgical success in eradicating the cancer, and that my nightmare of losing Mom was over.

By the time Lina arrived on May 10th from Hong Kong via Toronto, where Juliana was attending college and joined her in the bus ride to Windsor, Mom was resting quite comfortably in a post-surgical room on the hospital floor, having been released from intensive care earlier that morning. The mood was almost festive as we rejoiced over Mom's successful surgery. She was drifting in and out of consciousness, but we could tell that she and was enjoying our company and listening in on our conversations. At one point, Lina, who had just started to learn Reiki healing, put her hands above Mom's surgical site in the abdomen, then glided them in the air past Mom's feet, and finally shook them as if she was casting something off onto the floor. Vivian and I thought that was rather strange but also looked rather fun, and so, we both followed Lina with the same hand motions. Mom woke momentarily, and playfully chided us, "What are you doing? Stop doing that; you are making my belly feel cold." Lina smiled, and mumbled contentedly that Reiki had worked to combat the inflammation in Mom's surgical wound. Whatever Reiki was, I thought to myself, it apparently had an effect on Mom. Being a total stranger to alternative or energy healing then, I made a mental note to one day investigate further what I considered the strange Reiki phenomenon. Little did I know that in just a few more years, Reiki healing would become my almost constant companion.

Alas, Mom's recovery did not progress as uneventfully as in those first couple of days, dashing my hopes that she would be discharged home and that our lives would return to normalcy in just a few days, as if nothing untoward had happened. She started developing an irregular heartbeat and suffering other troublesome symptoms, and had to return to intensive care by week's end, and that triggered a downward spiral which looked very bleak at various points. By then, I was running out of patience with the utter inattentiveness, and downright incompetence and ineptness, of the nursing staff and the attending physicians. As we realized later, it was probably the overdosing of pain medication (morphine) which almost completely derailed Mom's recovery. She ended up being hospitalized for another two months before she could be discharged home. By then, she had lost much weight, and much life force had been drained from her, and she still had chemotherapy and radiation therapy to contend with in the months ahead. Mom would probably have been spared a great deal of her pain and suffering, if only I knew then what I know now. More than a decade later, from personal experience, I have become an "expert" on calling out the horrors that Western medicinal practices often inflict on its hapless patients.

I took tremendous comfort and pride in Mom's remarkable spirits as she endured more than six months of chemotherapy and radiation through the fall and winter of 2000. Her appetite slowly returned, and she was beginning to look like her old hale and healthy self by spring of 2001. She could not accept the colostomy, though; we were all hoping that at the one-year mark, we could convince the surgeon to remove it so that she could really feel "normal" again. I was counting my blessings that Dad could drive, taking Mom to her numerous therapy sessions and doctor's appointments. I taught Dad how to drive at the ripe old age of 72 years; he had never driven before then. It was obviously out of urgent necessity: Vivian abruptly decided to return to Hong Kong in May of 1995, and my parents had thus lost their "chauffeur." I could not be the dutiful chauffeur that Vivian was, and hence, had to press Dad into service. It turned out to be an excellent move, as Dad had become a reliable driver by 2000; he could drive himself daily to be with Mom during the three long months that Mom was in the hospital, and he drove Mom to her numerous medical appointments after her discharge.

As Mom continued to recuperate from her extensive surgery and extended hospitalization, and after she underwent the lengthy chemotherapy and radiation therapy regime, I saw a remarkable—nay, breathtaking—transformation in her. She had been, up until her bout with cancer, a strict disciplinarian, a taskmaster, an enforcer keeping tabs on everyone and everything. I supposed it was necessary for her to be so to keep her four children properly fed, clothed, and educated, and keep Dad performing as a fellow overachieving parent, even as all the while she was working full-time as a secretary to the managing director of a shipping company. Even after we grew up and went abroad to seek our "fame and fortune," Mom never relaxed her rigorous vigilance and exacting standards. She kept the home in immaculate condition, in spite of Dad's being a collector (read: hoarder) who regularly amassed assorted "collections," which in turn required Mom to find ingenious ways to make room to display and store his endless trophy finds. My sisters and I inherited the shopper-hunter-collector gene from Dad, and hence, we were all hoarders to varying degrees at various stages of our lives. Fortunately, we had also inherited the super-organizational gene from Mom, also to varying degrees. Mom continued to keep close tabs on us kids as we leapt out of the nest one by one, and sailed forth into life's great unknown. In other words, she ran a very tight ship. Mom seldom displayed affection or emotions. Not so, after her Round One with cancer. To my gleeful delight, she laughed out loud often; she even smiled for the camera whereas previously she detested being photographed. Thankfully, we thus now have many gorgeous, radiant photographs of Mom to remember her by. Instead of being stern and withholding, she became generous with praise and showed kindness and compassion at every turn. Instead of being critical and judgmental, she had become accepting and understanding. Her "feud" with Bev, though tamped down somewhat over the years, had simply vanished, wiping out much stress and grief out of my life, as one of the two bitter foes had stood down. It would be some years before I would fully appreciate how a life threatening disease could be so profoundly transforming and life affirming. Meanwhile, I simply basked in the warm and comforting glow of Mom's amazing metamorphosis.

Mom's surgery one-year mark came and went. Instead of scheduling the reversal of the colostomy, the oncologist informed us that the cancer seemed to have returned, and that we should adopt a "wait and see" attitude. That did not sit well with me at all. The denial side of me screamed, "The cancer couldn't possibly have returned; I did not hear that." The bravado side of me confidently proclaimed, "I *will* take care of that." The warrior-knight-combatant-lawyer in me—a role with which I was well familiar as I had played it in many a Past Life, as I would realize much later—swung into action, threw down the gauntlet, and geared up for war. I had heard of Memorial Sloan Kettering Cancer Center in New York City, famed for diagnosing and treating cancer patients. Costs no object (how very naïve I was then),

I single-mindedly wanted Mom to receive the best life-saving, cancer treatment in the world. I contacted the Center, corralled Mom's medical records for review, and by early September of 2001, all was set for scheduling an appointment for Mom.

It was a glorious Fall Tuesday morning with the deepest azure sky. I was to call Sloan Kettering once I got into my office that morning. It was September 11th, 2001, *the* "9/11."

Sending Mom, even accompanied by Dad, to New York City at that catastrophic juncture was decidedly out of the question. What about the Mayo Clinic? Mom and Dad were familiar with it as they were there in Rochester, Minnesota, with me and Vivian when my life hung in the balance in 1994. It was Mom's turn; the Mayo Clinic would save her life, it was meant to be. The Mayo Clinic scheduled Mom's visit right away after a telephone triage with me. Dad accompanied Mom; I should have gone with them, but my job was all consuming. If I knew then what I know now, I would have had my priorities correctly set: Mom's health and life would definitely take priority over any client's case I was handling. Heck, I would have spent much, much more time with Mom, even if it had meant a delayed promotion to partnership, or inciting Bev's irrational ire and jealousy. I now weep just thinking about the Christmases, the birthdays and New Years that I allowed Bev to talk me into "going away" on trips and vacations instead of spending them with Mom during those last few years of her life. It was not an excuse that I did not know or believe that Mom would really depart this world so soon. It was not valid justification that I did not realize Bev's intentions were *really that* mean-spirited—to keep me away from Mom and my family. My heart still aches with remorse today, and the "would have, should have, could have" still haunts me.

While Mom and Dad were at the Mayo Clinic in early October, I was in West Palm Beach, Florida, receiving what I thought was newfangled healing. Earlier that year, I read a TIME magazine cover story about "New Age healers," and was fascinated. I have a very complicated and rare spinal cord condition that has been giving me grief over the years. Surgery and Western medicine did not render satisfactory results. Hence, I was beginning to pay attention to alternative, holistic healing. I picked two healers lauded in that article: George Goodheart of Grosse Pointe Woods, Michigan, a chiropractor who founded applied kinesiology, and John Upledger, an eminent proponent and practitioner of Craniosacral Therapy. Both had long waiting lists, but probably because of 9/11 with quite a few patients cancelling their appointments, I was in for a course of treatment with Dr. Upledger in early October.

I loved my time away from home, away from the pressure cooker that was my job—and without consciously realizing it, away from Bev. Such respite was far and few between, however, which made each time-out all the sweeter and much cherished. Florida was not my favorite destination, but it was a gorgeous Fall week when I was in the West Palm Beach area. I took in the sunshine and crisp air, I had proper, delicious meals, and I slept soundly. I indulged in my leisure pursuits of browsing bookstores, camera shops and fountain pen boutiques. I drove and strolled around and took photographs whenever the mood or sights moved me.

Photography has been my hobby since early childhood. Dad was an avid amateur photographer; as soon as I could walk, Dad gave me one of his used cameras (it was probably a Rolleicord twin lens reflex) to accompany him on photographic excursions on Sundays. Dad and I had bonded as soon as I was born, and photographs tell the tale. In a photograph which has been hanging on the wall in my parents' home as long as I could remember,

I was not quite a year old, and Mom was holding me in her arms with the sweetest smile, while I had my arm outstretched, trying to reach the person with the camera taking the photograph—my Dad.

Throughout primary school and secondary school in Hong Kong, and even when I was attending Barnard College in New York City, you would always find me with my camera bag. Obviously, I had graduated from that trusty Rolleicord TLR to various compact rangefinders, to finally in the late 1960's, my very own set of Nikon F SLR with a couple of lenses, and then a spanking new Nikon F2 SLR body, all gifts from Dad for going away for college. At Barnard, I joined the Photography Club at Columbia, and started experimenting with developing my own black-and-white film and making prints. I was a photographer for the Barnard newspaper for a while. I had no idea what I was doing, nor whether my photographs were "good" enough, but photography in my life was simply a given. In retrospect, photography practically saved my life; conversely, without it, my soul atrophied, whether I realized or acknowledged it or not at the time.

In late September of 1977, at a lesbian social group called "Women Together," which met weekly in the basement of a church in a Detroit suburb, I met Bev. I was a first-year law student at Wayne State University Law School. My lover then, Barbara, was in Switzerland with her "friend," Simone (not her real name). I was new to Detroit, and simply wanted to meet other lesbians and make new friends. Bev and I started dating. She lived in a northern suburb, and I lived in a dingy apartment within walking distance of the Law School. By spring of 1978, Bev declared that "our relationship would falter" if I did not somehow get a car, as she had tired of driving downtown to visit me. That should have been a third-degree alarm bell, but I was—as usual in my much younger days—consumed with infatuation rather than making mature choices in picking a mate. I was very poor, being a "foreign student" (an immigration term of art), I was restricted in the type of employment I could engage in (basically part-time and on-campus). I made just enough for rent and food, and not much more, sometimes not even for books. My parents subsidized me to the best of their abilities when I was in college, but the subsidy petered out after I came out. They disapproved of my sexual orientation (as if I had a choice) and of my choice of partner (they were wiser than I on that point). My only "valuable possessions," then, were my beloved Nikon cameras and lenses. Time to sell them, I reluctantly concluded; I figured I could always buy new cameras "later." The car and "salvaging" my relationship were top priorities at that point. I was able to sell my Nikon gear in no time, and the sale proceeds were just enough for me to buy a highly pre-loved, lime-green Mazda "RX3" which limped along for only six months. That was replaced by an even cheaper Chevrolet pickup truck with a broken grille (gas was only 70 cents a gallon then), until I was almost graduating from Law School when I could qualify for a loan to acquire a used Chevrolet "Chevette."

I did not seem to miss my cameras in the ensuing ten years, as I was far too preoccupied with an overload of life's issues. In the summer of 1987, Vivian gifted me with a then state-of-the-art, point-and-shoot camera. I was overwhelmed by and very grateful for the generous present. That was the summer Lina and Juliana emigrated from Hong Kong to Windsor, and all of us decided to browse the annual Ann Arbor Art Fair. I did not even have a chance to shoot a roll of film with that camera before it was stolen at the Art Fair; the thief probably stealthily and masterfully cut the neck strap as I was wearing it around my neck. My photographic days came to an abrupt halt again. As I wrote the preceding sentence, the coincidence or irony is not lost on me: I am now living in Ann Arbor, but again, am unable to take pictures even though I now have an enviable collection of fine cameras.

After the loss of that brand new point-and-shoot, I was heart-broken and could not bring myself to purchasing another camera for another ten years. It was 1997, and Bev and I were celebrating our 20th anniversary with an 11-day tour of Italy. I figured I had to have a camera for the trip, and by then, I could afford a Leica compact film camera (one does not call that a "point-and-shoot"). A couple of years earlier, Bev had bought a "bridge" camera for my birthday, but I never quite took to that camera. It had been too long since I had worked with a camera. Still, I did not bother to peruse the owner's manual before the trip, figuring that any idiot could use a point-and-shoot camera. My uppity attitude cost me eleven rolls of film's worth of unforgettable moments from that memorable trip. Apparently, I didn't realize that a Leica was not your average idiot-proof point-and-shoot camera. Thoroughly humiliated, I started paying more attention to cameras and pho-tograph taking again. Nonetheless, I was simply too busy at the office to have any time for travels or picture taking.

The Millennium was approaching, and a last-minute air-line special found me and Bev in Albuquerque and Santa Fe, New Mexico, for a 4-day getaway for the Y2K. I brought along my Leica compact camera and an entry-level Nikon SLR. The turn of the century did signify the dawn of a new life for me, spiritually and metaphysically, though I did not realize it as such at that time. Those four days in New Mexico were magical: the mile-high, deep blue skies, the fresh, crisp air, the high plateau desert landscape, the scenery refreshing yet strangely familiar. We visited the Very Large Array and the Bosque del Apache National Wildlife Refuge, as well as the galleries on Canyon Road. I came home with what by my own standards were breathtaking photographs. That inspired me to take up photography as a hobby again.

2000 turned out to be an extraordinarily hectic year. In addition to Mom's hospitalization and surgery for colon cancer from April to August, I was back at the Mayo Clinic in March for a biopsy as my kidney graft seemed to be rejecting. Fortunately, it turned out to be only a medication issue. In August, Bev suddenly showed symptoms of what her local gynecologist believed to be inflammatory breast cancer. We rushed back to the Mayo Clinic in September; an excisional biopsy proved that it was not the dreaded disease but something quite benign. That scare set me back substantially financially; ironically, she was just three months shy of being eligible for coverage under my health insurance from my law firm as my domestic partner. That was par for the course—anything involving Bev was bound to be complicated, convoluted, costly, ruinous, or litigation-prone, or a combination of all of the above.

In turn, I had to postpone my own spinal cord surgery until late October. After I had survived yet another spinal cord surgery, I decided to reward myself with my first "serious" camera—a Leica M6TTL rangefinder with a Leica 50mm Summicron lens. I had lusted after that camera since I saw an advertisement in an onboard magazine during one of my business trips several years prior. Armed with my new "toy," I started seizing every opportunity to go outdoors to take pictures, on weekends and holidays; going on driving trips on long weekends; even taking time off for real vacations. Little did I know then that photography (along with my other lifelong passion—music listening) would literally save my life in the very trying ensuing few years.

When my spirits felt spent, I turned to music listening. Since my childhood, music had always served to nourish my soul, replenish my life force, and restore my inner equilibrium. In the late-1960's, Dad upgraded our stereo system to separate "hi-fi components," replacing that chunky "cabinet" that was our all-in-one stereo in the 1950's. After my homework was done, the young teenage me would sit on the floor in front of the stereo rack, headphones over my ears, grooving to music of all kinds. A budding audiophile was born and was coming of age. As soon as I could financially afford it in my adult years, I started assembling my own audio "reference" system. Music appreciation was a reflection of my rather extensive musical training in my youth, and music listening became a legacy of that musical past.

Following my then established life script, I took surviving my October, 2000, spinal cord surgery, and indeed life itself, for granted again. I carried on with my hectic professional life, continued trying to make sense of my personal life, vacillated between denying and worrying about Mom's cancer threat, and juggled competing demands for my time and energy, all the while being oblivious to my own body's desperate wails for healing and replenishment. Tending to Mom in her waning years, coping with Bev's confounding changes and increasingly mercurial temperament, and satisfying my firm's escalating demands for billable hours, productivity and profitability, all took a toll on my health and psyche. Moreover, around 2002, I became aware of an even more distressing phenomenon, one that seemed to belong to the paranormal, the metaphysical realm, perhaps even a foreboding. I began to sense something sinister in my home; yes—sinister. This lovely 60-plus-year-old Cape Cod that Bev and I had called home for almost two decades suddenly felt chillingly dark and dank. Everything seemed filthy, as if covered in a layer of grime. Even though Bev had not been employed for years, she would not help clean the home. I offered to hire a cleaning service, but she scoffed at that. She had from time to time cleaned other people's homes for her spending money. Without missing a beat, she volunteered to clean our own home if I would pay her. "What!? Come again?!" I thought to myself, incredulously. In addition to feeling mired in filth and swamped by pestilence, I felt claustrophobic and suffocated as if the ceiling was caving in on me. There was a very real sense of impending doom. However, being the left-brained lawyer that I was, those bizarre feelings were not something that I could acknowledge, let alone comprehend.

Outdoors photography came to my rescue. After a week of 12-hour workdays, as much as feasible, I would dash out the door on weekends to "roam the earth" and take pictures. I was fortunate to have that escape chute. On the other hand, it also meant I did not really have a home to which to retreat, nor a safe haven in which to unwind and rejuvenate. Bev had not, for quite a few years, been the reservoir of comfort, support and love that one would expect of one's life partner. The sustenance of an intimate relationship had dwindled to a trickle, if that. Over time, I had become conditioned not to expect anything from her, and our dysfunctional relationship languished by a thread, owing its existence to habit rather than any meaningful viability.

Revitalized not so much by the craniosacral therapy sessions with Dr. Upledger, but by the cool breeze off the South Florida coast and the embrace of the gentle Fall sunshine, I intensely monitored Mom's checkup at the Mayo Clinic from afar by cell phone. As luck would have it, the oncologist assigned to her case was a Chinese physician. Dr. Guangzhi Qu and Dad could communicate in Mandarin, while Mom, who was not fluent in that dialect, felt completely at home with a doctor who, as she put it in Chinese, had the "same sound and same breath."

Mom and Dad were apparently enjoying their stay in Rochester. Dad later showed me photographs he took of Mom's hop-skipping across the lobby of the brand new Gonda Building, holding an ice cream cone in her hand. It happened to be the grand opening of that magnificent addition to the Mayo Clinic during the week of their stay, and lunch-time concerts and free ice cream were part of the festivities. They also enjoyed the complimentary breakfast buffet and afternoon *hors d'oeuvres* offered with their hotel room; Mom delighted in being able to stock up on fresh fruits. I was thrilled that their experience at the Mayo Clinic then was much more comfortable than when we were huddling in a non-descript economy-hostel in 1994. Mom especially enjoyed her dinners at the local restaurant *Henry Wellington*.

The difference? Money, pure and simple. I was your stereo-typical hand-to-mouth solo practitioner in 1994, while by 2001, I was an income partner in a top-notch large, corporate law firm in Michigan, Dickinson Wright PLLC. However, everything has a price, and in a large, corporate law firm setting, the price was steep. The firm owned your entire existence—mind, body and soul, time, energy and devotion. On the other hand, the remu-neration was intoxicating, bordering on addictive. Yet, lodged in the undertow was the haunting reminder that there was always a price to be paid when you bargained with the devil. You gallantly carried on, rationalizing everything in the name of professional pride and responsibility, of serving your clients. My broad brush ought not tarnish the many fine, genuinely caring professionals I worked with at my firm who routinely donated countless *pro bono publico* hours to fend for the deprived and the oppressed. My firm was uncharacteristically compassionate and enlightened, with genuine emphasis on diversity and elevating minorities and women among our ranks. Still, call me cynical, but the nature of any sizable business enterprise is by definition soulless and heart-less and by necessity Machiavellian and even ruthless.

A PET-scan, which was then unavailable in Windsor, clearly revealed where Mom's cancer had spread—mostly to her liver. According to Dr. Qu, the cancer cells lit up like a Christmas tree on the scan. The even better news was that the Mayo Clinic could offer Mom state-of-the-art treatment—intraoperative radiation therapy—to counter the spread of her cancer. The cost of the pro-cedure was substantial, and Mom offered to pay for it out of her life's savings. It must have been the refreshing ocean breeze in

Florida that triggered my sudden stroke of brilliance: I figured that OHIP should pay for a medically necessary and appropriate procedure which was not available in Ontario. Within minutes, I put Dr. Qu on the phone with Dr. Yoshida, and within seconds, Dr. Qu informed me that Dr. Yoshida agreed to apply for OHIP funding for the procedure for Mom. That application was approved the following day for Mom to receive the life-saving procedure at the Mayo Clinic. I was ecstatic.

Mom would much later expressly, verbally thank me for saving her life. That was monumental. All my life, I had been striving to please Mom and gain her approval. No matter how much or how often or what I accomplished since early childhood, her approval had always seemed just out of reach, or she was deliberately withholding it to spur me on to attaining ever greater achievements. Perhaps she was the original, the quintessential "Tiger Mom." The upside was that her reticence in expressing approval became my surefire motivator to excel in all of my undertakings. I developed a "can do" attitude from a very tender age; willpower was my middle name, and perseverance was second nature to me. These attributes would serve me well as I was buffeted by life's myriad trials and tribulations. The downsides, however unintended, would have long lasting and destructive reverberations. I felt inadequate at times; that vulnerability clashed conspicuously with my innate sense of invincibility, leaving me oftentimes baffled and befuddled. At yet other times, my overwhelming desire for approval found me entangled in lopsided and toxic relationships in which I unwittingly allowed myself to be exploited emotionally and financially. In all fairness to Mom, I was such a hopeless idealist and romantic anyway that, even without my hunger to be approved and loved, I would have suffered self-conflagration anyway in many of my misguided *liaisons*.

Mom's acknowledgement resolved a huge piece of unfinished business between us. In fact, many of the epic mother-daughter struggles that had caused untold grief in our relationship were also reconciled during the last three years of her life. That was an enormous blessing for me, as I would come to realize with each passing year since her death. Back in late 2001, however, maximizing Mom's longevity was partly my filial duty, partly a conditioned response by the bravado me, and last but not least, my perceived responsibility so that Mom would still be alive when Vivian eventually returned from Hong Kong to "spend the rest of her life taking care of Mom," Vivian's then professed intention for several years.

Mom and Dad had to make another trip to the Mayo Clinic in late November for the surgery and intraoperative radiation therapy. In retrospect, I should have accompanied them, but professional obligations—there were *always* "professional obligations"—beckoned. The day Mom had the surgery happened to be the night my law firm was holding its 124th Annual Firm Dinner. Once a year, all 150 or so attorneys (the firm had grown to more than 425 attorney in 2016) from all our offices would gather for a black-tie-only formal dinner. When the call came from Dad, during the Dinner, that Mom was finally out of surgery and resting comfortably in post-op, I pumped my fist in the air triumphantly. And yet there was no one, there and then or later that evening, to celebrate with me my triumph, to share my excitement, my sense of relief, my feeling of fortitude. Bev was certainly not overjoyed that my Mom survived the surgery; quite the contrary. I was too busy lawyering (read: making money to make ends meet) to properly address such psychological assault and battery in my long-standing but increasingly flawed and toxic life partnership. I was seeing a psychotherapist weekly, and thus figured all was in check and well under control. As a matter of fact, I had by then been in therapy on and off for over twenty years. Obviously, I took very seriously Socrates' entreaty: "The unexamined life is not worth living." Most likely, I was simply an excruciatingly slow learner in grasping life's lessons. It would take a catastrophic event several years later for me to finally begin Lesson One of those essential life lessons. In the interim, the weekly therapy sessions would suffice as a release valve, a make-do patch.

In retrospect, I was too naïve to think that the Mayo Clinic surgery was the be all and end all, and that Mom would soon resume being the picture of perfect health. Mom was greatly weakened by the surgery. Follow-up care provided by OHIP was haphazard. A stent placed during surgery and which was supposed to be removed when Mom returned to Windsor, for instance, was overlooked and not removed until months later, causing Mom undue suffering. Nonetheless, I believe that surgery did extend Mom's life by almost two precious years during which she enjoyed excellent quality of life, notwithstanding OHIP's *faux pas*. On the other hand, I remained in denial, not realizing—or not wanting to realize—that Mom would soon enough not be with us on this plane. We all carried on with life: Lina and Vivian pursued their careers in Hong Kong and China respectively, Juliana attended university in Toronto, Dad was a superb caregiver by Mom's side, Mom continued to whip up her fabulous home cooking and keep their home immaculately, and I continued to be a hardworking and dedicated foot soldier for my law firm. If I could do it all over again, I would definitely have spent much, much more time with Mom, Bev's protests, snide remarks and derision notwithstanding.

Mother's Day of 2002 was particularly memorable. Instead of giving Mom an item purchased from a store, I gave her something I crafted. That was most unusual because I had not "created" anything since perhaps primary school days. Being a left-brained lawyer, arts and crafts was certainly not my *forte*, or so I thought. On a trip with Mom and Dad to a shopping mall in Windsor that spring, I happened to pick up a few charming pewter photograph frames with the inscription "I Love Mom." As if it was meant to be, I found perfect photographs of myself and my sisters that I took in recent years, and trimmed them to fit the tiny 1-inch or so opening in the frame. I was extremely proud of my burst of creativity. When I presented the frames to Mom on Mother's Day, she was visibly moved and delighted, and I could not have been more gratified. She prominently displayed them on top of the chest of drawers in her bedroom, where she could see and be with us while she rested and slept everyday.

Family portrait taken in December of 2002, in the formal sitting room of Mom and Dad's home, on the occasion of Dad's 80th birthday and Mom and Dad's 50th wedding anniversary. From l to r: Vivian, Vivian's (late) husband Edward ("Ted") William Fenna, the author, Dad, Mom, Lina, and Lina's daughter, Juliana. (Photograph by Mena Fung Ng and Lap Fai Ng—reprinted with permission).

2002 was an auspicious year in even more ways. Dad and I celebrated Mom's 75th birthday in August. In December, we had a huge celebration: Dad's 80th birthday and Mom and Dad's 50th wedding anniversary. Lina, Vivian and her husband, Ted, flew in from Hong Kong, and Juliana came in from Toronto. We engaged professional photographers to take family portraits in the ornate sitting room at my parents' home. Looking at those photographs now, I lament that I could not even take time out of my jam-packed work schedule to get a haircut so as to look more presentable for that special occasion. We hosted a feast in a large banquet room at a Chinese restaurant in Windsor for more than sixty of Mom and Dad's friends. The walls were decorated with Chinese calligraphy, scrolls of Chinese paintings, and Chinese poems that Dad's friends composed to celebrate his milestone birthday. Party favors for each guest included a crystal cube engraved with the Chinese character for "longevity" nestled in an elaborate brocaded gift box. It was truly a night to remember. The guests were gracious and uproarious in feting Mom and Dad. The atmosphere was festive and jubilant, as the food was sumptuous. Mom was resplendent, and joyous, while Dad was at his gregarious best. Bev sullenly arrived late for the feast, and left early without excusing herself to the celebrants or even informing me. As usual, I made excuses for her abrupt, unannounced departure.

The celebration continued a few days later in Toronto where we hosted another feast for friends and relatives residing in that city. Dad's best friend from childhood served as master of ceremony and regaled us with memorable and hilarious stories from their boyhood and youth. Little did we know then that that would be the last time many of our relatives and friends would see Mom in person. Bev drove up from Michigan by herself just in time to attend the feast, and drove back the same evening, a glum and discontented figure disappearing into the frigid December night.

While we were in Toronto for the grand celebrations, on a casual trip to a local shopping mall, after much hesitation, Mom bought herself a German-made frying pan by J.A. Henckels. It was frightfully expensive, but I figured Mom, the superb chef, was clearly qualified to use such professional grade cooking implements. That gave me an idea for Mother's Day the ensuing year: I presented her with an entire set of J.A. Henckels pots and pans. She fairly gasped upon opening the present. I had no inkling that I was celebrating the last Mother's Day with her. Thankfully, in the two short months, she did get to use some of the pieces in preparing her legendary home cooking for me and Dad.

After all the festivities and excitement of December 2002, January 2003 rolled around and it felt particularly harsh, bitterly cold, and brutally dismal. We all felt unusually subdued, after the exalted highs of the previous month. I remember visiting Mom and Dad one weekend, and while we were having lunch at an Italian restaurant, Mom suddenly brought up the subject of cemetery, her cremation and burial. While Dad sat next to me in stone silence, probably in shock or in denial, I barely managed to hold back my tears. Mom described to me a cemetery that her neighbors, Bill and Mary da Silva, had told her about. She did not give me the name or even the general location; perhaps she did not know, but I remembered every detail Mom related about that "perfect" final resting place. She added that one day we would drive by to take a look. Mom never mentioned it again, and we never did drive by . . . until the day before she passed away.

It must have been just a couple of months later when Dr. Yoshida informed us that Mom's cancer seemed to have returned again. I immediately arranged for Mom to go see Dr. Qu at the Mayo Clinic. I was thankful that Vivian could take time off work to accompany them to Rochester. It was late March, and the news was not good; Dr. Qu could offer Mom only a slot in a clinical trial for a very promising new drug for colon cancer. Mom adamantly refused, claiming she did not want to be a "guinea pig." I could not convince her otherwise, by reasoning, threat or guile. I was absolutely crestfallen; I simply could not conceive of someone not wanting to fight or resort to all available means to survive. That was utterly beyond my realm of comprehension. It would, once again, take a series of catastrophes some years later for me to appreciate "quality" over "quantity" of life. I would come to comprehend, much too late for Mom, the teaching that one does not so much as "fight against" cancer as one learns to "live with" cancer. If I had been more of a "peaceful warrior" then, I might have been a better adjunct to Mom in coping with her health challenges. No matter, it was meant to be: the "experimental drug" that Mom refused to try turned out to be Avastin, a most effective drug against advanced colorectal cancer. Most ironically and as if to add insult to injury, Avastin was fast-track approved by the FDA not even a month after Mom passed away.

Since Mom's return from the Mayo Clinic, I was subconsciously running away—from reality, from acknowledging Mom's imminent demise. I took full advantage of long weekends to go away, with Bev in tow, to San Diego in May, to New Orleans to attend a law conference in late June, and to Connecticut, Rhode Island and Cape Cod in early July. I was actually quite miserable during those mini-vacations, even as I enjoyed taking lots of photographs in the great outdoors and being away from my suffocating home and the pressure cooker that was my job. Despite my expending significant sums for upscale accommodations and gourmet meals, Bev seemed increasingly unimpressed by and dissatisfied with the all-expense-paid getaways. In New Orleans, for instance, she again wrongfully accused me of supposedly having "wandering eyes," and made quite a scene while we were having lunch at the Ritz-Carlton Hotel. Throughout our 26-plus-year relationship, she had berated me with such baseless accusations on a regular basis, and would then up the ante by throwing a royal fit. In an effort to avoid such unpleasant and unwarranted confrontations, I tried to maintain a "straight-ahead" gaze whenever I was with her in public. That, of course, did nothing to reduce my chances of being unjustifiably accused. Instead of realizing that our interaction was unhealthy and destructive, I was unwittingly enabling the abuser.

While Bev and I were still in New Orleans, Mom told me over the phone that her feet and ankles had suddenly become very swollen. I did not know then that was the first sign of her entering the end stage of her life. Still, I was extremely distraught by the news. I would have moved mountain and earth to enroll her in that clinical trial in an instant, but my hands were tied since she remained resolutely opposed to being a "guinea pig." My frivolous and aimless excursions those few months accorded me only temporary escape and illusory solace. I should have spent those precious, final months with Mom. Yet, how could it be "final" when all the while I was still subconsciously denying the finality? At that point in my life, death was not a concept that I could grasp let alone accept; I was a gung-ho "death denier." Since birth, I had always felt vibrantly full of life, to the exclusion of any notion of death—the absence of life. In truth, I could not have spent more time with Mom or talked with her more because that would have required that I accept her impending demise which to me was an unacceptable premise. I was in the prime of my life personally and professionally, notwithstanding my critically flawed relationship with Bev and my own medical issues in the background; death and dying was an alien concept.

There I was in Mom's room in the special hospice ward of the hospital, standard guard, ever vigilant. Somehow, that sentry duty felt very familiar; I could do it very well, as if I had done it many times before. Do you believe in Past Lives? I then had no notion of such phenomenon; the time for me to learn and understand would come much later.

I watched Mom intensely throughout the night, sending her the dogged willpower that I knew I had always possessed in abundance, willing her to live, and being fully prepared to interject myself between her and whomever or whatever that seemed intent to whisk her away. I was ready to battle any such malevolent intruder. Again, I would learn much later that Past Lives had much to do with that chivalrous and valiant stance.

Two or three times in the night, Mom called out, in a very faint whisper, for water. To this day, I feel certain that if I had not been there to give her water when she needed it, as she was obviously too weak to call for the nurse, she would have slipped away that night.

The night wore on, and I continued to stand vigil over Mom, and continued to stare down Death, keeping it at bay. Even though I was bone tired, I did not dare fall asleep until almost dawn, when I heard Mom snoring ever so gently in her deep slumber. What a sweet sound that was!

I awoke an hour later to the hustle and bustle of doctors and nurses making their early morning rounds. The sun was streaking through the blinds into the room. Mom awoke as well, fresh as a daisy! She could not have been more like her old self, asking me where she was, followed immediately by "What's for breakfast?" At that moment, all I heard in my mind was a rousing rendition of the "Hallelujah" chorus from Handel's "Messiah."

Dad arrived shortly after 8:30 a.m., totally surprised to find me in Mom's room, as he had no idea that I had spent the night there. He was elated to see Mom in good spirits and physically revitalized, and hurried to take over helping Mom with her breakfast. I could see that they were resuming their daily routine of more than fifty years: having breakfast together, talking about dreams they might have had the night prior, the weather, the agenda for the day, and so on and so forth. I felt triumphantly relieved, having discharged my duties faithfully and honorably. There was work to tend to; clients' cases could not wait. I hurried home to change into my lawyer's "uniform" and back to the office I went. It had been a tediously long and wearied twenty-four hours.

Nothing in life is ever a coincidence. Mom was rushed to the hospital on July 17th; when my secretary placed the call to Lina, it was already July 18th in Hong Kong, which also "happened" to be Vivian's last day of her 8-year lucrative stint with that U.S.-China joint venture company. That was the putative end point of Vivian's professional career, and the start of her declared commitment to henceforth devote her life to taking care of Mom.

I was at the hospital again early Saturday morning; Dad was there already. Mom looked well rested and cheerful, a far cry from just two days earlier when she seemed to be hanging by a thread. I left mid-day to pick up Lina and Vivian arriving from Hong Kong at the Detroit Metro Airport. When they emerged from behind the large opaque glass sliding door after clearing customs and immigration, I was startled by Lina's appearance. She had on what appeared to be a flowing robe, her hair was cropped extremely short, and one of her hands was clutching a string of Buddhist prayer beads. The only hint of her "Material Girl past" was the oh-so-exclusive Louis Vuitton backpack over her shoulders.

The last time I saw Lina was probably a year or so earlier when she came to attend a Master's level Reiki workshop at the International Center for Reiki Training in Southfield, Michigan. She stayed with Mom and Dad in Windsor, but during the workshop weekend, she stayed at a hotel near the Center; I drove her to and from the workshop when she could not otherwise get a ride. Her appearance and attire then were consistent with what they had been for decades. Lina was always very fashionably dressed, and a devotee of selective Designers with a capital "D." When I had a sudden above-turn and became a shopping maven in the early 1990's (in retrospect, of course there were reasons for my transformation), Lina was quite an influence in my acquiring a taste for the high-end.

Lina dabbled in what she called crystal healing soon after she repatriated to Hong Kong in 1993. She claimed the crystals got rid of her assorted ailments, real or imagined. I did not even know she was in less than ideal health. I did not pay much attention to her forays into what I then deemed New Age excesses and indulgences. She was then climbing the corporate management ladder, and was onto a highly remunerated career track. In retrospect, she was transforming right before our eyes, and it took only a few more years for her to completely change course. Just before Mom was diagnosed with colon cancer, she returned from Hong Kong a couple of times to take weekend Reiki courses at the International Center for Reiki Training. I did not know what Reiki was and did not particularly care to find out; I simply thought Lina had found a new hobby. In the ensuing couple of years, she continued advancing her Reiki training, getting "attuned" in Japan with descendant disciples of the founder of Usui Reiki, and eventually attaining Karuna Reiki master certification. In 2002 when she was visiting Mom and Dad, she gave me a "treatment" which did not make me feel better or worse. I tried to be respectful of what was obviously a serious pursuit for her, but thought it was a leap of faith for those believing in such "healing." For the then very pragmatic me, it was obviously still a bridge too far.

In early 2003, we heard that Lina had joined some sort of Buddhist temple. We were concerned that it might be a cult, but were relieved after learning that it was a recognized branch of Buddhism; it's Shingon Buddhism, or Esoteric Buddhism. Mom enlightened us with the fact that our maternal grandmother had also worshipped at a similar temple near her home when we were too young to remember. I was more amused than alarmed, thinking to myself that crystal healing and Reiki were nebulous enough, but Lina had to be involved with "esoteric" Buddhism; couldn't she just be a "regular" Buddhist like everyone else?

Lina was known for changing her looks periodically, a trait that Juliana apparently inherited. One would be well-advised to ask Juliana, for instance, what color she had dyed her hair before picking her up at the airport. Yet that time, Lina's aura—even though I was not sure what that word really meant—was different as she emerged from behind that glass door with Vivian. She had indeed changed profoundly, I thought to myself. She seemed more serious yet more serene; even her gait seemed purposeful. I instinctively braced for the worst, not quite knowing what to make of her latest and rather mystifying persona.

The drive from the Airport to the hospital in Windsor took more than an hour, as we had to clear customs and immigration across the Ambassador Bridge. I do not remember much about the drive or what we talked about; I concentrated on rushing them to the hospital for their reunion with Mom. Mom was, of course, ecstatic to see Lina and Vivian again. I am not sure if it was by choice or divine grace, I do not recall much since their arrival, other than several notable events. Perhaps my subconscious understood the grim eventuality that would befall our happy gathering; I had self-defensively numbed myself into oblivion; that week zipped by in a flash. I really should have taken time off work and spent that entire week with the rest of my family and stayed by Mom's side. As for Vivian's resolution to spend the "rest of her life" taking care of Mom? That lifetime turned out to be but a fleeting nine precious days. Alas, hindsight is always so painfully prescient.

Sunday, July 20th, a day after Lina and Vivian arrived, Mom was so energized that we felt she could use some fresh air and sunshine out on the rooftop terrace just down the hall from her room. Vivian seemed to have fun trying out different beds with castors for Mom to be transferred into. We enjoyed the little "outing" with Mom, but she did not much care for the heat and humidity outdoors, preferring the climate-controlled comfort of her room.

Lina, Vivian and Dad spent all day with Mom that week, going home only to sleep at night. I would leave work "early" (around 6 p.m.) and join them in the early evening. Lina told me several things that I could fully appreciate only months and years later. The fact that Mom survived through the first night after she was hospitalized, Lina explained, was because her fellow Buddhists at her temple interceded with their—I presume— prayers and incantations, so that Mom would stay alive until Lina and Vivian could arrive the following day. To color me skeptical about Lina's assertions is an understatement. I thought it was my standing vigil, staying close by Mom's side throughout that night, giving her water when she needed it, willing her to live with the sheer power of my unflinching determination, all of which stabilized and revitalized her.

Lina then told me something even more inscrutable. She had apparently been giving Mom Reiki healing as soon as she arrived at the hospital every morning, and she would continue doing so throughout her visit until she left at night. She revealed to me that she was "supported" by her fellow Buddhists back in Hong Kong as she gave Mom healing. I could see with my own eyes that Mom's swollen feet from the night before would return to normal as soon as Lina started Reiki healing, and her swollen abdomen (from the ever enlarging cancer tumor in her liver) would also shrink with Lina's healing. However, Lina cautioned, she could not continue to sustain Mom this way as there was supposedly a limit as to how long one could ask for Heaven's forbearance. I simply listened, not fully comprehending or believing what she shared with me.

Lina also related to me a dream that Mom had during that week. Mom told Lina, Vivian and Dad that she dreamed she was walking down a path, holding in front of her abdomen a rather heavy sphere or ball made of rattan, and she saw "dark" people, or people in shadows. Vivian explained it away as Mom's seeing dark-skinned nurses at the hospital coming into her room to care for her. Lina, however, told me that it was a vision, a sign, that Mom was on her way to meet her maker; "they" were calling her from "the Other Side." Again, I simply listened without fully understanding or assimilating those novel ideas.

By Wednesday, July 23rd, Mom's condition was apparently so stabilized that the doctor was planning on discharging her home. Was it Lina's Reiki healing, or the fact that Mom was surrounded by her loved ones, or something else altogether, that should be credited for Mom's dramatic turnaround? There were discussions of modifications and devices that would have to be instituted at the home ahead of her return. Vivian was extremely enthusiastic about Mom's going home again. However, Mom was very reluctant; it appeared that if she had to be discharged from the hospital, she would rather be transferred to a rehabilitation facility.

Mom also had a special request that day: she had a taste for Jello. One would imagine the hospital would have Jello galore, but apparently such was not the case. Hence, after work that day, I was stopping at various restaurants on the way to purchase numerous containers of Jello in a variety of flavors, rushing to the hospital before they melted in my Mercedes-Benz "ML320" in the hot July sun.

Toward the end of the week, Lina was preparing us—and Mom—for her intended return to Hong Kong the following Monday; she *had* to return to her job. Vivian, on the other hand, having just completed her employment with a very lucrative severance package (as the joint venture was being turned over to Chinese control), could stay indefinitely, and indeed, could take care of Mom for the rest of her life. Nonetheless, Mom apparently had other plans in mind. As I did not take much stock in Lina's Reiki healing, I did not worry about Mom's health or comfort after Lina intended departure. As it turned out, I did not have to fret over that at all.

Dad, Lina and Vivian had apparently been driving around on Thursday and Friday, looking at cemeteries and plots. Someone must have suggested that it would be a wise move; perhaps it was Mom who had urged them to search. By Saturday, I joined the search, not that there was any sense of urgency. Sketchy information from Dad's friends gave us names of three cemeteries. They were supposedly cemeteries in which many Chinese immigrants in Windsor had purchased plots. Those were the days before Google and GPS-on-every-dashboard. We had to ascertain the exact locations the best we could, using old-fashion foldout maps and navigational training from our respective Boy Scouts and Girl Guides days. We found the first two cemeteries, and indeed there were quite a few headstones with Chinese inscriptions. However, the location, the overall appearance and the ambience—if one may ascribe such attributes to a cemetery—were far from ideal; we cringed, drove away, and agreed that Mom would not have approved.

The last cemetery we were to visit was quite far from the other two, but as it turned out, very close to our parents' home. As soon as I turned the corner and drove up to the main entrance, I immediately knew that this was *the* cemetery that Mom told me about earlier that year: the wondrous, heavenly place for eternal rest. Aptly, the name of the cemetery was Heavenly Rest Cemetery. From a busy major thoroughfare, a quick turn onto another major road, and exactly as Mom had described it, one would as if by magic come upon a quiet stretch. Proceeding under the majestic arch at the entrance, a serene landscape unfolded before us: pristine, green lawn, pond with Canadian geese, shade trees, all perfectly tranquil and extremely well kept. "This is *it*; we found it," I muttered to myself. Everything was precisely as Mom had described it to me.

We easily located the on-site office on our right not far from the main entrance. A most pleasant "family counselor," as they were called, Chris Kavanaugh, greeted us. He showed us photos and diagrams of the various plots and "slots" that could be purchased for burial and cremation. We were particularly interested in their "family estates": a sizable piece of real estate for burial of up to sixteen, complete with marble headstones, marble benches, flower beds, and very attractive and individualized landscaping. Even though it was a huge cemetery, there were only three family estates available for purchase on that day. Chris accompanied us to view them, and one in particular was destined to be our "Chan Family Estate." It had a gorgeous 3-section light grey marble headstone that was vertically-oriented, and thus particularly suitable for Chinese inscriptions. Its location was also ideal: it faced south, and one side of the estate would always be open and unoccupied as it abutted an internal access road. Lina declared the *feng shui* to be agreeable, and we promptly returned to the office to complete the paperwork for the purchase.

We returned to the hospital in the late afternoon, excited and elated, to bring Mom the excellent news that we had located her "dream resting place," and had in fact purchased our Chan Family Estate. We showed her the brochures we brought back from the Cemetery, as well as photographs we took of the actual site and headstone. Mom seemed extremely pleased indeed, but she also appeared to be very tired that night. We were so proud of ourselves for a job well done; we left for dinner and let Mom rest for the night.

I was awakened early the following morning by a panic telephone call from Vivian. She had arrived at the hospital early to check on Mom, and found Mom in distress with very labored panting. As Vivian had driven herself in Dad's car, I had to pick up Dad and Lina before rushing to the hospital. I barely had time to tell Bev the nasty turn of events as I dashed out the door. Dad and Lina were anxiously waiting for my arrival and for their ride to the hospital. We spoke very little as I drove as fast as I could; all of us instinctively knew that the situation was dire.

As the three of us hurried down the hallway to Mom's room, I could see from quite a distance Mom's stirring in her bed as if she could hear, if not see, us approaching. We entered the room and found Vivian close to tears and Mom continuing to pant as if she could not breathe. We tried to calm Mom down, and Lina started her Reiki healing. At that point, Dr. Liang arrived, and instructed us to help Mom sit up a bit more in her bed. I could not tell whether it was Lina's healing or the change in Mom's positioning in bed, but Mom's breathing became calm and peaceful, and we, in turn, exhaled for a moment.

Mom did not seem her usual self though. She did not say anything nor open her eyes, but I knew she could hear us, and she certainly knew we were by her side. Mom told me that Jacques had told her that, near the end, she would not be able to see or speak, but she could still hear. We surrounded her, held her hands, and we talked to her. Dad and Vivian dabbed her lips with a water-soaked sponge. Lina and I talked about paranormal phenomena and things that I did not understand, but it was conversation to pass the time, to fill the void. We ordered in pizza, but I did not have any appetite for lunch. We stood vigil; we stayed very close to Mom every nanosecond from the moment we arrived, except for the few minutes when I had to go out to the adjoining rooftop terrace to make a phone call.

Around 12 noon, Bev called. As cell phone calls were not allowed in the hospital rooms, I indicated I would call her back right away as soon as I could step out onto the terrace. How thoughtful of Bev, I thought to myself, to call me to find out how Mom was doing and how I was holding up. I surely could use some moral support at that point; the tension and mournfulness of impending doom were stifling. Out on the rooftop terrace, under the noon day sun, I inhaled deeply the fresh air and dialed my home telephone number, anticipating a sympathetic ear and a comforting word or two. Bev answered; in a voice and tone colder than ice and steelier than a rapier, she hollered at me: "Your girlfriend called!" "What?" I couldn't believe my ears, "What girlfriend?" I was incredulous and confused. She then lunged into a jealous fit—as I was presumed guilty of infidelity—barked my supposed girlfriend's name and telephone number, and hung up without a word about my Mom or how I was faring.

I was sitting on a bench on the terrace. I simply, completely broke down, sobbing uncontrollably, in broad daylight, under the midday sun. I was wailing. I cried out for…what?! I did not care if anyone saw me sobbing; I could not stop sobbing. It felt strangely cathartic, in fact, to let the torrents of pain and hurt gush out. For the first time in 26 years, I finally and *truly* realized that I had no life partner and no meaningful relationship. What, if anything, did I have then? Nothing, absolutely nothing: no emotional support, no empathy, no sympathetic ears, no shoulder to cry or lean on. It had been that way for years; I was just too blind, too busy, or too much in denial or self-deception, to acknowledge that plain fact. Perhaps, too, I was a person of honor: keeping my "commitment," even though there was no love left to speak of or relationship worth committing to. Was I really *that* detached from reality? For those few revelatory, cathartic moments on the terrace, I was giving myself a much needed and understanding hug with my sobbing.

That rude awakening turned out to be a turning point that would redirect the course of my life's path. However, there and then, I did not have time for self-pity or introspection or plotting for my future; Mom was languishing in a hospital bed a few hundred yards away. I hurried back to be by her side, convinced that I could help her pull through yet once more.

I resumed my place at Mom's bedside; everything and everyone remained in place, as the vigil quietly continued. I, for one, did not believe Mom would really leave us; she looked fine and normal to me even then. Surely, our collective love and determination would rejuvenate her. At one point in the early afternoon, Lina pointed out how shallow Mom's breathing had become, and how each breath was farther and farther apart. I numbly acknowledged her observations without comprehending the significance of those signs. Lina also cautioned us not to indulge in melodramatic chest thumping sobs and wails when time came for Mom to depart. Buddhists believed that the family must let the dead embark on his or her journey to the next world; any interference with that process (by, for instance, a loved one's screaming or crying out loud) would trap the dead person's spirit in between two worlds, which would be torment for that departing soul.

Another hour passed, Lina had to use the restroom, and she specifically instructed me to closely watch Mom's breathing. I affixed my gaze, like a hawk. I watched Mom's face, so young, serene and beautiful. All of our contentious bickering, agonizing confrontations, gut-wrenching schisms spanning over several decades had been absolved in the past few years as she and I bonded to battle her cancer. She was such a domineering figure in my childhood and youth, and I was such a rebellious, independent daughter, that we simply could not become close. She lent true meaning to the term matriarch of the family. She was a strict disciplinarian. She displayed affection, if at all, only sparingly, and then only very coyly and obliquely. For my part, I felt I was an utter disappointment for her and a disgrace to the family: being a lesbian was a "crime" or "sin" from which I could never redeem myself. Hence, subconsciously, I tried to make it up to her by either chalking up academic, extracurricular, and professional accomplishments, or conversely, I kept subconsciously punishing myself by repeated and escalating self-sabotage. Yet, in her final few years as she was ailing, all that was forgiven, while I began to realize and appreciate the positive influence that strict upbringing had on me. I had always adored my Dad; he was the romantic, the lover, the optimist, the fun loving adventurer, the hunter and hoarder, galloping into the wild to conquer for more and more... with me in tow. But for Mom's droning into my head the virtues of exercising restraint and self-discipline, I would have lived a life as a spendthrift and wastrel with wild abandon, in total destitution and misery. As it turned out, I did unwittingly spend half my adult life as a spendthrift and wastrel, teetering on the verge of total self-annihilation—a walking wounded, a barely functioning dysfunctional.

Mom's breathing became extremely shallow and gentle and farther and farther apart. Mercifully, I had no notion that it meant Mom was literally breathing her last breaths. At 3:59 p.m., she suddenly seemed to want to say something, but it came out only as a gasp, and she breathed her last. Lina immediately pointed out to us that the very conspicuous swelling, the cancerous tumor, in Mom's liver also mysteriously dissipated immediately after Mom breathed that last breath. All of us were weeping quietly, being mindful of Lina's earlier admonition. Vivian was inconsolable, climbing into the hospital bed and lying by Mom's side. I heard Lina utter under her breath: "I am so glad I was able to help you, Mom, even during these last days."

Little did I know then that Mom's passing would bring about even more of a sea change in me and our family. I would come to not only understand but accept why she did not want to undergo that drug trial, and why she preferred to let life come to its natural conclusion than to rely on another—even if it's a family member—to "take care of" her. Alas, with the passage of years, I now give full credit to Lina and her fellow Buddhists for keeping Mom alive until Lina and Vivian arrived in Windsor and for that precious final week of family togetherness. Whatever Lina was conjuring up with her prayers, chants and healing, it mysteriously contained the tumor growth and general swelling—albeit temporarily—and thus giving Mom enormous comfort. Mom must have realized that, without Lina's daily healing, she would not fare well at all. Hence, she chose, even if subconsciously, to bid us all farewell before Lina's planned departure. I was very grateful to Lina and her Buddhist fellowship for enabling Mom to enjoy a family reunion for nine glorious days, and then to pass away with such serenity, contentment and dignity. I witnessed it personally, and it was nothing short of a miracle.

II.

Game Changer

Lina returned to her job in Hong Kong two days after Mom was laid to rest on July 29th at our "Chan Family Estate" in Heavenly Rest Cemetery. Vivian stayed with Dad for another couple of months before returning to her husband, Ted Fenna, in Hong Kong. Dad literally burst out in tears from time to time as he moped around the house, doing daily chores that he used to share with Mom. I took a total of two precious days off: one for Mom's funeral, and the following day when I was so exhausted that I could not even get out of bed. Otherwise, I was back to the grind that was my job. Everyone and everything *seemed* to resume the established routine. Yet, with the close of the "Mom dynasty," I could feel a shift, a tectonic shift no less.

For a few months after Mom's passing, I felt adrift. I was emotionally sauntering aimlessly as if lost at sea, missing *inter alia* the deft steering, solid anchoring and secure shelter that Mom provided, those same attributes that I used to think were hallmarks of her being overbearing and micromanaging. Dad, Vivian and I returned to the Chan Family Estate frequently in those first months to commune with Mom, to find solace. Bev made the sly remark, dripping with her blend of disdain and annoyance, that I was seeing Mom—and she was hearing about Mom—now that she was dead, even more often than when she was alive. I was offended and felt brutalized by that statement; however, as on so many other vexing occasions and as with so many other hurtful statements, I did not challenge her. I was, in a way, brainwashed; in truth, I was emotionally numb—I had to be in order to carry on.

Little did I realize that a revolution, no less, was brewing inside since Mom's passing. In between the ever present and pressing deadlines at work, I felt a constant and increasingly urgent call for me to return to Hong Kong. That was a very unusual and unsettling feeling. After all, I had not returned—and did not want to return—to Hong Kong often since I left in August of 1972 to attend college in New York City. It seemed that each of the few times I went back to Hong Kong, some "mysterious force" would wreak havoc in my life after I returned to the United States. With the passage of the interim decades, I believe I had finally gained insight to solving that "mystery." Meanwhile, there and then in the late summer of 2003, all I was thinking of was the loss of Mom to colon cancer. Along with that thought, I simply could not afford to lose my Down syndrome younger sister, Lilian, to breast cancer without seeing her and letting her see me again. When I recalled how I had somehow managed not to see her for twenty-five long years, I shuddered and wept in my heart.

The last time I visited Lilian was when I returned to Hong Kong for a month in the summer of 1978 to spend some time with Dad as he was recovering from surgery for kidney cancer. How did twenty-five years go by without my looking in on my beloved sister? Quickly and all too easily; when something was too painful to experience, we would find a way to postpone, avoid, overlook, or forget.

When Lilian was born, I was only 3-1/2 years old—too young to remember much of the very first years of her life or understand that she was born with severe Down syndrome. My earliest memory of Lilian was that she was a sweet sister and cute baby, and I loved her to pieces; but she was a very "difficult" child. She could not talk; she would grunt and scream loudly and throw tantrums. She had incredible physical strength, and thus was very difficult to restrain or discipline. I vaguely recalled Mom's telling me and Lina about Lilian's illness—that she was "retarded"—and that even Dr. Chau, our family doctor whom we then revered as "omnipotent doctor-god," could not cure her. As if it was any consolation, Dr. Chau gratuitously proffered that people with Down syndrome would generally live only to their 20's.

Mom and Dad both worked full-time to make ends meet, so that we could be properly fed, clothed, sheltered and have a decent education. Even though we had a live-in domestic servant (the archaic term was "amah"), Lilian was too unruly for amah to handle, as amah had to take care of me and Lina as well as clean and cook for the entire family. I do not remember the day or the circumstances when Lilian was sent to live with a childless middle-age couple; the husband was the delivery truck driver for the company with which Dad was employed at the time. In retrospect, it must have been extremely painful for me, and presumably for Lina as well, to see or realize Lilian's being removed from our midst. I was too young to understand that Mom and Dad had no viable alternative. I had probably associated Lilian's being banished from our home with her "misbehaving." I thus must have made a mental note to always obey my parents lest I be sent away as well.

I am surmising that it happened when Lilian was not quite 2 years old; what a traumatic experience for the 5-year-old me. I vaguely recalled the truck driver couple bringing Lilian home from time to time for dinner with us. I would comfort and convince myself that Lilian seemed happy, that she must have enjoyed riding in the truck all day. In the one or two years when Lilian was under the care of this couple, she ran away at least once or twice. I do not believe it was because she was mistreated; she was simply mischievous or being adventurous. For a child that young who could not speak, it was miraculous that she was found by the police and safely returned to our parents shortly after her "disappearance."

In the mid-1950's Hong Kong, resources and facilities for people with Down syndrome were scarce to nonexistent. Attitudes toward these *retarded* people ranged from neglect, to ostracism, to scorn, as if they were freaks of nature. Even at my tender age, I understood that the existence of Lilian was not to be mentioned in polite company. Her existence was not acknowledged, especially after she was removed from our home, as if it were shameful to have such a *retard* as our family member. I, of course, did not feel Lilian was a freak of nature nor did I feel ashamed to have her as my sister. I loved Lilian dearly; she was my sister, just as Lina was (Vivian wasn't born yet). Yet after Lilian was removed from our home, it seemed to me that even our parents started to disassociate themselves from Lilian, Mom much more so than Dad. They began to not acknowledge her existence in our everyday life, and there was a deliberate effort to fade her out of our lives. I felt extremely torn, saddened and outraged—my first brush with manifest injustice. Perhaps my passion to defend and fight for the underdog, the outcast, and the have-nots sprang from that moment of truth. Perhaps, subconsciously, even as a young child, I reckoned that I was one of "them"—an "outcast."

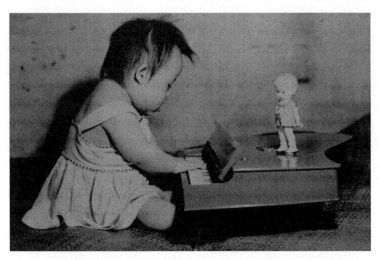

Author's younger sister, Lilian, at her toy piano.

As Mom's alienation (or my perception of her alienation) of Lilian became increasingly overt as I grew into my pre-teen and teenage years, my heartache also deepened. The conflict between my love for and loyalty to Mom on the one hand, and my love for and conviction to fend for Lilian on the other, became irreconcilable. I failed to appreciate, in my youthful exuberance for championing the cause of the disaffected, that the only way my perfectionistic Mom could accept her "failure" of having given birth to such an "imperfect" child was to disassociate herself from that "flawed" child. Therein lies the conundrum—my lifelong internal, subconscious struggle to love Lilian but not to offend Mom's sensibilities. At times during my youth and even into my adulthood, I wished Lilian would just go away or disappear, so that I would not have to confront my painful dichotomy. Mom never reconciled with her perceived "failure" of having given birth to Lilian; well into our adulthood, she still had difficulties acknowledging Lilian's existence. It was extremely heartbreaking for me to witness her struggles.

After a while, Mom and Dad must have realized that having Lilian cared for by the truck driver couple was far from being an ideal arrangement. Lilian managed to "run away" a few times, perhaps because the truck driver couple was not attentive enough. I had no idea how Mom and Dad found "Ding Ma," but when Lilian was perhaps four or five years old, she was sent to live with Ding Ma. Ding Ma was a very kindly, lovable, chubby, middle-aged Shanghainese lady. She had no children. She had a male friend who sometimes showed up; he was a tall, thin middle-aged Shanghainese man who made a living as a tailor. Perhaps he served as the male-figure guard and protector for Ding Ma in their rough-and-tumble neighborhood.

Our family was by no means well off, but Ding Ma was apparently very poor. While we lived in a one-bedroom low-income housing project, Ding Ma lived in a pigeon-hole of an efficiency apartment in a "resettlement housing project." Resettlement referred to placing refugees from Communist mainland China in minimally habitable, rudimentary apartment buildings. Hundreds of thousands of refugees inundated Hong Kong in the 1950's and 1960's after the Communists took over China in 1949. It also referred to resettling the "squatters": those desperately impoverished who dwelled in "tin sheds" (ramshackle huts stitched together with scavenged tin and other scraps) dotted across hillsides or wherever they could "squat." In numerous designated "resettlement areas," the Hong Kong Government built vast housing projects consisting of no-frills apartment buildings to shelter the refugees and the squatters. Each block was about five- or six-storey high, constructed of grey-beige concrete, giving them a very distressed, drab look. There was no elevator; "barrier free" or "accessibility" was obviously not a concern for the Government in building these "barracks" for the poor, huddled masses. Each barebones apartment unit was no larger than perhaps two hundred square feet, one next to another along long, open corridors. There was, of course, no indoor heat or air-conditioning. Restroom and bathing facilities were shared communal facilities in a central area on each floor. Residents cooked outside their units in the corridors, because the faucets were located outside the apartment; there was no room or provision for a kitchen inside the tiny efficiency. Many residents also hung their clothes to dry over the walls along the corridor, ironically and surprisingly enlivening the otherwise dreary shell of the building with splashes of color. I did not know if Ding Ma had to pay rent to the Government, but if she did, it must have been a pittance, perhaps only for the costs of the most basic utilities. There were "wet" markets, tiny neighborhood bakeries and local shops selling sundries on the street level. These sizable resettlement areas were a city unto themselves, distinguished by their notoriety just this side of lawlessness.

Once a month and usually on a Sunday, we would go to Ding Ma's to visit Lilian. I think that was also when Mom and Dad paid Ding Ma an allowance for taking care of Lilian for the month. I hadn't an inkling how much that was; it must not have been much, but probably constituted a "fortune" to Ding Ma. We would leave our home mid-morning, and arrive by lunchtime. Ding Ma's apartment was quite far from our home in the western district on Hong Kong Island. I remember having to take the bus to the cross-harbor ferry terminals, then taking the ferry to the Kowloon side, then taking another long bus ride to the particular resettlement area. As it was a very large housing project, once we got off the bus (at a bus stop that was the "central" drop off point for the entire housing project, but which was not very centrally located at all), we had to walk quite a distance to her particular building. Mercifully, Ding Ma's apartment was on the second floor, and we thus had to climb only a relatively short flight of stairs. Ding Ma had bound feet, which made it very difficult for her to walk. That was probably why the Government assigned her a unit on the second floor as opposed to the sixth floor—that was a nod to accessibility in the early 1960's Hong Kong. The fact that she had bound feet, I now understand, meant that she was a "lady," as opposed to being a member of the working or lower class, in her youth before she fled the Communists in mainland China.

I remembered those monthly visits vividly. They started when I was may be 7 or 8 years old, and ended when I left for the States for college in 1972. When we got off the second bus at the resettlement area, I could see, feel and smell abject poverty and a sense of resignation, if not destitution. It was as if we had landed in a different world. Those feelings were completely alien to me. Even though, as I have pointed out, we were not well off, our parents tried their best to provide me and Lina with a "proper" upbringing. They instilled in me a sense of propriety, integrity and upward mobility. I always felt special even as a young child: educated, cultured, civilized, and overall well provided for. I had unfettered optimism and hopes for an even brighter future. Yet once a month when we visited Lilian, I was rudely jolted to confront the vexing and painful dichotomy: why was I able to live such a comfortable life, while my own sister had to subsist in such sub-standard, deprived living condition? As our family moved up the economic ladder as I approached my teenage years, the contrast became even starker, and those visits became ever more emotionally torturous for me. There were times when I had to hide my tears as we left Lilian and Ding Ma for yet another month.

(l to r) Lina, Lilian, and the author, at Victoria Park,
Causeway Bay, Hong Kong, circa December of 1958.

Each visit always began with Ding Ma's welcoming us with
a delicious home-cooked lunch. Lilian was, of course, thrilled to
see us. Even with her diminished intelligence, she definitely could
recognize us and understand that we were family. In fact, I would
come to learn that her memory was spectacular. I enjoyed those
lunches tremendously; it was homemade Shanghainese fare. We
were Cantonese, and Shanghai cuisine to me was a gastronomi-
cal treat: hefty noodles in soup, a variety of meat and vegetable
dumplings and buns, and my favorite lion's heads (hefty pan-
fried pork meatballs). Even so, I often wondered why our parents
wouldn't take her and Lilian out for a restaurant meal instead, as
I imagined Ding Ma could not really afford to fete us. Obviously,
such gluttonous meals were not their daily affair. I also tried not
to consume all the dishes, so that they would have leftovers for
their next meals; but then I also wondered whether that was really
helpful as I did not recall seeing a refrigerator.

Ding Ma spoke Shanghainese only, a dialect that Mom, Lina
and I did not understand. Hence, Dad was the one to translate

whatever he and Ding Ma discussed. She talked almost nonstop throughout lunch, with Dad translating only one or two sentences. I was sure he would later give Mom the full account. I could see that Lilian was genuinely happy being taken care by Ding Ma. She loved Ding Ma, and obeyed her every command. In turn, the love Ding Ma had for Lilian was also clearly evident. Lilian was so enamored with Ding Ma's home cooking that for the rest of her life, she would demand Shanghainese dishes such as noodles in soup or dumplings whenever she was treated to a restaurant meal.

After lunch came the highlight of the visit for me, and I am sure for Lilian as well: we got to play ball. She obviously could not chat with me, nor could we play board games or cards or any sports such as badminton or table tennis. I could not remember how I discovered that this was something she could manage and enjoyed: she would fetch her hollow plastic ball which was smaller and lighter than a volleyball. We would go to a nearby side corridor-hallway, and stand at each end of the corridor about 8 feet apart, and roll that ball on the ground to each other. Back and forth, back and forth, we would play roll and catch ball. It delighted me to no end that she had so much fun with that simple game. We would play ball for "hours;" in reality, it was perhaps half an hour or so. Lilian and I really bonded over roll-the-ball; it was the most gratifying half-hour each month, in her life and in mine, while it lasted.

Mid-afternoon would come too soon to bring the visit to a close; it was time to bid Lilian farewell for another month. I always felt so forlorn walking away from her block and toward the bus. The feelings were a potent cocktail of rage (it was not fair that Lilian did not get to live the same life we did), sadness (that I had to leave her and would not be able to see her again for another month), injustice (Why?! Why?! Why?!), contentment (Lilian was finally taken care of by someone who loved her, and even though she was not physically with us—her family—Lilian was clearly happy), and then more sorrow (how I wished everything were different, and how I wished I had the power to change everything). Such emotional wrenching would only deepen with each passing year as our family moved up the socioeconomic ladder, as we moved from our one-bedroom apartment in low-income housing to a 3-bedroom apartment in the Mid-Levels (literally joining the middle class), and as I enjoyed being enrolled in an exclusive parochial all-girls school when I was in Primary 3 (the 3rd Grade).

As if to accentuate the stark contrast, after each visit, Mom and Dad would usually take us shopping at "Sincere," the large department store in Mongkok on the Kowloon side. We lived on Hong Kong Island, and very seldom traveled across the famed Victoria Harbour to the peninsula known as Kowloon and the New Territories, all of which (and an assortment of outlying islands) totaling 396 square miles made up the British Crown Colony of Hong Kong. Sincere was where Lina and I, and later Vivian, learned how to enjoy browsing and shopping, and even eventually got addicted to shopping. It had everything, from toys to clothes to kitchenware to furniture. Then there was "Koffee Korner," a fancy, little café within the store. In a good month when Mom and Dad had disposable income, we would have a treat—afternoon tea at Koffee Korner, complete with delectable pancakes (crepes, really) filled with fresh strawberries, and freshly baked cheese scones. The guilty pleasures felt so much guiltier when I had just been with and seen how the "have-not's" eked out a living.

There were also a handful of times when Dad would fetch Lilian to come home for a weekend stay. I had almost forgotten about those visits as they were utterly too painful to remember; I had thus relegated the memories of such visits to the deepest recesses of my recollection. I anticipated each visit with great joy, as I could play roll-a-ball with Lilian. I could also show her things in our home (which I considered her home as well), and play with her with all the toys and games we had at home. Reality was that Lilian would get bored easily and become temperamental. As much as I thought it was her home as well, it was a strange environment for her, and was probably quite stressful for her after a while when she would miss Ding Ma. Mom was not very motherly or hospitable toward Lilian, a fact that I secretly resented but could not do anything about or even acknowledge. All too soon, it would come time for Lilian to return to Ding Ma, and I would feel as if my innards were being torn asunder. Why did she, *my* sister, have to leave home? Why couldn't she stay with us? Those separations were altogether far too painful for the youngster me to experience and assimilate. I am quite sure those ghastly experiences made me cling onto people whom I should have left long ago; separation anxiety was my undoing growing into and through my adulthood.

When I left Hong Kong in 1972, I had no idea that I would be leaving for good, and thus, would not be playing roll-a-ball with Lilian monthly anymore. It was fashionable, at least for those who could afford it, to study abroad for a few years and then return to Hong Kong. Everyone presumed that I would follow the same trajectory. I was not thinking that far into the future; I simply wanted to get away from what I perceived to be a very stifling Chinese society, and to experience the personal freedoms in the United States that I heard so much about. My family could not afford to send me abroad for college, but I was awarded a full scholarship to study at Barnard College in New York City. Little did I know then just how fortunate and privileged I was.

In 1974, I returned home for the summer. I am sure I visited Lilian during those 3 months. I have no specific recollection, because I was then preoccupied with fomenting a feminist movement and raising feminist consciousness in Hong Kong. I was also busy with personal pursuits.

For some reason, I and my parents must have expected that I would return home every couple of years or so, but that turned out not to be the case. In 1976, my parents came to New York City to attend my graduation from Barnard, and hence, that was my excuse not to return to Hong Kong. In the summer of 1978, I had finished my first year of law school, and Dad had survived surgery to excise a cancerous kidney. That was good enough an excuse to send me home to Hong Kong again. I was there for just one month, but then and there, I knew for the first time that I would in all likelihood *not* be returning to Hong Kong; it was not my home anymore. I preferred to live in the United States, if only there was a way for me to become a permanent resident.

The realization that I would probably not return to Hong Kong permanently made that one-month visit in August of 1978 excruciatingly emotional. I visited with my maternal Grandmother whom I loved and adored. Growing up, we also visited her about once a month. Those monthly outings were joyous, as I would get to see and play with my cousin Grace who was four years my senior. She was the first-born of Fourth Uncle, one of my mother's three elder brothers (mother was the Seventh daughter). Grandmother would give us treats such as bits of dried scallop to gnaw on; that was a very expensive delicacy. She would tell us stories about *the* war: the Japanese invasion of China in the 1930's and the occupation of Hong Kong by the Japanese during World War II. My worldview was thus molded, during my formative years, by my Grandmother's war stories. Other times, we would listen to the radio together; Grandmother loved listening to the radio. This was before even black-and-white television was popular. I learned to appreciate Cantonese operas from these listening sessions.

Grandmother lived with Grandfather and their Ninth daughter on the ground floor, with Fourth Uncle and his family (Fourth Aunt, cousin Grace, her younger twin sisters Alza and Athena, and a younger brother Arthur) living upstairs, of an old, two-storey home in Tai Hang, the district east of Causeway Bay which in recent decades has become a bustling über shopping magnet and tourist destination. The home must have been very grand at the turn of the 20th century, as it was spacious by Hong Kong standards, and had a front yard and garden with an iron gate. It, however, did not have indoor plumbing or gas hookup for the kitchen; cooking was accomplished on an old-fashioned wood- or coal-burning stove. Electrical wiring was added much later; lighting was a lightbulb dangling at the end of a wire hanging from the ceiling. It also did not have interior walls. Rooms were divided by screens and panels. That was not unusual, as there were no interior walls in our one-bedroom apartment either; a lineup of wardrobes served as the demarcation between the bedroom and the living room.

I loved climbing up and down the stairs at Grandmother's house as it was literally an adventure. One could go upstairs the boring and cumbersome way: unlock and go out the backdoor on the ground floor, lock the backdoor, then go up the flight of cement steps, walk across a small overpass shared with the next door neighbor, knock on the entrance door, and then enter the second floor via that entrance door. The daring way to go up and downstairs was to use the narrow and steep ladder (it was too rudimentary to qualify as "stairs") from the ground floor kitchen up to the small rooftop terrace (it was the roof over Grandfather's living quarters), walk across the terrace, then climb another steep and narrow ladder from the terrace to a large window on the second floor, and climb through that window to enter. It was definitely quaint, charming, and challenging, especially when one was holding something, such as a lunch tray, in one hand.

Grandmother, then in her early 60's, climbed up and down those ladders regularly, and often carrying something in one hand. She was an amazing woman; in addition to keeping the ground floor immaculate, she kept close tabs on all her grown children and the growing brood of grandchildren. She and cousin Grace were very close. Grace told me that Grandmother used to take her to the Buddhist temple, which happened to be located just a few hundred yards from the home, for special Buddhist celebrations. Grace noted the temple's uniqueness—its tidiness and serenity—unlike most other Buddhist temples which were bustling with worshippers praying and making offerings, rendering the air thick with incense smoke. Decades later, I would learn that Grandmother's temple belonged to the same elite Buddhist sect as Lina's temple—Shingon Buddhism, otherwise known as Esoteric Buddhism. There are no "coincidences" in life; who would have guessed that, decades after Grandmother's passing, one of her grandchildren (and the least likely one) would attain the rank of Acharya in that exact Esoteric Buddhist tradition.

About once a year, Grandfather and Grandmother would host a feast at their home on special occasions such as Grandfather's birthday, and the birth of my cousin Arthur. I loved those feasts, not only because the food was absolutely delicious and plentiful, but I would get to play with Grace for the entire evening. There would be three to four big, round tables, each seating twelve people. Relatives that I would see only once or twice a year would arrive in droves beginning around 7 p.m. Those included Grandfather's siblings, their grown children (my many aunts and uncles), and their children (many more of my cousins). It was a very festive affair. Gourmet twelve-course dinner was prepared by professional chefs in Grandmother's kitchen. I used to watch with amazement as the chefs worked their magic, preparing gourmet dishes for fifty people over wood-burning stoves. The caterer not only prepared the food on site, but provided everything for the banquet—the tables and chairs, cups and glasses, dishes, chinaware, chopsticks, even the beverages. Those were the good old days. Dinner would be served around 9 p.m. I can smell the food just thinking about it: flash-fry whole cashew with shredded chicken and celery; crab meat with straw mushrooms; shark fin soup (very politically and environmentally incorrect); crispy roast chicken; steamed whole fish; braised duck feet with vegetables and large, whole black mushrooms, and so on through to two or three dessert selections, until everyone was positively stuffed.

In August of 1978, I trekked back to Illumination Terrace to visit with Grandmother. How she had aged in just 6 years. I still remembered the day I left for America when she and Fourth Uncle and Aunt and their family all came to the Airport to bid me farewell. I knew they were very proud of me, as I was the first one of my generation to go abroad for higher education. Fifth Uncle left for America decades before me, he got married, had children, and never returned home. I had never met him, but I would; after a few days' stopover in San Francisco to visit my friend Rebecca Chin who left for the States when we were in Form II (8th grade), I would be stopping over in Los Angeles to meet him, Fifth Aunt and my two cousins, Anne and Nelson, for the first time.

Grandmother's two-storey home was still as I remembered it; it was comforting that nothing much had changed there. Her eyesight had deteriorated, but otherwise she seemed hale and healthy. I do not recall whether we went out to have dim-sum lunch, or what specifically we talked about. I do remember Vivian was with me, as she was wearing a t-shirt with a picture of a skeleton on the front, and Grandmother thought the depiction was of a bunch of grapes. We laughed but didn't have the heart to correct her as we did not want to scare her and could not in any case explain why Vivian would wear "skeleton clothes." I also vividly remember returning home that evening, recording a cassette tape for Bev (we had met the year prior), telling her about my visit with

Grandmother and, with tears in my eyes, how I felt I would not be seeing Grandmother again as she would probably pass away before my next visit to Hong Kong. I knew by then that, like Fifth Uncle, I would not be returning home; Hong Kong was not my home anymore. What if I had returned to Hong Kong and sought my "fame and fortune" there, instead of getting tangled in what turned out to be decades of epic struggles in the United States? Idle fantasies and sheer speculation; it was not meant to be, and that was not how life unfolded. Grandmother did pass away in 1987, and I did not get to return to Hong Kong again until October of 1988. Hence, my hunch was spot-on—1978 was the last time I would see Grandmother.

I also visited Lilian during my short month in Hong Kong in 1978. Ding Ma had passed away by then. I was told that Lilian seemed to understand the concept of death; she attended Ding Ma's funeral and cried. I could only imagine her grief; she had spent her entire childhood and teenage years in Ding Ma's loving embrace and was well fed with Ding Ma's Shanghainese home-cooking. Before Ding Ma passed away, Lilian was transferred in 1976 to a dormitory set up specifically for girls and women with Down syndrome. It was run by a venerable charitable organization called Po Leung Kuk which had operated orphanages in Hong Kong for many years. Our parents were extremely fortunate in having the right "connection" to someone in the social welfare department who in turn was able to secure for Lilian one of only 50 or so beds in that dormitory. The dormitory was one of only a handful of boarding facilities specifically for people with Down syndrome. Back when, they did not classify the levels of Down syndrome disability in admitting residents to the dormitory. Lilian was severely affected by the chromosomal disorder, but some of her dorm-mates were able to speak and were even gainfully employed.

The dormitory was out of the way somewhere on the Kowloon side. Dad had to lead the way; it took a ferry ride across the Harbour and several bus transfers to get there. I had very little recollection of the facility or the visit itself; it was simply too painful to remember. By then I knew I would not be returning to Hong Kong permanently, and my next visit would be years in the unknown future; I would not be able to see Lilian for years to come. In other words, that was a farewell visit, for years to come. Lilian would not know or understand that, of course; and that was perhaps the saddest aspect of this agonizing situation. It is almost a cliché to say that it was heartbreaking, but it utterly, simply was. I only remembered trying very hard to hide my tears on the bus ride home from the visit; I did not want to unduly upset Dad. I did not realize that that pain would haunt me so that the only way I could cope with the separation was to forget Lilian altogether. Hence, I actually managed to *not* see her in my next visit to Hong Kong, even though I was there from October 1988 to January 1989. It was of course not deliberate or intentional; it was entirely subconscious. Between Mom's subconscious denial of Lilian, and my subconsciously not wishing to revisit the pain, I somehow found one excuse after another not to visit Lilian. I would suggest that I needed to see Lilian, and Mom would counter with how the weather was not ideal, that it was pouring rain or too chilly, for instance, or how it was too far away, or how I really did not have enough time to go visit. I did not insist, and I did not persist. Three months went by and I returned to the States, not realizing what I had wrought.

Several years later, during one of my therapy sessions, I happened to mention Lilian. My therapist, Dr. Sara E. Byer, was surprised that I had never mentioned Lilian, my younger sister with Down syndrome, until then even though I obviously had talked about all the other members of my family in the three or four years that I had been in therapy with her. I was in turn surprised that she was surprised, and brushed aside her probing follow-up questions. I nonchalantly told her that there were many people and events that I had not mentioned in my therapy. Being an experienced therapist, she would not let me "off the hook" that easily. My and our family's unspoken "secret" of benign "neglect" of Lilian was laid bare there and then. Just a few more probing questions later, I completely broke down in tears, sobbing uncontrollably, horrified that I, too, like Mom, had succumbed to fading Lilian out of my life.

For weeks afterwards, I would cry at the drop of a hat just thinking about Lilian. I was sick with irredeemable grief and regrets and shame. That did not mesh with the "macho attorney" image I thought I had to maintain during the day. At home at night, I let those tears flow freely. I could not believe how I managed not to see Lilian during the three months I was in Hong Kong in late 1988. It was totally unforgivable; I had no excuse for those years of benign neglect. Even more confounding was how Bev did not seem to understand my grief or offer any emotional support. I would realize much later that, over the years, it was I who had inferred or projected empathetic qualities that Bev herself did not possess. That episode was a much needed wake-up call, not so much about Bev's lack of empathy or moral support, but about our "family secret" named Lilian. In the ensuing months of weekly sessions, I worked with Dr. Byer, who was worth her weight in gold, through the traumatic effects of experiencing Lilian's being removed from our home, the hurt and pain of witnessing the increasing inequalities of our lives, the grief of our parents' growing disavowal of her existence, and rationalizing my own benign neglect of my beloved sister in the decades since my childhood. It was the unlocking of a floodgate of emotions—regrets, grief, guilt, rage, shock, sadness; incredible, immeasurable sadness.

Yet, nothing discernible happened or changed after that cathartic process, other than my feeling more in control of my emotions and my having a profound understanding of Lilian's significance in my life. Perhaps that was all I could handle at that time. That was also when Lina had returned to Hong Kong in mid-1993, followed by Vivian in mid-1995. Vivian resumed the regular visits with Lilian, allowing me to vicariously take comfort in believing that Lilian was once again being well looked after and well loved by her family. Every three weeks, Vivian would take Lilian out for a gluttonous lunch and shopping spree. Vivian would then supply us with an abundance of photographs showing a very happy and chubby Lilian eating up a storm and delighting in the new clothes and shoes and snacks that Vivian showered her with. With the advent of cell phones, I was even able to "talk with" Lilian during Vivian's visits. I was told Lilian loved listening to my (and Dad's) voice, as she loved listening to the radio (echoes of Grandmother's past). It was necessarily a brief, one-way conversation, as Lilian was either silent or would only "grunt" into the telephone. It was a fine, new routine; I felt reconnected to Lilian, and I even felt absolved from taking further remedial action or otherwise having to pay penance for decades of benign neglect.

That sufficed until Lilian was diagnosed with breast cancer, just as Mom was battling her colon cancer. It was another jolt of a wake-up call. Nonetheless, I was too preoccupied with "saving" Mom and with my professional obligations at work for me to do much other than monitoring from afar Vivian's heroic efforts in "saving" Lilian. Vivian was the only one who could conjure Lilian into taking umpteen mammograms, undergoing a mastectomy in early 2003, followed by 3 months of chemotherapy and then five weeks of daily radiation. Miracle of miracles, Lilian not only survived the horrific surgery and post-surgical treatments, she positively thrived. After the surgery and while she was still in the hospital, she had a prodigious appetite, demanding Vivian to bring her roasted chicken drumsticks and noodles in soup as snacks after each full meal. She regained her fighting weight and then some. Even more startling was Vivian's report that Lilian had somehow become smarter and able to speak many more words.

Vivian half-jokingly attributed that stunning development to the effects of her radiation treatment; if so, that would certainly be the most unexpected and unorthodox beneficial side effects of radiation. Call it a miracle or a hoax, I am now convinced that such unknowable events do happen all the time, to anyone and everyone. One simply has to turn down the noise, pay attention, and acknowledge their manifestation.

In early fall of 2003, Hong Kong—Lilian, actually—beckoned. No more excuses, no more delays, no more postponement, and certainly no more benign neglect. Work would never let up enough, there would never be a more opportune time, and I would never be in better physical health, to make the trip. Mom was gone, Lilian had just survived advanced breast cancer, and all of us were not getting any younger. I did not even care if "mysterious forces" would again wreak havoc when I returned from Hong Kong. If not now, when? "When" indeed. Thanksgiving was the answer when I checked my calendar. I could take that long weekend and stretch it out to a 2-week escapade so as to justify the expense and the long flight. It was also immediate enough that I could not change my mind, but just far enough in advance to give me sufficient time to wrap up critical cases. There was no way Bev could have talked me out of this trip even if she had tried. My mind was made up; twenty-five years was a ridiculously, shamefully long time for me not to have called in on my beloved sister.

News of my intended visit caused a stir, for I had not returned "home" for twenty-five long years. Buddies from my primary and secondary school days were elated in anticipation. We were and still are a tight-knit group. We bonded when we were mere children, and that bond held through our rebellious youth, ambitious young adulthood, and mellowing middle-age. Vivian was extremely excited, planning meals at restaurants and sightseeing outings for many of the days of my stay. Uncharacteristically, Lina also chimed in with two requests for me. First, she asked that I go to her Buddhist temple to pay respects to Mom; she had consecrated a "sacred space" in the temple for Mom so that we could visit with and pray to her. Of course I would be happy to pay homage to Mom at the temple. Even though I was not a Buddhist, it was very honorable and thoughtful of Lina to secure a place there for Mom's spirit to dwell. Second, she had made an appointment for me to see her two traditional Chinese doctors as soon as I arrived. I was a bit startled by that request, but figured that those herbal brews "prescribed" by traditional Chinese doctors were similar to Mom's chicken soup—they never hurt anyone. Even though I had no idea why I had to see those Chinese doctors, or what they could possibly do for me, I acceded to Lina's request.

Dad was already in Hong Kong; he left Windsor in October. He had not returned to Hong Kong since he emigrated to Windsor in 1993. Hence, it was high time that he visited with his friends and our relatives there, and of course, that he spent some time with Lilian again. Dad was staying at Lina's apartment. I was welcomed to stay there as well, but I figured it would be overcrowding if I also took up lodging there. Vivian lived with her husband, Ted, in an efficiency apartment. It was meant to be: I stumbled upon a hotel conveniently located in Wanchai with a tiny room available for those weeks at an incredibly affordable rate. The hotel room was so pint-size that it was actually quaint. It was barely large enough for a twin bed, a small wardrobe, a tiny desk and a minuscule counter where I could heat water for tea or coffee; there was a small bathroom along the narrow corridor leading from the door to the room; the corridor, incidentally, was the only space to accommodate my two suitcases. The hotel was centrally located within walking distance to the shops and restaurants in

Causeway Bay, and with easy access to public transportation such as the subway.

Two months went by in a flash, and it was time to embark on that long postponed journey. To express her displeasure with my making that trip, Bev announced well in advance that she would not be driving me to or picking me up from the Detroit Metro Airport. Her reasoning was that she detested my family's supposedly "using" me as a pack mule, lugging things for them back and forth; she declared that she would not be any part of such despicable practice of my "sick" family. Perhaps I was simply too used to her slights and insults to my family, and did not make much of a fuss. I did not have time to analyze her behavior, or to take offence or object to her unkind characterization of my family. Besides, her animus toward my family was not news; it had unfortunately been woven into the fabric of our relationship for some years, but had by then become particularly venomous. As usual, I simply went about fashioning a practical workaround, and accordingly made reservations for reasonably priced shuttle rides to and from the Airport. My more immediate concern was whether I could physically make the trip. Eighteen to twenty hours on a plane was grueling, especially when I had a spinal cord condition. The last time I survived that long flight was when I was fifteen years younger, when my spinal cord condition was not as dire, and when it was quite a few surgeries ago.

I left Detroit on Tuesday, November 25th and arrived in Hong Kong late in the evening the following day. I survived the flight, just barely, but I made it. Hong Kong was even more congested than I last remembered. The masses of humanity, the tightly packed high-rises, and the inundation of traffic all vied for space in the landscape unfolding before me. I felt quite overwhelmed just as soon as I got off the plane. The conversations around me in Cantonese, my native dialect, sounded at once familiar yet jarring. My surroundings seemed strangely unfamiliar, bordering on exotic. Fifteen years earlier, my plane landed via a singular runway jutting out into the Victoria Harbour and amidst jam-packed buildings surrounding the venerable Kai Tak Airport. Hong Kong was still a British colony then. In 2003, I was met by Dad and Vivian at the ultra-modern Hong Kong International Airport, purpose-built on Chek Lap Kok Island. Hong Kong had by then become "Hong Kong SAR, China." I was a stranger in my home country; even my Hong Kong identity card shown to the immigration officer at the Airport was woefully outdated and almost not recognized.

We took the airport express bus to my hotel in Wanchai. Along the way on that long bus ride, I tried to acclimate to the sights, sounds and views of the new Hong Kong. I did not recognize much, for everything seemed to have changed vastly in the interim fifteen years. When I was in Hong Kong last, there were very few freeways, there was no metro subway (called "MTR" for Mass Transit Railway), public areas were not as neat and tidy, and people were hardly as polite. It was almost midnight, yet many shops and restaurants were still doing bustling business. Having spent decades of my adult life in a tame and lame suburban Detroit neighborhood, I had forgotten how vibrant city life could be. I anticipated with trepidation and excitement spending the ensuing two weeks in this intoxicating mix of intrigue and nostalgia.

My first full day in Hong Kong, Thursday, November 27th happened to be Thanksgiving Day in the States. The highlight of the day was visiting Lilian at her Po Leung Kok dormitory that evening, and taking her out for dinner. Vivian had advised the caregivers there to prepare Lilian for the dinner outing, as she normally would when she took Lilian out for meals and shopping every three weeks. The dormitory had by then moved to Kwun Tong, still quite a distance from center of town on the Kowloon side. The modern and convenient MTR saved us several bus transfers and a ferry ride across the Harbour. For the last portion of our journey, we had to take a "light bus" (a 14-passenger van) to go up the small hill to a building where Lilian's dormitory was located.

It was a nondescript, mixed-use high-rise building, one of many at that location but decidedly more upscale than the drab structures in the resettlement housing project, and in a more civilized neighborhood. Dad, Vivian and I walked up a flight of stairs to the second-floor dormitory. By then, my heart was thunderously pounding with anticipation and anxiety. What if Lilian did not remember me? What if she did not recognize me? I would not blame her at all if she did not have a clue as to who I was. After all, I was the one who had abandoned her, even if only subconsciously and unintentionally, for twenty-five years.

We arrived at a large entrance door with an iron gate; the door was opened but the gate was locked. Even before we were at the gate, I could hear Lilian's voice (yes, I did recognize her voice) grunting and hollering excitedly. She could tell (from our footsteps?) that Vivian was arriving for their usual outing, and was calling the social workers-caregivers to unlock the gate. Dad and Vivian let me step in front of the gate first. The gate had many "slits," and I could see and immediately recognize Lilian standing on the other side of the gate. I started tearing up before a single word was said. Lilian stared at me for the longest time through the gate while she kept hollering for someone to open the gate. A caregiver came and unlocked the gate, and Lilian rushed out to hug Vivian and Dad. She kept staring at me. I did not know what to think or say; tears of joy came gushing out of my eyes.

As usual Vivian brought Lilian her favorite foods and snacks, new clothes, and sundries. This was apparently their routine, and Lilian couldn't wait to inspect her "loot." So off to the caregivers' office we went, with Lilian gleefully rummaging through her bountiful gifts. The caregivers would then check and store the items for Lilian. I was busy taking pictures to capture those precious and happy moments. Lilian seemed to be fully preoccupied and extremely pleased with her presents to notice my presence. I presented to Lilian my one present for her: a plastic ball similar to the one that we used to roll on the floor back and forth at Ding Ma's. I was hoping the ball would jog her memory about our time together in the years long gone by. She hurriedly carried the ball into her room and put it in her locker for safekeeping, without letting on whether she had any idea what the ball symbolized. Lilian knew from her routine with Vivian that a gluttonous meal was on the agenda, and so, she hurried us to leave the dormitory as soon as she was satisfied with her "haul" for the month.

Immediately noticeable to me was how remarkably more verbal and intelligent Lilian had become, exactly as Vivian reported shortly after Lilian completed her radiation treatment. Lilian not only thrived but fairly blossomed as a result of her radiation therapy. I could hear Lilian utter distinct words and phrases instead of just grunts in different tones. Astonishingly, she could vocalize simple phrases such as "Let's go," "I am in pain," "I'm okay," and many more. Simply stated, Lilian amazed and dazed me; she was "Exhibit A" for the adage that there are hidden blessings in every challenge.

Lilian bid farewell to her dorm-mates and caregivers as we left the dormitory and started walking to the light bus stop. I was startled when she walked next to me, took my hand in hers, and we walked down the hill together hand-in-hand. After a few more steps, she lightly pinched my arm. At first I was puzzled, but then it dawned on me that Lilian was trying to ascertain if I was "real," that she was not dreaming or hallucinating, that it was indeed her "big sister" who had returned at long last after twenty-five momentous years—practically half our lifetime. Thank goodness she didn't die in her 20's as Dr. Chau forewarned. Lilian not only remembered and recognized me, she had missed me. Tears streamed down my face.

For the special occasion, we went to a fancy Chinese restaurant in city center on the Kowloon side, instead of a neighborhood restaurant near the dormitory in Kwun Tong. Lina joined us at the restaurant. Dinner was sumptuous; after all, it was Thanksgiving, Chinese-style. We ordered Peking duck served tableside, several seafood dishes, as well as Lilian's favorites: chicken prepared in various ways, steamed whole fish, and of course, noodles in soup. Lilian's appetite was prodigious. She looked marvelously healthy, even on the chubby side. No one would have believed that she had spent the better part of the year battling cancer, and undergoing chemotherapy and radiation. During dinner, Lilian even played "food fight" with Vivian, and she was able to grasp humor in speech and behavior and react accordingly. Her leap in verbal skills and intelligence was nothing short of miraculous.

We took many photographs of that family reunion dinner; for the first and only time, we sent out a photo-card that Christmas with one of the photographs from that evening. Vivian told us that Lilian would usually holler and even scream that she wanted to "go home" after she had had her fill of the feast, even if others were still eating. However, she was uncharacteristically well behaved in that regard that night. Lilian "talked" a lot, too, that night; it was thrilling for me to hear for the first time in my life her verbally expressing herself.

After dinner, we walked back to the MTR station to take the subway home. I would take a different train after the first leg of the journey, and Vivian would take Lilian back to the dormitory in another train. When we were riding in the same train for the first leg of the trip home, Lilian suddenly gently touched my eyeglasses. I looked at her, and immediately understood what she was trying to say to me with that gesture: "What with these glasses? You didn't have them before." She was right, of course; I did not need to wear prescription glasses until early 1996. That simple gesture confirmed to me that Lilian indeed remembered me, knew exactly who I was, and even remembered that I did not wear glasses previously. She remembered everything . . . including the fact that I had been away for a long, long time. More tears swelled up to smear my eyeglasses. It was a very, very special night.

I could have returned to the States there and then, and I would have felt perfectly gratified and fulfilled. It was truly a day for Giving Thanks, and strictly speaking, mission had been accomplished. Yet I wanted to stay, forever if I could, so that I would not have to leave Lilian ever again. It was only Day 2 of my sojourn, and I wanted to enjoy Lilian's company and having many more meals with her in the two precious weeks before I *had* to return to work.

I awoke the following day feeling quite unwell. The stress of the previous weeks of trying to get ahead of my cases so that I could be away from the office for two weeks, the fatigue from the lengthy flight, the 13-hour time difference, and the emotional drama since my arrival, all conspired to make me call in a sick day. Nevertheless, I made it to the lunch date with my very special, dear friend, Pearl Wong Po Chu. She had just retired (for the second or third time) from her senior public relations position at Commercial Radio Hong Kong, and was looking forward to "exhaling" for a while, after which she would perhaps take on worthy consulting projects. Her official title at CRHK would only hint at her important role there. She was the muse and confidante of Winnie Yu Tsang, general manager of CRHK and one of Hong Kong's "movers and shakers" of our generation. The three of us were classmates from our primary (elementary) school days at St. Stephen's Girls' College (SSGC); Pearl and Winnie had been the closest friends since kindergarten at SSGC; they gave new meaning to "life-long" friends. Pearl and I, too, had very much stayed in touch over all those many years.

Pearl had a most colorful and bold career path. She started out in the highly competitive pressure cooker that was the garment-fashion industry in the 1970's and 1980's Hong Kong. In the mid-1980's, she joined Winnie at CRHK, and mingled with the Who's Who in the Hong Kong showbiz and entertainment scene. Ten years of maximum glitz and glamor later, she and her life partner Ellen (not her real name), whom she "married" in 1987 when marriage equality was still a pie in the sky, retired to Vancouver. Just a couple of years later, Winnie lured Pearl back to Hong Kong for an encore stint at CRHK. When we met up again that fine afternoon in late November, 2003, she seemed happy and content with her well-earned early retirement. Shortly after I returned to the States, Pearl invested in a bakery specializing in high-end pastries. She has always been a gourmet chef, but operating a bakery was not what I would have expected with her much envied Rolodex. Alas, that was a relatively brief whimsical diversion. In 2006, her beloved father passed away, which might have triggered her revisiting religion and spirituality. Pearl and I were baptized and confirmed together into the Anglican Church when we were in Form Lower VI (12th grade). I had strayed farther and farther away from organized religion, and Pearl seemed to me to be also a "nominal" Christian over the years. Her "rediscovery" of Jesus found her becoming very active with an evangelical congregation. I would learn a few years later that she confronted a spiritual crisis when the elders of that congregation pressured her to choose between serving Christ on the one hand, and honoring her personhood and her commitment to her lesbian relationship and life partner of more than twenty years on the other hand. After much soul searching and many prayers, including a "retreat" in Vancouver where she stumbled upon a gay congregation, my amazing Pearl enrolled in the Chinese University of Hong Kong in late 2008, taking a couple of divinity classes for taste, then jumped in with both feet. She was invited to spend her Fall 2011 semester as a guest scholar at the Yale Divinity School in New Haven, Connecticut. She and two other SSGC classmates from the East Coast came to visit me at the end of that semester, and we had a memorable reunion weekend. Pearl graduated with a Bachelor of Divinity degree in May of 2013. The title of her thesis was "Coming Out to Herself: A Lesbian Feminist Theology of Empowerment For Lesbian Christians in Hong Kong." Being a credentialed minister, she has been leading and ministering to a "queer theology" congregation in Hong Kong. Pearl is the shining star of "radicalization," in the best sense of that term, in my book.

Back in late November 2003 in Hong Kong, I was still trying to acclimate myself to my old hometown. The following day, a Saturday, found me rejuvenated enough for a full day packed with special highlights. In the late morning, Lina and Dad accompanied me to my appointment with Lina's two Chinese doctors. Their clinic was in Mongkok, a bustling area on the Kowloon side. We had to walk a distance from my hotel to the MTR station in Wanchai, then changed trains once, and walked quite a distance again from the Mongkok MTR station to the building where the clinic was located. Thankfully, it was a gorgeous Fall morning with crisp, cool air; making that trip in the sweltering humidity and heat in the summer would be quite taxing.

The clinic was a tiny suite on a high floor in a commercial building. It was staffed by two women doctors, their diplomas and licenses hung prominently on the wall in the small reception area. They were not just "alternative healers," but properly licensed practitioners of traditional Chinese medicine and acupuncture. There were two altars with Buddhist statues and incense burners, one on Dr. Cheung Wai Man's side and one on Dr. Lui Chiu Yu's side of the room. It didn't take long for me to realize that both doctors were also members of the same Buddhist temple where Lina was receiving her Buddhist training. I would later learn that Dr. Cheung was in fact also a high ranking archaya at the temple. Both doctors were about my age, and they were very friendly and casual, immediately putting me at ease. There were about four or five other patients, all women, in the clinic at the time receiving or waiting to receive treatment. Everyone was in the main room in the clinic, which was an open area with several treatment tables, along with desks for the doctors where they would "listen to your pulse," and write the prescriptions. Off to the side was a small room packed to the rafters with herbs; that was their on-site apothecary-pharmacy.

It was refreshing to see two women doctors practicing together, and it was particularly nourishing receiving healing in a traditional Chinese medical equivalent of a women's clinic. As I had no idea why Lina sent me to these doctors, I had no expectations nor did I know what to tell the doctors what I was there for. Of course, my medical and surgical history by then was quite lengthy, complicated and highly unusual. However, I did not think traditional Chinese medicine, with its typical herbal medicinal brews, would have any impact on my medical condition one way or another. I was seen by Dr. Lui who checked my pulse, and gave me the once over. She muttered something about my having excessive "internal bruises." Then she asked me how long I was staying in Hong Kong and whether I could come to the clinic for ten sessions. That would mean I would be going there everyday except Sundays. I chuckled, as that would be my daily "assignment" even while I was supposedly on vacation. I was also very puzzled about the need for the ten sessions. Since I was not planning on taking any side trips, and since I could have their first appointment everyday at 10 a.m., I figured I would still have the rest of each day to do as I pleased, I agreed to the ten sessions.

For my first session, as with all the remaining sessions, Drs. Lui and Cheung took turns in giving me their signature treatment modality: gently vibrating various parts of the body with their hands to access the internal organs, various meridians and pressure points. Where and how on the patient's fully-clothed body the doctors would "vibrate" was a mystery known only to them. The vibration treatment would last about 45 minutes each session. At the end of each session, Dr. Lui would prescribe an herbal brew for me for the day, which she would dispense from the on-site apothecary. Much to my delight and relief, the medicinal teas did not have to be literally brewed for hours anymore. In the olden days, one would have to put the assorted roots, twigs, leaves, and medicinal herbs with the prescribed amount of water in a special clay pot and boil and slowly simmer it down to a cup or ¾ of a cup as prescribed. In the modern day version, the numerous traditional herbs had been extracted and refined into powder. I was given a pack of powder mixture which would conveniently dissolve in a cup of boiling water. Traditional Chinese medicine, enhanced by modern manufacturing techniques, had updated to becoming consumer oriented and user-friendly. I did not feel or see any difference or improvement after my first session and even after I drank the herbal tea that evening. I wondered how the remaining nine sessions could or would prove otherwise.

After my treatment, we had a delightful dim-sum lunch, or "yum cha" ("drink tea") to be precise. On the agenda for the afternoon was meeting Lilian somewhere on the Kowloon side where some sort of special event was going to take place. It sounded very vague to me, but I did not inquire further as I was simply happy to be seeing Lilian again so soon. Lina and Dad led the way, and an MTR ride, a bus ride, and a brisk walk later, we arrived at what appeared to be a public recreational park, a patch of open space where people from the neighborhood could play basketball, soccer, tennis, or practice group tai-chi and enjoy other similar outdoors activities. For that afternoon, a makeshift stage had been erected at one end of the park. Under a large tent and in front of the stage were numerous rows of folding chairs. A number of "booths" took up a good portion of the remainder of the park.

Vivian had arrived ahead of us; we found her with Lilian and several of Lilian's dorm-mates at one of the booths. When I eventually managed to orient myself and looked around, I realized that this was not an ordinary outing or picnic for Lilian and her dorm-mates. The large banner above the stage, and the decorations in the booths, informed me that this was the annual awards ceremony for the disabled in the entire Kwun Tong District, billed euphemistically as "Kwun Tong District International Rehabilitation Day." Each nominee for the numerous awards had a booth in which his or her achievements were detailed on six-foot tall bulletin boards illustrated with photographs, drawings, news clippings, and essays. Lilian's booth was meticulously and attractively decorated by the social workers-caregivers from her PLK dormitory. The bulletin board was filled with photographs of her hospitalization for mastectomy, her undergoing chemotherapy and radiation therapy, and visits by Vivian, Ted, and Lina during her hospitalization and recovery, along with get well cards and messages from her dorm-mates. Someone penned a moving and uplifting account of Lilian's courageous battle with breast cancer. Lilian recognized herself in the many photographs and excitedly pointed them out to me. "Click," "click," "click"—I could not stop taking pictures with my cameras.

Soon the proceedings were called to order. The numerous nominees, friends and family took their seats under the panoply. There must have been several hundred excited people in attendance. Guests of honor, including several Hong Kong Legislative Council members and local social celebrities and political leaders, were introduced as they took their seats on the stage. There were speeches by politicians, social service department bigwigs, and acknowledgement of the governmental and corporate sponsors. The awards ceremony followed, and there were quite a few trophies to be handed out. One was for courage, another for creativity, and another for kindness, and so forth. One by one, the beaming awardee went on stage to receive the little trophy engraved with his or her name and the title of the award, to shake hands with the luminaries while photographs were taken. All of a sudden we heard Lilian's name over the PA system: she had won the "Reappearance of the Rainbow" award. Clearly, the award celebrated her bravery and resilience, and the marvelous miracle of her having survived breast cancer. We were so startled that neither Vivian nor I had our cameras ready, but we managed to grab a few shots. Dad walked Lilian up onto the stage. Lilian obviously understood that she was the star of the moment; she smiled valiantly, and bowed slightly in receiving her trophy. She turned around to face the adoring audience triumphantly, and held the trophy tightly in her hands against her chest for the photographers to snap away. When Dad walked her back to our seats under the panoply, the Chan clan could not have been more joyous and proud of our severely Down syndrome daughter and sister. Vivian had brought sandwiches and snacks and cold drinks. We enjoyed an impromptu, celebratory family picnic on this perfect, sunny fall day in a nondescript public park in Kwun Tong.

Several more awardees went up the stage to be recognized, but we were too engrossed in our elation to notice, until suddenly, Lilian's name was announced again. We were even more startled this time around: Lilian had won the event's overall championship award, aptly named "Overcoming Life's Obstacles" award. It seemed that Lilian also understood that this was an even "bigger deal." She followed Dad up the stage again. This time she was jubilant; she could hardly contain her pride and delight. She raised the special trophy almost defiantly and high up in the air as the crowd approved with thunderous applause. It was a moment to be remembered, for life.

A triumphant Lilian with her well deserved trophies.
November 29, 2003, Kwun Tong, Kowloon,
Hong Kong.

As for me, I could not believe my good fortune. After twenty-five long years, I had somehow chosen this particular time to return, which fortuitously allowed me to personally witness Lilian at the zenith of her life, in ways that really mattered and counted. Again, I could have returned to the States there and then, and would have been perfectly content forever. This homecoming trip of mine had already surpassed being remarkable; to describe it as unforgettable is too one-dimensional. As far as I was concerned, it had hit historic proportions, and it was only my third full day in Hong Kong. It was late afternoon, and the PLK social workers were corralling their charges for the return trip to the dormitory. We were all on such a high that it was difficult to bid Lilian goodbye. Reluctantly, I waved goodbye, and could hardly wait for my next outing with Lilian.

Lina, Vivian, Dad and I had one more stop to make before we called it a day: Lina's Buddhist temple. It was in Kowloon Tong, in the shadow of the landmark Lion Rock. It was in a rather upscale, tranquil residential neighborhood, where many other temples were also located. I figured that it must be *feng shui* that this area was such a magnet for places of worship. Lina's temple had recently expanded with the construction of new wings and sanctuaries. The master Buddhist presiding over this sprawling empire was Master Li, who was quite the local celebrity for his flamboyant and entrepreneurial style, his popular annual Chinese astrological predictions and books, and his extremely high-end *feng shui* consultations for the rich and famous, among his many talents and enterprises. He even had a retail location in the white-hot shopping district of Causeway Bay, doing a bustling business selling his special brand of Buddhist trinkets, jewelry and *feng shui* implements.

On that particular Saturday late afternoon, many disciples were at the temple getting ready for the evening's program of lectures and worship. My understanding was that Lina would spend the weekend there receiving religious instruction and participating in the Buddhist rituals. The disciples were wearing a uniform—a simple robe over their clothes—with a belt of different colors denoting their respective ranks. Everyone seemed very disciplined and polite, unlike many other Buddhist temples I had been to over the years where the crush of worshippers was often noisy and unruly, and the smoke from incense burning choked the casual visitor. The grounds were very clean and neat, the atmosphere was serene and pious. There were huge statues of many *bodhisattvas* just about everywhere one turned. They made it clear to all visitors that they were treading on "hallowed ground;" Dad and I understood that due respect must be paid, even as we were not Buddhists. Vivian, an avowed atheist, was quite uncomfortable being there, especially after she was told she could not take photographs; she liked to "document" everything with her camera. I was, and still am, not one for organized religion, regardless of the creed or faith, even though I am a baptized and confirmed Anglican. I was quite impressed with Master Li's brood, though.

Lina led us through the main sanctuary to a special wing where many small "altars" were installed. She showed us where she had consecrated one for Mom, and we bowed solemnly to pay respects. I paused for a moment to reflect upon how sorely I had missed Mom, and how strange it felt to be standing in a Buddhist temple—to which Lina belonged—to be remembering Mom who was an agnostic. Around me were the Buddhists who, just a few months earlier, had helped Lina to ensure Mom enjoy a smooth and tranquil transcendence to the Other Side. It was a surreal yet poignant moment.

By Monday morning, it was time for my second session with Drs. Lui and Cheung. There was nothing extraordinary about the session; the treatment was the same as the first session given two days prior. I was beginning to wonder if I was wasting time, energy and money by agreeing to undergo the ten consecutive sessions. I still felt fatigued and lacking vitality, and my legs were getting increasingly numb and uncontrollable again. Walking was becoming challenging, again. I had to focus to make sure my legs would not get tangled so as not to trip and fall while I walked. Still, that was a much needed two-week reprieve for me; at least I woke up knowing I did not have to face another extremely intense, stressful and taxing 12-hour workday.

I was a guest at Pearl and Ellen's well-appointed apartment Monday night, enjoying a gourmet home-cooked dinner, with a lesbian couple friends of theirs. The lavish meal and lively conversations lasted well into the wee hours of the night. It had been years since I stayed out late. Hence, when I awoke early Tuesday morning to go to my third session with Dr. Lui and Cheung, it was beginning to feel as if I were reporting for work. Besides, I was feeling quite unwell from the late night soiree; my "advanced age" was showing.

From my hotel, it was a good 10- to 15-minute walk to the MTR station. I had to transfer trains at Admiralty; the subway ride was about 35 minutes in all. Then it was another 15-minute hike from the MTR station to the building where the clinic was located. In contrast, my usual workday involved a 10-yard walk from my house to my car in the garage, a leisurely 10-minute drive in suburban traffic to my workplace, and another 30-yard walk from the parking lot to my office. I would not have guessed that my supposed "downtime" life in Hong Kong turned out to be much more physically rigorous. People in Hong Kong walked all the time and everywhere, compared with people in suburban Motor City who would *drive* everywhere. My pampered (euphemistically speaking) body had a hard time adjusting to the much more physically demanding lifestyle, especially during my first few days in Hong Kong. Hence, while I was waiting for my treatment that Tuesday morning, I bemoaned yet again the questionable investment of time, energy and money in making this daily trek for some nebulous "vibration therapy" and herbal tea. I do not recall what the agenda was for the rest of that Tuesday, but I am sure it was jam-packed with sightseeing and more sumptuous meals. I had been away for such a long time that I had become your average and typical tourist in Hong Kong—just about everything and everywhere was unfamiliar and fascinating to me.

Came Wednesday morning, it was time again for my daily outing to the Chinese doctors. For some reason, I had overslept that morning. In order not to be late for my appointment, I had to skip breakfast and tried my best to race to the clinic. I walked as fast as I could to the MTR station, I then practically "flew" down the long flight of stairs to the correct level for the train that would take me to Mongkok. Once I arrived at the other end, I again walked very quickly to the clinic, and made it just in time. As a rule, I disliked being late if I could help it. As I lay on the treatment table receiving my daily dose of "vibration therapy," I was suddenly overcome with shock and astonishment. What I had just described—how I hurried all the way to make my appointment with my Chinese doctors—was certainly most ordinary and mundane to the average person. However, in my case, what had transpired that morning was nothing short of monumental. For too many years, I had not been physically able to quick-step, let alone "fly" down a long flight of stairs. Yet, that was exactly what I did that morning in my mad dash to the doctor's clinic. What happened?! How could that be?! How did I manage to accomplish such impossible feat?! Could it really have been the result of my treatment with the Chinese doctors? Alas, there was no plausible explanation otherwise; it *had* to be the vibration therapy and the herbal tea. I shuddered at that stunning realization; the impossible had become possible—I was *cured*. It was not quite a few months ago when I was fretting about having to decide on a neurosurgeon for yet another spinal cord surgery; I then congratulated myself for having postponed that decision till after my trip to Hong Kong.

After the session, I made a point of quick-stepping and "flying" down the stairs at the MTR station just to make sure I was not hallucinating earlier that morning. No, I was not. Indeed, I felt as if I had suddenly become a combination of all of those comic book heroes and heroines with superpowers, able to fly through the air and leap tall buildings in a single bound. I had not felt so physically fit and vibrant for years. I felt free and unfettered; I felt powerful and unencumbered. All in one swell swoop, I was allowed to reclaim my lost youthful health and vitality. It was beyond empowering; it was transforming.

As if that morning was not spectacular enough, the rest of that day turned out to be extraordinarily memorable because I went back to visit my grade school and high school, SSGC. Vivian accompanied me on that nostalgic visit; she also attended SSGC, from kindergarten to 11th grade (high school graduation in our system), six years behind me. I suppose Mom saw and liked the fact that I was faring well at SSGC, and thus decided to enroll Vivian in that school as well.

The last time I saw my school was in November of 1988, when I was in Hong Kong for my immigrant visa interview at the U. S. Consulate. I went to SSGC with Bev for a quick visit, and was greeted by my school principal, Dr. K. E. Barker, and Mrs. Judy Chua, my Domestic Science (no—that is not a joke nor a misprint) teacher who by then was the headmistress of the primary school. Before that brief, nostalgic visit, the last time I was on campus was in June of 1972, more than 30 years prior, when I graduated from Form Lower VI (grade 12).

Vivian and I, joined by Dad, started our stroll down memory lane with lunch at our favorite hangout during my school years— Czarina Restaurant. It was a restaurant that served Western cuisine, or the Cantonese version of Western cuisine. It was frequented by SSGC students as it was conveniently located across the street from one of SSGC's main gates. As we lived not far from SSGC, our family would also occasionally enjoy dinners there. On that day, we, of course, ordered borscht, the restaurant's signature soup, and I had my favorite dish—grilled cheese spaghetti. After lunch, Dad set out by himself to visit and browse the nearby Fung Ping Shan Museum, one of the museums of the University of Hong Kong. We used to live across the street from that museum. Hence, that was a nostalgic side trip for Dad, while Vivian and I revisited our alma mater. I did not mention to either of them of my new lease on life—my suddenly being fleet of feet—I wanted to savor the delightful secret all by myself for as long as the miracle lasted.

I did not recognize my primary school at all. The original, quirky school building, sadly, had been replaced by brand new buildings. Gone were the oh-so-1930's bathrooms, stone interior stairs, and the dimly lit classrooms with rickety swirling ceiling fans. The stubby 3-storey building was replaced by a nondescript multi-storey building. I understood the need to have more classrooms to provide more students with a quality education. Hence, unfortunately, functionality and necessity ruled, and the charm and endearing eccentricity were sacrificed.

On the other hand, much of my secondary school, including the grand Georgian-style main building, remained exactly the same as I remembered it. In fact, the main building had been officially designated as a Historic Site, and will forever be preserved. SSGC was established in 1906 as one of the few schools for girls. Legend has it that during World Wars I and II, part or all of the buildings were requisitioned to serve as a treatment center for wounded soldiers, many of whom died of their injuries there. Naturally, stories of haunted rooms and corridors abound. Therein lay a certain degree of schizophrenia and tension. Here was an Anglican school, steeped in faith in the Almighty and educating young minds in the best British pedagogy traditions, with the school's principal and a fair number of teachers imported from the British Isles. The students, on the other hand, were 99.9% Chinese, born and raised with Chinese culture, traditions, and even superstitions. Growing up in that otherwise noble academic environment, I had always felt, subconsciously if not consciously, as if I had a split personality. At once, I wanted to be more English than thou, yet I reckoned that I could never be British enough, and thus, I was always haunted by a subtle and implicit but constant putting down of oneself. Add to that a societal order and system of government based on the imperialist colonial model of mid-19th century vintage, and you had a heady mix of benign subjugation and inferiority complex as a subject of an empire which had outlived its days of glory, the sun having finally set on the Union Jack. That sense of inferiority was insidious, stealthily lurking just beneath the surface, and sabotaging many endeavors in my early adult years.

As for the outlandish rumors of supposed ghost sightings at my school, I never put much stock in them. Mom, the devout agnostic, never pressured us to be believers or non-believers of any faith or religion. I, for one, prided myself on being "enlightened" by my studies in the sciences and humanities. Scriptures classes at SSGC were mandatory, but I was not at all religious for most of my years at SSGC. I viewed Scriptures as history lessons with a different bent. Spirituality, metaphysics, and otherworldly phenomena were definitely not within my realm of understanding then. With hundreds of us students streaming—and often screaming—through those hallways, I figured whatever ghosts there might have been, if they existed at all, would have fled a long time ago for a more tranquil environment.

Then one fine afternoon on a weekend, probably during my Form III or Form IV year (9th or 10th grade), I encountered the inexplicable. I was at the school that Saturday afternoon for orchestra practice, or choir practice, or another extracurricular activity. Whatever activity I was there for was over, and the school was quite deserted, and I was getting ready to go home as well. I was walking along the corridor outside a set of classrooms on the second floor, which overlooked the lovely and lengthy treed path leading from one of the gates to the school building. An outdoor tennis court was on one side of the path, and a swing-set on the other side. I had walked that path to school on a daily basis countless times. Something, or some noise, made me enter one of those empty classrooms and look out the window to see who was down on that path or in the school yard. From my vantage point, I had a panoramic view of the beautiful path, the empty tennis court, the trees and greenery, and the swing-set. There was no one around at all as far as my eyes could see. Yet, something seemed out of place: one or more of the swings were swinging wildly back and forth—with no one on them. It was a calm and bright afternoon, with no breeze whatsoever. I thought perhaps whomever was on the swings had probably just got off and walked away and out of my line of sight, even as the swings kept swaying from the momentum. I continued watching for several minutes; the swings did not slow down, but kept swaying to and fro with gusto—without a rider. I could even hear the "eek, eek" squeaks from the swaying swings. Then and there, I realized that I was witnessing something that defied logical explanation. There suddenly seemed to have a chill in the air, and a stillness and hush. Such was the stuff of legends at my venerable school. I left in a hurry, and from then on, I subconsciously avoided staying too late by myself at school and definitely not going to the restrooms by myself if it was late in the day. Thank goodness I was too young and brash to be really scared. Back then, I had no concept of the paranormal, metaphysical or spiritual; I simply refused to believe in the supernatural or superstition. My view then was very pragmatic: I had witnessed something inexplicable and illogical, but I had never mentioned it to anyone. I certainly did not associate it with any esoteric or profound theories such as the Universe or the Divine was demonstrating to me forces and phenomena beyond those that we understood or accepted on this plane.

On this fine afternoon in early December of 2003, there was no paranormal phenomenon on campus save for pure nostalgia. Vivian and I walked through those familiar corridors, peeked into some of the classrooms, even checked out the vintage "water closets." Thankfully, nothing had changed, not even the beige-yellowish paint on the walls. I loitered in the assembly hall (Kwok Siu

Lau Hall) where the entire student body gathered each morning. We sang hymns, listened to readings from the Bible and a short sermon, announcements by the Principal, and recited the Lord's Prayer, before each day of classes. That was also the hall where we staged school plays and concerts, and where the annual Speech Day was held, which was the approximate equivalent of commencement. The grand piano on the stage transported me back in time more than thirty years prior when I occasionally would serve as the pianist for those morning assemblies.

We walked up to the top floor of the main building, which used to be off-limits to students. It was the residence for teachers from the United Kingdom; there was also a formal "staff dining room" on that floor. The residence was no longer in use, but the formal dining room—oh, so Edwardian—was still intact. Adjacent to the dining room was what probably used to be a sitting room or game room to which the diners would congregate for after-dinner libation. It had become an archive, showcasing mementos from the school's fabled past. There was an armoire with glass doors full of trophies. I walked up to take a closer look, and there they were: the two trophies awarded to me, and engraved with my name on a silver plate, when I was the school's badminton champion in Form I and Form II (7th and 8th grade). It was flattering to see that at least my name was so enshrined for posterity.

There was another locked glass-door cabinet containing the booklets printed each year for Speech Day. The one for 1971 brought back memories of my winning the award for "Most Improved in English" that year. The award was perhaps HK$100 with which I could purchase books of my choice. I went to Swindon Books and selected several books, one of which was Germaine Greer's then newly published and controversial *The Female Eunuch*. The Principal had that book wrapped—because of the depiction of a naked woman torso on the cover—before presenting me my chosen books to me on Speech Day. Such was the uptight moral environment in which I came of age. In retrospect, that also marked my awakening as a budding feminist activist; lesbian activism would have to come later, not until after I had left Hong Kong. I had always espoused the belief that Sisterhood was powerful, and I had always been proud that I was a women-loving woman. Asserting or expressing those views, however, was an extremely lonely, punishing, and devastating experience for a teenager in Hong Kong in the early 1970's.

I took a goodly number of photographs that afternoon, covering just about every facet of the school grounds, including quite a few shots of the Domestic Science room just for old time's sake. Cooking and sewing, as a science or otherwise, were utterly not my *forte*.

There I was, standing on the nurturing grounds of SSGC, 31 years after I left with bitter sweet memories. I was an ambitious, promising and naïve youngster in 1972, eagerly and boldly leaving the mothership for the land of the free and home of the brave. I would have never dreamed of how my life would have turned out in those three decades. What transpired during those years was stranger than fiction; and unbeknownst to me, what was to come would take my breath away.

There and then, gazing at my old school building, I savored a moment of not so much personal triumph but personal entitlement. Thirty years hence, through trials and tribulations and circuitous detours, I was a partner in a prestigious large corporate law firm. I was finally enjoying the practice of law, and was well remunerated for my efforts. Even though my work life consumed my entire existence, and even though sustaining my and Bev's lifestyle still had me in the red financially, the long-term outlook was enticing and promising. I figured I would work harder yet, get more clients for my firm, and would in turn earn a bigger bonus which would eventually get me out of my financial straits. I indulged in the trappings of being a highly-paid professional. I had always reveled in availing myself of the finer accoutrements in life, chalk it up to my elitist upbringing in an exclusive parochial school surrounded by affluent classmates. From designer clothes and shoes to BMW sport sedans, from Prada luggage to Leica cameras, from Montblanc writing instruments to Cartier eyewear, I lived a pampered, entitled and privileged lifestyle of materialistic luxury. It was a lifestyle that was all too seductive and addictive, but one that I could not really sustain. A bigger paycheck simply encouraged me to spend even more lavishly, thus fueling a monstrously self-destructive vicious cycle.

The ever-so-Edwardian formal Staff Dining Room,
St. Stephen's Girls' College.

In retrospect, there should not have been any sense of personal triumph or entitlement; a wake-up call to curb my wanton spendthrift ways should have sounded instead. A more profound introspection would have revealed the fallacy of any sense of accomplishment: the youngster who smartly stepped out of those school gates in 1972, so full of fight and hope and promise, and all that could be said after 30-plus years was that I was just another partner in a large corporate law firm. Whatever happened to my resolution to be a champion and advocate for the oppressed, the disadvantaged and the defenseless? Plainly, that was a promise yet to be fulfilled. There seemed to have been a gaping discrepancy between dreams and aspirations on the one hand, and reality and expediency on the other. Lest I be too harsh on myself, life had been at once multifarious and challenging, engaging and enlightening in those forty-plus years. My dear readers, read on.

I continued my daily morning ritual of treatment with the two Chinese woman doctors. Before I underwent these "vibration therapy" sessions, even though I was not that old in chronological age, I had felt for many years totally spent and worn out. Hence, imagine my thrill as, for the first time in decades, I felt young, vital and energized again. The "reconstructed" me went on to relish the sights and sounds of Hong Kong, the many reunion meals with school buddies, and more sumptuous feasts with Lilian, all with renewed vigor and vibrancy. I even played the part of the consummate tourist, visiting must-see places listed on tourism brochures: Victoria Peak, Stanley Market, Lan Kwai Fong, and Ocean Park. I took countless photographs, quite a few of which enlargements had been hanging in my home. It was the first real and relaxing vacation I had in a long time. Traveling, or vacationing, with Bev was a very tense affair as I would never know when she would throw a fit over whatever. Typically, it would erupt from unfounded accusations that I was supposedly flirting with another woman on the street or in a restaurant. Other times, it was her enochlophobia. I could understand the throngs of humanity getting on the train at a Hong Kong MTR station, but a fancy street lined with high-end designer shops in Toronto? She suddenly refused to walk on that particular street because there were "crowds." I did not realize until after we broke up that her behavior was not normal or acceptable. For all those years and many extravagant trips though, I indulged her, and I suffered needlessly.

My surprisingly eventful homecoming was fast drawing to a close. I believe it was a Friday night a week before I had to return to the States when we decided to have dinner at Lina's new condominium apartment. She had just moved from the Kowloon side back to the Hong Kong side. For a family of Hong Kong Islanders, we had always viewed "the Kowloon side" with a bit of alienation or even disdain. Hence, Dad was delighted that Lina moved back to the Hong Kong side and set up residence on the "right" side of the Harbour. For this special family reunion dinner, Dad had ordered snake soup, as well as many of our favorite gourmet dishes, from one of his friends who was a restaurant master chef. Lina's condo was a bit off the beaten path, far away from the madding crowd on the eastern edge of Hong Kong Island; it took two bus rides to get to her condo complex. The buildings were very modern and impressive: ultra-high ceiling lobby with marble walls, sophisticated intercom system to screen guests, complete with uniformed security personnel standing guard. Her unit was on a very high floor, with a spectacular panoramic view of the inlet through which a flotilla of ships, boats, Chinese junks, and luxury yachts entered Victoria Harbour. I thought to myself: for a Buddhist, Lina lived a very charmed life; then I chuckled to myself: the Chan girls certainly seemed to seek and relish the highlife.

Dinner was sumptuous and delectable; we had so many dishes that we ran out of room on the dining table. We were eating up a storm, talking giddily and loudly over each other, laughing silly, and having the proverbial food fights; it was just like old times. Mom should have been there; it would have been perfect if we had had the time to fetch Lilian to join in the fray. It was so rare to have all three sisters together, with Dad, in Hong Kong, a place I had left 30-plus years prior with no regrets, and then returned—this time with no regrets.

I hardly noticed the background music being played on Lina's audio system. We were so engrossed in enjoying the food and our conversations that no one really paid attention to the background "dinner music." Toward the end of our gluttonous feast, we quieted down just a bit so as to reboot our appetite for the plethora of desserts. That was when I first heard, really heard, the "background" music that had been playing throughout our dinner. It was not music with which I was familiar, and I had been listening to a wide range of music since I was a young child.

Music listening was and still is so very important in my life that it borders on being my "religion." It lifts my spirits, soothes my soul, and feeds my core, surpassing the farthest reaches of my consciousness, and touching the subconscious and beyond—to the unknown and the unknowable. I remember when I was a mere child of four or five years of age, there would always be music—classical music—played every Sunday when I was doing my school homework. Mom or Dad would put an early-production 33-1/3 rpm LP record on the turntable that resided inside this "cupboard" which also contained a radio and loudspeakers. It was a fairly large piece of "furniture." I grew to be enamored with this piece of "furniture," and forever more, this budding audiophile would grow up to fall in love with audio gear, components and accessories, in the eternal pursuit of "perfect" reproduction of recorded music. Often times I was the only woman in the listening rooms or an audio show, "talking shop" with the guys.

I was too young to know the music my parents played on the turntable inside that "cupboard," but after I started my piano lessons at around six years of age, I learned that it was mostly symphonies, sonatas and concertos by Bach, Beethoven, and Brahms, the "classics" of the classical. Some years later, when Mom and Dad made more money, we began to ascend into the world of the middle class. No more low-income housing for us; we moved to a fancy, wholly respectable apartment in the Mid-Levels, within walking distance of SSGC, and downstairs from Dr. Chau. That was around my Form II or Form III year. With the new apartment came new stereo components, and for the first time ever, a television set. I would spend most of my evenings sitting on the hardwood floor in front of the stereo rack, Teac headphones glued to my ears, lost in my world of music. It was mostly rock 'n roll and pop then: the *Woodstock* soundtracks, lots of Beatles, early Elton John, Simon and Garfunkel, Carole King, Emerson Lake & Palmer, Deep Purple, Credence Clearwater Revival, Crosby Stills & Nash, and so on. Music was my link and exposure to the world and to the United States in particular. From those songs and soundtracks and news about the rock 'n roll world, I learned about the anti-Vietnam War movement, the hippies and the flower children, the nascent feminist movement, and the freedoms Americans ostensibly enjoyed. All that carved a deep impression on me; America was something and somewhere I aspired to be part of. Then there was the "Chopsticks," a female singing duo, Sandra and Amina, which was taking Hong Kong by storm in the late 1960's. I would listen for hours to their LPs, and watch their live performances on variety shows on television. They mesmerized me; I felt a powerful jolt of electricity between them whenever they performed. I responded to their interaction in a very special and personal way. I did not understand my reactions at the time, but those sensations also made a deep impression on me. In retrospect, it was of course my "gay-dar" tuning in to kindred souls. I learned several years later from rumors that Sandra and Amina got "married" in Japan. Thus, we were "fellow outcasts;" no wonder the resonance in me was so overwhelming. That was apparently the beginning of my emerging sexual identity; I was simply still too young and naïve to connect the dots.

After I went to the States, one of the first presents from Dad was an all-in-one turntable-receiver compact stereo. I had that in my dorm room throughout college and graduate school in the United States, playing many Stevie Wonder albums, from Motown to disco, from Carly Simon to Santana to the earliest New Age recordings. Obviously, sound fidelity was not of prime concern; the music must not stop playing for me. By the time I started practicing as a young associate, I spent my first "disposable income" on more "respectable" audio components. It was very modest Sanyo-type components, with very unpretentious Kenwood loudspeakers. But then I started reading avidly about high-end audio components, and within a few years, I would venture into the world of "audiophile" components, even though my budget could hardly afford them. B&W loudspeakers would take over my living room, and Krell power amplifier, Audio Research CD player and Cardas interconnect cables started to grace my audio rack. The listening sessions accorded me the only reprieve from a very demanding lawyering life, and solace from what was—whether I realized or acknowledged it or not—an emotionally troubling relationship.

The music that Lina was playing in her apartment that night was entirely alien to me. Once I started paying attention to it, the best way I could describe it was that it was ethereal; it was also strangely calming and soothing. It had the simplest instrumentation, with a female vocalist chanting in a language that was also unfamiliar to me. The melody was at once melancholy yet strangely uplifting. As I listened, I was captivated, then completely mesmerized, and before long, I started weeping quietly and uncontrollably. That mystery music had somehow managed to reach into the deepest recesses of my soul, and dredged to the surface all the hurt and pain that had been buried over the decades. At the same time, the music had also unlocked and unleashed all that was good and mighty that was my innate essence, but which had been glossed over, forgotten and abandoned in all those years past. There and then, in the midst of a festive family feast, I was experiencing a meltdown. Nay, it was an epiphany, an instantaneous metamorphosis, a spontaneous transformation.

I could not stop tearing up; I excused myself momentarily to compose myself and hide my tears. After dinner, we decided to tour the amenities in the complex that were provided exclusively for the residents, such as swimming pool, gymnasium, pool and game room, piano room, and to take a walk outside on the magnificent esplanade overlooking the sea. I did not remember much of the tour or the walk as I remained in a state of benign shock, with my head filled with the haunting melody and the uncommon lyrics of the mystery music. I felt estranged from myself as I did not know the new me who had emerged just moments earlier. Yet, on the other hand, I knew this person very well—it was the "old," empowered me from decades ago, before I ceded self-determination to another, before I resigned myself to "circumstances." In one mysterious swell swoop, I had reclaimed the dynamic and vibrant, loving and lovable, invincible and indomitable me.

As the momentous evening drew to a close, I asked Lina about the mystery music. She generously gave me the CD to keep: *The Chant of Metta* by Imee Ooi—The Chant of Loving-Kindness, sung in Pali.

The remaining days in Hong Kong flew by in a blur. Having dinner with Lilian one last time was heartrending. Lilian had no idea that she would not be seeing me again—for an unknown period of time—when she got into the taxi with Vivian to return to her dormitory. I cried. There had been a lot of tears throughout this homecoming trip. I did not know when it would be when I could see her again; I certainly hoped it would not be another twenty-five years. I promised myself that I would forgo all vacations so that I could tear myself away from work and return to Hong Kong on a "regular" basis to see her again.

The "new, old" me walked with a spring in my steps and a smile—actually, a smirk—on my face. It was a cliché to observe that I started looking at life very differently. How refreshing it was to welcome a brand new day, a completely new ballgame. As I was packing my suitcases for my return trip to the States, there was a faint but nagging notion that I tried hard to tamp down or ignore but could not: could it be that I was about to upend my life?

Dad saw me off at the Airport, the same place where just two weeks earlier I had arrived as a very tired and worn out individual. Dad took a couple of pictures of me as I was about to board the plane back to Detroit: I was grinning broadly, stepping out confidently, waving goodbye victoriously. What a stark contrast. Throughout the flight, in the subterranean of my consciousness, that nagging notion kept cropping up, however rigorously I tried to ignore or deny it: the frightful possibility of my upsetting the apple cart, thereby either making a complete mess of things or finally being able to turn a new leaf. Usurping the status quo could be positively cathartic or disastrously ruinous. I almost did not want the plane to land; I wish I could just turn back time to before that fateful dinner at Lina's apartment. Life was so simple—even if miserable—then.

I remembered the first time I landed at the Metro Detroit Airport: it was December of 1972, and I was flying in from New York City, via Toronto, to visit an SSGC classmate who was attending the University of Michigan in Ann Arbor. I looked down from the plane and thought to myself, "What an Armageddon of a wretched place—please let me never be stuck here." I got what I did not wish for: I ended up being "stuck" in Detroit since 1977. Call it destiny, call it karma, call it Divine Order, by any other name, I was meant to be in the Detroit area. If I were anywhere else, I would not have met Bev, I would not have encountered all that I did in the past forty years, and my life would not have unfolded quite so dramatically.

Detroit always seemed so desolate whenever I returned to it, especially after having spent a couple of weeks in a vivacious and dynamic city such as Hong Kong. It was Saturday, December 13th, three days before my milestone birthday. It was a typical Detroit wintry day—grey, overcast sky, cold, and yes, desolate. As Bev had declared that she would not pick me up at the Airport, I had reserved a ride on an airport shuttle home. The shuttle van pulled onto on my driveway, and Bev was opening and standing at the side door; all seemed normal and ordinary enough.

Yet the moment I reached the side door to enter my home, I knew it. It struck me like a thunderbolt: this was not my home anymore; I would be leaving it, leaving Bev, leaving twenty-six-plus years of everything behind. In a split second, the "before" and "after" became brutally demarcated. The impossible had, in an instant, become not just eminently possible, but the inevitable.

I wrote of "mysterious forces" which wreaked havoc in my life each and every time I returned to Hong Kong. It seemed that, with this 2003 trip, the troublemaking had reached an unprecedented zenith. How would I unravel entanglements twenty-six years in the making? I went into a sort of autopilot mode: shutting out emotions, and fully engaging my left brain instead. The "To Do" list was surprisingly abbreviated: find an apartment, find a moving company, and pick a date. The difficulty turned out to be masking my disinterest in "our" lives together in the interim.

We went out for dinner on my birthday, and it was extremely difficult and painful for me to pretend that I was still the same old me. Bev threw a birthday party for me at home the ensuing Saturday; all our close friends came to fete my milestone birthday, and no one was the wiser that anything was untoward. We went out for a movie on a frigid Saturday night; it was *The Lord of the Rings: The Return of the King.* As we walked from the parking structure to the cinema, she hurried ahead of me without waiting for me as usual, except that that night, the rejuvenated me was able to keep pace with her. She was so startled that she blurted out, "You *are* walking much better." I found a suitable one-bedroom apartment in short order and signed a lease, but I decided to wait until after the New Year before making my move-out announcement. We never fussed over Christmas, and so the Holidays came and went without a glitch. Of course, I told my therapist, Hazel Karbel, about my plans, and she advised me to have certain items pre-packed and close at hand, just in case I had to get out of the house in a hurry. That turned out to be a very sage piece of advice.

Bev wanted to see the musical *The Producers*, and so, I purchased tickets for us for New Year's Eve. We were inching ever closer to my target move-out date of after the first of the year, and I thought all seemed to be proceeding according to plan until the evening of December 30, 2003. As usual, I came home, late, from work around 9:30 p.m. After dinner and taking care of my personal e-mails, we went into our hot tub in the basement for a midnight soak as usual. About a year earlier, Bev decided that we (actually, she) needed a whirlpool hot tub. Without consulting me, she single-handedly cleared an area in the basement to accommodate a whirlpool that was about 6 feet in diameter plus motor and hose attachments. She surprised me with this monstrosity as a fait accompli, and the least I could do then was to take advantage of it to unwind at the end of a long workday. I would come to realize some years later that there might have been ulterior motives or other not-so-benign intentions in her installing the hot tub.

As we were taking our dip in the hot tub, she suddenly asked, "Can you be any colder?" I was taken by surprise; I did not realize my detachment was showing. It was time for a snap decision: do I continue to pretend, or…? I decided on the latter; there was no point in further postponing the inevitable or in masquerading the truth. I told her I was leaving, for good, and stepped out of the hot tub. It took her quite a few minutes to react, and even then, her initial reaction was surprisingly tempered. I went to bed, as I still had to work the following day. However, I did not get much sleep that night; as the gravity of my disclosure and decision finally struck her, she kept coming into the bedroom, interrupting my sleep, and asking me endless, senseless questions. It was a reprieve that I could escape to the office early the next morning.

It was New Year's Eve day, and many of my colleagues and staff members took the half workday off. I, on the other hand, wanted to stay at work and not go home if I could help it, but then there were the rather expensive *The Producers* tickets for that evening. I did not script the premature disclosure the night before, and hence, I was quite at a loss as to how then to proceed. I did not feel sad, or hurt, or forlorn; in fact, I did not feel at all. For the sake of self-preservation, I must have shut out all conscious emotions, knowing that I had yet to physically move out of my home.

I reluctantly returned home in the late afternoon. Bev had been lying in wait for me, assaulting me with a barrage of accusations, alternating with questions and. I simply wanted to go to the show, survive the New Year, and move out, even though by then I had no idea how exactly I could accomplish those in relative peace. Usually she would drive, but for some reason, I was the one driving us to the show that evening. I had to mentally block out her nonstop tirade, as I tried to hone in on the Masonic Temple without guidance from onboard GPS navigation. We had been to the Masonic Temple previously for other shows, but for some strange reason, I could not find the venue that night even as I knew I was circling in the general vicinity. It was not a neighborhood in which one would simply pull up "somewhere" and ask for directions. I was hoping Bev would help navigate, but she seemed only interested in launching her unrelenting invectives. Finally, I had to give up the futile exercise, and drove home instead.

Bev's verbal assault and inquisition only intensified as we headed home and escalated further after we arrived home. There was not an answer or a retort that would even momentarily lull her offensive. Then all of a sudden I heard these words: "Since you want to leave, go, leave *now!*" Yes, but of course; I could and should leave there and then. Because Hazel had prompted me just days earlier, I had actually rehearsed this precise scenario in my mind. I knew exactly the bare necessities that I needed to gather and load into my car. I knew I needed to get out of the house before she got hysterical, or became violent, or changed her mind. Twenty-six years, three months and four days from the evening when we first met; the last sight of Bev was her doing a half-baked tap dance-shuffle at the side door as if she were thrilled to see me leave. I hurriedly pulled out of the driveway and into the frigid New Year's Eve nightfall.

Free at last! Free at last! Free at last?

III.

Exceptionalism

It was a glorious decade to make one's debut into this world, the 1950's. Those were truly the simpler times, an idyllic time, a perfect time to frolic in the innocence of childhood. The post-World War II Hong Kong was a gem of a British Crown Colony, brimming with promise and optimism. The savage days of the Japanese invasion and occupation were fast receding in the collective memory. Chairman Mao Tse Tung and his Communist cadres had taken over China, and droves of refugees, many bringing with them knowhow and trunkful of cash and gold bullions, were fleeing the mainland for the beacon of freedom and opportunity that Hong Kong enticingly represented. Hong Kong—aptly named "Fragrant Harbour" in Chinese and endearingly renowned the world over as the Pearl of the Orient—was the destination of the era. The dynamism was palpable, and the possibilities inexhaustible.

Into this heady mix of peace and prosperity, juxtaposition of hopes and dreams, at the crossroads of the last hurrah of British colonialism and the blazing sunset of the Empire, I was born.

Ours was a humble family, hardly one of privilege, wealth or prestige. My paternal great-grandfather might have been a minor local official in the late Qing Dynasty, but not much was handed down through the generations. That was probably because my paternal grandfather was the son of a concubine who moved the family to Hong Kong from our ancestral village in Po On in southern Guangdong province. Dad and his two brothers received high school education, which distinguished him from the average worker-ant back in the days before academic credentials creep. I am not sure Dad's three sisters were allowed to enjoy the same privilege of higher education. My paternal grandparents had passed away some years before I was born. Grandfather's concubine, whom I called grandmother, was still alive, but I was not particularly close to her while I was growing up, partly because she spoke a different dialect which I could not understand. Dad's side of the family is very traditionally Chinese—patriarchal to a fault, unabashedly male oriented and male dominated. Yet Dad did not turn out to be a male chauvinist. Perhaps out of necessity of raising four girls, or owing to Mom's enlightened guidance, he was in fact a pioneer male feminist. He dutifully helped with housework assigned by Mom. He was genuinely respectful of a woman's opinions. He was also the "nurse" who gently applied Chinese herbal liniment on our bellies when we had a bellyache, until we were old enough to rub our own bellies. He was an enthusiastic cheerleader of all of my endeavors, and a proud parent of all of my accomplishments.

Mom's heritage is even more fascinating. She came from an equally large family with two sisters and three brothers. There were altogether nine children, but several died in infancy, a not unexpected occurrence in those days. The Second World War interrupted her studies, but she managed to finish high school after the War. My maternal grandmother was my grandfather's second wife; his first wife died some years earlier, and I do not know anything about her. As a "fill-in wife," Grandmother's children were not allowed to call her "mother;" Chinese superstition dictated that her children could only call her "aunt" lest the children not survive to adulthood. I could only imagine the psychological impact on the children, including Mom, of essentially not being able to acknowledge their mother. Perhaps that would explain Mom's rather fierce anti-religion sentiments; to her, religious beliefs and superstition sounded suspiciously similar. Being an agnostic was her way of rebelling against such oppressive superstitious "traditions." Being Chinese in the olden days definitely had its taboos and resultant constraints and burdens, as I would also discover as I grew up.

My Grandmother was the daughter of a hero, a real life rebel. I was told that my maternal great-grandfather was one of the fighters who took up arms against the corrupt and oppressive Qing Dynasty. He was martyred in one of the uprisings. There is a monument and historic marker somewhere in or near Guangzhou with his name and those of the scores of martyrs who were slain at that uprising. I had always felt extremely proud of my rebellious heritage, and I had always listened to and honored that warrior call in my genes.

Mom and Dad's wedding photograph,
January 3, 1953.

My maternal grandfather fancied himself a gentleman in the finest British tradition. I believe he inherited money and the ancestral home from his forebears whom I knew nothing about, and he thus lived a rather comfortable, gentlemanly life. His Western leanings allowed his daughters to have a high school education. However, it was obvious that his sons were his pride and joy, one of whom was given the opportunity to travel abroad for advanced studies; my 5th Uncle went to the United States and earned a university degree in engineering, and worked for NASA until his retirement. Grandfather was very old and crotchety by the time I was old enough to remember the visits to their home. I remembered him as a very stern, distant man. I was not that fond of him, while I was particularly enamored of my Grandmother, the daughter of a true revolutionary and hero. My grandfather passed away while I was about eight or nine years of age. I remembered Mom's outrage when she learned that, save for token gifts, grandfather provided only for his sons, but not his daughters, to inherit his estate even though it was by then not substantial anyway. Apparently, Mom had inherited the warrior genes as well.

When I came on the scene, Mom and Dad were living in an apartment shared with my paternal grandmother and Dad's younger brother (my 7th Uncle), his wife and their three sons. Dad, the giddy new father and avid amateur photographer, had documented my and Lina's early childhood in that venerable apartment with many stunning black-and-white photographs. There I was, crawling on the floor in my sleeveless tank top and diapers. In another photograph of me and Lina, she was sitting on a small Chinese drum beating it with a wooden drumstick, and I was sitting behind her, holding a round rattan crochet frame, quite seriously pretending it to be the steering wheel of a car.

The author, age 3 months, with Mom, on the rooftop terrace of the old walk-up tenement in Sai Ying Poon District, Hong Kong.

That apartment was a very old walkup tenement in Sai Ying Poon district, an unglamorous commoners' neighborhood on Hong Kong Island. It had very high ceiling and stone tile floors. Rooms were partitioned with portable screens and panels. The cooking stoves in the small, spartan kitchen burned wood or coal, just like the ones at Grandmother's. There was, of course, no central heating or cooling, just a table fan noisily whirling in the summer heat. As in most households in those days, there was an "ancestral altar" maintained by 7th Aunt and my paternal grandmother. It was important to honor and pay respects to one's ancestors, by burning incense and reciting sutras daily, and offering food and fresh fruits on special occasions at the altar. It was a practice derived from Buddhist beliefs. The consecration and placement of the altar were also critical, and high monks were paid handsomely for the installation of the altar. The auspicious placement of the family altar was said to ensure the ancestors' blessings of prosperity and longevity on their descendants. As a female descendant, I did not have any responsibility for the family altar, other than a perfunctory bow at Chinese New Year. As I was writing these pages, I happened to be reestablishing communications with my first cousin, one of 7th Uncle's three sons, Brian Siu Cho Chan, after almost 40 years of having lost contact. His first e-mail asked if I remembered our lives at "137 Queen's Road West" in Sai Ying Poon District. Indeed, I do; I do indeed.

This was Hong Kong before globalization: before the invasion of McDonald's and KFC's, long before the proliferation of Starbucks and Tim Hortons, and eons before the Internet and social media. I am not being nostalgic, but the archaic way of life was, in present day's parlance, much more impactful. Every so often, a young man would stroll up and down the street hollering, "Airplane Olives!" He was selling a favorite snack: a preserved olive in a paper wrapper. If you wanted to buy one, you would holler back from your balcony or window, "Here! Here!" and toss a 5-cent coin (less than one penny) to the vendor. No matter how lousy your aim might have been, he would always catch your coin. In return, he would hurl you a wrapped olive, no matter how high up your balcony or window happened to be. Drones have nothing on such surefire, instant-gratification delivery service. Recycling was accomplished with similar efficiency and aplomb. The recycler would come down the street yelling, "Buying broken brass and broken iron!" That's our endearing term for scrap metal— your charred woks, pots and pans and metal whatnots which had outlived their usefulness. Of the many ubiquitous street food vendors, the one who offered fried "stinky tofu" did not even have to waste his breath; the unmistakably pungent aroma would either repel one from three blocks away or have devotees flock to the vendor much like bees to nectar. Life's sad and somber moments played out on the street as well. With regularity, funeral processions would parade down the street, led by a funereal band with its piercing Chinese gongs and horns, followed by a column of Buddhist monks, trailed by loudly sobbing family members draped in mourning garb—full white muslin gowns. That was life in real time, life in a much simpler time, life in a truly authentic time.

One of my earliest memories involving that apartment was when I was at most three years of age. I decided to be a "good girl" and do some dusting as I must have observed Mom perform that task. I managed to fetch the feather duster and started dusting. Lina, who was about 1 year old, was just watching and not helping; I decided she was not a "good girl." After I finished the perfunctory dusting, I thought it would be considerate of me to play with Lina. We were standing on our parents' bed, and I reached into the small cabinet on the wall in which our toys were stowed and I took out a doll. I disliked playing with dolls, but I thought I would suffer it just to be sisterly. Lina suddenly lunged at me, bit my earlobe, and snatched the doll from me. From that day on, I decided I did not much like Lina—until we were both much older—and I never played with dolls again.

The author (right) at about 3 years of age, with Mom
and author's younger sister, Lina, at Victoria Park,
Causeway Bay, Hong Kong.

Other disparate snippets from my childhood years, as I would learn decades later, reveal glimpses of my Past; the significance of those apparently unrelated incidents oftentimes turned out to illuminate my Present. I was being potty-trained when I was sitting on the little pot one fine day in that vintage apartment. From the corner of my eye, I spotted a small centipede inching ever so threateningly toward me. I screamed at the top of my lungs for Dad. As I was sitting very close to the floor, the centipede appeared larger than life. I was also too young to realize I could just stand up, get off the pot and walk away. Perhaps I was trained to wait for Mom or Dad to come get me off the pot, and thus did not think of fleeing. Perhaps I was simply frozen in terror and could not even get up. Dad *finally* came to investigate what the fuss was all about; by then the multi-leg monster was much too close for comfort as far as I was concerned. Instead of rescuing me by immediately removing the life-threatening, offending monster, Dad walked away without saying a word. I was petrified, and for a moment, I thought I would never forgive Dad for child endangerment and abandonment. Nevertheless, he did more than redeem himself for defending me against many revolting cockroaches and assorted vermin subsequent to that centipede faux pas. Dad did return what seemed to be *eons* later with a hammer and a jar of oil. By then, the centipede was already crossing under my left foot, and I was delirious with fright. Dad explained later that a centipede soaked in a special oil made an excellent medicinal rub. That certainly did not ameliorate the scare of my life. From that day on, I have been deathly afraid of insects, even if it is a harmless little spider, let alone a menacing flying cockroach. Surely, I was too young then to realize that I suffered from entomophobia; I now believe that that phobia must have come from an earlier time—a Past Life. With the clarity gleaned and wisdoms gained from decades of living an admittedly unorthodox life, the pattern is evident and the evidence irrefutable, convincing me— the once hopelessly left-brained lawyer—of that seemingly far-fetched hypothesis.

I was about four or five years old when my mother's younger sister, 9th Aunt, visited us one day. I was thrilled when she took me for a stroll in the small market across the street. The market was typical of a local neighborhood outdoors market, chock full of vendors of all stripes, hawking everything from "street food" to pots and pans to clothing. From previous visits to the market, I remembered that there was a stall selling plastic toys, and for some "unknown" reason, I decided that I needed a plastic toy sword that day. I insisted on having the sword; I felt as if I would not survive if I did not have a sword that day. I was throwing a royal fit on the street, which was very uncharacteristic of me. 9ᵗʰ Aunt finally capitulated, and bought me a plastic toy sword. It was scandalous, because I was a little girl, and a little girl was not supposed to play with swords. However, in my mind that particular day, the sword was an absolutely essential item missing in my very young life. Throughout my young childhood, I insisted on having toy guns and knives and swords. As a matter of fact, in his recent e-mail to me after a hiatus of 40 years, my first cousin Brian reminded me how I liked to "play with guns" even at a tender age when our families shared that old apartment at 137 Queen's Road West. By the age of eight years, I had fashioned myself an "arsenal," my version of a gun rack, at the end of my bunk bed, displaying my collection of toy weapons. I never questioned myself why I wanted or needed these "weapons;" I simply felt the need to have them. I fancied myself the defender of the entire family against intruders and malcontents. Yet I was never a violent person; I could not harm an ant even if my life depended on it. I was glad Mom and Dad indulged my idiosyncrasy; I supposed they were trusting that I would soon outgrow my tomboyish phase.

I remember vividly my fanaticism one Chinese New Year when I was about ten years old. It was customary during the first few days of the Lunar New Year for families to visit friends and relatives to exchange gifts, *lai-see* (red-packet money), traditional New Year delicacies, and well wishes for health and prosperity for the New Year. In those years gone by, there were strict rules on what might or might not be said, and tasks that were and were not allowed to be performed, during those auspicious days. It was our turn to pay our New Year visit to Grandmother and 4ᵗʰ Uncle. I had just received as a gift a new toy pistol, one that came with a holster for wearing the gun hidden under your arm, much like the one worn by the famed FBI gang buster Eliot Ness. I was so enamored with my new toy that I insisted on wearing it to visit Grandmother. Mom, of course, was livid, but she could not make me take the holster and gun off. I think we finally compromised: I would take the gun off once I got to Grandmother's. Apparently, it was taboo to be bringing such "instrument of death" during those special Chinese New Year visits. I must have given Mom a heartache and a huge headache, but as far as I was concerned, I simply did not see any issue for concern. I was not harming anyone. I would never use "lethal" force anyway; the toy gun, I reasoned, would simply frighten away any thugs who might harm my family. I was just being true to myself—it was natural then for me to be "armed," so that I could protect everyone in my family.

Long before my college years, I had indeed outgrown my need for a personal arsenal. Mom could finally exhale; but of course, from her perspective, I had another serious issue which gave her an even greater heartache: by then I had come out as a lesbian. "Coming out" was not even a recognized nomenclature in those decidedly unenlightened days. In a Chinese society such as Hong Kong, being gay was perhaps the ultimate taboo; it brought untold shame to one's family, ancestors and posterity. Hence, Mom probably would have preferred my continuing to clutch onto my toy guns to my embracing such "deviant and perverted" lifestyle. Fortunately, the opportunity for me to go abroad for undergraduate studies came as a timely and face-saving excuse for me to gracefully "exit stage left."

During my first semesters in college, I excitedly signed up for archery and fencing. I considered them venerable forms of martial arts in which I felt, for some unknown reason, I should excel. Yet after a semester of each, I had to move on as I was clearly not going to make the school team. Likewise, some years later, I was thrilled that I had the opportunity to take horseback riding lessons. The notion of riding a horse seemed as natural to me as breathing. Yet, as it turned out, I had a hard time even staying on the horse. The sense of defeat was humbling and puzzling until many years later, I came to realize and understand that I was indeed adept at those combat skills—just not in this lifetime. As a matter of fact, it seemed that I was destined to finally outgrow my "warrior track" during this lifetime, for once and for all.

There are no "coincidences" in life. The realization that I had been a warrior in my Past Lives came to me after many seemingly innocuous and unrelated incidents which led me to but one conclusion. Why else would the four-year-old me—a girl to boot—insist on having a plastic toy sword? How else would one explain my fascination with toy guns and weapons, even though I was not the least violence-prone? Obviously, for this lifetime, I was no longer "in combat" literally, but yet, I somehow ended up being an attorney, sparring and dueling in court all the same. Of course, I do not have recollection of specific details of my warring days (except for one instance), but I feel that I had been, through the ages, a combatant in one way or another: a Roman centurion, a gladiator, a Viking, a knight (many times over), a *wuxia*; in other words, a warrior for all seasons. I had thus killed and been killed many times, maimed and been maimed, caused great pain onto others and suffered grievous harm myself. This lifetime is thus for me to redeem myself: the slaughter must stop with this lifetime.

The event that triggered such an unorthodox realization by an erstwhile left-brained lawyer came quite unexpectedly. In 1997, Bev and I celebrated our 20th anniversary. We decided to take a trip, and when asked "where to?" I blurted out, "Italy!" Four years earlier, for *my* 40th birthday, *she* decided that *we* should go to New Zealand, *her* dream destination. I managed to enjoy myself in New Zealand all the same, and even came back with a rather mystical experience. We went to New Zealand with two friends, Annemargret, a German whom I met when I went back to Hong Kong in the summer of 1974, and Penny, one of the legal secretaries at the law firm where I worked as a young associate in the 1980's. For that dream vacation, we rented a station wagon and drove for 22 days through much of the North and South

Islands, staying mostly at local bed-and-breakfasts. Thank goodness Annemargret was adept at driving on the "wrong" side of the road, from her driving days in Hong Kong which also followed the British traffic protocol.

Fairly early on in our sojourn, we were told that we absolutely had to go see a giant tree while we were exploring the northern reaches of the North Island. A tree was not high on our must-see list; however, since it was on our way back to Auckland from a gorgeous beach in the Northern Region—endless miles of pristine beach with not another soul in sight, and if I were spiritual then, I might have considered it nirvana—we decided to make a pit stop to see what all the fuss was about. That tourist attraction was well marked; we were directed to pull into a small parking lot on one side of the road. Annemargret and I stayed with the car in the parking lot, while Penny and Bev *rendezvous* with the tree. When they returned a short while later, they were both unusually giddy. It was then Annemargret's and my turn to encounter with the mysterious tree.

To view the tree, one would walk across to the other side of the road from the parking lot, and follow the signs along a footpath. It was a very short, leisurely 5-minute walk through a most ordinary park-like setting, with the most ordinary trees, shrubs and plants. Annemargret and I, chitchatting as we mindlessly strolled along that footpath, were frankly amused and incredulous that we had actually made a pit stop to see a *tree*. Then all of a sudden, I was literally "stopped dead in my tracks" by an overwhelming presence, an immeasurable power. The air suddenly felt much cooler, crisper and purified, and the atmosphere suddenly became sacredly silent. I felt as if I were walking into a zone that was not of this world. There in front of me stood a tree—if one must call it that—exuding an aura that commanded total submission. It emanated all-encompassing power. Its sheer girth and stature would be imposing enough, but it was its essence, its spirit, that had me awestruck. I had never thought I would describe a true in those terms. Gazing at its massive trunk, I knew and felt I was in the presence of a keenly sage and sentient being. In the short time while I was in its ambit, it had imparted upon me wisdom of the ages. I felt not so much dwarfed as I was humbled in the best sense of the word.[1]

For our 20th anniversary then, I decided that it was my turn to go to *my* dream destination. I could not explain why it should be Italy; it just was, as I had pined for seeing that country for years.

It was the rather typical eleven-day touristy tour in November, hopping rather breathlessly through Rome, Florence, Venice, Naples, Pompeii, and the other usual hotspots. I was not disappointed; the piazzas, churches and other frequented landmarks were splendid just as I had imagined. For a devotee of fine handcrafted articles, I was in shoppers' paradise. I bought limited edition fountain pens, Murano glass trinkets, and assorted leather goods; I even lugged a hand-built, full-size, all-leather suitcase home with me.

During that memorable trip, two inexplicable incidents stood out. The first was how I yielded only one precious photograph from those eleven days, after I had exposed no fewer than eleven rolls of film. Ostensibly, it was my being overly confident of my photographic skills. I had purchased a new Leica compact camera for the trip, but did not have time to read the owner's manual. After all, I reasoned, how difficult could using a point-and-shoot camera be. I thus did not notice that "Auto Focus" was not engaged properly, with the result that all, save one of a lion statue in Capri, of my pictures were out of focus. It was as if the Universe did not want me to have a graphic record of what I experienced.

---

[1] For those preferring empirical data, it was the famed New Zealand giant kauri tree known as the *Tāne Mahuta* ("Lord of the Forest," in the indigenous Maori language) in the Waipoua Forest of Northern Region. With a girth of 45.2 feet, the tree soars 168 feet toward the sky. Its age is estimated to be between 1,250 and 2,500 years.

The second involved what I experienced, at two locations specifically, which could not have been captured by my amateurish photography in any case. Rome was, of course, one of the highlights of the tour, and a Roman Catacombs was on the itinerary one morning. I had no knowledge of the Catacombs, and thus did not have any preconceived notion as to what we were about to view. The above-ground building and entrance were innocuous enough. Once underground, it became all too clear that all around me were open burial chambers for early Christians. "Why would anyone, other than avid archaeologists, anthropologists, and perhaps art historians, need to view such morbid places?" I asked myself rhetorically as I wound through the maze of tunnels and passageways, every hair on the back of my neck standing straight up. "This ought not be a 'tourist attraction,'" I grumbled to myself. I was uncomfortable to the point of being physically sick. I simply could not understand my revolting reaction to that locale. In retrospect, eerily, it was as if I had been buried there, and it was not under the best of circumstances. At the time, though, it felt most disagreeable.

The afternoon, by contrast, was an exhilarating experience. Again, I was not prepared for what I was about to view—the Roman Forum, a must-see for tourists—as my Roman history was sorely lacking. As I traced the steps of the ancients in those spectacular ruins, I was sure that what I felt and saw and heard was not shared by my tour-mates. I heard the deafening roar of the crowds and the thunderous stomping of column upon column of Roman soldiers marching in lock-step. I was practically blinded by the gold and silver of the soldiers' helmets, breastplates and shields shimmering in bright sunshine; I saw deep red color fabric billowing everywhere—on the troops' colors, on the men's uniform; and I felt gloriously victorious and triumphant. The sights, sounds and sense were vivid and overwhelming. I kept having to snap myself back to reality, reminding myself that I was merely strolling along ancient, lifeless paths of rocks and stones and dirt, strewn with skeletons of outdated structures which had largely collapsed centuries ago. It was not so much a *déjà vu*, as my experience with *déjà vu* had been that it would last only a second or two, a very brief moment of familiarity, of recognition. *Déjà vu* is likened to a freeze frame, while what I experienced at the Roman Forum was more akin to a short film, frame after frame, playing out before my eyes.

I had never mentioned to anyone my strange vision that afternoon in Rome in November 1997. Now, years later, it does not matter that I could be judged as deranged, delusional or worse; it now matters more to me that events in my life "make sense." My Inner Knowingness now told me that I must have been at the Forum thousands of years ago during one of the victory marches, one of those triumphal processions.

Long before being the four-year-old who insisted on having my plastic sword, even much longer before my "homecoming" in Rome, I was a young child with a sense of being very "special": I was exceptional. It was not a conscious concept of or belief in exceptionalism growing up; I simply *knew* I was exceptional. What were my "superpowers," you ask. That never occurred to me, but I think it was willpower. All I had to do was call upon my inner tenacity and imbued resources, and whatever I wished to attain would be accomplished. I would *will* something to happen, and it would manifest. Case in point: when I was in the 5th grade, the school held an intramural swim meet. Being highly competitive by nature, I was excited about the opportunity to compete; I relished a worthy challenge, and absolutely trusted my exceptionalism. I figuratively threw down the gauntlet and rushed to sign up for several individual and relay races. It did not matter that I did not know how to swim at all. I came home proudly announcing to Mom and Dad my latest courageous and ambitious gambit, and then asked them for help in learning swimming. It was only about one month before the races. We did not have the financial means to send me to the YWCA for swimming lessons; private lessons were totally out of the question. My enterprising Dad then recalled that one of his colleagues, Mr. Wong, who also resided at Sai Wan Estate, swam every morning for his exercise regime. Dad thus accompanied me every early morning to meet my erstwhile swimming coach at the swim "club" located within walking distance of Sai Wan Estate. The club was actually a jetty-like structure made mostly of bamboo poles, housing the most rudimentary showers and changing rooms, jutting out by the water's edge—the western stretch of Victoria Harbour. The ocean water was frigid early in the morning, which encouraged expeditious learning on my part. One month of swimming lessons was not quite enough to make me competitive in the individual events, but my audacious gamble netted me a gold medal in the relay. I came away from that success realizing that I could and should always push myself to the limits. As Mom had drummed into my head, in English, since I was an infant, "Where there's a will, there's a way." That had become my life's motto. Indeed, life seemed to be going so well for me that I subconsciously and surreptitiously developed a propensity for self-destruction, a bent for self-sabotage, starting in my early teenage years. It was as if I had to build myself an obstacle course simply to make life more difficult and thus more interesting.

Lina, Vivian, Mom and the author, on a Sunday outing, circa 1962. The author was aptly pointing to—and shooting for—a far-flung star.

Along with my willpower, I felt a special connection to a source of power, and I instinctively knew to use the power only for "good," and never to serve "bad" or selfish ends. I was too young to analyze or verbalize it. Decades later, I now understand that my connection to that "someone" or "something" was also why while others saw a giant tree and I reckoned a sentient being, when others viewed ancient burial niches and I sensed hauntings, and why while others saw broken arches and remnants of antiquated structures and I heard the roar of the crowds and the thunderous steps of the troops. Furthermore, my exceptionalism bestowed upon me a sense of invincibility, infallibility, perfectionism, all of which could be considered fine traits—until I faltered, and falter I did sometimes as, after all, I was only human. Whether the setback was major or minor, inadvertent or otherwise, the consequences of such momentary "fall from grace," as I would learn in my more grownup years, could be ceaselessly devastating, guilt-inducing, crippling, even paralyzing.

Yet, ostensibly there was nothing exceptional about me. Dad was rather short in stature, and not particularly the masculine muscular type. Hence, I was not tall in stature or naturally endowed with physical prowess for athletic achievements. I was not blessed with good looks either, even though Mom was a very beautiful woman. If I had been more traditionally feminine, I might have been somewhat alluring, but head-turning beauty would not describe me at all. Even my last name, Chan, is so garden-variety common that it is the equivalent of Smith and Jones combined amongst Chinese surnames. Yet I did my growing up totally oblivious to my apparent lack of the attributes typically associated with winners and leaders. In fact, in my childhood, I felt so sure of my superior abilities that I often assumed success was all but preordained. I proceeded through my early years as if I were destined to excel, to accomplish, and to be outstanding in all of my endeavors.

Ours was a liberated and feminist family, before those concepts were chic or politically correct. Mom had always worked full-time. Dad was a manager with a small Chinese import-export, trading company. To raise a family with four young ones, they both shared housework. Mom would cook, while Dad would slice and dice the ingredients and chop up the cooked whole chicken to put on the serving plate; Mom would do the laundry, and Dad would hang the clothes on bamboo rods for air-drying. When we got older, we all had to pitch in to help. One of my many assigned duties was the rather physically arduous task of scrubbing and waxing the hardwood floor.

Mom and Dad were both high school graduates, when that distinguished one from the vast majority who did not even attend high school. Thus, they were well positioned for induction into that white-collar middle-class comfort zone. Unfortunately, Dad was an unwitting victim of post-World War II politics. His chosen profession of being a merchant with T. O. Wong & Co., Ltd., a Chinese import-export trading company, a perfectly honorable profession by all accounts and in other times, became a liability after mainland China established itself as a Communist country in 1949. In the hysterical Cold War years after World War II and in the very British colonial Hong Kong, his employment with a trading company that did business with *Communist* China was reason enough to blacklist him. In fact, even though he served for many years with distinction in the Civil Aid Service (somewhat analogous to an unarmed version of our National Guard), he was not promoted above the rank of warden for that precise reason. He could not even find alternative employment because he was tainted by his "Communist affiliation." Fortunately, his employment with that Chinese trading company was stable until the mid-1970's when he was forced to retire after one of Mr. T.O. Wong's sons succeeded as head of the company upon the company founder's demise. Mom, on the other hand, found remunerative employment as the secretary to the managing director of Sun Hing Shipping Co., Ltd., a Hong Kong-based company which was then the sole agent for Zim, an Israeli shipping lines company. She toiled there until her retirement in the mid-1980's.

My childhood was not filled with the minutiae of the political implications of Dad's employment or his advancement, or the lack thereof, in the business world. Instead, it was a wondrous world of unfettered fun and boundless optimism. Mom's boss, Simon Lee, was a very astute businessman. He worked his employees hard, but several times a year, he would also host lavish events for his employees and families. I, of course, would not know just how hard Mom had to work, but I enjoyed the largesse of that employment. In the summertime, there would usually be an outing on the company launch (yacht). We would sail to an exquisite bay generally reachable only by boat, and spend the day swimming, with sumptuous food provided by caterers hired by the company. For children of the employees, it was pure, unadulterated fun. In the winter, there was usually a Christmas/New Year party. There would be comedians, magicians, clowns, and again, plentiful, delectable food.

Even though we had a live-in amah when we were growing up, Mom had trained us to be self-reliant from an early age, a trait that would prove to be a lifesaver years later. Thus, Mom was the exact opposite of the "helicopter parent." She was not the touchy-feely type of mother either; she did not particularly fuss over us. I also do not remember her reading us bedtime stories. Rather, she would encourage us to read from an early age. I remembered reading everything I could lay my hands on even when I was perhaps just four years of age: Chinese newspapers (I did not understand the word "rape" and asked Dad, and he would not respond to my curiosity), children's books, comics, Greek mythology, encyclopedia, and more. Dad, on the other hand, was the affectionate parent. In addition to rubbing our bellies with liniment when we had a stomachache, he would be the one, usually on Sundays, to ask which of us kids would give him a peck on the cheek. When Lina and I began to learn to write Chinese when we were about four or five years of age, he could not wait to teach us Chinese brush calligraphy. He would hold my hand and guide it through each brush stroke. Dad had outstanding penmanship with Chinese brush calligraphy, as I would realize when I was older. In fact, Dad instilled in me such pride in Chinese art, culture, and literature that I was practically Sinocentric from my tender age. I could not understand why we had to learn English, the language of "barbarians." In fact, learning Chinese was difficult enough for the young and curious me without tackling the barbarian's language. Cantonese, which was spoken by 99% of the population in Hong Kong, was strictly a spoken dialect. It could be written, but that would not be proper or formal Chinese. Written Chinese is Mandarin, which is an entirely different language. To compound the confusion, the pronunciation for any given Mandarin/ written Chinese character for a Cantonese-speaking person is completely different from that for a Mandarin-speaking person. Hence, even as we learned to write properly, that is, in Mandarin Chinese, it did not mean we could speak Mandarin. To add fuel to the fire, when the Communists came to power in China in 1949, they decided to adopt "simplified Chinese" characters as the official written Chinese. The Communists did not invent simplified Chinese; it was a way of writing Chinese characters from thousands of years ago. However, people in China and Hong Kong had been learning to write Chinese characters in the "traditional Chinese" style for centuries. Simplified Chinese and traditional Chinese writings were quite different. Growing up in Hong Kong, we were in fact forbidden to use simplified Chinese characters in school; it was frowned upon and the student would even be penalized for using them. Taiwanese use traditional Chinese characters, for instance. When Hong Kong's sovereignty was returned to China in 1997, simplified Chinese characters began to make their debut in the former British Colony. The former British subjects, including me, were at a disadvantage as we could not recognize the written Chinese characters. It was as if we had to learn Chinese all over again. Why do we Chinese people make life so difficult for ourselves?

As it were, even without the simplified-traditional Chinese characters divide, we Cantonese-speaking youngsters had a very steep learning curve. I remembered when I was in Primary 1 (first grade), one of my homework assignments was to write a diary entry. I happened to have scraped my knee that day, and wanted to record that monumental event in my entry. I instinctively knew that the proper noun for "knee" would not be the three-character nomenclature by which I called my knee. I asked Mom, and sure enough she wrote down a very complicated two-character noun that I had never heard of. From that day on, I remembered the proper Chinese noun for "knee," but I did not think I ever had to occasion to write it again in my life. Still, my world then was filled exclusively with Chinese people; writings and signage everywhere were in Chinese. I listened to radio broadcast in Cantonese (we did not even have a television set then). Mom's cooking was, of course, authentically Cantonese Chinese, except for her heavenly butter pound cake, insanely tasty Borsch soup and Portuguese chicken with rice.

And then there was the "Sunday march": every Sunday morning, Dad would put on a vinyl record (an LP or a 78 rpm) of marches, often a Sousa or a Scottish bagpipe number, and he would march around the apartment, with me following him in tight formation, for ten or fifteen minutes. I did not even consider it bizarre that a little Chinese girl should be marching like a good little soldier, nor what Mom and my younger sisters might have thought. That was our Sunday ritual, just for Dad and me. I now take it as a given that Dad and I must have been comrades serving in the same regiment in one or more of our Past Lives.

Of course, Mom ran a very tight ship and was a strict disciplinarian; she just did not hover over us. She encouraged us to venture out on our own. I had thus prided myself on being fiercely independent and self-sufficient from a very young age. I would ride the bus by myself to piano lessons, badminton practice, ballet lessons, Brownies and Girl Guides meets and a host of other extracurricular activities. I learned very early on that travels meant adventure, excitement and fun; travel meant freedom, and freedom, to me, had always been the epitome of living life.

Speaking of live-in amahs, they were mostly older Chinese women, except for the one ("Ah Yin") who took care of me when I was an infant, and the one ("Ah Kwon") hired when Vivian was born. I was too young to remember Ah Yin, but from photographs Dad took of me with her, she was quite good looking. I remembered Ah Kwon very well; I was but six or seven years old then, and I was strangely attracted to Ah Kwon. Of course, I did not understand my feelings then; I was far too young to conceive of sexual attraction, but it was definitely a physical attraction. I did not understand then that my feelings were not "normal" or "acceptable;" that would become abundantly—and agonizingly—clear to me in just a few more years.

From a very early age, I was blessed with the propensity for living life with unbounded optimism, augmented by that uncanny sense of exceptionalism. I awoke every morning with exhilarating anticipation of the day's excitement and adventure. Being the ultimate optimist, I was hardly ever disappointed; the cup was always not only half-full, but was *practically full*. My optimism begot wonderment begot more optimism. That empowering circle thus launched my life through an enchanting childhood, and more significantly, sustained me through many trials and tribulations later in life. It was fortunate that I was such a hopeless optimist, because we were of very limited means, and my parents could not afford to give us much in terms of toys or anything else that was not absolutely essential for sustenance. I distinctly remembered how disappointed I was one New Year's Day. We would usually get a gift on that day, often a toy that we had pined for during the year. I was perhaps six years old, and all Lina and I got that New Year was a slip written by Dad praising us that we had been "good girls," and our gift was a few balloons that we had to blow up ourselves. Mom and Dad must have been particularly financially stretched that year. A few years later, I learned how to ride a bicycle and was aching to have my own bike. Dad took me to a bicycle shop and I spotted one with which I fell in love. However, it was a men's bike, and the women's version had to be ordered. I did not understand why I could not have the men's version, but it seemed as if the store would refuse to sell Dad the men's version if I were the rider. It was as if they would be horrified and the world would end if

I were allowed to ride a men's bike. I remembered it cost "only" about HK$120, or roughly US$17; still, I understood that it was a "huge" sum of money for us. Dad gave me the impression that he had ordered one for me. Weeks and months went by, but the bike was nowhere in sight. Dad would tell me that the delivery date for the women's version had been delayed for one reason or another. I patiently waited, and waited some more, until I was eventually bursting with impatience. I would later come to realize that the delay was due to Dad's needing much more time than anticipated to save up enough money to buy me that bike. My lesson from that experience was, unfortunately, a thirst for instant gratification. In my adult years, I developed a taste for "high-end" materialistic goods, and my appetite for them had to be sated instantaneously, regardless of my financial ability or budget. That was, of course, a recipe for financial ruin, but that would be a lesson for another day much later in my life.

Another unintended consequence of my unbridled optimism and exceptionalism entailed, for better or worse, a complete inability to comprehend mortality. I did not have to grapple with the nuances and complexities of existentialist ruminations. Death, mine or another's, was a state of being that I could not acknowledge, let alone accept. As illogical and fantastical as it sounded, I for one would live forever. Life, no more and no less and above and beyond all else, is itself worth living to the fullest. Such zest for life helped me prevail in many a life challenge through the years. Hence, it pained me beyond words when Mom refused to enroll in the drug trial recommended by Dr. Qu to forestall her late-stage colon cancer, and instead allowed the cancer to claim her life four short months later. What I did not and could not appreciate then was quality versus quantity; that cliché of a concept was entirely lost on me then; it was very much a life lesson yet to be learned.

My early childhood was a period of pure bliss and fascination, marred only by very occasional hiccups almost too trivial to mention, if not for their far reaching ramifications in my adult years. I was enrolled in nursery school by age two or three years. One morning for some unknown reason, I did not feel like going to school; I did not want Mom and Dad to abandon me by dropping me off at school, as they did on all the other weekdays while they went off to work. They had to literally drag me onto the bus and into the school building, scraping my knees along the way. That behavior—a temper tantrum, as my parents probably viewed it—was very unusual for me, as I had always been a well-behaved child. I suppose I was struck by a sudden fit of "separation anxiety." Likewise, I was the only crying angel in the nativity play at nursery school. I did not remember my crying, but there was a photograph of me playing the angelic role; I was quite angelic then at age two or so, just that I did not want to be separated from my parents and my familiar environment and be thrusted onto the stage. The scientific-minded would most likely tag my separation anxiety as a mild, transient psychological disorder not uncommonly found in very young children. I, however, would conclude in retrospect that such "anxiety" had to come from a Past Life, as I could not imagine having experienced any traumatic separation by that young age which would have engendered such angst. Thankfully, that particular idiosyncrasy reared its ugly head only once in a blue moon. The next occasion when it struck was when I was about five or six years old, and Mom and Dad were late coming home from work one evening. I was so anxious that I went, with the hapless Lina in tow, to the lobby on our floor where they would emerge from the elevator. From that lobby, I could look 10-storey down to the long zigzagging flight of steps leading from the street up to the ground floor elevator lobby. I consoled myself by believing that Mom and Dad would "materialize" and come up the steps sooner if I affixed my gaze on those steps—that willpower of mine kicked in, apparently. It was getting dark and darker yet, and I was getting increasingly hungry; it was past our usual dinnertime. I panicked as I was getting angry, and ultimately became distraught beyond reason; by then, I was convinced that Mom and Dad had abandoned us and would never come home again. The fact that they did eventually show up did not ameliorate my innate separation anxiety.

Vivian, at about age 1-1/2 years, with Mom, at
Sai Wan Estate, Kennedy Town, Hong Kong.

The separation anxiety would manifest in subtler ways as I entered adulthood. The few times when my parents visited me in the States, or the even fewer times when I returned to Hong Kong, parting was worse than "such sweet sorrow;" it was unmitigated agony, and not infrequently with dire consequences. The feeling was one of my not being "whole" without my parents. As I came of age, that anxiety became the bane of my personal relationships. In essence, I overstayed my welcome and wallowed in destructive or even abusive relationships. I did not want to end a relationship, however ruinous it was for me, because subconsciously I could not bear to say "goodbye." Hence, I justified—ostensibly to myself—my unwitting masochism by labeling it honoring my commitment.

When I was about five years of age, we moved from the apartment in Sai Ying Poon. I was too young to know or remember, but I was told later that it was because that old tenement was being demolished, presumably to make way for a high-rise apartment building. Hong Kong was then in the thick of her post-War boom. With the influx of people and capital from mainland China and robust population growth in what became known as the Baby Boom years, real estate was emerging as a precious commodity, even more valuable than gold, silver or diamonds. Mom and Dad were fortunate enough to qualify for a government-subsidized apartment unit in what was known as a low-income housing project named "Sai Wan Estate" in Kennedy Town, a newer working class neighborhood west of Sai Ying Poon. These "estates" were springing up all over the Colony to house the working-class masses. Depending on the size of the housing project, there would be five or more multi-story apartment buildings, each with 20 or more units on each floor. The apartment units were of modest size and equipped with only the most rudimentary facilities. Each householder was assigned a unit based on family size.

Our unit was a rectangular box of about 400 sq. ft., including a tiny bathroom, a small kitchen, and a pint-size balcony. Those were the truly quaint days. There was electricity, and indoor plumbing meant basic cold water faucets and the proverbial hole-in-the-floor; there was no built-in bathtub or shower. We used a portable bathtub, and filled it with boiled water for hot baths in the colder months. When Lina and I were older, we could use the handheld showerhead hooked up to the faucet for showers. Of course, there was no central heating or air-conditioning, but we had many electric fans going in the summer months. It was up to the individual family to demarcate the various living areas. Ours was simple: a couple of floor to ceiling wardrobes served as the divider between the bedroom and the living-dining area. Just about every piece of furniture was foldable, collapsible and stow-able so that, during the day, the cot-bed would not be in the way of the living room, my sofa-bed would become a sofa again, and the dining table would be unveiled only during mealtimes. The balcony was where you would hang your clothes to dry on rows of bamboo rods on a rack up near the ceiling; clothes dryers were not popular then and were prohibitively expensive. After a few years, Mom did buy a clothes washer, the old-fashioned kind with hand-wind rollers to squeeze the water out of the freshly laun-dered clothes. Even so, it was a novelty amongst the neighbors, and the envy of other housewives. Mom had always fancied her-self running a modern, "Westernized" household, with the lat-est kitchen gadgets and appliances that her budget would allow at the time. Before the clothes washer arrived, amah would wash our clothes by hand, using a wooden washboard in a portable tub that otherwise served as our bathtub. The balcony also served as a small storage space for Dad's sundries, and for him to indulge in his passion for gardening with a few pots of plants and flowers. When I was older, about eight years of age, the balcony was also where I would shine everybody's shoes on Sundays. The small bal-cony was also where I was allowed to keep my "pets" for a while. Mom apparently did not like pets, and thus, we never had a dog or cat, and did not have any concept of pets until we were much older and living on our own. Sai Wan Estate did not permit pets such as dogs or cats; caged birds and small aquarium of fish were allowed. Hence, Dad had a small aquarium of tropical fish for a while, as that was the fad at the time. However, that did not last long as it proved to be too expensive to keep and was taking up too much room in our preciously limited living space. I was permitted to keep a tortoise and a box of silk worms for short periods because of "science projects" at school, but those creatures were banished by Mom to the balcony where, unfortunately, the tortoise committed suicide when it found a slit along the wall of the balcony and plunged to its death 10 stories below. I was fairly traumatized by that tragic death. My box of silk worms all died after they spun their cocoons. I still blamed myself for their not being able to metamorphose; chalk another traumatizing death-event up for my tender, broken heart. I did not want to have pets, ever, until Bev "forced" a caged parakeet on me some 20 years later.

Instead of keeping pets or tropical fish, Dad introduced us to what I thought was an even more fascinating hobby: model trains collecting; and not just any model train, but Marklin model trains. These were not ordinary toys; they were not made of plastic but metal, with every intricate detail represented to scale. I had no idea how expensive they were even then. I remember Dad started with just a few railroad track sections, an engine and a couple of passenger cars. Before long, he added curved track sections, train station and depot, tunnels, traffic lights, and all sorts of cargo and specialty cars. There were even engines with chimneys that spewed real smoke. In order to display and play with the trains, we would have to clear our small living room; all chairs and tables had to be folded up and temporarily stowed. I would help Dad assemble the tracks and lay out the station and landscape, and situate the various "people" at the station. Then came the delicate task of gently placing the trains on the tracks. We would then throw a switch and hope that we had connected everything correctly so that we could enjoy the trains running majestically on the maze of tracks we had laid down. For hours on many a Sunday, we would play with these model trains, making them go forward and backward, up the incline and through the tunnels, until Mom demanded that we disassemble everything so that dinner could be served. The hobby must have consumed too much of the "disposable income" that Dad did not in fact have, as Mom must have put a halt on his indulging in such an extravagant pastime. We stopped playing with the trains at some point; by then, I was too busy with my many extracurricular activities anyway. Fast forward to the mid-1990's when I stumbled upon a hobby shop and rediscovered Marklin trains. Sentimental memories of those happy days early in my life, playing with those model trains with Dad, prompted me to acquire and give Dad a new collection of Marklin trains and accessories; I was fortunate to have the financial means by then to do so. Dad proudly set up his new collection on a large table in the basement of their then new "dream home" in Windsor. That lovely finished basement was the repository of his wide ranging "collections," his "treasures." I felt very gratified that I was able to rekindle and share with him those cherished memories of my childhood, to which Dad was an outsized contributor.

While I thoroughly enjoyed playing with model trains with Dad—a typical guys' or father-and-son pursuit—I did not play with my younger sisters the typical "girls' games." I did not participate in their playing with dolls, having tea parties and preparing meals with toy cookware and kitchen utensils. Lina had *Barbie* dolls; interestingly, I was given a *Ken* doll which I nonetheless hardly played with. Mom really tried, but I stubbornly kept to my plastic swords and arsenal of toy guns. Another lasting legacy from that era was my penchant for acquiring only "the very best" with respect to material goods: not just any model train, but Marklin trains; not just any whatever, but a leading designer's or a world renowned brand of the whatever. However, since budgeting or saving was not my *forte*, and since I was not born into plenitude, nor was I a self-made millionaire, nor did I have a job that paid spectacularly, my expensive taste for the "finer things" in life left me in dire financial straits for much of my adult life. Couple my profligate ways with my knack for picking parasites for life partners, it was pure gracious fortitude that I did not perish by self-immolation but was instead given a second chance time and again to redeem myself.

Back at Sai Wan Estate in the early 1960's, Dad's interest in collecting grew in earnest; just about everything was "collectible" to him, even old newspapers. When his "collections" became sizable, he rented a tiny storage room on our floor off the side of one of the common areas. For hours on Sundays, he would disappear into his "store room." At that point in time, I was not particularly interested in his prized possessions, whatever they were. Unbeknownst to us then, all of his daughters had inherited his "hoarder gene." Mom was not so much a hoarder as she was an ardent and discriminating collector. She had exquisite taste when it came to buying furniture and furnishings, such as handcrafted rosewood furniture and Scandinavian dinnerware. She collected English fine bone china and Rosenthal porcelain. In the 1960's, the two large department stores in Hong Kong, Sincere & Co. and Wing On, periodically had special promotions of exquisite imported goods, under tantalizing themes such as A Week in Scandinavia, the Best of Germany, and A Taste of France. Along with Mom, my sisters and I were introduced to the world's delicacies and exalted accoutrements without as much as going near an airport, thanks to those department stores. We, therefore, grew up collecting "things;" accumulating and acquiring things while not letting go of anything was as natural to us as breathing. As I reached mature adulthood, divesting my "holdings" became a necessity due to unforeseen circumstances. I had been fortunate in being able to, just in the nick of time, recognize and reasonably tame the hoarder in me. Hoarding sates a false sense of security and abundance, and is highly addictive. It is likened to binging on "comfort foods." I can certainly empathize with those who feel the need to be cocooned by their possessions—even to the point of being inundated, overwhelmed and suffocated; but the uncontrollable urge to amass is in truth masquerading a deep-seated sense of inadequacy, lacking and deprivation.

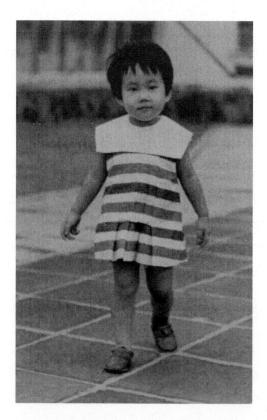

Author's youngest sister, Vivian, at 2 years of age,
at the rooftop playground, North Terrace, Sai Wan
Estate, Kennedy Town, Hong Kong.

There was another trait that I inherited from Dad—the "travel gene." Dad was required to go to Guangzhou (then called Canton) once or twice a year to attend large trade shows. I was too young to understand the concept of trade shows, or even traveling, for that matter, but I could see that Dad enjoyed those sojourns. I enjoyed them as well, because he always brought home interesting gifts for us. One of the most favorite items for Lina and me was jars of pure raw molasses; I think they were a specialty from Peking (Beijing). The molasses were ten times thicker than the richest honey or maple syrup, and tasted a hundred times more heavenly. Mom would dip into the jar with a chopstick and twirl it around and around until a delicious glob just the right size congealed, and we would lick on it for many pleasurable hours. There was another time when he brought back a leather suitcase; I absolutely fell in love with it. Mom and Dad immediately had a tailor make a canvas cover to protect it; years later, I was allowed to use it on my first overseas trip—to Japan. Then inexplicably, it disappeared. I did not realize until some years later just how much I had missed it, and I had been looking for a replacement ever since. I started collecting leather suitcases ever since I could afford them, but I still have not found an exact replica of that first-love; I am still searching.

Then there was the only family vacation we had when I was growing up: a two-day weekend trip to Macau which is about 37 miles southwest of Hong Kong across the Pearl River delta. That was years before Macau became the Asian Las Vegas, when it was still an incredibly quaint Portuguese colony in the backwaters. Vacations were considered a luxury in the 1950's and 1960's Hong Kong; I understood that our family was simply not well off enough to have vacations. Thus, when Mom and Dad announced the Macau vacation, I was shocked but was also excited beyond measure. I was about ten years old at the time. We took the hydrofoil, which was state of the art transportation then, to Macau; an old-fashioned ferry ride would have taken many hours one-way. It was also my first ever hotel stay, and it was luxurious, exactly as I had read about in the newspapers and magazines. The three of us kids even had a hotel room to ourselves. We rode horse-drawn carriages to the various tourist spots and historic sites. We had lavish gourmet lunch and dinner featuring the famed roast pigeon, fresh seafood and local specialties. For in-between snacks, we gorged on egg custard tarts and other pastries for which Macau was renowned. I felt utterly pampered, even as I was having an on-location geography, history and cultural education. We were supposed to have pancakes with fresh strawberries for breakfast at the hotel the following morning, but instead, we did not even have breakfast. I would learn later that Mom and Dad had exhausted their vacation budget. They did not bring enough cash or that was all the money they had for our one dream vacation; they did not have credit cards then. Nonetheless, I had decided from that one trip that vacations and travels would be my life's necessities when I grew up—whether or not my budget could afford them.

I have very fond memories of my years growing up in that Sai Wan Estate apartment. It was much newer and slightly bigger than the old tenement in Sai Ying Poon. More significantly, I had many playmates as most tenants in the housing project were families with young children my age. There were also several common areas that served as my play pans. There I happily spent my childhood as a very young "knight in training." There were more than twenty units on each floor, one next to the other, and thus there was a long corridor in front of the adjoining units. With the adjoining "Terraces" (other connecting multi-story apartment buildings in the housing project), some of the corridors stretched for "miles," perfect, in other words, for roller-skating, tricycle riding, and for us kids to tear up and down in general to have fun. There was also what passed for a "clubhouse." In reality, it was nothing fancier than a bare, large room on the ground floor of the administration building, which residents could rent to host parties or banquet feasts. Our apartments were so small that it would be standing-room-only if more than two or three dinner guests were invited. I remember well that Mom and Dad rented it for a few hours for my 11th birthday bash. It was such an honor for me that they actually spent precious dollars to rent the space and folding chairs, prepared the foods and drinks, and supervised game-playing at my birthday party. Once in a while, we would have two or three dinner guests—friends or coworkers of Mom and Dad. I loved those occasions because it meant we would have an extra sumptuous dinner: deep fried chicken, roast duck, roast pork, and other home-cooked specialty dishes Mom would serve up; when in season, we would also have steamed live crab and clams. It was definitely a gastronomic treat.

The Sai Wan Estate was where I learned to play a mean game of badminton, where I learned kite flying, played soccer before girls were allowed in the game, and where I could be just this side of mischievous as an active, athletic youngster. The only activities Mom vetoed were mahjong playing and tai-chi. She considered mahjong a form of gambling, and tai-chi a form of martial arts not suitable for girls. Hence, my sisters and I grew up as just about the only Chinese in Hong Kong who did not know how to play mahjong. Mom's puritanical view could have put me and my sisters in a decided disadvantage as Chinese women were supposed to provide entertainment (read: play mahjong) as hostesses for their husbands' house parties. Mahjong was also a favorite pastime for housewives. Fortunately, I was not a traditional Chinese housewife, or I would have been severely handicapped. I was very keen on learning tai-chi, and a neighborhood teenage boy was willing to teach me, but Mom put a quick and decisive *nyet* to that. I was sorely disappointed. I supposed Mom did not fancy my learning "kung fu," and with a stranger teenage boy no less. Those were the days before tai-chi was widely accepted as a form of healthful, meditative, low-impact exercise.

I do not recall the specific day I first picked up a badminton racquet and a shuttlecock, but I must have been prompted to try it when I saw other children swatting the birdie back and forth in the large common courtyard on the ground floor and in the small playground adjoining South Terrace. As soon as I had my own racquet and shuttlecocks when I was about six or seven years old, I begged other girls on our floor to play with me or let me join in their impromptu games. I was a natural at badminton, and became quite good rather quickly. Too soon, I was getting a tad too aggressive and in general too advanced for the neighborhood girls' pickup games. Just in time, I spotted an older girl and a couple of guys playing badminton in the courtyard on the ground floor; they were playing at a much more serious level. I took my racquet and boldly asked if I could join them. They agreed, and my badminton playing entered an entirely new level. The guys were the girl's older brother and father who did not want to rally with me at first. The teenage girl was already a much stronger and better player than I was. I started hustling for games on weekends, including with the girl's brother and father, and would play for *hours*, and would play until I was *beyond* exhaustion. That turned out to be extremely valuable training for me in terms of stamina and endurance, physically and mentally. When I was about eleven or twelve years old, I had the good fortune of having a classmate, Anna Yu Yuen Nar, whose well-to-do father played badminton with other well-off businessmen and a group of young men on Sundays. They rented the badminton court at the YMCA in the Mid-Levels just for their private games. Anna invited me—it was, of course, strictly by invitation only—and I started playing with the young men, and my game took another quantum leap. In fact, after a while, one of them exclaimed that I "played like a guy." I considered that the ultimate compliment. I did not care then that

I was not "ladylike," being so athletic and physically strong. As a matter of fact, by then, I was noticing increasingly that I was indeed not "ladylike" in many other ways, especially in the way I looked at and felt about other women. In the meantime, Dad had bought me a much better, professional-grade badminton racquet, and with that, I felt invincible. That dovetailed very nicely with the sense of exceptionalism I was born and grew up with. It was a boost to my ego that I was as well acing academically and excelling in a host of extracurricular activities. By the time I was in Form I and Form II (7th and 8th Grades), I won the trophies for the School's badminton singles and doubles two years in a row. My sense of sports superiority did not get somewhat deflated until I played in the Colony-wide tournaments against players from other high schools when I was in Form IV. I was eliminated by another young woman who was a much stronger and better player than I was; I was stunned and incredulous that I could be defeated.

In addition to badminton, I enjoyed many other extracurricular activities at Sai Wan Estate. There was soccer, a definite taboo for a girl to participate in during those unenlightened days. The neighborhood boys would play a pickup game at the small playground at the end of our Terrace. I would insist that I be a team member, and they would ignore me, but I would be a nuisance and refused to go away. Half the time they would let me be the goalie; they still would not let me kick the ball with the boys. Growing up a girl in a Chinese culture and community, I was aware of the many "don'ts" and "must not's" simply because of my gender. However, Mom and Dad never explicitly told me that I "couldn't" or "mustn't" simply because I was a person of the female persuasion, and hence, I proceeded to grow up without regard to limitations, restrictions or prohibitions imposed by traditions or taboos. Being excluded from the neighborhood soccer game at that tender age was my first taste of up-close and personal gender-based discrimination. It definitely made a compelling impression of manifest inequality and unfairness on this young lady's mind.

Fortunately, there were other activities from which the boys could not exclude me: kite flying being one, and "mountain" climbing another. There was a terrace on the rooftop of North Terrace. The favorite activity there was kite flying, throughout three seasons of the year except winter. Kites were very inexpensive then; they were also very flimsy, made of very thin paper with delicate bamboo "ribs." That was important as we were playing a very mean game of "killer" kite flying, requiring frequent replacements of kites. The key was in the strings: I learned from the boys to "sharpen" my lines with a mixture of broken glass and glue. The lines thus "weaponized" could be used to cut the lines of other kites in flight. In other words, the one with the sharpest, toughest line survived. I did not much like that destructive aspect of kite flying. I enjoyed watching the colorful kites drifting ever higher up in the glorious blue sky; it was liberating, soothing and exhilarating all at once. However, in order to enjoy kite flying and to ensure my kites survived, I had to "arm" my kites and lines accordingly. Those were essential and pragmatic lessons one learned in early childhood.

Then there was "mountain" climbing, another activity in which other girls did not engage. For me, though, it was natural to follow the neighborhood boys to explore the hillsides surrounding the housing project. In retrospect, it was indeed a very risky proposition, as I did not have proper hiking boots, clothing or first aid supplies—or cell phone in case of injuries or emergencies. I loved the thrill and adventurousness all the same, but Mom apparently did not like my running around with the boys, and in short order I was no longer allowed to wander into the "mountains." I did have other more genteel activities such as auditioning for a radio program, a very popular children's hour on Hong Kong Radio's Chinese channel. I qualified, and was picked to voice a witch in a children's story. I think I was picked for that role because I had a strong, deep voice for my age, and could do a "wicked" laugh better than anybody else around at that time. I was very proud of my achievement, as was Grandmother who was a devoted radio fan. I learned to appreciate Cantonese operas—decidedly an acquired taste—at an early age from listening to radio broadcasts with Grandmother. Mom and Dad were not amused, though, that I was tapped for that role; I suppose they were hoping for a role as a princess or just about anyone else but a witch. I remember that experience well, as there were many rehearsals before taping and airing. I learned to flip the pages of my script quietly without rustling the papers, and of course, I enjoyed being with the celebrated hostess of the program. That was my 15 minutes of fame at the tender age of seven years or so.

While I made many friends at Sai Wan Estate, so apparently did my parents. Mom had a lady from West Terrace, similar to an "Avon lady," who would come to our apartment from time to time to show and sell Mom Shisheido cosmetics, creams and lotions. Dad's coworker, who taught me swimming, lived with his family two floors above us. When Vivian was about four, we no longer had an amah. I was older by then, and could help look after my younger sisters. Moreover, at Sai Wan Estate, we had many "aunties" (neighbors) who helped my parents out. "Uncle" Michael and "auntie" Betty Tse from West Terrace had an amah and I would get fed a delicious home-cooked lunch before I left for school. Likewise, "uncle" and "auntie" Chan in Centre Terrace practically adopted Vivian. They had three children, the youngest son was about the same age as Vivian. Vivian spent much time at auntie Chan's who kept her well fed and helped her with homework. With a nod to Hillary, it does take a village, and Mom and Dad found their village at Sai Wan Estate.

I remembered very little about my kindergarten years, except that I must have been a good student. The teachers and fellow students seemed to like me. I attended an Anglican kindergarten school, St. Stephen's Church Kindergarten. I remembered those two years as a very serene and safe time period. When it came time for Primary 1 (1st grade), I was sent to a public school just a stone's throw away from our housing project, Sai Wan Estate, so that I could walk to school by myself. All I remembered of that school was that the students were extremely noisy and unruly. Not much learning was going on, as the teachers were too busy trying to keep order in the classrooms. I was not particularly interested in studying either, being distracted by badminton, mountain climbing, kite flying, and just about everything else but hitting the books. Then there were the street food vendors along the way. I had a small allowance of perhaps fifty cents a week, for which I had to keep an expenditure log. Mom thought she would train us from an early age to be fiscally savvy and financially responsible. Despite Mom's best intentions, that lesson was clearly lost on me as I was and still am deficient in money sense, often with disastrous results along my life journey. My modest allowance enabled me to indulge in an occasional snack of steamed rice noodle rolls with diced dried shrimp and scallion. Then there was the vendor making fresh baked egglettes—similar to Belgian waffles but they came out in a pan of little egg-shape bites. That was my all-time favorite. These egglettes are still being freshly baked and sold in Hong Kong; in fact, they have become quite a fad, a delicacy, selling not for pennies but quite a few dollars for a pan.

After one year at that public school, Mom and Dad decided something drastic had to be done before I would become a truant. For Primary 2 (2nd grade), I was sent to another school nearby, a Catholic primary school. They even hired one of the teachers there to be my private tutor; that was how concerned Mom and Dad were that I was falling off the wagon before I even got started. Education was apparently extremely important for children of upwardly mobile families; that was our only or best hope to break into the middle class and beyond. The trek to the Catholic school was much longer, and it involved walking by a cattle slaughter house. I still remembered the stench from the killings; I never dared look too closely. That did not make me a vegetarian or vegan, however; I suppose I never associated the killing with the delicious dishes Mom whipped up at dinnertime. You may also wonder why a slaughter house would be located in the midst of a residential neighborhood and practically next to a primary school. One quick answer was that the slaughter house existed long before the residences, apartment buildings and schools sprang up around it. Another explanation was that land use planning and zoning regulations were quite lax then. There was a *laisse-faire* attitude as this Pearl of the Orient, the emerging bustling metropolis, was then hurtling toward its post-World War II prosperity. Money- making trumped all other considerations, be they political, economic, or public health and safety. Hence, you would often find a tool and die shop in the midst of a residential block, and plastic flowers assembling home-factories were everywhere.

My Primary 2 year went by in a flash. The school was not as noisy, and the students were not as undisciplined. Nonetheless, I still did not have much interest in my studies; the concept of education being the key to upward mobility did not register with me, and the notion that academic excellence might lead to opportunity and prosperity did not even cross my mind. After all, I had badminton, kite flying and the rest of the lot of hobbies to keep me happily preoccupied and entertained. Besides, Catholicism was definitely not my cup of tea; it was too ritualistic and far too strict for this free spirit. I was not able to articulate it at the time, but the Catholic faith was altogether too oppressively patriarchal for this budding feminist.

Unbeknownst to me, Mom and Dad continued on their mission to find the "right" school for me. All I remembered was being whisked from school to school to partake in admissions examinations and interviews. I did not comprehend the purpose or the significance of those encounters. I only remembered one particular day of testing at another Catholic school, St. Paul's Convent, where I could not even read or understand the questions asked because they were all in the barbarian's tongue—English. That was rather humiliating. Suffice it to note that I did not qualify for admission to that school. I would learn later that St. Paul's Convent was Mom's alma mater. She must have appreciated the strict discipline of mother superior and the nuns who taught there. She sent Lina to that school from Primary 1 onward; Lina was thus thoroughly indoctrinated as a Catholic growing up, only to become a Buddhist *Acharya* decades later. Life's unexpected twists and turns could indeed be stranger than fiction.

I also remembered being interviewed at another school, and flunked the simple question of whether birds and cats were "good friends." Being the eternal optimist and pacifist that I was and am, and never having had cats or birds as pets, I saw no reason why they should not be "good friends," and thus answered affirmatively. Amazingly, despite that *faux pas*, I was admitted to the school for Primary 3 (3rd grade). That school was St. Stephen's Girls' Primary School (SSGPS), an Anglican school in the rather tony Mid-Levels District on Hong Kong Island. It was highly unusual for a non-public school to take transfer students; it must have been because that school was expanding and had capacity for additional students, and I had the good fortune to be at the right place at the right time. Chalk it up to serendipity. In fact, I still remembered a rather mystical experience when I was there for the admissions interview. I was walking up the wide flight of steps leading up to the floor where the interview room was located. The sun was shining through a doorway onto the steps, and the air felt strangely purified and invigorating. I felt as if I were entering hallowed grounds reserved specially for me.

Alas, the transformation of Liza Chan began there and then when I became a Primary 3 student at SSGPS. It was, indeed, meant to be.

From the moment I arrived at SSGPS to begin my Primary 3 studies, I instantly felt I "belonged." Even more than belonging, I felt a privilege and entitlement, as if I were specifically chosen to make my mark in life by being "formed" at that school. If there was such a phenomenon as unison of mind, body, spirit and purpose, I experienced that as soon as I stepped upon that wide flight of stairs again, going up to the classrooms on the second floor. My senses were heightened, my intentions sharply focused, and my innate drive to excel blossomed. My exceptionalism was at last allowed to be in full bloom.

First of all, it was an all-girls school. I had not previously been in an all-women environment. At the school, I felt instantaneously at ease; in fact I felt deliriously at home. I could finally breathe…and exhale. I had always gotten along well enough with the boys, but then again, in their company, I always had to prove myself, put up my guard, defend my turf, and otherwise show them that I was not "just another little girl." I did not fully understand then why I so delighted in the company of girls and women (the vast majority of the teachers were also female), but that obviously pleased me to no end.

I found my classmates utterly delightful: they were well behaved, well bred, and many of them had that upper-crust, aristocratic airs. That was what the English called *breeding*—that enigmatic quality that elevated one to the rarefied a-cut-above, ready to take on the world. Some may call that snobbishness, but that suited my exceptionalist *modus operandi* perfectly. It sounded almost chauvinistic, but in the presence of so many young *ladies*, I felt compelled to be on my best behavior, and to put my best foot forward. As I would learn soon, quite a number of my classmates were indeed from very affluent and privileged families. They were driven to school in their family limousine by private chauffeurs, complete with several amahs in tow. Since the school was located at the Mid-Levels, it was not possible for me to walk to school. Until I was old enough to take the bus, Mom and Dad had to pay for a "private taxi" (think *Uber*, almost fifty years ahead of its time) to take me—and five or six other children attending various schools in the Mid-Levels and packed like sardines in the car—to and from school. When I was old enough to take the bus, I found a classmate from the West Terrace, Connie Chong Yun Ching, to ride the bus with me everyday. None of us in the class realized then that we were fostering an enduring and profound bond of Sisterhood that would be cherished through the decades to come.

At SSGPS, we were required to wear a school uniform that was in the style of traditional Chinese pants and top; it was sky blue for the summer uniform, and navy blue for the winter version. A silver-color metal school badge (prefects in secondary school had a fancier, multi-colored school badge) had to be worn on the uniform at all times. The school's motto, "In Faith Go Forward," was stamped on the school badge. We would change into navy blue shorts and white shirt for Physical Education classes; attaching the school badge was required on that outfit as well. We were told by teachers to take pride in our school, that people would know and judge us by our school badge, and that we must not disgrace our school by misbehaving in any way while we were in our school uniform. Such was the discipline and moral compass with which we were indoctrinated—along with lessons from the Bible. The heretofore rebellious me snapped to attention once I became an SSGPS student. There was something about that school: the building, the students within it, the spirit of the place, which eminently agreed with me. I belonged, and I felt I had come home, finally; I could blossom to my full potential, at long last. Exceptionalism was given wings and at once took flight.

For the first time, I paid attention in class and I took an interest in my studies; shockingly, I actually wanted to excel academically. I was studying so hard that I was burning up with a fever when I was sitting for the final examinations at the end of my Primary 3 year. My efforts were not expended in vain: I placed within the top 3 of my class. I literally burst onto the scene, and never looked back. From then on, it was as if I had discovered my academic-excellence gene, turned it on and kept it on. Mom and Dad were obviously elated. To celebrate my accomplishments, Mom and Dad bought special celebratory "additions" for dinner: roast pork, barbecue pork, and roast duck. By then, I felt so thankful that I was a student at SSGPS that I would keep on studying diligently even without the enticement and reward of barbecue delicacies.

The curriculum at SSGPS was rigorous. There were the usual subjects such as English and Chinese language, civics, and arithmetic, but we also had classes in music, art/drawing, Chinese brush calligraphy, physical education, Mandarin speaking, and Scriptures. We were supposed to learn more than 2,000 Chinese characters and hundreds of Chinese proverbs by the time we reached Primary 6. As if that was not enough of a tall order, we also had to read, write and speak English, which was particularly challenging for me. I could not even pronounce the words in English, let alone compose a grammatically correct sentence. I devised a clever trick to help me remember the pronunciation by writing Chinese characters above each English word to prompt me phonetically. When Mom discovered my devious shortcut, she was furious and made me erase my laborious transliteration. Fortunately for me, classes at SSGPS were conducted in Cantonese and written Chinese. English, then, remained the bane of my existence; I simply could not accept why I had to learn such an inferior but difficult language. I loved my music classes, though, which was mostly singing, and I sang my lungs out. Likewise I thoroughly enjoyed my physical education classes; I wish we had a P.E. class everyday. Mandarin speaking, on the other hand, felt even stranger than English; it was to me a wholly irrelevant foreign language. It was not even on the curriculum of most other schools, except in the few Mandarin-speaking schools. Perhaps I should have paid attention in class then as Mandarin is now definitely very relevant. Drawing was also a stretch for me. I most certainly could not understand why we, who were deficient in the drawing department, were compelled to draw. Some of my classmates, such as Ivy Li, were superb at it and were the art teacher's favorites. Nonetheless, I persevered and muddled through Primary 6 after which, thankfully, there was no more mandatory drawing. Chinese brush calligraphy was a breeze, as Dad had coached me since I was four years old. It did not have much practical application then, and certainly not now, but it was considered mandatory for a cultured and well-educated Chinese. On the subject of writing, we handwrote our homework with No. 2 pencils and fountain pens—leaky pens, messy bottle ink and all—decidedly very quaint. Ballpoint pens were quite new then and were not allowed in school. Little did I know then that my love for fountain pens would be rekindled more than 30 years later on a 1996 trip to New York City. Scriptures classes were literally a different story, Biblical stories to be precise. I did not feel pressured to become a Christian, but it was unmistakable that I was in an Anglican school. Every morning we began the school day with an Assembly in which the entire student body gathered for hymn singing, readings from the Old and New Testaments, a short sermon, and recitation of the Lord's Prayer. I had no notion of or allegiance to any particular religion—good, bad or indifferent—as my parents were not churchgoers. I viewed the morning Assembly as a daily ritual without ascribing to it any religious undertone, and the Scriptures classes were to me another variation of a history lesson. In retrospect, my naïveté, as it was, saved me from the peer pressure of having to join an organized religion until years later. At SSGPS, we had two classes for each grade, morning and afternoon classes. For instance, I was in the morning class for Primary 3, and the following school year, I would be in the afternoon class for Primary 4. Thus, I would not know my classmates in the other class of the same grade. It would not be until several years later when we "ascended" to secondary school with a full day of school that we would know everyone, about 120 students in all, in our Form. During recesses—there were at least two 10-minute breaks each half-day of school—we would rush downstairs to the playground to play jump-rope (ropes made with stringing rubber bands together). Most of the time, I would go to the ping-pong room to play table tennis. It was entirely self-taught, but I was a decent player for my age. For a while, there was also a "milk break" about midway through our school day, when we would line up for a bottle of chocolate- or strawberry-flavored milk, courtesy of the Anglican Church or the government. In sum, SSGPS was simply charming, delightful, and wholesome.

The school was founded in 1906; the year was proudly inscribed on our school badge. Thus, when I was in Primary 6, the school, both primary and secondary, was celebrating its Diamond Jubilee year. There were special events, including Open Day for parents to visit us in class, and view our handiwork and the school's facilities. Selected homework and artwork were posted on the classroom bulletin boards for parents' perusal. There was, of course, a special and spectacular Bazaar. School bazaars were held annually. It was a charitable affair, a genteel carnival as only the English could orchestrate. For sale were arts and crafts creations, re-purposed items, artisanal presentations, homemade articles, even baked goods. You can well imagine how Domestic Science teachers and students were pressed into service on overdrive for our annual bazaars. Outdoors on school grounds were many games booths for visitors to try their luck with basketball shooting, knocking down bowling pins with a softball, hoops and bean bag toss, and many other similar family-friendly attractions. I remembered thinking then that by the time the school celebrated its 100th anniversary, I would be in my 50's. For a young teenager, that was a sobering thought and a measurement of time that could not be fathomed. As it turned out, I was able to attend the school's Centenary celebration in Hong Kong, but under circumstances that were entirely not anticipated.

I think it was a tradition at SSGPS to groom well-rounded students. It was also Mom and Dad's hopes and dreams for me to be multi-faceted. I was expected to participate—and excel—in a plethora of extracurricular activities in addition to acing academically. Piano lessons were almost *de rigueur* for upwardly aspiring youngsters. It must have strained my parents' budget to purchase an upright piano for Lina and me to practice our assignments. I think I started my piano lessons at the age of six or seven years. It did not feel natural to me, and I obviously was not a gifted pianist. I could not appreciate the sums expended and the sacrifice endured by my parents in order to pay for my piano lessons and to buy that piano. Still, as a dutiful daughter, I would attend my piano lessons every Saturday morning, even when I was delinquent in practicing during the week. My progress was erratic; there were periods when I was even brilliant, such as when I learned to play Beethoven, but not so much with Bach. By the time I was a young teenager, I had actually advanced through the Royal Schools of Music system and had passed Grade 7 for Practical Examination, and Grade 8 (the highest grade) for Music Theory. That, of course, did not mean I would qualify as a concert pianist or a composer, but that formal music training accorded me a comprehensive musical background and enabled me to enjoy a lifetime of music listening and appreciation.

Piano lessons were only the beginning. Dad convinced one of his younger colleagues, Lai Kim Man, to teach me to play violin. Once a week, I would go to Dad's office where "uncle" Lai would give me a lesson in the backroom. I definitely preferred the violin to the piano. Uncle Lai would in a few more years become a licensed traditional Chinese doctor and acupuncturist, and our paths would cross again many years later when his healing arts would restore my health on several critical occasions. In fact, he almost became my real uncle, because he dated my 9th Aunt (Mom's younger sister) in the 1960's. I had no idea why they broke up and I knew better not to ask. Because I could play the violin, I was "drafted" into the School Orchestra by the time I was in Primary 6 (6th grade). Hence, on Saturday mornings, I would dash from my piano lessons to School Orchestra practice. After about a year, I was "compelled" to learn and play the viola because the Orchestra was short on viola players while it had a glut of violinists.

To augment our training in classical music, Mom and Dad took Lina and me to concerts at Hong Kong City Hall on a regular basis. The 1400-seat concert hall at City Hall was brand new with then state-of-the-art acoustics. We attended performances not only by the resident Hong Kong Philharmonic Orchestra, but also performances by visiting world-class symphony orchestras and soloists. Classical music then was mostly pieces from the Baroque, Classical and Romantic periods. Until I discovered rock 'n roll, Beatles, Woodstock and the rest a few years later, music to me was Bach, Beethoven and Tchaikovsky. I enjoyed those evenings out; mingling with the ladies and gentlemen (in those days, concert attendees actually dressed up for the occasion) before the performance and during intermissions made me feel very grown-up and sophisticated. City Hall was not where the municipal offices were; it was akin to a cultural center. In addition to the concert hall, it houses an extensive public library, and an art gallery and exhibition hall. Dad was a regular visitor to the superb exhibitions, as his office at Union House was only a few short blocks away. He would drool over the antique scrolls, books and texts, Chinese water color paintings and brush calligraphy by renowned artists, antique jade and ivory carvings and porcelain on display. He also enjoyed the regular lectures presented on Chinese history, culture and antiquity.

My Saturdays in the early 1960's would soon become even more packed when I was allowed to join the Brownies, the junior division to Girl Guides (Girl Scouts in the States). I *loved* being a Brownie and later a Girl Guide; I was in the "Gnomes" patrol in the Brownies, and in the "Nightingale" patrol in Girl Guides of the 8th Hong Kong Island Company. I liked wearing my uniform (especially with my camping knife, compass and whistle), I enjoyed the activities (hiking and camping, in particular) and the skills taught (first aid and Commonwealth knowledge, for instance, but not so much sewing and hostess-ing). I remembered my first camping trip far away from town, in the rural countryside. Because we were women, we were not sleeping in tents outdoors, but in a dormitory on the camp site. Still, gazing at the mysterious night sky populated by tens of thousands of glittering stars, I felt so recharged, inspired and filled with awe and wonderment that I made a point of "communing with nature" as often as possible in my adult life.

Even then, I questioned what I perceived to be the sexist policy of the Boy Scouts and Girl Guides leadership. I felt insulted that Girl Guides were not taught the same camping skills as Boy Scouts. We were not trained to pitch our own tents, for instance. The Boy Scouts enjoyed extensive training for navigation and survival in the wilderness, while the Girl Guides were denied such knowledge. I did not understand why we were precluded, simply on the basis of our gender, from learning those useful skills for hiking, camping and outdoors adventures. Sexism was so ingrained in our society and culture back in the 1960's that it was not questioned let alone challenged. The unequal treatment between Boy Scouts and Girl Guides was yet another rude awakening for me:

that I would be severely constrained in a Chinese community as a woman, that there were formidable forces to keep me down and "in my place" as a woman in a Chinese society such as Hong Kong, or for that matter, even a British-influenced society such as Hong Kong. That was my reality in the 1960's; I certainly did not like it, and I most definitely did not think it was fair. I just did not know then what I would or could do about it.

Meanwhile, being a Girl Guide was as close to being self-sufficient and independent as I could get as a young woman back in those days. Hence, I enjoyed my Guides days even as I resented the built-in sexism. I especially relished the camaraderie and being in the company of other young women. As a matter of fact, I had my first serious crush on a woman when I was a young Girl Guide—on my Girl Guides patrol leader who to me was as beautiful as a Greek goddess incarnate. I would later come to understand that it was more than your typical teenage infatuation; it was in fact a preview to my sexual orientation which I was then too young to grasp or verbalize. It was also in Girl Guides when I first met a lesbian—a "butch"—but then again I was too young and naïve to articulate my own strong feelings toward women. In the meantime, I took great pride in becoming an outstanding Brownie and Girl Guide. I successfully completed all the requisite tests before, if I remember correctly, my eleventh birthday, so that I "flew" up to join the ranks of the Girl Guides. I, therefore, was awarded a "wing" badge on my Girl Guides uniform to proclaim that distinction. I also attained all the proficiency badges and passed all the mandatory tests before my sixteenth birthday and was awarded the esteemed "Queen's Guide" designation (equivalent of the American Eagle Scout), complete with a certificate signed by Her Majesty Queen Elizabeth II. Mom and Dad must have been particularly gratified because, after all, they met while Dad was serving as a Scout Master and Mom was a Den Mother to the Cub Scouts of the 13th Hong Kong Island Scout Troop. One overarching lesson I garnered from my Girl Guides days—above and beyond mastering the Morse code and building a fire with tree twigs and not more than three matches—was succinctly summed up in the Guides' motto: "Be Prepared." Be prepared, always, and even for life's most unexpected.

After School Orchestra practice and before the Brownies and later Girl Guides meetings on Saturdays, Lina and I would get a treat: lunch at the restaurant on the top floor of Union House in Central, in which Dad's office was located. Mom would walk from her office a few short blocks away and join us. Long before IBM Selectric electric typewriters were commonplace, most office workers in Hong Kong worked half-day on Saturdays; some still do now. I felt very sophisticated and grown-up at those lunches as Western food was being served, and I had a chance to practice using the appropriate flatware, from salad fork to soup spoon, from fish knife to dessert fork, and to demonstrate proper dining etiquette. On rare occasions, we would be invited by one of Dad's friends to lunch at a private club in Central. Adjacent to the dining room was the billiards room. Watching from outside the room, I was mesmerized by the distinct and crisp sounds when the cue stick hit the ball, the genteel décor of the room, and the elegance of the game. Yet I was told women were not allowed in the room, let alone play the game. I demanded to know "why," but Dad would only make vague references to cigarette smoking and wagering in the room which were ostensibly not suitable for ladies. It was the first time I was confronted with blatant gender-based discrimination; the game was off-limits to me for no justifiable reason other than on account of my gender. I was indignant: in a Chinese community, in a British society, I, as a woman, would have limits and restrictions imposed on me as to what I could do or could be. That did not sit well with me at all, even at that tender age.

After lunch at Union House was the highlight of my week: Brownies/Girl Guides meets, where we would learn and practice marching, rope tying, trekking, and what I deemed "military" skills for this young "knight" in training. When the fun ended, it was time for one more extracurricular class: ballet. It was certainly not my choice, but Mom and Dad apparently decided that it was necessary for a young lady to learn to be poised and wispy as a ballerina. Those attributes certainly were not my forte, and I was glad that I did not have to continue the suffering after three or so years of my ballet-pretending.

Saturday was also a day when charities were out in full force. I do not know whether it was a Hong Kong phenomenon or a British tradition, "flag day" was Saturday. Just about every Saturday featured a charity selling tiny paper "flags," printed with the charity's name, emblem or logo, for a donation of any amount deposited in the tin cans held by throngs of young and enthusiastic solicitors, strategically deployed at busy bus stops and bustling shopping areas. The most popular was the bright red paper poppy flowers sold on Armistice Day, commemorating the end of World War I. That was a must-buy. People proudly dangled the poppy on their lapels, flaunting their patriotism and support for the British troops and veterans and honoring those who perished in the Great War. Those were the days when life was definitely much simpler, decidedly black-and-white. There was no concern that the solicitors could be impostors scamming for money with their handy tin cans. Those were not collections taken for any political crusade, but fund-raising for decidedly uncontroversial causes such as prevention of cruelty to animals and research for better treatment for tuberculosis. The political landscape in Hong Kong underwent a sea change on account of the Tiananmen Square Massacre on June 4, 1989. There have been annual commemorative "6-4 marches" ever since, which in turn spurred many a civil disobedience demonstration, protest, and march on the Governor's House. Occupy Central and the Yellow-Umbrella Revolution of recent memory was a progeny of the nascent activism. However, fifty years earlier, in a time and place that seemed eons away from Tiananmen and the return of Hong Kong's sovereignty to China, Hong Kongers were a rather apolitical, pliant bunch, dutiful British subjects contributing to the burgeoning prosperity of the Colony, *Exhibit A* for the finest hour of British colonialism and its benevolent overlords.

Basking in the secure and nurturing enclave of SSGPS, I was thriving academically while I continued to hone my badminton skills and indulged in the smorgasbord of extracurricular activities. There was, however, a formidable challenge looming just ahead: at the end of Primary 6, we had to sit for a series of Colony-wide examinations to determine if we could advance to secondary school and if so, whether our grades were good enough to be admitted to the school of our choice. It was the first of two public examinations that would define a student's future, and her prospect for advanced studies and career options; the other public examinations awaited us at the end of Form V (11th grade). To prepare for the examinations, those who could afford it would attend private tutorial classes at night. It was the first time I experienced tension, pressure and stress. The drills were intense. The subjects tested were Chinese, English and Mathematics, and of the three, English was relatively the easiest, even though I still had to struggle mightily to make the cut. Math was tough, as it was not merely simple additions, subtractions, divisions and multiplications. If I remember correctly, we had to solve obscure problems using a slide rule, memorize equations for computing the surface area of irregular shapes, and figure out the arrival time of a boat traveling with and against the tide. Chinese was ridiculously brutal. We had to learn to write thousands of distinct Chinese characters and hundreds of Chinese proverbs, and understand the meaning and usage of each. During my Primary 6 year, I, along with ten or so other pupils, attended the tutorial classes for several hours a night during the week. They were held by Mr. Wong Kai, an uncle of a dear friend of my Dad's; his wife and three grown children would also take turns to teach at times. After the tutorial classes, I would return home for a very late dinner by myself, and half the time I was too tired and sleepy to even eat dinner. It was grueling even for a vivacious twelve-year-old. While I could not appreciate the significance or the nebulous concept of passing the examinations with high marks to ensure a bright future, I certainly understood the tragedy of not being able to join my classmates to advance to secondary school (high school) if I did poorly at the public examinations. The school of choice for me, of course, was St. Stephen's Girls' College, the even more exclusive, prestigious "extension" beyond SSGPS. Hence, I goaded myself to studying harder and harder yet. My hard work, focused efforts and dogged determination, and Mr. Wong's relentless drills, did pay off. Eye on the prize—SSGC, here I come.

IV.

Knight's Coming of Age

S t. Stephen's Girls' College molded, sculpted and polished the teenage me. It would be years before I would fully appreciate how those six years spent in that esteemed institution, from Form I (7th grade) through Form Lower VI Arts (12th grade), fairly shaped my life.

My first day as a Form I student at SSGC was exhilarating. I was wearing a new school uniform: same color scheme, but instead of traditional Chinese top and pants, it was a *cheongsam*, a traditional Chinese dress. I felt instantly much more grown up, even as I detested the inherent ergonomic restrictions of the garment. If I had stepped onto hallowed grounds at SSGPS, then I had stepped up into the consecrated embrace of SSGC.

The main school building was located only yards away from the primary school building on the same campus. However, as primary school students, we were forbidden to stray across the invisible boundary separating the two. Hence, the first day as a Form I student was my first glimpse at the fabled secondary school. The four-storey building had very high ceiling, and the classrooms were much larger and had a formal feel, as if to remind us that studious learning was expected. Even the air smelled dignified and rarefied. The assembly hall, Kwok Siu Lau Hall, was cavernous compared to the assembly area in primary school. Students and teachers from all seven Forms would gather for morning Assembly of hymn singing, sermon, Bible readings, announcements of the day by the school Principal, and prayers before the day's classes.

I was thrilled to be reunited with most of my classmates from SSGPS. The excitement of seeing so many familiar faces momentarily overshadowed the sadness of missing some of my best friends in primary school, including Elaine Tsui Yee Lin and Louise Choi Yuk Yung, with whom I would be reunited decades later. There were also a few new faces—students from other primary schools who chose to come to SSGC. For the first time, everyone—more than 120 of us—in the same Form was together, instead of being separated into morning and afternoon sections. We were divided alphabetically into three classrooms: Form I, Form IA, and Form I Alpha. Being a "Chan," I was in the Form I classroom with others whose first letter of their surnames ranged from A to about H. It was also exciting to finally get to know my classmates from the alternate section in primary school.

Our school day began at 8 o'clock in the morning and finished at about half-past three in the afternoon, followed by several more hours of homework. There was a lunch break around 1 p.m. The school was still serving lunch when we were in Form I. We would gather in Ho Tung Hall, our dining hall, sing a short hymn[2], and a hot, delicious lunch would be served to many tables of ravenous, talkative teenage students. It was strictly Chinese

---

[2] It was the well-known *Doxology: Praise God, From Whom All Blessings Flow*, lyrics by Thomas Ken (1674):
Praise God, from Whom all blessings flow;
Praise Him, all creatures here below;
Praise Him above, ye heavenly host;

fare—no hamburgers and fries or pizzas for us. We would hurriedly gobble our meal so that we could use the remainder of our lunch hour for fun, such as playing bridge, basketball or table tennis. From one of the school gates at Babington Path-St. Stephen's Lane, one would walk up the lovely, treed, and fairly long stone path up to the main school building. As I had described, there was a swing set near the top of the path, and during lunch hour, I would sometimes queue up for my turn on the swings, or chat with classmates in the garden by the path. On quite a few occasions walking up the path, I would see my classmate, the effervescent May Chien May Fung, enthusiastically waving at me with a toothbrush dangling from her mouth (she, the poster child for proper dental hygiene, brushing after each meal), from a 4th floor—the boarders' floor—window of the school building. She was a boarder when SSGC had boarding facilities for students from overseas, such as Thailand, Cambodia and Vietnam, as well as students from the farther reaches of the Colony. At its peak, the school had about sixty boarders. It unfortunately had to cease operations at the end of our Form I year when the headcount was down to about thirty boarders. May had remained our Class' most ardent cheerleader and booster since our graduation. She had tirelessly organized our reunions and hosted countless gatherings throughout the years to nurture our dynamic and empowering Sisterhood. We have another classmate, Anita Liu Chow, who as early as the 1980's, had the foresight to ensure our bonds would become even more enduring with the passing years. In those quaint days before computerized spreadsheets and apps,

---

Praise Father, Son, and Holy Ghost. Amen.

In Chinese:

我們會食同心感謝

一粥一飯來處不易

上帝恩賜同胞汗血

歡喜領受為人服役 阿們

before e-mails and Internet, and before social media, she undertook the monumental task of tracking us down—we were by then scattered all over the globe—compiling, and regularly updating and distributing contact information to Class members. In recent years, yet another classmate, Julia Wong Yee Lin, has taken over that herculean undertaking to ensure that we are but an e-mail or telephone call away from each other.

Those first days at SSGC were immensely stimulating. Everything seemed to be new yet familiar, while the familiar surfaced with a new twist. In retrospect, there were indeed many tacit dichotomies. We were encouraged to be creative and enterprising, yet the curriculum and classes were very structured. Individualism and free-spiritedness were lauded yet utmost respect had to be paid to Chinese tradition and the all-important unspoken English *breeding*. Boldness and originality were applauded yet convention and orderliness had to be adhered to. Perhaps we were being schooled in the wise ways of pursuing "Balance" in life, walking the Buddhist path of the "Middle Way," or living the Confucian ideal of moderation. To a bravado young teenage me, it was tremendously confounding at times.

If schooling at SSGPS was rigorous, then the pedagogy at SSGC was exacting and demanding. All classes, except Chinese Language and Literature, Chinese History, and Mandarin (which remained compulsory through Form II), were conducted in English. Classes included Mathematics, Geography, (European) History, Biology, Chemistry, Physics, English Language and Literature, hardly "fluffy" subjects one and all. Thankfully, we still had Music and Physical Education classes for a change of pace. Most of our teachers were very strict and serious lecturers. Pity the few younger, newer teachers then, as we would take full advantage of their relative inexperience; after all, as well behaved as we were, we were still a bunch of rambunctious young teenagers. We had quite a few teachers "imported" from England; I feared them the most because I—still—could hardly communicate in English. Presiding over these multifaceted proceedings was our school Principal, the formidable Miss K. E. Barker (those were the days before *Ms.*; a woman was either a *Miss* or *Mrs.*). She was the quintessential stern English headmistress. She did not even have to utter a word; one sideward glance at you and you would sheepishly confess to all your misdeeds and meekly beg for mercy, that is, if you still had any nerve left to form a coherent sentence.

Each classroom of students was assigned a responsible teacher. For my Form I year, it was Miss Poon Chor Ying, a very experienced Chinese literature and Chinese history scholar. She apparently liked me and my Chinese writings—we had to turn in a weekly journal in Chinese, among many assignments—and gave me high marks. I in turn adored her, and studied especially diligently my Chinese literature and history lessons. Chinese history was extremely challenging: 5,000 years of dates, places, names, warriors and emperors, dynasties, wars and countless historic events to commit to memory. It, however, dovetailed nicely with my Chinese superiority complex at the time, and more than compensated for my English deficiencies. Each class also had a class monitor, selected by the responsible teacher. She was generally someone who was considered a "model student," as she was tasked with keeping "law and order" in the classroom, though not always successfully. Additionally, each class was assigned one or two Prefects. Those were upperclasswomen (Forms V and VI students) selected by the Principal to be leaders and models for the younger students. They would visit their respective assigned classes on a weekly basis before morning Assembly. They were supposed to be available to reasonably assist us with our studies and academic issues. In reality, they became objects of teenage crushes. I most certainly had a hopeless crush on my Form I Prefect, Sophia Wong, who was then in Form Upper VI Arts. It was actually more than just a crush, though I could not articulate it at the time my strong feelings for her.

In the meantime, I had much to distract me from trying to understand or analyze my "strong feelings" for women. First of all, there were always tests and quizzes, and hence, studying took up many more hours than when I was in primary school. To my delight, there was an even greater range of extracurricular activities for me to try out. As the ping-pong tables were located in a covered playground just yards from my classroom, I played table tennis just about every chance I had, during recesses and lunch hour. The fact that I was at times outmatched by my classmate Sandra Lau Pui Sum did not deter me from trying to improve my game. Then there were basketball and volleyball. During my years at SSGC, her volleyball team was in the midst of a 13-consecutive-year run as the inter-collegiate champion. Our coach was the legendary P.E. teacher, Miss Siu Wai Ling, whom all of the athletically inclined students at SSGC worshipped. I was not on the school basketball or volleyball team, but I was on the Class teams. In Forms I and II, Miss Barbara Feathers (Mrs. Fonseca) coached me on the finer points of my badminton game. I joined the bridge club and the drama club, even though I knew next to nothing about either. It was no surprise that I was lousy at bridge; growing up, as you may recall, Mom allowed us to play only one or two "non-gambling" type card games. Dramas and plays, on the other hand, were staged regularly when we were in the lower Forms, and everyone was expected to participate. I was not particularly good at acting either. In the role of the king in a play when we were in Form I, I klutzily fell down as I royally descended some rickety steps from my "throne," astonishing my "ministers," including Rita AuYeung Tung Yi and Vivian Fung Wai Wan, who stood frozen and tongue-tied on the stage. I suppose we were too green for improvisation then, but it was experiences like that (the drama play, not the falling down) that cemented our bonds for life. I even took up French for almost a year. It was not offered at school, but at Maison Française. It was fashionable then for students to be fluent in a foreign language in addition to English. That proved to be an overreach for me; French was not my cup of tea, while years later, I discovered that I was more adept at learning the German language.

When I was in Form II, a new teacher, Miss Rosalind Stephenson (Mrs. Melis), arrived from England. She taught us geography, but she also introduced those of us interested to soccer and tennis. Needless to say, I immediately signed up for tennis (playing with my left hand so as not to "ruin" my right hand's badminton game), and was enthralled that I finally had formal coaching for soccer. I would practice early every morning hitting the tennis ball against a wall, kicking and chasing the soccer ball around in the playground all by myself. As for geography lessons, I had never been more attentive in class. I was strangely attracted to Miss Stephenson. It was not a crush but more of a fascination. I ached for her to notice me. It was as if she knew something that I did not know or that I wanted to know more about. My hunch was spot-on, as it turned out. She only taught at SSGC for a couple of years, but our paths would cross again in 1978 when I would learn that we had much in common.

It was around that time that the school recommended me for membership in the Hong Kong Youth Orchestra as a violist. I would travel to the Kowloon side, to a large hall at a technological college located in Hung Hom, for our weekly orchestra practice. If I remembered correctly, we would have a concert or two every year, at the concert hall at City Hall in Central no less, tackling an ambitious repertoire ranging from Beethoven's *Symphony No. 5*, to Mussorgsky's *Pictures at an Exhibition*, to Dvorak's *Symphony No. 9 (From the New World)*. Our Music teacher at the time, Miss Jacqueline Pullinger, was also in the Youth Orchestra as the lead oboist. I used to think that it was rather strange that we both should be in the *Youth* Orchestra. I did not realize just how youthful she was, even though she was one of our teachers. Miss Pullinger was a most unorthodox teacher, as I will detail later in these pages. I continued to play the viola in SSGC's school orchestra, of course, and we, too, would occasionally stage concerts at City Hall. I remembered a particularly grand project when I was in Form IV: we performed Gluck's opera *Orpheus and Eurydice*. Hours and hours spent with my classmates in school orchestra practice cemented our bonds: Vivian Fung Wai Wan standing behind me with her double-bass, Cheung King Kok, Leonora Chau Ling Yi, Joanna Lam Sau Tsen, and the twins Cherry Fung Yu Ching and Susan Fung Yu San in the violin section, and Diana Cheung Nan Yat the oboist.

In addition to its academic excellence, SSGC was also famed for her nonpareil school choir, led by the distinguished Professor Chao May-por, which placed first year after year at the Hong Kong Schools Music Festival. You can well imagine how we were seriously groomed from Form I onward to carry on that tradition. Proudly, I was chosen, as an alto, to be a member of the school's choir when I reached Form III or IV. Choir practice took up another chunk of my dwindling free time, but I thoroughly appreciated yet more immersion in music. Music indeed had an outsized presence in our lives growing up at SSGC. Folk songs— folk song singing, accompanied by acoustic guitar—were taking over Hong Kong by storm in the late 1960's. We did not associate the trend so much with the anti-Vietnam War movement as an "in" thing to do. Dad bought me a Spanish guitar and I taught myself a few chords, and that was good enough for me and a few classmates—Diana, Mona Chin Sau Hing, Cherry and Susan—to form our own folk singing group, "The Unicorns." Susan and I played the guitar, and all five of us sang our hearts out. We learned from sheet music by Peter, Paul and Mary and Joan Baez. Other classmates formed their combos, too. Vivian Fung and Jennifer

("Ah Fook") Luk, her friend from another all-girls school nearby, Sacred Heart Canossian College, formed their duo. Jennifer was hanging around us so much throughout our secondary school years that she had been "inducted" into our Class as an honorary class member; she had been joining us regularly for reunions and group activities. Seven schoolmates from upper classes formed "Tomorrow Seven" which had quite a following at the time. "The Unicorns" practiced when we had time; it was not as if we had to prove our worth or justify our existence. It was another excuse to be with each other outside of the classroom, and to be enjoying a wholesome, fun-filled hobby with friends. By the time we were in Form IV, we felt confident enough to enter the folk singing category of the annual Hong Kong Schools Music Festival. To our utmost surprise and delight, we placed second in a very competitive field; our winning number was the tried and true spiritual, "Go Tell It On the Mountain." As it was the height of the folk song craze in Hong Kong, we were immediately booked to appear on television shows and folk concerts. We were too green and unprepared to be "rock stars." Thankfully, the fame did not last too long or it would have spoiled us for life. Still, it was a heady ride with all the adoring fans, and if we were more serious about pursuing our fame and fortune, we would have been offered a recording contract.

In Form I, we had the good fortune of having Professor Chao, who led our School Choir to perpetual dominance at the Hong Kong Schools Music Festival, to be our Music teacher. In Form II, a new music teacher, Mrs. McAllister, took over the baton. Miss Pullinger became our Music teacher when I was in Form III; she had literally just got off the boat from England. In addition to continuing the tradition of and emphasis on vocal training, Miss Pullinger taught us to play the recorder. I started out, as with everyone else, on the soprano recorder, and was then picked to play the alto recorder in our all-recorders band. All of us loved Miss Pullinger, even if not everyone loved music or singing or playing a musical instrument. Unlike other teachers, she was very approachable, full of energy, enthusiasm and charm; charismatic would best describe her unique magnetism. She had quite a contingent of groupies—students who had a crush on her. We did not realize then that she was only a few years our senior, having just graduated from university herself. There was something else that we did not know when she first arrived at SSGC: she wanted to be a missionary, and Hong Kong ended up being her chosen locale for saving souls. As detailed in her best-seller, *Chasing the Dragon: One Woman's Struggle Against the Darkness of Hong Kong's Drug Dens*[3], she thought her destination was somewhere in India, but she sailed on; when the ship docked in Hong Kong, she knew she had arrived. Call us naïve, but we, her students, did not figure out until much later that she led a double-life: a perfectly respectable teacher at a prestigious parochial school by day, and by night and on weekends, she was God's messenger zealously evangelizing drug addicts and outcasts in the notorious slum of all slums, the Kowloon Walled City. I had some vague memories of going to her small apartment on Robinson Road, but I could not recall whether those visits were for band practice or for her to evangelize me and my classmates. Connie Chong also recalled her visiting us at Sai Wan Estate, of which visit I had only the faintest recollection. Connie had a born again experience during that visit by Miss Pullinger who pointed out certain "divine sightings" to Connie. Obviously, her evangelizing did not even leave any impression on me, while some of my classmates were called by Jesus. Starting when I was in Form III, I and some of my classmates were "recruited" by Miss Pullinger to assist in her missionary work. As she did not speak any Chinese then, she

---

[3] Pullinger, Jackie, with Andrew Quicke, *Chasing The Dragon: One Woman's Struggle Against the Darkness of Hong Kong's Drug Dens*, first published in Great Britain in 1980 (Hodder & Stoughton, 2006).

needed interpreters. Of course, it sufficed to note that, fifty-plus years on, she now speaks Cantonese even more fluently than I do, as I had spent most of those years in the United States. Some of the places we evangelized were very civilized; we would even be served a proper afternoon tea after the Gospel teachings and hymn singing. I found the English afternoon tea routine rather fascinating, but the crumpets, the wee sandwiches and biscuits were most definitely overrated. We, the Hong Kong Cantonese, were practically born foodies; the finer points of the rather bland morsels accompanying the English afternoon tea were lost on us.

My memory was quite foggy on our excursions into the proverbial forbidden city with Miss Pullinger. Perhaps I was subconsciously blocking them out as I could not believe that I had actually ventured into Kowloon Walled City. No self-respecting person would go near there, let alone a privileged teenage schoolgirl. Even the police would not patrol there or interfere with the illicit dealings inside those "walls." If my parents had known I was venturing into the Kowloon Walled City, they would have been livid. On the other hand, I must have told them as it was not possible for me to have unexplained "disappearances." The fact that I was traveling with Miss Pullinger, an SSGC teacher, must have sanitized the entire affair as a school-sanctioned outing and thus assuaged my parents' angst. I and a few of my classmates would accompany Miss Pullinger, mostly on weekends, into that forsaken underworld ruled by the Triads and densely populated by prostitutes, drug addicts and outlaws. She had established a mission there, a community center. We would lead hymn singing, she would read from the Bible, and preach the Gospels. I remembered well one time when I was acting as her interpreter, and she read from the Gospel according to John, Chapter 3, verse 16: "For God so loved the world, that He gave His only begotten Son, that whomsoever believes in Him shall not perish, but have everlasting life." I did not have a Chinese Bible with me, but all those years of

Scripture lessons came in handy: I did not have to interpret as I was able to recite from memory that particular Biblical verse in Chinese. I impressed even my classmates who were with me that day, especially since I was not even a Christian then. I am sure that the impoverished denizens must have thought that the young Caucasian woman was *mad* for trespassing into that den of sin, and that we, the kids, were foolhardy or insane to stray with her. After a year or so, she was able to find locals to interpret for her. She devoted to her mission work full-time after teaching a few years at SSGC. Even though Kowloon Walled City was finally demolished in 1994, Miss Pullinger had continued to save souls and heal drug addicts with the Spirit, and her mission and rehabilitation residences for the drug addicts had grown exponentially over the decades. She named her mission: St. Stephen's Society.

Music was not my only pressure cooker relief valve from the rigors of academic studies at SSGC; there was always sports, the active side of me that nurtured my physical endurance and honed my competitive spirit. Track was not my cup of tea, but field was where I comfortably dwelled. At the school's annual Sports Day, I competed in various "throwing" events. When I was at SSGPS, I was the champion in cricket ball throwing. At SSGC, I "graduated" to softball throwing, and then to shotput, both of which events I held the school record for years. Sports Day was also when you would find me running around with my camera taking pictures of my classmates, such as Anita Liu's preparing for her 100-yard dash, or of my less active classmates enjoying their picnic lunch or happily chitchatting. I did not realize then how natural, or important, photography was and would be for my well-being. I continued with my Sunday badminton practice with the guys at the YMCA until 1967, when riots and bomb threats erupted throughout the Colony. The Cultural Revolution was gathering momentum in Mainland China, and the leftists and pro-Beijing elements were emboldened to challenge the authorities in Hong

Kong. I witnessed confrontations between the riot police and pro-
testers in Central on quite a few occasions after my Sunday badminton practice. It was an extremely tense period in Hong Kong.
It so happened that the host of these Sunday badminton meets
was an editor or publisher of a leading leftist Chinese-language
newspaper, and not surprisingly, the badminton meets ended
when the riots became widespread by mid-1967. I remembered
well Miss Barker's addressing us at morning Assemblies; it was
the characteristic "stiff upper lip" approach to surviving the crisis.
Survived we all did, thanks in no small part to our gallant *Royal
Hong Kong Police Force*.

To make up for the loss of advanced badminton practice, I
stumbled upon a new interest which, for a couple of years, added
a new dimension to my assortment of extracurricular activities.
When I was in Form III, a performance by a schoolmate in Form
V on a *zheng*—an ancient Chinese musical instrument similar to
a zither—resonated with me deeply. The haunting sounds emanating from the *zheng* spoke to the contemplative side of me that
oftentimes was overpowered by my extroverted leanings and
undertakings. My journey to learning to play the *zheng* was unlike
playing any other musical instrument. The details are somewhat
hazy now, but procuring a *zheng* was not a simple act of going to
a store and buying one. Perhaps that would be too expensive for
my parents' budget. Instead, Dad located an artisan in the New
Territories who would build one for me. While my *zheng* was
being fabricated, through Dad's "connections" I found a teacher,
and a famous one at that. Leung Mo Sheung was a well-known
Cantonese opera singer, a woman playing and singing male roles.
When my *zheng* was built, I picked it up myself, traveling quite a
distance into the New Territories. I also had to make the three finger picks myself; perhaps that was part of the training as a *zheng*
player. I still remembered vividly the sweet aroma of my new *zheng*;
it was the special wood used. I traveled to my teacher's apartment

for my lessons, and the first lesson was nerve-wrecking, because I was going to meet a famous performer-star in person and because I had never played a Chinese musical instrument. Her apartment was huge, very tidy and richly appointed. She led me into a room where her *zheng*—a very elaborate and expensive one, probably an heirloom—was placed. She had handwritten the music for me to start my lesson. Unlike Western music, Chinese music was written in Chinese characters; that was very novel but presented quite a steep learning curve for me. The finger placement and movements in playing a *zheng* had nothing in common with playing the piano, the violin, the viola or the guitar. Miss Leung herself was most impressive. She came across as a very stern teacher and a very serious musician. In other words, she was one of the very few who intimidated me. There was also what I would call her "male persona" which alternately fascinated and again intimidated me: I felt I could identify with her and yet I was apprehensive about identifying with her. I definitely found in her a kindred spirit.

It never occurred to me then that my parents had to sacrifice somehow, somewhere, so as to pay for all the extracurricular activities for me and Lina, and later on, for Vivian. Perhaps Dad did not get new clothes and Mom used the beat up set of pots and pans year after year. Their altruism and foresight enabled my sisters and me to enjoy learning beyond strictly academic subjects. It was not as if Mom and Dad had any choice in any case, as most parents enrolled their children in at least one or two activities or classes outside of school. It was *de rigueur* if a student were to be considered truly well-rounded, aspiring and ambitious. Thanks to Mom and Dad, my upbringing in that regard had all the necessary and proper "credentials." In any event, money matters never entered my mind in my youthful days; that might explain why I was so ill-equipped to handle all things fiscal once I was on my own. Back in the 1950's and 1960's, Hong Kong was known as a paradise for bargain-hunting shoppers. Wages were ridiculously low then, but then again, everything from food to furniture to dining out was affordable if not downright cheap. The proliferation of high-end designer boutiques—the Louis Vuitton, the Hermes, the Gucci and the rest of the luxury brands gang—and the highfalutin life, which aided and abetted Hong Kong's claim to fame, became a hallmark only since the early 1980's.

Meanwhile, my timing, as usual, was off. By the time I was onto the *zheng*, I apparently no longer had enough "Chinese-ness" to play it well. I felt it a struggle to learn the instrument, an even huger struggle to find time to practice sufficiently, and an inscrutable puzzle to acquire the mindset to groove to classical Chinese music. It was then, when I was in Form III, when I underwent a transformation stunning even by my standards—me, whose life tended to accentuate on the melodramatic. Mrs. Katherine Chau Ma Pui Kin became our class's teacher for English Language and Literature. At that time, I was still barely limping along with my English studies. Mrs. Chau commanded my undivided attention from the moment she stepped into our classroom. She was elegant, she projected intelligence and exuded *savoir faire*, and she spoke English impeccably. To put it mildly, I was in awe. For the first time ever, English intrigued me; or was I intrigued by the mesmerizing woman who imparted such flourish on the barbarian's language? Her arrival on the scene sparked a rare round of soul searchinger H.

The analysis was straightforward, and the evidence was overwhelmingly lopsided, and thus, the conclusion came almost instantaneously. It was undeniable that, in my world then and there, English was king. In order to hope for a decent paying job and to advance in one's career in Hong Kong—a British colony—being fluent in written and spoken English was the bare minimum requirement. I was subconsciously holding out because of my Sinocentric pride. By remaining so handicapped in English, I was unwittingly sabotaging my own advancement. Pragmatism trumped Chinese chauvinism, and I resolved then and there to improving my English. Improved I did. It was as if I pounced on the accelerator pedal and never looked back. It was as if I had all twelve cylinders firing at full blast, and had gone from zero to sixty in two seconds flat. It was as if there was an "English gene" which was suddenly switched on in me. Mrs. Chau deserved much of the credit for my miraculous turnaround. I was inspired and captivated by her, and was motivated to diligently pursue my reading assignments, from John Keats to Elizabeth Browning to T. S. Eliot, from William Shakespeare to Charles Dickens to D. H. Lawrence and e e cummings. By the conclusion of my Form III school year, I was composing poems and stream-of-consciousness pieces—in English.

As noted in a previous chapter, when I was in Form V, merely two years after my "English awakening," I was awarded the "Most Improved in English" prize on Speech Day. I did not know if the school created that prize just for me, but I was pleasantly surprised and very gratified to be so honored. Speech Day was an annual formal affair when all the teachers donned their academic gowns to recognize and present awards to outstanding students for their diverse achievements. Of course, there would also be speeches by distinguished guests. When we sat for the "School Cert" at the end of Form V, a Colony-wide examination even more cut-throat than the one we endured at Primary 6, I garnered "Distinction" (the highest grade) in two subjects, one of which was Chinese Language and Literature. Many of my classmates were surprised, because even they had by then associated me with all things English and had forgotten that I had been a life-long "Chinese chauvinist" until just a couple of years prior.

Let there be no doubt or argument that quality and dedicated teachers beget inspired and accomplished students. All of my SSGC teachers were fine educators, but there were several who, with their wisdom, caring, wit and unique flair, left an indelible mark along the way in my academic pursuit. There was Mrs. Judy Chua who assuredly herded us through our cooking, baking and sewing disasters in Domestic Science, even as I thought the nomenclature for the class was an oxymoron, if not a thinly veiled euphemism to entrap me into "domestic servitude." Then there was the aristocratic and brilliant Miss C. L. J. Hallward (Mrs. Sworder) who imparted upon us lessons from European History when I was in Forms II and IV. Mrs. Alice Kiu-yue Lam, with a flamboyance all her own and who was our homeroom teacher in Lower VI Arts, took over European History when I was in Forms V and Lower VI Arts. Guiding me through the thicket of English Language and Literature in Form IV was the gentle and soulful, recent Hong Kong University graduate, Miss Angela Kwok, while Mrs. Angela W. Y. Cheung led our English Literature tutorials during my Form Lower VI Arts year. I count my blessings for having a stellar cast of mentors in my formative years; they had taught me well indeed, and I owe them all a profound debt of gratitude.

Alas, the law of unintended consequences reared its ugly head; at least that was so in my case. With my newly acquired fluency in English, I should indeed have better options for a quality post-secondary education, and I could expect brighter career prospects in Hong Kong. Soon enough though, it became painfully clear to me that I could never be "British enough." In a British colonial society, true power and prestige resided with the British elite, or at least with the Caucasian Britons. I could strive to be as British as I could aspire to be, but I would never be genuinely British; that was a "handicap" that I could never overcome. At best, I would become a "certified" Anglophile, hardly a desirable "status." In fact, the more determinedly I tried to emulate the British or to be "more British than thou," the more ferociously the stark corollary—inferiority complex—haunted me. It was a classic zero-sum game; there could be no winner in that quixotic endeavor. There was irreconcilable tension between my colonialism-induced inferiority complex and my personal exceptionalism. Moreover, as I would realize many moons later, that intractable sense of inferiority permeated and poisoned my personal and professional life. It would finally take the natural process of maturity, and a personal crisis in my fifties, to overcome that stumbling block. Nonetheless, it was a prudent decision on my part, as English became the unofficial universal language with globalization over the past few decades. Even though I could not ever be British enough, having a certain level of proficiency in the language had served me well. Much as Mom's "compelling" me to learn typing on my own when I was about fifteen years of age turned out to be another asset. In those days before everyone was texting or "personal computing" in one form or another, typing was a skill that enabled me to make enough chump change for sustenance when I was in tough financial straits as a foreign student in a foreign land. Not to spin too fine a point on this discourse, but English proficiency would not necessarily be a criterion for career advancement in Hong Kong nowadays, as the Chinese language is once again king since Hong Kong's sovereignty was returned by the British to China on July 1, 1997.

The reverberations from the leftists' riots of 1967-68 were felt even at our school. At the height of the riots, and for some time thereafter, several classmates left Hong Kong and emigrated with their families to "safe" countries such as the United States, the United Kingdom, Canada and Australia. During my Form II year, I "lost" my dear friend, Rebecca Chin Lai Kwan, to San Francisco; Margaret Szeto Kwan Yee, who was a rising star on the school's basketball and volleyball teams, also left us for New Jersey. With the takeover of mainland China by Mao Tse Tung's Communists in 1949 still frightfully fresh in their memory, many Hong Kongers, especially the well-heeled, hurriedly beat their retreat as the Chinese Communists' takeover of Hong Kong seemed threateningly imminent during those tumultuous months.

The exodus of Hong Kongers devastated the real estate market. Prices for apartment condominiums, or flats, were at a historic low. As our family was not moving overseas, we became one of the unexpected beneficiaries of the real estate bonanza resulting from the collective abandonment of this Pearl of the Orient. I had some notion that we were not in any financial position to buy our own flat, as we were still living at Sai Wan Estate, a low-income housing project. However, near the end of my Form II year, Mom and Dad were taking me with them to view the many flats for sale, all of which were located in prime and upscale residential neighborhoods. Even I could tell that the asking prices were insanely below market. After a while, I started fantasizing living in our own luxurious flat in one of those highly desirable and respectable neighborhoods. That was unfortunately not meant to be. Even at those Depression-era prices, Mom and Dad still could not afford to buy a flat. I learned later that Mom was counting on her employer to help out with a loan, but the head of that family-own company nixed the idea. Mom had never forgiven him for that slight.

All was not lost, though, because during those panicky days, there was also an over-abundance of vacant rental flats. Nervous landlords were begging for tenants, enticing potential renters with unimaginable lease incentives and rock-bottom rent rates. I did not know just how Mom and Dad came upon this absolutely exquisite flat in the exclusive Mid-Levels, within easy walking distance of SSGC, and located practically across the street from the main campus of Hong Kong University and the Fung Ping Shan Museum, one of Dad's favorites "hangouts" as I had noted. Mid-Levels was named for its location at about midway up Victoria Peak. It was fairly straightforward for gauging one's station in life in Hong Kong: generally speaking, the higher up on the Peak, the tonier the residential neighborhood, and the wealthier the residents. For an exception to scaling the heights of the Peak, if one was extremely affluent and desired true exclusivity while still having easy access to the razzle-dazzle of the City, one would then own a custom-built mansion—nay, castle—on a knoll on the south side of Hong Kong Island, in enclaves such as Repulse Bay, Deep Water Bay and Stanley, overlooking magnificent beaches and the spectacular seascape beyond, and where there would be no public access but a meticulously manicured landscaped private drive for one's customized Rolls Royce.

The first time Mom and Dad took me to view *the* flat, I was literally swooning with glee. It was a stand-alone 7-storey building with only two units on each floor. I was, up to that point, used to living in a massive apartment building with a multitude of indistinguishable dwelling units packed like sardines in a can. The entrance to this apartment building had walls of fine marble, and a very genteel name in Chinese for the building was tastefully etched on the marble. The air was pure and refreshing, and the surroundings were serene and exclusive. There was not a street vendor or market or shop in sight; instead, there were mature trees—how novel, *trees*—dotting the neighborhood. There was even a watchman at the entrance to keep out loiterers and intruders. We rode the private elevator up to the particular flat our parents were going to rent. Once we opened the thick wooden door to the flat, I was giddily impressed. Compared to our teeny "shoebox" at Sai Wan Estate, this flat was ridiculously capacious: it had a dining room, a living room which opened to a spacious balcony, a master suite, two additional bedrooms, another full bath with built-in bathtub, a sizable kitchen, a laundry/storage area, and servant's quarters (a tiny room behind the kitchen and laundry area). It even had a shiny, waxed hardwood floor, and plenty of windows to let in the sunshine and fresh air. I did not dare believe that we would be living in such decadence until the day the moving truck actually showed up at Sai Wan Estate. I also did not realize just how much "stuff" Dad had in his tiny rented storage room; it was well into the evening before the moving was finally completed.

The move to the Mid-Levels flat brought about subtle but profound shifts in our family dynamics and in my own perspectives. For the first time in my life, instead of sleeping in the living area on a "bed" which in the daytime was our sofa, I not only had a bedroom but my very own bedroom. It was small, barely enough to accommodate my twin bed, my desk (which looked out through a large window onto rooftop terraces of nearby apartment buildings), and a chest of drawers. No matter; that was a recognition of my special status as the first-born, while Lina and Vivian had to share the other, albeit larger, bedroom. I felt so pampered that I vowed to study even more diligently and strive to be an even more outstanding student. Thus, it was perhaps not a coincidence that my "English gene" was switched on around that time. Because of the proximity of our new home to SSGC, I could walk to school, and even had time to return home for lunch, which was decidedly a treat. The impact of living in the Mid-Levels, though, was a case of "the whole was more than the sum total of the parts." It was not simply the spaciousness of the flat, the gleaming wood floor, the fine bathroom facilities complete with hot water on demand, an air-conditioner in each room, all of which were unheard of amenities at Sai Wan Estate. It was much more than mere amenities. The move signified: "We have arrived." The middle-class status to which my parents aspired had finally been attained. With that came respectability and acceptance on a much higher rung on the social ladder. It was a monumental leap, actually. I began to understand the privileges and creature comforts many of my classmates were born into, now that I was living on the fringes of their neck of the woods. Of course, some of them lived in even larger and more lavish flats and glamorous penthouse suites. They could afford to dine at fancy restaurants, shop at exclusive boutiques with amahs in tow to carry their shopping bags, recreate in private clubs, with chauffeured luxury sedans at their beckon and call. I did not have any of those creature comforts, but from the perch at my new home, I got a glimpse of how the top-whatever-percent lived and played. To be fair, I also had a few classmates who hailed from the bottom-whatever-percent and who could ill afford even their school uniform. I believe the school fully or substantially waived their tuition and subsidized their books and supplies expense. I tried to be especially friendly with them, but I regret that I did not have the courage or the insight to be more empathetic. I should have, for instance, listened to them and cared more about their daily struggles which had to be downright insurmountable in our status conscious society.

For our little family unit which had been stratospherically elevated in one single bound, the changes were dizzying and dazzling. I remembered vividly the process of shopping with Mom and Dad for light fixtures for our new flat. I could not believe how insanely expensive each was. The point was that, all of a sudden, we had to decorate our home with complementary "appointments;" yet just months earlier and for years, a humble lightbulb or fluorescent tube sufficed for illumination. Beautiful, hand-crafted rosewood furniture arrived at our home a piece at a time: the sofa, the dining table and chairs, the telephone side table, and so forth. Even plates and bowls and dinnerware received ostensible upgrades, from the plebeian chinaware to exquisite porcelain and colorful Scandinavian sets.

Because of the larger, bright and airy kitchen, Mom's interest in cooking took a quantum leap. With new woks, pots and pans, roasting oven, and assorted cooking and baking gadgets, she served up delectable Chinese and Western fare from roast pork loin, Portuguese chicken, rotisserie chicken, borscht, to steamed fresh whole fish and my favorites, flash-fry vegetables fresh from the "wet market," and Mom's special butter-laden pound cake for snacks and dessert, and countless Cantonese version of comfort foods of the 1950's and 1960's. Dinner was always a happy and lively family togetherness affair. We took after our parents both of whom genuinely enjoyed food. Lina and I would often get into a friendly food fight: we were both growing teenagers with ferocious appetites. Lina could fairly "inhale" food such that she could finish an entire dish before anyone else could even get a glimpse of it. Fortunately, Mom's portions were very generous, and everyone left the dinner table stuffed. At Sai Wan Estate, our flat was so small that we would literally trip over each other. At our new home, however, we would go to our bedrooms to study and do our homework after dinner, while Mom did the laundry and ironing, and Dad would "disappear" in the servant's quarters which had become his storage room. We had not exactly drifted apart but we were not as physically tightly knit as in our previous dwellings.

Uncle Michael and auntie Betty Tse had also left Sai Wan Estate by then; they had also moved into a flat in the Mid-Levels, just down the street from us. Hence, they became even closer friends with our parents, coming over for dinner on a regular basis. Uncle Tse worked in the then nascent electronics-related field, and therefore had connections to audio retailers. On his recommendation, Dad invested in a stereo component system—separate components, and not an all-in-one unit that looked like an antiquated sideboard. I remembered well each piece in the system, as I watched Uncle Tse set up the system for us: a Lenco turntable, a Scott receiver, a Teac reel-to-reel tape deck (cassette decks and tapes were too avant-garde then), and a pair of floor-standing Wharfedale loudspeakers. I thought I was in music-listening nirvana. The significance of that first *real* stereo system in my life was not fully realized until years later: not only was a "quality" audio system an absolute necessity in my life, I started gauging the wellness of my life and defining my station in life by the quality and sophistication of my audio system. The "audiophile bug" bit me hard from the moment that component audio system moved into our Mid-Levels home. As I would learn later, a female audiophile was a rather rare bird; I was consistently the only woman "in the room" with other enthusiasts in pursuit of the objects of our obsession. When I attended high-end audio shows, where manufacturers showcased their latest and the greatest, I could tell that many did a double-take whenever I entered an exhibit/audition room ("A woman in our midst! How novel!"). I was used to being the odd-woman-out. In addition to audiophile gear since my teenage years, my passion for sports cars followed in the early 1980's, another typically male dominated pursuit. Then came fountain pens collecting in the mid-1990's; I would as a matter of course be one of only a handful of women in a sea of male collectors at pen shows held in major cities all over the country. Last but not least, since I rediscovered my passion for photography at the turn of the Millennium, I started collecting high-end film cameras and lenses as well. At photographic equipment shows, used camera swaps, and photography club functions, I would often be one of a tiny contingent of female devotees. That suited me just fine, as I had never been one to march lockstep with the masses.

There was, however, a darker side to all the dazzling lifestyle upgrades, courtesy of our move to the Mid-Levels. The acquisition of creature comforts and finer things in life had a price tag, one that was apparently too steep for my parents at that particular time. Soon after we moved in, I saw them engaging in heated arguments, something that I had never witnessed previously, in many a late evening when Dad returned from a business-related function or dinner. They made a point of going into the kitchen, farthest away from our bedrooms, before hollering at each other. However, I could see the kitchen from the window of my bedroom; even though I could not hear exactly what they were screaming about, I could see and feel that it was most likely about the runaway expenses. At those times, I felt a tremendous sense of guilt from enjoying all of our newly acquired creature comforts. I also wished I could help out with the family budget. The lasting lesson from that period, hence, was my resolution to make as much money as I could when I grew up, so that I could accord Mom and Dad all the luxuries they had obviously strived hard to provide for us. Therein sown the seeds of my materialism, for better or worse, and moral judgments be darned.

It was also after we moved to the Mid-Levels when I began to better understand and appreciate Mom. Dad and I bonded the instant I had any consciousness of my being; we had a natural affinity for each other. With Mom, on the other hand, there were never any shared interests or spontaneous sparks of affection. I supposed I had taken her very much for granted in my early childhood, all the while she was toiling in the background, sternly, silently, methodically, and thanklessly. Moreover, she was the parent who played the disciplinarian, and thus was hardly the "favored" parent. Dad was too gentle for that role; in fact, he would make himself scarce whenever Mom played disciplinarian. When we were tiny youngsters, Mom used to mete out discipline with a feather duster whenever we seriously misbehaved. She did not whack us hard; just the sight of the feather duster was enough for us to never transgress again. To the unenlightened young me then, there was nothing particularly attractive or beloved about her being. Then one day, as if struck by a lightning bolt, I suddenly saw and was awed by Mom's colossal role in keeping our little family functioning like a well-oiled machine, and everyone happy and together. She worked full-time as a secretary; full-time then meant weekdays as well as half-day on Saturdays. There was no down time for her after a full day's work at the office, as she had to plan everyday's meals, go to the "wet market" after work with Dad to buy ingredients and groceries to prepare dinner as well as the next day's breakfast and lunch for everyone. When she got home, she had to cook dinner for all of us. After dinner, she had to wash the pots and pans and dishes (few families had dishwashers then), and start a couple of loads of laundry. When the clothes were in the washer, she did the ironing (most clothes were made of cotton, especially our school uniforms and active wear). My sisters and I were "too busy" studying and completing our homework to help much with household chores. It would be well into the late evening before she could take a bath and retire to bed, only to start another day a few hours later, fixing us breakfast and preparing lunch that we could reheat, then off to the office she went again for another 8-1/2-hour work day. On weekends, she would take on additional tasks such as mending our clothes and helping us with special school projects. Her only recreation was on Sundays when she could take us to visit Grandmother occasionally or Lilian monthly, or enjoy a dim-sum lunch with friends, or go shopping for whatever the family needed. Once in a blue moon, she would squeeze in a movie with us, or attend a dinner banquet hosted by a relative or a close friend celebrating a birthday or a wedding. Though I was aware that we were of very modest means, Mom and her "magic" (read: hard work, budgeting, planning, scrimping) made life so that I never felt in need. On the contrary, even when we were living at Sai Wan Estate, I was always well-fed, well-clothed, well-provided for, and certainly well-educated, and very presentable. Hence, when I had a few moments to be less self-absorbed, and could instead momentarily focus on Mom's singular contribution to enabling our blissful and carefree lives, I was flabbergasted. She won me over completely; she was my new hero. I started helping out more with housework, and tried to make up for lost time by being with her as much as I could. I tried to learn the secrets of her cooking as she prepared our dinners and desserts, all the while as I endeavored to unravel the enigma that was Mom. She was not a demonstrative person, and did not verbalize her feelings; thus, it was only when I started being with her more that I realized that she was in fact very proud of me and my achievements.

When we were at Sai Wan Estate, we hardly ever dined out. After we moved to the Mid-Levels, however, Mom and Dad discovered this quaint neighborhood restaurant, Czarina Restaurant, located across the street from SSGC. From time to time, we would have a treat and enjoy a dinner there. I loved those treats as the food (Cantonese spin on Western—specifically, Russian, no less—cuisine) was usually outstanding, and I delighted in the fact that Mom would get a night off her cooking duties. There was a "specialty" at Czarina that made it worth the trip for her: the dinner roll. Czarina had apparently procured a very early commercial version of the microwave oven which transformed the humble dinner roll into a uniquely tasty, *über* comfort food. The delicately warmed soft roll became a sort of meal unto itself that enthralled Mom; one could say she dined at Czarina just for the dinner rolls. Imagine her gratification decades later when the microwave oven became as commonplace as a coffeemaker, and she could have her very own roll-warmer. As a matter of fact, Czarina was the *de facto* hangout for many SSGC students. Aspiring to be a "model" student, "hanging out" anywhere was not on my agenda. Besides, my allowance was so modest that I could not afford to hang out at Czarina in any case. It did make me wonder what, if anything, I had missed out by not having hung out there with my classmates.

My Form IV year was not a happy one. For the first time in my life, I felt enormous peer pressure to conform. My classmates and friends were starting to talk about boys and having dates with boyfriends. I felt lost, confused, abandoned, even betrayed, because I had absolutely no interest in boys. In truth, I did not even have any interest in forming any one-on-one personal relationship at that time. Besides, I was having too much fun with my classmates and friends in Girl Guides, the Youth Orchestra, and in various group activities. I had no notion of being attracted to the opposite sex; that did not exist in my world at all. Yet during our Form IV year, it was as if all of a sudden the boy-crazy gene (or more likely, hormones) got turned on in my classmates. May be I should have hung out at Czarina after all; I might then have been clued in to the what's and the wherefore's, and more crucially, viable alternatives, if any existed. Nowhere in my upbringing was there any mention of, let alone tutorial on, such relationships. That might explain why I was miserably inept with intimate relationships throughout my adult life, stumbling, hurtling from one disastrous liaison to another even more destructive entanglement. Dad had always doted on us kids as his "little girls;" the idea of our having boyfriends or eventually getting married could not have been farther from his mind when we were growing up. The ever pragmatic Mom, on the other hand, must have figured that such things were "natural" progressions in life: at the "appropriate" times, you would find a husband, you would get married, you would get pregnant and have children, you would become a mother, and there was nothing to talk about or to think over. However, those "life-progressions-according-to-Mom" did not at all resonate with how I felt or what I had in mind.

Nevertheless, there was the tremendous peer and societal pressure, and I felt torn by a raging internal dichotomy. As all my classmates were flocking to boyfriends and preoccupied with going on dates, and as the Chinese society expected no less of young ladies at that age, the pressure to conform to the norm was practically insurmountable. Yet, conforming simply for the sake of conformance ran afoul of my innate resolve to march to my own drummer. My upbringing dictated that I honor my abiding sense of self—self-reliance, self-confidence, self-sufficiency, integrity to myself. That left no room for unauthenticity, deceit, or expediency. On the other hand, I had up to that point in life prided myself on being a "good" daughter and a "model" student, and as such, I felt I could not do or be anything that contradicted the expectations of my parents and my teachers. To be "disobedient" or to disappoint my parents and teachers would run against every indoctrinated grain in me. Indeed, "approval"—needing and getting it—was drummed into me from my very earliest age. An extension of that need to be approved was to be "accepted." The unspoken rule was thus loud and clear and concise: you conform, you are approved and accepted, you advance, and you are rewarded. Mom was non-verbal with praise and non-demonstrative as to love and appreciation, and hence, my approval came only in the form of indirect acknowledgement, such as the addition of roast pork or roast duck at the dinner table. As the approval was meted out so subtly and sparingly, I was conditioned to accepting the law of diminishing returns: I would persevere even if there was little or diminishing or even no reward, which in the worst case scenario amounted to self-flagellation. Such Pavlovian aspect of my upbringing also engendered an urge to please others, so as to receive their approval and acceptance. That ostensibly innocuous yearning for approval and acceptance, paradoxically, turned out to be my Achilles' heel in adulthood. Whenever I, or my course of action or choices in life, did not receive approval or acceptance, I would—subconsciously, of course—punish myself by engaging in self-destructive behavior, sabotaging the self.

That pattern of self-defeating behavior, the proverbial vicious cycle, began with my boyfriend-dating dilemma. After much agonizing internal debate, I reluctantly convinced myself to give "it" a whirl, "it" being the mode of social behavior expected of me at the time. I surmised that if I went on a date, I might tolerate it or even learn to enjoy it. After all, how could I be sure if I did not give it a try. I did not remember how I found this hapless specimen for my date experiment; it might have been a classmate of a boyfriend of one of my classmates, most likely a student from St. Paul's College, a nearby all-boys school. I did not remember either what was on our agenda for that first—and last—date, but most likely we went to a movie or attended a concert. All I remembered was how utterly miserable and revolted I was; there was not a single redeemable moment during that torturous encounter. I kept wondering how I could survive if I were condemned to spending the rest of my life with *any* man, let alone bearing his children; no, I would not survive—and I did not have any death wish.

I should have been fully convinced by that experimental-date debacle that under no circumstance would or could I be enamored with any person of the male persuasion. I was indeed convinced, because emotions that intense do not lie or deceive. However, something even more ominous than not being approved by my parents lurked just beneath the surface; it hung in the balance between my continuing on a triumphant track to being a well-groomed success on the one hand, and beginning my self-inflicted descent to being a contemptible outcast on the other. Even though I had only a vague comprehension of the terms that I had accidentally stumbled upon, I instinctively understood that they denoted an abhorrent, condemned caste. It was a state of being to be avoided if humanly possible. It was around that time when I stumbled upon a novel when I was browsing at the Public Library at City Hall: *Ravages* by Violette Leduc. It was the first time I read about love between two young women. The revelation served as a validation of my feelings but also as a siren warning for my having those illicit feelings. Since I did not have any interest in, let alone any attraction to, members of the opposite sex, it seemed then that I would be categorized as one of those despicable outcasts: a homosexual, a sexual deviant, a sexual pervert, mentally ill, a psychotic, and a sinner, a term fraught with the worst religious connotations. That was before I realized that such outcasts were not merely ostracized but many were persecuted to the point of being physically assaulted, jailed, and even killed. In the cloistered shelter of an all-girls school, we were told that we could be all that we aspired to be. However, the wholesale subjugation of women was par for the course in the male-dominated, chauvinistic Chinese society. As if that was not enough for this uppity female to defy the established social order, being a member of the "homosexual caste" would certainly doom my future in the very close-minded community. I had to do all that I could to avoid that wretched fate.

Starting with our Form IV year, and in preparation for "School Cert," we had to choose between "Arts" and "Science" for our area of academic concentration. "School Cert" was our affectionate nick name for the Hong Kong Certificate of Education Examination. It was a series of Colony-wide public examinations held at the end of our Form V school year, and signified a student's graduation from high school (even though it was the equivalent of only 11th grade in the United States). More significantly, for those students who desired a college or university education, their HKCEE grades had to be high enough in order to advance to Forms Lower VI ("O Level"—Ordinary Level—in the British education system) and Upper VI ("A Level" for Advanced Level). For a chance to be admitted for a three-year course of studies at a university in the British system, one had to successfully complete the two preparatory years. For consideration to be admitted to a college or university in the United States for a four-year Bachelor's degree, completion of the Form Lower VI year was required. Accordingly, for the academically ambitious, the stakes could not have been higher to score high enough in the HKCEE so as to be admitted to Form Lower VI.

Of course my choice was "Arts," as my affinity for mathematics was nil, and my aptitude for physics and chemistry was nonexistent. As an Arts student, I was required to enroll in two Science subjects. Thankfully, Geography and Biology came to my rescue; they sufficed very nicely as science for the non-scientifically inclined. Because of the new "lines of demarcation," our three classrooms of students were shuffled accordingly: Arts students would have, for instance, English Literature classes together, regardless of the alphabet of their last names. Hence, several times during each school day, we would be switching classrooms in a mix-them-up. Happily then, I was able to know my classmates in the "A" and "Alpha" classes, several of whom have remained my lifelong friends, including Sandra, Anita, Flora Sun, Raina Tsung Pui Hung, Pearl, Fatima Wu, and Winnie.

I had always felt a special bond with Winnie since our primary school days; she was the only other tomboy in my class. We were seriously competitive at table tennis as if we were sworn enemies; she, being the smarter one, would beat me by cleverly distracting me or mischievously teasing me. Away from the ping-pong table, we constantly seemed to be in a kind of friendly jousting; perhaps that was the "rules of engagement" for kindred spirits. There was a tacit mutual understanding though. In secondary school, I was impressed by her creative talents, and her knack for showbiz, in writing and directing dramatic, comedic and musical skits which were performed by her classmates on special occasions, and rapturously enjoyed by the entire student body and teachers. By the time I began to wrestle with issues pertaining to my sexual orientation, Winnie was already embarking on her illustrious career. I remembered vividly during a class we had together, instead of listening to the teacher, she was writing under her desk on a Chinese manuscript paper (with little lined "squares," one for each Chinese character). I later asked her what she was scribbling, and she replied that she was composing scripts for shows on the Chinese channel of Commercial Radio. We were only sixteen years old then; imagine my envy and admiration that she was already able to make a living by selling her creative writings. I remembered just as vividly, a year later, while we were sitting in the cavernous Kwok Siu Lau Hall writing one of the "School Cert" examinations, Winnie abruptly stood up and walked out of the Hall. As far as I knew, she never returned to finish the examinations nor attend another class. Instead, she went on to become a wildly popular DJ for Commercial Radio Hong Kong, and then an even more stellar and celebrated host of a morning talk show on that radio station. She was also a much sought-after master of ceremony for top-tier pop concerts and variety shows. She then parlayed her radio showbiz credentials into her entrée into the movie business, with stints as an executive producer of Chinese movies. She rose to the top job at Commercial Radio, serving as its general manager until the early 2000's. Above all, she had been a mover and shaker in diverse arenas spanning the entire entertainment and cultural firmament of Hong Kong. She had always been a phenomenon; she defied being defined, and she certainly would not conform. The paparazzi had a field day whenever she was "caught" out shopping or dining with her latest glamorous girlfriend. I had a taste of life in the limelight when I was practically blinded by the blitz of camera flashes as we exited the restaurant after a dinner with her and some friends in the summer of 2006, and that was after she had already had her chauffeur escort her then girlfriend out the backdoor. Even when we were young teenagers growing up, I instinctively knew that we were both "outcasts." She knew it, too, but putting on the mantle of a fine and mighty renegade, she boldly charged on. I, on the other hand, was too indoctrinated into walking the path of a "good" daughter and "model" student, which in turn coaxed me into pausing to agonize over my sexual orientation.

That turned out to be my undoing, and sent me careening down a two-year masochistic detour. I foolishly postulated that my physical appearance might have been the culprit for my not having an attraction to the opposite sex and vice versa. To prove my theory, I decided to lose weight to look more "ladylike." I read about the low carbohydrates high protein diet that was all the rage then, and thought it was a good idea for me to try that. It took me perhaps half a year to come down to 100 lbs., but that was far too thin for my frame. Mom was understandably worried, and took me to see Dr. Chau. He had nothing to say to or offer me. I could not very well tell any of them why I was on this self-destructive course of behavior. At the time, I honestly did not think that I was being self-defeating; I thought I was trying my darnedest not to become an abominable outcast, and wished they could appreciate and thank me for my herculean efforts. I still did not feel any attraction to persons of the male persuasion in my new, slender body. Worse, the exercise made me even more aware of the futility of my attempts at forcibly altering what came natural to me. Nonetheless, since I had succeeded in slimming down, I thought I would ride with my new physique for a while, and see if or how my life would change. I did not feel good though; I was feeling weak and losing a lot of my "powers." "So, this is what being feminine is all about," I thought to myself, "what a wicked, rigged trick the male-dominated society played on women." That was a very lonely year for me. Outwardly, I was a shadow of my former self. My spirits took the harshest hit; I was uncharacteristically withdrawn, secretly agonizing over my dilemma, bemoaning how no one could understand, let alone help, me. Even I was beginning not to understand myself.

There was a respite from the doom and gloom in the summer of 1970—the excitement of traveling overseas for the first time in my life. I had joined the ranks of Queen's Guides by then, but I did not recall how exactly I and Ginny Lam Doi Chu, a classmate and a fellow Queen's Guide, were selected to represent Hong Kong at the Girls Guides' International Diamond Jubilee Jamboree held in Osaka, Japan. As the official representatives of our delegation, we had to present a "performance" at the jamboree. Instead of presenting the archetypical Chinese fan dance, it was decided that Ginny and I would present a Chinese version of "Beauty (Ginny) and the Fisherman (me)" *pas de deux* set to a traditional Chinese folk song. All I remembered was Ginny and I being coached the dance by our Physical Education teacher, Miss Siu. Mom made me a fisherman's outfit, bought a fisherman's straw hat, poncho and cloth shoes to complete the ensemble, and a cheap Chinese bamboo flute for my prop. We did not have much time to rehearse our "number," because it was, as I recalled, very short notice between our becoming Queen's Guides and being chosen to be the two official representatives. Lina was also a member of the delegation; in fact, the local English language newspaper (it could have been the *South China Morning Post*, *The Star* or the *Hong Kong Standard*) published a photograph of the two of us in our Guides' full uniform at Kai Tak Airport preparing to depart for Osaka. I did not recognize myself—the new slender me—and I was not sure I liked what I saw. I realized even then that another major downside to my having lost all that weight was that my memory and intellect were critically affected. I used to have a photographic memory; no longer, after I slimmed down. I also used to be a fast learner with a laser sharp mind of boundless mental reserve and prowess; no longer, as not only my body was a shadow of my former self, my mind was even more so. What sacrifice just for the sake of conformance, of fitting in; let that be a lesson for me for years to come.

The relatively short flight to Osaka was full of excitement. It was probably the first flight and first overseas trip for many of the teenage delegates. The amazing cohesiveness of the Japanese people impressed me upon our arrival at the base of our campsite which was up on a hillside. The Japanese host contingent had formed a human chain from the base all the way up to the campsite; our bags and luggage were passed from one to another up the hill and to our assigned tent, carefully and efficiently. Throughout the jamboree, meals, showers, and events were similarly well organized and proceeded without a glitch. The only "hiccup" I experienced was my unexpected intolerance for the traditional Japanese food served at the camp. Fortunately, the host had thoughtfully supplied each tent with a huge tin can of biscuits/crackers on which I subsisted. Communicating with our hosts was challenging and interesting. Challenging because most

Japanese did not speak much English and we did not speak any Japanese. Interesting because we could otherwise communicate by written Chinese as the Japanese incorporated many Chinese characters in their language.

It was a fine evening with a slight chill in the air when Ginny and I presented our "Beauty and the Fisherman." It was rather unnerving to be performing before such a huge audience in an open-air amphitheater. Thankfully, our *pas de deux* unfurled flawlessly. I could feel the gaze of thousands of pairs of eyes trained on our every move. I was relieved that we did not let our delegation down, and could finally relax and enjoy the jamboree festivities. An unexpected and delightful sequela of that performance was my sudden popularity among the young Girl Guides; I had a throng of adoring groupies following me. To be frank, I learned then that I loved being adored by women! In stark contrast, there was a handsome young Japanese man who was assigned to "serve" our tent, assisting us with whatever we needed to fetch or replenish. My tent-mates told me as much that he was enamored with me. I, on the other hand, harbored no attraction whatsoever to this charmer and couldn't run away from him fast enough. Those sentiments ought to have jolted my senses into abandoning my quixotic efforts to become more "feminine" and to conform as a heterosexual. Still, I clung on to my misguided self-styled feminization. I had failed to recognize that, while perseverance was generally a virtue and a fine character trait, it was decidedly misplaced in such a masochistic gambit.

When the jamboree drew to a close, our delegation was treated to a tour of historic and major cities including Kyoto, Nikko and Tokyo, and a quick but memorable visit to the spectacular "Expo 1970" in Osaka. Nikko struck a profound and nostalgic chord in me: I felt as if I had come home to serenity and bliss as I strolled along the stone paths lined with old-growth tall trees, an ancient sun filtering through their boughs and leaves. When it was time to return to Hong Kong after about ten days in this land of the Rising Sun, I was eager to go home for I was famished. I had not had food that I could stomach other than crackers, noodles in soup and Kentucky Fried Chicken in Tokyo. That incidentally was my very first taste of KFC; my first taste of the so-called American food made quite an impression—I liked it, or perhaps I was simply too starved.

That old, familiar feeling that I had while I was in Nikko makes me cogitate on happenstance that only *seemed* to be a coincidence. Echoes of my trip to Italy in 1997 beckoned. Mom used to dress Lina and me, when we were pre-teens, in colorful Japanese kimonos on special occasions. Perhaps we then became the cute little Japanese "dolls" that delighted Mom. I did not mind being dressed up once in a while as the costume was very exotic to me. Dad seemed to fancy Japanese decorations and furnishings when we were very young. A Japanese-style curtain made of strings of plastic beads was hung between the front entrance and the living area at our Sai Wan Estate flat. We occasionally ate and had tea using Japanese dinnerware and chinaware. Although I never had the opportunity to return to Japan since that jamboree, it turned out that Lina's connection to Japan deepened as she became a Reiki master, and especially since she joined her Buddhist temple where she eventually attained the rank of *Acharya*. She now makes pilgrimages to temples and sacred sites in Japan from time to time.

Form V was a maddening and tense year because of the looming School Cert examinations. It was also the year when I was named a Prefect, complete with a new, fancier school badge. Other, especially younger, students would recognize my "special status" by that badge. I felt as if I had to be a model Big Sister, an all-around model in general, and that was quite an onerous responsibility. I even had a Form I class to which I was the assigned Prefect, though I did not remember much about that particular undertaking. I was too consumed with studying for School Cert. I also had to take the SAT and TOEFL (Test of English as a Foreign Language), though at that time, I had no idea whether, or how, I would be attending university in the United States. It was "fashionable" for secondary school graduates, after completing Forms Lower and Upper VI as appropriate, to study at universities abroad, if their families could afford the expedition. The United Kingdom and the United States were popular destinations for those with financial means. After earning a bachelor's or higher degree, and thus ensconced with perceived superior foreign educational credentials, most would return to Hong Kong to be rewarded with a remunerative career and the proverbial good life. Of course, I yearned to earn at least a bachelor's degree. I would major in English, and I aspired to becoming a professional journalist, or better yet, a photojournalist, and moonlight as a film critic. Having such an exciting—even if not the most lucrative—career goal positively motivated me to give the School Cert my best efforts.

There was an enticing opportunity for me during my Form V year when the Hong Kong chapter of Lions Clubs International held a "Youth of Hong Kong" contest; the prize was an all-expense paid trip to Australia hosted by club members in various cities. I was one of the finalists, but my apolitical upbringing proved to be my shortcoming in the final round. When I was asked by the panel of judges about my views on apartheid in South Africa and on a certain ombudsman then appointed by the Governor of Hong Kong to resolve certain issues. Not at all versed in world or local politics or current affairs, I was clueless in responding to those weighty questions. I therefore lost the contest to a schoolmate one year senior, Mabel Fung. As a first runner-up, I ended up with a consolation prize, auspices of Mom's boss who happened to be the president of the local chapter that year. Although I was not the official "Youth of Hong Kong," Mr. Lee arranged a similar tour for me as a goodwill ambassadress for the Hong Kong Lions Club to Lions Clubs in several Australian cities.

My consolation victory lap through Down Under took place in August of 1971, a couple of months after the grueling School Cert examinations. Again, one of the hometown English-language newspapers published a story about my stint to Australia, accompanied by the most feminized photograph of me, ever. I was wearing a mini-dress, cuddling a small stuffed toy Koala bear, shoulder-length hair, wearing cosmetic makeup, almost anorexic, in general, looking very unlike what used to be me. My mindset then though was triumphant: I had finally succeeded in becoming feminine, and accordingly, any sexual orientation issue had been tamed—or so I thought.

Australia was a vast and peculiar country. The accent was unfamiliar, the people were an awkward cross between being friendly and proper, the cuisine consisted of lamb chops prepared 101 ways, and the landscape was unlike any I had seen up till then. It must have been my new "looks," and much to my chagrin, a member in the Sydney Lions Club somehow saw fit to introduce me to a prominent local Chinese family, and specifically, to its very eligible bachelor son. He in turn did his level best to impress his newest date, while I tried to hide my utter distaste by being coy and demure. He arranged for us with a group of friends a ski trip to Melbourne. I was not dressed for skiing at all, and between being frozen alive and revolted to death, I never skied again in my life. The tour otherwise proceeded smoothly enough. It consisted mostly of my wearing a silk brocaded *cheongsam*, and smiling beguilingly at many official dinners. Of course, I spent time with the koala bears, the wallabies and kangaroos; I even had the good fortune of attending a dirt track car race in Newcastle, and a concert by Neil Williams, my Sydney host and an Australian recording star. Incredibly, I still have the LPs he autographed for me. Mostly, the month-long visit went by in a blur; in retrospect, that was mostly because I was on such a "femme trip" that I was quite detached from reality.

By the time I returned to SSGC to start my Form Lower VI year after my Australian jaunt, I felt very secure and assured. Secure—academically—because I had performed well enough with my School Cert that my future advanced studies at a university seemed all but preordained. Assured, because the demons lurking behind issues surrounding my sexual orientation seemed to have been vanquished. Indeed, when I walked into my new classroom, I strode with self-confidence and a measure of maturity, eager to start a new academic year with singular focus. The class size was smaller, and I was with classmates who shared my passion for language and literature; no more pretending that I understood or liked algebra or geometry, photosynthesis or osmosis, fission or fusion.

One of my classmates was Pearl. In primary school, I only knew of her as we were in the opposite half-day section. In secondary school, she was in the Alpha classroom, hanging out with Winnie and Flora, while I was literally and psychically far away from their raucous classroom. In truth, I was simply too preoccupied with my academic and extracurricular agendas. Even though we were in the same room for English Language and Literature classes in Forms IV and V, for some strange reason, we did not become particularly friendly then. Here I was, cruising along as I started Form Lower VI, secure and assured, and there was Pearl, suddenly bursting onto the scene and straying into my sights. I delighted in my new found friend, a gentle soul who appreciated the same beauty in life as I did.

Pearl and I compared notes as we enjoyed the reading assignments from our English literature class. We composed and exchanged poems, and of course, she was a far superior poetess; I preferred prose. We loved music of all stripes, from pop to folk to classical to sacred. I think it was music that brought us to St.

John's Cathedral; we joined the church choir very early during the school year. St. John's Cathedral is an Anglican cathedral; it is the Diocesan cathedral of Hong Kong Island, and houses the seat of the Archbishop of Hong Kong. The venerable church was founded in 1849; it is strategically located in Central, surrounded by buildings and skyscrapers that epitomize the political and financial powers of Hong Kong. Pearl and I attended choir practice every Thursday night, and sang in the choir for both services on Sunday mornings. There were also outings organized for members of the church choir, which were very meaningful and refreshing. I did not remember being so carefree and elated since my Girl Guides camping days a few years prior. Those camping days were thrilling as I loved being outdoors, "roughing it" in what passed for "wilderness" in the highly urbanized Hong Kong, and above all, it was my opportunity to be "living with" women for a couple of days.

It was not religiosity that attracted me to the church choir. There was the music, our voices soaring and echoing within the arch and spire, there was the sanctity and serenity within that sacred structure, and then, in the final analysis, there was Pearl. Ever since I attended SSGPS, I had always had to study the Scriptures, and had always had to pray, sing hymns and listen to sermons at morning assemblies. Yet, I never associated those activities with religion *per se*, nor did I feel any pressure to convert to Christianity. Most of my classmates were church-going Protestants, but they did not proselytize or evangelize me. Anglicans especially impressed me as being polite and quiet; they kept to their rituals and traditions, and let others around them carry on with life. There was a Christian Union at SSGC, the students' organization for Christian fellowship. Up to that point, I stayed clear of involvement with that group, as I did not much care for Bible study or praying. Hence, my sudden involvement with St. John's Cathedral was very uncharacteristic of me and was surprising even to me. It was subconscious, but the only explanation was that I enjoyed being with Pearl. It did not really matter what I was doing as long as we were doing it together.

Since about Form III, I had been put on the roster as a pianist for morning assemblies; someone had to play the piano for our hymn singing. I dreaded being called to duty because playing the piano to lead 700-plus students in hymn singing was to me very nerve wrecking. There were so many gifted musicians in the school that they could tell if I had played even just one wrong note. Oftentimes, the pianist was not told in advance the selected hymns so that she could at least practice the night before. Instead, the pianist had to rely on sight reading the piano score, which was definitely not my forte and which aggravated my wrecked nerves. It was most refreshing then when in my Lower VI year, Miss Barker allowed us to, once in a blue moon, stray from the rather formulaic and staid agenda for our morning assemblies, permitting senior students to put on a "show." I did not recall how Pearl and I were chosen to take charge of one of those shows. The rock opera *Jesus Christ Superstar* was all the rage then, and that gave us the idea to build a "show" around that original soundtrack. Selected tracks from the album were weaved into a story with recitation of appropriate Biblical verses. It was a very bold, *avant-garde*, bordering on scandalous, production for our morning assembly steeped in reverence and tradition, but it was very well received. I relished accomplishing another creative project with Pearl.

After so many weeks of singing in the St. John's Cathedral church choir, it was not surprising that Pearl and I were persuaded to consider being baptized into the Anglican Church. We attended baptism classes together. Our baptism and confirmation were scheduled for January of 1972. I did not pay much attention to what my agnostic Mom thought of my newfound attachment to all things church related. I thought both of us viewed Anglicanism as harmless, more a respectable social club than a religion. After all, even Miss Barker attended service on Sundays at St. John's

Cathedral—very respectable indeed. As you may gather by now, the early months of my Form Lower VI year was the diametrical opposite of my irksome Form IV year. For the first time ever, I had found a gentle and genteel soul who was my intellectual equal, who shared my sense of beauty, wonderment and sensibility, and whose persona inspired me to aim and soar high once again. I felt I could breathe freely again, and could laugh with wild abandon again, and could simply be me again.

It was late October, 1971, and Pearl and I were staying late after school. We had probably taken on more than we should have. The project at hand was updating and decorating the bulletin board for Christian Union. I still remembered vividly where the board was located—outside a Form II classroom along the corridor on the second floor of the main school building. When I returned for my campus visit in December of 2003, the board was still there, at the same exact spot. It was early evening, but the sky was completely dark already; the air was crisp and invigorating with a hint of autumn chill. Hardly anyone was left on campus. Pearl and I were taking down the outdated postings and decorations, and were lining up the new materials that we had prepared for posting on the board. Nothing was out of the ordinary at all. Then, without any forewarning or fanfare, and not an inkling of what was to come, I was at once overcome with the sensation of love, an entirely unfamiliar but electrifying sensation. Perhaps it was an alluring and tantalizing glance from her, perhaps it was the sweet serenity of the evening, or perhaps it was the purity of two female hearts beating as one, which triggered a cascade of tenderness and ecstasy. A startling moment of elucidation: *I am in love!* I had never been in love before. Lyrics of the popular songs of the era about being in and out of love had always been an abstract concept if not an enigma to me. Yet there I was, dumbstruck, awed and overpowered in the magic and intensity of the moment.

When "it" actually happened—my being in love with a woman who reciprocated or who in fact sparked the ardor—officially making me the "outcast" that I had so desperately tried to avoid becoming, I welcomed and accepted my new reality with wide open arms. Being in love with a woman was so exhilarating, affirming and empowering that all consternation and condemnation were rendered wholly irrelevant and immaterial. I was liberated to be me; no more dieting, no more self-flagellation or self-sabotage, and no more self-doubt or self-denial. Even I did not fully realize then the momentousness of this milestone of coming of age. Our relationship was blissfully platonic. When one loved so unreservedly, purely and fervently, nothing could be lacking whether or not there was a physical component to the liaison. The intoxicating highs and the ecstatic euphoria would, for better or worse, shape my life script for many years to come. Pearl and I were baptized together, at St. John's Cathedral, on January 8th and confirmed the following day, a Sunday. To me, our love was sealed in the eyes of God. I recalled asking our pastor whether we could be married in the Anglican Church. He was gracious and told me to check back in another ten years. He was too optimistic by about ten years, but I would always remember his graciousness in not condemning but indeed honoring our love.

Meanwhile, I was on cloud nine, levitating with my feet nowhere touching ground. I wanted to shout from the mountaintop about how ecstatic and exultant I felt, and how powerful woman-loving-woman was. I believed that it was men's conspiracy to "outlaw" lesbianism, or else there would not be enough heterosexual women willing to "service" all the men on earth. The intensity of the passion and the profoundness of the longing with women in love were beyond what mere words could convey. When I was on that month-long home visit in the summer of 1978, I was introduced by Winnie to a friend of hers, Rita, at Rita's birthday party in what passed for a women's bar at the time. I took to Rita in an instant; she was gregarious, vivacious and charismatic, and all the young women in the party flocked to her. She was perhaps a couple of years older than Winnie and me. She had completed her university studies in the U.S. and returned to Hong Kong triumphantly, landing a plum job with the international marketing firm of Young & Rubicam. She personified the quintessential Yuppie before that term was even coined, well on her way to fame and fortune. She requested the DJ to play Dan Hill's *Sometimes When We Touch* for her birthday. The chorus struck me as particularly poignant in appreciating that intensity of a woman's love:

> *And sometimes when we touch*
> *The honesty's too much*
> *And I have to close my eyes and hide*
> *I wanna hold you till I die*
> *Till we both break down and cry*
> *I wanna hold you till the fear in me subsides*

Just a few short years later, I was stunned to learn that Rita had committed suicide, apparently over a woman lover. Perhaps it was a flamboyant dare that went awry, or perhaps the passion was simply too conflagrant. Winnie was still visibly shaken as she recounted the tragedy of Rita's untimely demise when several of us gathered in New York City for a mini-class reunion in September of 1986. So many years on, whenever I hear the song (I always hear it as if it were sung by a woman to a woman), I shudder, and ponder the power of a woman's love and touch.

In my youthful exuberance and naïveté, I had taken shouting from the mountaintop a step too far and too literally. In the heady days after my liberation, I must have imprudently shared the secrets of my joyous delirium with someone. My recollection was hazy as to the whom and the circumstances of my disclosure, but the next thing I knew was my homeroom teacher's reporting to Miss Barker who at once summoned my Mom to her office. I still recalled my shock when I saw Mom late that afternoon when she returned from her meeting with Miss Barker, her eyes red and swollen like a goldfish's from crying. I was honestly mystified by all the fuss and above all, flummoxed by their decidedly negative reaction to the single most beauteous and dynamic event that had ever happened in my life. Nevertheless, by then, it was obvious that I had committed an unforgivable *faux pas*. To my horror and untold distress, Pearl had started to distance and drift away from me. From the zenith of rapture and wonderment, I fell hard when Pearl started withdrawing from "us." Her excuse was that she was distraught dealing with her parents' impending divorce. My intuition told me that she simply could not handle the stigma, or the unexpected and unwanted attention, of being involved in a lesbian relationship. The irony would become glaringly stark when Pearl came out fifteen years later and "married" (it was before same sex marriages were widely recognized) a woman. The irony turned bitter sweet when, forty-plus years later, Pearl is now an ordained minister[4], championing "queer theology" and leading a vibrant LGBTQ group in Hong Kong. She cannot be more "out" today, and I cannot be more proud of her, but O, we have had so much, so very much, water under the bridge.

The unceremonious and abrupt end to our sacred bond pained me beyond imagining. The dreaded feelings of abandonment, from the days when Lilian was taken from our home, which I subconsciously interpreted as a punishment for her having "misbehaved," came flooding into my consciousness. There I was, being punished and abandoned for having "misbehaved." I had brought shame to my parents, displeased my teachers, hurt the

---

[4] To her credit, Pearl returned to school and earned a Bachelor's degree in divinity in her late 50's. Her graduation thesis was entitled "Coming Out to Herself: A Lesbian Feminist Theology of Empowerment For Lesbian Christians in Hong Kong."

only person who mattered the most to me, offended all conventional sensibilities, and in general totally upset the apple cart.

Crestfallen barely began to describe my then state of being. As I was wallowing in my despondent, forlorn morass, Miss Barker summoned me. Surprisingly, she did not want to see me in her office; rather, I would be going on an outing with her one weekend. I had never received that sort of invitation before, from Miss Barker or any of my teachers, nor had I ever heard of any student going on such a one-on-one outing. Needless to say, I was a nervous wreck, but then again, I was such a wreck already that spending the day with Miss Barker would not and could not have added much more "wreckage." I was bracing myself for her to give me a stern dressing down, citing chapter and verse from the Bible on how such relationships were sinful in the eyes of God, how I would be ruining my otherwise promising future with such depravity, and how I had to repent and reform for my own good. I was psychologically prepared to be assaulted with moralistic lectures and judgmental strictures. It was a sunny and balmy early spring weekend. At the appointed hour in the morning, I presented myself at school. We got into her private automobile (it might have been a *Morris Minor*), and she drove us to some place in the New Territories. I frankly did not recall where exactly we went, what we did, except that I remembered we briefly visited with one of her woman friends on Hong Kong Island in the late afternoon. Instead of giving me the third degree, admonition, and dire warnings, she in fact hardly spoke. We were mostly enjoying the drive, the scenery, and the very agreeable weather. There was no mention of lesbianism or homosexual relationships, and certainly no discussion of my role in or involvement with any such liaison. I was quite nervous in the beginning, waiting for the other shoe to drop; but as the day progressed and the proverbial Sword of Damocles never fell, I started to actually enjoy the outing. I would have welcomed it if she had brought up the taboo subject; I would have asked unflinching questions and argued my point of view. Perhaps that was exactly why she would rather not open that Pandora's Box. When I reflected upon the outing, I could not but conclude that it was a magnanimous gesture on Miss Barker's part. It could be that she was signaling to me her tacit understanding and acceptance, if not approval, of my sexual orientation. After all, in the late afternoon, she made a point of visiting her "woman friend" (who happened to be married, if I remember correctly, but that could just be a perfect front); that extremely subtle message was not lost on me. Even without what I interpreted as Miss Barker's backhanded blessing, I had by then resolved never to conform or compromise. That epic episode had seared into my heart and mind that I would fight for my—and our—right to love, the love that dare not speak its name, till my dying breath.

The school year was careening to a close, but I was in no mood to even care about how I was faring academically. Fortunately, my grades were respectable enough before that year, as were my college admissions test results. From the days of my exposure to American popular culture through music listening, I had always wished that I could pursue my university studies in that country. I recalled the hours I spent belly-laughing with Goldie Hawn and the rest of the *Laugh-In* cast week after week, learning to appreciate American humor and sarcasm reading *Mad* magazine, and informing myself in the affairs of the world as seen through the lens of *TIME* magazine. Despite my British-tinged preparatory education, the United Kingdom was not my first choice of destination for advanced studies. However, my family simply could not afford the extravagance of sending me abroad for higher education; it was more wishful thinking than a wish. As a shot in the dark, I had earlier that year submitted my applications, along with my request for financial aid, to three colleges in the United States. They were all Seven Sisters colleges; naturally, I preferred to continue my higher education in an all-women environment. I did not know that the Seven Sisters coordinated their admissions process, and one generally would not apply to more than one Seven Sisters college at a time. My ignorance about American colleges was not limited to procedural matters; I had only a very rudimentary understanding of their educational and political system, culture, history and society in general. What I knew of the United States was limited to what I heard in popular songs and what I saw in the occasional movies. Nonetheless, the United States appealed to me as the antithesis of the strictly traditional, conservative, and stifling society in which I grew up.

With the fallout from my unintended indiscretion, leaving Hong Kong under the guise of pursuing advanced studies abroad became at once urgent and a welcomed excuse for my graceful exit. It would save face all the way around. Timing was just about perfect as decisions from those colleges were expected in April. The first decision arrived right on time; I did not recall whether it was from Wellesley College or another Seven Sister school, but it was a rejection. For someone not used to being rejected or to countenancing failures, that was a rude awakening. I consoled myself by reminding myself that my applications were a very long shot anyway. Then came the second letter from the United States, and it, too, was a rejection. I choked. By then, I was under unbearable emotional stress; I was stumbling in a dense fog of grief and self-recrimination. My rendezvous with true love was brutally truncated, leaving me reeling from the whiplash. Then the third and last letter from America came from Barnard College in New York City. It was an *acceptance* with full scholarship. I gasped. There was not a sweeter word on earth than "deliverance."

According to Mom, the estate of my maternal grandfather was settled just in time, and Mom's share was just enough to pay for my one-way plane ticket to America. That was Chinese tradition for you—according to grandfather's will, the daughters received a token distribution, while the sons shared the bulk of his legacy.

The gloom and doom lifted posthaste, as the narrative nonchalantly pivoted from the unspeakable to the excited hum of preparing for my heralded trip. I had no idea then just how immensely fortunate and entitled I was to be a freshman at Barnard, with full financial aid to boot. The prestige, the privilege, the entrée, not to mention the finest education I was about to receive, all were lost on me at the time, and even for some years to come. I was only grateful then that my "exit stage left" miraculously materialized just in time. There was an educational organization that purported to prepare students for their studies abroad. I perfunctorily attended a couple of their meet-and-greets and tea parties, and sat through talks on the typical American university campus, the basics of maintaining our lawful foreign student immigration status, and life in America in general. In truth, those well-intentioned primers hardly prepared me for my new life in the States, let alone in a multifarious and dynamic city such as the Big Apple. It was somewhat helpful to meet other students heading for America. One, Shirley Wu, was also entering the freshmen class at Barnard. We had intended to stay in touch once we arrived at Barnard. In fact, Selina Wang Sou Chien, another SSGC classmate who left for the States with her family when we were in Form II, was also in my Class. It would turn out that I did not socialize with other Chinese students at Barnard but would map my own course in uncharted waters.

My date to set sail was scheduled for August 15th. Because the plane ticket allowed a few stopovers without extra charge, I requested stopovers in San Francisco to visit my classmate Rebecca Chin, in Los Angeles to meet my maternal 5th Uncle, his wife and my two cousins for the first time, and in Tulsa, Oklahoma to visit with Sophia Wong, my Prefect from my Form I days, who was studying to become a dietician. My parents must have been fretting over my imminent departure as the first chick to leave the nest. On the one hand, they must have been excited for and proud of me for having achieved such an accomplishment. On the other hand, they must have been worried for me and my life in a strange land, as I had never stepped outside of the ambit of their protection and provision. On yet another hand, they must have been relieved that I was bidding farewell to the disgrace of my making. Nonetheless, I could tell that they were already beginning to miss me. It was far simpler and straightforward on my end; I felt only fatigue—from months of suffering heartbreak and emotional stress, and excitement—from being able to live and continue my studies in a country whose proclaimed ideals I admired. I was too young to be capable of projecting beyond the immediate. That turned out to be a blessing, for if I could foresee all that would be lying in wait for me in the months and years ahead, I probably would have curled up and stayed put in Hong Kong, the intrepid knight in me notwithstanding.

Two months before I embarked on my fateful journey, and as if to mark the occasion with a morbidly memorable tragedy, Hong Kong suffered a natural disaster of historic proportions. Torrential downpours drenched the Colony for what seemed an endless seven days and nights. While that was not unheard of, what followed stunned the citizenry: massive mudslides in the densely populated metropolis buried hundreds, if not thousands. One of those horrific avalanches was unleashed just blocks from our home. The ground beneath a small free-standing garage located on the hillside above the Mid-Levels became so unstable from the rains that the garage became dislodged and slid down the grade. As the deluge gathered momentum and corralled more debris, it "snowballed" and knocked down multiple high-rise apartment buildings as it roared down its destructive path. The deadly rampage came to a halt only when it became too massive for further downward tear and as the grade became less steep, just a few hundred yards from our apartment building. Lina and I were babysitting for two separate families at a nearby high-rise apartment building where many officers of the British troops stationed in Hong Kong and their families resided. If the mudslide had swept down another couple of streets, it would have taken down that building as well, along with Lina and me. It was simply too frightening to contemplate. As it was, several of my schoolmates perished in that disaster, including a classmate, Grace Cheung Ka Yi. Grace was quiet and studious, and an outstanding pianist. She was supposed to be leaving for university studies in the States; unfortunately, she did not leave soon enough. The catastrophic mudslides of 1972 were recounted in James Clavell's bestselling novel *Noble House*. Along with his earlier epic, *Taipan*, Clavell put on full display his keen appreciation and depiction of the emergence of Hong Kong from what Lord Palmerston dismissed as "a barren rock" in the mid-19th century, to the dynamic and intriguing Pearl of the Orient that was Hong Kong in the 1960's and 1970's. For days afterwards, I would walk by the cordoned off area after school. I would look up the side of the hill that had been deeply gouged, scarred and truncated, and the mount of mud and debris eerily at repose. I would quietly weep for the souls buried within. Life is so fragile, I thought to myself; it could be snuffed out in an instant. I resolved to live life even more fervently, and death would not even dare draw near me. Such were the prerogatives of youth.

August 15th arrived none too soon. I was ready to leave my birth place that had nurtured and indulged me, but which I had outgrown, and which sadly could not accept me as I was. I was the first in my generation to travel abroad for studies; my maternal 5th Uncle mapped out that route some thirty years before me. The entire clan on my Mom's side came to the airport to see me off: my dear Grandmother, my 4th Uncle and Aunt and their four children—my cousins Grace, Alza, Athena and Arthur—and Uncle

Michael Tse, and of course, Mom and Dad, Lina and Vivian. I was wearing a brand new pink pantsuit, and around my neck was the solid gold medallion that my 3rd Uncle, who owned two jewelry shops, gave me for the occasion. No one cried; I certainly did not. It was supposed to be a joyous occasion; I was expected to have a triumphant homecoming after I completed my university studies. With just US$100 cash in my wallet, I took a monumental leap of faith and launched a thousand dreams.

V.

Land of the Free, Home of the Brave

When I stepped outside the airport arrival building in San Francisco, I thought America was truly a land of plenty, so much so that it could even afford air-conditioning to cool the outdoors. The air was refreshingly cool, pure and fresh as I took in a deep invigorating breath under the bluest sky I had ever seen. I had just arrived from the sweltering heat of Hong Kong in the thick of summer, where the air was thick with fumes from high-octane, leaded gasoline and a concoction of pollutants. Then I realized what felt like filtered, artificially cooled air was in fact natural, sweet, oxygen-rich air, free for all to breathe in; my very first impression of America: Yes, I belong here.

My three stopovers were each memorable in its own way. I was thrilled to see Rebecca again; she moved to San Francisco with her family four years earlier when we were in Form II. Yet I spent most of my three days in what turned out to be my favorite city, San Francisco, sleeping. I did not realize just how utterly exhausted I was from the emotional turmoil that year. I must have felt safe in Rebecca's home, with her parents and two brothers, to finally collapse and recharge. I next flew to Los Angeles to meet my maternal 5th Uncle whom I had never met. Growing up, I heard Mom spoke admiringly of him often; he was an engineer with NASA. Grandfather sent him to the States for advanced studies and he never returned to Hong Kong. When he spotted me at the airport, he exclaimed how I looked just like my mother. I also met for the first time my 5th Aunt (a Malaysian or Singaporean Chinese), and my cousins Ann and Nelson who did not even speak Chinese. I spent two days by myself at Disneyland which impressed me as being very "American" as portrayed in popular movies and television shows of that era: glitzy, overblown, self-aggrandizing, brash, but confident, idealistic, optimistic, and winning. That visit was the only one I had with 5th Uncle and his family, and I did not have the occasion to return to Los Angeles ever since. Southern California struck me as being quite otherworldly, as everything seemed artificial, superficial, and over-the-top. My last stopover was Tulsa, Oklahoma, an admittedly off-the-beaten-path destination where Sophia was pursuing her advanced degree in dietetics. Even though we corresponded regularly after she left for the States a few years prior, the interim years had proven to be too alienating. The one memorable event of that brief visit was my tasting pizza for the first time, and I thought it was all hype and definitely overrated. I would later revise my verdict after I had tasted Sicilian slice in New York City. Oklahoma would not make a suitable abode for me; I did not feel at home there.

At the end of August, I arrived on the campus of Barnard College, Broadway at West 116th Street, just in time for freshmen orientation. I did not harbor any preconception of my "home" for the ensuing four years, but my first impression was decidedly positive. I found the smallish campus in an urban setting very familiar, welcoming and not intimidating. Still, I could hear my heart pounding as I, with a small suitcase in one hand, checked in at my dormitory and made my way to my assigned room. It was on the top floor of the newest of the three residence buildings. As I entered my room, my roommate, Sylvia Wong, had already checked in and was busy unpacking her belongings. She was drop-dead gorgeous: tall and slender with an athlete's build, exuding allure, strength and vitality in equal measure, her long shiny black hair draping over her shoulders. I would learn in short order that she was of Chinese descent, born in the States but grew up in Peru. She spoke very little Chinese, but was fluent in Spanish. Interestingly, she had studied for one year, in Primary 3 or 4, at the school located next door to SSGPS; we did not know each then, of course. Barnard had paired us as roommates apparently because both of us indicated that we preferred not to have men visiting in our room, distracting us from our academic pursuits. At least that was her reason; my unstated reason was simply that I did not care to be around men at all.

The first couple of days on campus were a complete blur; everything was unfamiliar and thus quite overwhelming to me. One of the first things I noticed was my accent: I had a distinctively British accent, having been tutored by British-Hong Kong teachers to speak Queen's English. I stood out like a sore thumb whenever I opened my mouth; I sounded too formal, too standoffish. Those were the days before BBC-America, before the Brits "invaded" America, with the Beatles and the Rolling Stones being the notable exceptions. Some schoolmates found my accent "delightful," while others stared at me as if I were from outer space. There and then, I made the decision to drop my British accent and adopt the American accent so as to blend in. In retrospect, that was a harebrained move, as the results were definitely half-baked. I ended up with an accent that most court reporters-stenographers could not decipher when I became an attorney and was arguing a case in court. The transcripts would be full of errors from mishearing my speech. After more than forty years, I have come full circle; I am now amply comfortable with myself, and have for most of the time reverted to my somewhat watered-down British accent. Old habits are difficult to change, and as I have learned, some should never be changed at all.

Absolutely nothing in my upbringing or education in Hong Kong had prepared me for surviving in the United States, or living independently in New York City, or pursuing my undergraduate studies at Barnard. There was far too much freedom and far too many choices, for one who hailed from a society and an educational system with strict rules, prescribed roles, set scripts, and defined boundaries. For the first time ever, I had to select and register for my classes. My academic "menu" had always been dictated to me by my school and the Hong Kong educational system. I frankly had no idea how to even begin to pick my courses from that big, thick catalog. My pride prevented me from seeking counsel from the foreign student advisor or my class advisor. After all, it was only my first few days at Barnard, and I simply could not admit defeat that readily. Sylvia was most helpful in cluing me in about the mandatory freshmen required classes, and prompting me so that I did not miss registration altogether. Barnard, an independent educational institution, enjoyed cross-registration with Columbia University across the street. That added more confusion for me with even more choices to parse, along with a vastly expansive campus and a host of imposing, historic-looking buildings to get acclimated.

Even in the densely populated New York City, the air was much fresher than that in Hong Kong. I felt charged from the moment I arrived at this Morningside Heights neighborhood. Everything was unfamiliar but captivating, and everything seemed bigger than life than its counterpart in Hong Kong. I walked down the west side of Broadway from West 116th Street to 110th Street, and back up the other side of Broadway, with a detour to the venerable Cathedral Church of Saint John the Divine at 112th Street and Amsterdam Avenue. I stopped in momentarily, and was at once transported back to the many Thursdays and Sundays when Pearl and I sang in the church choir at St. John's Cathedral, our voices echoing through the hallowed arches. I did not worship there in the four years I was at Barnard, as the memories of St. John's Cathedral were too painful to evoke. There were bakeries, greengrocers, diners, bars, bookstores, records stores, ice cream stores, restaurants, and a diverse collection of mom-and-pop shops just in that short stretch of Broadway. Unfortunately, that unique klatch of local, independently owned businesses had by and large given way to the usual array of nauseatingly uniform and bland chain-stores when I returned in the late 1990's. So-called progress is sometimes not at all.

I remembered meeting Sylvia for breakfast one morning in the first week of classes at Tom's Restaurant, a classic diner on the east side of Broadway at 112th Street. We sat at the counter; I took in all the sights, sounds, tastes, pulse and rhythm of the eatery on a typical busy weekday morning. It was there and then that I fully realized I was no longer in Hong Kong, no longer restrained in any way, but was in a country in which I would be free to sculpt my own future. Subconsciously, I must have decided to do exactly the opposite of what I would have done if I were in Hong Kong. I resolved not to be obedient, convenient, or conforming. Unfortunately, some of those first decisions, under the guise of being rebellious and asserting my independence, were horrifically self-destructive. I started smoking cigarettes out of curiosity, and before I even realized it, I was hopelessly addicted. It would be another twenty-two years before I could finally quit. Another decision was to take full advantage of what the City had to offer outside the academic arena. Unfortunately, I took that one or two steps too far, by immersing myself in one liberation movement after another, and getting myself involved in one after another disruptive and destructive relationships, all to the detriment of my academic studies. Hindsight is so prescient.

There was no regret whatsoever for one unplanned side trip in those early days. I visited a couple of women's bookstores near Broadway around West 70th Street on a fine, sunny Fall Saturday morning. For some reason, I proceeded walking south until I stumbled upon Lincoln Center. I had heard of the superb concerts and performances at that world famous venue, but it was a poster promoting a musical that caught my attention. It was a performance of *Man of La Mancha*. I was fascinated, probably because of the depiction of a knight on the poster. Because of the availability of discount tickets for students, I could afford to attend a matinee performance. It was a very cozy venue; I felt as if I could reach out and touch the performers on stage. It must have been the Lincoln Center Theater. As soon as I realized the story was about a self-styled knight setting out to right the world's perceived wrongs, never mind his formidable foe was in fact a windmill, and never mind he might have been delusional, I completely identified myself with Don Quixote. It was as if the play was written for and about me, about my life's mission, my dreams and aspirations, my *modus operandi*, my travails, my triumphs:

> *This is my quest, to follow that star,*
> *No matter how hopeless, no matter how far.*

> *And the world will be better for this,*
> *That one man scorned and covered with scars,*
> *Still strove with his last ounce of courage,*
> *To reach the unreachable star.*

The fact that he expired when his dreams and hopes were snatched from him underscored precisely the need to obey our life's calling, to honor those hopes and dreams. That was the only time ever I walked out of a performance sobbing. About twenty-five years later, I would attend another performance of *Man of La Mancha*. It was a touring company with Robert Goulet in the lead role, and the venue was the Fisher Theatre in Detroit. Unlike the Lincoln Center Theater, the Fisher was huge and we had a full house for that performance. I went with Bev. Again, I came away from the performance filled with tears. By then, my life had changed quite dramatically, as will be revealed in the pages that follow. Little did I know in 1972 how my life journey would so faithfully trace the arc of that fabled "mad" knight.

I could not be blamed for being distracted from my studies right out of the gate. Growing up, I always ate whatever Mom had prepared and put on the dining table, except for small snacks here and there that I could whip up or purchase from street vendors. With my dormitory room came cafeteria meals which were surprisingly delicious. I discovered new favorites such as donuts; some mornings I would even miss my first class as I indulged in one after another freshly fried donut. There was one morning very early in the semester when I was enjoying my coffee and donuts when a dormitory staff member rushed to tell me that I had a telephone call from overseas. It was decades before mobile phones, and I had to dash to the switchboard to pick up the call. Besides, international calls were very costly in those days. It turned out to be from Mom and Dad; they were worried about me because they had not heard from me either by telephone or letters; there were no texts or e-mails back in those primordial days. I was obviously having too much fun with my new life, and did not realize weeks had gone by without my "reporting" to them. How quickly I had changed in asserting my independence. The other quick change was my weight: I gained all of my "freshman 20 (pounds)" in just the first few weeks. The rude awakening was in my finance management department. After purchasing books for my first semester and some incidentals, I had almost depleted the $100 I brought with me. I was panic stricken, as I had never had to worry about money previously; *everything* was provided for me then, or I would simply wait for the next weekly allowance from my parents. Even though we never discussed it, I would imagine that my parents would continue to give me an allowance. However, given that we were not rich and their income could never sustain my much higher cost of living in the States, I reckoned that my financial outlook was grim. Fortunately, the rules about foreign students working were not as strict then, and as long as the foreign student advisor authorized it, I could work up to 20 hours per week. I picked up babysitting jobs from Barnard's placement office listings, and worked for a short period serving ice cream at Baskin-Robbins, and another semester at Zabar's selling coffee beans, pastries and cheeses. My stint at Zabar's was elucidating, introducing me to the world of gourmet foods and the culinary arts. A fringe benefit for me was being able to sample delicacies that I could not otherwise afford at the time, including prying Gabrielle (not her real name) with her favorites: *Brie* and fresh *baguettes*, which I purchased with steep employee discounts. Mom and Dad did send me allowances regularly, with some notable periods of exception. In fact, they were extremely mindful of my needs and creature comforts. In the second semester of my freshmen year, Dad sent me a surprise gift of a compact stereo (turntable and AM/FM radio with speakers), which I treasured for years until I could afford my own audio system after becoming an attorney. They even sent me, at great expense via airmail, my *zheng*. However, my lack of money sense and disinterest in fiscal management had me constantly living beyond my means. For better or worse, the takeaway from this my early financial "crisis" was that I had to work in order to survive, and if I wanted more than mere sustenance, I had to work very hard. By extension, I fell for the fallacy of gauging the quality of life in monetary terms: the more money I could make, the more I could buy, and a more comfortable life I could enjoy. That materialistic view would underpin most of the endeavors in my working years, even as I held on to lofty, altruistic aspirations.

The early 1970's was a uniquely exciting time for political activism. I arrived in New York City just three short years after the Stonewall uprising, and as the gay rights movement was gathering momentum. The nascent lesbian-feminist movement was blossoming synergetically in tandem with the thriving women's movement. One could almost touch and feel the raw zest and zeal of those grassroots revolutions. Coming out of a cruel and unjust stigmatization and ostracization, if not outright persecution, because of my love for another woman, I plunged unreservedly into both movements with impetuous abandon. It was as if I came to America not to advance my studies, but to experience life in a way that bore no resemblance to all that came before. Within days of my arrival at Barnard, I had located the local lesbian-feminist group. The Lesbian Feminist Liberation met every Sunday afternoon at the Firehouse. It was a decommissioned firehouse, located at 99 Wooster Street in SoHo. That part of SoHo was not the über-trendy, high-end boutiques district that it is nowadays; it was populated largely by warehouses, lofts and studios, with a charm all its own. The Firehouse was the headquarters of the Gay Activists Alliance, a group for mostly gay men; LFL shared the facilities for its weekly meetings and monthly dances. My first visit to the Firehouse was on a Sunday when LFL was screening a lesbian movie. I opened the door to enter, and literally stumbled in the dark for a seat. When the lights came on, I was pleasantly surprised to find myself in the company of about a hundred women. That in and of itself was mind boggling and affirming; I had found my new "home." LFL was chiefly coordinated and facilitated ("led" was too hierarchical and patriarchal a term in those days of feminist consciousness-raising) by Jean O'Leary and

Ginny Vida, both of whom I admired greatly, as both were fearless trailblazers of the lesbian-feminist movement.

Being a movement activist was rather romantic. One could hold on to ideals, embrace grandiose visions for a goal, and be gratified with the belief that one was fighting the virtuous and righteous battle to benefit society, or at least a specific segment of society. That harkened to my deep resonance with *Man of La Mancha*. In those my exuberant youthful days fresh on American soil, I was thrilled to see that people in this country were actually free not only to express their opinions and beliefs, but to strive for equality where there was none, to seek redress where there was injustice, and to effectuate change where status quo was no longer acceptable. That was enough of a cue for me to fervently engage in advocacy, without consideration for implications or ramifications. The first two years in the States would turn out to be my fancy-free, naïve but passionate and earnest activist period.

To raise public consciousness for a positive image and understanding of gay men and lesbians (bisexual and transgender people were not yet expressly included in those early movement days), LFL and GAA organized speaking engagements. I did not believe there were even training sessions; I signed up as a volunteer speaker, and learned from the more experienced speakers as I went along. We spoke mostly at high schools. Our audience was by and large receptive, and the questions were sincere and innocent. Homosexuality was such a taboo then, and the general public's reception to our lot ranged from pathetically lacking, to antagonistic and worse. The speaking engagements served to spark a much needed dialogue, provided a forum for dispelling misconceptions, and accorded the public a chance to meet homosexuals in person. Additionally, LFL and GAA organized "zaps," our version of nonviolent civil disobedience, and my idea of indulging in a bit of mischievous fun. The "zap" actions predated the call for gays to come out and be counted, and long preceded flamboyant political actions by groups such as ACT UP. I was one of the "zappers" the night we patronized the ultra-luxe Rainbow Room atop Rockefeller Center. There were several pairs of us, in equal number of gay men and women, all dressed to the nines. We were welcomed and served without as much as half a raised eyebrow. When the band struck up, and the fabled dance floor began to fill up, we, too, descended on the dance floor and swayed to the music in male-female pairs. After a few minutes, following the signal from the lead pair, we changed partners and continued dancing with a same-sex partner. That, of course, caused quite a stir (we were then *lightyears* away from "marriage equality"). We were promptly ushered off the dance floor and out of the establishment. Still, the point had been poignantly made. In retrospect, that was extremely gutsy of me. If I had been arrested for disturbing the peace or similar offense, it could have resulted in my deportation and put an abrupt end to my studies in the States. Thank goodness the Rainbow Room management apparently respected our First Amendment rights, and we were cooperative in departing when requested. Civil disobedience should be so civilized.

I also decided to be the rabble-rouser on campus, barely three short weeks after I arrived as a freshman. The feminist movement was prominently represented at Barnard: there was the student group, Women's Collective, and Barnard had even established a well-staffed and well-resourced Women's Center. We also had several outspoken feminist professors to lead the charge. On the other hand, the silence was deafening with respect to recognition of lesbians rights. So, I decided to found the group Lesbian Activists at Barnard (LAB), which was duly registered with the McIntosh Student Center and recognized as an on-campus student activity group. I penned an article entitled "Three Cheers for Sisterhood," which was published in the campus newspaper, announcing the formation of the group and calling for participation at our organizational meeting. That served double duty as my coming out to my roommate and dorm-mates. As I had expected, everyone read the article, but none of my dorm-mates talked to me about it, but none ostracized me either. Homosexuality was still too sensitive a subject for polite company then, even on a progressive campus such as Barnard.

I was putting up LAB flyers at McIntosh Student Center when I was hailed by a young woman who wanted her own copy of the flyer. We struck up a conversation, and I found her quite fascinating. She was a sophomore at Barnard, and was born and grew up in France. The very naïve me did not even recognize at the time that Gabrielle was actually making a pass at me. The organizational meeting of LAB was attended by about a dozen students in attendance. We had a few more meetings through the school year, but there was not enough momentum to organize activities. Still, the existence of LAB enabled us to find each other for support and camaraderie. In the ensuing year, LAB became somewhat subsumed into the Women's Collective. There were increasing number of events for lesbian-feminists in the City, from the Gay Pride Parade (I served as a marshal in one of the early marches), to women's dances sponsored by LFL at the Firehouse (and once on Columbia campus, in the Lion's Den, no less), to women's concerts. Lesbian musicians and singers-songwriters, such as Alix Dobkin, Kay Gardner, Cris Williamson, and Meg Christian, were the raves of the day. Then there were the women's bars, mostly in the Village. *Bonnie and Clyde* was a popular hangout for lesbians. I did not patronize the bars often; I did enjoy the music and dancing, and the camaraderie as we would often go as a group.

I was hardly ever on-campus during my freshman year, given my extensive involvement with lesbian-feminist activities off-campus. I also made a point of not mingling with the Asian or Chinese students at Barnard or Columbia. To me, they could not and did not accept my lifestyle, and I could no longer be stifled as I was in Hong Kong. Hence, I might have appeared snobbish, but I did not even "hang out" with Shirley, the only other Hong Kong student to be admitted to Barnard that year, or my classmate from SSGC, Selina. I barely managed to attend classes, and I did also manage to join the volleyball varsity team. I played inter-collegiate games during my freshmen year, and Sylvia was one of my teammates. Somehow, we seemed destined to be friends for life. My first semester of dormitory life did not suit me well at all. Within days, Sylvia was the object of desire for half a dozen swooning Columbia College men; bouquets of red roses arrived and filled our room as if on cue. I was thankful that men were not allowed on the dormitory floor. With each passing day, the radicalized lesbian-feminist separatist me was becoming increasingly intolerant of the patriarchal and heterosexual world. Hence, the predominantly heterosexual atmosphere of the dormitory became unacceptably oppressive to me. By the end of the first semester, I was able to get out of the dormitory and into an off-campus apartment building, sharing a suite with five other women, with my own room. As if predestined, Sylvia and I reunited again when we became suite-mates during our senior year at Barnard. It was gratifying to see how much we had matured in just four years; by then, she was a most understanding friend in need, while I was less militantly separatist. From there, through graduation, and more than four decades of following each other's life's trials and tribulations[5], we had remained steadfast correspondents in the pre-email age. We even managed to get together no fewer than three times over the years. Nowadays, she is a best friend and

---

[5] Sylvia and her late husband, William, built their artisanal, hand-dipped ice cream store (Dragon Eye ice cream, anyone?) in New York City's Chinatown to phenomenal success through sheer determination, unflinching courage, and unimaginable hard work. She lost William to cancer three months before I lost my Mom to same. She could have sat on her laurels and stayed in retirement to enjoy the fruits of her labor, but instead, she returned to school in the last few years. The former biology major and aspiring marine scientist earned a second Bachelor's degree in Nursing, and is now working as a Registered Nurse. Kudos, my inimitable compadre!

confidante, a sage consigliere and a shoulder to cry on, and we are closer than ever with mobile phones, e-mails and texting at our fingertips.

Barnard presented me with quite a challenge academically; I had finally met my match. The students were all brilliant and competitive, over-achievers one and all. I would learn in later years that her roster of alumnae reads like Who's Who from showbiz to politics, from the healing arts to the performing arts. At SSGC, we students were by and large passive recipients of knowledge, listening intensely to our teacher's every word, taking copious notes, memorize and then regurgitate that knowledge. Here in America, in classes at Barnard, it appeared to me that the knowledge was being negotiated, debated, and argued over, and a certain percentage of our final grade was reserved for "class participation," a totally alien concept to me. Meanwhile, my academic plans were falling apart at the seams. After completing the mandatory Freshmen English class in my first semester, Professor Remington Patterson, chair of the English Department, nonchalantly informed me that I should enroll in the "Remedial English" class in the ensuing semester. I tried not to feel fragile and shattered or insulted and indignant, but my plans for majoring in English, and pursuing a career as a journalist, were decimated into smithereens then and there. Since my arrival in this country, I had not personally encountered any disparate treatment based on my race. Most people were often quite fascinated with my Chinese background. It was probably because there were not that many Chinese from overseas then. President Nixon had only recently returned from a historic visit to China, and Americans were only beginning to learn about China, its people and culture. Professor Patterson's comments singularly struck me as being not so subtly racist; he had made up his mind that my English was not up to par simply because I was Chinese and a foreign-born person. All the same, I felt devastated, and I was adrift, academically speaking. My best laid plans to be an English major and pursue a writing career had been completely demolished.

I also felt adrift psychologically, strangely ungrounded in that vast city. I had heard about psychotherapy when I was in Hong Kong, and had been intrigued by the notion. I wondered how talking to someone not a friend could be therapeutic. I knew it was popular in the United States, though it was taboo in Hong Kong; it insinuated that one had a mental illness that required treatment by a psychiatrist, a "mind doctor." Here I was, in New York City, far away from Hong Kong, and had no need to worry about such culture-based taboo. Since the health coverage at Barnard included psychotherapy, I hastened to sign up for sessions with our resident psychiatrist, Dr. Zira DeFries. It was not because I thought I had any mental, emotional or psychological issues to be addressed; it was strictly out of curiosity. However, after my first session with Dr. DeFries, I was "hooked." She was a petite lady perhaps in her 50's. As I would later understand, she was a classic Freudian psychiatrist, thus arguably precisely the "wrong" type of therapists for a radical separatist lesbian-feminist. No matter, we must have found each other engaging; I liked her letting me do all the talking with her hardly utterly a single word, and she must have liked me as a subject for her research and studies. As I would learn years later, when I visited her in 1996 after she had retired and was living by herself on Shelter Island at the far end of Long Island, she won international acclaim for her presentation at one of the American Psychiatric Association's annual meetings on the subject of "political lesbianism." She allowed that much of her observations, analysis and conclusions for that series of papers was based on her work with Barnard students of my era.

I remembered watching a TV interview of Barbra Streisand years ago in which she disclosed that she was in therapy for a number of years. When the interviewer, whose identity escaped me, exclaimed at the length of time she had been in psychotherapy, Streisand calmly retorted: "I am a slow learner." I obviously was an even slower learner; I continued with various therapists after I left Barnard, and ended up with a total of about twenty-two *years* of psychotherapy. I often joked that I should be conferred an honorary degree in that discipline, for having been such a long-term and steadfast consumer of psychotherapy services. In retrospect, those weekly sessions were an expensive (health insurance covered at most only half the costs) but necessary pressure relief valve for the insane level of stress I was experiencing on all fronts—work, home, family, and health—during most of my adult life. For each non-verbal Freudian therapist, I had several non-Freudian therapists who did not hesitate to impart their pearls of wisdom to whatever situation at hand. Some of those gems of an advice would turn out to be lifesavers while others were life lessons for me to ruminate over time. I do subscribe to the adage that a "good" therapist is worth his or her weight in gold. A "bad" one however well-intentioned, on the other hand, can do so much harm as to give new meaning to the admonition *caveat emptor*. My weekly therapy sessions would have continued to date, with one therapist or another, but for a chance *rendezvous* with meditation in August of 2004. More out of curiosity than any profound yearning for enlightened truth or inner peace, I took a lesson in mantra meditation with Dr. Nirmala Nancy Hanke (in a non-professional setting, she preferred to be known by her spiritual name, Nirmala), and unexpectedly became a daily meditator ever since. Precisely as she predicted, I no longer needed psychotherapy once I became a regular daily meditator. That was ironic and comedic, as Nirmala is a practicing psychiatrist. In the fall of 1996, Bev and I underwent couples therapy sessions with her for a few months. I reconnected with her in July of 2004, not for therapy, but for "spiritual guidance," which will be regaled in a later chapter.

Even with weekly psychotherapy sessions at Barnard, I had unwittingly set myself on a path of physical and psychological self-destruction, deconstructing all that had been so meticulously crafted and intently honed in the preceding eighteen years. My subconscious decision to devote my time and energy to the "movements" instead of academic pursuits could arguably be justified in lofty, quixotic terms of championing the cause of the oppressed. There was no rhyme or reason, however, to my hurtling from one disastrous relationship to another even more abusive or destructive. I could chalk any one of those dangerous *liaisons* up to inexperience or immaturity, but the serial masochism became apparent to me only in hindsight. My maiden relationship with Gabrielle would almost be comical if it was not so pathetic in setting the devastating pattern that followed. I was apparently searching for a reprise of the euphoria that came with falling in love with a woman soulmate, the pure ecstasy that I had experienced with loving Pearl. Instead of finding another soulmate, I found myself falling in love with love itself, even as the object of my desire was a totally wrong match for me. With Gabrielle, it was the quintessential puppy love, with my taking the relationship far too seriously. She probably found having a relationship with a woman rather exotic, and we had fun together for the better part of my freshmen year. She was genuine and sincere, for that year. She even parted with $500, a very substantial sum for a student then, to buy me a beat-up 1965 Oldsmobile "F85" from a junk car yard in New Jersey, simply because I so wanted a car. That wreck of a car lasted just a few months, but her ardency stole my heart. Nevertheless, after that first year, the "novelty" for her must have worn off and she started disassociating herself. It was as if the love affair was merely one of many titillating experiential excesses she indulged in, a casual and wanton incidence of youth. I was woefully unprepared for the rejection; my fear of abandonment certainly aggravated my trampled feelings and wounded ego. It would not be the last time I felt discarded as if I were yesterday's newspaper.

I flew to Toronto in December of 1972 to visit Pearl as well as several classmates from SSGC—Flora, Cherry and Susan and others—all of whom were pursuing their university studies there. Any hope of picking up where we left off with Pearl was purely fantasy on my part. I then flew to Ann Arbor, Michigan, to visit Vivian who was studying at the University of Michigan. I remembered distinctly, as the plane was flying low over the City as it prepared to land at the Detroit Metro Airport, the view out of my window. I had never met a city that looked like Detroit: block after block of deserted buildings and dwellings, bombed out windows, boarded up storefronts, unrelenting grayness, and unmitigated desolation. I made a mental note "never" to come to this forsaken land which time and humanity seemed to have cruelly abandoned. That is why the sages of the ages taught us to "never say never;" I ended up living in the Detroit area for my entire adult life.

In early 1973, Pearl came to New York City to visit me. We spent a lovely weekend together, exchanging poems, talking into the wee hours of the night. I even took her to the women's dance at the Firehouse. She requested the DJ to play a track by the Eagles, probably *Take It Easy*. She told me how Minnie Ripperton's *Loving You* reminded her of me. There was, sadly, no intimation that we could rekindle what we shared barely a year earlier. In fact, Pearl got married to a man, Peter, a guitarist in a local rock band, in the spring of 1973. I could not bear to attend their wedding. In the spring of 1973, Winnie also visited me at Barnard. We had a wild time. I drove us to Ann Arbor to visit with Vivian, but Winnie was more interested in returning to the City to spend more time with Christine, a friend of Gabrielle's who was then visiting from France.

My freshmen year came and went. I had no idea that I could not stay in a dormitory or my off-campus apartment during the summer months. Gabrielle came to my rescue by finding and helping me rent a tiny apartment in east Greenwich Village. By then, she had already drifted away from me; she hardly came to my apartment. The only diversion that summer was my joining a women's karate dojo where I finally received a form of martial arts training that I pined for growing up in Sai Wan Estate. Those three months of getting physically fit with other women, many of whom were closet lesbians, gave new meaning to the slogan "Sisterhood is Powerful." Nonetheless, after barely one year in the United States, I felt totally unhinged; I had completely lost my bearings, my purpose, my exceptionalism. I had successfully renounced all that was confining and stifling in Hong Kong, but I had not found meaningful substitutes for my new life in America. New York City suited me to a tee, but perhaps too much so; its dynamism had in fact overwhelmed me without my realizing it. I was so over-stimulated most of the time that I felt I needed to elude to a retreat whenever I had a system overload. Not having the financial means to take my leave as desired, I was quite burned out during the four years I was there.

I did visit Pearl again in Toronto in the summer of 1973, and beat my retreat with my heart and spirits even more broken; it would be years before that flame would be finally contained if not extinguished. In returning from that visit, however, an incident occurred that would fundamentally alter the course of my studies as well as career. At the Toronto International Airport, I was being cleared for customs and immigration to board my plane bound for New York City. The officer examined my proffered valid Hong Kong British subject passport containing my valid U.S. student visa and my Form I-20, Certificate of Eligibility, which evidenced my foreign student status at Barnard. For some reason, he wanted additional identification, such as a student ID card or a driver's license. I gladly pulled that out of my wallet. In the process, I noticed his fixed gaze at my wallet, specifically, the flap that contained my membership card in the Gay Activists Alliance. He rudely snatched my wallet and examined that membership card. The next thing I knew was being told that I would not be allowed to board the plane to reenter the United States. I was extremely shaken; I had been in the country for only one year, and I had never had any previous encounter with law enforcement. My memory is hazy as to whether he stated to me any reason for refusing to let me back into the country. However, it was very clear to me that it was because of my possession of that GAA membership card. I had to call Pearl to pick me up and return to her home. Her mother was most gracious in hosting me for a few more days, and accommodating the umpteen telephone calls I placed to my comrades in the Lesbian Feminist Liberation for assistance. They in turn put me in touch with a couple of immigration attorneys who counseled me *pro bono*, and who advised me to fly out to London, United Kingdom, stay for a week or so, and then return via another port of entry (I picked Washington, D.C.). The entire episode was extremely unnerving to me, not to mention that it was very costly and inconvenient. Not knowing the law, I could not and did not defend myself at the Toronto airport. In retrospect, it was a clear violation of the guarantees under the First Amendment—freedom of speech and freedom of association—on the part of the immigration officer. I now understand that many fundamental Constitutional and legal rights are somehow suspended or even eviscerated at the border. Besides, it would not have been a smart move to argue with or challenge the officer; it would have gotten me deeper in the mêlée. Apparently, a foreigner—an alien such as myself—could *advocate* "Gay and Proud" only entirely at his or her own peril. On the other hand, the officer was "merciful" enough not to have formally excluded me, or placed me under exclusion proceedings; he did not even mark my passport. It was probably chalked up as my having voluntarily withdrawn my application for admission to the U.S.

On yet another hand, I had an unexpected opportunity to tour London, though I would of course have preferred the visit to have been under less stressful circumstances.

That sobering and most unpleasant experience sparked my interest in the law. My one year of activism in the lesbian and feminist movements had also paved the way for my realization that, at least in the United States, the law was king. Every right and privilege was founded in the law, and mastering the law would be the key to success in the American society. Returning to the U.S. just in time to start my sophomore year, I took another required course: political science 101 with Professor Inez Smith Reid. She introduced me to the legal world which heretofore had never existed in my conscious awareness. She mesmerized me as a learned and well-tempered legal scholar. I decided there and then to major in Political Science, *and* to become a lawyer. It was easier said than done, because I had no inkling of the steep learning curve that decision would entail. Two other Barnard professors were instrumental as I loaded up on political science courses. Professor Hannah J. Zawadzka inspired my interest in geopolitics and foreign affairs, and Professor Peter H. Juviler, a legendary professor worshipped by many students, guided me through the thicket that was the studies of political science. He was progressive and open-minded to a fault; I picked him as my senior thesis advisor even though he was not a woman, and even though the subject of my thesis was the politics of parthenogenesis and matriarchy.

My sophomore year was a repeat of my freshmen year, *sans* Gabrielle. I had a couple of casual affairs, all incidents that I would rather forget. I did not plunge headlong into them "casually;" they were false starts for my well-meaning but misguided attempts at locating my next soulmate. My "movement" activities did not even lead me to forming any new, lasting friendship. New York City could indeed be very alienating, with everyone being preoccupied with his or her own very full agenda. I was on-campus a bit more than during my first year. I continued to take photographs in my spare time, using the two Nikon "F" SLR camera bodies and a couple of lenses that Dad gave me. I also joined the Photography Club at Columbia, and learned darkroom skills on my own. I enjoyed spending long hours in the darkroom developing my black-and-white negatives. I would in later years take photographs for the Barnard Yearbook, *Mortarboard*. To supplement my allowance from my parents, I worked as a typesetter for the Columbia campus newspaper *Columbia Daily Spectator*, in the year when Gail Robinson, a Barnard student, was the Editor in Chief. Starting with my junior year, I worked as a student assistant at Columbia Law School, assisting Jo Green Iwabe (a Barnard alumna), the editor of the alumni publications, and under the supervision of Dean Arthur O. Kimball, the Director of Development. While there, I briefly met U.S. Supreme Court Justice Ruth Bader Ginsburg who was then a professor at the Law School. With an education at Barnard, and a stint, however insignificant and peripheral, at Columbia Law School, you would imagine that the tentacles to my future legal education and career should have been well placed. In fact, I did not take advantage of any "connection" that might have existed. The privilege of having attended Barnard, in particular, was unceremoniously squandered by me, even if only subconsciously. I could and should have continued to pursue academic excellence at Barnard to ensure a promising academic and career future. Instead, I walked the path of a feckless renegade, the quintessential rebel without a cause. Lest I be too critical of myself, having my separatist feminist consciousness raised and my politicization were valuable, if not exactly bankable, experiences. To a significant extent, my reckless rebelliousness was a delayed reaction to Mom's perfectionistic parenting. While she demanded and expected excellence from me, she also made sure that my growing up was well planned in all respects, and well provided for within our means. It was a worry-free and supportive childhood for me, but by the same token, it was too regimented for my innate free spirit. I thus led a very sheltered life, wholly unprepared for life in the adult world. It would have worked out if I were a "traditional" female, as a suitable husband would have taken over where my parents left off. Instead, I was at the farthest opposite end on the "tradition" spectrum. Hence, once I was released from Mom's strict script, I went overboard with exploiting my personal liberties. Mom was not to be blamed for her well-intentioned Herculean efforts in nurturing me; it was I who careened from one extreme to the other.

My parents decided that it was time for me to have a home visit after two years in America. It was the summer after my sophomore year; Dad had just been promoted to directorship, and Mom had received a salary increase, and hence, they could afford my round-trip plane ticket. I was excited to return home for the first time, eager to show off what I had learned in my two years of being untethered from the mothership. I had heard that Barnard awarded grants for worthwhile summer projects. I applied just in time for mine: to promote feminist consciousness-raising in Hong Kong. With the $100 I was awarded, I purchased a film from a women's bookstore on the politics of rape from a feminist perspective. I chose that title simply because it was the only film within my award budget. The women's liberation movement had not yet reached Hong Kong; I was prepared to be one of the vanguards to agitate and educate.

It turned out to be a rowdy and utterly self-destructive summer for me. With hindsight, I could clearly see how a confluence of disparate circumstances conspired to orchestrate my "downfall." First and foremost, in two short years, I had completely outgrown my Hong Kong past; I no longer fit in my family or the Hong Kong society. That came as a total shock to me, and I was the worse for it because I did not understand the dynamics of my own growth. I only felt totally out of my elements; everything that was once familiar had become a stranger and worse, an irritant. I had naïvely thought that I would simply slip back into my familiar role when I returned home, and while I was at it, introduce my family and friends to the new me—the feminist side if not exactly the lesbian side. Instead, I found resuming the role of the dutiful, pliant daughter repugnant, all the while as I was not exactly free to assert my new-found feminist independence and empowerment, especially vis-a-vis family friends and relatives. I felt confounded and frustrated. It was certainly not the warm and triumphant homecoming that I had anticipated.

I proceeded perfunctorily with my consciousness-raising campaign. I held consciousness-raising sessions and showed the film to several Chinese community groups. The reception was not particularly heartwarming, and I could not claim that I had raised the feminist consciousness of too many women. Shortly after my arrival in Hong Kong, Mom's boss, Simon Lee, had generously loaned me one of his many cars, a red MG-B convertible sports car. I loved cars and driving, and was in seventh heaven with that loaner car. I learned then that most young women loved being driven—and seen—in fancy, fast cars. As for me, that little loaner car boosted my self-image immeasurably, especially in the arena of attracting women. I was by then more interested in whisking around town in that flashy, classic British racer than in preaching the feminist bible.

On a typical scorching hot and humid afternoon early that summer, I did not remember what prompted me to look into Dad's liquor cupboard, but look I did. I was never interested in liquors up to that point, but the heat drove me to try a cool glass of orange juice with a thimbleful of vodka added. That quenched my thirst on that sweltering afternoon; I also felt suitably relaxed. Alcohol consumption had always been the bane of existence for the males on Dad's side of the family. I remembered seeing my uncles and male cousins at family banquets and feasts downing whisky out of large tumblers as if they were drinking iced tea. I knew Dad also had somewhat of a drinking problem which Mom tried time and again to reign in. I had always congratulated myself that, being a female descendant, I had not inherited the "alcoholic gene;" but that was before that fateful summer afternoon in Hong Kong. Once I stumbled upon the allure of the potent potables, my precipitous downfall was not far behind.

Winnie was then on her way up the food chain at Commercial Radio. She would soon become a wildly popular host of a morning talk show and a successful radio DJ, and was well poised to garner even greater fame and fortune in the ensuing years. I visited her a few times at the studio. I remembered vividly the time she whispered to me as she was cueing up an LP: "This one is going to be a huge hit." The mesmerizing introit, with its purposeful crescendos, cascading into a haunting and majestic anthem of a love song, was quintessential Elton John at his prime. "Don't Let the Sun Go Down on Me" remains one of my all-time favorite songs. On another occasion, she invited me on the air, and that was when I realized I was a very clumsy radio guest. In 1974, she lived in her bachelorette pad—a small rooftop apartment, which was not to be confused with a "penthouse suite." I visited her often; we would commiserate into the wee hours of the night, finding consolation in Scotch and brandy, often finishing off a full bottle between the two of us. Other times, she would have private parties in her apartment, with more booze and, of course, attendance by a bevy of adoring young women.

I did find a feminist group in Hong Kong, and showed the film at one of their regular meetings. The group members were mostly non-Chinese, expatriates from the United States, United Kingdom, Australia and European countries working in Hong Kong, or whose husbands were posted to Hong Kong. I befriended a couple of women in the group: Annemargret, and Sally, an American and a part-time fashion model. Annemargret, who was a closeted lesbian (she was working as a nanny for a wealthy family), and I became fast friends. The three of us would often enjoy a night on the town, savoring fine foods and drinks, and once or twice, we joined Winnie's private parties. Once I started drinking, I discovered "night life." One of my cousins was a keyboardist with a band playing at a night club in a respectable hotel. I went there one night to listen to his band and was hooked; I found their singer, Delilah, captivating. Music, alluring women, and, of course, liquor constituted an intoxicating combination. By then, my summer in Hong Kong had degenerated into serial carousing and womanizing; I was mostly in a drunken stupor. I had no idea what my parents thought at that point. I was too grownup for them to control or even manage; all they could do was to enable me and grin and bear the consequences. It was most likely a case of my delayed teenage rebelliousness of the worst kind. I had never been one to do anything haphazardly. Likewise, I was at full throttle when orchestrating, however innocently, my own descent into self-conflagration.

Before the summer of wanton excess drew to a close, my parents treated me to a trip to several Southeast Asian countries. I ventured by myself to Singapore, Kuala Lumpur, Malaysia, and Bangkok, Thailand. Looking back, it was very audacious of me to be traveling alone in those countries as a young single woman. Nothing much stood out from that week-long trip, except perhaps my stay at a brand new five-star luxurious hotel in Kuala Lumpur. I was welcomed with a room there practically for pennies because it had not yet officially opened for business. The hotel was so opulent and my room was so decadently deluxe that I had not since been able to afford any hotel accommodation even remotely as lavish.

Back at Barnard for my junior year, without the superficial glitz and glitter but drowning in liquor all the same, I felt gloomy and frustrated, spent and lost. Throughout my childhood and youth, I sallied forth from triumph to triumph, sure of my purpose and direction. By contrast, there I was, dangerously floundering. Liquor, of course, had a lot to do with that doom and gloom, even if I was not consciously aware of my steady descent into the abyss. Not only was I unable to see a future, I did not even feel grounded enough for clear thinking about the present. The only decision I could make was to take a semester off in the faint hope that that would give me sufficient time to regroup. That turned out to be a misguided decision. Apparently, foreign students had to be enrolled full-time in order to maintain their nonimmigrant visa status. I hurriedly re-enrolled in several art classes such as wood engraving, lithography, and welding sculpture. By then, I had moved out of my Barnard apartment, and found a room to sublease in an apartment just a few blocks from campus. I did not realize I had a famous landlady/roommate: Joan P. Tower, the renowned composer of *Fanfare for the Uncommon Woman* and other award winning pieces. I remembered her fondly as a kind and gentle free spirit, and who was, understandably, extremely serious about her music. I would never forget her generosity in giving me a ticket to her recital at the Carnegie Hall. It might have been her first performance at that venue, but it was certainly my first visit to that renowned concert hall. For an impoverished student, that was a treat for which I felt extremely privileged and honored.

The year of my darkest hour trudged on. My sorely limited budget was stretched even thinner so as to support my liquor and cigarettes habits as well as rent payments. I often had to go without food. Not having any talent in creating visual art, even my no-brainer art classes presented challenges. Liquor increasingly became my only solace. Drowning in liquor, every aspect of my life was hurtling down the proverbial slippery slope. It was a classic vicious cycle. I remembered running for the Barnard seat at Columbia's University Senate that year. I had no idea what made me think that I should run or that I could be elected. It was probably a grandiose idea conceived in an inebriated state. I was so much under the influence most of the time that I was more an embarrassment than a credible candidate waging a viable campaign or getting the votes out. That was a low mark for how far I had strayed from any resemblance of reality. A classmate who won the seat, Jessica Zive, was magnanimous enough to name me an "observer" to the Senate. I was thankful for my friends in the Women's Collective, including Roz Richter, Jennifer Fox, Anne Caplan, Rachel Brody and many others, kindred spirits one and all. I wish I had reached out to them in those darkest hours, but my pride kept me on my misguided lonesome sojourn. Perhaps I did not even realize that I needed help. Beth Falk and Lisa Lerman, the co-editors of the *Barnard Bulletin*, kept me on staff though I did not remember writing any article for the paper. Perhaps I was the photographer, but then again, alcohol had a unique way of decimating one's memory.

On the personal relationship front, I was an unmitigated disaster. I kept "falling in love" with women who were not even gay, resulting in surefire if self-induced heartbreaks. Over and over again, it was as if I fell in love with the very notion of falling in love, or that I did so just for the sake of falling in love, even though there might not even have been any true love to speak of. Far too often, I ended up being exploited emotionally and financially by the other who took full advantage of my naïve loyalty and blind devotion. A brief respite came in the spring of 1975, when I met a classmate, Carol-Ann Allen. She was performing at one of Barnard's spring festival events, singing and accompanying herself on the guitar. She reminded me somewhat of Pearl, as she inspired me to compose poems again. It was as if a sliver of sunshine, of sanity, of normalcy were returning to my life. I relished associating with an intellectual equal again, allowing me to reclaim a measure of self-respect in the process. As it turned out, Carol-Ann was not "out" yet as a lesbian; she was still in the "confused," "unsure" or "questioning" camp. By then, I had finally learned my lesson to stay away from heterosexual women and women who were not "committed" lesbians. I had been grievously wounded and disappointed by those women who viewed our tryst as an accident, or a one-off adventure, or a novelty experiment. I, one who loved with unbridled passion and devotion, refused to be singed anymore. Nonetheless, my all too brief liaison with Carol-Ann gave me an opportunity to come up for air, to make me realize just how far down the proverbial rabbit hole I had fallen into. Carol-Ann and I would lose contact shortly after graduation from Barnard. I learned that she had left for the United Kingdom in the 1980's and was active in the anti-nuclear, anti-Thatcher movement. She telephoned me once out of the blue around that time, but we lost contact again thereafter. With Bev's possessiveness and jealousness, it was not prudent for me to reconnect with her anyway. It would be another twenty years before our paths would cross again.

Mom and Dad had a surprise for me in the summer of 1975—Vivian would be visiting and staying with me in New York City for more than a month. As she was my favorite baby sister, I was positively thrilled to have her spend time with me. That was her first visit to the United States, and I rolled out the red carpet to show her my favorite haunts in the City. I had a very limited budget, and thus, we could not afford to attend Broadway shows or have dinners at 5-star restaurants. Instead, we had a feast at my favorite Italian restaurant, Mamma Leone's, that served so much food that we fairly waddled out of the restaurant. Moreover, there were enough free-admission events and places to see and attend in New York City. I even initiated her to the fine art of street hawking my vinyl LPs on the sidewalk outside my apartment. With the few dollars we made from the sales, we gorged ourselves silly on ice cream and pizza slices. In retrospect, I believe our parents sent her to me probably because she was missing me. I had been gone for three years, and Lina had also left for her university studies in Regina, Saskatchewan. Vivian was probably having a tough time dealing with the separation which felt more like abandonment. I was too self-absorbed at the time to ponder on those finer points, but for the first time in a year, I was having a relatively sane time. I was simply happy, enjoying simple things in life with my baby sister.

Vivian's visit in fact brought me more than a breath of fresh air. I woke up one morning with my typical hangover. I was nauseous and groggy as usual, except that on that particular morning, with Vivian sharing my room and being there, as if struck by a thunderclap, I suddenly came upon a realization: my state of being was shameful and despicable, even though Vivian did not even seem to have noticed let alone minded my drunkenness; perhaps she was simply being polite and did not pick on my nasty addiction to liquor. From that moment on, I stopped drinking. It was not monumental and there was no drama involved. I did not have to throw down the gauntlet or swear on my ancestors' honor to stay off liquor. I simply ceased drinking liquor from that moment on. It was not a strict prohibition either; in the ensuing five years, I might have had a celebratory sip of champagne or a glass of wine on special occasions. Liquor simply ceased to be a part of my life, and certainly no longer at center stage as it was during my junior year. The last time I had any liquor was when I passed the Bar Examination, qualified to be licensed as an attorney in Michigan. It was one very fine day in November of 1980. One of the senior partners of the law firm, for which I had been working as a law clerk, invited me to a celebratory lunch. I did not flinch when we ordered round after round of cognac with our meal; after all, I used to gulp that stuff down as if it were a soft drink. By the time we returned to the office after that long lunch, I was drunk as a skunk, and could not even drive home. Since that day—and to Bev's dismay—I have never had another drop of liquor.

Regaining control of my mind—and my life—just in time for my senior year at Barnard was an unexpected gift of Vivian's visit. In one swell swoop, everything in my life seemed to get back on track again. I moved back into a Barnard apartment for seniors, reuniting with Sylvia and sharing the spacious apartment with three other studious classmates. Having totally wasted my junior year, I had to make up for lost time in order to graduate on schedule in May of 1976. That meant taking an extremely heavy load of classes both semesters, in addition to completing my senior thesis. For the first time since I arrived from Hong Kong three years earlier, my fighting spirit had returned and I was ready to shine again. I was happy to be "unattached" to anyone; and I was happier yet that I wanted to remain unattached for a change. I did not realize even then that I had this need to be "in love," as if I were not a whole person without a life partner. All would be well if I could indeed end up with a soulmate who was "perfect" in every way. The glitch was that I was not very good at picking a "perfect" partner. As a matter of fact, I had the knack, even if subconsciously, for picking those who would do me the most harm, as if I were staging my very own Greek tragedy.

Not quite three weeks into the semester, on one lovely Saturday night, several of us at Barnard decided to patronize a new local women's bar for some fun and dancing. I tagged along, figuring that I had studied quite enough for the week. The bar was packed, as it usually would be on a Saturday night. There were very limited options for lesbians to gather and socialize back in those dark ages. The music and the dancing seemed much more delightful and enjoyable for me without the intoxicants, or it might have been me who was feeling particularly vibrant that evening. As I was dancing with a friend, out of the corner of my eye I caught sight of a woman who captivated me. Now many decades later, I would learn and understand that we are attracted to certain people often because of our Past Lives or karma. These people might have been significant players in one of our Past Lives, such as our spouse, lovers, parents, siblings, comrades and best friends, or even enemies with whom we had "unfinished business." We are drawn to them instinctively, whether or not we recognize them from our prior lifetimes, when we meet them again in this lifetime. Hence, even though we seem to have no logical or ostensible reason to be attracted to them, we are rendered helpless in resisting the attraction. "Resistance is futile," as the Borg in *Star Trek* ominously threatened. That was exactly the case with this woman whom I spotted across the dance floor. She was not particularly good-looking or outstanding in any way that I could articulate. Yet, the attraction seemed to be mutual, spontaneous and irresistible. In short order she came over and asked me for a dance. Her name was Barbara, and she was a registered nurse. She was also ten years my senior. My best intentions to remain single lasted not even a month; it was an almost innate need, not just a yearning, to be with someone lest I not be a "complete" person. That need would be my downfall, over and over again, until I belatedly learned my life lessons.

Whenever I thought I was "in love," I loved intensely and passionately; half measures were not for me in these matters of the heart. That was, in retrospect, a surefire formula for relationship disasters. Any reasonable person would allow a trial period for getting to know at least the basics about the "object of desire" at hand, to ascertain whether she was indeed an "object" deserving pursuit and devotion. Reasonableness, however, had no place in my book; my *modus operandi* was to jump in with both feet, blindfolded, and let the chips fall where they might. With Barb, it was an illogical, overpowering attraction. She was a most unlikely soulmate for me, and we did not otherwise have much in common. Instead, I congratulated myself on happening upon someone who appeared to be gainfully employed, and a bit more mature than women my age who kept leaving me after a relatively brief affair. Her darker side would, to my horrors, unfurl in the course of our two-year entanglement. In those first few months, however, we were swept up in our rapturous romance.

I would soon learn that Barb had a "good friend," Simone (not her real name), who worked and lived in Switzerland, and whom she visited on a regular basis. I was of course thrilled that she proposed to pay for my trip to Switzerland to meet Simone over the Christmas holidays. That was such an exciting and exotic idea, especially for a poor student who could not even afford to attend a local concert let alone a vacation abroad. Switzerland impressed me from the moment I landed in Geneva. Everything was pristine, orderly, and very civilized. It was a peaceful society, and the scenery was exactly as enchanting as depicted on postcards. I felt very much at home in that country, for some strange reason. I took to Simone immediately, a very kind and intelligent soul. The feeling was apparently mutual and reciprocal, as she seemed particularly pleased that I had, as of three months earlier, been the light in Barb's life. She had a doctorate in Education and an advanced nursing degree, and held a very respectable job as the head of some institution. Her apartment was roomy and tidy. During the ten days or so when Barb and I were her guests, she took time off work to drive us around sightseeing, to visit her extended family in the idyllic countryside, and to Paris for a weekend. The few places we visited in Paris left a lasting impression with me: the Sainte-Chapelle, Place de la Concorde, Notre-Dame Cathedral, and the Avenue des Champs-Élysées. The drive to Paris itself was almost mystical; as we drove through the mountains, a crystalline light snow was gently blanketing the scenery unfolding around us. Joan Baez's "Diamond and Rust" was playing in Simone's car cassette deck. Barb and I also took the train to northern Switzerland, and we then proceeded by bus to view a glacier. I had been fascinated with glaciers ever since I learned about the last Ice Age in my geography class in secondary school. I was awestruck as I stood and walked on one. My Swiss vacation was, in sum, everything a dream vacation should be, courtesy of my new-found love and a very gracious hostess. Indeed, as I was being serenaded in the fairy-tale-like setting, I failed to discern even the obvious. There was one day when Barb seemed unusually quiet. I asked Simone whether something was untoward, and she mumbled something about Barb's being "sad" or "depressed." It was glossed over ever so deftly that I did not even give it a second thought, and everything seemed to return to normal the following day. Then there was the nature of the "friendship" between Simone and Barb. At that time, I naïvely accepted that they were the best of friends and thought nothing more of it.

Back at Barnard for my final semester, for the first time in four years, I felt very productive. I was finally accomplishing what I was meant to do when I was sent here for college. I was getting good grades, and the senior thesis was taking shape. There was a week in April when I did not sleep at all as I raced to finish my thesis and cramped for the finals. At least the relationship with Barb up to that point was positive such that I was able to devote my time and attention to my studies. I graduated in May of 1976, and my parents came all the way from Hong Kong to attend the commencement. They were proud of me, and I was elated that I made it to graduation despite all my missteps during those four tumultuous years. However, the upbeat, feel-good atmosphere soon gave way to acrimony as my parents completely disapproved of Barb. They saw in her serious flaws or deficits which I somehow was still unable to recognize. Barb drove us to Washington, D.C. for a couple of days of sightseeing. She was in one of her "quieter" moods to which I was accustomed by then; my parents apparently saw something much more troubling or even sinister in Barb's behavior. The visit to the capital, needless to say, was awkward, strained and disappointing. I then went with my parents to Toronto to visit some relatives and family friends. It was during this trip when Dad was practically in tears begging me to disengage from Barb at once. I had not a clue as to why they were so "against" Barb, other than their general notion of not accepting my lesbianism. Of course, I had no intention then of discontinuing our relationship. Mom and Dad went on to visit Lina in Saskatchewan before returning to Hong Kong. In the ensuing months, I would realize that Mom and Dad had adopted a "tough love" course of action, and ceased all financial support for me, in the hope that I would leave Barb or better yet, return to Hong Kong. That move unfortunately resulted in the unintended consequence of compelling me to be totally dependent on Barb financially, and thus, even more vulnerable to her whims and dictates.

I had focused all of my energy on graduating on schedule, which I managed to accomplish, but I was utterly unprepared for my "post-Barnard" era. When it was time to move out of the Barnard apartment shortly after commencement, I had nowhere to go but to move in with Barb. She shared an apartment near campus with another nurse. Barb also had two Siamese cats, Lila and Stinky. As I crowded into the small apartment, the dynamics of our relationship changed as if on cue. It was rather subtle at first as she became "moody" oftentimes. Devolving from those fickle moods, she became abusive, verbally and physically, a shove here, and a push and bump there. I made excuses for her changed behavior, blaming it on work stress which in turn made her irritable. She progressed to becoming domineering, overbearing and excessively possessive. I could not reach out to my friends as she would fly into a rage. It was stunning how quickly *my* behavior changed as a result of her tyranny; I was intimidated and I became submissive in short order. She would be particularly attentive and lovable after I acceded to her unreasonable demands and after each altercation, as if to reinforce my submissive or defeatist response.

In my mad dash to graduate from Barnard on time, I failed to plan for my future beyond my graduation. I had wanted to study law, but I had not even taken the LSAT, and it was obviously too late to apply to any law school. A plausible option was to work on a graduate degree, but where, what and how? At least I did have the foresight of having taken the GRE in my senior year. By then, I had no income, no actionable plan for the immediate future, and was pitifully dependent on Barb for a roof over my head and a couple of meals a day. She somehow decided that she—with me in tow—should return to the Detroit area, where her mother and twin sister resided. On the day the tall ships sailed into the Hudson River and New York Harbor to honor the nation's Bicentennial, Barb and I shipped out; I thus missed out on the historic and spectacular parade on water. Barb's twin sister, Kate (not her real name), drove from Michigan in a rented U-Haul truck to help us move. The resemblance of the twins was uncanny, and Kate, incidentally, was also a lesbian. The exit from New York City to relocate to Detroit was unfolding so hurriedly that I was mostly in a daze or in shock. We arrived at an old house somewhere in Detroit, the very forsaken city that I had, four years prior, promised myself never to set foot in. The house was located in a "bombed out" neighborhood. There were only one or two Chinese carryout restaurants fortified with bullet-proof glass partitions between the customer waiting area and the kitchen/sales area. We happened to arrive in one of the hottest summers on record, and needless to note, there was no air-conditioning in that old house. If memory served me correctly, the house was occupied by Barb's stepfather and half-brother, and it had to be vacated in a week in any case because it was slated to be demolished. Hence, it was just a pit stop for us. We next moved to Barb's mother's home in a Detroit suburb. Shockingly, she would not invite us to move into her home—we stored our possessions and slept in her garage. Clearly, the dynamics between mother and daughter were too fraught for me to decipher. Fortunately, garage dwelling lasted only a few days as Barb was able to rent a home in another Detroit suburb. It was there one afternoon when I found Barb lying in bed weeping for no apparent reason. Alarmingly, there was nothing I could say or do to relieve her seemingly sudden sadness and ceaseless crying. I, the eternal optimist by nature, was puzzled and frustrated. I had never seen her in that state, and she could not, or did not want to, explain to me the cause of her despondence. It was not until sometime later when I learned, presumably from Simone, that Barb was bipolar, a manic depressive. Those were not terms with which I was familiar, and there was no handy internet search engine back when for me to learn more about the disorder, but learn I eventually did. That would perfectly explain her violent behavior and drastic mood swings, but I still did not realize just how menacing her condition was, especially when she was inconsistent in taking her medications. In the previous nine months, it was possible for her to disguise or downplay her depression; once I moved in with her, deception was no longer a viable option for her. In her manic state, she was energetic, passionate and fun-loving, all qualities that I cherished, but she could also be impulsive and brash. When she was depressed, she became someone I could not recognize. In between, there were verbal outbursts and fits of physical violence. By then, I had unwittingly been conditioned to accept her "bad" behavior for the scraps of "good" times in exchange.

No sooner than our having moved into the rental suburban home when Barb announced that it was time for her to visit Simone again. I was to be shuffled off to nearby Ann Arbor to visit with my SSGC classmate, Vivian, who was studying at the University of Michigan. As it turned out, Vivian was far too preoccupied with her studies to play host. I was able to rent a room, sharing a house with several students; I was even able to borrow an old bicycle as my means of transportation around town. The helter-skelter series of moves within a month was dizzying and unsettling; I felt as if I were some sort of urban "refugee." More pressing, though, was planning for my future beyond that summer. Simone came up with a "rescue plan" just in time: she suggested that I look into attending graduate school in Texas because the cost of living was extremely reasonable in that State. Acting on her cue, I stumbled upon a university of which I had never heard—Texas Woman's University in Denton, Texas—and whose tuition was such a bargain that even I could afford with income from a part-time on-campus job. Best of all, it was not too late for me to apply. Applied I did, and I was admitted to their Master of Arts program. I flew down to register and stayed temporarily with several Chinese students in their rented house. As kind as they were to give me shelter, I knew I would not be able to get along with them as, by then, I had become too "un-Chinese." The transformation of this once Sinocentric me was by then complete. Their socializing mostly if not exclusively with other Chinese, and cooking and eating mostly if not only Chinese food, seemed too narrow-minded and confining. It was almost revolting for me to imagine how before long they would inquisition me as to why I did not have a boyfriend, or worse, try to match me up with Chinese men. So, I pounded the pavement under the blazing Texan sun for several days, scouting for a room that I could afford to rent. I was rewarded with a rather spacious home within walking distance of campus, and which I shared with two other women. Barb returned from Switzerland at the end of August just in time to relocate me to Denton. We loaded up her 1966 VW Beetle with my boxes and some of her possessions, and embarked on the long, tedious drive from Michigan to Texas, stopping for a motel stay and food only when absolutely necessary. Whether that was because Barb wanted to arrive at the destination as quickly as possible, or whether it was due to financial restraints, or whether it was yet another means of her exercising dominion and control over me, I was too naïve and compliant to object or rebel. Throughout that long drive, Barb was not in her best mood to begin with; when her trusty and overloaded Beetle broke down somewhere in Oklahoma with a cracked axle, life with her became downright miserable. Thus, when we finally arrived at my new home in Denton, and Barb left once more for Switzerland, I actually felt reprieved.

After thrashing about for four eventful years in New York City, I found the pace and pulse of the not-so-Dynamic-Denton, Texas, almost moribund. Besides, everything in Texas felt oddly foreign: the accent was entirely unfamiliar to me, as was the cuisine; the culture—political and social—was certainly not hospitable to an East Coast radical progressive. Some of my new woman friends packed throwing knives strapped to their ankles, and everyone wore cowboy boots *all* the time. Fittingly then, I came away from my transient hiatus in Texas a cowboy boot fancier. I still own two pairs of Lucchese handmade cowboy boots which I could afford only years after my stint in Texas.

It was plain to me that Texas, not just Denton, was only a way station for me. As such, I should complete my Master's degree program and hightail it out of there as expeditiously as humanly possible. To that end, I carried the maximum load of courses each semester, in addition to completing my thesis, so as to graduate with a Master's degree in two semesters. I also held a part-time on-campus job, as a graduate research assistant, in order to pay for my meagre living expenses. By then, financial support from my parents had completely dried up. In retrospect, that tactic was not so much for pressuring me to leave Barb than to compel me to return to Hong Kong. As far as they were concerned, my "overseas tour" had concluded with the Barnard graduation, and it was time for my "triumphant homecoming" to motherland, following the well-trodden path of so many other Hong Kong students who studied abroad. It never even dawned on me to return "home;"

America was increasingly becoming "home" to me, and I wanted to obtain my law degree yet.

My life in Denton was unexpectedly tranquil, even boring by New York City standards. Barb was not around, and hence, I did not have to contend with her "moods" and "drama." There was nothing to distract me from my arduous academic pursuits; nonetheless, trying to finish a Master's degree in nine months was admittedly ambitious. There were no movement activities in which I cared to participate; there were no women's bars at which to hang out; there was no shows, concerts, or entertainment that I could not live without, even if I could afford a ticket. Nothing much ever happened in and around Denton. Dallas-Fort Worth was about 35 miles south, but venturing there in Barb's rickety VW Beetle was too risky an expedition. Hence, by design or default, all my time and energy were devoted to my studies; I was paying full attention to my academic pursuits for a change, for the first time since my SSGC days. When I was not in class, I was at the library conducting research for my term papers and thesis, or at home studying for quizzes and finals. It was an incredibly uncomplicated life, for a change. It would have been downright dull if I were not so preoccupied with racing against the clock to finish my degree program in nine months. Two semesters flew by in a blink of an eye. I was a model student: aced each and every class I took, including my thesis which I successfully defended before a panel of professors. I do not recall exactly the title of my thesis, but it involved China and geopolitics, as my degree was in International Relations in their Government Department (the equivalent of Political Science Department at TWU). I did it— attaining my M.A. degree in just two semesters. I was euphoric. I should have realized then that I could accomplish spectacularly, and live a fancy-free life, free from having any so-called love interest. Unfortunately, being sensible did not come natural to me. A grimmer view would be that my psyche somehow doomed me for repeated self-sabotage; that self-destructive pattern would take me decades to undo.

I did not even linger for commencement exercises. Barb returned from Switzerland to accompany me on my posthaste escape from Texas. By then, I had been admitted, with a full scholarship, to New England School of Law in Boston. We made a pit stop in Michigan, and then drove straight through to Boston, ostensibly for a campus visit and to find affordable housing. Barb was in a particularly nasty mood throughout that arduous, long drive. At once, the horrid memories of the previous summer came flooding back; I was subjected to an ugly, double-downed reenactment of the abuse a year earlier. We did not even stop for motel stays, and we hardly stopped for food. By the time we drove into Boston, we were utterly exhausted, and she was irredeemably irritable. I never even saw the law school, because she unilaterally declared, as she pulled over and parked momentarily on a street somewhere in Boston, that there was no way I could afford to study and live in Boston. With that edict, she turned the car around and started our journey back to Michigan. I had also been admitted with full scholarship by Wayne State University Law School in Detroit. I immediately made a telephone call from a public phone booth—those were the quaint, pre-cell phone, pre-email days—to inform Wayne State that I was belatedly accepting their offer, and was on my way to Detroit to register. It seemed that fate, or some other invisible force, destined me to wind up in Detroit, the one place on earth that I had promised myself never to even visit if I could help it.

We found and rented a nice apartment within walking distance of the law school. For a brief moment, everything seemed to be settling down, with the exception of Barb's increasingly temperamental and violent streak. My understanding of bipolar was still too skimpy to recognize the classic symptoms of her disorder, and I, therefore, unwittingly allowed myself to be dragged along with every peak and trough of her dysfunction. We were in that lovely apartment for barely a month when she deemed it too costly. Not having a means of making a living nor any other financial resource, I could hardly argue otherwise. We found a very economical dormitory room for me to move in. However, after just a few days, my roommates reported to the "authorities" that I had too many boxes of possessions to be living in a dormitory room. Truth be told, I had definitely outgrown my dormitory days. By then, it was a cruel replay of the previous summer of random "homelessness" alternating with makeshift and transient relocations. Finally, she found an unbelievably inexpensive efficiency apartment for me not too far from campus. Since she was leaving her antiquated VW Beetle with me, I could—in theory—drive to and from school. In fact, I had become quite adept at mechanical improvisation: using a hair blow dryer to dry out the distributor cap so that the carburetor would function, and popping the clutch to start the car. Unbeknownst to me, the reason why the apartment was such a bargain was because it was situated in the heart of the infamous "Cass Corridor," now fashionably gentrified, but a seedy neighborhood populated by assorted unsavory characters back then. No wonder my 3-storey apartment building reeked of urine and was in such overall disrepair. No wonder the sales clerk at a tony suburb, where I treated myself to a carton of imported cigarettes, kept staring at my address imprinted on my check with which I paid for the purchase. He looked at my check, his face turned ashen, then looked up and stared at me, and then stared at the address on my check again, and returned his gaze at me again. I had no idea that my address could be an outright shock to white-flight suburbanites. Barb, being a native Detroiter, however, should have known that that was not an ideal neighborhood for me. In retrospect, her repeatedly uprooting me and placing me in untenable living environments reflected her conscious or subconscious efforts to subjugate me so that she could exert total dominance over the dispirited me—except that, thankfully, I was never the dispirited type. Even now, it is sobering, if not downright frightening, to recollect those chaotic and unsettling times.

Wayne State University Law School had a program for the new students who wanted to lighten their load during their first year of law school: we could take two of the required courses during the summer before fall term began. I happily opted for that head start. By then, it was time again for Barb to return to Switzerland to be with Simone. I was in fact relieved that she was leaving again. Our relationship had degenerated into unbridled tempestuousness, with not even much of an interlude of love or happiness for my trouble either. Even so, it never crossed my mind to call it quits. I should have been alarmed when I happened to learn another heretofore unfamiliar term: symbiosis. Barb's frequent and prolonged escapades to Switzerland prompted my suspicion that she had in fact been having a symbiotic relationship with Simone. The initial thrill of "loving" me had long since faded, and Barb, in all her manic-depressive glory, yearned to be with her symbiotic half all the time. I unwittingly became alternately the punching bag and the proverbial third wheel that kept getting in the way. Out of respect for Simone, I did not feel jealous or enraged. Even with that realization, my thick skull, coupled with my misplaced sense of honor and commitment, precluded me from even entertaining any thought of terminating the abusive relationship with Barb.

With Barb in Switzerland and not causing havoc in my life on an hourly basis, I was once more able to devote my full attention to my studies. I did very well with my two summer classes, Torts and Criminal Law. A very kind and understanding Professor Kevin Tierney gave me a copy of the criminal law casebook from his collection. He had no idea how enormously grateful I was, as I could barely afford to buy my law books. I learned then that "small favors" meant so much to those who did not have much, and thus, when I had more, I tried to share and give as much as I could. During that summer term, I found the study of law intellectually stimulating and emotionally fulfilling. Even without the turbulent—and that is a hugely euphemistic characterization—relationship with Barb as a wakeup call, I really should have realized that I would do so much better in life without falling or being "in love." It was most likely my perceived lack of love and approval from Mom that subconsciously prompted me to seek substitutes. My perceived need was so overpowering that I would endure untold indignities just so as to be sated with the tiniest dose of love and approval. Hindsight, aided and abetted by twenty-plus years of psychotherapy, could be such sweet revenge.

When the fall semester rolled around, with a full academic load typical for a first-year law student, plus my twenty-hour per week on-campus job as a student assistant at the Law School Placement Office, I was feeling the crunch. More alarming was my realization that I was facing an extremely steep learning curve. America prides itself on being a nation that venerates the rule of law, and the supreme law of the land being the Constitution. The average American student is well acquainted with the Constitution and the Bill of Rights since grade school if not earlier. By the time he or she enters law school, that student is ready to tackle the finer nuances of the lofty Constitutional framework and to parse the rights it guarantees to all. I, on the other hand, was ignorant of the Constitution and the Declaration of Independence until my Barnard days as a Political Science major, when I took courses in party politics, electoral politics, governmental bureaucracy, and other political science "basics." As my undergraduate and graduate theses were on alternative political subjects (radical feminism and comparative geopolitics), my lack of in-depth knowledge of the fundamental tenets of the American legal and political system was not a handicap. I could probably tell you more about the French Revolution than the American Revolution; more about

The Crimean War than the Civil War; and more about the assassination of Archduke Franz Ferdinand of Austria than of Abraham Lincoln. At the law school level, however, there was no safe harbor for my relative ignorance of American history, its political and legal systems, and those pesky unalienable rights of life, liberty and the pursuit of happiness. How rights are derived from the Constitution, how a Constitutional provision is interpreted and applied, the separation of powers and checks and balances of the three branches of the government, the interplay between the Federal and State governments, and the bifurcated Federal and State judiciary systems, are enormously complicated to the novice and uninitiated. In other words, I had a great deal of catching up to do in a very short period of time. As I tried to wade through the thicket that was the study of law, it turned out not to be what I expected it to be. It was not about pursuing the laudable ideals of righteousness, equality, or justice, but more about perfecting the technicalities of winning an argument or scoring a point. I would become even more disillusioned as a practicing attorney, when I realized that the entire exercise was much more about increasing billable hours and chasing the almighty dollar than fighting for the downtrodden or upholding Constitutional guarantees.

I had not been active in the movement when I was busy finishing my Master's degree the previous year. Hence, early in the fall semester at law school, even though the rigorous studies was taking up all my waking moments, I thought it was time for me to survey the local lesbian-feminist scene. I looked for women's bookstores and found only one which seemed to be closed whenever I telephoned. Then I stumbled upon a women's group called "Women Together." It listed only a telephone number; in the bad old days, utmost discretion was the operative mantra. I telephoned repeatedly over a period of weeks, but no one ever answered. Just as I was about to give up on contacting the group, a woman finally answered my call one evening. The tactful questioning on her part was obviously to screen me. When I just as obviously passed her "lesbian *bona fides*" test, I was given the location and date of the upcoming meeting.

The meeting was held in the basement of a church in a northern suburb of Detroit. No one would suspect that a bunch of lesbians were gathering "next door" in a typical middle-class neighborhood. I would soon find out that it was strictly a social group with no overt or covert political agenda. About twenty to thirty women, most of them about my age or slightly older, got together every Tuesday night to socialize and discuss topics of interest. There were group outings such as hay rides in the fall and screening of lesbian-themed movies, and private parties and barbecues were held occasionally at members' homes. After each weekly gathering, the group would adjourn to a nearby Denny's-type restaurant for coffee and snacks. It was a refreshing experience for me, for a change, to gather with lesbians just to socialize and have fun with no activistic pretensions. That first night I attended the gathering, on September 27th, was by all account a fairly typical weekly meeting, with all of us sitting in a large round circle. I did not recall the topic for discussion that night, as I was too preoccupied getting acclimated to my new surroundings and new friends. As I looked across the circle, a woman caught my eye. She looked sullen, sitting there rather glumly and emotionless, yet for some unknown reason, I found her magnetic. After the meeting, I joined everyone at the restaurant; we were seated at a long table. When I sat down at an empty seat, I found that sullen woman sitting directly across the table from me. Serendipity? Hardly. I learned later that she had noticed me the moment I arrived at the meeting; in fact, she had immediately commented to the friend who brought her to the gathering that she was going to buy me a new briefcase at Christmas. I was carrying my briefcase that night, a well-used hand-me-down from Simone. By the time we arrived at the restaurant, she watched where I was seated, and then literally pushed her way so as to grab the seat directly across from me. Hence, like Gabrielle before her, she was "hitting on" me, with my being the usual clueless. We struck up a casual conversation. Her name was Bev, and she was heartbroken as her lover of a couple of years had just left her for another woman. I mumbled something along the lines of: "Some breakups, we never ever get over," and that remark apparently impressed her as being profound and demonstrating my understanding of her grief. That was also her first attendance at a "Women Together" meeting. In retrospect, I wonder whether, under the guise of finding lesbian friends in my new hometown, I was if ever so subconsciously looking for a way out of my relationship with Barb. I should have learned by then that I would be much better off without any relationship involvement while I was completing my education. On the other hand, and perhaps instinctively, I knew I needed an "excuse" to leave Barb while I also needed backup support once I started that process.

Another month went by without any upheaval that would ordinarily have been attendant in Barb's wake and par for the course if she was in town. That was bliss enough, even as I improbably settled in my dodgy Cass Corridor efficiency, became increasingly efficient at starting the crotchety VW "Beetle" in the chilly mornings, and struggled to live on a shoestring budget, courtesy of my $3 per hour part-time on-campus job. By then, my parents had resumed support in the form of CARE packages, which were eagerly and gratefully received, not the least for my favorite foodstuff and clothing items, but for the showing of their love and concern. Even in Barb's absence, I would from time to time be tangentially snarled into her sister Kate's three-ring circus. Crises would erupt as if on cue, ranging from her not having money to put gas in her car to calamities involving her pre-teen daughter. I was thankful that I was not expected to be her savior, as providing a modicum of moral support was taxing enough.

One of the "Women Together" members was hosting a Halloween costume party at the end of October at her stupendous McMansion in an upscale suburb. I attended with a foreign student from Germany whom I befriended at Wayne State University. There I found Bev again, dressed in a slinky mini-skirt number, supposedly posing as a streetwalker. I did not wear any costume; I hardly had enough money for my basic wardrobe, I certainly did not have the budget for a frivolous Halloween costume. Having barely survived my Domestic Science classes at SSGC, sewing my own costume was also out of the question. Throughout the evening, Bev kept "bumping into" me, each time appearing more inebriated than the last. As the party drew to a close, exhausted from dancing and hearty partying, we found ourselves sprawled on a couch having getting-to-know-you conversations. She telephoned me late morning the next day, and we continued our conversation. I would find out much later that the repeated "chance encounters" at the Halloween party were deliberately deployed by her; it was her full-court press to attract my attention and to make a more than favorable impression. She succeeded, or I was gullible; by then, I was irretrievably attracted to her. As I came to know more about her in our first few dates, there were at least half a dozen times I saw flashing yellow—even red—lights, and should have scrammed the other way. Unfortunately, I did not do so, consistent with my self-sabotage propensity and my passion-trumping-reason *modus operandi*. She was married, to a man, even though she repeatedly assured me that there had not been a valid, existent marital relationship between them for years, and that they remained married in name solely for the sake of their child. She had a nine-year-old daughter; she married and gave birth when she was only seventeen years of age. She claimed to be a licensed physical therapist, but I would learn much later that she only had a GED, never attended college, and worked as a massage therapist making house calls. I would not characterize her as an intellectual. I would also learn later that her spiritedness at the party was not just in keeping with the party spirits, but was in fact her worsening dependence on the bottle. Despite so many nettlesome complications and duplicitous pretenses swirling about her life, I self-deceptively chose to accentuate on what I deemed her positive qualities. She lived in a decent enough renovated ranch in Troy, an up-and-coming affluent suburb north of Detroit; she drove a late-model car, appeared to be gainfully employed, did not exhibit any tendency toward physical violence and had nary a hint of manic depression. She was also energetic, enterprising and fun to be with, and above all, she was an "established" lesbian and not a curious heterosexual woman looking for idle diversion or casual experimentation. She exuded *chutzpah* which I found captivating. It would be years before I realized that her outward bravado was a façade and to overcompensate for her deep-seated insecurity and sense of ineptness. Obviously, my bar was set pathetically low. Once I was smitten, I overlooked inconvenient inconsistencies, made excuses for her shortcomings, and ignored clangorous alarm bells. Worse, I allowed myself to become her enabler. It was as if my mission in life were to please her, to make her every whim and wish come true, to indulge and oblige her, to salvage and otherwise rectify her *faux pas*. I would have done fabulously if I had pampered myself so, instead of being at her beck and call.

In the decades since, I have come to believe that destiny or karma (you may substitute your preferred nomenclature) dictates with whom we cross path, and surely, with whom we "fall in love." People come into our lives for a reason or a purpose, if even they themselves are not aware of the reason or purpose. It is not that "resistance is futile;" quite the contrary, we should welcome such happenings, and accordingly exercise our free will and choice. My hypothesis is that such relationships proffer an opportunity for us to learn essential life lessons. Similar relationship dynamics would keep recurring, even across lifetimes, to haunt us until we learn our necessary lessons and satisfactorily resolve the issues. Unfortunately, in my younger days, time and again, I failed to learn. I kept repeating the same "crash and burn" vicious cycle. I would viscerally react to a magnetic attraction (a product of karmic ties from the Past), throw caution to the wind, and before I knew it, I was burned to a crisp. With each succeeding relationship, I was likened to jumping out of the frying pan into the fire. Hence, even though there was not any articulable rationale for or ostensible benefits to my getting hooked up with Bev, I felt "committed" for life once I started down that path. Years later, one of my psychotherapists half-jokingly mused that I could consider just "having fun" with the person (presuming, of course, we were consenting adults) and not carrying on as if I were bonded or married to her for life. Alas, it would take me many, many more years before I finally realized and heeded the self-destructiveness of my impetuousness.

In those early days and months, Bev was pure fun. We both enjoyed dancing, and would go to the women's bars on weekends to bop and sway to the music. Afterwards, we would get a hearty midnight snack at a local diner, as we both had prodigious appetites. As I was an impoverished student, it would often be her treat for those humble but satisfying meals out. I did not realize that to others, I could be an attractive "investment" because of my earning potential as a practicing attorney; I simply could not see that far ahead. I still remembered our first date: dinner at a local Chinese restaurant. Apparently, she wanted to impress me that she enjoyed Chinese food on a regular basis. It was a rather lame compliment, as I hardly patronized Chinese American restaurants; I could not afford to dine out, and in any case, I was pining for more authentic Chinese cuisine. Dinner was followed by another treat: a movie. It was *Star Wars, Episode IV: A New Hope*, which was then taking the world by storm. Enjoying that movie, *with* buttered movie popcorn, was a luxury for me. *Mea culpa*—I was not only an easy prey but also a cheap date.

However, even in those early, carefree days, there were ominous signs which I either overlooked or ignored. She seemed not to care much for my law studies, and later, my legal career. At first I thought it was admirable that she was not associating with me merely because I was a law student or was going to be a lawyer, as I certainly did not attach any pretensions to that status. In retrospect, it was in fact her inability to deal with her own perceived inferiority and lack of formal education that prompted her to downplay my credentials, subtly belittling my *raison d'etre*. Unfortunately, the youthful, impressionable me began, as if by osmosis, to downplay my law studies. Almost imperceptibly, I started slacking off at law school. I started drifting again, my aspirational compass began to fog up, and I had once again lost sight of my goals and purpose in life.

One night in late November, I visited Bev at her home. We had probably had dinner at the local Chinese restaurant again, and played pool at her home. It was an unusually frigid November night, with light snow. I had no experience driving in cold weather, let alone snow and ice. I had heard from friends that one would need to put snow tires on the car to prepare for the winter. I had asked Barb about it, but she insisted that I wait till she returned from Switzerland in December when she would take care of it. Uncomfortable with that supposed reassurance, I went ahead and had four brand new snow tires put on the trusty old "Beetle" just that morning. As I was traveling on the Interstate going home, I did not realize how treacherous the freeway had become in the icy condition, especially on the overpasses and bridges. By the time I saw other cars skidding every which way, it was too late for me to do anything else but to try to steer, brake and slow down. I had never experienced anything as frightening, as I had absolutely no control over the car at 55 miles per hour on ice. I would steer it one way, but it would become an over-correction, and it would skid the other way. After a series of attempts at controlling or stopping the car, I had no choice but to give up and confront the possibility that my life might be over in a few more seconds. I let the car go wherever it wanted. It ended up plunging into the ditch in the median between the north and southbound free-way. If it had plunged the other way, I would have jumped off the overpass and plunged to my death with the car. The brand new snow tires helped, too, I was sure; I was glad I did not listen to Barb that one time but used my own sound judgment. The car careened, bounced and bucked to a halt at the bottom of the pitch dark ditch. A kind and brave gentleman rushed toward me to see if I was alright; the police followed, and in due time, I was taken to a nearby Big Boy's. I was shaking like a leaf. I telephoned Bev to come fetch me. I was expecting her to be at least understand-ing and comforting. Instead, she appeared irritated, annoyed, and greatly inconvenienced. I spent the night on the couch at her home. I could not sleep, as I was thoroughly traumatized by the accident, but also mystified and sorely disappointed by Bev's detachment and nonchalance. That should have been a third-alarm wakeup call for me.

Barb was scheduled to return from Switzerland just before Christmas. I naïvely thought that all would resume as before the diversion with Bev, which I convinced myself was just an innocent fling. Needless to say, I discovered to my horror that nothing was the same anymore when Barb reentered the scene. I was no longer in love with her; in fact, I did not even like her as a friend. I did not plan for a breakup; I had no experience with initiating a breakup. Just a couple of days after she returned, I could not pretend any longer. One night in my humble dwelling, I must have mumbled something about breaking up. I should have anticipated this, but I did not, and that oversight was almost fatal. She flew into a blind rage, chasing me through the tiny apartment and finally cornering me in the kitchen. She pushed me on the floor, and I thought of the knives in the kitchen drawers and feared I would be dead the next second. Instead she sat on me and started choking me with her hands on my neck. I could have been just as dead without the knives, I thought to myself. Somehow, in my last gasp, I managed to move my arms just a tad, and that apparently was enough to momentarily jolt her out of her insanity. I jumped up and dashed for the door. Unfortunately, the door opened inward toward me in a short and narrow hallway, and she was chasing right behind me. There was no escape. As a desperate move, something or someone told me to turn around and yell: "I love you!" Miraculously, upon hearing that, she broke down and snapped out of her murderous rampage. I hastily gathered a few items, and left the apartment. Into the cold night I walked to a nearby store and telephoned Bev, relating to her my harrowing narrow escape, and asked for a ride. Again, she sounded annoyed and greatly inconvenienced. While I was waiting for Bev by the street curb, the police scout car circled back a few times to see if I needed a lift or shelter. It was obvious that I did not belong to that street corner at that time of the night in that notorious neighborhood. When Bev finally arrived, instead of demonstrating concern and empathy in light of my close brush with death at Barb's hands literally, Bev again seemed detached and distant. I thought that was her testing me to see if I was tough enough to deal with life's hard knocks. If I had been more sensible and aware, I would have realized that she was incapable of "rescuing" me. She was expecting me, and others, to do *for* her rather than putting herself out for others. It could have been a psychological or emotional deficit on her part, or it could have been a personality trait of selfishness and self-preservation above all else. In any case, if I were looking for a supportive and empathetic life partner, I had definitely struck out. There would be several more crunch times for me in our 26-plus years together when I was basically left twisting in the wind. Why then did I not move on? Hindsight, once again, is so instructive.

For my personal safety's sake, it was imperative that I moved at once. It took me just a day to find a small efficiency apartment within a short walking distance of the Law School. That was important as I no longer had a car; the VW Beetle was Barb's. I secured a small financial subsidy from my parents as the rent, though just $100 per month, was more than my very meagre income could support. The building superintendent was kind enough to let me "borrow" a used twin bed and a small desk from their inventory room. I was at long last truly on my own; I felt safe. That sense of security was shattered one night a few months later when Barb paid me a surprise visit. I did not buzz her in, but met her downstairs in the apartment building lobby. Even agreeing to meet her in the lobby turned out to be a mistake; I did not realize that she could be so insane as to try to wrestle my keys from my hands and tackle me onto the floor. I was not afraid of her then, and we got into a physical scuffle. There were bystanders, but they seemed too stunned to intervene. Barb finally ran away, and I was black and blue with bruises from her unprovoked assault. The last time I ran into her was a few years later when Bev and I went to the "Underground," a women's bar, one weekend. Barb was there with a couple of women. We did not acknowledge each other, and Bev and I left very soon after we arrived.

I did not realize that my spirits had been seriously wounded by the breakup with Barb, and the emotional drain from the rather unsupportive relationship with Bev. I was merely going through the motion of getting by in Law School, putting in my part-time hours doing secretarial and clerical work in the Placement Office to make just enough for subsistence. My future looked grim, courtesy of my immigration status, even as I vowed to myself not to be discouraged. As a foreign student, I was not allowed to work off-campus, and thus, could not clerk during the summer or part-time during the school year. I could not afford to volunteer or intern as I needed my on-campus employment to make my modest ends meet. Without any clerkship experience, finding a lawyer job upon graduation was difficult enough. In my case, I would also have to find an employer who would not mind sponsoring me for one of the employment-authorized nonimmigrant classifications. Returning to Hong Kong after I graduated from Law School was, by then, completely out of the question. If I had not become involved with Bev, there might have been a slim chance that I could have considered repatriating to Hong Kong. As it was, I had to correspond with the State Bar of Michigan numerous times to be certain that I, as a foreign student and a nonresident alien, was legally permitted to sit for the Bar Examination for admission to practice law in Michigan.

Life, in the meantime, with Bev was rather interesting because it was quite different from my prior experiences. There was a strange sense of stability, contrasting with my volatile life with Barb in the previous two years. One of the first things she requested was for me to repaint the interior walls of my efficiency apartment. Such decorative projects would have never crossed my mind. I thought it was such a waste of resources, time and energy, but my humble apartment did feel cozier and look less drab after the repainting. We were diametric opposites in more ways than I could enumerate, but I enjoyed her companionship in exploring and enjoying life's simple delights together. We ate out often at inexpensive neighborhood diners and restaurants, enjoyed movies at matinee showings, and patronized the women's bars every so often to dance the night away. At one of the bar outings in those early days, Bev introduced me to one of her former flames, Betty Jo (she prefers "Jo"). I was fully prepared to be disagreeable, but Jo and I took to each other instantaneously and became fast friends over the years. I felt as if I had known her for ages; there was a strong sense of camaraderie. She was quite a bit older than me, and had a storied past. She served a stint as a young registered nurse in the Navy, and enjoyed her career as a psychiatric nurse in various mental institutions. When we met, she was a uniformed County deputy sheriff. As if that was not dazzling enough, she had a spiritual awakening in the 1960's, and became a devoted follower of her guru, Mr. J. Oliver Black. She bought a cabin near Mr. Black's "Song of the Morning Ranch" outside Gaylord, Michigan, so as to facilitate her participation in the activities at the retreat. Often times in my conversing with Jo, she would drift onto her "astral plane," speaking of blue lights and other phenomena which I did not comprehend. I would have to wait till she returned from those other planes so that we could resume our conversation on this plane. Perhaps Jo knew it when we first met, but it would take me decades yet to acquire the awareness that perhaps we did know each other from *across* the ages, and that perhaps we were indeed fellow warriors.

Since I did not have a car, Bev had to drive from her cushy suburban neighborhood to my apartment in Detroit. She first complained of not having a safe place to park her car. There was a bank of lockable garage units next to my apartment building; so I stretched my budget and rented one for her to safely park her car while she visited me. After a few more months, she tired of driving, and issued an ultimatum that unless I acquired a car, "our relationship would falter." As I had written earlier, the only "valuables" I had at that time was my beloved set of Nikon SLR camera bodies and lenses which Dad gave to me. I sold those and scraped together just enough money to buy a very used Mazda "RX3," which had to be unceremoniously junked after only six months, because its highly touted rotary engine had stopped rotating. For a few hundred dollars, I bought from my auto mechanic a beat-up Chevy "C10" pickup truck, the only vehicle that I could afford. It came with dual gas tanks, as it gave new meaning to gas-guzzling. However inefficient or unreliable, at least I had a means of transportation to drive out to Troy and spend time with Bev. What I failed to heed was how the pattern of my indulging and enabling her started from the very onset of our relationship. My character flaw of being overeager to please was too glaring and too tempting for just about anyone not to exploit. In those early days, at least there was a *quid pro quo*, however uneven. When I arrived at her home, I would be greeted with smiles and zest. We would enjoy our time together, whether it was playing badminton in her backyard, shooting pool in her rec room, strolling in the neighborhood park, going out for an ice cream or grabbing a bite to eat. Occasionally, her husband, Dave (not his real name), would also be home. There was no question that Dave knew and accepted my relationship with Bev, because he and I had a conversation about it. Bev wanted to maintain the appearance of their marriage until her daughter, Melanie (not her real name), turned eighteen years of age. In other words, Bev had not come out to Melanie. I did not agree with nor condone Bev's stance on maintaining the façade of her so-called marriage; on the other hand, I did not want to interfere with her raising her child. I wished the entire affair did not pose such a quasi-moral conundrum, but I stepped into it, and I knew I had to be extremely discrete for the ensuing eight years or so. Again, my much older and wiser self would have never willingly or intentionally stepped into that morass, and would have otherwise extricated myself pronto. As it was, Dave and I were polite with each other; he thought I was definitely a step-up from the lovers Bev took on who preceded me. I was not flattered; I was always very guarded with Dave. Not infrequently, on a Saturday or Sunday night, Bev, Dave and I would sit down for several rounds of Scrabble. Bev called it "killer Scrabble," because Dave and I were seriously competitive at it; most times I won. I also beat him, badly, at badminton, and thus, he quit playing after a couple of tries. When he was home, he mostly occupied himself with various projects in the garage, the most ambitious of which was building a steel-hull sailboat, which was ultimately unfinished. The strange dynamics worked somehow in maintaining superficial truce and harmony where all of us had our dance steps strategically choreographed.

It was sometime in 1978 when Bev expressed a desire to belatedly get a college degree. I, of course, seconded that notion enthusiastically. She wanted to major in Criminal Justice so as to become a licensed private detective. Granted, it had no relation to her prior work experience, nor did she exhibit any particular attribute that hinted at her becoming an outstanding future female Sherlock Holmes. I thought her ambition to return to school was laudable, and her choice of career path bold and unorthodox. Almost reflexively I stepped into the enabler role again. I helped her with her papers and projects. I edited her papers, corrected grammatical errors, and neatly typed them up for presentation. To her credit, she did graduate with a Bachelor's degree in Criminal Justice from Wayne State University in about four years. What I did not anticipate was how the enabling dynamics once established, it became a bottomless pit. After graduation, it was time to apply for her private detective license. Before doing so, I advised her to form a corporation for liability reasons. I was a newly minted attorney by then, and of course, I was expected to take care of forming her corporation, and applying for her license, along with securing the license bond, and obtaining a permit to carry a concealed weapon. When those were accomplished, I even had to order stationery for her new company. I did not view those tasks as "enabling;" I thought I was simply helping my significant other when and where I could.

I was a bit startled when she requested that I accompany her on her first surveillance case. It was physically very taxing for me to work a full day as an attorney, and to play detective by night as well. The kind of surveillance she was engaged to do was not particularly dangerous or exciting as glamourized in the movies, but it was tedious, time consuming and physically draining. Fortunately, she had been retained perhaps only two or three times in her entire private detective career. Nevertheless, she kept renewing her private investigator license (i.e., she had me renewing her license) for years and decades, even though she was not practicing as such. At the time, I felt it was thoughtful of her to invite me as "part of the team" on those surveillance assignments. It took me years to realize that, despite her bluster, she was in fact very unsure of herself and her abilities; the apparent swagger was to overcompensate for her innate insecurity. When push came to shove, she would recruit a backup, a substitute, or she would simply fizzle out and disappear. She could not even owe up to her own "misdeeds." Hence, there were numerous times when I had to bail her out, so to speak. Very early on in our relationship, we attended a Chinese new year banquet. She struck up a casual conversation with a total stranger at our dinner table, and the next thing I overheard was her daring the stranger to a swimming race. I thought they both had a bit too much to drink, and so, I interjected to neutralize the "duel." Refusing to take my cue, Bev kept egging him on and upping the ante, and the stranger accepted her dare. After the dinner, she confessed to me that she did not know how to back down. She did not even telephone the stranger to apologize or to call off the "shootout at high noon;" instead, she simply did not show up at the appointed hour and appointed location. In the first years of our relationship, she was still working as a massage therapist making house calls. From time to time, when she did not feel like working; she would ask me to call the client on her behalf to cancel the appointment. Obviously, I did not mind as it was not much trouble for me to make those calls. I should have been more discerning and paused to cogitate on her pattern of behavior and what it signified. I had not really had a "play mate" before, and thus, I focused on our fun times together, overlooking and dismissing all the flashing red lights and yellow warning signs.

In early 1978, news came that Dad was forced into retirement as a result of a changing of the guards in upper management at his company. That was followed by the even worse news that he had to have surgery to remove one of his kidneys. I was not told the diagnosis at the time, but found out years later that he had cancer in that kidney. Mom was still working full-time, all the while spending time with Dad in the hospital after work, and nursing Dad back to health after the surgery. I was still too immature in these matters to comprehend that my parents had to be in crisis mode, and that I should have rushed to their aid. They finally sent for me that summer; I would return to Hong Kong for a month, ostensibly to cheer Dad up while he continued to recuperate from his lengthy hospitalization.

It turned out to be an extremely emotional homecoming for me. In stark contrast to my previous trip in 1974, this was a very sobering and even somber visit. On a certain level, I had grown up a great deal in four years; I was no longer throwing caution to the wind in pursuit of a renegade lifestyle. I had finished my first year of law school, and was only two years away from becoming a lawyer. I had settled down, acknowledged my responsibility, and even vaguely, my calling. On another level, I had not matured at all. I should have been more considerate of my aging parents' circumstances. Dad had retired and was ailing, and Mom was nearing retirement age, and supporting Dad all by herself. I should have seriously considered repatriating to Hong Kong upon law school graduation, and getting a job there as a legal consultant if not as a lawyer. I could then have taken care of my parents personally and financially. Needless to say, those thoughts never even crossed my mind. I was too adverse to the stifling patriarchal society that was Hong Kong; I was too smitten by Bev to consider walking away from that relationship which had only just begun; and I was lured by the real or imagined prestige and fortune of being a practicing attorney in the United States. Quite on the contrary,

I was increasingly anxious about strategizing for remaining in the United States after I graduated from law school. From time to time, I do wonder, even fantasize, how utterly different my life would have been if I had opted to return to Hong Kong after my education abroad.

When I arrived in Hong Kong, I found Dad to have almost completely recovered, kudos to Mom, her healing soups and tender loving care. Vivian had graduated from high school by then, and was attending secretarial school. Within days of my arrival, Mom, Dad, Vivian and I went to visit Grandmother. She was thrilled to see me again. Her health was reasonable for someone her age, but her eyesight was very poor and failing. I had the overwhelming feeling that after that visit, I would not see her alive again. I was horribly upset by those thoughts. I recorded a cassette tape to send to Bev, in which I was sobbing uncontrollably, telling her about my visit with Grandmother and how I was afraid I would never see her again. Yet there was nothing I could do about that seeming inevitability: my desire to live permanently in the United States might require me to stay in the country for a substantial period of time. As it turned out, my hunch was spot on. Grandmother passed away in 1987, and I could not return to Hong Kong until October of 1988.

Of course I checked in with my SSGC buddies; Winnie was on top of my list. By then, she was already a rising star at Commercial Radio as the host of a highly popular and successful morning talk show. We went out one evening for dinner and entertainment. She came to pick me up in her spanking new electric blue Porsche 911SC, a stunner of a luxury sports car. She picked up a few more young women, all of whom piled into the tiny racer. We had a lavish dinner, with liquors freely flowing; I was practically a teetotaler by then. She then took us for a hair-raising spin at blistering speeds on steeply winding roads through some exclusive enclaves around the upper reaches of Victoria Peak. Some would say that was exactly what the "good life" looked, smelled, tasted and felt like, and what success was all about. That was when I realized I had mellowed precipitously in just four years. With each hairpin zigzag hugging the hillside in her zooming and overloaded Porsche, I was praying for my dear life. I simply wanted to survive Winnie's mini *Le Mans,* just so as to live another day in my roach-infested, dingy apartment in Detroit, and cruise the mean streets of Motor City in my embattled Chevy pickup truck.

I also tracked down Annemargret. We met for lunch, and she introduced me to her charming girlfriend, a Hong Kong Chinese woman named Rose (not her real name). They met while working at a hospital where Annemargret was a nurse and Rose was a nurse's aide. It was wonderful to see Annemargret being so happy and doing so well. She was also working occasionally as a photography fashion model. She, too, had settled down from four years earlier. In fact, in just a few more years, she would be venturing into the food service business and become a successful restauranteur.

Sadly, heart wrenching farewells awaited me. Lina married Joseph Li in 1976, and they returned to Hong Kong in mid-1977. They were living with our parents, until the birth of their daughter, Juliana, in July of 1977. A very raucous falling out erupted between Joe and our parents, and Joe moved his family out to an apartment on the Kowloon side. It was a very contentious split, with hard and hurt feelings on both sides. Mom and Dad had been deprived of seeing or being with their daughter and granddaughter ever since; it was a heartbreaking family ruckus. Mom and Dad suggested that I visit Lina and my new niece, and I thought that would only be the proper thing to do; perhaps I could break the ice with my visit. They lived quite far away and it took me a ferry ride and several bus transfers to reach their home. I finally found the apartment and rang the apartment doorbell. Lina came to the door, opened it a crack, and peered through the bars of the iron gate outside the door; she looked cold as ice and waved me away. I could hardly believe the treatment I was getting from my own sister, even though I was not personally involved in whatever that came between our parents and Joe. I started weeping uncontrollably, and refused to go away. After a short standoff, a man stepped up to the door, and told Lina to let me in; it was Joe. Once I was in the apartment, Joe was even superficially nice to me, offering me tea and making small talk. It was embarrassing, but I could not stop tearing up. In those few minutes, I knew everything. It was Joe who controlled everything and everyone. For some reason, Joe, who was reportedly a psychology major, decided that our parents were "evil" and a "bad" influence, and should be shunned. Lina, the poor dear, was extremely conflicted, of course; but for that particular time period, she chose to stay with him and Juliana. Juliana, barely a year old and barely walking on her own, waddled out to the living room. She would not have any notion of who I was or would she even remember the brief meeting. Lina tore off tiny bits from a slice of white bread and fed her the morsels. She was very pretty; I would learn later that she wanted to be a princess when she grew up. In the meantime, I was trying to hold back my tears, and sipped my tea with our beautiful little princess.

There was an even sadder farewell awaiting me. Dad accompanied me to visit Lilian during that short month while I was in Hong Kong. Ding Ma had passed away a few years prior, and Lilian was fortunate enough to become one of a very limited number of residents at a Po Leung Kuk (a charity organization in Hong Kong) funded and operated dormitory/boarding school for mentally handicapped girls and women. The dormitory was located on the Kowloon side and quite far away. I did not recall the location or the surroundings, the dormitory or even the visit itself. It was all an ineffably painful blur. I was mindful of the fact that I might not be able to return to Hong Kong for a long, long time. Worse, since I wanted to emigrate to and live in the United States eventually, I would not be able to visit Lilian on a regular basis. That visit, then, was a true farewell. Lilian was thrilled to see me again, of course; she had no idea of the impending prolonged parting. I only remembered quietly weeping on the bus all the way home, and I would never forget that searing separation agony. It would turn out to be another twenty-five long years before I would see her again.

VI.

The Chin Case

With a very heavy if not broken heart, at the end of that intense month, I returned to the United States, my hoped for home for the future. It was my turn to feel sorely conflicted. The depth of my sorrow over missing—nay, losing—my loved ones in Hong Kong practically crippled me. Yet I could not see giving up my promising future in America. I started my second year of law school in an ambivalent haze tinged with grief. More than being adrift, I was rudderless. My usual zest and zeal had slipped away while I wallowed in my subconscious indecision. It was proven true once again that, each time I returned to the States from Hong Kong, my life would somehow descend into disarray and turmoil.

Almost one year spent with Bev had "domesticated" me to vicariously leading a suburban life a la Michigan: emphasis on not rocking the boat, very middle-of-the-road, and some, especially New Yorkers, would call it mind-numbingly dull and boring. We would occasionally go to see a matinee movie, attend shows and concerts when we could afford them, browse local fairs and festivals of all stripes but mostly arts and crafts and culinary, and indulge in bland but satisfying comfort foods. We continued with the Women Together gatherings, but patronized the women's bars less and less. We could not afford to go on vacation or trips yet, or even drive "up North" as so many Michiganders did as a weekend ritual. The down side was that I had drifted far from political activism and altruistic goals and ideals; I was beginning to live a self-serving life of materialism and consumerism. By the end of the second year of law school, I had saved enough and earned enough credit to purchase a very used Chevrolet "Chevette" 2-door coupe with manual transmission and no air-conditioning. As lowly as that vehicle was, for a burgeoning automobile enthusiast without financial means, it was by far my "best" car and I loved it. Bev managed to literally break the manual transmission when she was driving my car one day, and I had to borrow money from a very understanding friend for the repairs. Of course, Bev blamed it on the age of the car. That established a lopsided pattern in our relationship: whenever she made a mess of something, it was up to me to clean up after her.

One day for no particular reason and without warning, she presented me with a pet: a parakeet in a small bird cage. I had never had a bird as a pet; in fact, I had not had any pet other than the short-lived tortoise which leapt to its death from our balcony at Sai Wan Estate. Bev pronounced that everyone had to have a pet in order to be a "decent and normal" human being. I was compliant enough to swallow that hook, line and sinker, even though I could barely feed or care for myself at the time. I felt very responsible for and protective of my new pet. I fed it a variety of expensive seeds and supplements. It kept me company while I studied. One morning I awoke to find a small cockroach invading the bird cage, the bird was not perturbed but I was livid. Then and there, I decided to move; I had had it with these pests. I did not have many options as a poverty stricken student, but in short order, I found a very inexpensive basement apartment in one of the working class suburbs. It was a very bare, repurposed space in the basement of a rundown old house, but at least my parakeet and I no longer had to contend with roaches. Besides, it was geographically closer to Troy, and hence, shortening my commute to spending time with Bev. I thus increasingly became a suburbanite, and rocking-the-boat activism was increasingly a faint memory of the past.

Three years of law school was drawing to a close, whether or not I was ready for that closure. I still had no idea what specialty, if any, I would pursue in my law practice. In fact, I had no idea what practicing law would entail. It seemed that just about every classmate had secured a law-related job, but I delayed my job search till the very last minute, because my prospect for being hired was next to nil. I did not want to confront that sorry state of affairs. If I were not under the impression that I had found "the love of my life" in Bev, and if I did not think I had a promising future in the legal profession in America, I would not have had such a daunting dilemma. I would have simply packed up my meager possessions and flown back to Hong Kong. Conversely, if "marriage equality" were the law of the land at that time, Bev and I could have gotten married (of course, she would have to legally divorce Dave first), and I would have been eligible for applying for permanent resident status (the much touted and sought after "green card") as the spouse of a U.S. citizen with the right to work. Alas, that was a fanciful moot point as same-sex marriage was not only decades away, the social and political climate in the late 1970's and early 1980's was decidedly homophobic, unabashedly oppressive and discriminatory toward gays and lesbians. To add insult to injury, homosexuals were classified as "sexual deviants" who were subject to exclusion and deportation under the immigration laws and regulations existing at the time.

Without getting unduly mired in legal technicalities or jargons, following is a primer of my untenable immigration predicaments at the time. As a foreign student, I was eligible for a twelve-month period of "practical training" upon graduation. I thus applied to the Immigration and Naturalization Service (INS) and obtained such employment authorization. I then embarked on a series of job interviews, but most prospective employers became disinterested as soon as I informed them that I was not a U.S. citizen and had only a one-year work permit. That was before I even told them that they would have to sponsor me and apply for further employment authorization in order to continue employing me. That further period of authorized employment, in H-1B nonimmigrant status, would still be considered "temporary;" the foreign worker with the requisite credentials could be employed as a professional or in a specialty occupation for a maximum of six years under then current law. In order to permanently reside and work in the United States and receive the green card, my employer would have to sponsor me to obtain "labor certification" from the U.S. Department of Labor, which essentially certified, through an intensive and convoluted application process, that no U.S. person could perform the job offered to me. After the labor certification could be approved, I would have to be approved by the INS as an immigrant, and even after that, I would still have to wait for the availability of an immigrant visa. Needless to say, there were countless potential pitfalls and red tape lurking with each twist and turn of that protracted process. Moreover, each country was allotted a set number of immigrant visas in various categories each year, and therein lay the rub. Hong Kong, then being a dependent colony, had an annual total visa quota of only 600. As one can well imagine, there were far more than 600 eager prospective immigrants each year waiting in line for visas to relocate to the United States. In short, even if I were able to jump through all the loops and hoops of securing a sponsoring employer, obtaining labor certification and immigrant petition approvals, my place in that formidable queue was somewhere in the range of fifteen or more years out. In other words, after my six years as an H-1B temporary worker, I would have to leave the States to wait for my turn for an immigrant visa, or if I remained, I would have become an "illegal alien," hardly a viable option for an attorney, an officer of the court.

After a goodly number of futile job interviews, I went for yet one more with a small general civil practice firm in Southfield, a northern suburb of Detroit. I was interviewed by one of the senior partners, James A. Hiller, who hired me on the spot as a law clerk. He was apparently not fazed by my temporary immigration status, or my lack of legal work experience for that matter. He might have told me years later that he was intrigued by my rather unconventional and multifaceted background. The other three partners were Barry L. Howard, Sheldon G. Larky, and Daniel J. Hoekenga. In addition, there were two young associates, Marc M. Susselman and Susan A. Ciullo, and Of Counsel, Moe R. Miller. Another law clerk, Deborah G. Holefca, was also hired about the same time. Debbie and I were assigned legal research and writing projects. It was also our duty to drive across counties to file pleadings with various courts. For me, it was a much welcomed training period. I was also taking special classes to prepare for the State Bar examination, a nerve wrecking two-day affair scheduled at the end of July. Thus, my life had been very intense since my law school graduation in May; so much was at stake. The Bar examination was held in Lansing, the State capital, about 95 miles away from Troy. I had to book a hotel stay for the night. Bev must have viewed that as a getaway, a mini-vacation, and decided to come along, *with* Melanie in tow. I must have been insane to concur with her request, another one of the countless instances of my ill-advised catering to her whims at the expense of my own welfare and well-being. That indulgence would only worsen as our relationship droned on. As it turned out, the duo was indeed a dreadful distraction during those two harrowing examination days. They were not very considerate of the enormous mental and physical stress I was under. I did not even get a massage from Bev at the end of the first day of grueling testing, and it was difficult to get a good night's sleep with three people in the small hotel room. It was a miracle then, or perhaps it was my steely determination and laser-sharp focus that enabled me to pull through the examination. I did pass the Bar examination when the results were announced in November. On November 24, 1980, Sheldon moved for my admission; the Honorable Gene Schnelz of the Oakland County (Sixth Judicial) Circuit Court administered the oath, and I was admitted to the practice of law in Michigan as a licensed attorney.

Thus began a new chapter for this fledgling attorney, except that I had absolutely no idea how to be an attorney. My firm seemed to have supreme confidence in my abilities, as I was immediately assigned real clients, with real motions to draft and argue in court. The firm did not have any formal in house mentoring or training program. Sheldon was meticulous in coaching Debbie and me the "nuts and bolts" of preparing pleadings, procedural technicalities, and the practical aspects and protocols of court appearances. Dan, whom I respected as a brilliant lawyer specializing in public sector labor law, patiently reviewed and corrected my draft legal briefs and pleadings, allowed me to tag along occasionally when he appeared in court for oral arguments, and enlightened me on the finer points of substantive law. I would also learn, much later, from Moe the ways and means of a transactional practice, and counseling clients in buying, selling and operating closely-held businesses. The first time I appeared in court to argue a motion, opposing counsel was gracious enough to discretely signal to me when it was my turn to address the court. I still have in my mind's eye the photograph of me taken in the firm's law library very shortly after my Bar admission. I was sitting at the huge conference table, hunched over a yellow legal pad, pen in hand, flanked by shelves of law books, with a small pile next to my legal pad, looking studious, serious and as "lawyer-like" as I could pretend to be. On the inside, I was shaking like a leaf.

About a month before the Bar examination results were announced, I decided to move once again. I found a cozy one-bedroom apartment in Clawson, a suburb just south of Troy. That was the first decent abode I had since arriving in Michigan; it had central air, common laundry facilities in the basement, and a private parking lot. It was a gamble, as there was no way I could have afforded the rent, as modest as it was, if I did not pass the Bar examination. Once every so often, I allowed my brash and risk-taking streak carry the day.

As a young associate, I was finally earning more than chump change. In truth, I had no idea at the time of the sacrifices I would have to make in order to earn a decent living as a lawyer. A corollary of that simple truth was that I was so *laissez-faire* about money most of my adult life that I always ended up living beyond my means. I started down the spendthrift way just a few months after becoming an attorney. On a typical frigid, grey-sky day in February, 1981, Bev called me at the office to announce that she was sick and tired of the dreary Michigan winter. She had looked up on the map for the southern-most point in the United States, Florida, and wanted to vacation there. The "love of my life" wanted an escapade in the Sunshine State, and of course, my reaction was "your wish is my command," even if I did not exactly verbalize it. Many, many moons later, of course I recognized the probable source of my undoing. My very rudimentary understanding of Imago relationship therapy[6] suggested a culprit in my relationship with my Mom. That relationship had been a challenge since my early childhood. It was as if I could never please her enough or reach the ever rising pedestal to which she had expected me

---

[6] *See,* Hendrix, Harville, Ph.D., *Getting the Love You Want: A Guide for Couples, 20th Anniversary Edition* (Henry Holt & Co., 2007).

to ascend. Subconsciously, I yearned for her attention, love and praise, which were doled out only sporadically and very sparingly. That in turn conditioned me to over-perform, resulting in my eagerness to please almost at any cost so as to get a dollop of love and appreciation. Bev, then, became a stand-in for my Mom in a sense; unwittingly, she became the avenue for me to attempt reforming my relationship with my Mom. The warped logic went as follows: if I would be able to please her, she would then love me, and my deficit would then be erased. Pitiful.

I had never gone on vacation before, not counting the family weekend outing to Macau when I was a child, and the trip to Switzerland with Barb to visit Simone. The idea was so novel and decadent: we would drop in on a city and simply loaf, eat, shop and play to our hearts' content. Without any experience in vacation planning, I hastily reserved a flight, a rental car and a motel room to and in Miami. The rental car suffered a flat tire in an iffy neighborhood within the first few hours of our arrival, but fortunately we made it to a Hertz location for a replacement car. My random choice of a motel was far off the mark. Hence, as we drove by the fabulous Fontainebleau Hotel on Miami Beach, I hopped out of the car and grabbed a room for us for two nights, the exorbitant costs be darned.

I enjoyed my first vacation so much that I planned a second, to New York City, for June of 1982. I was so eager to show Bev my old haunts and hangouts that I had a packed itinerary meticulously planned down to each half-hour bloc of time for our weekend stay. Almost comically, I sprained my ankle the first evening we arrived. We had a dinner reservation at a hoity-toity French restaurant, and we thus had to dress up for dinner. I was not accustomed to negotiating the City's uneven pavements on heels as we walked to the restaurant. My ankle swelled up like a football for the remainder of our vacation, relieved only somewhat when I could apply medicinal liniment purchased in Chinatown. In the meantime, at our dinner at one of the "last bastions of grand luxe dining in New York," Bev had probably given the chef heartburn when she ordered lamb chops from the evening's menu, but specified that they be "burned," that is, *tres* well-done. We also had lunch at the Russian Tea Room, and of course, authentic Chinese meals in Chinatown. When I was a student at Barnard, I was nowhere near these rarefied eateries. For balance, I did take Bev to a Nathan's Famous to chow down a bowl of chili and a hot-dog. We also met up with Roz who was then a staff attorney with Lambda Legal. She was the true, brave trailblazer, a vanguard in those early days of the gay rights movement, long before it was fashionable to advocate for the gay community, ages before it was rewarding to champion LGBTQ causes, and certainly eons before it was "trendy" to be gay.

In the three years before I became a lawyer, we each paid our own way when we went out; occasionally, she would treat me to a meal or a movie. After I started working full-time, I was expected to pay for everything when we went out, and our vacations were no exception. Little did I know that that was a pattern-setting vacation for years to come in our relationship: my footing the bill for expensive luxury hotel stays, rental car expense, unbridled shopping, and gluttonous and pricey meals. She would pick up the tab for a meal here and there. The only notable exception that I can recall was when she paid for my plane ticket for our New Zealand extravaganza which was *her* choice for my 40th birthday celebration. The saving grace came in the trips we took in the last three or so years of our relationship. That was when my passion for photography had been rekindled. Whether we were in cities or countryside, taking photographs allowed me to commune with nature and accorded me a respite from an increasingly oppressive and depressive home environment, and which in turn richly replenished my spirit and nourished my soul.

Shortly after our Miami vacation, splurging felt so good that I decided to treat myself to a "decent" car. I chose a modest Honda "Prelude" coupe, with manual transmission, sunroof, air-conditioning, and custom red pinstripes on the sides of its satin-silver body. It was my first brand new car, and as far as I was concerned, it was my Lamborghini. Of course I could not pay for it in cash, but by then I had learned that with a full-time job, I could buy on credit just about anything. Once I started down that path, though, a dangerous precedent was set. After years of almost ascetic living as a foreign student, I felt as if I finally deserved to live the "good life," even if largely on credit. After all, I had lived a reasonably comfortable life during my childhood and my teenage years; the deprivations during my foreign student years were an anomaly. I was not hopelessly frivolous with my money; rather, the salary of a brand new associate in a small-size local law firm was not that lucrative for one to be living the "good" life. After paying for the necessities, there was not much left that could be considered disposable income. No matter, after the new car, I also wanted a better component stereo system, for instance; and that system required periodic upgrades, as a constant stream of shiny new components paraded onto the market to entice this budding audiophile. In other words, I was beginning to get quite seriously in the red financially even early in my professional career.

While I clearly appreciated and enjoyed the spoils of my labor, the labor itself was punishing indeed. The practice of law was nothing even close to what I had imagined what and how it would be. After just a couple of months, I instinctively knew that lawyering was the wrong profession for me, but under the circumstances, it was too late and impossible for me to find and push the "reset" button. Worse than the long hours at the office, worse than the tedious, monotonous and tiring research and writing, worse than the physical stress and strains of lugging "tons" of files dashing through court corridors and from crowded courtroom to even more crowded courtroom in high heels and skirt, to my surprise and dismay, I loathed being in an adversarial and confrontational environment. I had a very naïve and myopic vision of the profession when I dreamed of becoming a lawyer. I was enamored with the ideal of being able to protect, advance and champion the rights of the disadvantaged, the deprived and the oppressed. Somehow I had overlooked the often mundane processes involved in pursuing and accomplishing that lofty goal. Perhaps if I had joined Legal Aid or another nonprofit legal organization, I might not have minded the constant combat as much, as I would presumably be inspired and motivated by the worthy cause. In my day-to-day practice in that Southfield law firm, however, as the "low woman on the totem pole," I worked on whatever was assigned, from contract disputes to collection for nonpayment to probate estates to divorce proceedings to personal injury litigation, and everything in between. I had never been bothered by competition, and I had always welcomed a legitimate challenge. It was not the combat or the game itself that I detested. It was the perpetual disharmony, the never-ending series of heckling and bickering, the ceaseless taunting and posturing, the unrelenting tension, all of which ran against my peace-loving nature. My decision to go to law school grew out of a quixotic moment of idealism, and of the unexpected turn of events derailing my majoring in English. I could engage in advocacy on an intellectual level, but I obviously had a hard time disassociating my emotions from the slugfest with opposing counsel down in the trenches even after the day was done. Unlike other litigators, I did not and could not get any thrill out of being a constant combatant, fighting just for the sake of fighting, in court or even on paper by way of motions and briefs. I did not relish my role as a "hired gun," or worse, a mercenary. An attorney's work is much more taxing and demanding than it appears. The attrition rate is abnormally high for what many outside the profession deem merely a paper-pushing desk job. There is tremendous wear and tear mentally and physically when one is constantly arguing, bickering and haggling. Competition among lawyers and law firms is fierce as there is an abundance of practitioners, while good paying clients are hard to come by. I had seen quite a few fellow attorneys literally "wither away" after engaging in a lengthy trial or age prematurely while still in the prime of their lives. It would be quite a few years before I would discover "non-combat" law practice, in the form of a transactional practice and administrative law practice, which offered somewhat of an escape chute and some measure of redemption and reprieve.

I felt trapped. On the one hand, my workaday grind was stiflingly stressful and joyless. On the other hand, I had already incurred substantial expenses, and financial obligations left me with no choice but to keep faithfully slogging for those precious paychecks. Moreover, if I wanted to remain in the United States, job performance was critical so as to persuade my firm to sponsor me for employment, and legal immigration status, beyond the one-year Practical Training. Hence, the dice was cast, and the situation had all the makings of an indenture. Furthermore, since homosexuality was still on the books as a ground for deportation, as unbearable as it was, I had to fully retreat into the "closet" if I wished to attain permanent resident status in the future. Accordingly, I was "trapped" geographically as well. I had to stop going over to Windsor for my favorite *dim sum* lunch and Chinese grocery shopping. Even though it would take only fifteen minutes of driving over the Detroit River via the Bridge or Tunnel, the destination is a foreign country. That self-imposed restriction on my movement was to preserve my eligibility, however unlikely, for permanent resident status under a rather obscure provision in the Immigration and Nationality Act. One of the requirements under that provision was continuous physical presence in the United States for seven years. Bev seemed not to be particularly empathetic or supportive. I chalked it off as her being busy with her life, working as a massage therapist making house calls, raising her daughter, and attending college part-time. I also thought that perhaps she had faith in my self-sufficient ability to cope with adversities and overcome obstacles. That was exactly how Mom would have expected me to carry on as well. One of her favorite admonitions was: "God helps those who help themselves." I was too young then to appreciate the irony of such religious-tinged guidance coming from my unabashedly agnostic Mom. The last time I heard that chastisement was after she returned from her meeting with Miss Barker about my falling in love with a classmate. Sexual orientation issues aside, total self-reliance was clearly bred into my DNA.

Meanwhile, after not quite a year of toiling as a young associate, my health had already taken a toll. By autumn of 1981, I started having sharp burning chest pains, and I would frequently be overcome with sudden fits of fatigue. I had been very strong and healthy all my life, and hence, I did not even know where to turn for medical help. I arbitrarily picked a walk-in clinic and saw a doctor who thought I had costochondritis; he might have prescribed a pain medication. I next saw a hematologist referred by Bev. He did not think I was suffering from costochondritis, but the laboratory test results indicated that I had some sort of autoimmune disorder, and he recommended that I follow-up with a rheumatologist. That consultation in turn, thankfully, ruled out systemic lupus erythematosus, but the rheumatologist detected something awry with my kidneys. It was then off to a nephrologist I went. In the short span of less than a year, I devolved from being a perfectly healthy and normal twenty-something, to someone whose calendar was laden with a slew of medical appointments and tests, complete with ominous sounding diseases and disorders hanging over my head. After another round of doctor's office visits, and a battery of laboratory tests, culminating in a kidney biopsy in May of 1982, the results were shocking. I was informed that both my kidneys were about one-third damaged. The technical term for the disease was glomerulonephritis, or inflammation of the tiny filters in the kidneys known as glomeruli. In my case, I apparently had some form of autoimmune disorder which caused my immune system to attack my own organs. Irony of all ironies, I was indeed committing self-sabotage and self-destruction, even physiologically. It would not be until 1988 before my nephrologist could confirm that the cause of my glomerulonephritis was vasculitis, inflammation of my blood vessels resulting in organ damage. I was prescribed oral Cytoxan, a cancer drug, in an attempt to halt the disease's progression. I took Cytoxan for about two months, which turned my fingernails blue; it had no beneficial effect on my glomerulonephritis, but instead, its side effect was premature menopause. In the meantime, my nephrologist took a wait-and-see attitude, and by the beginning of 1983, he prescribed Medrol, a corticosteroid, presumably in an effort to tamp down the inflammation and slow the destruction to my kidneys. As a result, I discovered I am extremely sensitive to pharmaceuticals. Within weeks of taking Medrol, my face had turned into the typical Cushingoid "moon face;" I almost could not recognize myself.

My rather unexpected medical condition was still merely a sideshow at that point, an irksome inconvenience as I continued my fledgling legal career. As my unrelentingly stressful law practice drudged on, I would find temporary respite only in the leisure activities that I enjoyed with Bev on weekends and holidays. By then, we seldom patronized the women's bars, as they were located in neighborhoods that were becoming increasingly unsafe. We continued to participate in Women Together's meetings and private parties. Bev had a very generous and kind heart back in the days. There was a nursing home for the elderly nearby in Clawson, and she volunteered to hold Bingo games for the resident ladies on Saturday afternoons. Of course I was recruited to join her in that charitable effort. When she deemed the prizes provided by the nursing home to be too shabby, at our own expense, we bought and furnished more enticing and desirable prizes from local dime stores. We continued that weekly routine for several years. Across the street from the nursing home, we noticed one day, a new establishment opened for business in a small standalone building: a women-only gym named "Spunky's." The owner, Bev, nicknamed Spunky, was the trainer; she was assisted by her teenage son and daughter. Spunky, who was not gay, founded the gym so that women could have our own space and place to work out, free from intimidation and harassment by men in a typical gym setting. Her gym most certainly soon attracted an enthusiastic but discrete lesbian clientele. Bev and I signed up as members right away. Bev worked out there regularly; I would do so whenever I had an evening when I was not too exhausted from the day's work. From time to time, we would also attend body building shows in which Spunky was a participant. Spunky's was quite a change-of-pace diversion and a welcomed women-oriented hangout. Also across the street from the nursing home was a florist from which, on one fine summer day, Bev bought a one-off life-size replica knight in shining armor. It was a knight in full regalia, even if not as authentic and elaborate as the ones you may find in the Arms and Armor section of a historic museum. Bev christened him "Herman," spray-painted his thin metal coat of armor and lance in black color, and even had him rustproofed at a local automotive shop. I was slightly bemused by her unorthodox purchase. Decades later, I would gain insight as to why she was so enamored with that knight replica.

When my Practical Training period was about to expire, my law firm sponsored me for an H-1B visa to continue my temporary employment—a three-year reprieve for me, with a possible three-year extension. Hence, life seemed to have settled down somewhat, even with assorted built-in deadlines, lurking obstacles, and the daily grind. To mark the occasion—a lame excuse, really—I decided it was time to upgrade my "chariot." The Toyota "Supra" sports car had just debuted, and I simply had to have it. It was definitely a reach for me financially. My new car arrived from Japan in early summer of 1982: white exterior with reddish-brown leather interior, 5-speed manual transmission, and as fully loaded as could be. In my mind, it announced, "I have arrived." It did cross my mind, but only fleetingly, that I might appear to be unpatriotic or tone deaf to be driving a Japanese import vehicle at that particular juncture in time. We were in the thick of an economic recession. Detroit, and its automotive industry, was especially hard hit. Tens of thousands of automotive workers had been laid off, many of whom blamed the importation of cheap Japanese cars for luring away customers from American-made cars. I thought it was irrational and too simplistic to scapegoat the Japanese, or any one people or any one country or any one cause, for our economic hardship. Unfortunately, my pacifistic views would soon be proven misplaced.

I do not recall who initiated the reunion, but in about February of 1982, Pearl and I went to Boston to visit Vivian Fung. Since I last saw her in 1976, Vivian had moved from Ann Arbor to New York City, divorced her first husband, moved to Boston and obtained her advanced degree in architecture from MIT. There she met Ted, who was then pursuing his Ph.D. in some esoteric micro-technology field; they owned a charming apartment in Boston. One of the intended purposes of the weekend trip was to lend emotional support to Vivian whose pet dog, which had been her constant companion since secondary school, was seriously ailing. Sadly, by the time we arrived at Vivian's apartment, her pet had expired. Pearl and I did our level best to comfort Vivian, who was totally distraught. We tried to keep the conversation light-hearted but not frivolous, reminisced about our SSGC days, and changed the subject every so often so as to give Vivian a respite from her grief. As we chatted away into the wee hours of the night, Vivian suddenly suffered what seemed to be an anxiety or stress attack. Ted, Pearl and I immediately accompanied Vivian to the Massachusetts General Hospital's emergency room. We were received by a very kindly psychiatrist; Vivian insisted that Pearl and I stay with her while she talked with the good doctor. Vivian was simply overcome with emotions, having just lost her long-time pet companion, all at the same time reuniting with two of her closest friends. It must have been two or three o'clock in the morning when we left the hospital. Pearl and I proceeded to our hotel where we shared a room. Before we turned in, recollecting the events of the day, I recalled remarking to Pearl that I had never seen Vivian being so fragile and vulnerable. Pearl wisely observed that that was precisely part of Vivian's unique charm and tender-ness. Pearl was right; I would understand only years later that being in tune with one's feelings is essential for authentic living. When we met up with Vivian at her apartment the next morn-ing, she was looking and feeling better. My memory is fairly hazy as to what we did that Saturday. There were sumptuous meals, of course, and we browsed exquisite boutiques near her apartment. I purchased for Bev a lovely V-neck sweater, her favorite. Mostly, we talked non-stopped in Vivian's apartment. Other than briefly meeting her several years earlier when she was on a business trip to the Detroit area, I had not seen Pearl for quite a few years. The small reunion at Vivian's, for some strange reason, seemed to have rekindled our intense, deeply buried but hardly forgotten feelings. We caught each other's stolen glances, and the air was palpable with words unspoken. By the end of the day, it was at once comical and embarrassing when Vivian blurted out: "This is too painful; you two should just get on with it already." Haplessly, neither Pearl nor I could join in that refrain. I was "committed" to Bev already at the time. Pearl was not even out then; she had divorced Peter a few years prior, but had been dating men. We were, fatefully, the quintessential two ships passing in the night.

The sweet reunion was all too short, and I dreaded going home. It must have been my sixth sense: instead of a warm welcome home, when I went to deliver the sweater to Bev, she opened her door and threw the sweater box back at me with such force that I fell backwards. She was insanely jealous and furious. I had not done anything unfaithful; if I was at fault at all, it was only that I would not deny my true feelings which took even me by surprise. I had thought that after a full decade, emotions would ebb and memories would fade, but that turned out not to be the case. Aside from that incident, throughout our lengthy relationship, Bev's jealousy fits were legion and brutal. We could be happily having breakfast together at a local diner when suddenly she would fly into a blind fury because she was certain that I was "flirting" with the waitress. That unjustified accusation not only spoiled our meal out, but sadly also conditioned me to guard against any wayward glances, intentional or otherwise, when we were out so as not to rile her ire. It was not so much jealousy as her brute attempt to exercise despotic control over me. Hindsight, and maturity, is so illuminating.

In the spring of 1982, there appeared to be a ray of hope for my immigration dilemma: the Simpson-Mazzoli Act was introduced for possible enactment. That piece of proposed immigration reform legislation focused primarily on amnesty for certain illegal aliens, strict employment authorization verification, and imposition of employer's sanctions for hiring illegal aliens. However, there was a little known provision in it for updating the "registry date," which could be my savior, immigration status-wise. It gave aliens who had resided continuously in the United States since the registry date the opportunity to apply to become permanent residents, if they met other eligibility requirements such as possessing good moral character and not being otherwise inadmissible.

That provision had been in our immigration laws since 1929; the last time it was updated was in 1965, bringing the registry date to June 30, 1948. If the registry date could be updated to a date after my initial entry to the United States in 1972, I would be eligible for applying for the "green card." I drafted a letter pleading my case and sent it to all 435 members of the House of Representatives. I followed up with countless telephone calls, and in June or July of 1982, I was my own one-woman lobbying corps descending on Capitol Hill. By then, I had been in contact and working with one of the staffers on the Joint Committee on the Judiciary. She had kindly facilitated my meetings with the staff of the Congressman for my District, as well as several members of Congress who were instrumental in getting the bill reported out of the Judiciary Committee. I was intrepid in my single-minded mission to resolve my personal immigration conundrum. I was crestfallen when the bill died in the House that year, and again in the following session of Congress in 1984.

It was about the fall of 1982 when Mom wrote and asked, on behalf of my youngest sister, Vivian, whether I would take her in and help her as she desired to pursue post-secondary education in the United States. She had graduated from high school and secretarial school, and had been working as a secretary for a couple of years. The fact that she wanted to pursue advanced studies in order to have a more rewarding career was laudable. As I had noted, she is my favorite, baby sister, and of course, I applauded her ambition and wholeheartedly supported her plans without hesitation. She indicated that she would continue her full-time work for a year, save up money to pay for her tuition, and prepare to apply for admission to Oakland Community College. I was very excited that after eleven years in the States by myself, I would be joined by a family member. I had always felt that Mom cut her, the youngest child, greater slack than she did for Lina or me, though I did not mind that at all. Vivian reciprocated with total adoration for and dedication to Mom. Lina and I were disciplined very strictly by Mom when we were growing up, from behavior to etiquette to academic and extracurricular performance. Yet, Vivian was allowed to, for instance, stand in front of the full-length mirror to stare at and perhaps talk to herself, in the middle of our family dinner. She was such an obedient, sweet and caring kid that no one in the family could possibly find fault with her. In anticipation of Vivian's arrival, it was time for me to seriously consider moving to my own home. It was my good fortune that my "cold call" to a real estate company connected me to LaVerne, a realtor then in her 50's. She would become a good friend and business partner with me and Bev in just a few years. Meanwhile, she patiently showed me one "starter home" after another, as I had an extremely modest budget. By late spring of 1983, my offer for a small ranch-style home in Troy was accepted, and Vivian and I would move in shortly after she arrived from Hong Kong in August of 1983.

Against this backdrop of mundane routine of life in the Midwest, an unprecedented bombshell exploded in early spring of 1983, transforming the Asian American polemics and political landscape, and my life, forever more.

A telephone call came in at my office in the afternoon of March 20, 1983; Henry Yee, the inimitable "unofficial mayor of Detroit Chinatown" was calling me. I do not recall how our paths crossed in the first instance; we were business acquaintance. I did remember having been invited to his Chinese New Year banquet at his restaurant, "Forbidden City" in Chinatown, a couple of years prior. He sounded uncharacteristically excitable, asking if I had read the newspapers about the lenient sentences handed down to the two white men who had killed a Chinaman. "No," I replied; I had not read the papers and was not aware of such an alarming, tragic event. Ever since I moved to Michigan in 1977, nay, ever since I came to the United States in 1972, I had never made a point of seeking out and socializing with other Chinese. In fact, Sylvia from Barnard was just about the only Chinese I had befriended in the States. I came to the United States for the American experience—whatever that meant, from time to time—but not specifically or necessarily for the Chinese American or Asian American experience. After all, no one would dispute that I had had sufficient "Chinese experience" growing up in Hong Kong amongst a population of some four million Chinese. Hence, I was quite detached from "the community" in Greater Detroit; I was not known in the community nor was I familiar with the community, and I was certainly not a member of the various community organizations.

Henry continued and told me about a community meeting scheduled for that evening at Golden Star Restaurant in Ferndale, and asked that I attend. I did not know what to make of the request, as the entire event seemed so out of context for me. Nonetheless, I checked with one of the senior partners about my attending the meeting; he was supportive and even suggested that I leave work earlier that afternoon to prepare for the meeting. I left work a bit earlier that afternoon, and telephoned Bev to tell her about the tragic news that I had learned from Henry and about attending the community meeting. She vociferously protested and objected; she resolutely did not want me to attend the meeting, contending that any controversy involving Chinese people would be messy turmoil from which I might not be able to extricate myself. I was taken aback; her usual jealousy and possessiveness aside, it was the first time she had interfered with my work-related undertakings. I also felt torn. On the one hand, I felt attending the meeting was my duty just as any other work assignment; on the other hand, there was not any attorney-client relationship established or even anticipated, and thus, I was not legally obligated to attend; and on yet another hand, if I contravened Bev's stance, I would have provoked and be subject to her rage and worse. We argued back and forth, and got to a point where I felt if I had insisted on attending, she would have thrown a royal fit and accused me of secretly "meeting my girlfriend" there. Finally, I yielded, deciding that the then rather nebulous incident and impromptu meeting were not worth inciting such havoc in my private life. After all, it was not an "official" work assignment, I rationalized. Bev was delighted that I relented, and "rewarded" me with spending the evening with me working out at Spunky's and having dinner out afterwards.

Thus, my dear friend and comrade, Helen Zia, was very magnanimous and flattering when she recalled and recounted in her seminal treatise, *Asian American Dreams*[7], that community meeting, portraying me as "the only Asian American woman practicing law in Michigan" who spoke up and said, "I'll meet with Kaufman," while the other attorneys in attendance at the meeting demurred, supposedly because "such an act might jeopardize their jobs." I did offer to meet with Judge Charles Kaufman, but it was at another time and place the next day. I was indeed somewhat of a rare bird during those "Stone Age" days, to be a Chinese and a woman engaging in the private practice of law, not to mention my lesbian sexual orientation and my status as an "alien" with no right of permanent abode in the United States. To the best of my recollection, there were only about five other Asian attorneys licensed in Michigan at the time. The most senior was Harold Leon, who was a senior partner in his own firm, handling exclusively insurance defense cases. The rest were Baby Boomers like me, in our late twenties and early thirties. Ann O. Lee and James W. Shimoura were also employed with insurance defense law firms. Roland Hwang was with Ford Motor Company, and Kester So was an associate attorney with a large corporate law firm. It was understandable that they were not at liberty to take on the legal representation of any interested party in that controversy.

---

[7] Zia, Helen, *Asian American Dreams*, 1st ed. (Farrar, Straus and Giroux, 2000), p. 65.

Nevertheless, each of them gallantly played an important and steadfast support and consultation role, enabling the nascent "movement"—nothing short of the political awakening of the Asian American community—to take the country by storm.

The morning after that community meeting, and shortly after I arrived at my office, one of the senior partners, Dan, came to my office. He was almost body-blocking the doorway to my office as he held up that morning's *Detroit Free Press*, with a prominent front page story on what would become known as the Vincent Chin case. Referring to the travesty, he intoned: "*What are you going to do about this!?*" It was a rhetorical question, leaving no room for answer, or any other answer but the one he was expecting. I had never felt smaller; it was the first time I could be viewed as having committed dereliction of duty (even if not in a strict, legal sense), and worse, having been caught doing so. I had also never felt so ashamed, having done nothing for the cause as a Chinese myself, while an Occidental forthrightly expressed righteous indignation for my people. I almost wanted to blame Bev, but I was too honorable for that; I took full responsibility for my action and omission. Dan wanted to know what transpired at the community meeting the night before, and all I could do was mumbled something incoherent in response to the query. By then, Jim had also joined the brief discussion, and they both charged me to call Henry immediately to offer assistance.

It was manifest destiny, then, that I would be involved in the Chin case.

I became a "woman on a mission" right there and then, feeling woefully guilty about not having attended the meeting the previous night, while being enormously grateful for the second chance given. I contacted Henry by telephone and learned that they were planning on meeting Judge Kaufman, who handled down the ridiculous, disproportionately lenient sentence, the following day or the day after; he specifically mentioned that a Helen

Zia would also be attending the hoped for meeting. I promised him that I would meet them at the appointed time and date outside the Judge's courtroom. I hurriedly conducted preliminary legal research in the interim, and prepared my arguments in the event the Judge granted us an audience. To Bev's credit, from that point on when the outrageous miscarriage of justice in the Chin case had been made widely known, she no longer objected to or interfered with my activities relating to the case. I would not have allowed her to do so in any event, as the case had by then become my formal assignment from the firm.

At that time, I only had the barest of facts of the case, but even those were enough to make one shudder and wonder. How could it be? What went awry and how? Above all, what could be done legally to rectify the manifest unjust outcome? In the evening of June 19, 1982, Vincent Chin, a 27-year old Chinese American, went with three friends to a bachelor's party at a strip club in his childhood neighborhood of Highland Park to celebrate his upcoming wedding. An altercation erupted in the bar between Chin and Ronald Ebens, an automotive plant supervisor and his stepson, Michael Nitz, a laid off automotive worker. Chairs were thrown and heated words exchanged, and they were all ejected from the bar. After a few more verbal exchanges in the parking lot, Chin and one of his friends, also a Chinese American, ran for their lives. They fled on foot for about three blocks, and thought they had found refuge at a busy McDonald's restaurant along a major thoroughfare. They sat outside the restaurant, waiting for their other two friends to drive by and pick them up. Ebens and Nitz, who had apparently been cruising the area in their car searching for Chin for about half an hour, spotted him at McDonald's. They ambushed Chin; while Nitz held Chin down, Ebens swung his baseball bat at Chin's head, savagely striking it four times. Chin died of his wounds four days later. Ebens and Nitz were charged with second degree murder, which was incredulously allowed to be plea bargained down to manslaughter. In March of 1983, Judge Kaufman sentenced both men to three years of probation, and each a fine and court costs of $3,780 payable over three years. Case closed, as far as the State trial court was concerned—mere dollars for a Chinaman's life.

Once the sentence in a criminal case has been entered by the judge, it is well-nigh impossible to revisit that sentence, absent exceptionally extraordinary circumstances. It was a shame that the Chin case, or Chin's mother, Mrs. Lily Chin, did not receive legal representation or cohesive, meaningful community support, or appropriate public attention prior to sentencing. By the time the stunningly lenient sentence was handed down, it was a heartbreaking case of the proverbial spilled milk, as far as the State criminal case was concerned. While the two killers were hustled through the Wayne County criminal justice system, there was no organized court watch, nor provision for crime victim impact statements. In those dark and unenlightened days, Asian Americans constituted less than one percent of Detroit's population, which amounted to carrying little or no political clout whatsoever. Then there was also this "tradition" among the characteristically docile Chinese of not wanting to "make waves" unnecessarily, trusting instead government officials, such as prosecutors and judges, to be fair in dispensing justice. It was widely known that Wayne County (3rd Judicial) Circuit Court, where the criminal Chin case was decided, was an extremely busy court; judges, prosecuting attorneys, court personnel were all seriously overextended. Criminal cases were routinely plea bargained down so as to quickly cycle them through the system. Lacking all the pertinent detailed facts at that time, the outcome in the Chin case at the State criminal court level seemed to me to be at the very least the culmination of one oversight compounding another, error begetting error, and missed opportunity upon missed opportunity, a travesty of justice bred of so-called practicality, limited resources and human foibles. Nevertheless, none of that could excuse the lack of appropriate and proportional punishment for an unjustifiable and intentional act directly resulting in the loss of a human life, especially one that was tinged with overt racial hatred and motivations. For the Chinese, especially those of the older generation, Judge Kaufman's sentence was particularly offensive, for it ran afoul of millennia of Chinese "tradition": the accepted "rule" of "a life for a life." As feudal as it may sound, it was really an intuitive, uncomplicated, and straightforward edict in traditional Chinese lore: you knowingly take a life, you pay for it with your own life. Hence, I could only imagine how unfathomable it was to Mrs. Chin—and insulting to the honor of the Chin ancestors— that those two killers were not even sentenced to a jail term.

On the morning we were to meet with Judge Kaufman, I arrived at the courthouse early to wait for the arrival of the contingent. Already standing in the corridor outside the courtroom waiting was a Chinese woman about my age; she introduced herself to me as Helen Zia. When Henry mentioned her name a couple of days prior, I was expecting her to be of Pakistani descent because of her last name; I was recalling the then General and President Muhammad Zia ul-Haq of Pakistan. Henry arrived in short order, accompanied by another Chinese gentleman, Kin Yee. I did not know Kin but would soon learn that he was the head of the Chinese Welfare Council and On Leong Merchants Association.[8] I do not believe Mrs. Chin was in attendance that morning. We proceeded into the courtroom, and asked the Court Clerk to advise the Judge of our arrival. We were rebuffed, and were told that the Judge was unavailable, even though Henry asserted that he had made an appointment in advance. There was no point in lingering in that empty courtroom, and thus, Henry

---

[8] For an excellent primer on the various Chinese community, business, social and cultural organizations, including the Chinese Welfare Council and On Leong Merchants Association, *see*, *Asian American Dreams*, *ibid.*, pp. 61-62, 65-66.

suggested that we adjourn to Carl's Chop House to strategize over lunch. If my memory serves me correctly, a few other members of On Leong joined us there. The meal was stupendous; I mused to myself that Henry really did not need to wine and dine me, as I would have worked just as hard for the cause without being fed. We discussed our legal options, coalition building efforts, as well as coordinating the hoped for resources responding to our clarion call.

From that moment on and for the ensuing four months, my life felt as if it had been put on hyper-drive. Hours, days, weeks flew by in the blink of an eye, and yet time seemed to have stood still all at once. There was no time for reflection or pontification, not a moment for second guess or rumination, no time to even exhale. Even my experience in the 1970's as a veteran of the feminist and gay rights movements did not prepare me for the tidal waves that swiftly swept the case to national and international prominence. There was even an episode in the *Twilight Zone* television series prominently alluding to the Chin case.[9] Nothing in my formal educational or legal training prepared me for the intense scrutiny by the media, the community and the public that the case received almost overnight, nor the multitudes of tasks, many of which were unfamiliar to me, to be undertaken and accomplished urgently. It had to be part youthful exuberance, part sheer *chutzpah*, part benevolent ignorance, and part pure conviction in a just cause that propelled us to tread those uncharted political and legal waters so fiercely and fearlessly.

My new friend, Helen, became my soulmate-in-arms in very short order. In those early days, I was not yet aware of her journalistic credentials, but was beginning to learn about her community and political activism involvements also in the 1970's. I was in awe

---

[9] *Twilight Zone*, Season 1, Episode 21, entitled "Wong's Lost and Found Emporium," aired November 22, 1985.

of the series of press releases that she prepared under utmost time and logistical constraints. They were cogent, concise, convincing, and always timely. No self-respecting journalist or member of the media could resist "picking up" the tantalizing newsworthy nuggets that she dangled with those press releases issued on behalf the American Citizens for Justice, the organization formed specifically to spearhead the Chin case efforts. Without her deft liaison efforts with the press, I very much doubt that we would have received such positive publicity and widespread support for the case, at least not at such lightning speeds, in those pre-fax, pre-Internet, and pre-social media days. Helen and I were akin to a *doppelgänger* of each other, working in tandem. I focused on the legal aspects, while she was the eyes and ears of all things Chin case. She masterfully juggled public relations duties and, along with others in the ACJ leadership, handled the unenviable task of "herding cats" with the historically fractious Chinese community,[10] making sure that everyone stayed focused on the stated purposes and objectives. In time, Helen would also take on the role of confidante and companion to Mrs. Chin as she traveled the country to greet and thank supporters, and for television interviews and other public appearances. For instance, Mrs. Chin, accompanied by Helen, made a memorable and high-profile appearance to plead for justice for her son on *The Phil Donahue Show*. Watching Helen tenderly wiping away Mrs. Chin's tears on the show, you can tell she cared for Mrs. Chin as if her own mother. In truth, from my observations, the feelings were mutual, as Mrs. Chin cherished Helen as if her own daughter. There were many other similar heartrending public appearances by Mrs. Chin, putting an inconsolable mother's face to the case of alleged hideous hate crime and egregious miscarriage of justice.

---

[10] *See*, e.g., *Asian American Dreams, ibid.*, pp. 75-77.

After consulting with my senior partner, Dan, we proposed to ACJ that a motion be filed with Judge Kaufman to seek resentencing. Admittedly, that was a rather unprecedented request and a long shot, but we did not have many viable legal options. On a parallel track, we also recommended that ACJ appeal the sentence to the Michigan Court of Appeals. My colleague and a senior associate at the firm, Marc, who was a brilliant appellate attorney and brief writer, was given that tough assignment. Conducting legal research and drafting legal pleadings were not particularly demanding for me, even in a time crunch; after all, that was what I was trained to do. However, doing so under the glare of the media, while fielding a constant torrent of inquiries from the press, and attending ACJ meetings and various strategy sessions, was arduous. Barely a third-year associate attorney, I was just about as green as they came in the legal arena. There was nothing in my legal training that prepared me for such a heady assignment, or for discharging my duties as an attorney under such intense community fervor and scrutiny. No matter, the cause was abundantly righteous, and the grievous harm to be redressed most compelling; I was determined to give my assignment of a lifetime my all.

On a typical "motion day" at Wayne County Circuit Court one Friday in April, 1983, we appeared before Judge Kaufman to present oral arguments for our motion for resentencing. I was grateful that Dan had not only reviewed my pleadings before submission, but he had also agreed to appear with me and lead the oral arguments. Being the one who had asked me what I was going to do about the injustice, I sensed that he was thrilled to have the opportunity to speak his mind for the record. The courtroom was packed with ACJ members, supporters and the press. To be frank, I hardly remembered much of that morning, and certainly not of our specific arguments, or questions from the bench. The emotions were raw, the stakes were high, and the atmosphere was highly charged. The Judge took our motion under advisement, and ultimately and not surprisingly, denied our motion. I do recall attending an ACJ community meeting the following day, a Saturday. I arrived late, as I had slept in that morning, being utterly exhausted from weeks of ceaselessly tending to case-related tasks since that Carl's Chop House lunch. Having been put on cortisone medication, which I did not tolerate well, early that year for my kidney condition was also fatiguing. As I walked into the hall, I was stunned to receive a standing ovation. I genuinely did not feel that I had done anything to deserve such an honor; it was very gracious of the community. A sense of foreboding haunted me later with the thought of the let-down everyone would feel if our justice system should fail us again despite our colossal collective efforts.

By then, there was widespread belief among supporters that the killing was racially charged and motivated. That may well have derived from accounts by Vincent's three buddies who were with him that fateful evening, and from news stories by investigative reporters who had interviewed one or more of the dancers at the strip club. The focus of our legal efforts then shifted to the viability of a Federal civil rights violation investigation and prosecution. I was charged with conducting the necessary legal research, gathering relevant information and materials, and compiling a report for presentation to the U. S. Department of Justice's Civil Right Division. My law school education and legal training, again, did not exactly provide concrete guidance or precedent for such an endeavor. My meagre efforts were a footnote at most, but during this phase of the Chin case movement, a multitude of powerful political forces was harnessed and coalesced. The historic movement culminated in the announcement, by William Bradford Reynolds, chief of the Civil Rights Division of the U.S. Justice Department, and Leonard Gilman, U. S. Attorney for the Eastern

District of Michigan, in September of 1983, of Federal grand jury indictments against Ebens and Nitz for civil rights violation.

En route, as far as my involvement in the case was concerned, trials and tribulations abound. If the atmosphere surrounding the case was intense when the motion for resentencing was prepared and heard by the Court, the Chin case had by late April, 1983, become a cause célèbre, reverberating internationally. Even friends in Hong Kong contacted me as they read about the case in the local newspapers. The pressure was almost unbearable for me to expeditiously complete the report to be submitted to the Department of Justice. There were also demands for public appearances. I left those mostly to Helen and the contingent of ardent ACJ supporters. However, there were numerous exceptions, the pace-setting demonstration in Kennedy Square and the march on the Federal Courthouse being one. Mrs. Chin made a most compelling appearance at the Square addressing the throngs of fervent and peaceful demonstrators, appealing for justice for Vincent and expressing her profound gratitude. The historic demonstration received widespread press coverage, including photojournalists from New York, and representatives of the press from the West Coast, most likely courtesy of the support from Stewart Kwoh,[11] an attorney and activist from Los Angeles, and the various Chinese America organizations based in San Francisco.[12] If I am not mistaken, television crews from NHK, the Japanese national television network, were also present.

I joined Helen on a couple of radio talk shows, fielding listeners' pointed and probing questions.[13] I was also invited to speak to members of one or two large African American organizations, to draw an analogy between our efforts to seek justice in the Chin case with their time-honored civil rights struggles, and to seek

---

[11] *See, Asian American Dreams, ibid.*, p. 81.

[12] *See, ibid.*, p. 76.

[13] *See, ibid.*, pp. 68, 74-75.

their support and build solidarity. For me, it was hardly a publicity blitz but more of recalling my good old days of consciousness-raising. Then, there was the lively discussion, held in my firm's conference room, between the volunteer attorneys and the invited guest of honor, Prof. Robert A. Sedler, my Constitutional law professor at Wayne State University Law School.[14] I was then already in the thick of compiling my report for the Department of Justice. Professor Sedler lectured and contended that the Civil Rights Act did not apply to any race other than African Americans. It was an honor for us, and especially for me, to have such a refresher and input from a distinguished Constitutional legal scholar, but it was all academic well enough; we *had* to push that proverbial legal envelope. If it had not been attempted before, then it was sufficiently meritorious for us to then and there advocate extending civil rights protections to all races and ethnicities.

Some weeks before I argued the motion for resentencing before Judge Kaufman, I met Mrs. Chin. I might have first met her at an ACJ meeting, but more likely, our first meeting was at her home in Oak Pak at her invitation. I was anxious as I had no idea how I could convey my condolences sufficiently and appropriately. Mrs. Chin surprised me then as she came across as a very warm and understanding, as well as a very dignified and composed woman. She also almost felt motherly to me. It was good fortune that my mother tongue is Cantonese, and she thus had no difficulty understanding me. Her Chinese dialect was Taishanese, which was slightly different from Cantonese, but close enough that I could also understand her. Over time, she even made an effort to speak her Taishanese with more of a Cantonese intonation to accommodate me. I believe at our first meeting, she mostly expressed gratitude for my assistance, and we might have conversed about my family and background in Hong Kong. In

---

[14] *Ibid.*, p. 72.

turn, I must have explained to her the multi-pronged legal efforts then in planning, the formation of ACJ and its outreach efforts. Little did I know that that would be the beginning of a beautiful and memorable friendship that spanned almost two decades till her untimely passing in 2002. Even more surprisingly, Mrs. Chin and Bev hit it off fabulously from their very first meeting. Again, I have no recollection of exactly when or where that was, but I surmised that Bev might have come along on one of the non-work related get-togethers with Mrs. Chin in the early summer of 1983. Back in those days, Mrs. Chin would often prepare *dim sum*, dumplings, pastries, and other delectables to treat friends, supporters, and volunteer attorneys working on the case. Mrs. Chin genuinely took to Bev; it was natural affinity. They managed to communicate somehow, with Mrs. Chin speaking very broken English, and Bev mouthing very simple, short phrases augmented by much gesturing. After a while, Bev would visit Mrs. Chin from time to time to keep her company and entertained. Bev would help Mrs. Chin cook and bake; under the guise of learning to make dumplings, Bev would end up eating more than apprenticing. That apparently delighted Mrs. Chin greatly, perhaps because it was such a welcomed diversion from her unknowable sorrow and unmentionable grief. So their friendship blossomed, quite apart from the angst and travails of the Chin case movement. Bev and I never directly came out to Mrs. Chin as life partners, and she never asked. Then again, unlike some of my older relatives, Mrs. Chin never grilled me as to why I was not yet married (to a man). Obviously, she knew that Bev and I lived together (as of mid-1986), as she had been our overnight guest on quite a few occasions. She simply accepted us as a pair.

Amongst the many activities and functions on behalf of the Chin case cause, one stood out to me. I was asked by Henry and Kin to accompany the Detroit On Leong contingent on its homage to On Leong's headquarters in Chicago to seek support for the Chin case efforts. It was probably in May or June of 1983. As a Hong Kong-born-and-raised Chinese, I was not familiar with the history, politics and dynamics of Chinatown and its inhabitants in the various U.S. cities. I had vaguely heard of the *tongs*, the triads, and other seedier elements operating within the fabric of Chinatown communities. It all sounded more a fable than reality to me. As Helen pointed out in her *magnum opus*, Vincent, who worked part-time at Golden Star Restaurant, was a member of On Leong from the younger generation.[15] According to Henry, Chicago On Leong wanted to know more about the killing and death of one of its "brothers," and hence, our trip to Windy City. I had been to Chicago's Chinatown once or twice previously as a casual visitor. Every visitor is familiar with the ornate arch-gate that spans over Wentworth Street as one enters Chicago Chinatown. Nonetheless, on previous visits, I did not notice an equally ornate building tucked among numerous shops and restaurants; it was On Leong's headquarters. It was a 3- or 4-storey building, the interior was decorated and furnished with classic, traditional Chinese décor. There were traditional blackwood and rosewood furniture pieces, altars, wall hangings of brush calligraphy; the atmosphere was solemn and fiercely traditional. As I entered the building with Henry, Kin and other members from Detroit On Leong, we were greeted by an official who oversaw our signing in on the official register. If my memory has not failed me, we had to sign in using the supplied Chinese calligraphy brush and ink. Tradition must be kept and respect must be paid. That, or it was purposely administered as a litmus test of the visitor's Chinese authenticity. My brush calligraphy was very rusty, but I managed to sign in with my Chinese name. Apparently, one also had to make a "tithe" upon entering; Henry and Kin covered me in that instance. We then had an audience with the chief of Chicago On Leong. My

---

[15] *Asian American Dreams, ibid.*, p. 62.

memory is fairly hazy about the specifics, but I believe we met him on the second floor. Everyone was extremely respectful of the chief, bowing and almost kowtowing. I then realized I more than stood out like a sore thumb. I had the sense that, most probably, no woman had ever set foot in that building until that day when I descended upon it out of necessity. The men, mostly older, did not know what to make of me—a very young female attorney who happened to be Chinese and who could speak Cantonese, and who also happened to be the "Chin case lawyer." Our consultation with the chief of Chicago On Leong was relatively brief. Mostly, Henry and Kin updated him on the latest, and there was not much need to mull over the legal fine points and nuances. I was then told we would adjourn to a nearby restaurant to meet with the membership over lunch. Since there was time before that engagement, I was allowed to roam and tour the building on my own. One level after another, my impression was confirmed that the building, the architecture, the layout, the decorations, and the accoutrements were all designed to enshrine this bastion of male dominance and to glorify patriarchal exclusivity. There was also a sense of secrecy, as if the walls were whispering inaudibly. My mind wandered to the real or imagined intrigues that I read and heard about various Chinese secret societies and their fables and foibles. I certainly did not belong there, had no place or business there, and probably would not have been welcomed there otherwise. It sent shivers up my spine. I also wondered, though, realistically for how long such patriarchal tradition could continue to thrive in our fast changing world. I could not help but also felt a measure of pity for those older gentlemen who were entrenched in their male-centered ways, so oddly out-of-pace with time and reality. I left the building and walked onto the sidewalk under a warm sun, all too happy to have left an environment that felt stifling and oppressive. The lunch meeting at the nearby restaurant was very well attended. In fact, the enthusiastic and concerned audience was so large that it spilled over to another restaurant; I had to make my presentation twice, at the two separate locations. I had no idea as to what Chicago On Leong decided in terms of support for the Chin case; I trusted that Henry and Kin continued to liaison with their counterparts and brethren.

Claims of race-based motivations in the Chin case swelled almost from the very start when Judge Kaufman's probation-and-fines sentence was meted out. We heard and read reports that racial slurs and epithets were supposedly uttered by Ebens against Chin. There were also allegations of Ebens' apparently mistaking Chin for a person of Japanese descent, and thus blaming Chin for the massive automotive layoffs in the United States, especially in the Detroit area. My task then was to corral any and all relevant information and potential evidence relating to any racial animus or motives on the part of the two killers. I decided to visit Fancy Pants, and hoped to meet and talk with as many as possible of the dancers who performed or who were present that night. I was hoping to identify one or more witnesses who might have heard words, if any, exchanged leading to and during the altercation. My visit was in the daytime, and even so, I was quite unnerved. Highland Park, where Fancy Pants was located, had fallen into disrepute as a neighborhood; it was certainly not your family vacation destination. Even under broad daylight, I tensed up as I drove into the parking lot of the strip club. There was an air of forlornness, abandonment, despair, living on the edge. Besides, I had never been in a striptease club before in my entire life.

I had never previously conducted any "investigation" either. I only had recollections of law enforcement and private detective investigations seen in movies and television shows to fall back on as a general guide. As I no longer have access to my files and notes, I can only rely on my memory in relating these accounts. I introduced myself to the manager of the club, who allowed me to speak with several dancers. I might have visited Fancy Pants more than once, so as to meet with different dancers on different days. I believe Helen had joined me on one of the visits. Other than Racine Colwell, a couple of the other dancers claimed they did not hear any verbal exchange between Ebens and Chin. That could be because words exchanged, if any, were beyond their audible range, or words were not exchanged between the two until Colwell's turn as a dancer on stage, who thus was in a position to hear the verbal exchanges. Colwell agreed to be interviewed by me at her home where I would have more time, and fewer intrusions and noise, to hear her account of the pertinent events. The specifics I learned from Colwell were, of course, detailed in my report to the Department of Justice. By the time I met her, Colwell had been interviewed by various newspapers and television networks; what she reportedly overheard that night had already been widely published. She steadfastly maintained that she clearly heard Ebens voicing to Chin: "It's because of you motherfuckers that we're out of work."

After my visit to Fancy Pants, I drove around the several blocks in the vicinity, trying to retrace the steps Vincent and his Chinese pal took in fleeing the two assailants. I found the McDonald's restaurant, and pulled into its parking lot. I walked around the premises, imagining myself sitting on the planters in front of the restaurant, anticipating to hail my buddies driving by with the car. Then I looked at my parked car, and chuckled nervously to myself. I was either being tone deaf or death defying uppity to be tooting around town, at the zenith of anti-Japanese sentiments in Motor City, in my rather flashy Japanese-made Toyota "Supra" sports car. The truth was that I was simply a budding car buff who had bought the "wrong" car at the "wrong" time. Those were very uptight days, and that was an understatement.

As the Chin case gained ever escalating fame or notoriety, depending on one's perspective, increasingly appearing in the news reports were various and sometimes conflicting renditions of the events of that heated night, especially with respect to racial comments or slurs reportedly hurled or overheard. My information gathering process had come to a point when it was necessary to have in-depth interviews with the three friends who were in Vincent's celebration party that night. Once again, hindsight proved to be so instructive yet unforgiving. Because of time constraints, and for expediency's sake, I did not give it a second thought when I asked all three of them to come in to my office for a group interview. Now, many moons later, the much older a somewhat wiser me tells me that such a "group interview" was a horrid idea. I do not believe any experienced lawyer worth his or her salts, in the process of ascertaining relevant facts of a case, would have proceeded with such a group inquiry. It was not unlawful or criminal or unethical professionally, but it just was not a suave move. I was simply too inexperienced as a lawyer then, and it was definitely a ham-handed interview as a result. However, my intentions were earnest, honest and pure: a focused effort to gather relevant facts wherever they might fall; there were absolutely no ulterior motives or hidden agenda. As a matter of fact, to document my openness and impartiality, I tape-recorded the interview, as I had done with similar interviews with Colwell and other potential witnesses in the case. Those were *not* secret recordings; I informed each interviewee of the recording, placing my very humble office-issued Dictaphone in plain view, and obtained his or her recorded verbal consent for the recording before each session. There was also a practical aspect to the taping: it was for my own edification; I wanted to be able to concentrate on the interview give-and-take without having to be distracted by taking notes. As copiously as I could have made my notes, I was concerned that I could have inadvertently left out important data. A seasoned trial attorney would interject at this point in noting that such recording might be tactically highly undesirable; but then again, it was certainly not against the law or even any moral code.

The taped interview with Vincent's three pals lasted for hours into the late evening. I was gratified that I learned minute details about what transpired that evening, as recalled by the three who were present with Vincent. I recounted in my report as best I could all the relevant specifics gleaned from these gentlemen. Indeed, there were inconsistencies in what was heard and said and done, and most pertained to insignificant minor collateral points. Perspectives differed, witness' memories could play tricks, and any number of variants could have given rise to the differing accounts. The gist of my comments to them was to tell the truth to the best of their recollection, and to be responsive to the question, if ever they were called to testify. My only other suggestion to them, as I recall, was that they did not have any legal obligation to speak to the press when requested for an interview. While this did not pertain to the Federal case, a distinct impression I garnered from their narratives was that the killers should have been charged with first-degree murder in the State court in the first instance. There was, in my view, sufficient evidence of premeditation. There was about half an hour between the parties' ejection from the bar and the ambush of Chin at McDonald's. Thus, while Chin disengaged from the altercation at the bar and fled for safety on foot, instead of cooling down, Ebens and Nitz were set on a rampage to hunt down and inflict mortal bodily harm on Chin. The sad reality was that the County prosecuting attorney's office had apparently, routinely and nonchalantly, agreed to the plea bargain to manslaughter. To compound the oversight (euphemistically speaking), a prosecuting attorney did not even attend the sentencing to present the aggravating circumstances to argue for just punishment and lengthy jail term for the killers.

As it was always the case, if I had more time, I could have tried to locate more potential witnesses, or conducted further follow-up inquiries. As it was, my report was completed just in time for our appointment with Assistant Attorney General

William Bradford Reynolds, the chief of the Civil Rights Division of the Department of Justice, in July of 1983. I accompanied the contingent on that trip to Washington, D.C.; our delegation included Henry and Kin, Mrs. Chin, and representatives from ACJ. Speaking strictly for myself, the meeting was quite anticlimactic; it was polite and formal. I believe the Department and the FBI had by then already commenced their investigations for a potential Federal civil rights case against the two killers. My legal responsibilities had thus been discharged, and I quietly returned to my private law practice, and to my not altogether uncomplicated private life. Of course, I continued to participate in ACJ's functions from time to time as a private individual, and not infrequently, visited with Mrs. Chin as a friend.

Indictments were handed down by the Federal grand jury in November of 1983, against Ebens and Nitz for violating Chin's civil rights. The trial was held in Detroit in June of 1984, with U.S. District Judge Anna Diggs Taylor (who, incidentally, is a Barnard alumna) presiding. The jury returned a verdict of guilty against Ebens, and Judge Taylor sentenced him to 25 years in prison. We all exhaled, and for a moment, it appeared that a measure of justice was finally done. Alas, the elation would turn out to be illusory and short-lived. Ebens' attorneys promptly appealed his conviction to the Sixth Circuit Court of Appeals in Cincinnati, Ohio. As the world knows by now, Ebens' conviction in the Federal civil rights case was ultimately reversed and remanded on appeal in September of 1986. The appeals court concluded that Ebens did not receive a fair trial, citing various procedural and evidentiary errors, the most glaring of those ruled errors, as far as I was concerned, was the accusation that I had supposedly "coached witnesses." The Appendix to the Court's opinion[16] contained deliberately selective excerpts from the transcripts of

---

[16] *United States v Ebens*, 800 F2d 1422 (6th Cir. 1986), Appendix A.

my tape recordings of the group interview with Vincent's three friends, purporting to highlight my transgressions. My infamy thus, however undeservedly, resides for eternity in the canons of American jurisprudence.

In preparing for trial in the U.S. District Court in Detroit in 1984, the U.S. Attorney's office did ask me to review the accuracy of the transcript of the tape recordings. I learned that the transcript was prepared by transcribers hired by Ebens' attorneys. Not surprisingly, the transcript was full of errors and misleading transcriptions. It was my accent—still somewhat heavily British-tint then—that apparently threw the transcribers off, as well as my British (as opposed to American) manner of speech which somehow appeared far more "sinister" and "conspiratorial" on the pages of that transcript. As I have mentioned earlier, that was not unusual at all in those pre-BBC-America, pre-globalization days when most people were not familiar with a British accent. Transcripts of my court appearances, when I was arguing clients' cases, were routinely full of errors because the stenographer or court reporter was not accustomed to my English accent. That, or if I were to be cynical, seeing that I appeared Chinese, the court reporter decided implicitly that I must have been speaking "Chinglish," and thus, consciously or subconsciously made a mess of the transcript of my oral presentation.

At the U.S. Attorney's office's request, I listened to my tapes again and dutifully marked all the errors in the transcript, and then turned in my marked-up transcript. I had naïvely thought that the transcript would then be corrected, or at least challenged, but in fact it was allowed to be used, "as is," to impeach the witnesses and as "evidence" of my having "coached witnesses." For instance, at one point in the interview, I noted: "Now, if you don't agree, like I explained to them earlier, you definitely remembered certain things happened, say, it's a black car and you definitely remembered it's a white car and we kind of..." In the Appendix, the next word was "(inaudible)." In the original transcript that I reviewed, it somehow had the phrase "fudge it." Neither version is correct, because "fudge it" was not even a term or expression that I knew. As I no longer have access to the tapes, I cannot recall what I said at that point, but it would have been something along the lines of telling the truth as he or they remembered it. Dan had patiently listened to all the tapes at the time. Granted, he was hardly impartial, but he concluded that he heard nothing untoward or incriminating in the tapes. If suffices to add that Dan was, of course, familiar with my accent. If I had intended to "coach the witnesses," why would I have openly tape-recorded the interview? I would have had to be either utterly insane or a complete imbecile to have done so. I submit that I was neither. There might have been very clumsy questioning and remarks on my part, but there was absolutely no "witness coaching" intended or insinuated. In retrospect, as I have reiterated, it was bad judgment on my part to hold a "group" interview out of expediency and time constraints to gather relevant information as expeditiously as possible. However, a neophyte's *faux pas* does not a case of witness influencing make.

I had prepared to testify at the first Federal trial, presumably as to the tape recordings or the error-filled transcript, but I was never called as a witness. When the case was remanded, and the retrial commenced in April, 1987, venue had changed to Cincinnati, a locale that was all too sympathetic and favorable to Ebens, as Helen aptly noted.[17] Again, I was told to stand by as a witness. I stayed in a hotel room near the courthouse, chain-smoking cigarettes, feeling totally misunderstood, maligned, and stressed out. I would telephone my colleague, Marc, from time to time to seek his counsel and for a shoulder to figuratively cry on. I believe it was the second day when the U.S. Attorney informed me that I

---

[17] *Asian American Dream, ibid.*, p. 79.

would again not be called as a witness, and that I could return to Michigan. Perhaps they decided that they did not need my testimony after all to clarify the tapes, or they might have thought that I would not have made a "good" witness—lawyers are generally lousy witnesses as we tend to be too argumentative. Hence, I never had an opportunity to present or explain myself to the jury, or to correct the mis-transcriptions, or to rebuff the negative inferences swirling around the tape recordings. The jury then proceeded to acquit Ebens.

In the many years since that insult-upon-injury acquittal, I have had much time to reflect upon my involvement, however insignificant, in the Chin case. I often chastised myself for having unwittingly provided the sorry excuse that the defense exploited to absolve Ebens. Granted that there were other technicalities and procedural nitpicks which the defense attorneys exploited in advocating for their client, I admonished myself for my missteps, however innocent or even harmless. I was a perfectionist, and had always been; as such, my having contributed, however indirectly, unintentionally or innocuously, to the most disheartening outcome in the Federal civil rights case was simply unacceptable and inexcusable. The blow to my psyche was verily devastating. I was bred and raised by Mom to excel always, and to succeed always; reaching the goal may occasionally require a do-over, but failure was inconceivable. In this case, there could be no do-over. Despite my best efforts, I had irredeemably "failed" Mrs. Chin, the movement, and myself. That was the reason why I had not, through the many decades, given any interview or speech, made any public appearance, or collaborated with the various scholars, writers and filmmakers studying and documenting the historic case. It is not because I harbor "guilty" feelings; not at all. I had performed to the best of my abilities, and had given the case my unreserved all. My conscience in this matter is crystal clear, my honor is intact, and my integrity unblemished.

There is another reason—an admittedly quirky and highly personal one—why I never sought and did not want any recognition, let alone accolades, for my participation in the case or to reprise my role as the "Chin case lawyer." To delineate my point, I pay homage to the great Sir Sidney Poitier. There are poignant passages in his memoir, *The Measure of A Man: A Spiritual Autobiography*,[18] with which I found deep resonance. Though born in Miami, Florida, Poitier spent his early childhood on Cat Island, The Bahamas, which was then, as was Hong Kong, a British Crown Colony. Poitier's Cat Island was a spit of land 46 miles long and 3 miles wide. There was "neither plumbing nor electricity," but there were "gorgeous beaches and a climate like heaven, cocoa plum trees and sea grapes and cassavas growing in the forest, and bananas growing wild."[19] In other words, there was everything that a boy needed to grow up properly. He called it "my Cat Island curriculum."[20] It is not that he disregarded his race or his skin color, but his Cat Island curriculum had put those in unique perspective and context.

Poitier moved with his family to Nassau, the capital of The Bahamas, when he was ten-and-a-half years old; at age fifteen years, he was sent to Miami to join his brother ten years his senior. His formative years on Cat Island, though, would reverberate throughout his fabled life, culturally, emotionally, and racially. Nearly sixty years after he left Cat Island, a dear friend asked him a "very telling" question: "On Cat Island . . . when you looked in the mirror, what did you think about the color of your skin?" Poitier's retort was sheer brilliance:

---

[18] Poitier, Sidney, *The Measure of A Man: A Spiritual Autobiography*, 1st ed. (HarperCollins Publishers, 2000).

[19] *Ibid.*, p. 3.

[20] *Ibid.*, p. 13.

The question opened doors that helped me to understand that special place. I told him, first of all, that I had no recollection of having seen myself in a mirror at that time. I couldn't remember having ever seen a looking glass in our house, or any other kind of glass anywhere on the island (except maybe rum bottles on the shelf of Damite Farrah's shop). No glass windows, no glass doors, no stores with glass fronts. Our family didn't drink from glassware; we drank from enamel cups. Reflections, of course, from pond water, baking pens, various other kinds of metals. That's what I had. That's all I had. Occasionally glimpses from reflections. Never was I able to recall having seen myself in a mirror. So I never got a fix on my color. No reason to. With no frame of reference to evidence its necessity, the issue never arose. There was one guy in Arthur's Town, a doctor, who was white, and Damite Farrah, the shopkeeper, who was white. These guys were different-looking, yes. But neither represented power. Therefore, I never translated their color into that. Or control . . . or hostility . . . or oppression . . . or anything of that nature. They were just there, and I never wondered why they were white and the rest of the people were black.

So in answer to my friend's question, I didn't think about the color of my skin. Not any more than I would have bothered to wonder why the sand was white or the sky was blue.

But outside the island of my early years, a world was waiting that would focus on my color to the exclusion of

all else, never caring to go beyond that superficial char-
acteristic to see what else I might have to offer.[21]

As Poitier acknowledged, the world outside Cat Island, unfortunately, was not as idyllic and color-blind, and, of course, in his adult life in the United States, he had encountered racism and experienced disparate treatment because of the color of his skin. How he countenanced racial oppression was equal parts dignity and poetry. When he arrived in Miami, it struck him that "Miami shared a climate and lifestyle with the Caribbean, but its culture and mores were of the American South, 1940's Jim Crow style, and nothing had prepared me to surrender my pride and self-regard sufficiently to accept those humiliations. In fact, it was quite the opposite. My values and my sense of self were already fully constructed." Case in point: on one of his first assignments as a delivery boy, he was sent to a wealthy home in Miami Beach. He knocked on the front door to advise the lady who opened the door that he had come to deliver the package from the drugstore. The lady ordered him to "[g]et around to the back door where you belong." Poitier politely explained: "But I'm *here*. Here's the package you ordered." The lady slammed the door in his face instead. He could not understand what the problem was, and left the package at the door. A couple of nights later when he went home, everyone at his brother's house "was lying on the floor, huddled together as if they were in a stage of siege." Apparently, the Klan had been there looking for Poitier earlier. Everyone was terrified except him. Poitier elucidated his sanguinity with these insights:

> *In Nassau, while learning about myself, I had*
> *become conscious of being pigeonholed by others, and I*
> *had determined then to always aim myself toward a slot*
> *of my choosing. There were too many images of what I*

---

[21] *The Measure of A Man, ibid.,* pp. 29-30.

could be. Where I could go. Too many images of won-
derful, accomplished, interesting black people around
and about for me to feel bad about my color.

In Miami, this strange new society started coming at
me with point-blank force to hammer home its long-es-
tablished, non-negotiable position on the color of skin,
which declared me unworthy of human consideration,
then ordered me to embrace the notion of my unworthi-
ness. My reply was, "Who, me? Are you fucking crazy?
Me? You're talking to me?

. . . I have no evil designs; I'm a well-intentioned,
meaningful person. I'm young, and I'm not particu-
larly headstrong—though I can get pretty pissed. I'm a
good person, and nothing you say can undo that. You
can harp on that color crap as much as you want, but
because of the way I was raised, I don't have a receptor
that's gonna take in any of that.

Of course, over time, osmosis brings a lot of that
sewage to you, and some of it does seep in, you know?
But having arrived in America with a foundation that
had had time to set, the Jim Crow way of life had trouble
overwhelming me.[22]

Poitier illustrated his point in recounting yet another incident which deeply resonates amidst today's hue and cry with the
Black Lives Matter movement and accusations of police bru-
tality against African American men. In trying to retrieve his
clothes from the dry-cleaner in the black people's part of town,
he was told they were not yet ready, but that he could try picking
them up at the plant which was located in a "white, middle-class

---

[22] *The Measure of A Man, ibid.*, pp. 40-42.

neighborhood." Unfortunately, his clothes were still not ready at the plant, and worse, the buses had by then stopped running, and he was stranded and "extremely out of place." He tried to cautiously hitch a ride home, but the vehicle he thought contained a black family was in fact an unmarked police car. Poitier was forced to go into a dark alley, while the cops followed in the car with gun cocked and pointed at Poitier's head. A dialog ensued in the car: "What should we do with this boy?" "Find out what he's doing over here." "Should we shoot him here?" Poitier was scared out of his mind, "but mad too, furious at what appeared to be their need to belittle me." Finally, after Poitier explained about the snafu with the dry-cleaning, and complied with the cops' order to "walk all the way home without looking back once," his life was spared. Reflecting upon that close encounter, Poitier had these pearls of wisdom on rage, injustice and peace:

> *Did I always have that peace? No. Wasn't I an angry young man when I played the teenager in* Blackboard Jungle? *Certainly I was a different young man when I was nine or ten, and when I was twelve or fifteen, and when I was twenty-seven. So how did I deal with my rage? I dealt with it in ways that were shaped by my early life, my family surroundings, my friends, the fact that I was a member of the black community that was indeed the majority of people in the country. All those things interplayed with each other over my early years to put a certain kind of youngster on that boat heading for Florida in 1943. And when that kid got to Florida and Florida said, "Oh, wow! Let's sit this kid down and tell him, or show him, or explain to him what the rules are," it was too late. You see, by then I had already fashioned*

my own rules—rules quite contrary to what Florida was then saying to me.[23]

So, what do Poitier's contemplations on the color of his skin have to do with me? Just about everything having to do with my attitude toward my race and ethnicity. I would not be as presumptuous as to compare myself to the noble Sir Sidney, but I, too, had my "Hong Kong curriculum." Before I arrived on these American shores at the ripe old age of eighteen years, I was quite fully formed and molded in my ways, "with a foundation that had had time to set." Because I was a member of a Chinese community "that was indeed the majority of people" in Hong Kong, with "images of wonderful, accomplished, interesting [Chinese] people around and about."[24] As you may recall, it was not too long ago that I boasted to be a Sinocentric. Hence, I also did not and do not "have a receptor" to take in any of "that color crap." Being raised and educated in a British colonial system, my beef, if any, was with my benevolent British colonial overlords. Not with the individual overlords, such as my British teachers or the occasional governmental officials, *per se*, but with the *system* which bred inferiority complex, and hence, implicit subjugation, in us the colonial *subjects*. Paradoxically then, race and color of my skin were never consciously an issue with me all my life. I count on my lucky stars that I have not had any brush with overt oppression by reason of my race. *Ergo*, I could not address oppression or relate to discrimination based on race or ethnicity on a personal level. I can and do certainly empathize on an intellectual level, but the exercise is decidedly academic. How, then, did I acquit myself in the Chin case (pun intended)? Deeply personally, zealously, and

---

[23] *The Measure of A Man, ibid.*, pp. 129-32.
[24] We proudly call ourselves "Hong Kongers" in the nowadays post-1997 Takeover era. It is exhilarating to watch the younger generations in Hong Kong rising up to demand true and full independence and democracy for the former British Colony.

with unflinching commitment. I sublimated my relative estrangement from racial politics into sexual politics. I did have compelling personal experience with discrimination, and have suffered oppression, based on gender and sexual orientation. Hence, for me, it was a simple and straightforward psychological substitution: I treated it as if Vincent were killed and deprived of his civil rights because he was a woman, or because he was gay. In truth, all hate crimes bear the same vile hallmarks of ignorance, intolerance and violence, whether the animus stems from race, color, creed, ethnicity, national origin, religion, gender, sexual orientation, sexual identity, age or disability.

In the afterglow of the case, however, I did not feel comfortable having or receiving any purported credit assigned to me, nor did I wish to engage in any activity that might be interpreted as seeking recognition. Racial injustice, when all was said and done, was not my primary or personal crusade; feminism and LGBTQ rights have been my calls to arms. I would, therefore, feel inauthentic, even opportunistic, as if I were an imposter, if I were to take even more than just one very muted nod for my humble part in the Chin case. There were many selfless and courageous champions who railed, and continued to strive, against anti-Asian, anti-Chinese sentiments and discrimination. Many of them were named in Helen's *meisterstück*, but there remain many, many other unsung heroes and heroines. To them, we owe our debt of gratitude for leveling the playing field and exorcising racism for the tens of thousands of young Asian Americans coming of age.

For too long, it has been too searing for me to revisit my "failure," on such an epic scale and under the harshest limelight, that was my fateful involvement in the Chin case. Mrs. Chin had never ever, even for a split second, intimated any blame on my part. Nonetheless, I had silently asked for her forgiveness, not for any wrongdoing but for my having "failed;" and she had graciously absolved me, far more powerfully than with words, with her loving friendship and trust in me. Therein rest my closure and mind at peace.

VII.

Land Baroness

After returning from Washington, D.C. to submit my Chin case report to the Civil Rights Division of the U.S. Department of Justice, life for me quickly returned to the pre-Chin case normal—not smooth, calm or easy, but normal. My youngest sister, Vivian, was arriving in August, 1983, to embark on her college studies. Because of her joining me in Michigan, I had purchased a very modest "starter home," a plain and simple 3-bedroom ranch in Troy, for us to move into; the closing was scheduled for early September.

It turned out to be too many unknowns and changes to my life all at once, with consequences that were not anticipated and which spelled vexing troubles. I had loved Vivian to pieces since the day she was born. Hence, I was overjoyed when she decided to come live with me while she furthered her education in the States. During the first couple of weeks after she arrived, we had a wondrous time catching up since I was last in Hong Kong in 1978. I also enjoyed introducing her to suburban life in Detroit, getting her ready for school. One of the mandatory lessons was driving instruction. She had never learned to drive, but she would have to in order to get to classes at the West Bloomfield campus. I could hardly believe it when she was really hesitant about learning driving, and asked me instead why I could not drive her to school. In suburban Detroit, unfortunately, public transportation was spotty, and one had to drive, I explained; I could drive her once in a while, but not on a daily basis. That minor incident should have clued me to issues that would develop soon in our interaction. I had not saved up enough to purchase a car for her, and thus, had to resort to renting a "wreck" from an acquaintance, Riley. Riley fixed up vintage huge American cars from the 1960s and 1970s; they were all on their last legs and barely running, but they were extremely economical to rent. Vivian, all of 5-foot, had to prop two or three cushions behind her back in order for her leg to reach the pedals to drive. I volunteered to be the driving instructor, and when she got a bit cocky after driving for a while and would not listen to my advice anymore, I had to pay to complete her driver's training with a Sears professional instructor. A couple of months later, I had enough money to buy her a very used Volkswagen "Dasher;" I figured a sturdy German-made vehicle should be better for her safety. I would learn a few years later, when she could afford buying her own cars, that she actually preferred the cushy, softer Japanese-made cars.

As a first-time homeowner, I had plenty to learn in short order. I did not know that there would be field mice in the garage in the winter. The mice chewed through some cables in my "Supra," cutting off heat in my car. Worse, they chewed through some other cables in Vivian's "Dasher," which caused her brakes to malfunction. She was born under a lucky star, thankfully, and she was smart and calm enough to maneuver the car to a safe stop after a harrying jaunt through traffic. Then there was lawn mowing, which was a chore that had never previously crossed my mind as a city dweller all my life up to that point. My ranch was small enough, but it sat on a relatively oversized lot. A lawn mower would have taken hours for just one cut. My senior partner, Jim, was generous enough to loan me his simplicity riding mower, alleviating much grief from this joyless task. Not having had "Shop 101," it was a wake-up call to me just how expensive it was to hire contractors to fix major and minor disrepairs in or around the house. That prompted me to start cruising the Do-It-Yourself aisles at Sears, accumulating tools and how-to manuals. One of most expensive items was repaving my crumbling circular drive-way (yes, for a starter home, I had a circular driveway) with new concrete; that was definitely not a Do-It-Yourself project though. The repaving was done just in time for me to take photographs with my new car on the driveway. My law firm had instituted a lease car program in early 1984, allowing each attorney to lease a "company car" within a prescribed budget. I loved my "Supra," but I figured the lease car program was in lieu of a salary raise, and thus I had better take advantage of it. Sadly, I parted with my "Supra," and chose a black Dodge "Daytona" with manual trans-mission. So as to make it closer to the trim-level that I had in my "Supra," at my own expense, I installed a custom audio system in it with a Harman Kardon head unit and ADS power amplifi-ers and loudspeakers. It is plain to see how I easily and always spent beyond my means: I *had* to have it, whatever *it* was, and so, I put it on credit. Hence, my debt load inconspicuously and mindlessly began to pile up higher than Mt. Everest. As with the parakeet, Bev surprised me with another pet, my "house warm-ing pet," a Siamese cat we named Mousy. He coexisted in uneasy truce with the three or four parakeets which I was then keeping in a floor-standing cage. The birds kept Mousy entertained, while Mousy kept Vivian company, as I, as usual, put in long hours at the office.

There was just one noticeable glitch even during those very early days after Vivian arrived. Even though I promptly intro-duced her to Bev, Vivian was very cool to her; they did not warm to each other at all. I chalked it off as Vivian's being reserved, and trusted that in time they would get to know each other better and get along well. How wrong I was. It was not long thereafter that things started unraveling between Vivian and me. At the time, I did not have a clue as to why we could not seem to see eye to eye. Coming fast at the heels of my Chin case challenges, such unexpected upheavals on my home front were most distressing. It pained me to no end to see that I was obviously unable to provide a joyful home for her, and yet I could not see nor understand how or where I might have erred. I was very distressed, confounded dismayed, and emotionally distraught for not getting along with my favorite sister. Our interaction continued to degenerate in the course of that first year. It was around this time that I restarted weekly psychotherapy sessions with a psychiatrist, but those sessions were not particularly helpful. Nonetheless, it served well enough as a sounding board for the multiple dilemmas with which I was confronted on the home front and at the office.

With the passage of time and maturity, I was finally gaining some insight to that regrettable interlude in my otherwise life-long fond sisterly relationship with Vivian. I had unrealistically expected a more mature baby sister coming to join me as my closest confidante and companion. Instead, I had on my hands a still somewhat sheltered and dependent younger sister. I had overlooked the fact that, while I had had eleven years of rough-and-tumble surviving on my own, that was the first time she had left the "nest." She had until then lived all her life with Mom and Dad, with just about everything well provided for. To compound matter further, I had changed more than even I realized. I had outgrown and was no longer the same Liza who was a part of that nuclear family unit which marched in lockstep in sync mostly with Mom's agenda. Vivian adored Mom to a fault, and followed Mom's ways and means to the letter. Hence, from Vivian's perspective, I had strayed and sorely disappointed her by not being the compliant family member, and by not adhering to established family routines and practices. I also did not realize then that ours was a very insular family unit, perfectly happy and content among ourselves, and not keen on accepting "outsiders" into its ranks. The biggest outsider of all, of course, was Bev; and by default, Bev became the scapegoat for the row brewing between Vivian and me. If I could have stepped into Vivian's shoes, I would have understood that she perhaps had expected me to exclusively devote to her and *our* life together. She did not expect that I would have *my* life, encompassing work, pastimes, a significant other, and freedom to roam. On the other hand, from my perspective, she seemed to be elbowing her way into my life, and implicitly demanding my conformance. My apparent conflict with Vivian was in no way her "fault;" she was simply being herself as how she was raised in our family. On the other hand, I had had twelve years of living away from those family dynamics and its unspoken code of conduct, propensities, eccentricities, and idiosyncrasies.

Without even realizing the root cause of our difficulties living under the same roof, I instinctively determined that I would not and could not give up my free will and my way of life. It broke my heart and caused me months of internal struggle and consternation, but I believed it would be good for her to become more independent and self-reliant; after all, she was in her twenties already. It pained me to no end to face the fact she might have to move out of my home. I was, of course, not abandoning her; I fully intended to continue looking after her, just not under the same roof. After her first school year was over, she went to Toronto to visit and stay with some family friends in May of 1984; that gave us both a respite from those emotionally tense and hurtful months.

In early spring of 1984, Bev and I also embarked on an unusual trip which was a diversion that I needed, and a chance to leave my Vivian conundrum behind for a week or so. Bev learned that a police department in Denver, or a suburb of Denver, was recruiting plebes, and she wanted to apply. With her bachelor's degree in Criminal Justice, she met the minimum prerequisite. Since her licensure as a private investigator two years prior, she had but one or two minor cases. Her college degree thus seemed wasted. I never questioned whether or how she would or could relocate to Colorado; being evermore the faithful enabler, I applauded her "ambition," gassed up the car and off we went. We took turns at the wheel and drove 24 hours nonstop to arrive in Denver. I still remember vividly how I immediately took to the fresh air, the blue sky, and the high mountain altitude. I felt liberated and revitalized, recharged and energized; I would revisit that "high" sixteen years later on our Millennial foray into New Mexico. The qualifying examinations spanned two days. I could tell that, by the end of the first day of written and oral examinations, that Bev either did not do well or her heart was not really into vying for admission to that police department. The second day consisted mostly of physical and performance tests. We both knew she did not fare well at all in that category, as she could not jump or run well as she was simply not athletic or physically active. I was quite disappointed, but only for a brief moment; I rationalized it away with how in a thousand ways this was not a job meant for her. We spent the ensuing couple of days for rest and recreation, visiting the Coors brewery, and driving up Pike's Peak. We had fun together, and I was just thrilled to be away from the office, from the law practice that I found increasingly drudgery.

The particulars of my debacle living with Vivian must have reached our parents who were understandably perturbed and concerned. They announced that they would be coming to stay with us that summer. By then, both of them had retired and were operating a small shop in Central, selling Chinese and Oriental home furnishings and furniture, home décor items and other collectibles. Mom had always dreamed to be a shopkeeper, and I could only imagine her delight tending shop. To spend the summer with us, they would have to close up shop for almost three months. I was excited to welcome them as they had not visited the States since my graduation from Barnard eight years earlier. What I had failed to appreciate was the primary objectives of their visit: to mediate and arbitrate any disagreement between Vivian and me, and to persuade me to allow her to continue living with me.

My humble starter home easily accommodated our parents; compared to the pigeon holes that passed for flats and apartments in Hong Kong, my basic 3-bedroom ranch was downright capacious. The family reunion was absolutely joyous for the first couple of weeks. Mom was serving up her fabulously delicious home cooking. Dad was fantastically interested in what seemed to him newfangled items such as riding mower, and tools and gadgets at the local hardware store. A neighbor across the street had a litter of domestic shorthair kittens to give away. I was captivated by one kitten in particular; Mom gave him a good once-over, and approved my pick. I christened him "Smokey;" we were the best of buddies until he passed away from old age in March of 1999, after which I would not have another pet again. My parents enjoyed grocery shopping at the local supermarkets which to them were cavernous and extremely well-stocked. We especially enjoyed our outings to tour "dream home" open houses, and marveled at the scale and opulence of those newly-built "McMansions." We embarked on a road trip to Pennsylvania to visit a family friend, and Vivian drove them up to Toronto to visit with relatives, as I could not leave the States.

The first sign of trouble came soon after the first week of my parents' arrival. I waited until they were sufficiently acclimated to their new living environment before I raised the specter of introducing them to Bev. I might have suggested having Bev over for afternoon tea, lunch or dinner, or even meeting her in a restaurant to share a meal, whichever they would feel more comfortable with.

Mom demurred, and conveniently ignored my request. When I renewed the proposition a couple more times, I was met with the same resistance and stone silence. Bev was clearly *persona non grata*. I was too naïve to have thought that Bev would and could be readily accepted into our "inner family circle." Moreover, I was foolishly blind to the fact that Bev had become my parents' scapegoat for my not getting along with Vivian and wanting her to move out of my house.

Life for me was, as can be well imagined, very exasperating that summer. I could not explain to Bev why my parents would not meet her, or why she could not come over to my house, but she was gracious enough not to insist otherwise. Life muddled through until one day that summer when Mom and I had our tête-à-tête, our personal summit meeting. It covered all sensitive and taboo subjects ranging from my lifestyle (to wit: lesbianism), to the risks of contracting AIDS, to why I would not let Vivian continue to live in my household. To my defense of my lesbian lifestyle, Mom retorted sharply, in English no less, "Do not prose-lytize me, and I'll not proselytize you." As for Vivian's continuing to live with me, I tried to explain my need to live my life without undue interference—however unintentional or well-meaning—such that I "had to draw the line somewhere." Mom in turn chided me, in English again, with "We Chinese people do not draw lines." The discussion exhausted and emotionally drained both of us. I believe ultimately Mom quietly respected my standing up for myself, and would not impose her will on me any further. Not long thereafter, we started looking for an affordable apartment for Vivian. We soon found a reasonable enough basement apart-ment in a nearby suburb, and started moving her in toward the end of August. I was emotionally distraught at the specter of hav-ing to practically chase my favorite sister out of my home. On the other hand, I could not see any other way out in order for me to honor my personhood. It was an extremely painful decision, and it clearly took a toll on my psyche and perhaps even my physical health. I could only imagine how equally emotionally jarring it was for Vivian to be compelled to live on her own, torn away from her "big sister," when all she knew was that she had done nothing to deserve the cruel outcome. Mom and Dad returned to Hong Kong at the beginning of September, leaving Vivian and I to fend for ourselves. Vivian and I reminisced how we cherished our summer spent with them, and how we had missed them sorely already just hours after they departed Michigan. When one is in such a tight-knit family, growing up and asserting one's independence is no mean feat, requiring courage, self-assuredness, and steadfastness. Oftentimes, back in those young adulthood days of mine, I still felt the dilemma of "can't live with them, but can't live without them" toward my parents and their influence over my life. It would require maturity—years of growing up—for me to comprehend and reconcile those internal conflicts.

It was early September, 1984, and life finally seemed to return to normal for me for the first time in more than eighteen months. I had completed my duties in the epic Chin case, and I was living by myself again, with a cageful of parakeets and two cats. Bev could come over to my house again. In stark contrast to images of valor, gallantry, intrigue, allure, prestige and affluence with which lawyers were associated in television shows and movies, my day-to-day work life as an attorney was decidedly mundane and largely unglamorous. It was thus on an ordinary Thursday morning, October 18, 1984, when something extraordinary happened.

It was a gorgeous autumn day in Michigan; the leaves had taken on glorious colors, the sky was strikingly blue, and the sun was gently warming the crisp and invigorating air—my favorite time of the year. I was at my office preparing a motion scheduled for oral arguments the following day—the usual Friday "motion day" in Wayne County Circuit Court. It was around 11 a.m. when all of a sudden I felt an "electric current" sensation coursing up my spine. It was sudden, totally unfamiliar and unexpected sensation. Since nothing of the sort had ever happened to me before, I paused momentarily from my work to regain my composure, after which nothing seemed to be out of place. About fifteen minutes later, I was struck by another and stronger "electric current" sensation rolling up my spine. Since the sensation was so unmistakable and strange, I could not ignore it at that point. When it happened again for the third time about another fifteen minute later, I told myself perhaps I was too tired or coming down with a 'flu, and that it might be wise for me to go home to rest for a couple of hours before continuing work on that motion.

I gathered up the pleadings and documents, and carried that file with me as I left for home. As I drove home, which was about a half an hour drive from my office without traffic, the "electric shock" sensations occurred more and more frequently. Instead of every fifteen minutes, it became every ten minutes, then five minutes. Worst of all, I was about mid-way home when the sensation became painful. The sensation became jolts of the most excruciating sharp pain taking over my spine, my back. I had to pull over and collapsed on the steering wheel after one of those particularly painful jolts. I had telephoned Bev before I left the office to wait for me at my home. By the time I somehow made it home, I could barely stagger out of my car, totally consumed by sharp, blinding pain coursing up my spine every five minutes or so.

It was obvious that I needed immediate medical care. We did not think of calling an ambulance, but rather, I had Bev drive me to the emergency room at the nearby Beaumont Hospital. Even though it was a very short drive, I was doubling over in unspeakable pain along my spine and losing consciousness. By the time we arrived at the emergency room, the pain had just about knocked me out. Bev told me later that the triage nurse, seeing a by then rather disheveled Oriental woman slumped over in the hospital wheelchair, asked if I could speak English, and Bev supposedly screamed at her: "Better than you do!" That was perhaps my one encounter with a racist slight, but I was in too much pain and heaving in and out of consciousness to realize it.[25]

I believe the emergency room doctors gave me intravenous sedatives as well as very strong pain relief medications, and I was admitted to the hospital. I gave my file, which I had clutched under my arm all the way to the hospital, to Bev for immediate delivery to the attorneys at my office so that they could adjourn the court hearing set for the following day. For the ensuing couple of days, I was given heavy pain relief and sedative medications. A neurologist who examined me thought I had meningitis. Things seemed to have calmed down somewhat when the spinal taps (lumbar punctures) started, almost as if every hour on the hour. It was a painful procedure whereby the doctor punctured my spine, with only topical anesthesia, to withdraw spinal fluid for testing. I was so inexperienced with hospitalization, and the medical and healthcare world in general that I did not know I could refuse the taps or to request a halt to them. I was raised to view doctors as "gods," as they supposedly knew everything about the body, diseases and cures. Their pronouncements, whether parsed as an observation, a recommendation, or an order, were to be obeyed, and, accordingly, it would be prudent of me to be a "good and compliant" patient. It was Sunday evening when the waves—nay, tsunamis—of blinding, cutting pain started rolling

---

[25] I can recall encountering one other incident of subtle racial bias, and it took me quite by surprise. A legal secretary with my former firm in Southfield was chatting with me one day about the motorcycle that she had just acquired. I knew hardly anything about motorcycles, and politely inquired more about it. She was clearly enamored and enthused with her newest acquisition and was thus unguarded with her speech. She responded with something along the lines of "Of course, it's a Harley-Davidson; I don't want any 'rice-burner.'" That was the first time I realized that she might have harbored racial bias if not racial animus; ironically and sadly, we had enjoyed an extremely fine work relationship otherwise.

up my spine again, except that this time, it was even worse than the pain I suffered three days earlier; it was a "twenty" on a pain scale of one to ten. The doctors finally, after several long, agonizing hours, gave me a very potent morphine injection to silence my piercing screams.

When I awoke Monday, I was in a total haze and hangover from the morphine. The doctors at long last seemed to have a clue as to what was wrong with me. They alluded to the fact that they kept getting "bloody taps," while spinal fluid was supposed to be clear and free of blood. Once in a while, a spinal tap might have punctured a blood vessel and rendered the fluid bloody, but that should not be the case with the many spinal taps that they had performed on me. Therefore, they concluded that I had suffered a subarachnoid hemorrhage. In layperson's terms, for unknown reasons, I had bled in and into my spinal canal, the space between my spinal cord and the arachnoid, a spider-web-like membrane that wrapped around my spinal cord. It was similar to a brain aneurysm, except that my bleed occurred, in my thoracic area or mid-spine instead of in my brain. It was and is a rather rare condition. As we know, brain aneurysms can be deadly. It had to be karma that I survived my hemorrhages; apparently, it was not time yet for me to depart this world.

A transfer to Henry Ford Hospital in Detroit, where I had been followed for my renal condition for a few years, was determined to be appropriate for further evaluation and treatment. A battery of tests—more aptly labeled "torture, Medieval-style"— awaited me at Henry Ford Hospital. In addition to more spinal taps, there was the myelogram. Only local anesthesia was administered while the radiologists strapped me onto an examination table that could be tilted in all directions. Supposedly, I had to be conscious for this particular torture to give the doctors "feedback" as they dug and probed. After a lumbar puncture, a medical dye was injected into my spinal canal, and I was being tilted every which way for the dye to course up and down my spinal canal; x-rays were then taken, which supposedly would reveal any blockage or abnormality in the spinal canal. The doctors suspected the cause of my hemorrhages to be arteriovenous malformation, a congenital defect represented by a tangle of blood vessels that disrupts blood flow in the brain or elsewhere in the central nervous system. To locate the suspect AVMs, the doctors administered another torture called angiogram. Catheters were inserted and threaded through my arteries and blood vessels and x-rays were again taken. However, they had to abandon that procedure as they did not have catheters small enough for my vessels. They never did find any AVM. I was too unfamiliar with the medical world then; I should have declined all such risky "diagnostic" tests and procedures. As I would learn in later years, not only were some of these invasive procedures potentially harmful to the patient, the test results were often inconclusive. Even when the sought after results were obtained, oftentimes there was no available treatment or cure. It was truly the epitome of academic exercise in futility, and not infrequently, at the expense of the patient's comfort or even life. With the advent of and advancements in magnetic resonance imaging (MRI) and other non-invasive scanning techniques, we are only beginning to come out of the barbaric age of probing and violating patients' bodies.

After about two weeks, the emaciated and battered me was discharged from the hospital with pain medications, but no definitive diagnosis, and certainly no prognosis or treatment. In less than one month, I felt as if my life had been mercilessly turned upside down. I did not know what to make of my hemorrhages. Would I hemorrhage in my spinal canal again, I wondered. As it was, I felt "cut down" to size and extremely vulnerable; I no longer felt invincible, at least not physically, as I did when growing up. I was barely thirty years old, otherwise poised to enter into the prime years of my life. How could something so unfathomable, painful and destructive happen to me without any rhyme or reason? Even though I returned to work right away, I was in an emotional slump for the ensuing couple of months, feeling sorry for myself on the one hand, and bemoaning what I perceived to be the end of my professional career on the other hand. In retrospect, it should have been plain to me that my body was telling me the simple message that whatever I was doing, my lifestyle, my personal and professional life, my circumstances, were literally "breaking" my back.

Smokey, my cat, was such a pal; he comforted me by snuggling up and practically sleeping on my face. My family also rallied to my aid. Mom wrote me lengthy letters with advice about foods and soups that would aid my recuperation. She urged me to consult with Uncle Lai who by then was a licensed Chinese medicine practitioner and acupuncturist in the San Francisco area. Uncle Lai would write a "prescription," and Mom would accordingly send me the packages of prescribed Chinese medicinal herbs for me to brew tea to restore my "chi" (life force). Vivian visited often and brought homemade soups. When I regained enough strength, I resumed my weekend visits with Vivian every other week or so. We had lunch together, and sometimes we shopped together, but mostly we talked incessantly to catch up on each other's life. It was gratifying, even though it had only been several months, to see her living her independent life astoundingly well. She was such a safe driver that I did not have to worry about her outings. She enjoyed clipping coupons, catching sales and shopping for bargains. She was obviously much more financially savvy than I was, spending her money far more sensibly. She was also doing very well academically at Oakland Community College. In just two short years, she would transfer to Walsh College and graduate with a Bachelor's degree in Professional Accountancy.

In the aftermath of the subarachnoid hemorrhages, I experienced aches in my mid-back and weakness in my legs. The psychological toll was actually even higher than the physical distress; the uncertainties and apprehension of what might come next constantly haunted me. I underwent another myelogram in the spring of 1985, and was told that there were scarred tissues in my spinal canal from the bleeds, which might have accounted for my pain and discomfort. MRI was just making its debut then; I had one taken at the University of Michigan Health System, but was told the scans were "like very grainy pictures," and did not yield much helpful or definitive information.

There was another startling change which manifested sometime after the hemorrhages. It was very subtle at first, but after a year or two, I began to notice that I had difficulty recognizing Chinese characters, and even more so with writing them. A similar amnesia also affected my not insignificant musical training; I could no longer read music, which was almost second nature to me. I recalled a telephone conversation in Cantonese with my parents when I was still hospitalized after my subarachnoid hemorrhages. I meant to say a certain word, but apparently a totally different word came out of my mouth instead. Mom understood what I was trying to express, and gently pointed out the discrepancy. Except for that telephone conversation, speaking Cantonese, thankfully, had not otherwise been permanently affected. I did not think much about that peculiarity at the time. However, in the course of a few years when my ability to read Chinese or music did not return, I realized that had to be the result of the damage wrought by the hemorrhages in certain parts of my brain. I deeply mourned my loss. I now can read Chinese only, and marginally, with enormous effort and concentration; it should not be so otherwise, given the fine and extensive education I had had with the Chinese language. As for reading music, those little dots and dashes on the music score might as well be a foreign language. I am grateful, though, that I am not a professional musician, and that my hearing is intact so that I can continue to indulge in my hobby as a self-professed audiophile, and continue to listen to, enjoy and "get lost in the music." In the final analysis, I should count my blessings that the hemorrhages did not wipe out my English language abilities or my legal training, as that would have meant a disastrous and premature end to my means of livelihood.

In May of 1985, I decided to pay Uncle Lai a visit, as we had talked often enough on the telephone about my symptoms. Bev tagged along for the week-long visit; we stayed at his and his wife's lovely home in Daly City. Twice daily, I went to his acupuncture clinic, just a few miles away, for treatment. When he had time after the afternoon treatment session, we would cheerfully discuss wide-ranging subjects from health, healing to music to Buddhism. In between sessions, Bev and I enjoyed the sights and tastes in and around San Francisco, one of my favorite cities. We also visited with Flora and her then husband, Bob; we stayed overnight in their spectacular condominium near Fisherman's Wharf. We had the good fortune of meeting Flora's father who also happened to be in town; he was a respected and successful banker in Hong Kong before his retirement and emigration to Toronto.

The healing with Uncle Lai was close to miraculous. After numerous acupuncture, cupping and "gua sha" (scraping) sessions, I felt totally revitalized; he literally gave me back my life—quality of life. Even my colleagues noticed the difference; I walked with a bounce again, and smiles had returned to my face. Unfortunately, the aches and pain in my back returned a few months later, and I became restless again, wanting—rather, wishing—all such "defects" would go away forever. I should have left well enough be, in retrospect. Instead, I pursued with my doctors again about viable treatment for the aches and pain in my back and the so-called scarred tissues in my spinal canal. They in turned suggested that I consult with certain specialists at the Cleveland Clinic. Bev and I drove to Cleveland in September of 1985. I brought with me all of my myelogram films and other tests results to meet with the specialist who advised me that there were only three renowned experts nationwide specializing in my particular rare condition; of the three, he recommended neurosurgeon Dr. Robert Spetzler in Phoenix, Arizona. I was elated, believing that I had finally located my "medical savior" to make me whole again.

After Dr. Spetzler reviewed my films, scans and medical records, a date was given to me for admission to the hospital in Phoenix with which he was affiliated. It was early November 1985, when I flew to Phoenix by myself. I was full of anticipation and hope for definitive answers, for my prognosis, and for appropriate treatment to alleviate back pain and to prevent future hemorrhages or complications from the previous bleeds. The first order of business, once I was admitted to the hospital, was yet another myelogram. Dr. Spetzler then informed me that the test showed a "complete block" in my thoracic spinal canal; I believe he indicated the T-9 area. He recommended laminectomy spinal cord surgery to investigate and presumably remove the blockage. After the surgery, he told me simply that he had removed two or three arachnoid cysts, about thumb-size, in my spinal canal which were impeding spinal fluid flow. When I asked how those cysts came about, he explained that they were most likely formed after my subarachnoid hemorrhages the year before. That was not what I was expecting to hear: in addition to worrying about whether I would suffer another hemorrhage, I then also had to worry about formation of arachnoid cysts. Little did I know then that things would in fact become worse, much worse. In the meantime, I recovered from that spinal cord surgery fairly quickly and effortlessly enough. It was not until almost a year later when I realized my legs had become very weak; I almost tripped and fell when I tried to quicken my steps crossing the street one day. I was prescribed a month or two of physical therapy, after which my legs seemed to function fairly normally again.

Since about late spring in 1985, there was another unusual project that, thankfully, distracted me from my back pain and related discomforts. Bev's home was located on one of two adjoining small residential streets remaining in an area that was rapidly developing, as high-rise office and commercial buildings sprang up all around. Word came that a substantial commercial real estate developer was interested in assembling and purchasing those residential lots to develop as a commercial parcel for office buildings. In years past, I had acquired three vacant lots on her street, and thus, was an interested party in the potential development proposals. I was also a familiar face to most of the neighbors, having been around for more than eight years. Dave and I and a couple of neighbors took it upon ourselves to canvass the neighborhood, hold neighborhood meetings, and share ideas about the potential commercial development, pros and cons. By early summer, we had formed a representative committee, and began meetings and negotiations with the developer's in-house counsel. By early fall, an offer to purchase was proffered by the developer to all of the lot owners and homeowners, contingent upon everyone agreeing to sell at the same time. After a few more weeks of haggling, all but one or two holdouts accepted the offer. It sounded simple and all too easy, but I and others worked very hard in those months to keep neighbors informed, liaison with out-of-town owners, and maintain unity among more than two dozen householders. There were many junctures at which the entire endeavor could have been derailed by a recalcitrant homeowner, an uncooperative neighbor, or unreasonable demands.

The stakes were admittedly high for me. If the sale could be successfully consummated, I would have sufficient money to pay off my consumer debts, and still have an appreciable amount left for investments. That would be a much welcomed reprieve and breakthrough for me, fiscally speaking. Otherwise, as my debt load was getting unmanageable, I could fall into financial ruins in short order. The real estate bonanza, if it materialized, would be a financial lifesaver for me. For Bev, the situation could not be more melodramatic. Bev had always planned on divorcing Dave once her daughter, Melanie, attained the age of eighteen years; she had announced and reiterated that intention over the years. As if on cue, in early January of 1986, a few months before Melanie turned eighteen years of age and in the midst of Michigan's frigid winter, Dave unceremoniously moved out of the home. Melanie chose to follow her father. Bev was in a panic, as she was not prepared to be financially independent, let alone to take over paying for the mortgage, utilities and the myriad of other expenses to continue living in that home. She had apparently been reducing her work-load and dropping clients in her massage therapy business. Tacitly, I was expected to be the enabler and rescuer once again. I could not well financially sustain two households, and hence, there was only one viable option. Even though I had just returned from my spinal cord surgery in Phoenix two months prior, I boxed up my belongings, moved in with Bev, and rented out my own home. With that arrangement, at least she did not have to worry about freezing or starving. Thus, ensuring the pending sale conclude on time was even more critical for her survival post-divorce, as she and Dave had already agreed on property division upon the sale of the home.

The pressure was on then for the pending sale to proceed on schedule, as Bev and I each had our compelling reasons to root for its timely closing. Early spring of 1986, was a busy sea-son for me, but that turned out to be only a preview of just how I would be consumed with multi-tasking in the ensuing few years. In addition to my full-time work as an attorney, I had to attend a series of hearings before the City Planning Commission and City Council on the developer's rezoning request. The entire exercise of parcel-assembling and sale proposal could have been unhinged if City approvals were not obtained. By then, Bev and I had also decided to dabble in investment real estate if and when the sale was consummated, as we each would have some money to invest. Moreover, we started looking for our home together, because we would have only 90 days to vacate once the sale was closed. I contacted LaVerne, the knowledgeable and friendly realtor who helped me find my starter home three years earlier. She was excited for Bev and me, and started working tirelessly to show us potential properties for our future home, as well as prospects for investment properties.

It was March of 1986, and we were still two months away from the target closing date; in other words, our real estate bonanza could still be a bust. LaVerne showed us a small, older bungalow with an oversized lot located just off a major thoroughfare in the heart of Troy. It was listed for sale at a very attractive price. Bev and I simply could not pass that up because of what we perceived as its potential for commercial development, given its prime location. Neither of us had any cash on hand. As luck would have it, Dad informed me that one of his longtime close friends, whom I called "Uncle" Woo, had a sum to lend. Uncle Woo was going to loan it to my parents toward their down payment for a condominium home in Hong Kong, but that purchase fell through. It was extremely unlike me, but I took a gamble that our real estate bonanza-in-the-works would indeed manifest, so that I could repay the loan with interest to Uncle Woo, as well as pay off the balance on the land contract in two short months. I could not even imagine what would have happened or what I could have done if my bet turned out to have been imprudently placed. Bev and I bought the bungalow in both of our names, equally, even though I alone procured all the funds for the purchase. We started a running tab then, for funds that I advanced or loaned to Bev for real estate investments and for her other expenses. It was understood that such loans and advances would not accrue any interest. Over the many years, that running tab had chalked up alarmingly high balances, been paid off a few times, remained outstanding most of the time, and it formed the basis for my burdensome responsibility for fronting most if not all of her financial outlays during our relationship.

The gods were smiling upon us as the group sale of the two residential streets did consummate in mid-May, and I was able to discharge my financial obligations to Uncle Woo and the seller of the bungalow in a timely manner. I made a mental note to myself never to undertake such high-wire-act transactions ever again; the risks and exposure were disproportionately lopsided, and the psychological pressure was horrendous. We were pleasantly surprised when, shortly after we purchased the property on land contract, a self-proclaimed developer contacted me to negotiate a potential sale. He apparently had plans to assemble nearby lots and develop the parcel for commercial developments. After the developer and I engaged in negotiations for a couple of weeks, he tendered an offer to purchase with a very attractive purchase price. Yet Bev must have felt jaded as our maiden venture into real estate investments appeared to her to have born fruits all too readily and easily. She demanded an even higher purchase price from the developer, despite my best efforts to dissuade her. The developer then abruptly cut off negotiations and withdrew his offer. I figured that Bev had perhaps overreached and overplayed her hand. There was nothing else we could do but to rent out the house as soon as feasible to derive a small income from our investment.

A couple of months later, I was in for a nasty surprise. Bev and I were served with summonses and a complaint filed in the Federal District Court, no less, in a suit brought by the sellers of the bungalow. My perusal of the complaint greatly alarmed me. It was not your garden variety complaint filed in a local trial court alleging one or another claimed mistake or misdeed in that buy-sell transaction. Rather, the crux of the complaint was that we, in purchasing the property, allegedly violated provisions of the Racketeer Influenced Corrupt Organizations Act (RICO), the infamous piece of legislation that brought down many a mobster. Our potential liability under RICO, if plaintiffs were to prevail, would have been treble damages. That would have meant filing for personal bankruptcy for both of us. Moreover, plaintiffs were represented by attorneys from a respectable large national corporate law firm. I did pause for a moment to wonder how the plaintiffs could have afforded to hire those high-powered lawyers. Perhaps there was someone else who put them up to and financed them for the legal showdown? I would never know, even as I had my suspicions. I shuddered after the complexity and gravity of the complaint before me sank in. Bev perhaps could not fully appreciate the severity of the down side or the ramifications of that nettlesome legal tangle, or she might have had too much confidence in my ability to ward off those foes. I, on the other hand, knew I needed legal assistance. The adage that whomever represents himself or herself has a fool for a client was certainly not lost on me, especially when the opposing combatants were admittedly formidable. I knew whom I needed there and then: my colleague, Marc, who had been a steadfast friend, wise counsel during the Chin case retrial, and a stellar legal scholar. Marc had by then left the firm to pursue further advanced studies, a graduate degree in Public Health at the University of Michigan. He was kind and generous in agreeing to take on our defense if I would help conduct legal research, do the "leg work" necessary for filing and the like, and help draft and prepare pleadings. I was only too happy that he agreed to serve as the "general" in this fight; I would gladly serve as the "foot soldier." Over the ensuing ten months, Marc and I worked together to prepare and file a number of pre-trial dispositive motions. Marc's outstanding legal analytical mind shone as he literally picked apart plaintiffs' complaint, count by count. His legal strategy succeeded in persuading the Court to dismiss all the counts in the complaint save two, the RICO claim and a claim for imposition of a constructive trust on the property. The RICO allegations were convoluted and complex, but it required even more intricate and elucidative arguments to debunk them. As even a layperson would understand, it is no mean task to be able to obtain a dismissal of the lawsuit before trial. Marc achieved precisely that, in a David-versus-Goliath contest that was sheer brilliance.[26] It may be cruel irony that no developer approached us again to purchase that property for development; we finally managed to sell it eighteen years later after Bev and I had parted company. As it was, that lawsuit was only a warm-up preparing me for future legal frays as we waded ever deeper in the investment real estate swamps.

By the time we received the sales proceeds from the group sale of the two residential streets, Bev and I were busy closing on several homes in Troy that we bought for investment. As only a relatively small down payment was required when buying on seller-financed land contracts, we were able to maximize our capital. That was the mid- to late-1980's when "zero-down" real estate investment was all the rage. That was the era of Gordon Gekko's touting "Greed is good," and Donald Trump's *The Art of the Deal* passing for a novice investor's bible, even though that was not my cup of tea. The properties we bought were all older homes with around 1,000 square feet of livable space, quite ideal for renting out to single professionals or young families. One notable exception of an acquisition was a larger than 5-acre parcel with two very old cinder-block bungalows. When we ran low on capital, we joined forces with our realtor, LaVerne, who by then was a good

---

[26] *McMullen v. Christenson*, 678 F. Supp. 1277 (E.D. Mich., 1987).

friend, as partners; it would be either an equal one-third split, or LaVerne would hold a one-half interest with Bev and me each holding one-quarter. In the span of just a few years, and at the height of our real estate investment venture, we bought, rented out and were managing ten homes, including a condo in Bloomfield Township and a home in Auburn Hills, as well as 1-1/2 street block of vacant residential lots in Troy. In 1988, I was even able to purchase the apartment below my parents' in Hong Kong, and asked my parents to manage it for me. By then, they had closed their retail shop in Central, and had been working as real estate agents. That condominium purchase turned out to be a smart and timely acquisition, as will be detailed in these pages.

With my own home having been rented out in January of 1986, and Bev's home being sold to make room for office buildings, we had to look for a home for ourselves, even as we scouted many rental homes for potential investment. LaVerne showed Bev numerous prospects in our price range, but nothing impressed her until one fine afternoon when Bev excitedly telephoned me at my office to urge me to go and view a certain home for sale located in the northwestern corner of Troy. When I pulled up onto the driveway, I saw a charming, older 1-1/2 story Cape Cod, located on more than 3 wooded acres by a brook. A few hundred yards across the street was the Lloyd A. Stage Nature Center. It was a highly desirable residential neighborhood in Troy, with many new subdivisions of imposing McMansions dotting the landscape. The interior of the home was cozy and quaintly decorated; the stairs leading up to the second level had a charming solid oak banister. A sizable wooden deck stretched out from the back door, and looked out onto the vast backyard and the deep woods beyond, all part of the homestead. The asking price was somewhat beyond what we had budgeted for, but with LaVerne's deft negotiations, we purchased and moved into our new home in mid-June. Hercules, Dave's 120-pound massive mastiff dog, moved in with us, as Dave nonchalantly announced that he no longer wanted him. By the end of that summer, Bev and Dave had finalized their amicable divorce. Hercules was trained by Dave to be particularly unfriendly and antisocial; accordingly, he barely tolerated my existence. I had to be very much on guard whenever I was home alone with Hercules.

There was a sea change in our lives and routines after our real estate bonanza from the group real estate sale. First of all, after my surgery in Phoenix, my legs and back were too weakened to engage the heavy clutch for the manual transmission in my Dodge "Daytona." As much as I detested it, I had to swap my company car with a colleague, and ended up driving a nondescript Pontiac "6000 LE" sedan. In just a couple more years, the firm's leased car program would be discontinued, and I would end up driving a very used Nissan "Sentra" that I bought from LaVerne and her husband, Mike. It was a long way—downscale—from my Toyota "Supra," but I was then bent on conserving money for more real estate investments. I was as usual very generous with Bev, though, on the other hand. In the spring of 1987, when I was at the Nissan dealership for some routine maintenance for my humble "Sentra," I noticed a special promotional lease program for the Nissan "300ZX" sports car with a T-roof, Bev's "dream car." Without hesitation, I leased a flaming red one for a 5-year term, drove it home and surprised and thrilled the "love of my life" to no end. That was one fast and easy enough way how I parted with my hard-earned dollars.

Then there was Bev's casual announcement one day that she was stopping work as a massage therapist. There was really nothing much I could say or do in response as it was her decision. I presumed that she must have found it too physically straining as she was then in her mid-30's. To my query as to what she would then do for a living, she indicated that she would clean houses. There were many affluent homeowners in our neighborhood who would need and could afford regular house cleaning services, and thus, she should not want for clients. Of course, I thought it was such a waste of her education and abilities for her to resort to physical labor for her occupation. As it turned out, she pursued house cleaning only part-time, and then only sporadically. After just a few years, she stopped doing that altogether, and instead, proclaimed that she was writing a book; there will be more on that topic in later pages. I was naïve in believing that income from our numerous rental homes would provide her with a financial cushion; I was wrong. As our properties were fairly highly leveraged, outlays often exceeded income. Thus, our investment properties were terrific for generating tax deductions, but not so much for producing income. As such, her running tab with me kept running higher and higher. I was not concerned about it for a good number of years as I thought we would keep having real estate bonanzas which would enable us to more than pay off our respective debts. On the conscious level, I did not begrudge her economic dependence on me, as I reasoned that being a life partner meant supporting her through thick and thin, even though we had understood that our relationship was supposed to be an equal partnership. I further reasoned that she—the one seemingly with the Midas touch—contributed to our partnership in-kind and in other ways such as scouting and strategizing for our real estate investments. Over the years though, I not only felt the financial burden but also begrudged the lopsided unfairness. Once the seed of inequity was sown, it silently and insidiously became toxic to the relationship. Gradually but surely, I also subconsciously dismissed that disconnect with denial, yet all the while wondering and bemoaning what could have come between us.

There was yet another bone of contention that I unwittingly internalized. After we moved into our new home, Melanie came over to visit her mother quite often. They would enjoy sitting on the back deck, playing badminton in the backyard, swinging in the hammock, and in general, having a swell time. I was glad for them that our new home was so conducive to fostering mother-and-daughter togetherness. However, subconsciously, there was a deep sense of resentment fermenting in me. It was understood that Vivian was not allowed to come over to visit. Bev also started badmouthing my family members, even though I tried to defend them. After all, one cannot really or easily change another's opinion, and I could not change Bev's mind or opinion. It all stemmed from the very awkward and difficult times we had when Vivian first arrived in the States, and my parents' not agreeing to meet Bev when they stayed for the summer of 1984. That there was "bad blood" between them was an understatement. Still, there I was, caught between my beloved family and the "love of my life." I was offended and miserable, but I refused to acknowledge my misery. Instead, I pretended that I was living in "paradise" for the first time in my life, as I shared my life with a longstanding significant other, owned my home and real estate holdings, and had an established professional career. In the ensuing years, the gulf between Bev and my family would deepen and widen, and my internalized conflict would grow ever more tormenting.

My day-to-day life also went through a seismic change after we started playing "land baroness." Essentially, I was juggling two full-time jobs. My day job, fortunately, had become slightly more palatable because I had discovered "non-combat" legal work. Our firm's Of Counsel, a semi-retired experienced attorney, Moe R. Miller, took me under his wings and introduced me to the world of business transactions. He had many family-owned and small businesses as clients, mostly party stores and liquor stores. He taught me the high art of counseling clients in a buy and sale transaction, the fine points in reviewing commercial leases and negotiating with landlords, securitizing assets for the seller, financing for the buyer, and efficiently coping with the mountains of paperwork in consummating the transaction. He would ask me to accompany him to closings, when oftentimes the buyer and seller were still haggling over inventory valuation, allocation of the purchase price, and a myriad of details that could derail the closing. I enjoyed that transactional practice, and I was quite adept at it. Above all, at the end of all the posturing and huffing and puffing, I especially relished the classic happy ending as the parties shook hands when the transaction was finally closed. Little did I know then that Moe had shown me the way to building my own practice just a few short years later.

My "night job," on the other hand, was much more arduous because it was new and different to me: managing and maintaining ten rental homes. As those were older homes built in the 1950's or earlier, much needed to be done before we could even rent them out. Bev would usually "move in" first with her cleaning supplies, paint and paint rollers and brushes. She would spend almost a week repainting and cleaning the entire interior. I would change into my work dungaree and work boots every evening after work and dashed over to one or more of our rental homes. Hauling my two heavy tool boxes and a menagerie of hand and electrical tools, I would play handywoman, fixing everything from a toilet tank to door locks to plumbing leaks. It was strictly "Shop 101 on the fly," learned as I did. Then there was the 5-plus acre parcel, mostly of which was covered in thick weeds. Troy had weed abatement ordinances; if we did not keep the weeds shorter than the designated height, Troy would have merrily sent in their commercial mowers and charged us an exorbitant fee for their "services." Hence, during the summer, I would spend the entire Saturday or Sunday every week mowing five acres. I became very tanned and physically fit, which made my desk-bound colleagues at the office wonder. One should also not forget that our home was situated on 3-plus acres. Granted that only slightly more than one acre was "tamed," but mowing and weed-whacking around our vast green patch took another few hours weekly in the summer.

In another five years, Bev would suddenly become paranoid, for lack of a better word, about her imagined "intruders" trespassing into our woods in the back acres. She demanded that the shrubs and underbrush be cleared so that she could "see through" the woods and detect whatever trespassers might be doing in there. I could not persuade her otherwise; she was throwing a fit every other day over it. She was enraged beyond reason, and she was on the verge of getting into a nasty verbal fight, if not a physical one, with some neighbors during the day while I was at the office. We could not afford a lot clearing crew, and hence, I had no choice but to take out my gas-powered professional grade weed-whacker and started clearing the back acres. I was, however unwittingly and unwillingly, the ultimate enabler once again. It was hard, back-breaking, sweaty work. Over that summer, I succeeded in clearing a sufficiently extensive area of the woods to assuage her fury and paranoia. The shrubs and underbrush would only grow back the following year, but I refused to weed-whack them again as my physical health was by then not in the best of shape.

In addition to conquering weeds and shrubs, as a landlord, there was the constant paperwork for me to keep up with for bill paying, rent collecting, record keeping, tax reporting and on and on. Of course, as the lawyer between the two of us, I also had the responsibility for preparing all leases and related documents to comply with applicable laws and regulations. When tenants failed to pay rent on time or were destructive to the premises, it was also tantamount upon me to prepare and serve notices to quit, file complaints and appear in court to evict tenants. In fact, anything remotely related to anything legal was within my province of responsibilities, and that certainly encompassed negotiating and reviewing real estate sale and purchase agreements and closing documents. While Bev would have completed her share of the work after the first week or so of a vacant property coming on-line, my work continued nonstop throughout the year.

There was always someone moving in or moving out, and repairs, paperwork and bookkeeping to be tended to. I was breathlessly busy. I did not mind the grueling work at the time, because our initial experience with real estate investment had been most positive and rewarding, reaping us a very respectable return. Hence, the Pavlovian effect had taken hold, and I was spurred on by the expectation of more real estate "bonanzas" to come; after all, I thought, the real estate boom in Troy was only beginning.

There was a lovely surprise at the end of that fast-paced and momentous summer of 1986. I received a telephone call from Pearl one day out of the blue. As we happily chitchatted along to catch up on the latest—we talked only once every couple of years if that—she dropped me a bombshell: she had recently fallen in love with a woman, Ellen, and had finally found happiness in a relationship, after her marriage and divorce and dating a plethora of male suitors. "Finally!" I thought to myself, "What had taken you so long?!" Still, I was absolutely thrilled for her—and for myself, in a vicarious way.

As things turned out, Winnie and her partner at the time, Judy, were going to New York City in October to shoot a movie on location; Winnie was in charge of Planning for the film. The movie was *An Autumn's Tale*, starring international star Chow Yun-fat, co-starring Cherie Chung and Danny Chan. The film would later win the Hong Kong Film Award for Best Film, Best Cinematography, and Best Screenplay. For his role in the film, Chow won his second Golden Horse Award for Best Actor. Several SSGC classmates thus decided on having an impromptu mini-reunion in New York City. Not only did I get to see and talk with Pearl, who looked resplendent just as a woman in love (with a woman), I also reunited with Sylvia for the first time in ten years, since our college graduation. Sylvia joined one of our dim-sum lunches, with her four young children in tow. It turned out to be a fabulous gathering; quite a few classmates with whom I had lost contact showed up, including Margaret Seto, Selina, Anita, Emily Tong. Of course, Vivian also came down from Boston to join the fray. We listened intensely to Winnie as she recounted, almost in tears, how Rita's suicide shook her to her core. Of course, there was much laughter as well as we window-shopped in mid-town Manhattan, and talked nonstop until the wee hours of the night. We enjoyed many gourmet meals, the most memorable for me was the dinner at "Pig Heaven" on Third Avenue. When I returned home from the reunion, Bev did not shove me in rage and jealousy that time, probably because I had told her that Pearl had found a life partner. Pearl and Ellen married in 1987; it was not a "legal" marriage *per se*, but it was celebrated as a very formal, elaborate and elegant affair. Even though I was unable to attend because my immigration status at that time would not permit me to leave the United States, I was enthralled when I viewed the video-tapes of the festivities. Both Chinese and western traditions were observed in their wedding ceremonies, with their many women friends attending in tuxedoes and evening gowns. That trend-set-ting wedding remained the talk and envy of the community for some years.

Speaking of immigration, there was yet another delightful surprise awaiting me before the close of 1986. Against all odds, the Immigration Reform and Control Act, formerly known as the Simpson-Mazzoli Act which had failed to pass Congress in 1982 and 1984, was signed into law by President Ronald Reagan on November 6, 1986. At first blush, I was despondent when I learned that, while the law did update the Registry Date, the updated date was January 1, 1972—eight-and-one-half months *before* I first arrived in the United States; in other words, I had missed my eligibility by just eight-and-one-half months. Such insult upon injury, I thought to myself. However, to my glee and elation, another provision in the law increased the immigrant visa quota for Hong Kong from a measly 600 annually to 5,000, an almost nine-fold increase. I believe that provision was enacted as members of Congress were mindful of Hong Kong sovereignty's being slated to revert to China in 1997. Accordingly, the increase was a humanitarian measure to accommodate the anticipated "mass exodus" from Hong Kong. The quota increase meant that the decades of backlog should fairly quickly evaporate. My application for labor certification had been approved for several years, but I was waiting, "forever," for the availability of an immigrant visa. With that significant visa quota increase, my wait should thankfully be cut short dramatically. How short? By October of 1987, my turn was up; that was considered lightning fast. I was scheduled to appear for an "adjustment of status" (from non-immigrant to an immigrant) interview in December. A friend and fellow attorney who specialized in immigration law, Charles Owen, was kind enough to represent me *pro bono* at that interview held at the District Office of the INS in Detroit. We both knew that my adjustment application could not be granted because of a technicality—that I had by then exhausted my legal periods of stay in the United States—but we appeared to ask for discretionary relief so that my application could be held in abeyance while the file was promptly forwarded to the U. S. Consulate in Hong Kong for visa processing. I would have to apply for immigrant visa issuance at the Consulate in Hong Kong, and then return to the States to be "admitted" as an immigrant/legal permanent resident. With Chuck's capable representation of me at the interview, all proceeded well as planned without a glitch. My decade-long immigration nightmare was at long last almost over, pending the procedural and technicality step of a trip back to Hong Kong.

I was not the only one with immigration in mind. Lina announced in late 1986, that she wanted to emigrate to Canada, with her daughter, Juliana. By then, she had divorced Joe, and had patched things up with Mom and Dad. She left Regina, Saskatchewan, and returned to Hong Kong in 1977 when she was pregnant with Juliana, without completing her bachelor's degree. She felt it was time to pick up where she left off, education-wise. Originally, she had planned to relocate to Toronto, but at the last minute, she changed her mind and decided instead to call Windsor her new home. Vivian had by then fairly blossomed, was thriving and enjoying her independent life, and faring well academically. I could not have been more pleased and proud; the heartaches and recriminations of her first year in the States were all but forgotten and forgiven. Once Lina decided to relocate to Windsor, just across the river from Detroit, Vivian was excitedly preparing to welcome Lina and Juliana whom she hadn't seen for about four years. She found a very affordable two-bedroom upstairs apartment for them in an Italian neighborhood. She would even shop for groceries and necessities for them when they first arrived in early June, 1987. My first meeting with Juliana was most memorable; I was at Vivian's apartment when they arrived. Our course, she had no recollection of my visiting her in Hong Kong when she was one year old. To her, having another aunt whom she had never met was a very novel idea. She did not warm up to me at first, but by lunch, she had already accepted me as part of the inner circle. Juliana was just turning ten years of age then, but she learned English very quickly in school. She was the only exception in my family whom Bev liked and welcomed. Bev had invited her to our house for overnight stays at various times. During the day, she and Juliana would play badminton, or take a walk in the park, or take in a movie. On weekends, we would visit local museums to view special exhibitions, dinosaurs being Juliana's favorite.

Lina enrolled in the University of Windsor and majored in Business Administration, while working part-time as a waitperson at a popular Chinese restaurant. By then, Vivian had generously given Lina her Nissan "Stanza," so that Lina and Juliana could get around. The four of us got together once a month, usually on a Sunday. It would be a full day affair, starting with brunch, and on to shopping, then more eating and shopping, and a late dinner. I cherished the family togetherness, our conversations, and our sisterly squabbles; we were all so young and vital then. Who would have guessed that we, the three sisters, would have the opportunity to be so close together at that stage of our lives. In retrospect, those were very happy, carefree days. Of course, I missed Lilian, but missing her had always been a sad misgiving and a sorry given of my existence.

In the late summer of 1987, Bev and I, along with throngs of friends and well-wishers, bid a tearful farewell to Mrs. Chin as she departed for her hometown, Kaiping in Taishan County, China. Both the Federal retrial and the civil wrongful death suit had by then concluded. She did not want to remain in the States to be reminded of her irredeemable loss. We would miss her heart-warming smiles, her righteous and unflinching spirits, and of course, her home-cooking. I promised to write to her, even though I had not written a letter in Chinese in years. With a very heavy heart, we watched her disappear from our midst and onto that jet plane that would carry her to her new-old chosen home a vast ocean away.

1988 was undeniably a memorable year. In June, Vivian graduated from Walsh College with a Bachelor's degree in Professional Accountancy. Mom and Dad flew in to attend her commencement. Vivian had by then moved to a lovely apartment in Wixom, a suburb northwest of Detroit. For the first time, our entire family was together since I left Hong Kong in 1972. It was a very special and joyous summer. At my request, Bev was considerate enough to leave our home for a day, so that Mom and Dad and Vivian could visit at my home. As far as I could remember, that was the only time they were at my house. Bev and my "clan," as she deridingly called my family, were still bitterly at odds with each other. That acrimony was a constant source of distress and friction for me. It was a Hobson's choice, but I could not very well side exclusively with Bev or my family. The untenable position that Bev's stance had put me in was destructive and painful.

Upon her graduation, Vivian, just as I did some years prior, was granted one year of Practical Training. She was hired as a junior accountant with a public accounting firm in Detroit, while she studied and sat for the series of examinations to qualify as a Certified Public Accountant. Meanwhile, she had decided to continue her studies to attain a Master's degree in Professional Accountancy. A year later, she was hired by AAA Michigan as an Internal Auditor. Like me before her, her employer applied for H-1B nonimmigrant status for her, which allowed her a maximum of six years of employment authorization.

While our family was enjoying our reunion the summer of 1988, I knew that I would be returning to Hong Kong to apply for my immigrant visa at the U.S. Consulate. I was waiting for the Consulate's notification of the appointment date. That notice came in mid- October with an appointment date in early November, 1988. I was ecstatic beyond belief; that was the last step in my prolonged quest for permanent resident status—the "green card." I wanted to stay for a more extended period of time with that particular trip home, so as to spend more time with my parents. Moreover, knowing that I would become a U.S. permanent resident and eventually a citizen, I wanted to "soak up" everything Hong Kong for one last time. I asked my firm for a three-month sabbatical which was granted. Bev wanted to go with me. I thought it would be an excellent opportunity for her to see and understand my background, my hometown, and my people. I was not thinking of how she and my parents would get along; I optimistically believed that everyone would at least be cordial and polite. After all, it was a joyous occasion of my finally getting the "green card."

Bev and I left for Hong Kong in late October. It was the first time in ten long years since I had been back to Hong Kong. We were welcomed by Mom and Dad when we landed at the airport. We took a double-decker bus from the airport on the Kowloon side, going through one of the tunnels, to the Hong Kong side, and arrived at my parents' apartment in the Mid-Levels, located practically across the street from SSGC. I could tell Bev was already in culture shock from the bus-ride. Everything seemed strange and unfamiliar to her; truth be told, everything seemed different to me as well. To her, the masses of humanity, the noise, the lights, the jam-packed buildings, were an assault to her senses and sensibilities. In fact, one afternoon as we were going to take the subway somewhere, she adamantly refused to ride the escalator to the lower platform, because throngs of people were swirling around her and rushing toward the escalator; she stood there frozen, or she had completely freaked out.

My parents' apartment was a typical smallish Hong Kong flat. It was beautifully furnished with exquisite rosewood and blackwood furniture pieces. It was also tastefully decorated and accented with many Chinese artifacts from jade to porcelain to vintage ivory. The walls were covered with exquisite Chinese brush calligraphy scrolls and Chinese water color and ink paintings. I slept in one of the two bedrooms on a small couch; Bev slept in the living room on another couch. The first week went by uneventfully enough with everyone behaving guardedly. Bev was polite enough and enjoyed the sights and sounds, the meals out, and Mom's home cooking. However, after the initial week, all hell broke loose. Mom and Bev started snarling at each other. Bev claimed Mom slammed the door close on her. Bev in turn showed her displeasure by refusing to talk to Mom and Dad, and not cooperating in general. Things deteriorated very rapidly from there. What was I thinking about when I agreed to bring Bev with me?! Obviously, I was not thinking clearly at all. There was only one solution to that increasingly antagonistic standoff: I had to situate Bev somewhere else pronto. Bev would have been happy to go back to Michigan there and then, except that we had made arrangements with Mrs. Chin to rendezvous in Hong Kong, and we would then take an 18-day guided tour of China. That tour was scheduled to commence in mid-November, after my interview at the U.S. Consulate. It dawned on me that I owned the apartment a floor below my parents'; it had been rented out to a British couple. I do not remember whether it was I or Mom who came up with the idea of asking my tenants to let Bev stay at their spare bedroom (actually, the servant's quarters) for a few weeks. We asked, and the British couple graciously agreed to take in Bev. That was one real estate investment of mine that turned out to be a lifesaver; World War III averted.

It was perhaps my third visit to the venerable building on Garden Road in Central that housed the U.S. Consulate, a building that represented hopes and dreams to many over the years. With my appointment letter, I did not have to queue up for hours for entry. My previous visits to the Consulate were to apply for my foreign student visa. Those visas, being nonimmigrant visas, were highly discretionary. It was incumbent upon the applicant to demonstrate convincing nonimmigrant intent; that is, he or she will return to his or her home country after the "temporary" visit to or stay in the United States. The interviews for my foreign student visas years prior turned out to be uneventful enough; even so, I was justifiably nervous, as one unintended misstep could have meant complications or denial of the visa. In stark contrast, I was rather enjoying my visit to the Consulate this time around. I felt that I had earned my "green card," after years of angst and uncertainty; I had paid my dues. I do not remember much about the interview itself; it obviously went very smoothly. It was more a formality than any substantive screening of me as an applicant. I was not nervous, and the immigrant visa was duly issued. It was almost anticlimactic.

Mrs. Chin arrived in Hong Kong from Kaiping in early November, and we had a joyous reunion. She looked healthy and much more relaxed; the stress and strains on her face had lifted. A year of being away from the Chin case tragedy, being with her people, eating local foods, and living a simple life, had ostensibly been good for her. Bev and I did correspond with her on a frequent and regular basis since she left Michigan. She wrote to us in Chinese; I would translate Mrs. Chin's letters to Bev, and in turn, Bev would write a few paragraphs in simple English which Mrs. Chin could understand. I would reply in Chinese even though Chinese writing was becoming more and more laborious for me; I had to increasingly rely on my trusty English-Chinese dictionary.

We embarked on our China tour with an express train ride from Hong Kong to Guangzhou. I was told that Mom and Dad had taken me with them on a China trip when I was perhaps three years of age, but of course, I had no recollection of that expedition. China then was still very much an insular country; foreign investments and travelers were only beginning to trickle in. Looking back, it was fortunate that I made my China tour then, before the onslaught of globalization which has totally altered the face of not only China's large metropolitan cities but also the countryside. I was able to see China as it had been, more or less, for thousands of years. Guangzhou is the provincial capital of Guangdong Province. It has been a bustling city for dynasties; it is the hub for Cantonese-speaking Chinese. Other Chinese cities and locales may be famous for their scenic beauty or historic sites, Guangzhou has always been feted for its cuisine. One simply cannot have a bad meal in Guangzhou. It was thus a very belly-pleasing way to start our China tour. We visited one of the war memorials commemorating the martyrdom of 72 revolutionaries who fought against the Qin Dynasty in the Huanghuagang uprising in the early 20th century. As I strolled through the site, my thoughts turned to my maternal great grandfather who was a martyred revolutionary in another uprising in Guangzhou of the same era. I patted myself on the back for having hailed from such a very fine and proud warrior pedigree.

We boarded a domestic flight the next day bound for Guilin. It was refreshing, if not startling, to see the ground crew paddling their bicycles on the tarmac to service our plane. We were there to admire the ethereal scenic landscape formed by eroded limestone, famed throughout the ages the world over. We took a riverboat cruise down the idyllic Li River as it wound through the limestone rocks. As we glided along the River, we watched as the cooking staff fish from the River, then chop and hack, slice and dice the undeniably fresh ingredients as they prepared our lunch on deck. I had to admit that I lost my appetite just a tad, being more accustomed to cooking with and eating the not-so-fresh supermarket-dressed ingredients. There were many hawkers on the cruise boat, selling everything from typical tourist souvenirs to jade (most likely colored stones) chops with one's name custom-carved in ornate Chinese characters. Wherever we went, we were swarmed by panhandlers young and old.

From Guilin, we flew to Shanghai. There was a comic moment on board as flight attendants handed out the Chinese equivalent of the peanut snack packs to the passengers. Inside each pack were a few candies and a couple of crackers, and something that resembled a small piece of chocolate. The Westerners on the plane wondered aloud, probably out of an abundance of caution garnered from past mishaps, what gastronomic delight awaited them. For those pining for a chocolate fix, I was the bearer of unwelcomed truth: it was in fact a Chinese snack delicacy—a piece of marinated and preserved duck gizzard, definitely not for the faint-of-heart Occidental. I heard shrieks and moans up and down the aisle of that small jetliner. Shanghai was far too large and fascinating a city for us to explore in only two days. What I remembered most vividly was our visit to the Jade Buddha Temple. The jade Buddha statues were impressive indeed, but what was more captivating was when a large column of monks in their flowing saffron and grey robes filed in for worship. They were chanting sacred sutras as they proceeded to the main hall; their chants, accented by the occasional bell clanging softly, were serenely mesmerizing. Bev might have had an epiphany of sorts there as she reminisced and spoke glowingly about those monks even years later. On the more down to earth level, the street vendors of Shanghai tempted us with aromatic pan-fried scallion pancakes, fresh steamed dumplings, and very filling Shanghai meat and vegetables buns. We merrily ate our way through the city those two days.

Hangzhou, a few hours train-ride south of Shanghai, was next on our agenda. Our tour guide was beyond apologetic as he explained that an unintended mix-up had resulted in his not being able to procure First-class train tickets for the entire tour group of more than twenty. Most of us would have to be relegated to the notorious "Third Class Hard Seat" sections of the train. The group rightfully decided to give the few First-class seats to the elderly, Mrs. Chin included. Bev and I headed for the Third Class Hard Seat compartment. What an eye-opening experience that was! First of all, there was no seat at all; the few "hard seats" available in the compartment were occupied by locals who had the smarts to board the train much earlier on. Hence, it was standing room only for us. The floor was beyond filthy; it had not been cleaned for eons. En route, passengers were coughing and sneezing and worse, spitting on the floor at whim. I kept shifting my standing legs, as if that would help fool myself into thinking that I had somehow transported myself to a more sanitary environment. If breathing were optional, I would have temporarily suspended my breaths so that germs could not invade my body. The train-ride somehow stretched out to last much longer than just a few hours, probably because of traffic; most of the time, it was immobile or grinding on sluggishly on the tracks. When we at long last arrived at Hangzhou, the hotel awaiting us was the most modern, exquisite, and luxurious thus far, as if to reward us for having survived Third Class Hard Seat. Bev and I jumped into the bathtub almost with our clothes on; our skin was breaking out from the unimaginable filth on the train-ride. Our foresight to have brought with us antibacterial soap saved the day. Our reward for having survived Third Class Hard Seat was a most elegant dinner at the hotel that evening. We were entertained, as if we were royals in ancient palaces, by a consort of musician playing traditional Chinese musical instruments; enchanting Chinese music wafted through the air as we enjoyed a first-rate feast. Hangzhou is famous for its breathtakingly beautiful West Lake. We enjoyed taking lots of photographs at the Lake the following day. The picturesque Lake was obviously very popular with the locals. There must have been thousands of families there enjoying the scenery, and everyone was angling for the best backdrop for snapping photographs. We also visited a historic pagoda, one of many that we would encounter on that tour.

We crisscrossed the country again, flying west from Hangzhou to Xian. The air was so thick with smog in Xian that the firmament was of an indescribable color day and night. The highlight of our visit to Xian was the famed Terracotta Army of Emperor Qin. The discovery of the Terracotta soldier sculptures in 1974 stunned the world, much as the unveiling of King Tutankhamun's Tomb in 1922 did. I had learned about the controversial Emperor Qin in Chinese History classes at SSGC. Yet nothing quite prepared me for the overwhelming awe I experienced when I came face to face with that Army. The Terracotta Army museum was built on site and over the excavation site itself. Once I stepped inside the building, the vast expanse before my eyes was an endless formation of warriors, arms and armament, archers, and horses and chariots. Even though they were only clay sculptures, I distinctly felt their collective power and energy as if they were alive. I believed that was the intent of the Emperor and the designers of the 38-square-mile necropolis: the deployment of a mighty and triumphant army, with vigorous undying spirits, that would guard and remain at the command of the Emperor in eternity. I admired the rows after rows of the gallant fighters from afar, basking in the very "yang" energy all around me. Visitors could only view the "pits" from the skywalks erected above; sample individual sculptures were displayed in the adjacent museum for visitors' closer examination. I felt a strange kinship and chilling familiarity with the battalions standing at attention in those pits. I would relive that sense of "having been there" at the Roman Forum in Italy nine years later, only by then, my sensations were even keener and more palpable. It took years before I could reflect upon and begin to understand the sensations which came over me at the Terracotta Army pits and the Roman Forum; it was not your run of the mill *déjà vu*, but a profound resonance on a soul level.

We were besieged by peddlers selling desktop-size clay Terracotta soldier replicas as we returned to our tour bus. They were sold, at very reasonable prices, in bundles of five or so warriors in various battle-ready poses. I could not help but buy a bundle to give out to friends as souvenirs, keeping the archer for myself. Our next stop on the tour was the Banpo Prehistoric Village nearby. It was an archeological site revealing the lives of Neolithic people settled in that part of China more than 5,000 years ago. I found the museum displays captivating, as it was a matriarchal society, but also somewhat eerie because one could readily see the primitiveness and harshness of lives in prehistoric times.

Beijing, in all its glamor and glory that had for millennia been the epic-center of the Middle Kingdom, was our last stop before returning to Guangzhou. The tour had a very ambitious agenda for our three days there. We somehow managed to visit many of the obligatory major points of interest, even if we were only whisking by each, including Tiananmen Square and the Mausoleum of Mao Zedong, Temple of Heaven, Thirteen Tombs of the Ming Dynasty, the Great Wall of China, the Forbidden City, and the Summer Palace. I learned about the Forbidden City and the Summer Palace in some detail in my Chinese Literature and Chinese History classes at SSGC. At the time, China was ardently Communist and sealed off from the Western world. As a teenager, I used to daydream and imagine the majesty, splendor and romance of those fabled imperial sites and structures. To be standing on the grounds of the Forbidden City, and strolling down the Long Corridor in the Summer Palace for me was nothing short of astonishing. The same sense of my "having been there" flashed again when our tour bus was driving down the 4-mile long Sacred Way to the Ming Tombs, lined with oversized statues of warriors and mythical beasts. By the time we ascended the Badaling section of the Great Wall, the echoes from the past were ricocheting vibrantly off the chambers of my psyche. Perhaps a tad too vibrantly, as I was by then quite overly sated with the sights and sounds of almost eighteen days on the road. The tour was the first time I had the opportunity to relate to Mrs. Chin completely outside of the context of the Chin case. It was refreshing that neither one of us even once mentioned anything remotely related to that tragedy. That was an auspicious beginning for a new friendship. Mrs. Chin, as I had noted above, was very fond of Bev; during the tour, Mrs. Chin enjoyed giving friendly advice while Bev was tempted to overspend on souvenirs. The dozens upon dozens of photographs we took of each other reside in my photographic archives, and are my most treasured souvenir.

Upon the conclusion of the tour in Guangzhou, and Mrs. Chin welcomed Bev and me to stay with her as her house guests; Bev stayed on with Mrs. Chin for about two weeks while I returned to Hong Kong after a few days. Mrs. Chin lived with her relatives in a very tidy, bright and airy flat. It was on the third floor of a small, single-unit residential building, attached to other similar buildings. Those few days spent with Mrs. Chin left in me a very loving and lasting impression; she was an extraordinarily warm and generous hostess. On a couple of mornings, we accompanied her as she went shopping for fresh food and ingredients for lunch and dinner that day. We would walk to the nearby "wet market," where one could buy live fish and seafood from the catch that morning, the freshest vegetables from local farms, live chickens and just laid eggs. She treated us to dim sum lunches at the newest and poshest Chinese restaurants. She kept telling us how reasonably priced everything was compared to prices in the States. We had to "fight" with her so that we could pay for some of the meals. We also enjoyed a day trip to a nearby town, Foshan, a short train-ride away. Dinnertime was reminiscent of my young childhood days when we were living with our extended family. While the flat was practically empty during the day as everyone was off to work, there would be ten or fifteen family members gathering at a large round table sharing the evening meal. Just as I remembered it in my childhood days, dinnertime was a very essential communal occasion to strengthen family bonds.

When Bev returned from her stay with Mrs. Chin, she decided to leave Hong Kong as soon as she could reschedule her return flight. I concurred as there was obviously an irretrievable breakdown in any friendly relationship between her and my parents. Besides, it was not advisable to impose upon my tenants to accommodate her for another month. Before she left Hong Kong, we were invited to dinner with Winnie; Pearl and Ellen were also in attendance, together with several mutual friends. Bev and I had met Ellen earlier on at a Halloween party. I took to Ellen right away. She exudes confidence and competence, maturity and stability. Winnie whispered to me, after I introduced Bev, her first impression of Bev; Winnie's edict when translated roughly to English was "she's one tough cookie." To me, Bev was just the opposite: malleable, empathetic, caring and reserved. Of course, time would prove Winnie right, but it would take me many more years before I realized just how arduous life was with Bev.

Hong Kong had changed a great deal in ten years since I last returned for a visit. There were new highways, tunnels connecting Hong Kong Island and the Kowloon peninsula, and of course, new skyscrapers, and many more residential high-rises. I had changed, too, in those interim years. I accompanied my parents one day to the large "wet market" in Central to shop for groceries. That was almost a daily ritual when I was growing up. Yet as I entered the three-story building that day, I immediately became uncomfortable as my sense of smell alerted me to the slaughtering and butchering being carried on there. On one floor were the meat stalls. In addition to fresh slabs of raw meat hung and dangling from large metal hooks, there was also a severed head of a cow on the floor. The smell of blood was overwhelming, and my stomach turned completely upside down. On another floor were the seafood vendors, hawking live fish, shrimp, crab and the like. From the corner of my eye, I caught the ghastly sight of a vendor hacking a live turtle. That did it; I had to get out of that killing field at once. I had been to that market countless times as a child; it was inexplicable how I was apparently not perturbed by the same activities way back when. I was even more pathetic when Dad treated me to a meal at a neighborhood outdoor sidewalk food stall one day. Growing up, I loved the food from those stalls, everything from congee, fried pastries, rice rolls, to stir-fried noodles. Every item on the "menu" was fresher than fresh, chopped, diced and sliced, and cooked as you ordered and gawked right before your eyes. There was, by the way, no "menu" per se; one simply *knew* the perimeters and asked, if one must, whether a particular dish was available on a particular day. Food was served piping, steaming hot on rugged, wooden tables (*sans* tablecloth) strewn across the sidewalk; patrons were seated on simple wooden or metal stools around the tables. Eating at those stalls used to be a special treat for me when I was young. After the meal, Dad and I were supposed to go shopping, but I had to hail a taxi to rush home immediately. The food obviously did not agree with me at all that time around; it was perhaps too "fresh" for my Americanized stomach.

During those three months in Hong Kong, not only did I have plenty of time to catch up with many classmates from SSGC, to my great delight, I was also able to reconnect with Annemargret. She was faring very well in business, and was still living happily with Rose. Annemargret was the general manger of a chain of very popular Italian fast food restaurants called "Spaghetti House," as well as a Mexican restaurant, which she would purchase and own in a couple more years. She showed me a large scar on one of her forearms, and told me her valiant rescue story. Rose was leaving the apartment for work one morning, while Annemargret was just waking up. For some strange reason, or perhaps because their dog was barking, Annemargret decided to get out of her apartment and when she got to the elevator landing, the elevator doors were just closing when Annemargret caught a glimpse of Rose looking frightened inside; there was a man in the elevator with her. Annemargret stopped the elevator doors from closing, and soon and easily enough realized the man was a would-be robber. Annemargret hollered at him as she caught him in the act and rescued Rose. Annemargret was physically strong enough to tackle the robber, but she did not realize he had hidden a meat cleaver on him, which he yielded and started slashing at Annemargret. He fled after cutting her forearm, leaving her bleeding and wounded. I thought that was such an act of chivalry, and I respected Annemargret immensely for it.

I even had the opportunity to enjoy a lunch with my former Chinese Literature and History teacher, Miss Poon. She happened to be a member of a group of mostly retirees, including my parents, who walked for physical exercise and practiced "Luk-tung" (somewhat similar to Tai-chi) every morning. She heaped praise upon me for whatever she learned in the news a few years prior of my role in the Chin case; I demurred, naturally. Clearly, I had time to rekindle friendship with many during that visit, yet, each time I mentioned that I wanted to visit with Lilian, there was somehow always a reason why I should or could not do so on whichever particular day. It was either because my parents had a prearranged engagement with or for me, or the weather was not agreeable, or some such. Horror of horrors, three months came and went, and I returned to Michigan without visiting Lilian even once. In retrospect, it was partly my parents', especially Mom's, issues with Lilian, namely, their inability to accept her disabilities, projected onto me that subconsciously led to my grievous omission. However, I should also shoulder responsibility for my lapse; the heartache of my last visit with Lilian in 1978 was simply too painful, and thus, I was subconsciously avoiding a repeat of that trauma and heartbreak. It would be another fifteen years before I would see Lilian again—in late 2003, when we had been apart for a full twenty-five long years.

I returned to Michigan in mid-January of 1989, this time as an immigrant, a permanent resident, a "green card." The transformation began at the port-of-entry, namely, the Airport in this instance, where arriving passengers were inspected by immigration and customs officers. Instead of the usual "third degree," as my immigration documents classified and identified me as a member of the professions, I was politely addressed and welcomed by the officer as he processed my admission. Finally, at long last, I was coming "home" as a legal permanent resident; no more angst about extending my "temporary stay" or "employment authorization." In due time in five years, I would be eligible for naturalization as a U.S. citizen.

Bev picked me up at the Airport. After being away for three months, I was quite ready and excited to be home again, especially when Bev and I had been apart for more than a month. By that evening, though, I sensed something untoward. Bev had changed. The paradigm shift in our relationship was unspoken, almost indescribable, very subtle, yet unmistakable. Things between us would never be the same again. She went to bed early that night while I needed to stay up a bit. I remembered kneeling beside her bed, tears involuntarily welling up in my eyes, feeling shattered, mourning the loss even though I could not quite articulate that "loss." Even while my feelings for her had not—at least on the conscious level—changed, I knew deeply that whatever happened, and whatever had caused that happening, would and could not be reversed. It was not as simplistic or as straightforward as its being the result of her having been cold-shouldered by my Mom in Hong Kong. Something, which I would never know, happened during the month when we were apart, and set in motion a rift that would not heal, a gulf that would not be bridged, a path with no return.

VIII.

Double Jeopardy

My life resumed its routine in short order after my three-month hiatus in Hong Kong. I was back to my attorney day job, and landlady-ing at night and on weekends. Just when all seemed settled enough, after only a few months, the several senior partners of my firm apparently were, for whatever reason, calling it quits. As the firm was on the verge of falling apart, I decided to move on and seek an in-house counsel position with a large corporation, a line of work that I thought I could better tolerate. As I was updating my resume, and preparing envelopes for mailing, Bev stood by my desk and gently inquired: why don't I consider going on my own, setting up my own practice? If not now, when? There would never be a "good" or "better" time, and now is as good a time as ever. I paused and contemplated for a moment, and promptly concluded that she was right; it was time for me to strike out on my own. Monumental, life-changing decisions, or what turned out to be such, are sometimes made quite breezily.

I had no business background or management experience, but as I only had to "manage" myself, I figured that setting up shop and drumming up business should not be too complicated. I started looking for office space, and soon found an office sharing arrangement in an ideal and centrally located office suite in Royal Oak, a northern suburb of Detroit. I would sublease an office from an older attorney who practiced with his son and another sub-tenant, a young male attorney. My rent included the use of their law library, photocopying machine and conference room. Starting out, I had no provision for hiring even a part-time secretary or law clerk. With a desktop personal computer, a laser printer, Word Perfect™ program, a no-frills time-keeping and billing shareware, a two-line telephone, a facsimile machine, a desk, a chair, two client chairs, a file cabinet, and my trusty briefcase, I hung up my shingles. My parents were very excited for me, and helped me with getting Chinese language business cards printed, complete with my Chinese "chop," a square-shaped stamp with my Chinese name in stylized characters, printed prominently in red as my "logo." I did not have any business plan, per se, but with my bilingual capability, it was logical that I developed a practice to serve primarily the Chinese-speaking community. Just before I launched my solo practice, I sought out one of my mentors, Sheldon, who had left the firm a couple of years prior. We met for lunch at his favorite Chinese restaurant in Southfield, and he came bearing gifts: a pack of yellow legal pads, a few boxes of paper clips, a couple of pads of Post-It® Notes, and most significantly, he specifically pointed out, a stash of "No. 9 return envelopes" which I must include with my bills for clients' convenience and to encourage their prompt payment. He was also very complimentary, noting that I supposedly had a "sterling reputation" amongst my peers in Oakland County. That was high praise indeed, coming from Sheldon who was a former president of the Oakland County Bar Association. As a solo practitioner himself, he gave me many valuable pointers, and one, in particular, turned out to have far-reaching ramifications. When I shared with him the type of legal services I intended to provide, ranging from real estate, wills and trusts, to business transactions, he sagely advised: "Immigration, don't forget immigration. You are uniquely qualified to provide legal services in that field." Frankly, I had not thought about practicing immigration law at all in my solo practice. That was because I wanted to run and stay away from the INS District Office and INS officers as far as possible. I had had it with them, given my own immigration travails which, thankfully, had by then been resolved favorably. I did not want to even hear the word "immigration," if I could help it. As it turned out, Sheldon was spot on, of course; there was indeed a substantial demand for immigration legal services as I developed my solo practice. More significantly, my immigration legal experience would become my lifesaver, literally, in a just few more years.

News spread quickly in the Chinese community that I had set up my own shop. Moreover, my parents helped with printing Chinese language lunar year calendars, with my law firm's contact information prominently displayed, and mailing them from Hong Kong to my clients and potential clients as a promotional gift. The response was positive and enthusiastic in terms of business development. Moreover, there were still only a handful of Asian American attorneys in private practice in Michigan in the late 1980's, and hence, competition was practically nonexistent. My practice was off to a gratifying start. As my overhead was relatively low, even with a modest-size clientele and fewer late-nights at the office, I was making more money than when I was employed as an associate. For a pleasant change, I felt as if I were "cruising along" in life, gliding down "easy street" for the first time in a long time.

As if on cue to celebrate the auspicious occasion, Chrysler and Maserati jointly developed a stunningly magnificent convertible sports car which came on the market around that time. It was the "Chrysler TC by Maserati." I *had* to have one. I purchased a 1989 model which ended up being one of the very few, limited production version of that remarkable vehicle. It had a fire-engine red exterior, and under the hood was the true-blue 200hp 16-valve 2.2 Maserati engine, and not the Mitsubishi 3.0 L V-6 engine, mated with a 5-speed Getrag manual transmission. In short, it was my dream car. Bev had her Nissan "300ZX," and I had my "TC."

By all appearance, we were living the proverbial yuppies' good life. In reality, I was beginning to pile up debts again. Our rental homes did not generate a positive cash flow; they were in fact a cash drain as most highly leveraged real estate investments would be. With our clutch of rental houses and blocks of vacant residential lots, we had the façade—and a false sense—of financial security. To make matters worse, our real estate investments did not always pan out as planned. Such was the case with our purchase of a 1-1/2-story house located in a designated "historic district" in Troy. It had been occupied by the previous owner to operate her business, "Anita's Darn Yarn Shop." Bev had the grandiose idea that we could make it my law office if we were successful in requesting "special use" from the City Council. Unfortunately, despite our best efforts, we could not convince City Council that my proposed use as a law office was "historic" enough. We ended up having to rent out a very old home that required constant repairs.

Shortly after I returned from Hong Kong, Bev started winding down her sporadic house-cleaning work; she decided to write a book instead. Being the consummate enabler, I wholeheartedly seconded her unusual project, even as I then became the sole breadwinner by default. She showed me a chapter that she had just finished. It was a humorous take on an episode in our daily life; I do not remember specifically, but perhaps it was about one of our dining out misadventures. It was very succinct, only about three double-spaced typewritten pages. I was not impartial, but I liked the refreshing humor, and I thought it could be a promising endeavor. In the meantime, I had just added yet another task to my full load; I was apparently expected to properly "type-set" her compositions into my computer. While I was at it, I would serve as the editor, fine tuning sentences, correcting grammatical and punctuation errors and misspellings.

Bev's book project would leisurely stretch over the ensuing four years, one short chapter at a time. It might have dragged on for a few more years but for an unexpected catalyst in the fall of 1993. At the urging of a few gay male friends, I purchased a pair of tickets for us to attend the annual dinner of the Human Rights Campaign held in November at the Renaissance Center in downtown Detroit. A silent auction was planned in conjunction with the dinner as a fund raiser. Somehow one of the dinner organizers contacted Bev who, with her typical bravado, proffered her then nonexistent book as one of the items for the silent auction. I did not even have time to panic, as we had less than two months to turn her yet unfinished manuscript into a self-published book. I learned in a great hurry about obtaining copyright and ISBN bar code, book printers, and book distributors. She had drawn a picture, with matchstick figures and child-like rendering of house, cat, trees, and so forth, for her book cover. I was feverishly typesetting and laying out the text, as the printer would be printing the book exactly as I had printed the pages out of my humble laser printer. We decided to use the corporation that we had formed several years earlier—Speculators, Inc.—as the publisher. The name of the corporation was obviously tongue-in-cheek, as we wanted to own the label "speculators" that some in the Troy City Hall derided us as such in connection with our legitimate real estate investment activities. She used her *nom de guerre* in the lesbian community as the author for her book. As she requested, I thus helped her obtain a legal change of name, adopting her *nom de guerre*, before the book was published. Last but not least, I had to obtain a home equity line of credit to finance the self-publishing project. The night before we went to press, Bev was arguing with me over the mail order page at the back of the book, insisting that the printed retail price of the book include postage. I was beyond emotionally and physically exhausted by the time we handed the laid out pages over to the printer. A few days later when I recovered somewhat from the mad dash, I suddenly realized that my name was nowhere to be found in the book; I was referred to only by an assortment of pet names. Subconsciously, I supposed I was still ambivalent about re-emerging from the closet then. I was ready to "stand up and be counted" again, but my largely Chinese clientele—my bread and butter—might not take kindly to my politically correct and courageous stance.

As it turned out, the book printing took a tad longer than expected, and we did not have an actual book to display at the silent auction. We attended the formal-wear dinner, and were proud and gratified to see our "announcement" of the book included in the silent auction displays. As we were lingering at the auction tables, we ran into the famed LGBTQ rights vanguard, Urvashi Vaid, who asked us about the book. Bev remarked she might be too "serious" to appreciate her book of humor. Urvashi, without missing a beat, quipped: "My life partner is Kate Clinton [the wildly popular lesbian stand-up comedienne]." But of course, Urvashi understood humor. Speaking of which, around 1990 and 1991, Bev also decided that she would venture into the uncharted waters of stand-up comedy. I was totally bewildered by that twist in her career path, if one would call it that. She was quite serious at it, and had prepared "routines," mostly for her solo performance, with a few skits for performances with her daughter. She actually appeared once or twice on "open mike afternoon" at Comedy Castle, and actually took up "gigs" at various bars and clubs in the area for a period of time. It was not by any means a lucrative undertaking, and I was mostly scratching my head,

haplessly clueless, during that phase of her "career development."
Thankfully, that phase lasted only a couple of years.

Shortly after I set up shop in Royal Oak in April of 1989, tens
of thousands of Chinese university students began to occupy and
protest for democracy in Tiananmen Square in Beijing, China.
Their protests would end in bloodshed on June 4, 1989, in the infamous Tiananmen Square Massacre. The heavy-handed suppres-
sion of pro-democracy demonstrations shook Hong Kongers to
the core. The sovereignty of the British Colony was due to return
to China on July 1, 1997, with a supposed guaranty by the Chinese
authorities that Hong Kong would enjoy a high degree of auton-
omy for at least fifth years thereafter—the so-called "one country
two systems" principle. My sisters and I received a telephone call
from our parents shortly after the Massacre. It was not unusual
to be talking on the telephone with our parents on those Sundays
when we sisters got together. What took us by total surprise was
Mom's declaration that they would like to leave Hong Kong just
as soon as Lina became eligible to apply for their emigration to
Canada, that is, after Lina's naturalization as a Canadian citizen in
about a year. We had never imagined that our parents would ever
want to leave Hong Kong where they were born and had lived all
of their lives. How would or could they adjust to life in a Western
country at this rather late stage in their lives? How would they
fare without having their life-long relatives and friends nearby as
their support system? They had to be genuinely fearful of the 1997
Chinese takeover to have made that drastic decision; of course,
it could also be that they wanted to be living with or close to the
three of us in their old age. Lina and Juliana were indeed natural-
ized as Canadian citizens the following year, and Lina proceeded
to submit applications for our parents' and Vivian's emigration
to Canada as family reunification. I had permanent residency in
the U.S., and thus did not care to emigrate to Canada. However,
I shuddered to realize that Lilian would be left behind in Hong

Kong all by herself. Vivian assured and comforted me by pointing out that Lilian would continue to be well cared for by Po Leung Kuk, as long as she remained a resident of its specialized dormitory for mentally impaired women.

When Lina graduated with a Bachelor's degree in Business Administration in 1990, our parents came to Windsor to attend her graduation ceremony. It was a very joyous time when our parents arrived for that occasion, as we three sisters seemed to be hitting our strides. Lina would continue on with graduate studies to attain her MBA degree; Vivian was enjoying her work as an internal auditor at AAA Michigan, while finishing her Master's degree in Professional Accountancy, while my solo practice was fairly well established and flourishing by then. As par for the course, Bev did not care to be part of our family festivities, nor did Mom make any overture toward including Bev in our family affairs. I simply continued to steer as deftly as I could on those treacherous grounds between the two antagonistic camps.

As I settled into my solo law practice, I had a moment to reflect upon the fast-paced few years since Bev and I launched into our real estate investments and moved in together in our home sweet home. So very much had happened and changed in those three years. Much had been accomplished, yet I felt a strange void. I felt as if I had been chasing after some elusive prize, all alone, all by myself. I was supposed to be in a committed, longstanding, loving relationship, yet day by day, I felt more and more estranged. The fun we used to share, the caring we used to give to each other, the common bond and common purpose, all seemed to be slipping, fading away. My life with Bev at that time consisted of seemingly endless hard work around the clock, rewarded by an occasional meal out and acquisition of materialistic possessions, and constant financial juggling. That sad state of affairs was more than I could believe or accept, and hence, I intuitively shifted to a self-protective state of denial. Music listening, along with a growing interest in high-end audio equipment, thankfully provided a much needed distraction. As the world was being swamped by CDs, hunting for and collecting fine vinyl LPs became my pastime. In the midst of my doldrums, I received a telephone call from my dear friend, Helen, one fine day in late 1989 or 1990. Helen left Michigan in 1985, if I remember correctly, for the fast lane in the Big Apple, to work as a journalist, including a laudable turn as an editor with *Ms.* Magazine. I could not exactly say I was surprised when she told me she had of late fallen in love with a woman colleague (not at *Ms.* Magazine). For some reason, I had always presumed that she would come out one of these moons. I was bemused that my instinct—my "gay-dar"— was spot-on, and I was absolutely thrilled for her. She sounded deliriously happy. I remembered very well finding and falling and being in love with one's soulmate, a state of pure nirvana. For a moment there, I was carried away to days gone by, vicariously basking in Helen's euphoria.

In the early summer of 1990, I received what many would consider a plum assignment from one of the senior partners in my former law firm, Barry Howard. Barry had left the firm very early on, in 1981, and established his own law practice. In 1989, he was appointed by the Governor as a Circuit Judge of the Oakland County Circuit Court. In a highly contested divorce case pending before Judge Howard, the couple owned and operated a significant number of rental investment homes. I was appointed the receiver in the case to conserve and manage the marital assets, specifically the rental homes, pending resolution of the divorce proceedings. I was extremely excited to receive the appointment, as I thought Bev and I would work well together to manage those rental homes. After all, we had several years of experience from managing and maintaining our own real estate holdings. Alas, I was sorely and surprisingly disappointed. As most of the rental homes were located in a marginal neighborhood, Bev refused to even visit and inspect them, let alone getting them ready for leasing. In fact, she was reluctant to help me even with running simple errands. I was left to fend for myself. I did, of course, engage contractors where appropriate for needed maintenance and repairs, but the assignment turned out to be an onerous one. Many of the rental properties were quite distressed, and it bothered me greatly to see paying tenants suffer in silence as they felt powerless to demand decent and more humane living conditions. For the ensuing few months, I worked very diligently as a receiver to conserve, maintain and manage those properties while addressing, as best I could and within my mandate, the tenants' legitimate grievances. It was a very sobering and humanizing experience for me.

Something rather odd and interesting happened to me in early spring of 1991. My arduous receivership duties had been satisfactorily completed some months earlier. My practice was humming along. A large percentage of my clients were owners and operators of local Chinese restaurants. The proliferation of Chinese eateries in just about every neighborhood meant that I had a steady stream of clients needing legal services as restaurants changed hands and new ones were being launched. Out of the blue one day, I decided to go shopping, not shopping for essentials, but shopping for leisure and pleasure. That notion had never occurred to me before. Other than shopping for cars (which happened only once every few years), audio equipment (which required upgrades only once in a great while), and hunting for LPs as a hobby, I used to shop only for necessities such as food, clothing and daily sundries. For no particular reason on that particular day, I made a trip to Somerset Mall, the upscale shopping mall in Troy. I thoroughly enjoyed that outing, browsing and window shopping, which opened my eyes to the myriad of "nice" things available, if one could afford them. In just a couple of months, even my sisters noticed and teased me about my abrupt change. I started appreciating and desiring the "finer things" in life. I started paying attention to my wardrobe and accessories; I began shopping designer's and high-end merchandise. In retrospect, I believe there was a simple explanation for my transformation. I was shopping as a means of compensating for what I perceived to be lacking. I was pampering myself with material comforts—even excesses—in a pathetic and vain attempt to make up for the ever dwindling quotient of love in my relationship, and to sate the emotional void on the soul level.

It was another ordinary late afternoon at my law office in June of 1991; if I remember correctly, it was June 11th. Again, I was seated at my desk, working on a case. All of a sudden, a stroke of by now all too familiar "electric current" coursed up my spine. I must have muttered a swear word or two under my breath. It was happening again; "lightning" struck again. What I had hoped and wished would be impossible and unthinkable, happened again: another round of subarachnoid hemorrhages. Why me!? Why now!?

Methodically and calmly, I called 911 for an ambulance, and I then called Bev to let her know that the unthinkable was recurring. When the medics arrived, they were nonplused to see me, seemingly perfectly healthy, fully conscious and composed, and ready for my ambulance ride to William Beaumont hospital nearby. By then, the "electric currents" were striking me every 10 minutes or so, just as they did seven years ago. I knew that they would very soon become sharp, painful back stabs, and would soon bombard me just minutes apart. I patiently explained my rare medical condition to the flummoxed medics; I almost had to convince them to take me to the hospital. At the emergency room, even as I was doubling over in excruciating pain, I had to repeatedly educate the nurses and the doctors as to my admittedly esoteric medical history and the eruption of subarachnoid hemorrhages at hand.

It was as if I was resigned to my fate; that second episode, that recurrence of subarachnoid hemorrhages was endured almost as a matter of fact. I was again transferred to Henry Ford Hospital after a day or two at Beaumont Hospital. There was a marked difference, though, in my treatment during that hospitalization. There was no spinal tap, and the doctors did not administer myelogram or angiogram. I was given intravenous pain medications and sedatives, and was put on a liquid diet and bedrest. For about ten days, I rested and slept most of the time. When my condition had apparently stabilized, I was discharged home without much fanfare. I do not remember Bev's visiting me at the hospital. In fact, she had visited me only once during my hospitalization seven years prior. I do not remember feeling slighted or neglected, but then again, I must have sublimated my hurt feelings by rationalizing that she perhaps had an aversion to hospitals. I still remember that, lying in my hospital bed and in my drug-induced haze, I was frantically placing a telephone order for a birthday cake for her as I thought I would not be discharged in time to celebrate her special day with her. I also remember vividly how, in my greatly weakened state shortly after my discharge, I drove to Somerset Mall and bought her a Louis Vuitton handbag for her birthday; I almost passed out at the store. I had, miracle of all miracles, survived yet another bout of subarachnoid hemorrhages. However, I was extremely weak and had lost a great deal of weight. Slowly but surely, I bounced back physically in just a few months, and life and work resumed as if nothing out of the ordinary had intervened. Little did I know then that I would hardly be getting off scot-free quite so handily.

In October, I won a lucky draw sponsored by a local radio station; my prize was two-free-nights' stay at the fancy Grand Traverse Resort and Spa in Acme, just outside of Traverse City, Michigan. I was very excited about the trip, because my two previous forays "up North" were colorful, figuratively and literally, and intriguing. In early September of 1989, Bev urged me to take off a week to enjoy a vacation stay at Jo's cottage near Kalkaska. She could not come along as someone had to stay with Hercules. She had stayed at the cottage a few times with Jo, and talked often about the outdoors activities and restaurant meals they enjoyed there. That was the very first time I ventured outside the Tri-County Detroit area. I met Jo at the cottage, and we drove to the Song of the Morning Ranch in Vanderbilt, near Gaylord. Jo was then an active member of that spiritual retreat founded by the late J. Oliver Black. It was an eye-opening experience for me to meet some of Jo's friends, who lived in geodesic domes on the retreat grounds, and practiced meditation and yoga. For the left-brained lawyer that I was, such spiritual pursuits seemed rather esoteric and novel to me. I met Mr. Black and listened to one of his talks during my visit. Strange as it may sound, he passed away just a short week later; he was elderly but he appeared very vital when I last saw him.

The Labor Day weekend was drawing to a close, and Jo had to leave the cottage to return to work. She gave me a brief orientation on her cottage, the community and surrounding area, and I was left merrily on my own. That week spent at the cottage, in a completely unfamiliar environment, was an entirely new experience for me. Caressing my morning cup of coffee on the front deck, surrounded by thick stands of tall pine and spruce trees with the sun's rays streaking through their boughs, my environs felt at once serene and surreal. There were no telephone interruptions, and no extraneous noise emanating from television or radio. I was communing blissfully with nature, and nothing else but nature. Yet, I was somewhat spooked the night before, my first night by myself at the cottage. Again, for a left-brained lawyer, a nominal Christian, and not possessing any superstitious mind, it did not make any sense to me when I felt what I did after sundown. I felt as if there were numerous eyes, or multiple presences, watching me through the windows from about five to ten feet outside the cottage. I was not afraid nor did I sense any danger, but the "presence" was unmistakable to my senses. I was able to sleep through the night well enough, and tried to dismiss those strange senses the following morning. Subconsciously, though, I must have wanted to run and stay away from the cottage. Hence, early every morning, I would hop into my car and take extended road trips all across the northern lower Peninsula; one day, I even drove as far as Sault Ste. Marie in the Upper Peninsula. Those road trips opened my eyes to the spectacular beauty of the Great Lakes State. I fell in love with Lake Michigan along its north-eastern shores, from the Traverse City area north to Mackinaw. Driving across the Mackinaw Bridge, I was awestruck when I had a glimpse of the majestic body of water that was Lake Superior. When I returned to the cottage from driving all over for a full day, the "eyes" would be on me again at night. On the last day of my cottage stay, a Saturday morning, I had already packed my bags and loaded up my car for my return trip to Troy. As a courtesy, I decided to run a load in the clothes washer to launder the bed linens and towels that I had used during the week. I had operated that clothes washer a few days prior, and it was functioning uneventfully. Yet that morning, the water was mysteriously filling up the washer in miserly trickles, taking forever for that load of laundry. In fact, the water was barely dripping for the rinse cycle. The load was progressing agonizingly slowly as if to detain me there. As I alternately sat and paced, waiting for the wash to complete, a pall of melancholy overcame the cottage. When the laundry load was at long last done, I hurriedly locked up the cottage, dashed to my car, and sped out of the driveway for my long drive home. Weeks later, I casually discussed with Jo my odd "encounters" at the cottage. She was empathetic but assured me that she had never experienced similar "presence" there. She proffered a rather unorthodox explanation that perhaps what I sensed was the lingering spirits of the animals that the hunters who used to occupy the cottage had slaughtered. She added that she would cleanse the aura with appropriate incantations next time she returned to the cottage. I simply chalked the entire episode up for an inscrutable, and not necessarily supernatural, experience, and was very grateful to my friend for an overall enchanting vacation.

I was again gleefully traveling "up North" in the fall the following year, in perfect time to marvel at the incomparable Michigan fall colors. My parents arrived from Hong Kong to attend Lina's university graduation, after which we had weeks to enjoy togetherness and family activities. Vivian and I accompanied our parents for a splendid weekend escapade, roving from Traverse City, Charlevoix, Petoskey, Harbor Springs, to Mackinaw City. I remembered vividly how we enjoyed not only the breathtaking scenery, but also browsing in local boutiques, purchasing handcrafted Native American blankets and trinkets, and acquiring gorgeous stained glass creations by local artists. That family trip was a particularly cherished memory; everyone was still relatively young and in robust health, and we were happy and full of hope for the future. Both Lina and Vivian would be receiving their graduate degrees and embarking on a remunerative career, and our parents would be joining us in Windsor in the not too distant future when they emigrated from Hong Kong.

When Bev and I were readying for our free weekend stay at the Grand Traverse Resort in October of 1991, "up North" had a different array of treats awaiting me even as that was my third outing to the area three years in a row. One of the nicest perks of having my own law practice and being my own boss was that I could take time off work whenever I wished. We explored the Sleeping Bear Dunes National Lakeshore area, and hiked the sand dunes. It was an exhilarating, albeit somewhat eerie, experience; I was perhaps overwhelmed by the magnitude and desolateness of the dunes. We visited the Grand Traverse Lighthouse, and took in several local cider mills, feasting on fresh, warm donuts and chasing away the fall chill with hot apple cider. Of course, we shopped as well, at the hotel and the upscale boutiques in Harbor Springs.

We discovered a charming restaurant on Old Mission Peninsula overlooking the magnificent West Arm Grand Traverse Bay, and enjoyed a sumptuous dinner with the most glorious sunset as backdrop. If ever there was a perfect weekend getaway, that was it; it was heavenly.

Monday, October 21, 1991, the day after we returned from up North, I went back to work as usual, except that there was something unusual. My toes started tingling slightly. At first, I thought it was the weather turning colder, and I thus put on a heavier, warmer pair of socks the following day. To no avail, the tingling continued, and in fact it was becoming more and more prominent and noticeable. After about a month, the tingling became numbness. More alarmingly, the numbness started to slowly but surely spread upwards, from my toes to my feet, and to my ankles. I thus made an appointment with my neurosurgeon, Dr. Ghaus Malik. He did not have a clue as to the cause of the numbness, and ordered an MRI of my spinal cord. By the time of I returned in January of 1992 to review the MRI results with Dr. Malik, I could barely feel my feet below my calves. Dr. Malik could not come up with a diagnosis from the MRI scans, or he was rather vague with his comments on what, if anything, was revealed by the MRI. I then received a referral to consult with a neurologist, Dr. Nancy Futrell. By early spring of 1992, the numbness had traveled upwards to above my knees, and yet, I still did not have any definitive answers, let alone treatment. Because of the ever expanding numbness, I was beginning to lose control of my legs and balance when walking. By sheer determination, I continued to walk, without any assistance or assistive device, by carefully placing one foot in front of the other, even though I could not feel where my legs were any longer.

For my birthday in 1991, Bev for some strange reason decided to give me as my birthday present a course in handgun use and safety with a certified instructor. I must have expressed at some point a measure of fascination with the registered handgun that she owned, a Walther PPK semi-automatic pistol. I was and am in fact quite deathly afraid of firearms, despite my apparent obsession with *toy* guns and swords in my childhood, which obsession I now attribute to influences from my warrior Past Lives. Years earlier, Jim, a senior partner at my Southfield law firm, gave me a 22-caliber rifle as a gift. I believe I shot with it only once when Annemargret and Rose came to visit Bev and me in early 1992, when we went to the indoor shooting range for target shooting just for fun. I gave it away to a friend years later.

Curiosity made me attend those classes nonetheless. I was in a class with about ten others, mostly young men. We were instructed in the basic structure and operation of a firearm, and the instructor emphasized safety above all. Supplementing the classroom instructions were about two or three practice sessions at a local indoor shooting range. We used rented protective equipment and handguns. By then, my legs were quite weak and numb from ankles on down, but I managed to pass the targeting exercises as well. At the end of the course, I was awarded several certificates evidencing my basic knowledge in the safe handling and use of firearms. When we graduated, the instructor urged us to take the advanced course. I had no particular interest in advancing my "studies;" besides, my legs were so numb then that I would not be able learn and perform advanced maneuvers such as aiming and shooting "on the move." Nonetheless, I thought it would be interesting to purchase a handgun strictly for the purposes of practicing what I had learned about target shooting. I viewed it as a means of sharpening my eyesight, aim and hand-eye coordination, much like a sport or game.

I went to the Troy City Clerk's office one day to apply for a permit to purchase a pistol. Much to my surprise, even though I had passed the written test and was otherwise qualified for the permit, I was informed that U.S. citizenship was required for the issuance of the license. I felt decidedly slighted personally, but looming over the horizon was the larger issue of the unlawful, disparate treatment based on national origin or alienage, a "suspect classification," in legal parlance, which necessitated "strict judicial scrutiny." I would have loved to have been a U.S. citizen then, but the law required a period of five years as a permanent resident before I could apply for citizenship. I had been a permanent resident for only three years at that time. I cogitated for a few days on my having been denied an application for the permit simply because I was not a citizen, and decided that the law was unfair and unconstitutional. I believed the State had no compelling governmental interest in requiring U.S. citizenship for the issuance of a permit to purchase pistols. It was not at all my desire to own a pistol that motivated me to pursue the matter. Rather, to me, it was a classic case of the principle of the matter that dictated I take up the fight and attempt to rectify the injustice on behalf of all "aliens," especially as this impacted on the larger, general battleground of "alien's rights."

In the ensuing weeks, I contacted the Troy City Attorney, and representatives at the Michigan State Police, to ascertain whether they indeed intended to enforce what I viewed as an unconstitutional provision of the statute. They professed to be following the letters of the law, and could not allow me to apply for a permit to purchase a pistol. Hence, I filed suit in the Oakland County Circuit Court to challenge the U.S. citizenship requirement of that statute. During the pendency of that suit, members of the National Rifle Association contacted me several times, ostensibly to offer support for my legal efforts. Of course, I declined their offer as they had completely mistaken my intentions and stance on the issue at hand; I was and am not for gun rights, but I was and am for *alien's* rights.

I remembered that during my oral arguments before Judge Jessica R. Cooper, when the case was heard on a motion for summary disposition, I had the occasion to make reference to the woefully unjust internment of Japanese Americans during World War II, invoking the ghosts of *Korematsu v United States*.[27] The Judge took the motion under advisement, which meant she did not render a decision from the bench right away. Life is indeed sometimes stranger than fiction. As soon as I returned from my swearing-in ceremony as a citizen of the United States on the morning of October 20, 1994, I hurriedly telephoned Judge Cooper's clerk to advise the Court that my case against the City of Troy might be moot because of my newly acquired citizenship, only to be told by the clerk that the Judge had just issued her opinion that morning. Judge Cooper's written opinion arrived in the mail shortly; she had granted summary disposition and ruled in my favor. Undaunted, the City of Troy appealed Judge Cooper's decision to the Michigan Court of Appeals, which proceeded to affirm the lower court in 1996.[28] I never did purchase or own a pistol, and other than that one time with Annemargret and Rose in early 1992, I never again set foot in any shooting range. Chalk one for alien's rights; principles matter, always.

I had been consulting with Uncle Lai by telephone since the numbness in my toes began and as it progressed up my legs. He could not guarantee any results, but he urged me to again try acupuncture and treatment with traditional Chinese medicine.

---

[27] *Korematsu v United States*, 323 U.S. 214 (1944).
[28] *Chan v City of Troy*, 220 Mich.App. 376 (1996).

Recalling my favorable response to his healing in May of 1985, I took him up on his offer right away and hopped on the next plane out to San Francisco in April of 1992. It was heartwarming to see Uncle Lai again and spend a week with him. In addition to intense treatment everyday, we listened to music in his home, and he shared his views on a wide range of subjects from classical music recordings worth collecting to wisdoms and teachings from Buddhism. Unfortunately, my legs did not improve from the week's treatment, and the numbness and mobility impairment continued unabated. Bev was thoughtful enough to procure a quad-based cane for me when I returned from San Francisco, and I had to use that to steady my gait since then. By late June of 1992, I was unable to drive my "Chrysler TC by Maserati," as my legs were no longer stronger enough to engage the clutch to shift gears. I also did not have sufficient control of my legs to coordinate between the brake and throttle. Bev had to drive me to and from my office.

Amazingly, between January and June of 1992, I was determined enough to be able to make two previously planned trips with Bev. The first one was in January to attend a law-related conference in Dallas. We drove instead of flying down there, and spent altogether slightly more than a week, enjoying a few extra days as our vacation. That trip was the first time I felt Bev was not her usual happy and enthusiastic self when we went on vacation. We dined at fancy restaurants and shopped to our heart's content, yet nothing seemed to please her for more than a fleeting moment. Perhaps she was worried about my impaired walking. The other trip was, I believe, around May when we went to Washington, D.C. for my swearing-in ceremony for admission to practice before the U.S. Supreme Court. I had a miserable time during that trip, as I had lost just about all sensation in my legs, and walking became very daunting even with my cane. Instead of waiting for or assisting me, Bev became impatient and blaming, much to my chagrin. Those two trips would become a harbinger of all the trips to come for the remainder of our relationship. Except for the two overseas trips to New Zealand in 1993-1994, and to Italy in 1997, she was at best not engaging and at worst moody, temperamental and verbally abusive during our weekend or week-long vacations and trips. Those vacation trips were hardly inexpensive, as she shunned anything less than above-average. Hence, increasingly and frustratingly, I was spending more and getting less. Nevertheless, I sorely needed those hiatuses from work periodically. So, I tried to eke out as much enjoyment as I could from an untenable situation.

It was around May, 1992 when my neurologist, Dr. Futrell, informed me that I had residue of an oil-based color dye inside my spinal canal. I did not at all understand the significance or the ramifications of her pronouncement. I responded half-jokingly with a query as to whether she meant that I had a "colorful" spinal canal, but Dr. Futrell did not further elaborate or comment. As it turned out, it was no joking or laughing matter at all. Because of the rarity and complexity of my condition, she referred me to a colleague, Dr. Patricia M. E. Moore, a neurologist affiliated with Harper Hospital/Detroit Medical Center. Dr. Moore ordered an MRI of my entire spine in July of 1992. When I returned to her office the following month to review the MRI results, I was in for some stunning and upsetting news. She informed me that the MRI revealed that numerous arachnoid cysts had formed along the length of my thoracic spine, roughly from T4 to T11. The cysts were situated inside my spinal canal, specifically inside the spider-web-like membrane of the spinal canal, and were compressing on my spinal cord. As my spinal cord was being "squeezed" by those cysts, the cerebral spinal fluid could not flow normally, and the neurological signals could not travel unimpeded, up and down my spinal cord, and I was, therefore, losing sensation and strength in, and control and coordination of, my legs. She advised that surgical removal or decompression of the cysts should be tried as soon as possible. The neurosurgeon with whom she had been working had apparently just left the employ of the Hospital, and she stated that she would locate a suitable and qualified neurosurgeon in short order. I do not recall whether she explained to me at that time how those arachnoid cysts came about.

It would be early September before I could consult with the neurosurgeon to whom Dr. Moore referred me. My cane-assisted walking had by then been reduced to a slow and labored shuffle, and the numbness had crept all the way up to my waist. The neurosurgeon put my MRI films on the lightbox, and showed me how the numerous arachnoid cysts, increasing in size progressively along my spinal canal, from my upper-mid-back area toward my lower back, were compressing on my spinal cord. In some areas, my spinal cord was so severely "compressed" by the cysts from both sides that the cord was almost severed. He then gave me a neurological examination, checking my reflexes, and sensation in my legs. He asked rhetorically how I was still able to walk, and I replied as a matter-of-factly: "By putting one foot in front of the other." He then continued, "Since you are going to be wheelchair-bound anyway..." I almost did not even hear the rest of his sentence, as tears started rolling down my cheeks uncontrollably. Wheelchair!? What a strange and outrageous concept; I had never associated myself with any device or equipment intended for the handicapped. "Am I becoming a handicapped person!?" was one of the many questions cropping up in my suddenly heightened state of mind. After I regained my composure, I asked for more specifics about his proposed surgery. That was when he calmly informed me that once a spinal cord was injured or severed, the damage could not be undone. Since my spinal cord had been severely compressed by the arachnoid cysts, it would not "rebound," and thus, it was extremely unlikely that I would regain any sensation or leg function such as strength, coordination and mobility. However, *since I was wheelchair-bound anyway*, he thought it was worthwhile to attempt decompressing the arachnoid cysts, perhaps in the hope that the effort might prevent them from completely severing my spinal cord.

Stunned did not even begin to describe my reaction, and crestfallen did not adequately characterize my bundles of emotions. There was not any silver lining to be found in my neurosurgeon's pronouncements. Wheelchair, severed spinal cord, paralysis, and loss of leg function, were not "acceptable" terms to me, yet it was clearly not up to me to *not* accept. Since I was not given any other option, or even more than half a thin ray of hope, I decided to disregard the grim picture, continue to carefully place one foot in front of the other, and keep on walking in the meantime until surgery day.

Surgery was scheduled fairly promptly for September 28, 1992, at the University of Michigan Hospital in Ann Arbor. I did not harbor any unrealistic expectations, but then again, I also did not despair; hardly. I supposed I was confronting the situation with equal parts stoicism and bravado. When I came to, I was out of the operating room and in a stepped-down recovery area. I believe it was there and then when my neurosurgeon appeared by my bedside with a broad smile. In my post-anesthesia haze, I heard him say to me, simply, that my spinal cord remarkably "bounced back" as soon as he decompressed the cysts. Obviously, that was not supposed to happen. A medical miracle, a spiritual miracle, verily a miracle had taken place. Vivian came to visit me at the hospital numerous times, and I remembered her pushing me in a wheelchair to go outside to take in fresh air and the gorgeous fall colors. In the distance from the Hospital was a hillside full of trees with blazing colors. Vivian and I even enjoyed the "hospital food" at the cafeteria. I truly felt it was a time of hope and renewal for me; I was blessed with the improbable and impossible.

My neurosurgeon decided that I did not even need inpatient rehabilitation, but prescribed a month or two of out-patient physical therapy for me. As soon as I was discharged from the hospital after about a week, I was walking quite normally, without needing a cane, even though my legs were very weak. After the prescribed course of physical therapy, my legs regained some strength, and sensation was also returning to my legs. I could tell that there was still impairment to my mobility, balance and stability. For instance, I could walk but could no longer run, nor did I have complete or normal control and coordination of my legs. However, since I was not a professional athlete or in a line of work that required peak physical performance, my then level of ambulation was more than sufficient for my daily life. I resumed my private law practice and continued to manage our investment rental homes. However, I was devastated to realize that I no longer had enough strength in my legs to drive my "Chrysler TC by Maserati." Even after the prescribed course of physical therapy, my legs simply would not cooperate enough for me to operate that fine sports car. Abandoning my "TC" was unthinkable, and thus, I did not contemplate further on its future. In the meantime, I purchased for myself a consolation car—a Mercedes-Benz 190E—and had brake-and-throttle hand-controls installed in it, as recommended by one of my doctors, so that I could safely drive with my hands without using my feet. Bev drove me to an empty parking lot on a weekend, and I tentatively drove slowly around the parking lot with the hand-controls. It felt very awkward at first to be accelerating and braking the car with my left hand and using only my right hand for steering. Nonetheless, in a very short time, driving with the hand-controls became second nature to me. Still, it was quite humbling but I had to swallow hard and move on. Eventually, after more than a year, my legs still had not regained enough strength to drive my "TC." That was when I realized I would never be able to drive a car with a clutch and manual transmission again. I cried inside me for days for that loss, as to me, driving meant driving with a manual shift. However, I would cry even more when I had to face the fact that I could not afford to keep my "TC;" I was too financially strapped to keep it or to properly store it. I was forced to sell that car, an act that was almost too painful for me to recall even now.

With my new lease on life came a series of changes. A rent increase for my shared office space in Royal Oak prompted me to look elsewhere. I ended up sharing a small suite in a Troy high-rise office building with a woman attorney. I was only a short drive from the office, which allowed me even more time to window shop at the nearby upscale mall, Somerset Collection. By then, shopping had definitely become one of my favorite weekend activities, whether Bev wanted to tag along or not. It was refreshing to be sharing office space and resources with a woman, after working with mostly male attorneys for more than ten years. She did not hire a clerk or secretary either, and thus, we were the only two people in the office when we did not have clients. We supported each other, served as the other's sounding board, splitting expenses equally, such as rent, lease payments for the photocopier and copier papers. For the first time since I started practicing, I enjoyed the peace and quiet, freedom and harmony of that particular setup.

Shortly after my spinal cord surgery, a young gentleman claiming to be a residential developer contacted me, proposing to purchase the blocks of vacant lots in Troy that Bev and I owned with LaVerne. When we purchased those lots, we figured that they would one day be developed because of their location in the "center" of Troy. However, we did not anticipate that a development purchase proposal would land on our lap just a few years after our purchase; the purchase proposal was thus a very pleasant surprise. It took better part of half a year to negotiate and agree on all of the terms of the purchase, and for the developer to satisfy numerous stipulated contingencies, and for the transaction to be finally closed. It was the second time Bev and I were fortunate enough to enjoy yet another real estate bonanza. Unfortunately, both of us somehow managed to spend much more money and much faster than we could make money. Obviously, I was still not learning my life lessons. It was also about that time when Bev decided that we should start divesting our real estate holdings with LaVerne. Her reason for divesting was personal and quirky, but I did not mind scaling back our rental homes business, as it was getting physically too demanding for me to be landlady-ing in addition to my law practice. My partial paralysis in 1991 and subsequent spinal cord surgery in 1992 did take a toll on my physical strength and overall health.

It was also around that time that I unexpectedly learned more about my arachnoid cysts. One evening when I returned home from work, Bev excitedly sat me down to watch a television segment that she recorded earlier that day. She said she started recording as soon as she saw some people on that show limping and shuffling the way I did in late 1991 and through most of 1992. The news story was about the injuries caused by an oil-based color dye called Pantopague used in certain medical tests and procedures, including myelograms, and that there were class actions filed against the manufacturer of that color dye which had since been withdrawn from the market. That prompted me to conduct my research about Pantopague, the pending lawsuits, and how any of it related to my spinal cord condition. In those pre-Internet days, I had to actually go to a public library to search for my answers. What I unearthed stunned me. It turned out that it was the myelogram administered at the hospital in Phoenix in November of 1985 during which Pantopague, an oil-based color dye, was used. I was apparently very unlucky in that instance, as it was very late for that hospital to be using that dye which had almost been completely phased out by then. My previous myelograms at

Henry Ford Hospital, for instance, used a soluble water-based color dye which would not remain in my spinal canal. In contrast, Pantopague, being oil-based, would not dissolve and could not be completely removed by the surgeon during a spinal cord surgery. Thus, residue of the color dye remained in my spinal canal, a fact that was observed from the MRIs taken in 1992 before my spinal cord surgery. Also extremely unfortunate for me, as I suffered my second subarachnoid hemorrhages in June of 1991, the blood from that bleed mixed with the residual Pantopague in my spinal canal, sparking an inflammatory process—arachnoiditis; that causation had been confirmed by reliable and accepted medical research. The numerous arachnoid cysts in my spinal canal were in turn formed as a result of that inflammatory process. On the one hand, I was gratified to finally learn and understand the causation of my spinal cord condition; on the other hand, I was distraught because the die was cast—the Pantopague would forever remain in my spinal canal, and thus I was doomed to suffer recurrence of the cysts and the sequelae. I did not recall my neurosurgeon giving me any prognosis; he only advised me to consult with a neurosurgeon as soon as possible should I again experience numbness in my toes or feet. I did retain counsel to seek just compensation from the manufacturer of Pantopague. My attorney advised me that his investigations indicated that the pending class actions against that manufacturer were not well organized or active. Therefore, I did not join the class action suits, but filed my own claims against the manufacturer. It was not until mid-1997 before I reached a settlement with the defendant; the amount I received was very modest, especially considering the severity of my injury. However, since such product liability lawsuits were considered by plaintiff's attorneys as costly and difficult to prevail, most of them would advise their clients to accept if there was a half-way decent settlement offer. By then, I simply wanted to hold my head up high, refuse to even think about the possibility of recurrence, and move on with life.

The biggest change, yet, was when my parents emigrated to Canada. Lina's application for their immigration to Windsor had been approved, and by early 1993, my parents had sold their condominium home (my condominium in Hong Kong had been sold a year prior), and they were packing up their possessions, bidding farewell to their life-long friends, and enjoying one feast after another with relatives who wished them *bon voyage*. They arrived in March of 1993. Our family reunion was understandably a very exciting and joyous occasion. However, Bev, on the other hand, was extremely circumspect, and that was a gross understatement. The "bad blood" between her and Mom apparently was still as fresh and fierce as if it were incited just yesterday. Because of that antagonism, I often felt extremely torn between my parents and my life partner, especially when it came to allocating time spent with one or the other, or even simply talking about one in front of the other. Even though I tried to pace my visits with my parents as far apart as reasonably acceptable, Bev was still grumbling aloud about my being "sucked into" my "clan," a pejorative term she used for my immediate family. That dichotomy, that discord, would only deepen with passing years. I was grateful that my very sage therapist, Dr. Byer, had advised me a few years earlier in no uncertain terms that in my case, I should not and must not choose one over the other, that my family would always be my family which should and could not be abandoned by me. But for that advice, the pressure from Bev to slight and disassociate from my family members would have been so great and persistent that I might have made a serious life mistake that I would have deeply regretted for the rest of my life. Dr. Byer had another piece of prescient advice for me. When I told her that Bev had stopped working or trying to earn a living at all, but was instead writing a book, she wisely observed that writing a successful (read: money making) book was extremely difficult. She personally knew some very talented writers who, nonetheless, could not make a living solely from their writings. Her observations would turn out to be prophetic, as we would soon be burdened with almost ten thousand copies of Bev's book in our basement, and an equity line of credit to payoff.

The first order of business was for us to help Mom and Dad find and purchase a suitable home in Windsor. Their possessions, all neatly packed in cartons and stuffed into containers, were due to arrive in just about a month. On one fine Saturday, I remembered the realtor taking us to view a home in the South Windsor area. As soon as we walked in, all of us immediately knew, after having viewed many unacceptable homes in the past week or so, that that was *the* new home for our parents. It was a split-level house, and was only a few years old. The realtor realized that our parents were very particular, and figured that that house might meet their high standards because it was the builder's own home. As such, the builder-owner had used a far higher grade of materials, details were meticulously tended to, and there were many handcrafted, personal touches throughout the home. Indeed, first and foremost, the four-level home was cavernous enough to accommodate our parents' considerable collection of rosewood furniture pieces and Dad's vast collections of sundries, and even to display much of his collection of Oriental paintings, calligraphy scrolls, and other trinkets. Mom would have a large, open kitchen to stow her beloved collection of cookware, silverware and tableware, and to fix up scrumptious meals for us. There was also enough space for her wardrobe; she did love fine clothing. Mom was also thrilled that it had four bedrooms, which meant she could "assign" the three extra bedrooms to Lina, Vivian and Juliana, just in case any of them should choose to live with them. Even though on the outside the home did not look ostentatious, it had a sizable formal sitting room and formal dining room. It also had a front yard with a well-kept green lawn, a front porch on which they would place a porch bench, and a sizable backyard for Dad to finally indulge in horticulture. Mom pronounced it her "dream home."

The timing was perfect, as the 18-wheel tractor-trailer with the many containers of their possessions arrived at the door just days after they closed on purchasing that home. I took a day off work to "help," but mostly I was just observing, while Dad was excitedly taking photographs of the entire proceeding. I was awed by the number of cartons and furniture pieces unloaded from that mammoth truck. It took Mom and Dad several months of full-time devotion to unpack and situate all of their possessions. Vivian would drive them to the stores to buy additional curio cabinets and cupboards to display Dad's collections. She also spent just about all of her time when she was not at the office, especially weekends, tending to all of their needs. By the time they settled in, that home had been transformed; it was gorgeous inside out. It was warm, welcoming, finely and tastefully decorated, and richly furnished. Mom's home cooking, whenever we gathered, was indisputably the magical finishing touch. I was gratified to see our parents so fulfilled in their golden age, materialistically and emotionally, surrounded by their grown, loving children, each with her established professional career, and their sole grandchild who was also coming onto her own.

Curiously, even before our parents' arrival, Lina had informed all of us that she would be repatriating to Hong Kong. My sense was that she might have felt she could not live her life independently with our parents in close proximity. Mom tended to be somewhat controlling, perhaps even domineering, at times, even though she was well-meaning. My take was that Mom simply wanted to ensure our family and every member within run like a well-oiled machine, with every detail planned in advance, tended to, and executed perfectly as intended. Of course, Mom was the planner and designer. Dad loved not having to fret over his daily needs and concerns, as Mom took care of him down to the socks he would wear on any particular day. For us grown kids, however, I could see how Mom could be bordering on being over-bearing at times. Indeed, Lina left Windsor a few months after our parents were situated, leaving her daughter, Juliana, with them. Juliana would stay in Windsor for just a couple more years before she would leave for Toronto to attend Ryerson University. Lina in the meantime fairly prospered in Hong Kong, landing on well-paid managerial positions with Standard Chartered Bank, then with Hong Kong Bank (HSBC), and in the early 2000's, with an up-and-coming enterprise at the forefront of e-Commerce. It would be around the mid-2000's when she wound abruptly change course, quit her senior management job, become a Buddhist Acharya, and practice as a Reiki healer on a full-time basis with her unique brand of "Enlightenment Reiki."

I had always been close to my Dad, and he was obviously elated to be finally living if not with me, very near me again. I visited my parents at least once a month; I would have preferred to be with them more often, but the diatribe from Bev was sim-ply much too much for the trouble. Each time I was over at their house, Dad would spend hours showing me pieces from his col-lections of "everything." My contribution to their home, of course, was a decent audio system. I set up and connected all the com-ponents for them in their recreation room/den, which Mom had made very cozy for television watching and music listening. That was where Mom faithfully followed the 1994-1995 O. J. Simpson trial on television, eagerly awaiting each day's installment.

In 1993, Bev and I still had a number of rental homes to tend to, including that very old bungalow that was involved in the RICO lawsuit. The long-time tenant had just vacated that sum-mer, and we had to go in to clean up and fix up. I remembered fondly how Dad sat with me in that empty house for hours, on the several occasions when I held the house open to show prospect tenants after it was readied for re-letting. We enjoyed lovely conversations and reminiscences. A few weeks earlier, when Bev and I were working on the house, there was a rather peculiar occurrence. Bev told me one evening that, when she was repainting the interior walls in the house earlier that day, she heard a voice which seemed to be calling her. She asked who it was, thinking it might have been a potential renter, but no one answered; she got up to look around but could not find anyone, even though she was certain she heard the voice. She told Jo about the incident, and Jo was very alarmed, sternly warning Bev not to follow that voice if it ever came again, because it was from what she called "earthbound entities." In fact, Jo was so concerned that she told us she would come to "cleanse" the house. It must have been the next day or so when Jo met Bev at the bungalow; I was curious and thus, took a few hours off work to join them as well. Jo came with bundles of some sort of dried leaves; I was told they were sage smudge sticks. She lit one up, and as smoke billowed from the stick, she waved it gently around and to the left and to the right, while chanting some sort of incantations. I observed from a few feet away, and followed her as she went from room to room waving the smoking sticks. I had never encountered anything quite like that scene, but as she waved and chanted, the walls and the rooms literally and vastly brightened and opened up before my very eyes. Was it magic, or was it sorcery, or was it something beyond my realm of understanding? I was and am not one to "label" anyone or anything, but decided that my eyes and senses did not deceive me. Hence, I had indeed witnessed something extraordinary and which defied rationalization.

Well into December, 1993, Bev's book was ready to be shipped from the printer's. We had ordered a first print run of 10,000 copies; we had no idea how well it would sell, and had no idea that 10,000 copies might have been too ambitious or wishful thinking. In anticipation of the publication and distribution of her book, Bev finally, formally came out to her daughter. Melanie was reportedly totally taken by surprise that her mother was a lesbian; she incredulously asked her mother, "With whom?" Bev had to supply what we had thought was the obvious answer: "With Liza." Apparently, we were more discrete than we realized, even though we had by then been together for sixteen years, and had been living together for the last seven of those years. About a week before the books shipped out, I obtained about two dozen advance copies from the printer for the surprise publication party that I was throwing for Bev. Fortunately, two very good long-time friends of ours, Ann and Linda, volunteered to host the party. As luck would have it, I was friends with a gay male couple, Dave and John, who ran a private catering business as a sideline. I engaged them for the party, and they did not disappoint and served up absolutely exquisite delectables. Without my friends' help, I would not have been able to pull the party off. Bev was completely surprised when I drove her to our friends' condominium, under the guise that we were paying our friends a routine visit. There, she saw her book in print for the first time, was swarmed by about twenty of our invited friends who celebrated the special occasion with us. She was enthralled to autograph her book for the first time at that party. A few days later, the books arrived at our home by freight. We had lined up several friends to help unload the cache; even my Dad came to lend a hand. The books were packed 64 copies to a carton; hence, there were more than 150 cartons to unload. Our living room was filled with those cartons of books. It would be months before we cleared a sufficient area in our basement to stow all those cartons on wooden pallets. There they would stay for the ensuing fifteen years.

We learned the hard way that book selling was all about marketing and distribution, especially the latter. We had taken the initiative of mailing out complimentary copies to gay and women's magazines, publications and bookstores all over the country. We did not know that most bookstores would not buy directly from the author or the self-publisher. Hence, we had to sign up with two book distributors, Inland and Book People, and give them their usual "cut" for each sale. Some local bookstores as well as individuals who heard about the book did order directly from us. I thus had yet another new night job: processing orders, issuing invoices, packaging the books, and taking the packages to the Post Office or UPS for shipping. For the first year or two, we never passed up any opportunity to promote the book. For instance, when Bea Arthur was in town for her one-woman show, which we attended, we sent her a copy, and she in turn sent to Bev a lovely handwritten note (on the hotel stationery where she was staying) about how she had thoroughly enjoyed the book. Even when we were on vacation in New Zealand for my 40th birthday, we brought with us enough complimentary copies to deliver to women bookstores we happened upon along the way.

Our monthly-long sojourn in New Zealand spanned both the North Island and South Island. To describe the trip as memorable is a drastic understatement. The landscape, scenery, people, food and culture were so unique and diverse that they filled my senses to overload. Bev and Penny spent some time during the year prior to the trip studying maps and reference books, and drew up an itinerary. We then worked with a New Zealand tourist/traveler coordinator to reserve bed-and-breakfast accommodations in the cities and towns where we expected to stay overnight, along with a couple of hotel stays, and to secure a rental vehicle. The flight was long and seemed almost never-ending. By the time we disembarked, we were literally on the other side of the globe and in a different hemisphere. Auckland and many of its very friendly 1.4 million inhabitants greeted us with smiles everywhere we went. Life in New Zealand seemed very orderly and leisurely. Its denizens seemed very happy and content, as they were pampered with natural beauty from pristine beaches to invigorating geysers to Alpine glaciers. We were fortunate to have Annemargret traveling with us, because she turned out to be the only one who could drive us around: without hand-controls, I could not drive, and neither Bev nor Penny dared drive on the "wrong" side of the road. With our own vehicle, we had greater flexibility with our itinerary, lingering longer where we found a place or things of interest, and skipping along when necessary. There were too many towns and cities we visited on that driving trip, but a few places and incidents stood out. We took a dip in the sulphur hot spring pools in Rotorua. We took long walks on the almost deserted Taiputuputu Pahi Beach near Paihia, in the Northland Region. We enjoyed a show featuring traditional Maori dancing and music, followed by a traditional Maori dinner. New Year's Eve was spent in a luxurious hotel in New Zealand's capital, Wellington, where we also stocked up on the colorful hand-knit "Coogi" sweaters. A ferry ride took us to the South Island which is twice the size of North Island. Where North Island was much more cosmopolitan and urban, South Island was all about outdoors recreational and sport activities, scenic natural beauty and expansiveness of open space. Even though we spent almost three weeks on South Island, we still did not have time to reach the southern-most town, Invercargill. We had very memorable times hiking up to view the Franz Josef Glacier on the northwestern region of South Island, watching brave outdoorspeople Bungee-jump and paraglide in Queenstown, and cruising on a ferry in Milford Sound, rimmed by spectacular steep rock face, waterfalls, and the famed Mitre Peak. Our last stop was Christchurch, a bustling metropolis, where we enjoyed gourmet dining and shopped for more handcrafted souvenirs before we headed home. While on a train ride from Picton to Westport to begin our driving trip on South Island, Annemargret had an opportunity to talk with me privately. She very delicately hinted to me that Bev might have a drinking problem. It took her several tries before I even caught on to the subject of her friendly concern. I was astonished, because I had not even remotely considered that possibility. I thanked Annemargret for bringing it to my attention, but I must also have indicated to her that I did not believe that there was any such problem. I, being the consummate enabler and denier, proceeded to disregard Annemargret's astute observations and warning. I myself had practically stopped drinking liquor since the summer of 1975, and not a drop since November of 1980 after I passed the Bar examination. I was aware that Bev enjoyed her glass or glasses of wine, and it was a regular item on my grocery list. Since it was not "hard" liquor, I had thought that a small amount of wine with dinner was not a cause for concern at all. After all, Bev used to indulge in hard liquors and cocktails when we first met, and thus, a glass or two of wine seemed "tame" and an "improvement" to me, rather than an alarm bell. Annemargret's prompting haunted me for several months after the trip ended. It took me that much time to finally appreciate Annemargret's "word to the wise." I was too much of a habitual enabler, and was too close to Bev, to realize or acknowledge the truth. On that New Zealand trip, whenever we stayed at a hotel or had lunch or dinner at an eatery that served alcohol, Bev would as a matter of factly ordered wine with the meal, or as her afternoon "tea." However, there were many days and nights when we were in remote towns and villages, or staying at a bed-and-breakfast where no liquor was served. She would almost be frantic, urging us to look for a liquor store in town. Additionally, whenever we were in a larger town or city, she would make a point of "stocking up" on her travel stash of wine. That behavior clearly manifested Bev's reliance on and addiction to alcohol. It was classic alcoholic behavior, easily discernible to Annemargret yet so opaque to me. Just as it did not dawn on me for years that Bev always somehow wanted a trip or vacation away from home on my birthday or during holidays, so that I would not be able to celebrate those special occasions with my family. By the time my eyes were opened to her devious ploys, it was too late as Mom had already passed away, even as I tried to make up for lost time with Dad. In retrospect, I deeply regretted it, and I only had myself to fault for my myopia and stupidity.

It was mid-January, 1994, when we returned from New Zealand, and I had much to catch up on at the office. However, something was not quite right with my health and stamina; I seemed to be running out of energy and fatigued too easily. When I was leaving the Wayne County Courthouse one morning in February, I almost passed out from a sudden and unexplained "weakness" as I was walking to the parking structure for my car. I found a bench and sat down and rested for a few minutes to catch my breath before I could move on. I thought I was perhaps working too hard after my lengthy vacation in New Zealand, and had overtaxed myself. However, at a routine return visit with my nephrologist later that month, I was in for the shock of my life. The doctor informed me that my blood tests revealed an alarming and sharp rise in my creatinine level, indicating serious decline in my kidney function. My kidney function had been stable since the doctors discovered that they were both one-third damaged by glomerulonephritis in May of 1982. The sudden decline was unexpected and worrisome indeed.

My nephrologist advised that I undergo chemotherapy treatment in an attempt to arrest further decline of my kidney function. I was so shell-shocked that I almost could not even breathe. Ultimately, as we further discussed my condition and options, I accepted her recommendation. There and then, I would have done just about anything to save my kidneys. Other than the unusual fatigue and breathlessness, I did not have any other symptom. I could not feel my kidneys, declining or otherwise, and I did not experience any pain. The chemotherapy treatment plan called for an initial round of three monthly doses, and it would be administered intravenously on an outpatient basis. The first dose was in mid-March. I had never had any chemotherapy previously; sitting for several hours for the drip to finish, then driving myself home even as I felt nauseous and exhausted, was quite distressing. After the second dose in April, my nephrologist was encouraged that the creatinine level, though still high, seemed to have stabilized. By the time I received the third dose in May, I was beginning to crumble physically, both because of the chemotherapy itself, and my loss of kidney function. It was around that time that a long-time client of mine had managed to secure tickets and treated me to a Barbra Streisand farewell concert at the Palace in Auburn Hills. I remembered my staggering up the many flights of steps to our bleachers, and I was utterly spent by the time I reached our seats. Thankfully, my client also happened to be a registered nurse, and she had the foresight of bringing with her fluids and snacks to replenish me. I did not even realize then just how seriously ill I was, and how much worse my health would get.

I learned a great deal toward the end of that period of precipitous decline of my kidneys. My ankles started swelling up. My blood pressure shot through the ceiling, which was extremely unusual for me. I was also becoming anemic, apparently because the kidneys were also responsible for making hemoglobin, which they were no longer manufacturing. I started getting injections to boost my hemoglobin count. I also had to strictly limit my intake of protein, as it could not be processed without my kidneys. Even though I was prescribed diuretics, excess fluid still built up in my body. After the third chemotherapy session, my nephrologist gave me the bad news that chemotherapy had basically failed to halt the rapid deterioration of my kidneys. I was diagnosed with end-stage renal failure. How ironic that Dad had cancer in one kidney in 1978, and it was then my turn to have kidney troubles. Dad recovered fully after removal of the diseased kidney, but there I was, with *both* kidneys failing and being in a much dire situation than he ever was in. My nephrologist then briefly described to me the various dialysis modalities available, and gave me a handful of materials to read so as to come up with a decision on my dialysis of choice—soon.

That diagnosis was not something that I could believe, let alone accept. As for dialysis, I could not even get my mind pass the term or concept itself, let alone contemplating the ultimate reality of my being hooked up to a machine for hours on end, everyday or every other day. Yet, at that time, reality was all too honest; I was waning, failing, whimpering. Out of the blue, Bev asked why I had not considered consulting with the fine doctors at the Mayo Clinic. I had, of course, heard of Mayo Clinic and its almost mythical, sterling reputation, but I did not even know where it was located. In just a few short days, I would learn more about the Clinic, and that the original Clinic was located in Rochester, Minnesota, a mere 11-hour drive from Troy. When I contacted them by telephone, I was promptly given a priority appointment at the end of May.

With my nephrologist's referral letter in hand, Bev and I set out for the Mayo Clinic. By then, I had purchased a pre-owned Dodge "Caravan" minivan, and it would serve us well on numerous long road trips for the ensuing few years. As we were eager to arrive at Mayo Clinic well ahead of the scheduled first doctor's appointment, we chose not to stopover in Chicago, but drove straight through to Rochester. Once we proceeded past Chicago and its western suburbs, we were traversing mile after mile of open fields and rural areas in Wisconsin and southeast Minnesota. I had never been to these parts of the States, and found the small towns in the heartland along the way quite charming. Thus, I was surprised to see tall buildings as we approached downtown Rochester, after being mostly in the countryside for the past six hours or so. We checked into the brand new Radisson Hotel, and turned in early because I was exhausted, and my medical appointments would start very early the following morning.

I was quite nervous when I waited in the small examination room to see the doctor; I had no idea what to expect. Would he confirm the diagnosis? Perhaps he had a new advanced medicine or procedure that could salvage my kidneys. My first impression of the Mayo Clinic was that it was extremely well run, efficient, and very professional. Before I arrived, I had been furnished clearly illustrated maps of the various buildings on campus, and useful information on lodging, dining and the community. All of the buildings comprising the Mayo Clinic at its downtown campus, as well as commercial buildings downtown, were connected either by skywalks or tunnels. That enabled patients to walk, say, from the Radisson Hotel to the Mayo Building with relative ease, and sheltered from the elements during the harsh winter months.

I did not have to wait for long before my doctor came into the examination room and introduced himself. He was dressed in the "uniform" for all male Mayo Clinic physicians: in suitcoat, dress shirt and tie, with his name prominently displayed on a rectangular badge pinned to the left breast pocket of his jacket. After he reviewed my nephrologist's letter, results from the latest round of laboratory blood tests, and a physical examination, he calmly and very politely informed me that I had to be admitted to the hospital right there and then. While I tried to remain calm, I felt devastated; this must be very serious, I thought to myself. I vainly protested with a comment that did not even make sense at that point: "But I can walk," to which he replied: "but you don't have a kidney." I must have subconsciously considered my regaining leg function two years prior a monumental achievement that would overcome all travails. I could only muster enough wits to ask a silly question as to whether I could have lunch before my hospital admission. He answered in the affirmative.

Bev and I drove to Saint Marys Hospital which is part of Mayo Clinic, located about a mile west of downtown. The Hospital impressed me; unlike other hospitals at which I had been an inpatient, Saint Marys was quiet, spacious, bright and airy, and projected an aura of caring and serene healing. As usual, I underwent a number of blood tests and scans, though nothing too invasive or torturous. Fortunate for me, I was under the care of a nephrologist who was apparently very senior in rank and very knowledgeable and experienced; he was always followed by a throng of young and attentive residents. I think it was the second or third day of my hospitalization when he came in to give me the good and bad news. I remembered that conversation as if it took place yesterday. He began by saying, "My seniority dictates that I sit down," whereupon a resident pulled up a chair for him. The bad news was not a surprise, actually. He told me that my kidneys were beyond "resuscitation," and that there was no point in continuing with the chemotherapy. In his words, the chemotherapy was "beating a dead horse." He then gave me the diagnosis of "microscopic polyarteritis nodosa," commonly referred to as "PAN." It signified the inflammation of my many microscopic arteries, which inflammation destroyed both of my kidneys. He opined that PAN was most likely also the culprit that caused my two subarachnoid hemorrhages in 1984 and 1991. The best news was that he predicted that "since PAN had claimed my two kidneys, the disease had run its course," and that I should not experience any further subarachnoid hemorrhages. Knock on wood, his prediction has held thus far, twenty-plus years later. Now for the really good news, since I was "otherwise in good health," he continued, I should "consider a kidney transplant." Really!? I was "otherwise in good health?" And what was a kidney transplant, I wondered, and how could that be accomplished. After he further elaborated on the kidney transplant, I realized then that it was a viable alternative to dialysis. I did not know that such a wonderful life-saving option existed. The crux was to find a suitable donor. He explained that my immediate family members, except for Lilian who had a mental disability, could be potential donors. He described the blood tests that would determine the best match for me. His parting advice, before my hospital discharge, was for me to "conserve my energy" until the transplant. I did not understand or appreciate how valuable that advice would be until a month or two later. Mayo Clinic nurses and coordinators "walked" me through the transplant process from identifying potential donors, to the rigorous and thorough physical and mental examinations the potential donor will undergo at Mayo Clinic, to the surgeries to remove and graft the kidney, to post-transplant care for both. They emphasized that there would be two completely separate teams of doctors and specialists in each transplant case, so as to safeguard the health and welfare of the donor and the donee fully and independently. I was, needless to say, hugely impressed with the entire proceedings.

My mission then was to solicit potential donors to submit blood samples for testing. I wanted to live first and foremost, and there was nothing else on my mind then but to expedite the process so that I could get a kidney graft to bypass dialysis and ultimately to cheat death. My younger sisters, Lina and Vivian, both immediately submitted blood samples, as did Bev. Mom and Dad thought they were too old to be donors, and I agreed, as the transplant surgery might be too hazardous for either of them. In just a couple of weeks, my transplant coordinator telephoned to give me the good news that, while the blood sample from Lina showed that we did not "fight each other," Vivian's stood out as a shining star: we were a "perfect match," a "six-antigen match" in medical parlance. Vivian was absolutely elated, and I was greatly relieved. Vivian wanted to help me—indeed, save my life—in any way she could, and she was welcoming that opportunity. What a sister! She was thus scheduled for a week of very comprehensive testing and examination at Mayo Clinic in mid-July.

Bev was invited for her first book reading and signing by a women's bookstore in Asheville, North Carolina, in late June. I had been eagerly anticipating attending that event with her, and my kidney problem was not going to sidetrack me. I had also invited Dad to come along; Bev did get along with Dad, even as she and Mom were at loggerheads. The three of us took our time in driving through some lovely country en route to Asheville. It was the first time I had seen the Smoky Mountains. Dad and I also enjoyed shopping for folk handicrafts in Tennessee. When we arrived, it turned out that the hotel I had booked for us was a landmark. We had a luxurious stay there, taking in exquisite seafood buffets, relaxing in hot tubs, and taking in the genteel scenery. Dad quipped, "So, it's quite marvelous to be a rich person," referring to being treated like royalty at that resort hotel. I took it as a compliment that I could afford to treat him to some creature comforts. The book reading was fairly well attended. I did not recall if we sold any book that evening, but we were informed by the owners of the bookstore that the book had been selling quite well, and that was why they scheduled the book signing. Bev was understandably nervous, but she handled the event well enough for a maiden appearance; it was an enjoyable evening for all.

By early July, I was in the thick of suffering the symptoms of kidney failure. Not only were my feet and ankles swollen, my energy level had dropped to abysmal levels. Moreover, I was not able to eat, even though I felt my hunger. As soon as I started eating, I would literally lose my taste and appetite for food. I felt nauseous, and even my favorite foods seemed not to agree with me. Food somehow tasted so awful in my mouth that I had to stop eating after just a few bites. It was punishing, because I was famished, and yet I could not eat. All I could do was to stare at the food on the table tempting and teasing me. It was a strange and frustrating experience, to say the least. By the time Vivian passed all her tests at the Mayo Clinic in late July, I was barely hanging by a thread. Vivian told me much later that the Mayo doctors declared her "disgustingly healthy." However, I would learn after the fact that her doctors were originally not in favor of her donating the kidney supposedly because her veins and blood vessels were so numerous and delicate that the surgery to remove one of her kidneys would be extremely challenging. Vivian told me that she literally threw a royal fit, and refused to get up from the floor until her doctors agreed to proceed with the transplant. As a result, she was assigned their top transplant surgeon to conduct the difficult and tricky surgery. I was also told later that because her kidney was so close to her heart, to be safe and not risk damaging her heart, the surgeon had to basically cut her entire abdomen open to harvest the kidney, instead of the usual modest slit on one side of the body. Vivian suffered and endured far beyond the call of duty all in the service of saving my life, and I literally owe her my life.

The transplant surgery was scheduled for July 28th. The transplant coordinator informed me that I would need to remain in Rochester for thirty days after the transplant surgery, so that the transplant team could closely monitor and adjust my immunosuppressant and related medications, and to promptly address any organ rejection issue that might arise. I was in too sad a shape to endure the 11-hour drive, and hence, I would fly there. Bev would drive there, and then fly back to Michigan after our surgery, leaving the minivan there for me to use during the post-surgery thirty days. Vivian was already in Rochester, having just completed the donor's tests and examinations, and she would await there for my arrival. Mom and Dad were understandably eager to come along, as two of their daughters would be undergoing major surgeries. However, Bev agreed to let only Dad join her drive to the Mayo Clinic. When I informed my parents of Bev's "edict" by telephone,

Mom hung up on me; I did not blame her. By then, I was far too weak to be arguing with Bev, or to play umpire between her and Mom. Fortunately, Bev reconsidered and agreed to drive both of them. Mom surprisingly did not make a fuss, but started packing for the road trip. As it turned out, it was almost comical to see how much Mom packed—it filled our minivan to the brim—from pots and pans to electric rice cooker to three seasons of clothing and bed linens—as if they were moving to Rochester.

During the few months when my health started failing, my law practice suffered a lull as well. As a result, I was not in the best financial shape. I had paid for Vivian's stay at the Kahler Hotel, which was the least I could do for her love and generosity. However, I could not afford hotel accommodation for all five of us for two or more weeks after the transplant. Instead, I reserved a suite in one of the numerous "lodgings" in town whose room rates were definitely budget-oriented. Hence, when Bev arrived with my parents, she picked me and Vivian up, and we proceeded to check in at that lodge. To my dismay, I had obviously chosen the "wrong" lodging. It was much closer to Saint Marys than to Methodist Hospital, another Mayo Clinic hospital, where the surgeries would take place. Worse, it was a very run down building with very outdated fixtures and furniture. I thought it was too late to seek alternatives as our surgeries were scheduled for the following day. It took hours for us to unload the minivan and get my parents situated in their room. Bev later filled me in on their drive and the events after Vivian and I were admitted to the hospital in the evening of July 27th. That was when I smoked my last cigarette, by the front entrance outside Methodist Hospital. Some days prior to the transplant, Vivian had half-jokingly asked me not to "stink up" her kidney with cigarette smoke. She probably did not think I could really quit that nasty and unhealthy habit of twenty-two long years, but quit I did. I had tried quitting in years past without success, but for saving my life, hers was a very sage request that was all for my own good besides.

Bev recounted to me that she and my parents did not engage in much conversation on the long drive to Rochester. They proceeded as if they were an army unit on the move: orderly, precise and efficient. Every so many hours, Bev would stop at a service plaza or rest area for them to use the public facilities, stretch their legs, or grab a quick bite. My parents were very polite and cooperative. On the day of surgery, Bev picked them up to go to the hospital. It was then when Mom told her that she was breaking out in hives; Mom apparently was allergic to something at that lodge. By then, Bev had found and was staying at an economical inn within walking distance of Methodist Hospital. She urged my parents to move there. Mom was hesitant and skeptical at first, but agreed to go take a look. My parents liked what they saw, and Bev spent hours that day moving them and their considerable baggage to the new abode.

That move turned out to be a blessing in more ways than one. Its location was truly within easy walking distance of Methodist Hospital. During the more than ten days when Vivian remained hospitalized, Mom and Dad would take the five-minute walk to the hospital to spend the day with Vivian. I would join them after my daily medical appointments. Simple cooking was permitted in the rooms at that inn. I would drive Mom and Dad to a local supermarket to buy the items Mom needed to fix up simple meals in their room. Above all, Bev's altruistic act in delivering Mom from her misery from the original decrepit lodging, and then physically helping them move into the much more agreeable accommodation, unexpectedly and dramatically changed Mom's attitude toward Bev by 180 degrees. I would see from that moment on that, as far as Mom was concerned, Bev was no longer persona non grata; quite the contrary, Mom could not be nicer or kinder to Bev as if Bev could do no wrong. Unfortunately, the feelings were not reciprocal or mutual on Bev's part. As Mom increasingly warmed up to Bev, Bev became increasingly alienating and contemptuous of my "clan." She castigated, harangued and resented me for doing anything for or spending time with my family. I constantly felt the stress of having to avoid provoking Bev's ire toward my family. I was, to say the least, in a very unhealthy emotional environment.

After Vivian and I were admitted into Methodist Hospital the evening of July 27th, we were separated and were assigned different rooms. She had a roommate, Kathy, who was scheduled to donate her kidney to her brother, Kevin, the following day as well. As Kathy was about her age, they took to each other immediately, and Vivian would keep up that friendship with her fellow-donor for years to come. Both Vivian and I were wheeled into the pre-operation station early the following morning. We were lying next to each other while the nurses and medical technicians prepared us for the transplant surgery. Vivian was very excited and animated, and was trying to engage me in conversation. I tried to respond to her, but I was so weak by then that I kept drifting in and out of consciousness and could not carry on even a casual conversation. The next thing I knew I was in post-operative recovery already. I would learn later that the surgeries had taken an entire day, which was rather unusual for this type of surgery. Vivian's surgical team took such great care in harvesting her kidney that it took more than half a day before my surgical team received the kidney graft. I had been under anesthesia all that time, as was Vivian; as a result, both our lungs had "collapsed." Even though collapsed lungs were not exactly a life threatening event, I was told, it took us extra efforts to recover during our recuperation. The transplanted kidney was placed in my lower left abdomen; my own two withered kidneys did not have to be removed. I remembered being transported to my room on the hospital floor, and for the first 24 hours, they were "flushing" my new kidney with fluids intravenously. The doctors and nurses told me that my new kidney was very strong and healthy, and was functioning mightily; it was "really kicking out," as they put it. I was down to 90 lbs. when they weighed me, courtesy of not being able to eat for about three months. The swelling in my ankles was gone, and by the time anesthesia wore off, I felt absolutely fine for the first time in more than half a year. In fact, I did so well that I was discharged on the third or fourth day. Bev had by then flown back to Michigan. I rushed to see Vivian. She was not roomed with Kathy. Mayo Clinic's policy was not to place two organ donors in the same room so that they could not "compare notes" with each other. In Vivian's case, that policy was very foresighted, as Kathy was discharged from the hospital in less than a week, while Vivian had to remain hospitalized for about ten days, struggling to recover from her very major surgery. I, on the other hand, rebounded so phenomenally as to defy logic. Just one day after my discharge from the hospital, I felt so energized that I walked all over the downtown area for hours; I had so much vitality that I needed to expend some of it. One of the nurses in the transplant clinic, while driving downtown that day, spotted me walking spritely; she was dumbfounded as she figured I would still be bed resting from the surgery.

When Vivian was finally discharged from the hospital, she was in a piteous state with much pain from the large surgical incision across her abdomen from side to side. We borrowed a wheelchair from Mayo Clinic to transport her as she was in too much pain and was too weak to walk. Dad would push her wheelchair as we went out for meals and shopping at the many fine stores in the downtown area. I really felt bad for Vivian; for her magnanimity, she was "rewarded" with such suffering and such a difficult and lengthy recuperation. In fact, for the first few months, I harbored a tremendous sense of guilt. I had always prided myself on being self-sufficient and self-reliant; it behooved me not to borrow anything from anyone, not even a pencil. Yet there I was, "borrowed" a kidney which I could never return. It ran against my every grain and fiber. I had stopped my therapy sessions with Dr. Byer in mid-1992, when I could no longer drive. Around the time of my kidney transplant, I had resumed therapy with a different therapist, Doug Lachman. Even though I did not have a specific issue in mind in working with my various therapists, the underlying dilemma had for years been the conflict between my family and Bev, leaving me in the untenable position of being caught in the middle. After the kidney transplant saga, with my Mom's above-turn attitude toward Bev, my therapy pivoted to focusing on dealing with Bev's subtle but undeniable changes, and her ever intensifying animus toward my "clan." Meanwhile, in one session with Doug, he offhandedly helped me resolve my crippling guilt feelings about needing and receiving the kidney graft. His words were: "Think of the donated kidney as one of god's kidneys which has just got rearranged." That brilliant thinking instantaneously relieved all of my guilt feelings. Of course, I have remained ineffably grateful to Vivian for literally giving me a part of herself to save my life. Every year since 1994, I have written her a Thank You note on July 28th, and every decade, I had given her a keepsake to signify my undying gratitude. Thanks to Doug's insight, my guilt feelings have long been supplanted by an enduring sense of grace, gratefulness and lovingkindness.

In mid-August, I drove Mom, Dad and Vivian to the Rochester airport for their flight back to Detroit. As Mom aptly noted, we were fortunate that the transplant happened more than a year after our parents arrived in Windsor. Otherwise, it would not have been as easy for them to help us both through the proceedings if they had just landed as immigrants. I had tears in my eyes as I waved them goodbye at the airport, as they disappeared into the gangway to board their plane. I felt totally overwhelmed how my life had been saved from the very precipice by my family, especially Vivian, and how a nightmare had become a dream filled with promise. How could I ever sufficiently express my gratitude, let alone begin to repay for the gift of life?

I had to remain in Rochester for the remainder of the month as the doctors had to closely monitor my progress and medications. During those first thirty days post-transplant, I had time to reflect on how I had survived two catastrophic health challenges in just two short years. One could not help but be somber and circumspect.

During my month-long stay in Rochester, other than attending my medical appointments and laboratory tests in the morning, I had plenty of time to drive around to visit nearby towns and outposts. I enjoyed the countryside, the hearty Minnesotan cuisine, and the simple life of the locals. However, my favorite pastime was browsing at the small music store near downtown Rochester for used LP's to add to my collection. Even though compact discs had taken over as the recording format of choice, I remained a stubborn loyalist to the vinyl format because to my ears, it sounded so far superior to the two-dimensional digital wannabes. I would continue to hunt for vinyl records in the ensuing few years, attending swap meets and used LP shows. I have thus amassed quite a sizable collection, which had remained my pride and joy, especially joy as I felt emotionally and spiritually recharged after each listening session. By the end of August, my doctors were satisfied with my progress, as I did not have any sign of organ rejection, and I was thus allowed to go home with my large "basketful" of medications. Bev flew in to make the drive with me back to Michigan. I was expecting Bev to be quite excited to see me after a separation of almost a month, and especially since I had once again been given a new lease on life. Instead, she seemed very distant. I remember treating us to dinner at a rather exclusive (read: expensive, gourmet, artisanal) restaurant in town the day she arrived. She had always enjoyed fine dining, yet that evening, she was unusually quiet, and did not even inquire about my state of health post-transplant; the exquisite food and the charming setting did not as much as bring half a smile to her face. I defensively and instinctively shifted into my usual denial mode, making excuses for her that perhaps she was tired from the flight.

When I returned to my office, I felt as if I were a stranger and a trespasser there. For better part of that year, I had either not been able to devote fully to my practice because of my failing kidneys, or was not even at the office because I was at the Mayo Clinic for an extended period of time. Still, life had to go on somehow. That meant getting the word out to clients and the community that I was back on the saddle at long last. That also meant continuing our efforts to promote Bev's book, and managing the few rental homes that we had not yet disposed of. Vivian had finally fully recovered after almost two months, and had returned to her internal auditing position at AAA Michigan. She had also resumed catering to our parents, helping them with everything from grocery shopping to running errands. With my renewed health and vitality, I continued to spend a weekend day with our parents at least monthly. I wished I had made more frequent visits, Bev's slights and ridicule notwithstanding. It took years but I have finally forgiven myself for that unenlightened decision of not having spent more time with my parents before it was too late; I chalked yet another one up for life lessons.

IX.

Bliss

In March of 1995, Bev and I embarked on an ambitious promotional tour for her book. It was prompted by an invitation for a book reading and signing event from a women's bookstore in Saskatoon, Saskatchewan. If we were going to drive all the way to Saskatchewan, we figured we might as well make it our grand Canadian book tour. We contacted numerous women's and gay bookstores in several Canadian cities to offer book reading and signing by the author, and then mapped our route accordingly. All told, we made stops in Toronto, Ottawa, Montreal, Winnipeg, Saskatoon, Edmonton and Calgary, before heading south to Montana to head back home. At the cities where we did not have a prearranged book reading event, we visited selected bookstores to drop off complimentary copies of the book for review and promotion.

That self-financed, month-long expedition was an eye-opener for me in two ways. Canada is a vast country, and it is mostly "empty space" between major cities, I would discover. We drove miles on end through complete wilderness and open space with not a soul in sight. As we were traveling in late winter, the land felt frigid and remote. By the same token, each of its cities had a charm of its own. We particularly enjoyed Montreal, with its fine cuisine and unique shops and boutiques that were not the typical, monotonous chain franchise affair. Obviously, we hardly sold enough books to even remotely cover a fraction of the considerable costs of the trip, but the experience of traversing that vast expanse of land was reward in itself. Besides, the book reading at the Saskatoon bookstore was very well attended; the enthusiastic and attentive crowd of more than fifty women was decidedly heartwarming on that wintry evening.

The second revelation of the trip came very early on; while preparing for our first book reading, I noticed something odd about Bev's behavior. I was quite startled when she started treating me as if I were her servant. In retrospect, she was indeed very detached and distant during the entire tour, but on the day of a scheduled book reading, she became downright mean and demanding. She would holler at me to fetch for her or buy this thing or that, be it a drink, food, special soap or lotion, or whatever she thought she "urgently" needed. At first I thought she was just getting butterflies in her stomach preparing for the very first reading, but that abusive behavior continued throughout the trip and certainly before each book reading. By the time we were half-way through the tour, I felt utterly used, hurt, alienated and betrayed. However hard I tried, I could not come up with an answer as to how or why her attitude toward me could have changed so drastically and suddenly. By the second half of the tour, I was eagerly looking forward to going home and returning to my office for some peace of mind, sanity and perspective.

Shortly after we returned home in April, Vivian asked to meet with me for lunch one weekday, which was a bit out of the ordinary. At the time, she seemed very well settled with her professional career as well as on the home front, spending much time with our parents. We met at one of my favorite Italian restaurants in Troy. I would have never guessed what she was about to announce. She asked for my opinion on her going back to Hong Kong since she would be running out of her employment authorization in H-1B nonimmigrant status in a couple of months. I was almost speechless, as that would be a very sudden and drastic move on her part, especially since our parents had by then settled in Windsor for more than two years. I outlined the numerous viable options she had, short of returning to Hong Kong, in terms of immigration status and employment authorization. In sum, I was certainly not in favor of her heading for Hong Kong at that time. To no avail, I would learn there and then that she had actually made up her mind to repatriate to Hong Kong; she was just asking me more or less rhetorically. In fact, she proceeded to book her plane ticket the following day, and it was all a *fait accompli*. If I was shocked, I could hardly imagine how Mom and Dad must have felt on hearing Vivian's draconian decision. It was the ultimate irony: Mom and Dad took the trouble to immigrate to Windsor so as to be with the three of us, and within two years, two of us had opted not to be with them. The kidney transplant protocol at the Mayo Clinic called for the donor and donee to return for a complete checkup before the first anniversary of the transplant. Since Vivian would be leaving for Hong Kong in mid-May, we hurriedly made the checkup appointment for early May. We both passed the examinations and tests with flying colors, and I especially relished the opportunity to spend those couple of days with Vivian in Rochester, a city that held so much hope, joy, and precious memories for us.

Vivian's professed plan was to spend at most a year or so in Hong Kong. However, in the meantime, I had my work cut out for me. I could not very well fill Vivian's shoes in terms of driving our parents for shopping, errands, and doctor's appointments as she did almost on a daily basis. I did try to go over to their house every two or three weeks to help with errands and shopping. Mom loved shopping for fresh vegetables, fruits and groceries at Nino Salvaggio's. Often, we would stop at the nearby Barnes & Noble first to browse and listen to newly released albums at their "listening stations," followed by soft ice cream cones at the local Dairy Queen. That would be our Saturday afternoon treat. Nonetheless, I could not very well let Mom and Dad be completely housebound, anxiously waiting for me to give them a ride or to bring food to them every other week or so. Hence, out of necessity, I came up with a bold solution: let Dad learn to drive. He was then 72 years of age, and had never driven previously. Dad was understandably excited about learning how to drive, while Mom was equally understandably nervous. For the second time, I was the driving coach for the preliminaries, and then it was off to Sears driving school Dad went. Dad was such a trouper; in just a few months, he successfully passed both the written and road tests and was licensed. Truth be told, there were many unnerving moments during his apprenticeship, while I was sitting in the front passenger seat trying to maintain calm and decorum. Nevertheless, after the first year and with almost daily practice, Dad became a very reliable and careful driver, and we could not be prouder of him. Vivian had left them her Nissan "Quest" minivan when she left for Hong Kong, but I thought a smaller car would be easier for him to handle. I thus purchased a pre-owned Ford "Escort" station wagon for him to use. However, that vehicle somehow did not agree with him, and he had more close calls with it than I cared to acknowledge. Hence, I sold my Mercedes-Benz "190E" and kept the "Escort" for myself. That was quite a downgrade—from a Mercedes to a Ford "Escort;" in my younger days, I had always been known for my extremes.

The truth was that I sorely needed to economize at the time, because my practice had taken a steep dive just as my financial outlays had become astronomical. The grim situation actually started when my kidneys were failing in early 1994. With my absence from the office for an extended period of time for the transplant surgery, followed half a year later by the Canadian book tour, many clients and potential clients probably had thought I had discontinued my law practice. Moreover, by then, I had competition; there were a couple more Chinese attorneys engaging in private practice and thus, I was no longer the only game in town. On the expense side of the ledger, all the plane tickets for flying back and forth between Detroit and Rochester, rents for the lodgings, the grand book tour, and last but not least, annual return visits to the Mayo Clinic for checkups, had completely drained my financial resources at a time when I hardly had any income. Rumors also might have played a role. After the transplant, I had to take multiple medications to prevent organ rejection, one of which was cortisone which I did not tolerate well at all. My face became horribly swollen and misshapened. Clients who saw me during that time period must have thought I was suffering from some sort of deadly disease, and word must have spread like wild fire in the community that I was not in any shape to be lawyering.

On a more serious and personal level, after being on cortisone for more than two years, I began to suffer one of its worst adverse side effects: depressed mood. I had never felt depressed in my life; on the contrary, I had always been an eternal and ultimate optimist. Yet that drug made me feel so totally and strangely hopeless that it even made me question the point of having the kidney graft to save my life. Fortunately, my nephrologist who had been following me since I returned from the Mayo Clinic, Dr. Leslie Rocher of William Beaumont Hospital, was an extremely knowledgeable, enlightened and compassionate physician. He took the bold and unusual step of allowing me to wean off cortisone, given the fact that my kidney graft had been very stable and functioning superbly with not even a single incident of rejection up to that point. That made a huge difference in my quality of life. It took almost another year to complete weaning off the medicine and for my body to adjust, but I was finally able to be "me" again, and enjoy the health and benefits that the kidney transplant was meant to bring. Even so, I suffered yet another horrendous side effect of the immunosuppressant, cyclosporine, when I had a grand mal seizure in April of 1996. I had just met with a potential renter for the condominium we owned in Bloomfield Township. It was late in the afternoon, and on my way home, I stopped by a supermarket to pick up a few grocery items. The last thing I remembered was my standing by the tables with an assortment of potatoes. When I came to in the hospital, I was told I had a seizure, lost consciousness and fell down on the floor. I broke a couple of ribs, and amazingly, bystanders and the medics picked up and kept my wallet for me with not a cent or credit card missing. That incident called for yet another trip back to the Mayo Clinic for a thorough checkup. The Mayo doctors confirmed that there was no other plausible cause for the grand mal seizure but that it was triggered by the immunosuppressant, cyclosporine. I had never suffered a seizure previously, and thanks to my lucky stars, I have not suffered any further seizure.

There was, on the other hand, a silver lining in the medication saga, and which was made known to me by my neurosurgeon during one of my routine return visits. He was thoroughly impressed with my leg function and full recovery from the spinal cord surgery of 1992. He remarked that the several immunosuppressant medications I was taking to prevent organ rejection were also anti-inflammatory in effect. Hence, they worked to rein in the inflammation in my spinal canal and kept the growth of my arachnoid cysts in check. Of course, I delighted in having the unexpected benefits, but he also noted the severe long-term adverse side effects of those medications. In the meantime, I took the good along with the bad, and let the chips fall where they may, as taking the immunosuppressants for the rest of my life was and is not optional for me. As it turned out, over more than twenty years since the transplant, Dr. Rocher had pared my immuno-suppressant medications down to just one. I have certainly been counting my blessings.

In June of 1996, I decided to return to New York City to attend our reunion at Barnard College for the first time. It was our Class's 20th reunion. Another reason I wanted to make the trip was to visit with Dr. De Fries who had retired by then, and was living on the far eastern tip of Long Island, on Shelter Island. We had kept up our correspondence over the years, and I felt that it was high time that I paid her a visit in person. I had originally planned to drive to New York City, but with my grand mal seizure just two months prior, I decided to fly instead and rent a car for my drive out to Shelter Island. I could hardly recognize my old campus neighborhood as everything seemed to have become highly gentrified. The greengrocers were gone, so were the second-hand bookstores and record shops, and the no-frills delicatessen which was the destination of so many midnight ice cream and hero sandwich runs. It was wonderful to see numerous classmates, especially Sylvia, Selina and Roz, again after all those years. Sylvia was a successful entrepreneur with a boutique ice cream shop in Chinatown. Selina was an actuary with a national insurance company. Roz was on her rise up the "judicial ladder," as a prominent judge in the New York court system. I did not want to talk about my legal career or my solo practice, which was then on the verge of total collapse.

There were two particularly memorable events during that short trip. I did drive out to Shelter Island to visit with Dr. De Fries; it took a rather long drive and a ferry ride to reach that remote island. She welcomed me with homemade sandwiches for lunch. I brought her a present: a Tiffany sterling silver a caduceus ballpoint pen with her initials engraved on the barrel. We spent the afternoon reminiscing our days at Barnard, and what she thought of our rather rebellious Class. We talked much about her highly acclaimed research, analysis and papers on "political lesbi-anism." She also shared with me some of the poems she had com-posed. It was a very special afternoon to be with her again after twenty years, with both our perspectives having evolved much, to share precious memories and recollections. Unbeknownst to both of us then, it would turn out that we would not have another chance to meet again. By 2001 when I returned to New York City for another reunion, she had already moved to Florida. Even though I was in Florida in October of 2001, sadly she could not meet with me because she was suffering the last stages of breast cancer which took her life a few months later.

On a brighter note, that trip unexpectedly led me to a delightful discovery. After having spent half a day browsing and shopping in mid-town, on a lark, I decided to take the subway to the Wall Street area just to wander and explore. There I stumbled upon a pen shop, the venerable Fountain Pen Hospital, which I would learn was celebrating its 50th year in business. What a novel idea, I thought to myself, a pen shop; of course, I could not resist going in to investigate. I was welcomed by a kindly gentle-man named Harry. I had not seen or used a fountain pen since my primary school days. There in the store, in one large display case after another, were hundreds of fountain pens in all shapes, sizes and descriptions. I was captivated and mesmerized; I took my time in surveying their vast collection. One pen in particular held my attention; I kept returning to it. To me, it was stunningly beautiful. I was never one to fancy jewelry, but if I did, that pen was far more alluring than any jewels I had ever laid eyes on. It also had a steep price tag to boot. It would be the next day before I decided that I could not do without that pen. I hurriedly tele-phoned Harry to purchase it, which purchase sparked my pas-sion for collecting—and writing with—fountain pens in the years hence. The pen that began all pens for me was created by Omas, a renowned Italian pen maker, to commemorate 100 years of radio transmission as invented by Guglielmo Marconi. Several versions of the "Marconi" fountain pen were produced in limited numbers; the one that stole my heart happened to be one of the rarest: the "Elettra" model.

When it was time to go home again at the end of that fun-filled weekend escapade in the Big Apple, I found myself dragging my feet, not wanting to be home, not wanting to confront whatever that was plaguing my home life with Bev. I would rather stay at the office and work, or go shopping—again. Since we returned from the Canadian book tour, the widening silent rift between us could no longer be denied. The refrain of that familiar Carole King song came rushing to mind: "*One of us is changin', or maybe we've just stopped tryin'. And it's too late, baby now, it's too late, thought we really did try to make it. Somethin' inside has died, and I can't hide, and I just can't fake it....*" The only difference was that I did not move on, still thinking and hoping that it was not "too late." I was too naïve, too romantic and too loyal; I stubbornly refused to acknowledge and accept reality. Yet it was agonizing for me to remain in limbo, "stuck" in a dying relationship. For almost a year, I was foolishly hoping that Bev would be the one to take the initiative to put an end to our senseless suffering. Since she took to loudly and routinely complaining about me, my supposed shortcomings and my "clan," I had imagined that she would be unhappy enough to move out of my life and end the relationship. Of course, she did no such thing, and why would she? By then, she had not worked for a living for almost a decade, while I was conveniently providing her food, shelter and clothing, vacations and automobiles, all without expecting anything from her in return. Even if there was no love or meaning left in the relationship, my being the breadwinner and bill-payer served her well indeed. There was no incentive whatsoever for her to disturb the status quo. I, on the other hand, still hung on to the notion that we could or should somehow salvage the relationship. I thus suggested that we consult with a therapist specializing in marriage counseling. I was, by then, working with a marvelous therapist, Hazel Karbel; I would end up spending almost the ensuing eight years seeking her counsel weekly. During some particularly trying times in the early 2000's, I also consulted with a superb psychologist, Dr. Ralph Schillace, who apparently had unique insight into relationship dynamics. He had steadied my "ship" quite a few times when I was in troubled waters with my interactions with Bev.

Bev was initially adamantly opposed to counseling, but reluctantly agreed to give it a try, because the therapist was recommended by Jo. Jo was a member of The Lighthouse Center in Whitmore Lake, Michigan, a group of mostly women who advocated non-violence and practiced meditation. One of the group's leaders was also a practicing psychiatrist, Dr. Hanke. We started our weekly sessions with Dr. Hanke in September of 1996, but even I could tell after just a couple of sessions that it was an unmitigated waste of time and money. Bev was simply going through the motions; her heart and mind were not anywhere near analyzing, addressing or resolving issues in our relationship. After just three months, she unceremoniously announced one Saturday that she no longer wished to see Dr. Hanke. I attended that weekly session by myself and bid Dr. Hanke farewell. I would give couples counseling one more try some months later with Dr. Susan Darlington, a psychologist referred to us by a gay friend. Once again, it was largely meaningless for Bev to participate; nothing was learned, gained or improved. It became clear to me that she went along only hoping to see the therapist "change" me, or "find fault with" me, or otherwise justify her condemnation of me and my "failings." Perhaps I was simply worn down, or perhaps I was too fancifully optimistic, after almost a year of futile couples therapy, I proceeded to make the irrational decision to stay with the relationship. In other words, I put up and shut up. At least it was a decision, albeit an ill-advised one, such that at least in the meantime, I no longer had to deal with my constant internal struggle. In retrospect, that decision was not as nonsensical as it seemed. It hailed from my deep-rooted aversion to abandonment. I would suffer just about any indignities just so as to avoid a separation, a parting of ways, which I apparently internalized as being abandoned and unloved.

As if my personal relationship troubles were not disheartening enough, my finances were a total disaster since my kidney transplant. With dwindling client base and evaporating income, I managed by the skin of my teeth to stay afloat for almost two years by "extreme juggling." I might be a decent lawyer, but I was not particularly adept at business development, growing my practice, or expanding my clientele. The "loot" from our real estate bonanzas had long been spent on frivolous indulgences; I had to borrow funds just to pay the capital gain taxes on the sales. By mid-1996, I had no savings to speak of, and had maxed out my credit cards and credit lines. I was at wit's end as to how I could financially sustain Bev and myself; filing for personal bankruptcy was then not entirely out of the realm of possibilities. Before resorting to that drastic step, however, I dusted off my resume, and began sending it out to scores of potential employers. I received no reply, and certainly not any invitation for a job interview. I was then in my early 40's, mid-career, and did not have a substantial book of business, nor any particularly outstanding accomplishment in the legal field to attract a prospective employer's interest. Bev did not proffer any viable suggestion nor did she volunteer to find a job to help out with our living expenses. I went into my office everyday just to pass the time, as if to convince myself that I was gainfully employed. I was desperate, and destitute; my immediate future looked grim indeed.

One fine day in late September, 1996, I was in my office as usual when a telephone call came in from a stranger who asked if I handled immigration matters. A few more questions from the gentleman later, I realized that he was not the typical client looking for an immigration attorney. The caller, David Galbenski, through his company, Contract Counsel, was in the business of providing attorney services to law firms and corporations on a temporary, per project or contract basis. How he ended up calling me was pure serendipity. The State Bar of Michigan, the professional organization of which all licensed attorneys in Michigan were required to be members, published a monthly *Journal*. In those pre-Internet days, the April issue was the "Directory issue," which listed all licensed attorneys in good standing in the State and their contact information. In the year prior, the State Bar announced a new feature for the Directory issue: the "gold" pages which would follow the alphabetical attorney listings. For a very modest fee, an attorney could elect to be listed under one or more specific area of practice in the "gold" pages. I hurriedly responded and had my name listed under three categories: immigration, real estate, and I believe, business law. Galbenski had a client who had an urgent need for an immigration attorney. Immigration was such an off-the-beaten-path field then that he did not have a ready roster of candidates to call upon for that assignment. The "gold" pages debuted in April, 1996, in perfect timing for Galbenski to locate me; I was one of only a handful of attorneys who were listed under immigration law in those "gold" pages.

I had obviously passed his initial screening by telephone; he then asked to meet me for an in-person interview. I was hesitant and skeptical at first, as I could not be certain that it was not some sort of a scam. Besides, the proposed employment arrangement was rather unusual, or at least it was not the type of engagement with which I had previous experience. However, since I was desperate for work and money, I agreed to meet him at his office the following day. It felt odd that I was appearing for a job interview when I had not even applied for the job, and when I had only the skimpiest information about the proposed employment or assignment. He pored over my resume, and we chatted for half an hour about my relevant experience. When I left his office, I was still very tentative about the entire affair. It seemed somewhat mysterious to me: who was his client? What exactly did he or his client expect of me? How would I be compensated? How many hours or days of the week would I have to devote to the assignment, as I still had to tend to my own private practice? All my questions would be answered the following day. Apparently, he found me acceptable and recommended me to his client. Galbenski then revealed to me that his client was the large corporate law firm, Dickinson, Wright, Moon, Van Dusen & Freeman (known as Dickinson Wright PLLC since 1998), and that I was to meet with and report to the head of their immigration practice group, Larry J. Stringer, at their Bloomfield Hills office the following day. My jaw verily dropped onto the floor at that instant. Dickinson Wright was a premier large corporate law firm in Michigan with a sterling reputation. The firm hired only the top five or ten percent of graduates from selected law schools as associates. It ranked among the top three law firms in Michigan, with about 150 attorneys at that time.[29] Galbenski explained that I would actually be an employee of his company, Contract Counsel, and be assigned to Dickinson Wright as a contract attorney for the designated project. When he informed me of my hourly-rate remuneration, I had to contain myself so as not to show my giddiness. Almost by accident, I not only found gainful employment in the nick of time, but a well-paid job to boot. To be working for such a prestigious law firm was not just a plum assignment, but a dream come true for me. Granted that it was only a temporary,

---

[29] Dickinson Wright PLLC has since grown by leaps and bounds. It is now the largest law firm in Michigan (with locations in Detroit, Troy, Ann Arbor, Grand Rapids, Lansing, and Saginaw), and employs more than 425 attorneys, with offices in Austin, Columbus, Ft. Lauderdale, Las Vegas, Lexington, Nashville, Music Row, Phoenix, Reno, Washington, D.C., and Toronto, Canada.

contract-based assignment, I was gratified to have been given that opportunity. Incidentally, when I was a teenager, a fortune teller in Hong Kong once told me that I would come upon money when I reached age 42 years. I did not remember his other predictions for me, but I remembered that specific one, because I was so young then and 42 years of age seemed so far in the distance future that I could not even grasp the concept of my having money then. The fortune teller was amazingly spot-on.

I met with Larry Stringer the following day, a Friday; I liked him right away and knew I would work well with him. Our meeting was brief; he asked me to commence work the following Monday. The project involved obtaining the appropriate visas and employment authorization for more than a dozen Japanese executives and engineers, together with their accompanying family members, to staff a new office in the metro-Detroit area. It had a rather pressing deadline of less than two months. While he had two associates working in his practice group, they were too loaded with work for existing clients to take on that substantial project. After meeting Larry, I telephoned Sheldon for his counsel. Sheldon was thrilled for me, upon hearing my new employment and assignment. He frankly stated that if Dickinson Wright needed a domestic relations (which was one of his specialties) lawyer and offered him a position, he would drop everything and run to the firm which, he added, had a very fine reputation. His only concern was my health; he wondered out loud whether I could "hack" the hours. That was the least of my concern at that point, however, because I was finally enjoying robust health two years after my kidney transplant and having been weaned off cortisone. Besides, it was not as if I had a choice anyway, as my own practice had been in a nosedive for too long already; it would be so novel to receive a paycheck again. After the call, I fondly recalled how it was Sheldon who told me way back in 1989 when I started my own practice to include immigration law; how that gem of an advice bore fruit seven years later and saved the day.

Over the weekend, my mental state oscillated between euphoria and reticence, wondering if I could really handle the assigned project successfully and within the time constraints. By Monday morning, however, I was resolutely ready to tackle whatever came my way, as the assignment was an opportunity of a lifetime. The firm's Bloomfield Hills office was located in a very exclusive neighborhood, about six miles from my home in Troy. That office relocated a few years ago to a much larger space in Troy, even closer to my former home. The stand-alone three-story building was situated on an idyllic wooded lot frequented by cardinals and jays, bunnies and even whitetail deer. Larry welcomed me and showed me to my office, which looked out onto the woods. The first order of business was computer training. I was one-on-one with one of their trainers and spent the entire morning learning all about their "system," from word processing, to time-keeping, to other internal protocols and processes. In the afternoon, I was introduced to the two associates in the immigration practice group, Linda Armstrong and Julie Emerick, as well as their Director of Japanese Business Development, Yukiko Sato, and legal assistant, Hiromi McCarroll, and a couple of legal secretaries. Larry explained to me the project in greater detail, handed me a thick pile of file folders and relevant documents, and I was on my own and off to the races.

It turned out that I had to be at Dickinson Wright full-time for the ensuing two months in order to meet the project's deadline. I would check into my own office at the end of the day to take care of my own clients. Fortunately, I had so little work in my own law practice that I could easily manage the workload in the evenings and on weekends. Working at Dickinson Wright was a completely new and different experience for me as an attorney. What astounded me first and foremost was the remarkable and wide-ranging support provided to the firm's attorneys. There were very capable legal assistants experienced in specific practice areas assigned to assist attorneys in the respective practice groups. The legal secretaries also impressed me as being very professional and efficient, so much so that each legal secretary was assigned to assist two or more attorneys.[30] Picking up overflow work and preparing complicated documents were the responsibilities of the word processing department with its specially trained personnel augmenting the legal secretaries. There was also an energetic team of mailroom clerks to handle photocopying, sending, receiving and distributing facsimile documents, sorting mail, shipping and binding briefs and reports. When a conference room was reserved for a meeting with clients, for instance, it would also be well stocked with fresh coffee and tea service, soft drinks, ice bucket, and if requested, light refreshments; it seemed all so very refined and civilized. Of course, there was a contingent of trained messengers to run errands and file pleadings with the courts. There was even an in-house private investigator, an in-house marketing department, as well as a travel agent to make appropriate arrangements for business trips. Their Information Technology department was fully staffed with Help Desk personnel, trainers, and systems analysts. The law library at the Detroit headquarters was situated on the top floor of a high-rise building with a spectacular view of downtown Detroit, the Detroit River and Windsor just beyond. Even the law library at the Bloomfield Hills office had a very comprehensive collection and was overseen

---

[30] During my tenure at Dickinson Wright, I was capably assisted by two legal secretaries: Mary A. Schnitzler, followed by Dianne L. Sortzi. They were my link in many respects to the rest of the firm. They knew the in's and out's of how the "system" at the firm worked, who to contact to get things processed, and which "button" to push to accomplish a specific task. Needless to say, they were superb at performing all the typical secretarial tasks, and even specialized in "packaging" our pleadings for filing with the INS (and its successor, United States Citizenship and Immigration Services) and other governmental agencies.

by professional librarians. A sizable billing department with its many professionals handled time keeping, billing and collection, and various management reporting functions. Contrast all of these amenities with my solo practice where I was the attorney, legal secretary, law clerk, receptionist, office manager, mailroom clerk, accounting and messenger all rolled into one. Even at the Southfield firm with which I was an associate for nine years, the only support I had were legal secretaries for typing, and law clerks for court filing. There were about 60 attorneys working out of the Bloomfield Hills office at the time; getting to know most of them even just by sight or by name was a chore in and of itself. As a large and complex organization, on the other hand, everything took much time and processing through multiple levels, a thicket of channels, and myriad departments, before anything could be approved or implemented. One must also learn which level, channel or department to resort to so as to initiate the process in the first place. Furthermore, Sheldon was prescient when he expressed concern about my health in undertaking the project assignment for Dickinson Wright. I was leaving the office one evening later than usual, sometime after 6 p.m. Julie, one of the immigration associates, was still in her office working intensely. When I casually asked why she was not going home yet, she replied as a matter of factly, "It's *only* six-thirty," as if the evening was still young and she still had many more hours of work ahead of her that evening. "Long" hours meant *really* long hours at a large corporate law firm.

With such a comprehensive array of logistical, technological and personnel support, I had no excuse but to perform my very best to successfully complete the project well before the deadline. It was hardly a walkover though, as the project was not the type of immigration matter typically encountered by a solo practitioner or even a small general civil practice law firm. The client was a multi-million-dollar multinational corporation. The individuals slated to be transferred to the United States were senior corporate executives and highly skilled professionals accustomed to receiving and expected premier and prompt service at the highest competency level. All I's must be dotted and all T's must be crossed perfectly and in flawless synchronicity. Millions of dollars were potentially at stake, allowing no room for any glitches or second guesses. It was especially a high-wire act when one considers that we were in many respects at the mercy and discretion of immigration examiners and consular officers issuing visas. There were many variables not within the immigration practitioner's control; all we could do was to have a "Plan B" at the ready for the "just in case" even under the best of circumstances.

Fortunately for me, all went exceedingly well without a glitch and ahead of schedule. By the end of November, my project was winding down, and I was fully expecting to be released from the assignment any day. Instead, one morning in early December, Larry came into my office with practically a wheel-barrel of client matter files. Apparently, he continued to need my services to work on other and additional immigration matters for mostly Japanese corporate clients. In fact, most of the files had very urgent deadlines. I was pleasantly surprised, as that meant my paychecks would continue for a while longer. I also felt gratified as that was a clear indication that Larry approved of my job performance thus far. I, therefore, continued to work diligently on the additional files assigned to me. Yet the more files I completed, the more I was assigned. I congratulated myself for having had sixteen years of hard-earned practice experience which enabled me to remain calm and collected even while working under considerable time and clients' expectations pressures.

In early January 1997, Larry stunned me with his decision to offer me full-time employment as Of Counsel with Dickinson Wright's immigration practice group. I remembered asking Mom and Dad, when I telephoned them later that day with that piece of good news, to pinch me next time I saw them so that I would know that the job offer was a reality, and if it was a dream, not to ever wake me up. It would take another full month before the hiring decision was approved by all "levels." February 11, 1997, was the day I officially became a Dickinson Wright attorney. For the first time since I was sworn in as an attorney and an officer of the court in November of 1980, I was unreservedly happy and proud to be an attorney. As an attorney in the immigration practice group, I focused entirely and exclusively on immigration cases, mostly business- and employment-related immigration matters. I sometimes viewed it whimsically as "human logistics," facilitating the transfer of foreign business executives and specialists into and out of the United States. It was by and large a "non-combat" type of lawyering that I belatedly realized that I much preferred. In fact, the goal was to avoid any litigation or appeal, but to accomplish each "human transfer" smoothly and on the very first application. It was as non-adversarial as lawyering could be, because we were not exactly "fighting" the governmental agencies and officials, but were following the laws and regulations in obtaining specified benefits for non-citizens. It was more advocacy, which I enjoyed, than confrontation, which I abhorred. In short order, I would also discover that I reaped enormous emotional satisfaction from each case successfully completed. Each time I was successful in obtaining employment authorization in or a visa to enter the United States for an alien, I would recall my own imbroglio with INS and the countless hurdles I had to clear in order to stay and work in this country. Thus, each alien I was able to assist was akin to a sort of sweet "revenge" for the immigration grief that I myself had to endure and overcome. There were many times when I had to personally appear at the INS District Office or at a port-of-entry to represent an individual, such as a prospective employee of our firm's corporate client. In the olden days when I myself was an alien, I would try to avoid those appearances if I could at all help it, because it would mean I was applying for some immigration "benefits" and thus subjecting myself to the whims and mercy of the examining officer. As an attorney, and by then a United States citizen, representing an alien at those same hotspots, I was often greeted with respect and courtesy by the immigration and customs officers. How the tables had turned.

What I appreciated even more was my colleagues at the firm; they were truly of a different breed. Far from being cold-hearted corporate mouthpieces or calculating mercenaries, I found them to be caring individuals with a strong sense of decency and rectitude, and of the highest professional caliber.[31] The firm and its attorneys also took seriously our responsibility to provide *pro bono publico* legal services. That made my very long work hours at the office not only bearable but even enjoyable and meaningful.

---

[31] Let me count the many ways that I personally have been impressed by and have benefited from my esteemed colleagues' professionalism and magnanimity. Henry M. Grix, who prepared my last will and testament as well as that for Mrs. Chin, and his spouse, Howard W. Israel, have been generous activists, financially and personally, for LGBTQ and other enlightened, progressive causes for decades. Henry's younger colleague in his Estate Planning and Administration practice group, Judith Fertel Layne, not herself gay, has been an outspoken and steadfast advocate for the LGBTQ community. Amy A. Stawski, in the Family Law practice group, had been a friend and sage legal counsel. When Bev threatened to sue me for galimony, Amy assured me that could never happen, declaring: "Go ahead, [Bev], make my day!" Then there was the late Maryanne Kickham (née Zack), who advised me, prepared and recorded the quit claim deed for Bev to transfer her one-half interest in one of our investment properties in accord and satisfaction for her debt (the "running tab") owed me after we parted company. Maureen H. Burke, a seasoned real estate attorney, drafted and recorded another quit claim deed for me in a later transfer from Bev when our dealings with each other were admittedly tense. Throughout my tenure at the firm, I had enjoyed the enchanting friendship and unflinching support of Elise S. Levasseur, my comrade-in-arms. Cynthia A. Moore, Monica J. Labe, Kathleen A. Lang, Julia D. Darlow, Bernadette M. Dennehy, Deborah L. Grace, James A. Samborn, Dennis W. Archer, Larry J. Stringer, Roger H. Cummings, Timothy H. Howlett, Mark R. High, William E. Elwood, and Thomas D. Hammerschmidt, Jr., to name just a few, were the finest attorneys with whom I had the honor and privilege of associating in the practice of law.

In sum, this turn of events leading to my employment with Dickinson Wright was the ultimate reversal of fortune for me in a matter of just four or five months. It was pure, unadulterated bliss gracefully endowed, for which I was eternally grateful.

Finally getting a sense of accomplishment and recognition in my professional life, and cruising along with what I clearly was well-suited to handle, was only one side of the coin, the shiny side. The personal life side of the coin, the tarnished side, continued to be agonizing. Even as unhappy as she claimed to be, Bev showed no sign of quitting the relationship. I had, on the other hand, by then convinced myself to persevere and try to resolve our issues, if only I had a clear understanding of what those issues really were. Since I was working long hours at the office, usually from 9 a.m. to 9 p.m., the only time I had to interact with her was on weekends. More and more, we would just be going through the motions of "doing something" together. It could be a meal out at one of our favorite restaurants, or taking in a movie. Since she did not much care for window shopping, I sometimes would go by myself to browse at the Somerset Collection. In retrospect, and speaking strictly for myself, I felt very miserable and completely lacking emotionally, and that was why I shopped, or wandered, or searched for or purchased something and anything in a futile attempt to fill an ever enlarging void in my life.

Out of that misery, however, I managed to find solace in long-standing and newly-found pastimes. Ever since I became an attorney and was able to afford more than a compact all-in-one stereo in the early 1980's, I had been gradually and systematically upgrading my audio components. Victor Iagnemma, the operational director under Sid Hiller, Jim's father, who owned and operated several local supermarkets, became my audiophile buddy and mentor. I learned much about high-end audio components from him, even though I could not afford those exquisite pieces with stratospheric price tags. I subscribed to audiophile magazines, and on weekends, would often be the only woman "hanging out" at the local audio stores, auditioning their latest and greatest audio gear. With the advent of compact discs, and the apparent demise of vinyl LPs, I became an avowed contrarian and began hunting for and collecting LPs. There were used record stores to patronize, and LP shows and swap meets to attend. I was quite amused when LPs apparently had been making an impressive comeback in recent years. On most Sunday evenings, you would find me totally immersed and engrossed in music listening which worked to recharge me for another grueling week of long hours at the office.

On another front, since I bought my first fountain pen in New York City in June of 1996, I also started collecting writing instruments. I discovered the world of pen shows which were held in major cities at various times of the year and usually on weekends. That gave me the perfect excuse to travel which in and of itself was another one of my passions. Bev also became interested in fountain pens, and she often accompanied me on those road trips. We had attended the pen shows in Chicago, Washington, D.C., Columbus, and of course, Michigan. In July of 1999, I took Dad with me to the Miami Pen Show, and I remembered that cherished vacation with him as if it was yesterday. We stayed at the 4-star hotel where the show was held. Dad particularly enjoyed the pristine pool in the hot and humid afternoons. He quickly became popular with many of the vendors at the show; he was just such an outgoing and gregarious gentleman. As a connoisseur of all fine things, he was fascinated by some of the very exclusive limited edition pens highlighted at the show. Incidentally, a couple of years prior, I stumbled upon a toys and collectibles shop in Southfield; it had a sizable inventory of Marklin toy trains. For his birthday that year, I gave Dad a "starter" set of Marklin trains, rails and accessories. I had no idea whatever might have happened to the set that we played with when I was a young child, but obviously, nostalgia beckoned me there and then. Dad was so delighted with that gift that he cleared his large rosewood table in his "paradise" (some would call it his "man cave"—the finished basement of his home) and set up the Marklin train set there. In the spring thereafter, I drove Mom and Dad to the shop, and you can only picture their glee as they chatted away with the older couple who owned the shop, and as we picked out more Marklin trains to add to Dad's collection. The moral of this story is simply that the "simple joys of life," however each of us choose to define them, are priceless.

I rented a car and drove Dad around, taking in the diverse and pulsating city that was Miami and its environs. We took an airboat tour of the Everglades, drove up to Boca Raton, and then south to Miami Beach. Standing on the Beach, Dad masterfully took a series of photographs, intended to be "stitched" together to make a panoramic picture of the colorful, art deco buildings by the beach. Dad and I both took loads of photographs on that vacation, and that was also when I realized just how outstanding my Leica "Minilux" compact camera was. After the debacle of my yielding only one photograph out of eleven rolls of exposed film on my trip to Italy in November of 1997, the Miami trip was the first time I had the occasion to try that camera out again. The colors, vividness and sharpness enthralled me. Dad was clearly the better photographer, but the camera he was using was simply no match for the Leica. One more trip later, taken at the turn of the Millennium, would make me a Leica devotee for life.

In my early days as an attorney, I was filing some pleadings one day at the Wayne County Circuit Court. Lining up at the Court Clerk's office, I noticed a drawing, taped to the side of one of the clerks' desk, of some turkeys with the following caption: "How can I soar like an eagle when I work with turkeys?" I did not view it as a mean-spirited indictment of her co-workers, but admired that deputy clerk's courage, candor and sense of humor.

At Dickinson Wright, I harbored the exact opposite sentiment: how could I not soar when I worked with such a distinguished convocation of eagles? At their Immigration Practice Group, I started out working on immigration cases for mostly Japanese automotive suppliers. In April of 1997, I was handpicked to undertake a different assignment; immigration cases for a very substantial Canada-based Tier-1 automotive supplier, with operations in Europe and increasingly in Asia, became my primary responsibility. The volume of work grew exponentially over the years when I was with the firm. Indeed, my tenure at that firm was the golden era of my professional career in more ways than one; I blossomed there, I belonged there, and I felt at home there.

The firm necessarily was a bastion of traditions, having been founded almost 140 years ago by two young lawyers of Scottish ancestry. My initiation to one such tradition was my first attendance at the firm's Annual Dinner held in November of 1997, at the venerable Detroit Athletic Club. Nay, this was not your ordinary office holiday party. The formal invitation specified "black tie" dress code, and indeed, male attorneys strutted out in their full-regalia tuxedoes. Back in the "good old days," the Annual Dinner was a noble idea to gather around Thanksgiving to celebrate the year's triumphs and tribulations, regale your fellow warriors with "war stories," eat (lavishly), drink (with wild abandon), be merry (and even good-heartedly mischievous), and in general, enjoy a sumptuous evening of fine dining with all the trimmings and without having to be lawyerly serious as one had to be for the other 364 days of the year. It was in truth still a rather stuffy and male-oriented affair, complete with cigars and cognac after the gluttonous feast, with a whiff of debauchery tossed in for good measure, if legends were to be believed. As I would learn, each Annual Dinner had an organizing committee comprising volunteer or designated attorneys. A "theme" would be chosen by the committee each year, which was usually a tongue-in-cheek but all-in-good-fun sort of décor or *leitmotif* for the evening. In recent years, with more women joining the firm as attorneys, the admittedly traditional—and male-oriented—Annual Dinner could pose a challenge or two for the female law practitioner. First, the dress code: women attorneys by and large attended the Annual Dinner in high heels and elegant evening gowns, as *dictated* by the "black tie" dress code. I personally, however, found that tremendously ironic and entirely unsatisfactory. Female attorneys, as professional and competent as any of their male counterparts, had to attend the gala as "ladies" essentially, with all the frailties, fragilities and negative connotations that that much maligned term entailed. I thus decided to blaze my own trail, rock the boat, raise the bar, up the ante, set precedent and, indeed, break with tradition. I was able to purchase for myself a lovely tuxedo for women, offered by a well-known female fashion designer no less. The tuxedo shirt was a tad more difficult, until I found a custom shirt maker. I decided that I did not look reasonable at all with a bowtie or cummerbund, and hence, I dispensed with both. Instead, I went with studs. Over the years, I was able to collect several sets of gorgeous, sterling silver and gold studs to complement my tuxedo shirt. I had an existing collection of cufflinks for my French-cuffed shirts. For my Annual Dinner tuxedo shirt, I usually wore the pair of cloisonné enamel cufflinks bearing the Columbia University (of which Barnard is an independent campus) emblem. For the 2001 Annual Dinner, I was obviously in a flamboyant and renegade mood; in place of my usual black patent leather wingtips, I strode into the fray in my pair of Lucchese bright red leather dress cowboy boots. No one had ever said a word to me about how I should conform to "tradition" and don an evening gown; I gave my colleagues, male and female, due credit for being most enlightened.

The agenda for the Annual Dinner was set down by tradition, with minor variations here and there. Therein lay a couple more "curve balls" for the women attorneys in attendance. About mid-way through the multi-course, sit-down formal dinner came the call for the "Toast to the Firm." I was told that it was a traditional Scottish toast: all celebrants would get up from the dinner table, step up onto and stand on their respective chairs, and then place one foot on the table while raising their glass in toast. Try doing that in your slinky evening gown, even as most women attorneys had no choice but to ditch their high heels before even attempting such a high-wire act. The women lawyers of Dickinson Wright were an intrepid bunch, obviously. Alas, when all the feasting, toasting and merriment were finally done, next on the agenda came "Cigars and Cognac," to the astonishment of most women attorneys who would by and large flee to and seek shelter at the dessert tables (multiple tables) before retreating to the exits. All jesting aside, the Annual Dinner was a tradition worth observing because it was very bonding and empowering. No spouse, secretaries, or assistants in attendance, just hundreds of one's brothers and sisters at bar, under one roof, breaking bread together, and celebrating each other. The firm may have to rent an aircraft hangar to host the annual event when it grows even larger, but then the theme for the evening could aptly be "Top Gun."

Vivian returned from Hong Kong for visits often enough, but in April of 1998, she returned with a "special guest," Ted Fenna, a Briton some years her senior. They originally met when Vivian was in her early 20's and working as a secretary in the same firm in which Ted was an engineer and partner. When Vivian returned to Hong Kong in 1995, they reconnected and fell in love. He proposed to marry her, and I could not be happier for Vivian, as I could see how very fond she was of Ted. For our parents, however, it took Ted a bit of time to work his charm, given the age and racial differences. During that very joyful visit, I drove all of them to tour my office in Bloomfield Hills one Saturday, after a sumptuous lunch at The Capital Grille at Somerset Collection. To this day, I was so glad that Mom and Dad got to see where I worked, and how proud I was of the firm. They in turn were very impressed with practically everything about the firm and my physical office, facilities and amenities. I had never paused to wonder what might have been on my parents' mind as they roamed the firm's premises; but if I had, I would imagine that they would have exclaimed with glee and pride: "My daughter, the lawyer!" After the office tour, I drove them through the tranquil and grand Cranbrook campus nearby, and dropped in on the Cranbrook Art Museum with its collection of Eames furniture pieces which Ted particularly admired. I was driving a Dodge "Grand Caravan," which I leased for Bev's use as she was so enamored with the pre-owned Dodge "Caravan" that we had for a few years for schlepping to and from the Mayo Clinic. The "Grand Caravan" was perfect for chauffeuring the entourage in comfort, especially for our trip up to Toronto to visit friends and relatives, and to fill up on authentic Chinese meals and groceries.

Two short months later, Mom and Dad and I attended Vivian and Ted's wedding in Kent, the United Kingdom. Vivian was resplendent in her silk brocaded Chinese gown in brilliant colors, adorned with tasteful, solid yellow gold jewelry that Vivian handpicked for the occasion. That wedding gave me the rare opportunity to vacation with Mom and Dad; at the time, though, I did not realize just how precious that week was spent with them in and around London. As it turned out, I would not have another chance to be with them exclusively for an entire week, enjoying each other's company as well as the local cuisine, sights and sounds. As we arrived a couple of days before the wedding day, Ted played host by driving us around Kent to show us the city center, as well as several of the 180-plus world renowned Kent gardens in full bloom. Mom, Dad and I left Kent the day after the wedding for London. In addition to covering the usual tourist beat, the highlight of our visit was Mom's reunion with one of her best friends from high school who had emigrated to the United Kingdom more than 40 years prior. She lived quite a distance from London, and we had to take a train and a taxi ride to arrive at her home on a soggy London afternoon. I would always remember fondly those several fun-filled days exploring London with Mom and Dad, mostly on foot, from the British Museum to Westminster Abbey to the Tower of London, and from Buckingham Palace to Trafalgar Square. Life's treasured moments are treasured often in hindsight. I bought a classic English bridle leather portfolio briefcase at "Swaine Adeney Brigg," one of the many fine purveyors located inside the Piccadilly Arcade. It is now a keepsake that brings back vivid memories of that enchanting vacation with my parents.

After more than two years of putting in very long hours day in and day out at Dickinson Wright, just as Sheldon had forewarned me, my stamina and endurance, if not my overall health, took a toll. I was not stressed out, but was beginning to feel chronic fatigue. Looking back, it would have been beneficial if my home and personal life were at least supportive so that I could have sufficiently replenished as I plowed on. At that point in our relationship, Bev had become a consummate consumer. She had not had gainful employment for more than a decade. We had divested most of our rental properties by then, and thus, there was not much for her to clean or paint. She was never much of a chef, and I had never asked her to cook for me, and she did not. She would do housecleaning for pay, if asked for instance by Jo, but would hardly ever clean our own home. I had suggested that I pay for a house cleaning service, but she retorted that if I was willing to pay for such services, I might as well pay her. That led to a Mexican standoff, as I thought it ludicrous for me to have to pay her to clean our own home on the one hand, while she adamantly refused to allow any housekeeper to come clean up on the other hand. I was simply too busy at work, and I spent most of my time at the office in any case, to have time to do any cleaning or even to harp about the unkempt state of our abode. In the late 1980's and through the late 1990's, we used to host a house party at least once a year, and that would be the only time she would give the house a once-over. However, since then, we hardly invited anyone over, because she did not bother to clean, which in turn inhibited our inviting guests over, and the vicious circle thus became self-perpetuating.

I did not realize, or perhaps I did not want to acknowledge, that I was only going through the motions when we dined out occasionally, and when we took trips and vacations, all of which she participated in sometimes perfunctorily and other times nonchalantly. As my professional life was blossoming brilliantly, my personal life was quietly and unceremoniously descending into the abyss. Subconsciously, I was compensating for what was lacking, and rewarding myself for my working hard, with material possessions even as my budget would not accommodate such extravagance. To make matters worse, I unwittingly double downed on that self-destructive behavior by also showering Bev with material goods. It was as if the purchases would paper over the growing void and schism in our relationship. A case in point: we went to see the movie, *The Lost World: Jurassic Park*, when it was released in 1997, and I was mesmerized by the beefed-up Mercedes-Benz SUV featured in the movie. As a movie promotion, there was even a replica model of the vehicle displayed for a time in trendy downtown Birmingham. That prompted me to pay a visit to my local Mercedes-Benz dealer, and of course, without much effort, the salesperson was able to convince me to reserve my very own Mercedes-Benz "ML320." I managed to pass up my turn to purchase in the fall of 1997, but I did buy the 1998 model. That was quite a reach from a Ford "Escort" station wagon. I enjoyed that SUV tremendously while I had it. It was gargantuan and solidly built in Stuttgart, Germany. I was able to conquer all snowdrifts and just about all obstacles that stood in my way. The OEM customized Bose sound system onboard was surprisingly superb, allowing music to resonate sweetly and vibrantly within the vehicle's cavernous interior. My "ML320" braved a snowstorm as I drove myself and Elise to a meeting with clients at a plant located in Ontario, Canada, a two-hour drive away in fine weather. We literally carved through ice and snow on the frozen highway, with semi-trailers flipped over left and right and dotting the snow-covered landscape. Our clients were duly impressed as we arrived unfazed and composed, despite the inclement weather. After a few years, with gasoline prices trending into the stratosphere, I decided to sell the vehicle. Moreover, it was the vehicle I was driving back and forth umpteen times to the hospital where Mom was diagnosed with colon cancer and stayed for almost three months recuperating from her surgery. It was laden with too many memories of sadness and hopelessness for me. No need to grieve for me though, as I then proceeded to purchase one of my all-time dream cars: a 2001 BMW "325xi," complete with bordeaux leather interior, and a Harman Kardon premium audio system. Just to make sure that I broke my bank even-handedly and thoroughly, I had advanced the money the year prior for Bev to purchase her dream car, a 2000 Volvo "V40" station wagon.

I could not be happier when the lease ended for the Dodge "Grand Caravan" to make way for the Volvo, as I had a most bizarre and unpleasant experience with that minivan in the fall of 1999. Jo had rented out a condominium she owned in a suburb west of Detroit. Her tenant had suffered a heart attack and died in the home. Jo then decided to sell the condominium, and asked Bev to clean it up and repaint the interior walls so that it could be shown to prospective purchasers. Over the years, Bev had the habit of lugging home odds and ends that tenants left behind in our various rental homes—bits of carpet remnants and all sorts of scraps. We did not need and had no room for any of such leftovers, yet she could not help herself from scavenging. I was not a superstitious person, but certain Chinese folklore was ingrained in me by virtue of my having grown up in a Chinese community. One of the taboos was knowingly bringing into one's home something that had belonged to a deceased person who was not a member of one's own family. Hence, I literally begged Bev not to bring home anything from that condominium. She acknowledged my plea by mumbling her agreement. About a week or so later, I happened to be either getting something from or putting something into the minivan when I was overwhelmed by a foul smell emanating from the minivan's back cargo area. I was not particularly alarmed as I understood Bev had to transport all sorts of cleaning materials and painting supplies in the minivan for her work on the condominium, which project she had just completed. It was a weekend and since I had time, I decided to clean up the area right there and then. As I wiped and scrubbed the cargo area with detergents and cleaners, and vacuumed the carpeting, the offensive stench became increasingly nauseating and overpowering. Even though it was a very cool fall day, I was perspiring profusely as I cleaned. Stranger yet, I felt a "mask" or film of indescribable filth clinging on to my face and arms as I cleaned. I hurriedly finished the cleanup, and practically jumped into the shower, urgently trying to wash the malodorous grime, real or imagined, off my body. I was convinced then that Bev had hauled *something* home from that condominium, though she repeatedly denied it. Whatever that *something* was had certainly left its malevolence in our minivan *and* somewhere in our home. I did not want to linger on that thought, as the memories of that close encounter of the inexplicable kind were haunting enough.

For the first few years after my kidney transplant in 1994, I returned to the Mayo Clinic annually for checkups. I would make a long-weekend vacation out of each of those driving trips, with Bev joining me and stopping over in Chicago *en route* for a day or two of extravagant shopping and fine dining. We would browse the shops along the Magnificent Mile, enjoy a spot of tea at the Four Seasons Hotel, and indulge in the gluttonous Sunday brunch at "The Signature Room At The 95th" atop the John Hancock Building. We were living the charmed life, even if just for the week-end. While I felt extremely grateful for being able to afford such creature comforts, Bev seemed to be increasingly blasé about it all as if nothing delighted her anymore. Instead of curbing my extravagance, I upped the ante by arranging even more costly trips in the hope of pleasing her. She in turn grew more ho hum and entitled, increasingly taking for granted such luxuries as par for the course. In June of 1999, for instance, I was attending a law-related conference in Seattle. I made that an almost week long vacation, with a driving day trip to Vancouver. The hotel accommodation was first-rate, as were our meals at various notable eateries, as was the shopping, courtesy of the proliferation of fine boutiques in the vicinity of our hotel. Yet she did not seem to enjoy any of the amenities. Whatever happened to the good old days when we used to delight in the food and each other's company when we were grabbing a bite at the lowly neighborhood diner? It was such eureka moments when I realized just how much she had changed over the years. Those occasional weekend trips were my only chance to "recharge" from the intense 12-hour work days throughout the year, yet I felt even more emotionally drained after each trip because of her lackadaisical attitude and grudging presence. Even worse, she would throw a tantrum without any rhyme or reason or provocation. I recall one of our driving trips to Toronto when I was totally flabbergasted by her "moodiness." We had just finished a sumptuous brunch at the Four Season Hotel, and were about to take a stroll window-shopping in the Bloor-Yorkville area. No sooner than our having stepped out of the Hotel when she all of a sudden refused to proceed. Startled, I asked her what might be bothering her. Her response was "the crowds;" there were supposedly "too many people" on the street for her. Then, I recalled an earlier time when this behavior exhibited itself. It was when she went to Hong Kong with me in late 1988, and we were at a subway station, walking toward a platform to board the train that would take us to our destination. A crowd had just disembarked from the train and was walking toward us. She froze and refused to proceed. I ended having to hail a taxi instead of riding the subway. There in Toronto, the crowd was not even half as massive, yet she adamantly refused to budge. Call it phobia or tantrum, her condition had clearly worsened in the interim years. Since the mid-1990's, she had become increasingly reclusive. She would insist on my driving her home if she was suddenly not in the mood to attend whatever function we had set out for. That happened when we were invited to a reception for donors who supported a certain LGBTQ organization. That also happened at one of my office holiday parties. We had practically arrived at the door of the event when she demanded that I turn back and drive her home.

As the Millennium New Year drew near, Bev indicated that she wanted to do something special to mark the occasion. In retrospect, ever since my parents settled in Windsor, Bev had always somehow had an excuse for me to be away from home so that I would not be able to celebrate special occasions with my parents, be it my birthday, or holidays such as Christmas or New Year. I did not realize the subterfuge at the time partly because I was admittedly too eager to go on trips in order to get a break from my hour-intensive job. I had since been very remorseful, but it was too late to regret; I could only lament and forgive myself for the road not taken which should have been. I was very busy at the office the few months before the Millennium New Year, and did not have time to plan a special trip as Bev requested. Just a few days prior to the New Year, on a lurch, I searched for last minute airfare specials, and Albuquerque, New Mexico, popped up on my screen; I had never been to the Southwest, and New Mexico sounded exotic enough for our Millennium weekend getaway.

Sealing the deal was the availability of four-star hotel accommodation at bargain basement rates in both Albuquerque and Santa
Fe. I surmised that my good fortune resulted from trip cancella-
tions by those who were wearied of traveling, given the hype and
jitters about "Y2K."

Off we went for a four-day stay in those two cities in New
Mexico to ring in the Millennium. We spent the first day in
Albuquerque, strolling around Historic Old Town, and sampling
local cuisine which was decidedly chili-dominant. Bev was not
particularly enthralled with the sights, sounds and flavors that city
had to offer. It looked as if we were going to have a dud for a vacation again. We decided to move on to Santa Fe the following day,
and her mood improved visibly. I felt particularly rejuvenated, as
I took to the high blue skies and cool fresh air of New Mexico. The
hotel we stayed at in Santa Fe was superb and centrally located. We
were within easy walking distance from the town center, where we
enjoyed several delectable meals in between browsing the stores.
We were thrilled to stumble upon a boutique operated by a crafts-
woman who handmade measured-to-fit custom leather shoes and
boots. We each ordered a pair of shoes from her. We spent almost
an entire afternoon on Canyon Road, traipsing in and out of the
many exquisite art galleries, admiring the diverse art pieces on
display, from bronze sculptures to glass creations bursting with
colors. Lunch at a recommended restaurant amidst the galleries
was magnificent. We could have easily spent a week on Canyon
Road if we could spare the time.

On New Year's Eve day, we visited Bandelier National
Monument to view the fabled cliff dwellings, rock paintings and
petroglyphs. It was almost dusk by the time we drove back to Santa
Fe. I remember vividly the sight and sensation as I gazed upon the
brilliant sunset; the firmament was a palette of glowing orange,
red, purple and gold. The last sundown of the millennium flamed
out spectacularly, as if to foretell and usher in the mysteries yet to

unfold in the coming millennium. It was a divine moment, crystalized in time and space in my consciousness.

Two side trips made during our stay in New Mexico left a profound impression on me and unexpectedly became a catalyst for change. We visited the Bosque del Apache National Wildlife Refuge, and the Very Large Array in successive days. I had never felt closer to nature than when I was at Bosque del Apache. From that excursion, I recognized the significance of what I termed "communing with nature" in my life. In the late afternoon as if on cue, thousands of light geese and sandhill cranes darkened and covered the sky as they returned en masse to the water at the Refuge to roost for the night. It was a sight—and sound—to behold. I tried to capture the spectacle, but the images recorded by my modest camera equipment on hand could not do justice to the majesty and splendor of the moment.

The three-hour drive from Santa Fe to reach the Very Large Array was fascinating enough in and of itself. We exited the interstate freeway and headed west on US-60 which was more akin to a country road. The further west we drove, the more deserted our surroundings. There were hardly any signs of civilization on this high desert plateau which is a part of the Colorado Plateau, specifically, the Plains of San Agustin, 50 miles west of Socorro. It was as if we were journeying into a different plane, a vastly unfamiliar dimension. It was also eerily silent as we neared the Very Large Array. Once we arrived and stepped out of our rental car, the silence was resoundingly deafening. It is impossible to describe the sound of silence, except that it felt as if we were no longer on the third planet from the Sun but had been teleported to outer space lightyears away from our galaxy. My body also reacted to the ethereal environment; it became lightened, rejuvenated and empowered. Before us and as far as our eyes could see were the giant, white "dishes" tilting upwards toward the sky beyond, peering into the infinite, imposing, all-hearing, all-knowing. The dishes were radio antennas, each 82 feet in diameter; a total of 27 radio antennas were arranged in a Y-shaped configuration forming the Very Large Array. There were tracks on the ground for deploying the antennas. I walked up close to the base of one of the antennas; staring up at it, everything else was dwarfed by the antenna. In that instant, I seemed to understand human's innate longing to comprehend the secrets of the universe, our existentialist quest for universal kinship, and indeed, our quixotic search for the true meaning of life.

I had brought with me on that trip two cameras: a Nikon "N60," an entry-level single lens reflex camera with a stock medium zoom lens; and the Leica "Minilux" compact camera which, as I had learned the hard way, was not your usual simple point-and-shoot camera. I shot many of the same scenes and subjects with both cameras, not as a deliberate experiment to compare the two, but just because I was having fun. When the rolls of film were developed and photographs printed, I gasped at the ones taken by the Leica. Confirming my realization from the trip to Miami with Dad more than a year earlier, the images captured by the Leica immensely outshone those with the Nikon, granted that it was only an entry-level Nikon SLR. The Leica photographs exuded life, spirit, soul. The photographs of the Very Large Array taken with the Leica "Minilux" grasped, preserved and reproduced viscerally what many master photographers hailed as "spirit of the place." I was intrigued, and more crucially, my interest in photography was at once rekindled. That reawakened love for outdoors photography would turn out to be my lifesaver in the tumultuous and vexatious few years to come.

I plunged into my 12-hour workdays again upon returning from New Mexico, except that my eyes seemed to have been opened wider, my sight sharper, as my heart and soul having been nourished by the beauty and magic that I experienced at the dawn of the new Millennium. As it turned out, I needed all the replenishment I could get to endure a year 2000 that almost blind-sided me. In January, I made a weekend trip to Boston to partici-pate in a mini-reunion with several of my SSGC classmates. I had missed a reunion the year prior, and had thus promised to make up for my absence at the next reunion. The highlight of the Boston reunion included a tour, led by Vivian Fung, of the Harvard Law School Library and the Warren B. Rudman U.S. Courthouse in Concord, New Hampshire. Vivian was a member of the architect team that designed the renovations for the Library and the con-struction of the Courthouse. We were awed by Vivian's accom-plishments. After a weekend of catching up on the latest with each other, fondly reminiscing over old photo albums, and sharing many fine meals, we concluded the gathering and flew out of town just ahead of a fierce New England nor'easter.

I should not have unpacked my bags as I had to make an unexpected visit to the Mayo Clinic in March. The values from the routine laboratory tests for my kidney function suddenly went awry. Fearing a rejection of the kidney graft, I rushed to the Mayo Clinic to have a thorough checkup. Fortunately, the aber-ration was determined to have been caused by a recent change in my immunosuppressant medications, and not implicating an organ rejection.

In early spring, a senior partner of the firm who had since become a good friend, Henry M. Grix, passed on to me the wel-comed news that the firm had in the previous year decided to extend health and medical coverage to life partners of its employ-ees. Henry was one of the partners introduced to me very early on when I was working as a contract attorney. I recall running into him one morning at the office, and he was spotting a very colorful bowtie. I reflexively exclaimed with what I meant to be a com-pliment: "Oh, you look beautiful!" I then realized I might have offended him with the adjective "beautiful," which was commonly perceived to have a feminine connotation. I was relieved when he responded with a big grin and a delightful "Thank you!" I would learn much later that he was openly gay, and he and his life partner, Howard W. Israel, had been vociferous and staunch supporters of LGBTQ rights and other progressive causes. Both Henry and I had missed the open enrollment period in the year prior, but we hurriedly filed the requisite affidavit so that our respective life partners could enjoy coverage in November of 2000. My filing of that affidavit momentously marked my official coming-out at the firm.

Barely a month later, my world turned upside down with Mom's diagnosis of colon cancer, followed by extensive surgery, and her prolonged hospitalization due to a protracted recuperation. It was the first time I had to confront mortality head-on, even if it was not my own mortality. I was not equipped to deal with death; I could not deal with death, whether mine or another's, and whether as a concept or in reality. Hence, I shifted into denial mode for self-protection, from the moment I was informed of Mom's cancer diagnosis. I now wonder, of course, whether I would have treasured the time spent with Mom more if I were not in denial, and whether I would and should have spent more time with her if I had been able to acknowledge that her time on earth was limited. Again, I can now only lament and forgive myself for what could or should have been.

While Mom was very slowly recovering in the hospital in late spring into early summer, my own health was raising alarm bells for me. I was again beginning to experience numbness in my legs, starting at my toes, and moving on to my feet, and up my calves. I was familiar with that tell-tale numbness; the inflammatory process in my spinal canal was again rearing its ugly head after an eight-year hiatus. I remembered my neurosurgeon's admonition to consult with him as soon as I experienced any symptom that might implicate spinal cord issues. By then, the neurosurgeon who successfully operated on me in 1992 had just left Michigan for Medford, Oregon. He had left me in the care of his colleague, Dr. William Chandler of the University of Michigan Health System. Because of Mom's health situation, I did not consult with him until the summer. An MRI was taken, and Dr. Chandler confirmed that I needed spinal cord surgery again. I was not informed at the time, but the surgery was not to decompress the arachnoid cysts, but instead to surgically install a shunt to drain a syrinx (a fluid-filled sac *inside* my spinal cord) that was causing my numbness and increasing difficulty in walking. Alas, I had to postpone scheduling my own surgery because Bev suddenly developed symptoms that looked suspiciously like inflammatory breast cancer. In fact, a local gynecologist with whom she consulted gave her a preliminary diagnosis of exactly that ferocious and fast growing cancer. It was late August, and we hurried to the Mayo Clinic for the second time that year. We had a couple of very tense weeks, before the surgeon at the Mayo Clinic performed an excisional biopsy and determined that she did not have inflammatory breast cancer, but a benign intraductal papilloma. That was certainly welcomed news, but the cruel irony was that it happened just three months shy of the effective date of her health and medical coverage through my firm. As a result, I had to pay for the medical visit and surgical procedure entirely out of my own pocket, and it was not an insubstantial sum.

With Bev health issues resolved, and Mom having been discharged home from the hospital and undergoing chemotherapy, I could finally schedule my spinal cord surgery for late October. Before the surgery, in September, I made a point of visiting my local camera store to place an order for my very first Leica rangefinder camera: a Leica M6TTL camera body, with a "standard" lens, the Leica 50mm Summicron f/2.0. I had seen an advertisement for the M6TTL in a magazine several years earlier, and had fallen in love with it; it was almost as if it was calling out to me. However, it was priced well beyond my budget then. Since my very positive experience taking pictures with the Leica "Minilux" in Miami and New Mexico, I had been saving up to take the plunge.

My spinal cord surgery with Dr. Chandler proceeded rather uneventfully. I awoke from the surgery feeling a sharp pain down my left knee, but Dr. Chandler assured me that it was temporary nerve pain that would dissipate in a few days, and so it did. At the time, I did not know that the operation was to place a shunt to drain the syrinx, and not to decompress the numerous arachnoid cysts. I did not even know the technical distinction between a syrinx and an arachnoid cyst. After a month or two of physical therapy, I was off to the races again. The numbness and paralysis in my legs had receded, and I could walk spritely enough. In fact, I felt so fit in 2001 that I did not even have to install the hand controls in my new BMW "325xi;" I could drive it using my right foot and enjoy shifting gears again with its clutch-less manual shift. I was back at work in less than two weeks, in good time to receive the exciting news that I had been named a member (partner) of the firm effective the first of 2001. That was a most gratifying and significant milestone for me, personally and professionally. Membership did have its privileges. I would come to realize that as a member, even as a very junior one, I commanded more attention and respect, from staff members as well as fellow attorneys. However, with my membership came more responsibility. I was appointed by my Practice Department Manager, Tim Howlett, to serve on the Technology Committee; it was an honor which I humbly accepted, even as I did not think I had the necessary "technology" credentials or background. As a member, I was also expected to develop business opportunities and bring in clients to the firm, and contribute to the firm in other ways. I took those responsibilities very seriously, and thus worked even longer hours, and paid even more meticulous attention to meeting my corporate clients' needs and demands. There were many non-billable activities a member was expected to undertake, including staff training, improving practice policies and procedures, business development and marketing related activities, and the list went on *ad infinitum*. Hence, my job was fast becoming all-consuming, time-wise and energy-wise. Nevertheless, it was a distinct honor and no less a personal pride to be a member of such a distinguished law firm.

Because of the surgery, and my increasing workload, I did not get a chance to put my new Leica through its paces until my trip to San Francisco in May of 2001, and to New York City a month later. Taking photographs with the Leica rangefinder on those two trips made me realize that I am more a rangefinder photographer than an SLR photographer. It was natural, akin to second nature, for me to shoot with the Leica M6TTL, whereas I used to have to "fight" with my Nikon SLRs. With the Leica M6TTL, photographing anything and everything was an unmitigated joy. San Francisco was the locale for our SSGC class reunion. More than 20 classmates from various States and Canada participated in a weekend of rekindling our bonds, sightseeing, and gourmet dining a la Bay Area. It was at that reunion that I reconnected with Rebecca, Connie and Diana with whom I had lost contact for almost thirty years. I also made a point of getting together with Uncle Lai and Janet in Chinatown for afternoon tea. The trip to New York City was to attend the 25th reunion of our Barnard Class. It was a joy to see Roz again; I visited her at her barrier-free condominium that she shared with her life partner Janet, and we enjoyed a sumptuous dinner in the Chelsea neighborhood. Roz and I marveled at the tea reception for LGBTQ alumnae and students, which was an official event of the Reunion. Contrast that with the uptightness we faced in the unenlightened days when we were students at Barnard, and how being a lesbian was then such a taboo, we had most certainly come a long way. It was also thrilling to see Sylvia again after five years. Her children were grown by then, but unfortunately, her husband was then battling cancer, just as my Mom was waging her battles as well. I had plenty of time during that weekend to roam all over Manhattan and visit my old haunts in the Village. I shot many frames with my Leica M6TTL, including a photograph of the World Trade Center as viewed afar from the East Village. Little did I know then that those landmarks would be tragically and atrociously brought down, along with almost 3,000 souls, three short months later. It was also on that trip that I visited the Leica Gallery, and a retailer that sold very fine and exclusive Fogg camera bags that were handcrafted in France by Nigel Fogg and bee berman. I bought my first Fogg bag, a "B Minor," then and there, and my "romance" with the Fogg bags had thrived ever since, with my collection of Fogg bags filling up much of my shelf space.

Once I started taking pictures with my Leica, I simply could not stop; my love for photography had been fully reawakened. I signed up for an introductory photography class offered by a local community college, as I had never had proper instruction in the art and science of photography. I also participated in a black-and-white film developing class with a well-known local photographer, Dennis Greaney. On weekends, instead of shopping and squandering my hard-earned money, I had a new pastime: driving around, almost aimlessly, and stopping whenever and wherever I felt the call to get out of the car and take as many frames as the spirit moved me. Our occasional vacation trips became my full-fledged photography excursions. I would travel with a large Fogg camera bag holding one or two Leica camera bodies and several Leica lenses, together with my trusty Leica "Minilux." Those trips not only gave me the opportunity to hone my photographic skills, but served as a refreshing diversion from the daily grind that was my work life and the increasingly stifling home life. Being outdoors and making photographs reinvigorated me and resuscitated my creative spirit which I had subconsciously suppressed during my lawyering years. As my relationship with Bev became ever more estranged, and the emotional void became ever more distressing, travel photography and music listening—not necessarily in that order—became my solace and salvation. Meanwhile, my collection of Leica camera bodies and lenses had grown rather exponentially since the purchase of my first Leica M camera body. Moreover, I was tickled pink to be able to replace the Nikon cameras and lenses that I reluctantly had to sell in the spring of 1978 to fund my car purchase: an F body and an F2 body, a standard and a telephoto lens (and many more legendary Nikon lenses since), and above all, the same 1960's vintage Nikon F leather system camera case, all in pristine condition. I remembered fondly my weekend photographing in the Grand Traverse and Sleeping Bear Dunes area in the fall of 2001, where I photographed barns and covered bridges, quaint cottages and breathtaking lakeshore scenery. Earlier on that season, I was roaming and photographing in and around West Palm Beach when I was there to undergo craniosacral therapy with Dr. John Upledger. For Christmas and New Year in 2001, Bev and I took a week-long West Caribbean cruise, and visited with Jo on the Gulf side of Florida after the cruise. In the fall of 2002, we enjoyed a weekend in Vermont. My therapist, Hazel, was quite concerned that I would enter into a civil union with Bev while there, given all the relationship issues that I had been discussing with her for years. I knew even then that under no circumstance would I entertain such a notion. In May of 2003, we ventured out to San Diego. In June, I attended a law conference in New Orleans and stayed a couple of days beyond the conference to enjoy the sights, sounds and tastes of that city. Even though on most of those trips, Bev was her usual disengaged self, and she sometimes even picked a fight with me just to be irksome, I found blissful refuge behind the lens. I came away with quite a few images from those trips that I found very spiritually rewarding, such as tranquil lake scenes from Vermont, impressions from various missions outside San Diego, and quirky street scenes from New Orleans.

Mom's health began to seriously falter while I was in New Orleans; yet she was vital and vibrant just days earlier when I visited with them on Father's Day. I rushed home, but there was sadly nothing more I could do to help her, as she had declined to participate in the drug trial that Dr. Qu recommended as a last resort. Instead, I burrowed myself deeper in denial and escapism, and traveled with Bev to New Haven, Connecticut, Rhode Island, and Cape Cod for the July 4th holiday.

I do now regret my wanderlust, and wished I had spent those precious days and hours with Mom instead. Even though I had captured what I considered breathtaking images at Cape Cod, those photographs could have been made any other time, but there was no way to recapture the lost time with Mom. There was more than a year's time between Mom's full recovery from her April 2000 surgery and completing her course of chemotherapy, and her second surgery in November of 2001, when she was in relative robust health and we shared many happy days and quality family time together. Vivian came back to visit very often. We would drive to exquisite tea houses off the beaten path to take tea. I remembered vividly the day we spent strolling through Point Pelee National Park, about six miles south of Leamington, Ontario, and about 38 miles southeast of Windsor. I had taken many photographs on that day, one of which Mom liked a great deal—a beach scene looking out onto Lake Erie. An enlargement of it is hanging on the wall next to my desk in my study, as well as on the wall leading up to the upper level at my parent' home. If it was any consolation for my lost time with Mom, I was able to make many memorable photographs during those two to three precious years before Mom passed away, and which served to "mark" the time and events for me. I had also entered some of my photographs in several international photography contests, and a few had scored points close to Honorable Mention. Mom and Dad were proud of my admittedly amateur efforts, and displayed many of my prints on the walls in their home. Most amazingly, Mom, who never liked to be photographed, started smiling and posing for me. As a result, and thanks to my "non-intimidating" Leica cameras, we now have many alluring and charming photographs to remember her by, taken in her last vital years.

Ever since her cancer diagnosis, Mom had undergone a remarkable transformation in the remainder three years of her life. She became much more relaxed, easy-going and smiled often. She was no longer uptight, and no longer judgmental or critical of people or happenings. She became much more "in the moment," and was fully present in all conversations, activities and events. Nothing seemed to bother or upset her anymore. It was as if she had decided to give up her tight reins over everything and everyone all of the time, and instead, to go with the flow blissfully. Even Dad, the happy-go-lucky guy that he had always been, gleefully remarked to me that Mom had an above-turn change for the better and much jollier, and it was obvious that he was absolutely thrilled with the metamorphosis. I believed her dramatic and positive change in personality and attitudes enabled her to keep her advanced cancer at bay for more than three years. As I had noted, since my kidney transplant at the Mayo Clinic, Mom had fully accepted and completely warmed up to Bev; it was as if Bev could do no wrong. On the other hand, and most ironically, Bev became increasingly hostile to Mom and my family as a whole. That "thaw" on Mom's part in 1994 had made my life much less stressful on the home front as I was no longer torn between Mom and Bev. During the last three years of her life, Mom was even more accommodating of my lifestyle and of Bev's presence in my life. It was a tender and redemptive reconciliation with Mom which I had never dreamed possible, but one which I welcomed with a deep sense of gratitude. To have experienced such unconditional, mutual absolution before her passing was pure grace.

Just as we were circling our wagons again in the summer of 2001 when Mom's cancer recurred, I was dealt another blow when news of Mrs. Chin's ailing with cancer reached us in late August. Since her return to China in 1987, Mrs. Chin had come back to Michigan to visit with her relatives, friends and supporters several times. She had made a point on each of those visits to spend time with me and Bev as our house guest for at least a couple of days. She enjoyed cooking, and we were only too eager to wolf down her homemade delicacies. We would drive over to Windsor for *dim sum*, and enjoy sizzling steaks at Ruth's Chris Steakhouse, one of her favorites. During one of the visits, we went on a "Star of Detroit Dinner Cruise," sailing along the Detroit River from downtown waterfront. When our riverboat cruised by Belle Isle, Mrs. Chin regaled us with tales of how, in the olden days, she and her family whiled away many a happy Sundays there with other young Chinese American families. She was so very vital and vivacious all those years, and it was inconceivable that she should be battling cancer. She returned to Michigan that August to undergo a thorough checkup, to receive a definitive diagnosis, and to be apprised of her treatment options. Bev and I hurried to William Beaumont Hospital as soon as we received the shocking news. Tears welled up in her eyes as soon as she saw me and Bev coming into her hospital room. We were elated to see her again, but were very sad that our reunion that time had to come under such adverse circumstances. We would learn in a few days that Mrs. Chin had elected not to undergo surgery even though her tumor was theoretically operable. Apparently, the success rate of the surgery was not optimal, while the operation could be disfiguring. Mrs. Chin was frank in explaining her decision: she did not really have anyone to live for, since her husband had predeceased her and her son, Vincent, had been so senselessly killed; she saw no justification for undergoing such a risky and extensive surgical procedure. She told me that she was not afraid of dying; her only wish was not to suffer much pain. I respected her decision, and deeply admired her courage and dignity. She did elect to receive radiation treatment. Helen Zia flew in shortly after Mrs. Chin was discharged from the hospital, and it was obvious that Mrs. Chin was greatly cheered and comforted by our company. She treated us to a sumptuous lunch at a restaurant in Farmington Hills serving authentic Chinese cuisine. In the ensuing few months, Bev and I visited her regularly. She had maintained her wry sense of humor and care and concern for others, even while her own health was failing. She asked me often about how my Mom was faring in her fight against cancer; I did not have the heart to tell her that Mom's cancer had returned. In the spring of 2002, her condition took a turn for the worse, and she had to be admitted to a nursing home in order to be properly taken care of, especially for more effective pain control and management. By then, I had my hands full dealing with Mom's protracted recovery from her second operation at the Mayo Clinic, and my ever increasing workload at the office. Bev visited Mrs. Chin a couple of times in April and May, returning to give me the sad news that Mrs. Chin was seriously ailing. As I was setting aside time to visit Mrs. Chin, Bev urged me not to go so as to preserve my memories of Mrs. Chin as I last saw her—still coherent, sentient and vital. I was then still someone who could not cope with the concept, let alone the reality, of mortality, of death. Bev's admonition gave me an excuse of sort not to have to confront Mrs. Chin's imminent demise, a horrifying fact that I could not accept, especially with my Mom's intensifying mortal combat with cancer lurking in the background. Of course, I do now regret not having visited Mrs. Chin one last time before she expired in June of 2002. As with so many missteps in my life, I can only find consolation in the belief that I had learned valuable life lessons from that particular blunder. Hundreds attended Mrs.

Chin's funeral; Helen spoke for so many of us when she delivered a heartrending and loving eulogy. Just a couple of weeks later, I would return to the cemetery where a group of about thirty gathered to pay respects and observe the 20th anniversary of Vincent's untimely and tragic death. It was a very mournful summer, almost a harbinger of heartbreaks to come.

I would not know then that Mom would be with us for only one more year. I was literally buried with work, so much so that I did not even have time for a haircut before our elaborate celebrations for Dad's 80th birthday in December. In retrospect, that was Mom's finest moment; she was absolutely radiant at both birthday feasts in Windsor and Toronto. When the festivities were over and my sisters returned to Hong Kong, Mom's mood turned very somber. Starting in January of 2003, she began giving me "instructions" relating to her funeral, cremation and burial, and started giving away her prized possessions. I could hardly hold back my tears when she gave and entrusted me with her beloved collection of sterling silver jewelry, and the Cartier ballpoint pen with which I gifted her in January of 1989. She started marking items around her house, mostly clothing, with Post-It notes with our respective names as recipients. In May, after discussing with me, a local attorney was retained to prepare their last wills and testaments. I kept taking short trips, in a vain effort to run away from the grim reality of Mom's imminent departure. When all was said and done, and even with whatever left not said or done, July 27th was the end of our "Mom's era." Life would never be the same without her. Indeed, it spurred me to return to Hong Kong just four months later to reunite with Lilian after twenty-five long, unforgettable, eventful years. It was also during that three-week stay in Hong Kong when I received healing that miraculously restored my overall health physically, emotionally and spiritually. The healing gave me the clarity and discernment that I needed to chart my course forward, and it bestowed on me the inner strength, stamina and courage to finally put an end to the pain and suffering from wallowing in an emotionally abusive and destructive relationship. Bev and I had shared much carefree and joyous time in our younger days, for which I was thankful. For whatever reason we and our circumstances had shifted, and changed so drastically as to be causing pain and hurt, it was high time that we disengaged. It was karma that we met, fell madly in love, built a home, shared many fulfilling years, and then drifted further and further apart. Thus, it was also karma that I parted company with her there and then as a last ditch effort to save my own soul before it became irredeemable.

X.

Mortal Combat

New Year's Day, 2004, was the first full day, after more than twenty-six years, when I was single, alone, on my own again, having "escaped" from my home and Bev the night before with my beloved cameras, my briefcase, a pillow, a blanket, a water kettle and a mug. I stayed at a hotel in Troy, as I could not yet live in the unfurnished apartment that I had rented. I had probably spent that day talking to several long-time friends on the telephone, and went mindlessly shopping for essentials for my apartment. Everything was still a blur to me, as I did not expect events to have unfolded quite that rapidly. I had thought I would inform Bev of my decision to leave about a week after the New Year, but everything became unexpectedly accelerated the night before New Year's Eve.

I returned to work on January 2nd. Upon hearing that I had broken up with Bev and moved out of my home, Elise gave me a big, warm, empathetic hug. I really appreciated and needed that outpouring of moral support.

Bev and I had agreed that I could return to the home on Saturday morning, January 3rd, to retrieve some of my belongings.

It was thoughtful of her to have left the home that morning, so that the two movers and I could pack and move my possessions efficiently. In about four hours, we packed and moved my clothes and shoes, photographs and photo albums, a select few of the numerous pieces of rosewood furniture that my parents gave me, the twin bed from my childhood, my desk and chair, two file cabinets, my reference audio components and audio rack, my pair of reference loudspeakers, my collection of fountain pens, briefcases, leather bags and luggage, and above all, my sizable vinyl LP collection that I had been lugging with me since my college years. Packing and moving thousands of LPs took much time and effort. I eyed my substantial collection of compact discs, but decided at the last minute to leave that so that Bev could at least enjoy some music, as I had also left her the secondary audio/video system in our den. In other words, I left behind the bulk of my worldly possessions, including my *zheng*, my guitar from my Unicorns days, many boxes of books, diaries, my senior and Master's theses, Chinese carvings and wall hangings from my parents, and a trunkful of fine Chinese porcelain vases and artifacts. I simply could not take much with me to my tiny one-bedroom apartment. Bev and I were still on speaking terms then, and I thought—naïvely, in retrospect—that I would have plenty of time and opportunity later to retrieve the remaining items, when I would have rented a suitable storage space. As the movers loaded up the last boxes, I followed in my car as we proceeded to my new apartment. Lina kept telephoning me that morning throughout the proceedings until I and my belongings were safely at my new apartment. She was concerned that I might change my mind and not follow through with my move-out, or that certain unknown, unwelcomed external forces might sidetrack me or otherwise interfere with my moving plans. She should not have worried, as I had no intention of surrendering or abandoning my new found and hard won freedom and my reclaimed life.

Believing how Bev loved that house, I figured that she would never leave it. I thus had no plans for compelling her to vacate or for the sale of the home. As it would turn out, I was too kind-hearted and considerate. I continued to make the mortgage payments, and pay for real estate taxes and homeowner's insurance, but it would be up to Bev to pay for utilities and upkeep. For a few years, she had even sent me monthly checks representing her half of the mortgage payments. I thought perhaps she had found a job, and thus could afford to continue living in the home. I would learn the upsetting truth much later in the fall of 2009.

For the first few weeks after I moved out of my home, Bev and I agreed to undergo couples counseling once more to see if there was any realistic possibility of patching things up and salvaging our relationship. I found a psychiatrist, Dr. Jean Ross, whose office, coincidentally, was next door to the office suite where I had my private practice before joining Dickinson Wright. It was extremely tense and awkward for me to see Bev again at Dr. Ross' office, and I was quite sure that the misgivings were mutual. We managed about three sessions before Bev stormed out of the room in a fit of fury and bombast, uttering some menacing threats, and left me fairly shaken and embarrassingly weeping in the doctor's office. Plainly and painfully, our bonds had degenerated and disintegrated past the point of no return. Dr. Ross calmly reminded me to seek legal counsel as I prepared to leave. I had managed to compose myself by then, and in turn reminded her: "*I am* a lawyer." That was meant to be more a reassurance to myself than an appropriate response to her well-intentioned advice.

In a huff, Bev had "returned" to me, at one of our sessions with Dr. Ross, all the jewelry I had given her in our twenty-six-plus years together. In mid-February, she called me to retrieve the jewelry, and the Montegrappa sterling silver "Dragon" limited edition fountain pen that I had given her in 1995. I, of course, had no issue with her requests. She came by my apartment one evening. It was a very brief visit. She stood just inside my apartment door, took a quick look around, picked up the jewelry and the pen, gave me a hug, and left. In April, she called and wanted to meet me again. I should have declined, but perhaps I thought we needed to meet and talk about the remaining real estate that we owned as well as her plans for our home. We met for lunch at a local sandwich-and-soup diner. No sooner than when we had fetched our food and sat down, she became agitated and visibly upset, and abruptly left the restaurant. I would see her one last time in October when we attended a closing on the sale of a vacant lot that we owned in Auburn Hills.

Life on my own was emancipating but also came with a steep learning curve. I had always felt or believed that I needed someone to love, and someone who loved me in return, in order to live a full and complete life. The breakup with Bev was my first step out of that familiar territory and away from that trajectory, and removed from that perceived comfort zone. Accordingly, in the initial months after the breakup, there were still times when I felt as if I were missing someone or something, that there was a void to be filled. Over much time, I would learn to obliterate that void with a healthy and loving sense of self. In the immediate aftermath of the breakup, though, I was still reeling from the agony of a failed relationship, of missing a vital part of me that had been there for most of my adult life, of wondering whether I would or should ever find another soulmate and fall in love again. Those initial months were very unsettling times; I felt almost anchorless. Thankfully, travel and photography once again came to my rescue.

I began to understand how forlorn Dad might have felt the first months after Mom passed away. He and I visited Mom's gravesite often. He would talk to her at length, just as he had always discussed with her while she was alive, the day's events, news and updates about relatives and friends, and simply whatever else was on his mind. I visited Dad often, taking him with me to shop for furniture for my apartment, for instance. In May, he went on a 3-week European cruise with his friends in his Chinese calligraphy and literature class. My sisters and I were greatly relieved when his mood brightened visibly after that cruise. In June, he went with me to a family outing sponsored by my firm: a day at the Greenfield Village. We both enjoyed taking pictures as we strolled from one historic building to another. The sumptuous catered lunch provided by the firm was icing on the cake. It was difficult for both of us not to recall the last time we were at the Village: it was years earlier, with Mom and Vivian in tow, on a July 4th weekend. For the July 4th weekend that year, I drove us to Toronto to visit with friends and relatives. We had a marvelous time filling up our tummies with authentic Chinese food, and stocking up on Chinese groceries. I bought myself an electric rice cooker at a shop inside one of the rather unique "Chinese shopping malls" there. Unlike previous trips to Toronto, I made a point of driving beyond the metropolitan area to take in the countryside. Something rather odd happened that weekend, though. On the second day of our three-day stay, I suddenly felt unwell for no ostensible reason. I felt weak and slightly dizzy, nauseous with an upset stomach. Yet it could not have been an influenza virus that I had contracted, nor was it food that disagreed with me, because the discomfort came on very suddenly, and after half a day or so, the symptoms disappeared just as mysteriously. Dad went to Hong Kong again that fall, and stayed with Vivian for another three months. He had an excellent time there, visiting and dining out with old friends, checking out his old haunts, shopping till he dropped, and spending quality time with Lina, Lilian and Vivian.

A surprise telephone call came in March from Carol-Ann, with whom I had lost contact for almost thirty years. The last time I heard from her was in the 1980's when she called me from the United Kingdom where she had been working and living for a few years. The last time I saw her was on Barnard campus when we graduated in 1976. She was living in North Berkeley, and practicing as a licensed psychotherapist. Catching up with my long lost friend gave me a perfect excuse to go to San Francisco again, a trip that could not have taken place if I were not single, as Bev would have thrown a jealousy fit. The truth was that I needed a breather from my work, from the fallout of my breakup, and from the Michigan's grey and frigid winter. Around that time, my legs started to feel slightly numb and weak again; I needed a diversion so that I did not have to think about the treatment I should pursue to prevent further decline. I really did not have many options as returning to Hong Kong for another few weeks for treatment would be extremely difficult, given my obligations at work.

Carol-Ann and I immediately recognized each other as she picked me up at the subway station near her home. We were only a slightly older version of our youthful selves. It seemed as if nothing much had changed in the interim decades, except that I would have never imagined her, an English major and musically gifted, as a successful therapist. She first took me to the local farmer's market, and bought fresh vegetables and steamed crab for lunch. North Berkeley apparently was a foodie's town, a gourmand's haven. That fact would be underscored when we later had artisanal coffees at a local café, and gourmet noodles at a Japanese restaurant for dinner. I also visited her office—a very tastefully decorated and serene, safe space; it was obvious that she loved and was very proud of her practice. Her home was very charming and warm; again tastefully decorated, several excellent photographs that she took were hanging on the walls, with a lush garden that she lovingly tended to in the backyard. At one point, she volunteered her counsel, remarking that I should not carry on burdens that were not mine. That gratuitous but astute observation and advice was much appreciated. She impressed the heck out of me—a twenty-plus-year therapy patient—as a therapist. One day was hardly enough to learn all that had happened in each other's lives in the past thirty years. We promised to reconvene in the near future to continue our conversations.

While I had quite a few former classmates in the Bay Area, I only had time to visit with Flora and her husband, Bob, on that weekend trip. They took me on a driving trip to the Redwood Forest to stroll amongst the giant sequoias, and then on to the Russian River region where we had a delightful seafood lunch amidst breathtaking shoreline scenery. Needless to say, I took many photographs on that scenic drive. In the evening, Bob the chef treated us to a fresh seafood, homemade pasta dinner. Flora was a patient and understanding listener and a sage longtime friend. She helped put in perspective the myriad of pieces from my life recently torn asunder. On the last day of my weekend vacation, I rode the cable car downtown and then to the Castro District, wandering, feeling free, and totally unscripted. On the morning of my departure, I came across a small camera shop near my hotel, and spotted a pre-owned Contax film SLR camera body that I had been searching for. I purchased it as a very auspicious souvenir from that much rejuvenating trip.

For no particular reason it seemed, work was particularly onerous that year. Without any pressing home-front issue to distract me, I was working harder than ever. My job involved more than shuffling papers behind my desk at the office. Oftentimes, I had to travel to the ports of entry, such as the Detroit-Windsor Tunnel, the Blue Water Bridge, or the Detroit Metro Airport, to assist individual clients with their application for admission. Other times, I had to be at the District Office of the INS/USCIS for hours on end for filing or to represent a client being interviewed by the authorities. I even had to fly to South Carolina on one occasion to represent a client at a hearing. I also had to meet with clients from time to time at their offices and manufacturing facilities in Michigan and in other States. Yet the harder I worked, the more there was for me to work on, and so went the vicious circle. By the time another two months went by, I desperately needed another getaway in order to come up for air. It was the Memorial Day weekend, and I decided to explore the Grand Rapids, Michigan, area, and in particular, the increasingly trendy town of Saugatuck which I heard was very gay-friendly. It was early afternoon by the time I arrived at my hotel in Grand Rapids. After a very satisfying lunch at the hotel, my cumulative fatigue overcame me; instead of taking a drive around town to sightsee, I slept until the next morning. Feeling revived and refreshed the following day, I drove to Saugatuck and enjoyed a day of gallery hopping, shopping and taking pictures. That was the first trip when I felt I was truly on my own; Bev was not tagging along, obviously, and I could linger or move on or pause to take photographs as I pleased. I relished my liberty. I spent quite some time at a shop that sold CDs, enjoying listening to the superb selection of albums being played in the background while I browsed the bins of CDs. On the last day of my mini-vacation, I drove south to Muskegon, exploring an area I had never visited previously. Somehow I came upon the Muskegon State Park, and it called out to me. It turned out to be a magnificent stretch of beaches along the eastern shores of Lake Michigan. It was early in the season, and the beach was deserted. I bathed in the quietude of the pristine beach, gentle sun, azure sky, and the Lake stretching out to the horizon. It was a perfect communion with nature, and I came away with many memorable photographs.

I did not even remember what prompted me to sell my BMW "325xi," and lease an Audi "A4 Quattro" in June of 2004. Perhaps it was a subconscious effort to be rid of the old and to symbolically turn a new page. Around that time, I had also started looking at rental storage facilities, to prepare for retrieving and storing the remainder of my possessions from my previous home. It had been half a year since I had been single, but I was still feeling rudderless; mostly, I buried myself with work. Thus, I was excited about participating in the outdoors photography workshop with Dennis Greaney in late June. It was a glorious Sunday with bright sunshine, billowing and picturesque clouds that provided a dramatic and vivid backdrop for our scenic photography. Dennis led us, about a dozen amateur photographers, through several landmarks around downtown Detroit: the Detroit Institute of Arts, the abandoned Michigan Central Station, Philip A. Hart Plaza and the Dodge Fountain, and the James Scott Memorial Fountain on Belle Isle. For a change, I left behind my rangefinders but brought with me two Leica R6.2 SLR camera bodies, a wide-angle lens and two zoom lenses, and of course, my Leica "Minilux." It was time for me to learn to "tackle" my SLRs. I had always wondered if I had the stamina to withstand the rigors of a full-day workshop. Hence, it came as a pleasant surprise that I not only survived the workshop, but had thoroughly enjoyed the learning experience, and had been able to capture many satisfying images. I expected to join Dennis' other workshops, especially his photography excursions to Michigan's Upper Peninsula and Lake Superior.

Shortly after Dad and I returned from our July 4th weekend in Toronto, I received a very attractive offer to purchase the vacant lot that Bev and I owned in Auburn Hills. I contacted Bev to discuss accepting the offer, but uncharacteristically, she did not return my e-mails or telephone calls. After a few days of silence, I started panicking. I somehow imagined that she was so distraught over our breakup that she might have harmed herself. I telephoned everyone I could think of who might know of her whereabouts. Even her daughter, Melanie, had not heard from her for a while. A week or more went by, and my panic turned into feverish third-degree alarm. I even called the police to see about reporting a missing person. Finally, I asked Melanie to meet me at the home one Saturday to see if we could enter the house. Bev had apparently changed all locks, and I could not get it with my old keys. A locksmith was called, and arrived with a police officer. The locksmith was able to unlock the door, and the officer went in to investigate while we waited outside by the driveway. He came back out and declared: "[Bev] is not missing; she knows where she is, just that we don't know where she is." He said that the house had probably been vacant for a while as there were cobwebs here and there. I was extremely offended when the officer would only let Melanie in the house supposedly because she was Bev's daughter, while I was treated as a stranger, even though I asserted that I owned the house and the address was on my driver's license. No matter, the locksmith (whom I paid for) gave Melanie the new keys, and she in turn gave them to me and we entered the house together to investigate.

It had been more than seven months since I last set foot in the home. Nothing much had changed. Bev had moved some furniture around, the numerous wooden carousel storage units for my CD's were missing, and the CD's were instead piled on some metal shelves. We found the computer hard drive in the basement, and took it up to the study to connect it, hoping that it might contain clues as to Bev's whereabouts. We would soon realize that Bev had apparently dropped the hard drive into water, in a deliberate effort to disable it and obliterate all data. So, indeed, her "disappearance" was planned and intended. Where was she and where did she go? When I walked into the living room, something on the coffee table by the fireplace called to my attention. I do not now recall what I saw specifically, but there was something "arranged" on the coffee table. Whatever it was gave me the impression that it was some sort of deliberate and calculated array of objects arranged in a particular manner for some particular intended purposes. Of course those objects were not on the coffee table when I used to live there. I did not understand what it was that I saw, or the significance of the "arrangements." I simply had the intuitive knowingness the instant I encountered it that it was an intentional "arrangement." Think Stonehenge, even though I do not mean to imply Bev's "arrangements" in any manner attained or aspired to the same scale or degree of profound significance. I checked the garage, and Bev's car was not inside. The police officer was correct then in determining that she had gone somewhere, intentionally not letting us know of her whereabouts.

I had been invited to dinner that evening by two long-time friends, Cathy and Mary. I almost wanted to postpone the gathering as I was too distraught over Bev's "disappearance;" thankfully, my dear friends convinced me to keep the engagement. It turned out that I would be greatly comforted by their company, the fine dinner, and our lively conversations. I had some true friends in need indeed.

I had telephoned Jo in Florida to ask if she knew of Bev's whereabouts. She did not return my call until some weeks later, at which time I would learn from her much about Bev's "disappearance." It would be almost late July before I finally heard from Bev. She had by then received news of the impending offer, and was, of course, very interested in securing her share of the sale proceeds. She told me on the telephone that she was returning home shortly, and would sign to accept the offer. I would learn from Jo weeks later that Bev had in fact driven to Jo's condominium community in Florida just before the July 4th weekend, even though Jo had made clear that she would not exactly be welcomed there. As soon as Bev arrived, she forbade Jo to tell me that she was living there in a rental condominium. Thus, when I telephoned to inquire, Jo found herself caught in an untenable position. It was quite clear that Bev had elaborately orchestrated her "disappearance" so as to see what my reaction would be. In time, Jo would confirm to me what I had known for some years: that Bev had changed very drastically, so much so that even Jo was not sure of "who or what was in that body."

I was strangely rattled by the entire episode surrounding Bev's "disappearance." Something perturbed me. It could well be my dismay at my having been upset by her disappearance. It could also be the unsettling feelings I had while I was at my former home, especially my inscrutable encounter with whatever was arranged on the coffee table. It was as if there was something ethereal or metaphysical about the whole sordid affair, and which was beyond my realm of comprehension. It spooked me on the one hand, and on the other, it spurred me to find out as much as I could about the mysterious. Dr. Hanke came to mind. She was a psychiatrist, and thus, someone who could proffer counsel and perspective. More significantly, I knew she had been an active member of the Lighthouse Center in Whitmore Lake, which I then understood to be a non-denominational center for meditation and spiritual devotion. The Center was founded by the late Chetana Catherine Florida; I had been to the Center once or twice in the 1990's as Jo's guest. I thus imagined that Dr. Hanke would have insight about phenomena in the spiritual realm, with which I was completely unfamiliar.

I had lost Dr. Hanke's contact information from more than seven years prior, but Jo had her telephone number and put me in touch with her, and an appointment was scheduled for the last day of July. I remember that Saturday vividly. Late that morning, I went to look at a storage facility near my apartment in Troy. As I parked my car in the parking lot, a call came in from Lina. She had just returned from a pilgrimage to certain Buddhist temples and sacred sites in Japan, and was greatly alarmed by news of my being spooked by Bev's staged disappearance. Her view was that it was a classic ploy by Bev to manipulate my emotional strings, and I haplessly fell into the trap, lock, stock and barrel. We talked for such a long time on the telephone that I did not have time to look at the rental storage facilities, and was almost late setting out for the long drive to Dr. Hanke's. Re-tracing that route had an eerie sense of déjà vu; almost eight years ago I was making the trip with Bev during an extremely strained period of my life, financially and emotionally. So much had changed in those interim years. I recognized Dr. Hanke right away, and she was glad to see me again. She was a most intelligent and empathetic listener. At the end of the hour, she pointed out that I should not be working with two therapists at the same time; I was and had been working with Hazel Karbel for quite a few years. Hence, I made a decision to continue with Hazel as my therapist, while I would informally consult with Dr. Hanke on matters of a spiritual nature. She gave me some literature about the Lighthouse Center and encouraged me to attend the upcoming events. I left her office feeling unburdened for the first time in over a month; I even felt famished. I stopped at a fast food restaurant for a late lunch, and ate ravenously, before driving over to Windsor to pick up Dad for a visit with Mom—it was three days after the first anniversary of Mom's passing. Dad and I lingered at our Chan Family Estate for hours, talking to Mom, clearing weeds around the newly planted trees, taking photographs, and simply whiling away a lovely summer late afternoon and reminiscing with Mom whom both of us had missed sorely and desperately.

I did visit the Lighthouse Center in mid-August to attend a talk by a visiting guru, the Jain Master Gurudev Shree Chittrabhanuji. The attendees sang chants and meditated before the talk, activities which were alien to me, while the talk also seemed rather esoteric to me. No matter, I found the atmosphere at the Center very serene and the members enthusiastic and welcoming. Out of sheer curiosity, I signed up for an introductory class to meditation scheduled for late August. Even though I had been baptized and confirmed as an Anglican, I had not attended church for decades. I had come to accept myself as a lousy "worshipper." I did not fancy following any guru or religious leader, or observing religious beliefs and rituals that I deemed were necessarily patriarchal, or being a part of any organized religion that by definition was to me confining and oppressive. It turned out that I was the only student for that month's meditation class. Nirmala (she preferred to be called by her spiritual name, as I was not consulting with her in a professional capacity) was the instructor who gave me a one-on-one three-hour primer on mantra meditation in the Jain tradition. I had never imagined that I could sit still doing nothing for even a minute or two, let alone meditate for 20 minutes everyday, optimally twice a day. Nevertheless, I gave it a try, and started meditating as instructed every morning for 20 minutes before I left for work. I kept up the practice initially for the sole purpose of seeing whether I would derive any discernible benefit from such an inactive activity.

Fall had always been my favorite season; the cool, crisp air and the brilliant, glorious colors positively revitalized me. For that Labor Day weekend, I again drove to my favorite part of the State—the Grand Traverse area. For the first time since I left my home with Bev, I began to genuinely feel my personal and emotional freedom, and it was an enchanting realization. Perhaps that was a result of my daily meditation: to gradually be relieved of the ghosts of the past and be enabled to appreciate the exhilarating possibilities of a new phase of my life. I enjoyed that weekend trip so much that I followed up the ensuing weekend with a more ambitious driving trip: exploring the southeastern shores of Lake Huron by crossing over the Blue Water Bridge from Port Huron to Sarnia, Ontario. The scenery along the drive was achingly beautiful, and I stopped often to take photographs. As a result, I did not make it very far up north, and had to turn back when I reached Goderich because of time constraints. I had planned to take a week off work in the following summer and return to explore the area, driving all the way north and east to Georgian Bay.

In September and October, I returned to the Lighthouse Center to participate in their picnic and drumming circle event, a puja, another visit and talk by Gurudev Shree Chittrabhanuji, and an intensive meditation Friday evening when we meditated for more than two continuous hours. Nirmala also enrolled me in her chakra class, a weekly session that ran for eight consecutive weeks on the seven chakras. It was clear to me by then that, even though the Center honored all religions, many members of the Center followed the Jain religion whose central tenet was *ahinsa*, or nonviolence. Many members were vegans, in keeping with their faith to be nonviolent, including nonviolence toward animals. I certainly did not consider myself a devotee or follower of the Jain faith or any other organized religion for that matter. I simply thought practicing meditation and learning about chakras and other spiritual precepts might enrich certain aspects of my being that might have been neglected. What I considered the best photograph taken by me thus far was, incidentally, taken after the Candlelight Meditation at the Lighthouse on September 19th. I was leaving the Lighthouse at dusk, driving along the south shores of Whitmore Lake. When I rounded a bend, the last rays of the sunset were simply mesmerizing. I pulled onto a private road, jumped out of my car and pulled out my Leica M6 range-finder with a Leica 35mm Summilux lens. With the last remaining slivers of light, I shot several frames, holding the camera as steadily as I could without a tripod. When the film was developed and 4"x6" prints made, what I captured took my breath away: a slender but robust tree with its almost bare branches silhouetted against a placid Whitmore Lake, faint dots of lights emanating from the far side of the Lake, the firmament was the gentlest amber fading into grey-blue. I obtained an oversized enlargement of that frame mounted on a poster-board. It had been hanging on the wall and over my audio system, for me to gaze upon whenever I listened to music, to remember that twilight when I felt so alive, vital, liberated and in perfect alignment and harmony with the infinite power.

The cruel reality was that by August, my legs were acting up noticeably again, and I could no longer hide in denial by distracting myself with overworking or embarking on road trips. Numbness had started at my toes and feet, and I well knew that it was time again to have an MRI of my spinal cord. It was late September when I saw Dr. Chandler, my neurosurgeon, to review the MRI results. Almost nonchalantly, he informed me that that shunt he installed in October of 2000 might somehow have malfunctioned, and that fortunately, there was a "simple mechanical solution" to that problem. I would need to have surgery again so that he could "revise" that shunt or install a new one to drain the syrinx. That was the first time I heard the term "syrinx" as opposed to arachnoid "cysts" which were first successfully decompressed in September of 1992. I was not concerned at all because, obviously, the syrinx had been successfully drained as well in October of 2000. It sounded to me a relatively straightforward surgery to revise or replace the existing shunt. Surgery was scheduled for November 3rd.

Work was going very well for me meanwhile. My load was heavy, but my corporate clients were pleased with my legal services and I was rewarded with ever more business from them, and the firm's management took notice. It would turn out that at the end of 2004, I was being considered for equity partnership. I was personally informed by our Chief Executive Officer that although I had barely missed making equity partner that year, and I stood an extremely good chance for being named equity partner the ensuing year if I kept up the pace and scale of my contributions to the firm. As a consolation prize, I was allocated a generous bonus for 2004; I felt most grateful and honored for the recognition.

I attended an immigration law related function with my colleagues early in October; Larry and I drove together to the event. When we left in the early evening, he noticed that I could barely walk. The numbness had spread and expanded very rapidly this time around. Since August, it had already crept up my legs, and I could barely control my legs in walking or balance myself while standing. I told him honestly that my spinal cord surgery had been scheduled for early November, and all should be well afterwards it as was in 2000 and 1992. About a week later, I would meet Bev one last time, when we closed on the sale of the vacant lot. We were cordial to each other, but I felt awkward nonetheless. We did not talk much, and after the closing, she wanted to see my new car, my Audi "A4 Quattro." She followed me out to the parking lot. I tried my level best to walk "normally," but she, of course, noticed and exclaimed: "What's wrong with your legs?" I did not answer; she should know well what could possibly be wrong with my legs, and probably much more as I would years later suspect. She looked at my car, and mumbled something about our meeting again in the future, and we parted company. We would never see each other again.

Dad left for Hong Kong again in late September to be with Lina, Lilian and Vivian, and to enjoy his friends and gourmet meals for about three months. I drove over to Windsor weekly to check on his house and visit Mom at Chan Family Estate. It was late October when I called upon one of Dad's neighbors to keep an eye on the house; I did not tell him that I was having surgery, but rather than I would be out of town and would not be available to check on the home for a couple of weeks. I in fact had a trip planned for the last weekend in October. I had been a member of the Leica Historical Society of America for several years, but had not had the time to participate in any of its events or attend any of the annual meetings which usually featured lectures and workshops by world renowned photographers. I was determined to attend the annual meeting that year, held from October 28th to the 31st in historic Williamsburg, Virginia.

About two weeks before taking that trip, I had an unusual experience while participating in an intensive meditation at the

Lighthouse Center. During an intensive meditation, an experienced meditator led attendees to meditate on each of the seven chakras for twenty minutes each, starting with the root chakra and ending at the crown chakra. I was a novice meditator, and had learned to meditate only on the heart chakra; nonetheless, I stayed through the entire session, meditating on the heart chakra. Toward the end of the session, perhaps while the others were meditating on the throat or third eye chakra, a sense of horrific dread, doom and fear suddenly arose and overcame me, leaving me literally trembling in my seat. It was most unusual, because I was not a fearful person, consciously or subconsciously; just about nothing would faze or upend me. Yet there I was, shaking like a leaf and down to my core, gripped and overwhelmed by a bone chilling terror of unknown origin and nature. I finally steeled myself enough to conjure up a vision of my wielding a mighty imaginary sword and slashing my way through and out of the unknown frightful morass.

The LHSA annual meeting was as fun-filled and educational as I thought it would be and then some. First of all, I met many fellow Leica photographers, including a couple of friends I had made while attending camera shows in the past few years, Mark Theken and his wife Keka, and Igor Resnick, as well as Sherry Krauter who had been expertly overhauling and adjusting my Leica cameras. John Botte, author of *Aftermath*, a photographic account of 9/11, was the keynote speaker; I would have the opportunity a year or two later to purchase one of his Leica M6 camera bodies. There was also an equipment loan program whereby we could sign for and try out Leica cameras and lenses. I rushed to sign up for a brand new Leica R9 camera body with the acclaimed Leica 21-35mm ASPH f/3.5-4 wide-angle zoom lens. On the guided tour through Williamsburg, I shot and fell in love with that camera body and lens combination, even though an SLR camera body normally would not be my preference. It was during that walking photography tour that I realized my legs were in dire shape; I could not run to the shuttle bus when the rains started, and I could barely walk up the stairs to the second-floor dining room of the historic restaurant where our lunch was being served. Still, I enjoyed the many excellent slide shows and workshops presented that weekend. On Sunday, at the members' trade fair, I was able to purchase from a fellow member a limited edition Leica camera body and lens, the "Ein Stück Leica," for which I had been pining for some years. That trip confirmed for me that, after being on my own—sometimes floundering—for ten months, I was truly beginning to chart my new course, savor my new freedom, relish my new life, and cherish my new future. And my future at that point looked very bright and upbeat indeed.

I returned to my office on Monday, November 1st, and had only two days before my surgery to finish up some cases, and otherwise delegate and leave proper instructions for my legal assistants and secretary to carry on during my anticipated one to at most two weeks' absence for my spinal cord surgery and recovery. I drove over to Nirmala's office after work on Tuesday. She had kindly offered to drive me to the Hospital early the following morning for the surgery. I slept on the couch in her office that night; I was able to doze off for just a few hours, it seemed, before the alarm clock rang. At the crack of dawn, Nirmala arrived to pick me up for the early morning surgery.

Surgery was almost routine to me by then. The next thing I knew I was already recovering in the post-op step-down unit. I was thankful that I had made it through yet another spinal cord surgery. A new shunt had been placed to drain the syrinx which was enlarging inside my spinal cord at the T12 level. I knew I had to lie flat in bed for at least 24 hours, and if my surgical wound was healing properly and if I did not suffer any complication, I should be discharged in three or four days. That was precisely what happened; all went smoothly enough and by the weekend,

I was discharged. Nirmala insisted that I stay at her home for a couple of days so that she could watch and care for me. Around November 8th, she drove me to her office to pick up my car, and I drove myself home. I had to attend another closing that week on the sale, finally, of the property that was the subject of the RICO lawsuit almost twenty years earlier. After that sale, Bev and I only had the condominium in Bloomfield Township and our home to be disposed of.

The experience from my previous spinal cord surgeries had me psychologically prepared for weakness and pain during at least the first week of recovery. Physical therapy should follow shortly thereafter, and in about one to two months, I should be good as new. Hence, I was patient with myself, walking and doing just about everything else very gently and deliberately. However, at about eight days out of surgery, something seemed to have gone awry; my legs remained rather weak, my balance was off, and I was unsteady on my feet. Another few days went by, it became unmistakable that my legs were in fact worsening; numbness had returned once again to my feet, and I was becoming increasingly uncoordinated in my gait. Alarmed, I immediately contacted Dr. Chandler office for an appointment. It was mid-November when I was seen by his chief resident. By then, my walking had become very labored again. After he conducted a neurological examination, he was of the opinion that I should immediately undergo a second surgery to "revise" the shunt. Apparently, for unknown reason, the shut installed just two weeks earlier did not "take," and was not working properly to effectively drain the syrinx. He then tried his best to convince me to be hospitalized right there and then for my own safety's sake, while I await the surgery to be scheduled. I was stunned to hear that the newly installed shunt had failed already, but I was in no mood to be confined in a hospital again. More crucially, I did not have any confidence in having Dr. Chandler conduct the follow-up surgery. He first operated on me in October of 2000, and that gave me relief for barely four years; the surgery I had just had with him on November 3rd was even worse—it worked for merely one week, if that.

I left the clinic feeling disappointed and distraught. The first and foremost order of business: I had the good sense to have brake-and-throttle hand controls installed in my Audi so that I could continue to get around town safely. I telephoned Jo shortly after that clinic visit to update her on my latest leg dysfunction. Ominously, she remarked: "You ain't seen nothing yet." With that cryptic comment, she urged me to "stay in the Light," and stay close to the Lighthouse Center and Nirmala, for "protection." I had always fancied myself an intrepid fighter, and accordingly, I approached and tackled all of life's challenges with bravado, daring and unflinching conviction. No obstacle was allowed to stand in my way. Yet, what I was confronting was unprecedented, as all of my previous surgeries had been uneventful and successful. I was mulling my options for days on end, but I realized I did not have too many days left to vacillate or ruminate; my legs were failing fast. Clearly, something had to be done, perhaps I indeed needed another surgery. That prospect did not exactly faze me, but by whom and where?

I was invited to Thanksgiving dinner with several members of the Lighthouse Center. In chatting with one of the members, who was a licensed psychologist, about my recent ineffectual spinal cord surgery, I also recounted similar surgeries I had had in the past. It dawned on me, there and then, that I should return to the neurosurgeon who successfully operated on me in 1992 and who was then practicing in Medford, Oregon. He had saved me from being "wheelchair bound" twelve years earlier, ergo, he had to be the one to save the day once again. That decision felt right to me logically and intuitively. I telephoned him the following Monday and he remembered me well. I briefed him on the unsuccessful surgery that I had with Dr. Chandler three weeks earlier, and how I would like him to surgically salvage the situation. He remarked that I did not have a syrinx in 1992; he decompressed my numerous arachnoid cysts but did not have to shunt any syrinx. It became clear to me then that my T12 syrinx came into being in 2000, requiring the surgery to shunt it in October of 2000, and again, earlier that month. He was at first hesitant about my flying out to Oregon for him to operate on me; his concern was the difficulty in my returning to Michigan should there be any complications from the surgery. The possibility of complications could not be farther from my mind, as I was simply thrilled to have found my "savior," my neurosurgeon who I firmly believed would make me "good as new" again. I explained to him that I had no confidence in Dr. Chandler, and I did not know of any other neurosurgeon in whom I could place my trust for such a critical surgery. He finally acquiesced, and we set December 3rd as the date for a clinic visit, and Monday, December 6th for surgery. I had my MRI scans flown to him in the meantime by overnight express courier.

I was greatly relieved after that telephone conversation. I had complete faith in him, as he had performed my spinal cord surgery brilliantly in 1992. Nirmala offered to accompany me to Oregon for the surgery, and I did not decline her offer because my walking, as well as my stamina, was quite compromised by then. I was walking with a single straight cane for support and balance, and I could certainly use her assistance on that trip which was just a few days away. I hurriedly made our flight, hotel and rental car reservations. I packed my favorite Leica rangefinder and lens in my suitcase with about a week's worth of clothing. I had every expectation that I would enjoy taking a few road trips along the fabled Oregon Pacific coast during the week or so when I would be recovering after my surgery. In about two weeks at most, I figured, I should be back in Michigan and returning to my office well before Christmas.

The flight to Medford was long and tedious; we arrived Thursday late afternoon, well in time for the appointment with my neurosurgeon early the next morning. While walking to his office, I tripped and fell before Nirmala could grab me to break my fall. My legs were getting very uncooperative and weak. It was comforting to see my neurosurgeon again since he left Michigan about five years prior; he had not changed much. He had already reviewed my MRI scans. After a quick neurological examination, he explained what he proposed to surgically accomplish on Monday. He would once again try to decompress as many of the arachnoid cysts as feasible along and up my spinal canal and stopping where it would be unsafe to further proceed. Secondly, he would replace the malfunctioning shunt with another that would drain my syrinx to my pleural cavity where he hoped would provide a better draw and drainage. Thirdly, he would add certain material to my dura, the covering of my spinal cord, thus enlarging the space to allow my spinal fluid to flow more freely. I nodded in agreement. I trusted him and his expertise completely, as I knew from previous experience that he was very cautious, meticulous and mindful in his surgical decisions and procedures.

After the clinic visit, I underwent certain routine pre-op and laboratory tests as instructed. In the afternoon, we went to a view the hostel where I expected to stay for post-op recovery. I found the accommodation very satisfactory, and left my suitcase with them so that I would not have to lug it with me from the hospital after my discharge. As we had a weekend before my surgery, we drove up to Eugene on Saturday to visit Nirmala's son who was a senior at the University of Oregon. We had a very tasty lunch at a students' favorite hangout, followed by a quick tour of the campus, and a movie of which I have no recollection. We spent the night at the Eugene Hilton Hotel, and took our time driving back to Medford on Sunday. Sunday night before I retired to bed, Nirmala gave me a one-on-one tutorial on the crown chakra, as I would be missing the weekly class on that last chakra the following week.

We arrived at the hospital very early Monday morning for my scheduled surgery. I was in high spirits, as I was eagerly looking forward to having the surgery that should finally restore my health and leg function. Nirmala and I were cheerfully jesting and chatting away while I waited in pre-op; even the nurses who were preparing me for the operation were amused by our carefree banter. Soon enough, I was being wheeled to the operating room as I waved at Nirmala with a thumbs-up.

I awoke very briefly in the post-op step-down unit, but lost consciousness again until after I was transferred to my room on the hospital floor. It had to have been a rather lengthy operation, and it took me much longer to come out of my anesthesia. When I regained sufficient consciousness, I vaguely realized something was horribly wrong: I could not feel or move my legs at all.

I passed out again. More time had lapsed, and when I opened my eyes, my neurosurgeon was standing by my bed. He calmly informed me that he was successful in performing all three procedures that he recommended during our clinic visit the previous Friday. He commented that my spinal fluid flow was so impeded by the arachnoid cysts that it was not until he reached the T4 level before he encountered normal spinal fluid flow. I smiled and was, of course, delighted to hear that he had accomplished all three objectives of the surgery. He then picked up my left leg slightly, which was lying on the bed lamely, and gently let it go from his hands; my leg simply drooped and fell back onto the bed. He shook his head and did not say anything further, and left the room.

To my horrors, when I finally regained full consciousness, there was no mistake about it: I had lost control of my legs and all sensation from waist down. Nirmala was visiting me; she was softly chanting by my bedside, hoping to soothe me as she, too, realized something awful had occurred with the operation. She had to leave shortly to return to Michigan, as it was Tuesday already.

In the first five or six days after the surgery, I was focusing on recovering from the stress and strains of the operation; it would take me a while before I even began to grasp or understand my new reality in terms of leg function. During those days, I mostly convinced myself that it was merely a transitional condition, that my body was simply "in shock" from the extensive surgery, and that I would regain control of and sensation in my legs soon enough.

After six days in the hospital, it was decided that I should be transferred to another hospital with inpatient rehabilitation facilities. I was placed in a wheelchair, and onto a specialized van with a lift platform, and then transported to that other hospital in Medford. By then, I had also called the hostel to have my suitcase delivered to me at the hospital as it was clear that I would not be checking in at the hostel any time soon.

That was the first time I was a patient on an inpatient rehabilitation floor. In the past, I had always been able to walk on my own two feet right away after each spinal cord surgery. Typically, I would be prescribed outpatient physical therapy for a month or two after each surgery, and my legs would then be sufficiently strengthened and my balance restored accordingly. However, there I was in inpatient rehab, trying to learn about and get accustomed to my "new" legs which were, for all intents and purposes, not functioning. I would, in short order, find out that I could still stand up with assistance and could walk only with a walker, but not otherwise. My "walking" at that point was probably an automatic reflex phenomenon. Having been able to walk for all fifty years of my life, my legs were still able to go through the motions, placing one foot in front of the other, probably out of habit or some sort of built-in memory. As I had no control over or sensation in my legs whatsoever, the walker was my critical support for strength as well as balance and stability. In inpatient rehab, I underwent at least four hours of physical and occupational therapy everyday. I had to learn, for instance, how to walk myself to the bathroom and safely use the facilities. I learned to walk up and down a small step with the walker, though my stepping down was decidedly hair-raising. It was a shock to my system not to be able to simply get up and go wherever I wanted, or get up and do whatever I intended to. It was a huge adjustment and just about every move had to be relearned. The magnitude of the changes necessitated by my physical limitations was more all-encompassing in reality and practice than mere words can convey. My neurosurgeon had been checking in on me everyday. I remembered during one of his rounds, he mused aloud whether it was worth the extensive surgery that I had undergone, and I hastened with my rejoinder of: "Of course, it was," as if to console him. After a few days in inpatient rehab, I encountered more complications. I started having excruciating, blinding, stabbing pain up and down my spine every other hour or so. I bravely endured that pain for a couple of days before my neurosurgeon finally figured out that, even though he had taken all the necessary precautions during the surgery, I had somehow contracted aseptic meningitis. The "fix" was the administration of an epidural. I recalled my neurosurgeon instructing the doctor who performed the procedure to place it as low as possible in my sacral spine area. The unspeakable pain did dissipate after that procedure, but I have been wondering about its long-term effects on my spinal cord, sensation and functions. Again, there were no good options, and that epidural was yet another necessary evil.

Anita, Flora, Sylvia, Ann and Linda and many other friends had been following me since my operation and calling me regularly to check on my progress and to cheer me on. By then, I had also notified Larry at the firm of my predicaments, and that I would probably need a medical leave longer than the two weeks that I had initially anticipated. Everyone in my practice group was most caring and accommodating, and stepped up to fill in for me, covering my cases and keeping clients informed and well served. Flora, in particular, insisted on visiting me. She drove herself all the way up from the Bay Area to Medford just before Christmas, not an easy drive at all in the winter. There I was, lying rather vulnerably in my hospital bed, while just nine months earlier, Flora, Bob and I were strolling through the Redwood Forest and enjoying lunch by the Russian River. It was sweet and very thoughtful of Flora to return from Walmart with bags of snacks and fresh fruits, Christmas decorations which she put up in my hospital room, and even a pair of comfortable yoga pants for me. What a friend in need she was.

After about three weeks in inpatient rehab, I passed the "test" to be discharged to return home. During those weeks, I had plenty of time to cogitate on my latest predicaments. I never did ask my neurosurgeon what happened, or what went awry, or what my prognosis might be, or a million other similar questions. That was because I was, understandably or otherwise, in serious and total denial at the time. Above all, I did not particularly want to hear the truth, even if he or anyone else knew what the truth was. Denial was the only defense I could muster and the only posture I could assume to preserve my sanity, dignity, faith and hope. My disability happened too abruptly, too unexpectedly, too mercilessly, and altogether too unjustifiably. I would fetch my Leica camera from my suitcase and caress it, tears streaming down my cheeks, day-dreaming of the Pacific coast road trip that I would not be taking after all. I could hardly believe that my days of being "free" were over after just eleven precious, short months after I walked out of my former home.

There was no owner's manual, instructions or guidebook for me to chart my course forward. I knew that I had to move, once I returned to Michigan, from my second-floor apartment to a ground-floor unit. I knew I needed to be followed by a neurologist or neurosurgeon once I returned home. I also knew I needed someone to assist me with some of the mundane daily living activities such as grocery shopping, apartment cleaning, and taking the trash out. Beyond those immediate needs, I had no idea how my life would unfold, and thus, how or what else to plan for my future. My plan to retrieve the remainder of my belongings from my former home to be placed in storage, clearly, also had to be shelved for now. Dad had by then returned to Windsor from Hong Kong. Vivian volunteered to immediately fly to Detroit to help me with my move. I flew back to Michigan just before New Year's Eve, and spent the afternoon with Dad and Vivian viewing barrier-free apartments available in my apartment complex. That would be the very first time, of countless times to come, when I appreciated the existence of the Americans with Disabilities Act (ADA). We quickly picked a two-bedroom apartment on the ground floor, and I managed to reserve movers to help me pack and move on January 2nd, which ironically, was exactly one year after my move from my former home. Vivian was a saint; she not only helped me with the packing, she also unpacked for me, and helped me furnish and get situated in my new apartment. It was quite a shock to me that I could not do anything at all for my move, as both of my hands had to be on the walker, which precluded my fetching or carrying any item. I was moving all too slowly anyway to be of much help. Juliana also arrived from Toronto for a few days; she helped me set up and reconnect my audio system, which was the most important task on my agenda as far as I was concerned.

I had been consulting with a neurologist, Dr. Alicia Prestegaard, for several years for my migraine headaches. I called her while I was still in Medford to ask if she could also follow me with respect to my paraplegia, and she readily agreed to do so. Thus, I met her at her clinic a few days after I moved into my apartment. Dr. Prestegaard was most patient, and indulged me with more than an hour examining me and my legs, and gave me a prognosis complete with sketched drawings. She was of the opinion that "only" my peripheral nervous system, as opposed to my central nervous system, had been compromised. Thus, she believed my nerves would heal and regenerate, but it would be a very slow process, as those nerves supposedly regrew only about an inch per month, and I had quite a few feet to go for my legs. Obviously, there was no medicine for my condition, no secret potion to expedite the healing process. I had been prescribed an extremely small dose of Baclofen when I was at inpatient rehab to relieve muscle spasms. Dr. Prestegaard repeatedly remarked to me: "You are very brave." While I was flattered by the compliment, in truth, I felt somewhat bitter. It was not my choice at all; I certainly did not opt to forego my legs just to prove or to receive accolades that I was "brave."

By mid-January, Vivian had returned to Hong Kong after ensuring that I was well-settled in my barrier-free apartment. There I was, my first moments of contemplating on living my new life on my own as a "cripple." Occupational therapy was well and good, but in practice, I often had to improvise and devise my own ways and means in order to accomplish the even simplest task in daily living. With both of my hands on the walker, for instance, I had no way of carrying my food from the microwave oven to the dining table. It took me a while to figure out that I could "leap-frog" my plate from counter to counter, spot to spot, in the kitchen, and finally onto the dining table. It suffices to note that every task took much, much more time and energy. It was a mighty struggle just trying to put on a sock and shoe on my foot that had no sensation and with toes that would not cooperate. I had to engage a home caregiver from one of several new agencies springing up in the area. It was then still an emerging service sector, and the industry had not yet been consolidated into several major franchised providers. My caregiver came weekly for two hours, alternating between grocery shopping with my prepared shopping list, and light housekeeping such as vacuuming and dusting, and taking the trash out. Speaking of trash, there were days when I stared out the window from my study, watching neighbors taking the trash out to the dumpster. I would have given a million dollars, if I *had* a million dollars, just to be able to walk across the parking lot again and deposit my bag of trash at the dumpster. I cried many a times upon those thoughts. I had to train myself to be very organized; the motto from my Girl Guides days of "Be Prepared" became my guiding principle. If I were out of toothpaste, for instance, it was not as if I could just hop into my car and drive to the nearest drugstore to replenish my stock. Hence, I had learned to anticipate and always be well prepared in advance. It is astonishing how we take so much for granted in our daily lives, until we can no longer have those items or do those tasks.

In those early days, I was still able to attend my weekly sessions with Hazel. I had to walk, on my walker, the long way to my car, because I was not steady or safe at all in stepping down from the sidewalk to the parking lot. Hence, I would walk from my apartment door, down the sidewalk and over the curb cut to the parking lot, and then to my parked car. My gait was very labored and slow, and each step consumed an enormous amount of energy. Stepping up to or down from something as mundane and otherwise insignificant as the sidewalk could be a fall hazard for me. Same with opening doors to building and stores; the walker was always "in the way," and taking one hand off the walker to open the door could be another fall risk. I had never previously paid attention to those automatic doors triggered by a motion sensor, or those doors equipped with a push button for automatic door-opening. Those simple "conveniences" became necessities when one is physically disabled. Alas, I was beginning to see and experience the world vastly differently. Things that we would otherwise not think twice about, such as steps and stairs, and bathrooms that were too cramped to accommodate my walker, could indeed be a challenge for the physically challenged.

I had also started twice weekly outpatient physical therapy and occupational therapy at Troy Beaumont Hospital shortly after returning to Michigan. All seemed to be proceeding smoothly enough when in late February, my legs suddenly became wobbly and more unreliable. I requested an appointment with Dr. Prestegaard right away, and her in-house physical therapist in turn referred me to a new physical therapist: Stephanie Herrle at Providence Park Hospital of St. John Providence Health System in Novi, a western suburb of Detroit. Working with Stephanie, who specialized in rehabilitation from spinal cord injuries, twice a week, my legs became increasingly stronger even if sensation was still nonexistent below my waist. Ironically, even though I had lost sensation from waist down, I still felt "pain." Usually by mid-afternoon, a very unbearable and fierce "burning" sensation would grip my hamstrings, and I would have no choice but to lie down for a nap. My doctors would later inform me that it was neuralgia, or nerve pain, that was plaguing me. Nonetheless, those were rather encouraging couple of months, as I continued to strengthen my legs, while waiting patiently and watching for signs of regrowth of my peripheral nerves.

I was hopeful that I could recover fully and return to work in just a few months. However, by March, as I was still shuffling along with my walker, I could not blame Larry for hiring another attorney to take my place and handle the workload. Larry was decent enough to visit me with the new attorney at my apartment to ensure a smooth transition. In the meantime, my firm's human resources department assisted me with applying for and obtaining disability benefits. It felt very strange not to have to go to work.

To prevent my mind from becoming too lax, I volunteered to help coordinate a meditation conference that the Lighthouse Center was hosting in April. Those activities helped keep my mind off the snail-like pace of my healing. However, they also made me realize my pitiful state of not being able to do much more than making a few telephone calls, keeping a few lists, and undertaking a few mindless clerical tasks. What a rude awakening and sudden fall from grace.

As I bided my time for the supposed regeneration of my peripheral nerves, another setback occurred in early May. I was blindsided when all of a sudden one morning, my legs became extremely weak and unstable, and even the walker could not give me sufficient support to avoid fall risks; I also started losing control of my bladder. I called Stephanie to inform her of my new symptoms, and she decided that I should be in a wheelchair to be safe. I was wary, because I had heard somewhere, sometime ago that once one got into a wheelchair, one would "never" be able to get out of a wheelchair. Nonetheless, I did not really have a choice; my legs at that point were too unreliably wobbly to stand or walk even with the walker. A rental wheelchair was delivered to my apartment swiftly. It was a very clumsy and clunky manual wheelchair with many heavy metal parts, and not a custom wheelchair made to my measurements and requirements. I did not need a powered or electric wheelchair as my arms were still able to push the wheels on the chair. It took me a few days just to learn on my own how to navigate in my wheelchair, and to coordinate the use of the wheelchair with my walker. I did not realize that there would not be any tutorial on the proper use the wheelchair, let alone living my life being confined in a wheelchair. That turned out to be yet another steep learning curve, taking much time and experimentation. As I could no longer walk safely even with my walker, I had to stop my sessions with Hazel, as well as my outpatient physical therapy sessions with Stephanie.

I refused to be discouraged by the fact that I was "condemned" to a wheelchair. I held fast to my firm belief that my nerves were healing, as Dr. Prestegaard had assured me, and I would be restored my full health and leg function in just a matter of months. I tried to maintain some form of "normalcy" in my life, or even just a pale imitation of my former normalcy. On a day when I felt strong enough, I would walk with my walker to my car, parked just outside my apartment, and take a drive as I used to enjoy doing. I might even stop by a fast-food drive-through to indulge in a wholly unwholesome meal. However, harsh reality would sink in soon enough when I arrived at my destination, usually at the lakeside of a nearby small lake. Instead of being able to "roam the earth" and take photographs at will, I had to err on the safe side and stay in my car, peering at the scenery only from the very restricted vista of my car window. Moreover, it was impossible to take a decent photograph when both of my hands had to be securely on the walker, or from the very limited vantage point of the car window. *C'est la vie!*

Meanwhile, Lina urged me to learn and memorize the Heart Sutra, reminding me that she had sent me a year prior a CD of her Master Li's reciting the Sutra in several languages and formats. She never explained why I should learn the Sutra, and I never questioned why I should. She sent me the text of the Sutra in Chinese; though it consisted of only 260 Chinese characters, it was extremely difficult to memorize and far too profound for me to understand. That Sutra is reputed to be the best known and most popular Buddhist scripture in Mahayana Buddhism. I listened to the CD and decided to learn it in my mother tongue, Cantonese. It took me about five days to memorize it; I thought that was rather pathetic on my part, until I would later realize that not everyone could learn and memorize it in just a matter of days. One could chalk it up to karma, whether or not one could learn and recite the Heart Sutra. Ever since then, I had been reciting the

Sutra several times a day. While I do not have objective proof that such practice had been beneficial to me in specific ways or had brought about fame or fortune, reciting it had served to calm and steel me in times of turmoil, pain and adversity.

Jo telephoned me excitedly one day in May, relating how a Chinese healer visited her gated community over the weekend, and taught residents a form of alternative healing that he had developed—Tong Ren healing. The healer had allegedly been able to heal someone in her community with advanced cancer. She then gave me the healer's name and telephone number. It was Tom Tam from the Boston area. I knew Jo had been involved with all sorts of alternative, natural, and energy healing modalities over the years. I had listened to her singing praises of various healing regimes with bemusement. Yet she seemed particularly impressed with Tom Tam and his Tong Ren system of healing. That introduction came at a very opportune time, as I was still smarting from the setback I had just suffered earlier in the month that had me confined in a wheelchair. If I could, I would return to Hong Kong to receive treatment by the two Chinese women doctors who miraculously "cured" me just a little more than a year earlier. I was desperate then, I would admit it. Thus, I called Master Tam right away, and it turned out that he also spoke Cantonese, and we thus hit it off with ease. I would start reading some of his books about Tong Ren healing, but it suffices to note that it was a form of energy healing, similar to the more popular and widely-known Reiki. Best of all, like Reiki, the healing could be dispensed at a distance, for instance, over the telephone. Hence, I started healing with Master Tam twice weekly by telephone. He was so sure of himself and his healing system that he unequivocally pronounced that I should be able to not only walk on my own again but be able to run to his clinic in about two months. As he was a very busy person, having a clinic practice as a licensed acupuncturist in Boston in addition to holding Tong Ren healing classes several days a week, he passed me on to one of his top disciples, Laura DiGregorio, to continue my distant healing sessions. I absolutely adored Laura. She was a couple of years younger than me, and she exuded empathy, compassion and competence. By August, my condition had ostensibly improved. Even though I was still not able to walk on my own two feet, contrary to Master Tam's bold predictions, Laura's distant healing amazingly had restored my bladder control, and my legs had at least halted their downward slide.

Meanwhile, in mid-May, I was jolted by the bad news that our condominium in Bloomfield Township had suffered a flood. We had listed the condominium for sale almost a year prior, and did receive a very attractive offer at the beginning of 2005. However, Bev was in one of her typical difficult and uncooperative moods and flatly refused the offer, and hence, the properly remained vacant. Apparently, one of the water pipes broke, and soaked through the apartment. It took a while before a neighbor noticed the flood, and notified management. I was livid. First, the property, being vacant, did not have appropriate insurance coverage. Second, being confined in a wheelchair, I was not able to visit the condominium, which was on the second floor, to inspect the damage or oversee remedial repairs. Third, the remedial repairs had to be paid out of my pocket. Bev was totally nonchalant about the incident, expenses or the repairs. In short order, I engaged SERVPRO to remedy and make repairs, including any water damage to the unit downstairs from our unit. If Bev had agreed to the sale earlier that year, I would not have had to incur the substantial expense. That was archetypical of my life with and business dealings involving Bev: if anything appeared to be too smooth-going or easy or effortless, she would somehow find a way to throw in a monkey wrench so as to make life miserable just for the heck of it. There was another intriguing aspect about that condominium. I did not notice, when we bought the condominium in the spring of 1996, when I had my one grand mal seizure, that it could very well be the apartment where Barb's mother resided when we visited her once or twice in the summer of 1977. I was very new to Detroit then, and was not paying attention to the address because Barb was driving. However, I did recall that it was in Bloomfield. One day in 2004 when I was inspecting the unit, and the sun was striking through the front room window casting a certain light that triggered a sudden recollection and recognition in me: all at once I remembered and realized that I had been there before, and that I had walked up those stairs before—when I visited Barb's mom in 1977. Nothing in this world is ever coincidental; it sent shivers up my spine when I came to my realization.

Even though more than two months had lapsed since I began distant healing with Master Tam and Laura, I was still not able to walk on my own two feet. Master Tam urged me to consider traveling to Boston to receive healing with him in person. His Tong Ren system of healing had brought about enough health benefits in those months that I thought in-person healing with him should work miracles. Vivian again volunteered to fly in to drive Dad and me to Boston. I was extremely hopeful about that trip. It was early October, and the drive from Detroit to Boston, via Ontario and Niagara Falls, could not have been more pleasing with the spellbinding fall colors. During the week that we were in Boston, I received daily acupuncture treatment as well as Tong Ren healing from Master Tam personally. I also joined a couple of his classes, or collective Tong Ren healing sessions. I finally met Laura in person; she was even more charming and caring in person. At the end of the week, I could not honestly say that my condition had improved in any noticeable way. Before we embarked on our return trip, Anita, who was then in Nashua, New Hampshire, and Vivian Fung who was then residing in Boston, treated us to a fabulous dinner. I continued distant healing with Laura after I returned from Boston. I refused to be disappointed by the lack of progress from the week-long in-person healing with Master Tam, even though that *was* an unmitigated disappointment. I remained "hopelessly optimistic," waiting for the regrowth of my peripheral nerves, and convinced that I would regain mobility in due time; I just did not yet know how, or exactly when.

Almost a full year had flown by since I became a paraplegic. Obviously, my hoped for full recovery and the regeneration of my nerves, had taken much more time than I had expected. I would have never imagined that I would be stuck in a wheelchair at the prime of my life. Professionally, I was at the top of my game, poised to reap the fruits of my many years of labor to be named equity partner. Personally, I was just beginning to hit my strides, having bravely and resolutely liberated myself from more than thirty years of self-destructive and emotionally abusive relationships. Yet, there I was, my life, my accomplishments, my shining future, all abruptly halted and snatched away by the catastrophic paralysis and crippling disability. It was too cruel, too unreasonable, too undeserved. "No! I won't bend, I won't bow, and I most certainly won't yield!" I defiantly declared to myself. One of my favorite poems learned in secondary school became my battle cry:

Do not go gentle into that good night.
Rage, rage against the dying of the light.[32]

It was also then when the idea for this memoir seeped into my consciousness—after listening to an interview of Joan Didion by Terry Gross on "Fresh Air," a National Public Radio syndicated program. Didion had her "Year of Magical Thinking" after the sudden death of her husband; in a parallel universe, I had my "year of magical being," after my breakthrough and liberation from decades of unwitting emotional enslavement. It would, however, be several more years before my first feeble attempts at

---

[32] Dylan Thomas, "Do Not Go Gentle Into that Good Night," written in 1947, first published in 1951.

writing, and even more years yet would have lapsed before the substance of the book began to crystallize, and when I was finally inspired to proceed with the admittedly self-indulgent project.

By mid-December of 2005, as if to add insult to injury, I suddenly experienced more weakness, spasms and pain in my legs, which sent me back to the hospital for another round of MRI and observation. Incredibly, the MRI scans did not show any significant change, and the neurosurgeons accordingly decided that I did not have any surgical options. I was discharged home and prescribed a course of in-home physical therapy. I was also referred to a Physical Medicine and Rehabilitation specialist, Dr. Anthony Chiodo, for follow-up visits. My physical therapist was Susan Johnson, and I took to her immediately. We were in the midst of a typical snowy, frigid, grey Michigan winter, but her twice weekly visits with her healing touch brightened my spirits. It was in early February, 2006, when I had a remarkable dream followed by events that baffled me. In my dream, Mom was strolling through a beautiful park with Maxine; they were chatting away happily, as the sunrays streamed scintillatingly through the trees. I was gratified to see Mom being so happy. Maxine was a lymphatic massage therapist whom Mom worked with for a period of time while she was battling cancer in 2001 and 2002. Mom saw Maxine one last time just weeks before she passed away. I had met Maxine briefly only once. About two weeks later, on February 20th, I happened to telephone my long-time friend Mary to chit-chat. Mary gave me the shocking news that Maxine had passed away unexpectedly and peacefully on February 11th. That would have been around the time of my dream of Maxine strolling in the park with Mom. Even stranger yet, at some point later in our telephone conversation, Mary suddenly said to me, "And Maxine will heal you, too." I was startled, and puzzled by that statement. Mary would later tell me that she did not recall making that statement at all. That chain of events was simply too bizarre for me to dismiss, yet I could not make any sense out of it. It was perhaps the first time I was made aware of "supernatural" happenings, or at least unexplainable circumstances.

As if to challenge my preconceived notion of rationality, that is, all things had a rational basis and explanation, another bizarre dream came in March or April of 2006. It was more a haunting revelation than a dream. In that dream, Bev and I were brothers and Roman centurions. We came upon an inheritance which we were to share equally, but she/he wanted the entire loot. She/he lunged for me with her sword, but I, for some reason, could not bring myself to fighting her/him or defending myself with my sword. We were both in full armor and fully armed. I ran instead, with Bev giving chase. She/he caught up with me—and killed me, presumably stabbing me in the back with her/his sword, but in my dream, I did not really see that last scene as it was probably too horrific for me to experience my own death almost 2,000 years ago. That dream rang very true to me; it was as if the dream was a replay of what in my soul I knew to have happened. Before those two dreams, I did not recall ever having dreams of that nature—prophetic dreams, dreams with a message, and dreams that revealed something that happened in a Past Life, even though at the time, I was still not that convinced of the existence, nor did I understand the notion, of Past Lives. Over the years, I had had several more dreams about Bev and Smokey, my cat; some were repetitive dreams with the same theme. Gradually, I was learning the symbolisms in my dreams, which helped me understand events in the past, which in turn led to a greater appreciation of the present and even the future. While I could try to interpret my own dreams and draw inferences and wisdoms from them, this particular occurrence defied any rational explanation. When I was briefly hospitalized at the University of Michigan Hospital, I was moved into a private room late at night on December 15th, 2005. As soon as I was situated in that room, I saw that the wall clock in front of me had stopped momentarily. Out of that clock came a stream of images of faces of people whom I did not know. The faces looked ancient, dressed like horsemen in the high Steppes. After a rush of face images coming out of that clock, a most beautiful, serene woman came out. I was absolutely mesmerized. I called her "clock woman." I was not on any hallucinating drug or even prescription pain medication at the time, and thus, I could not attribute my "vision" to medications. Lina told me later that whenever a clock stopped, it signified supernatural forces at work. I would see that "clock woman" again on April 10, 2008, when I was again in a hospital. I was lying flat in the hospital bed, having physical therapy. My inpatient physical therapist was helping me exercise my toes when the wall clock in front of me suddenly and literally came flying off the wall. It was about 11:20 a.m. My physical therapist and I were both stunned. She picked up the clock and placed it in a Plexiglas shelf on the wall. She left the room, and about half an hour later, I happened to glance in the direction of the clock, and the "clock woman" appeared briefly. These supernatural incidents simply defied explanation or rationalization. Over the years, I had finally learned and come to simply accept and respect them, and try to learn from any symbolism, sign or message they might bring forth to me.

Just about then in early 2006, Lina urged me to return to Hong Kong to receive traditional Chinese and alternative healing. She was positive that I would be fully healed if I could just make the trip and come home as soon as possible. The 20-hour flight one-way was so fatiguing and daunting even for an able-bodied person, that I had never considered the possibility. I kept saying to myself and out loud that I would return to my two Chinese women doctors in Hong Kong when I regained mobility. Susan, my physical therapist, however, wisely asked rhetorically and challenged my thinking during one of her visits why I thought I had to wait. That prompted my re-evaluation, and it did not take me more than a day to decide to return to Hong Kong pronto. In late January, 2006, I saw Dr. Chiodo for the first time at his clinic. He gave me a thorough neurological examination, but did not have any medicine or advice for me, other than beckoning me to return to see him after my trip to Hong Kong. In early February, Dad, who was a robust 83-year-old then, pushed my wheelchair and accompanied me to Hong Kong. I had planned to stay there through May; I figured that three months ought to be a sufficient period of time for me to benefit from the traditional Chinese and alternative healing. As luck would have it, I was able to sell our condominium in Bloomfield Township just before I left for Hong Kong. Bev finally agreed to the sale, even though the purchase price was pitifully less than the offer she rejected a year prior; I supposed she really needed the money then.

Memories of my last visit to Hong Kong barely two years earlier were still very fresh in my mind, as our plane at long last touched down at the Hong Kong International Airport. Instead of my walking out of the terminal, Vivian met us and helped Dad push my wheelchair and fetch our luggage. Winnie, ever so kind and considerate a buddy of mine, had sent her chauffeur with a minivan to pick us up at the Airport and give us a ride to Vivian's apartment. Everything seemed familiar as I recalled my stay in late 2003, yet everything seemed so different and alien because of my new perspective—from about 3-1/2 feet off the ground, and fixed in a seated position. There was a unique "Hong Kong feel" that greeted me every time I returned to my home country. Even before interfacing with the throngs of humanity and tackling the onslaught of the masses, the sounds were the first thing I noticed. Everyone around me was speaking Cantonese, and the sounds emanating from television sets and radio stations in neighborhood shops and apartments were also Cantonese and Chinese music. Then there was the enticing aroma of food, Cantonese food of all stripes. There were so many restaurants and eateries everywhere that one could always smell something delicious just walking down any street. It all summed up as a warm "welcome home" to a native daughter.

Vivian's apartment, like most in Hong Kong, was small-ish. She had made a huge effort in rearranging furniture and her worldly possessions so that I could at least reach the bedroom and bathroom with my walker. Within two days after my arrival, I presented myself at the clinic of Drs. Lui and Cheung once again. Instead of my "flying down" the stairs at the subway station to board a subway train, Dad had to push my wheelchair through bumpy pavements, crowded streets, elevators located way out of the way in subway stations, and unexpected steps everywhere in order to arrive for my appointment. Dr. Lui was very understanding, caring and encouraging. She told me how she had successfully treated other patients who could not walk for one reason or another. I was told to return for daily treatment. After my first session with her, several of my SSGC classmates had arranged to meet me for *dim sum* lunch at a nearby restaurant. Fatima had arrived from Los Angeles, and had come to the clinic to help Dad push my wheelchair to the restaurant. She had been calling me almost every week since I returned from Medford, to encourage and cheer me on. Several of my SSGC classmates, Pearl, Sandra, May, Annie Chan Mei Ying, and Isabella Chong Siu Hung were at the restaurant waiting for me. I could not hold back my tears seeing all of them again under the circumstances of the day, as I felt pitiful, embarrassed and vulnerable all at once. Of course, my long-time friends were most considerate, caring and loving. It would turn out that they would play a major role in my healing journey.

For almost three weeks, Dad took me to Drs. Lui and Cheung every morning. It was also quite expensive as the treatments were not covered by my health insurance. It seemed that there was no miracle cure this time around, and I was still as numb as could be from waist down with painful leg cramps and spasms. Dr. Lui counseled patience, but Lina was not pleased at all with my progress or the lack thereof. Around that time, Dr. Cheung herself had to be hospitalized for surgery. I had not shown any improvement at all after three weeks, and that was enough evidence for Lina to call a halt to the exercise. Instead, Lina introduced me to "KK" (her English name was June, and her last name was Suen), a massage therapist and self-styled alternative healer. Just about then, Dad was complaining loudly and repeatedly about his knees, that they were getting weak and bothersome. Hence, when KK arrived at Vivian's apartment for my first appointment, Dad wanted her to treat his knees first. I let Dad have my appointment, and KK would return in a couple of days to treat me.

During my first treatment with KK, she noted that Dad's knee problems were very minor and typical of osteoarthritis suffered by older people. I, on the other hand, she thought, was suffering grave injuries. She was of the opinion that my legs were "atrophying" and had to be saved before they reached a point of no return. Her healing methods were a type of *qigong* massage therapy. In later sessions, she also occasionally used heat from a small fire that she sparked with alcohol. It was all quite mysterious, but that was the nature of folk, alternative Chinese healing. She would come every other day for a two-hour session. We talked quite a bit during those sessions. I would learn that she was a clairvoyant, and could "see" things that most people cannot. She would tell me some of the things that she "saw" in and around my body. I kept an open mind, and was not alarmed by her quirky healing ways and means. She was a Buddhist, and would bring me "sacred" water from her temple from time to time, and even gave me a few mantras for personal safety. Lina was not pleased with those "extras" from KK, warning me never to accept mantras from "unknown" sources.

In March, the Buddhist temple of which Lina was a member and was in fact fast rising in the ranks, had an anniversary celebration. Dad, Vivian and I were invited as guests. On that anniversary day, the venue was packed with hundreds of its members and disciples dressed in monk's robes. The guests of honor were several very high-ranking monks from a venerable Shingon Buddhist temple in Japan. Master Li appeared in a very ornate monk's robe, and led the procession and worship ceremony. Afterwards, there were performances by *kung fu* troupes which put on a show including lion's dance, dragon dance, and other martial arts extravaganza. I, in my wheelchair, seemed particularly out of place and taking up far too much space, as I was everywhere I went in the very densely packed Hong Kong. I was very proud that I was able to chant along when the congregants recited the Heart Sutra, a fact that several of Lina's fellow Buddhists noted and complimented on. Lina later told me that Master Li saw me in my wheelchair and commented to her that I would indeed heal, but that it would "take a long time." If only I knew "how long." In those first years, if I had a dollar each time someone remarked that I would be able to walk again on my own two feet, I would have been a millionaire several times over already.

In about March, May had referred me to a Chinese traditional medicine doctor and acupuncturist, and a professor at Hong Kong University, who was renowned for healing people with mobility issues, such as patients who had suffered strokes. Hence, in addition to healing with KK and for about two months, Dad would push my wheelchair twice a week, through subway stations and bustling streets, over to Central on Hong Kong Island to receive acupuncture treatment by that Chinese doctor. My friends from SSGC, including Isabella, May, Annie, Sandra, Pearl, Susan and Raina, often joined me for lunch afterwards. I felt endlessly grateful for their steadfast moral support, love and friendship.

I was also enormously grateful to Vivian for sheltering me and Dad, putting up with my wheelchair and walker, laundering our clothes, keeping us well fed, and keeping Dad well entertained. Ted was in the United Kingdom at the time. Dad would sometimes go out on his own, to meet with friends and to browse and shop. I mostly stayed in the apartment, *wishing* I could be out and about. There was, however, a huge bonus to my being in Hong Kong at that time: being with Lilian again. One of the unexpected blessings of my paraplegia was the opportunity for me to spend much time with Lilian, as if to make up for lost time in the previous decades. If I were still working as a full-time attorney at Dickinson Wright, I doubted very much if I could have spared the time to travel to Hong Kong and visit Lilian but once every few years, if that. Yet there I was, spending quality time and sharing meals with Lilian about once every three weeks, for months on end. As I could not travel the distance to Lilian's dormitory, Vivian would go to pick her up and bring her to the apartment or to a restaurant nearby. I would never forget the first time she saw me again, after more than two years, in Vivian's apartment. She recognized me right away, and made a big fuss and grunted heartily as she rushed toward my wheelchair with a big smile, then excitedly started pushing my wheelchair. I had no idea where she learned how to push a wheelchair. It was another one of life's most precious, priceless moments.

My daily life at Vivian's apartment in Hong Kong was not very exciting at all, since I could no longer, as I could and did in late 2003, come and go as I pleased to explore venues and take photographs. I tried to completely focus on my healing, repeatedly reassuring myself that I would "soon" be able to walk on my own two feet again. The sessions with KK continued into May, and even though I still could not walk on my own, my health and stamina seemed to have improved. During one session we discussed my ill-fated surgery of December 2004. She was understandably surprised that I had not filed suit against the neurosurgeon. Of course I had considered that option, but had repeatedly arrived at the same conclusion: no, I would not sue the neurosurgeon. My rationale at the time was three-fold. First, I was absolutely convinced that my paraplegia was "temporary," "transitional," and that in due time "soon," I would fully regain my leg function and be able to walk on my own two feet again. You may characterize that as denial in the extreme, but that was honestly how I felt and believed. Second, my neurosurgeon had successfully operated on me in September 1992, saving me just in time from the brink of paralysis, and I had thus been able to enjoy twelve very productive, happy years, perhaps some of the best years in my life. I felt very grateful to him, and therefore, I simply could not bring myself to suing him for whatever happened at the December 2004 surgery that had me wake up a paraplegic. Last but not least, it was as if I had tacitly made a pact with my Maker, a "bargaining," if you must; for not pursuing my neurosurgeon for damages and compensation, I asked that I be restored my full health and leg function. Time slipped by very quickly as I struggled to heal and recover, while the statute of limitations for filing suit ran. In making my decision not to sue for medical malpractice—not that I would necessarily prevail in any such lawsuit—I had failed to consider the "what if's." What if I never regained leg function? What if I would remain a paraplegic confined to a wheelchair for life? What if I ran out of money to live on, how would I sustain myself? The financial picture was in fact quite grim, as I was no longer able to work for a living while not having adequate provision for my forced "retirement;" I did not expect to be compelled to stop working at such an early age. No matter, I now have to live with the consequences, anticipated or otherwise, of my fateful decision way back in those relatively early days.

Dad returned to Windsor as scheduled in May of 2006, while I extended my stay for a couple of months. Lina was again not pleased with the progress of my healing with KK, and urged me to seek treatment with another Chinese healer she had found. I was, of course, disappointed that I was still not able to walk on my own, but I continued to keep my faith. The healer whom Lina wanted me to work with was Dr. Tang Li Cheng whose healing methods were quite unorthodox. While he was a licensed Chinese traditional medicine doctor, he was famous for his "wet cupping" healing methods. In brief, he made small punctures on different parts of the patient's body, depending on the patient's ailments, allowing tiny droplets of blood to flow from the punctured areas, while he used a vacuumed bamboo "cup" (by lighting a small fire to burn up the oxygen inside the cup) to suction briefly on the punctured areas to supposedly promote healthy and healing blood circulation. I was extremely skeptical, but KK had conceded that she had given me all of her healing know-how, and thus healing with Dr. Tang became my only option. Before my scheduled departure from Hong Kong, I bravely tried a couple of sessions with him. Though I did not notice any immediate benefit or improvement, I did not react adversely to the treatment. However, it was time for me to return to Michigan. I had spent a substantial sum healing with the numerous alternative healers in those six months, but I remained confined to my wheelchair, and the supposed regrowth of my peripheral nerves showed no sign of growth at all.

Back in Michigan in August of 2006, life continued with my return visit to Dr. Chiodo, and resuming physical therapy with Stephanie, though I did not resume distant energy healing with Master Tam or Laura. Dad came over from Windsor to visit me at least monthly, getting rides from friends. It was so cruelly ironic, as I had fully expected to undertake many more trips with Dad, just as we had in past years enjoyed our trip to the Miami Pen Show and our driving trip to Toronto. Yet, before I could even schedule one more trip after our Toronto trip in July of 2004, I was for all intents and purposes "out of commission." We talked on the telephone a great deal, frequently and regularly; I had always confidently assured—in fact, promised—him that I would be well and walking on my own "soon." It must have been around October when Lina again discussed with me about continuing treatment with Dr. Tang. As I did not see any likelihood of a breakthrough with physical therapy, I readily agreed to return to Hong Kong to resume treatment with Dr. Tang. I made the flight back to Hong Kong in early November, and without Dad accompanying me. Of course, it was insanely inconvenient to travel overseas as a paraplegic in a wheelchair. I had to rely on and pay for porters at the airports to help with my luggage and pushing my wheelchair, and at times on kind-hearted fellow travelers. For instance, one may not give any particular thought to grabbing a bite to eat at airport stopovers. In my case, unless there was a full service restaurant for me to patronize, I had to ask for help even with the simple task of carrying my plate and drinks onto a wheelchair-accessible table. Paying for merchandise could be downright humiliating if the counter did not have a "cutout" allowing me in my wheelchair to be seen by the cashier and facilitating my cash payment or signing for a credit card purchase. On the plane, while I could slowly and cautiously walk to the restrooms with my walker—dicey as it was through the narrow aisles—I could not take the walker with me into those pint-size bathrooms. I had to hang on with dear life to grab bars and hold my breath, hoping I would not fall down through the entire exercise. I had my very athletic much younger days to thank for my "residual" strength, balance, coordination and agility as a paraplegic.

Vivian again selflessly welcomed me to and accommodated me in her apartment. My SSGC classmates gallantly rallied to my aid. In particular, Susan and Raina accompanied me and pushed my wheelchair to each and every one of my appointments with Dr. Tang. May and Sandra generously made available to me their chauffeured minivans for my trips to Dr. Tang. Otherwise, it would have involved a lengthy subway ride with train changes, plus a taxi-ride to get to Dr. Tang's clinic from Vivian's apartment. Once again, I was filled with hope as I began my course of "wet cupping" treatment with Dr. Tang, twice weekly. And once again, I delighted in being able to be with Lilian again every three weeks.

2006 also happened to be the Centenary of SSGC. I was fortunate to have returned to Hong Kong just in time to participate in many of the 100th Anniversary festivities. I attended the Centenary Concert at the Cultural Centre, featuring stunning performances by the school's choirs and orchestras and the alumnae choir conducted by my classmate Rita. Remarkably, the highlight of the Concert was a near-professional performance of excerpts from the musical "My Fair Lady" by our secondary school students. That fund-raiser was followed by the official Centenary Dinner, a formal dinner for more than 2,000 alumnae, students and current and past teachers at the Hong Kong Convention and Exhibition Centre. Our class decided to celebrate the occasion with a custom-made silk jacket. More than thirty of us attended the Dinner in our highly visible silver silk jacket, and we were quite the center of attraction. Miss Barker, along with a couple of our former teachers, Miss Hallward and Mrs. Feathers, traveled from the United Kingdom to join in the special celebration. By the time we concluded the high-spirited evening by singing our school hymn[33] and "Auld Lang Syne," there was not a dry eye in the hall. Miss

---

[33] *We build our school on Thee, O Lord,*
To Thee we bring our common need
The loving heart, the helpful word,
The tender thought, the kindly deed.

We work together in Thy sight,
We live together in Thy love:
Guide Thou our faltering steps aright,
And lift our thoughts to heaven above.

Pullinger was also invited and was in attendance. She in fact came over to our tables, and asked that we organize a group visit to her Christian mission, St. Stephen's Society. May accomplished that task with flair; in early December, a group of about twelve of us traveled to her mission located quite far away from the city center. There, with residence facilities, she provided shelter and spiritual healing, support and religious education for drug addicts to kick the habit and rehabilitate. We also visited another facility where she and her followers conducted worship and had their various workshops. I purchased a number of t-shirts made by the members as souvenirs. In another couple of weeks, a smaller group of us would attend a play performed by members of her mission and based on her best-seller "Chasing The Dragon."

In late January 2007, Lina traveled to Japan with her Master Li and numerous fellow senior Buddhists to participate in a tonsure ceremony to be officially recognized as an Acharya of her Buddhist temple. She told us that it was considered good karma for the entire family when one member could become a Buddhist monk. I fully concurred and was very proud of her spiritual achievements. Shortly thereafter, she wanted me to learn Reiki healing, not so much for me to heal others, but to self-heal. By then, Lina was a Reiki Master several times over, having achieved that level of training and having been "attuned" several times as

---

Hold Thou each hand to keep it just,
Touch Thou our lips and make them pure;
If Thou art with us, Lord, we must
Be faithful friends and comrades sure.

We change but Thou art still the same,
The same good Master, Teacher, Friend;
We change, but, Lord, we bear Thy Name,
To journey with it to the end.
Dear Lord we pray, Thy Spirit may
Be present in our school alway.

such including once in Japan by the descendant disciples of the founder of Reiki, Mikao Usui. She gave me quite a few books to read and learn the Reiki healing techniques. When I finished studying, she "attuned" me for advanced level of Reiki healing. I had been giving myself Reiki healing on a daily basis ever since. Over the years, Reiki self-healing had ameliorated somewhat my neuralgia, and given me stamina and endurance to pull through the few times that I was severely challenged health-wise. Above all, it had helped calm and center my mind, putting me in touch with the "inner knowingness" within me.

Meanwhile, it was obvious that "wet cupping" with Dr. Tang was not yielding any positive results. In fact, Uncle Lai had been concerned about my undergoing "wet cupping;" he thought I was too weak and too underweight for that type of treatment. Lina had yet another healer to refer to me: Dr. Tong Hon Cheung. He was also a licensed Chinese traditional medicine practitioner, and his specialty was qigong healing. I started healing with him in about February. As he lived nearby Vivian's apartment, he was kind enough to make house calls on Sundays so that I would have to travel to his clinic in Wanchai only once weekly. Again, Susan and Raina accompanied me on those clinic visits, with Sandra's chauffeur giving us rides, rain or shine, and it poured buckets when it rained in Hong Kong. I got along famously with Dr. Tong, as we both loved photography and thus had lots to talk about during my treatment sessions. His qigong "massages" worked wonders on my overall health while my legs were also much less spastic after three months of healing with him. It was again time for me to return to Michigan as scheduled in May of 2007. Dr. Tong asked me to consider committing to healing with him for one year; he was of the opinion that my "occasional" healing—a few months here and there at a time—was not conducive to optimizing results.

A jubilant Lilian, flanked by (l to r): Dad, Vivian,
Lina and the author. November 29, 2003, Kwun Tong,
Kowloon, Hong Kong.

Given the positive results from sessions with him in those
three months, I agreed with his recommendations, and started
planning for my move to Hong Kong. I decided to live on my own
during that year, and my SSGC classmates swung into high gear.
Pearl, May, Annie, Isabella, Sandra, Susan, Raina and others were
out in full force to scout for an affordable "service apartment" for
me. As luck would have it, they found a tiny efficiency apartment
in a residential building located practically across the street from
Dr. Tong's clinic. It was May who wisely advised me to terminate
my apartment lease in Michigan and put my possession in long-
term storage, so as to avoid paying rents for apartments on two
continents. I thus started winding down my affairs in Michigan:
returning to the dealer my Audi "A4 Quattro" as the lease expired;

not renewing my apartment lease when it expired in August; locating movers and storage facilities to store my worldly possessions; forwarding my mail to Ann and Linda; and arranging for prescriptions to be mailed to me while in Hong Kong. In late August, the movers came to pack up my possessions for long-term storage. I spent that night at a hotel, and left for Hong Kong the following day with two suitcases out of which I was to live for the ensuing year.

Vivian had thoughtfully stocked up the pantry at my service apartment even before my arrival. It was very small, sparsely furnished efficiency apartment not much bigger than the size of my bedroom in Michigan. It had a very tiny bathroom with a shower stall, and a very narrow and small kitchen. It had a stove, microwave oven, and refrigerator, and that was all that I needed to survive. As I was still able to walk a few steps with my walker, I could use the bathroom and the shower with a shower chair. I did have to improvise to level the threshold between the kitchen and the rest of the apartment for my wheelchair to access the kitchen. Life as a paraplegic in a wheelchair was always very challenging, especially when I was placed in a new environment, or had to adapt to a new routine. Hence, it took me a few tries before I got used to preparing meals for myself and taking a shower in the new apartment. Laundry had to be done at a nearby drycleaner which charged by the pound for laundering and folding my clothes. Susan and Raina would drop off my bags of soiled laundry when they came to take me to Dr. Tong's clinic, and pick up the laundered clothes when they accompanied me back to my apartment after my appointment. Lilian was delirious the first time she saw me again when we met for dinner; Vivian took a photograph of us, both of us grinning from ear to ear, in the restaurant. I now look at that framed photograph everyday, and I silently smile and cry all at once every time.

My SSGC friends gathered a couple of times at my tiny apartment just to cheer me up and keep me company. We ordered carryout food, and enjoyed an afternoon of lively conversations and camaraderie. In September, Helen Zia happened to be in Hong Kong, en route to Shanghai where she would be spending half a year researching for a writing project. She dropped by my apartment for a visit, and we had a wonderful time catching up with each other as I had not seen her since Mrs. Chin's funeral in June of 2002.

I had been in Hong Kong for about a month, and life was just getting to be routine when one day in late September, I noticed a sudden weakening of my legs. My legs became increasingly weaker and even less coordinated in the course of just a few days. The abrupt change greatly alarmed me, as I was becoming very unsteady and unreliable when standing up or walking even with my walker. After a few more days and the deterioration continued, I had to think of the "unthinkable": I needed to return to the States right away before I became unable to travel safely by myself. Another few days went by and there was no equivocation: my condition had continued to decline rapidly. I broke the news and my decision to my sisters and my SSGC friends. Everyone was startled and saddened, and I, in particular, was most disappointed. I had hoped that my one-year stay in Hong Kong for healing with Dr. Tong would be *the* magic cure for my paraplegia. I congratulated myself for not having signed a one-year lease for my service apartment, so that I could terminate the rental at month's end. I felt awful that Vivian had to lug all the provisions that she had furnished at my service apartment back to her apartment. Worst of all, I felt shattered when I met with Lilian for dinner one last time. She had no idea that she would probably not see me again, but I had a strong hunch that I would not be able to see her again after that evening. She had been losing weight the past year. I had a premonition that her cancer might be returning. I also had a premonition that I would not be able to fly to Hong Kong for a good long time; I would turn out to be correct on both counts. So, there we were, sharing a last meal; instead of being able to spend another year with her, I was saying to her my last "goodbye;" it broke my heart. Two nights before I left Hong Kong in mid-October, I invited as many of my SSGC friends as I could gather for a nice dinner at a fine restaurant, to thank them for their unwavering support and to bid farewell. I gave them each a souvenir: a lanyard that I had custom-made with the imprint of "The Miracle Team," and a card bearing a photograph that I took in December of 2003 of the formal staff dining room at SSGC. It was an extremely emotional evening for me.

My plan was to go to the Mayo Clinic, as soon as I arrived back in Michigan, for a neurologic examination. As I no longer had a home in Michigan, I had to stay at a hotel upon my return. To my chagrin, the earliest appointment I could obtain at the Mayo Clinic was in mid-November. Hence, I moved into an extended-stay hotel to wait out the month. Living out of my suitcases in a hotel, and as a mobility hampered paraplegic, was quite maddening. However, my optimistic nature, and my determined, strong will to survive and thrive helped me through the days. Nirmala was kind enough to offer once again to accompany me to the Mayo Clinic. The workup at the Mayo Clinic was very thorough as always. A new full-spine MRI scan was taken. I had my kidney checkup completed as well while having my neurological issues addressed. I was examined by a neurologist, followed by a Physical Medicine and Rehabilitation doctor, and lastly, by a neurosurgeon. Thankfully, the PMR doctor had prepared me psychologically for "negative" news from the neurosurgeon. He predicted correctly that their neurosurgeons were very "conservative," and that, in all likelihood, they would decline to operate on me. That was precisely what the neurosurgeon informed me: he could not see how another operation could successfully drain the syrinx or relieve or reverse my paraplegia. Meanwhile, the PMR doctor had already referred me to a neurosurgeon whom he had seen accomplish "some amazing things" surgically. It was Dr. Andrea Halliday in Eugene, Oregon.

The visit to the Mayo Clinic turned out to be yet another disappointment, as I came away with no resolution for my increasing leg weakness or my paraplegia. I was not discouraged, though, and upon my return to Michigan—and back at the extended-stay hotel—I contacted Dr. Halliday's clinic to arrange for an appointment with her for possible surgery. It did not faze me that I had to fly to Oregon again. I was on a mission then; if only I could find the "right" surgeon who could and would operate on my spinal cord, just as in the past years, I would wake up from the surgery walking on my own two feet again, just exactly as had happened at least twice in the past. I would spare no expense, and would go any distance, to have my mobility restored. I had come this far, and had tried so many healing modalities and alternative healing regimes, that there was no way I would stop searching for my cure just because the Mayo neurosurgeons were not optimistic about my prognosis and declined to operate on me.

I found myself with one suitcase (the other suitcase having been deposited with Nirmala for safekeeping) and my walker arriving in Eugene in mid-December. I checked into the Eugene Hilton Hotel where, exactly three years prior, I had stayed one night the weekend before my fateful spinal cord surgery. I had engaged a home caregiver through an agency to assist me on an hourly basis. I was filled with renewed hope as I arrived at Dr. Halliday's clinic, only to be informed that she had an emergency case and could not see me that afternoon. I returned the next morning, and while I sat in the tastefully appointed waiting room, my mind was racing, wondering whether Dr. Halliday would find my condition operable. My answer came shortly when I met her in the examination room. I liked her immediately; she was the first female surgeon I had worked with, and she positively exuded competence and confidence, warmth and empathy. She had reviewed my MRI scans, and was of the opinion that she could and should decompress several arachnoid cysts that did not show up in previous scans. She did not directly address my question about shunting my T12 syrinx. She gave me a choice of having the surgery before Christmas or after the New Year. She was concerned that if I underwent the surgery before Christmas, she would be on vacation and not be available should there be any post-surgery complications. I was so eager for the "surgical fix" that I opted for the earlier date, and accordingly surgery was scheduled for December 18th. I was hoping to get this entire episode done and over with as expeditiously as possible so that I could return to Michigan and restart my life.

Again, spinal cord surgery seemed routine to me by then. I went through pre-op testing and laboratory tests, and showed up at the hospital punctually on the appointed day. Again, I was in high spirits, looking forward to benefiting from the surgery, especially when Dr. Halliday came so highly recommended by a Mayo physician. The surgery was uneventful, and I awoke in due time without undue pain or discomforts. However, the biggest disappointment was the realization that I was still a paraplegic after that surgery. Unlike when I awoke from previous successful surgeries, I still could not move, control or feel my legs as I lay in my hospital bed. All my hopes and dreams of reversing my paraplegia were snuffed out, even after an operation by such a distinguished and acclaimed neurosurgeon. I really did not know what steps to take next for my further healing, after having thrown a great deal of money, time, and physical and psychic energy at it in the three years since I was wheelchair-bound.

I was discharged from the hospital in a few days with a return appointment to see Dr. Halliday at her clinic after the New Year. I returned to the Hilton Hotel to lick my wounds. Little did I know then that there would be more literal wounds for me to tend to. Just one day after my discharge, I started feeling unwell. My legs turned to mush, and I almost could not even walk with my walker to the bathroom. Hence, on Christmas Eve, I checked myself into the hospital emergency room. Dr. Halliday had by then left for her vacation, and her colleague tended to me. It was soon determined that my stitches had somehow come apart, and I had an infection in my surgical wound. Of course, I was hospitalized immediately and was given intravenous antibiotics. The substitute surgeon also decided to perform a lumbar puncture and drain. He had explained to me the procedure using other terms. If I had heard the term "lumbar puncture," I would have never consented. I had no idea what it was that he was trying to drain from my spinal canal, but that lumbar puncture had totally debilitated me. He ordered the nurses to jack my hospital bed almost up to the ceiling, which supposedly would promote better drainage by increasing gravity from "hoisting" me at that height. It sounded and looked ridiculous, and it was indeed ridiculous. I remembered feeling life being drained out of me drop by drop, along with hope, faith, trust and the little optimism I had left. Those were several very dark days for me. It was the first time ever when I could not muster enough strength to endure, nor did I have a clear enough mind by then to ask that the procedure be stopped. I simply languished, in pain, and hoping to somehow survive long enough for Dr. Halliday to rescue me. Finally, delightfully, on the third day of the New Year, Dr. Halliday appeared. She was livid about the condition I was in; she reminded me that she had warned about complications from the surgery while she was on vacation; she knew that no other surgeon was qualified to handle my very complicated case in case of post-op complications.

Dr. Halliday scheduled me for immediate surgery to correct whatever caused the infection and spinal fluid leakage. After the surgery, I was sent to inpatient rehabilitation floor for recovery. That was the second time I was in inpatient rehab, and hence, I knew to expect at least four hours of physical and occupational therapy everyday. I was physically extremely weak, and worse, I could not understand why I could no longer stand up even with my walker; my legs were worse than useless. Thus, in physical therapy, in addition to strengthening my upper body and arms, I was taught to use a transfer board. I did not like the transfer board at all, and I could not understand why I had to use it. My physical therapist explained that I had to use it because my legs could not bear weight at all, and thus, I would not be able to transfer otherwise without the transfer board. It was all too new to me, too surprising, too shocking. Moreover, I started having horrific migraine headaches almost daily.

It must have been well over two weeks since I had been in inpatient rehab. I remembered one night I awoke and could not fall back asleep. I asked for help to get into my wheelchair, and pushed myself to the elevator lobby. There I sat in my wheelchair, in the wee hours of the night, staring emptily into the distant space. I felt incoherent in mind and speech. I felt drained of my last ounce of life forces. I had given my best and my all, in terms of financial and human resources, to recovering from and reversing my paraplegia, but clearly, that was not enough or effectual. How events unfolded was not at all how I had anticipated when I excitedly embarked on my journey to Eugene a month earlier. I had never before consciously given up hope or trying, but there and then, I reckoned that I had finally reached the limits of my forbearance and willpower. I had nothing more to give to myself, and my spirits were as abysmal as I had ever experienced. I asked an aide to help me back into bed. With a sense of complete resignation, I lulled myself back to sleep.

Another few dreary days went by when Dr. Halliday came to my bedside and shared with me her view that she should operate on me once more to correct and adjust my spinal fluid flow. She honestly told me that she had finally figured out that the culprit was the flow of my spinal fluid, or at least the rate of the flow. I trusted her completely, and thus consented to yet another spinal cord surgery, the third in less than a month. The surgery again proceeded uneventfully, and after a brief recovery period in the step-down unit, I was transferred back to the inpatient rehab floor. It was the first full day after I returned to inpatient rehab, and I was wheeled to the gymnasium to have my daily physical therapy session. Surprisingly, I felt well and stronger that morning. The biggest surprise, however, came when I tried to transfer—I was once again able to stand up while holding on to my walker; in other words, my legs could bear weight again. Dr. Halliday was a genius; it was indeed a matter of regulating the flow of my spinal fluid. Even my migraine headaches went away. Everyone in inpatient rehab was astonished, as if I had practically transformed myself overnight, and came alive after that operation. I remained in inpatient rehab for about another two weeks. My legs were strengthened, and I could again walk quite a few steps with my walker. Dr. Halliday wanted me to remain in Eugene for at least another month to ensure that my condition was really stabilized. The occupational therapist and social worker were trying to look for suitable accommodation for me without much success. I then decided to return to the Hilton Hotel and camp out the month there. As one could well imagine, this had been a very expensive trip for me, not that my three-plus years of alternative healing had exactly been affordable. My physical therapist had also noticed that my wheelchair had a bent axle, probably from rough baggage handling during my several trips to Hong Kong. As such, it was unsafe for me to be using it especially on public streets. They had a collection of donated used wheelchairs, and I was fitted with one that suited my petite physique. It was a Quickie "2HP" wheelchair with a Day-Glo orange frame. I was transformed once I got into that pre-owned wheelchair. Even though it was well worn and used and its tires kept losing air pressure, I could push myself, navigate the streets, and even go up and down inclines and turn on a dime. It was a much cherished, new-found freedom of movement for me.

I was prescribed outpatient physical therapy three times a week at the gymnasium located just one floor below the inpatient rehab at the hospital. Oftentimes, I would arrive half an hour earlier to strengthen my legs on the Nustep recumbent cross trainer stationary bike, as my physical therapist encouraged me to do. I was issued a guest pass to ride on Eugene's excellent para-transit system, my very first experience with such transportation which provided door-to-door service. I would call in advance to reserve a life-van to pick me up at the Hotel and drop me off at locations within the service area of Eugene's public transportation system. If it was a medical appointment, I could call when I had completed the appointment (a "will-call" ride) to pick me up for the return trip; a lift-van would usually show up within 10 minutes of my telephone call. The lift-vans were vans equipped with a power lift-platform that my wheelchair could roll onto. The lift would rise up to the cargohold level for my wheelchair to roll into, and lower to the street-curb level for my wheelchair to disembark. Once inside the van, my wheelchair was securely tied down to the floor of the van by four sturdy metal anchors-fasteners, and I would be seat-belted securely as well. As the para-transit system was mandated by the ADA, the fare was extremely economical at about $2 per trip. The system worked particularly impressively in Eugene: the lift-vans were clean and inviting, and their drivers were professional, courteous, and punctual. Hence, in addition to attending physical therapy sessions and doctor's appointments, I would go to a local supermarket about once a week to procure ready-cooked meals and snacks. The Hilton Hotel furnished my room with a tiny refrigerator, just large enough to hold a carry-out meal or two and a few pieces of fruits. In retrospect, I was quite the survivor in those months; I ate at the Hotel's restaurant at times, and order food delivery other times. It was not an ideal diet, but I made do. There were also several fine restaurants, and an upscale shopping center with a gourmet shop, within wheelchair-rolling distance of the Hotel, and occasionally I would patronize those to jazz up my diet a bit.

After a couple of weeks of physical therapy, my physical therapist suggested that I consider having craniosacral therapy which was a very gentle therapy that might encourage better spinal fluid flow. Stephanie had treated me a few times with craniosacral therapy, and of course, I had a week of craniosacral therapy with Dr. John Upledger himself in October of 2001. Karen Lackritz was the therapist highly recommended, and hence, I started weekly sessions with Karen. Karen indeed had a superb healing touch and temperament. Just spending the hour with her, without more, calmed and soothed all discomforts and pain, physical and psychological. As I continued to recover from my surgeries and rebuilt my strength, I returned to Dr. Halliday's clinic for a follow-up office visit in early March. It was then when I noticed some pronounced pain in my back as well as increased loss of sensation. An MRI of my spinal cord was ordered, and to my dismay, Dr. Halliday notified me that a couple of new arachnoid cyst had cropped up in my spinal canal. As incredible as it sounds, surgery was once again scheduled for early April; that was my fourth surgery in Eugene in as many months. The surgery again proceeded without incident, but again, I did not wake up from it with regained leg function or sensation; I was still a paraplegic. By the end of April, Dr. Halliday ordered another spinal MRI for me. She was reviewing the scans in real time even as the MRI was proceeding, and ordered the technician to undertake additional specific scans. After her careful and meticulous review of the scans, with a sense of satisfaction, she advised me to "go home" as my spinal cord then had "never looked better." She added that I had a "long rehabilitation ahead" of me. I had no idea what she meant by that at the time, but I would later understand that she was probably expecting me to regain leg function in due time.

Staying in Eugene for almost half a year, undergoing four spinal cord operations and incurring substantial financial outlays, were not anticipated at all. It was even more jarring when I looked back and realized that it had been almost four *years* since the onset of my paraplegia. I had struggled mightily, and I had sustained my optimism and dignity, through those years. Unfortunately, Dr. Prestegaard's theory about the regrowth of my nerves was far off the mark. Otherwise, I should and would have regenerated *yards* of my nerves during those four years, more than enough to enable me to walk on my own two feet again. I was disappointed, of course, but by no means giving up hope of regaining full leg function when the time would be ripe. In particular, I considered it a blessing that I survived all those spinal cord surgeries and complications. I was still alive; I had learned valuable survival skills as a paraplegic in a wheelchair from various physical and occupational therapists; I was still breathing; I still had functioning body parts sufficient to carry on with life; and my mind, alas, was still intact. Hence, my cup was not only half full, but indeed was practically, virtually full. I hailed my hard-won victory in those critical rounds of my mortal combat. I had emerged stronger, wiser and even more determined than ever to beat the odds.

XI.

The Peaceful Warrior

A nn Arbor, Michigan: an oasis for progressives, an enclave for die-hard liberals in a State that was not known for trail-blazing but for its Motown, as in music and cars. I had always wanted to seek refuge in Ann Arbor, but work and life kept me bogged down in the buttoned-down Troy. Returning from Eugene in May of 2008, with my worldly possessions still in storage, I could resettle anywhere I reasonably wished, which made for a perfect time to finally make the move to Ann Arbor. From my temporary quarters in the extended-stay hotel, I engaged a home caregiver to assist me with apartment hunting. It was meant to be, as I found my new home in just one morning, after touring numerous apartment complexes in the city. It was another ground-floor barrier-free apartment, airy, bright and cheerful, in an ostensibly well managed complex. Above all, it had an open floor plan with an oversized living room; my mind's eye could visualize the ideal placement of my audio system, and a hoped-for home theater.

In early June, the 18-wheeler with my storage cartons arrived at my new apartment and disgorged its contents. I felt a sense of settling down, after years of physically and psychologically drifting, in search of the "miracle cure." I also happened upon a couple of new caregivers, Remedios (Reme) Tillman and her life-partner, Eric Pylkas, who were not affiliated with any agency. Without their help, my move-in and unpacking would have been much more chaotic and time-consuming. Eric, in particular, and I got along famously; he was also very handy and thus, assembled my furniture and bookcases and connected my audio system, which I enjoyed doing myself before I was confined to a wheelchair. Eric would continue to assist me, about once a month, with grocery shopping, running errands, and odds and ends around my apartment. My surgeries, physical therapy and alternative healing in Eugene had clearly revitalized me; I was able to handle quite a bit of unpacking and putting items away in between calling for Eric's help. It still took almost two months before I was well situated in my new abode. Even Dad pitched in; he hung on the walls throughout my apartment, perfectly and ever so artistically, the many photographs that I took during the few years before my paraplegia.

Like Eugene, Ann Arbor also had a para-transit system with lift-vans. Unlike Eugene, it was not as well run, the vans were much older and quite unsanitary, and the ridership experience was altogether much less pleasant. Ann Arbor also did not have a "will call" policy for lift-vans; it offered "will call" return trips only to passengers who could transfer and thus could ride in a passenger car or taxi. Since it was difficult for me to transfer, I required a lift-van. That in turn meant that if I had under- or over-estimated the duration of a doctor's visit, I would either have to miss my ride and wait "forever" for an available lift-van to pick me up, or whiling and wasting hours waiting for my return ride. Indignant with the inequities, I filed a complaint under the ADA with the Michigan Department of Civil Rights about the disparate treatment between transferable and non-transferable passengers. After the complaint languished for almost two years, the Department ruled against me. While I was convinced that my complaint was meritorious, I did not pursue it further as I had learned to pick my fight, to fight smarter, and to conserve my energy. This exemplified the implicit attitude that, merely because I was physically disabled, I should be thankful for the availability of the para-transit system, and that I was not entitled to complain about inefficient or poor service. I do not suppose that under normal circumstances, able-bodied customers would have tolerated wasting such an inordinate amount of time and putting up with ineffectual logistics and disorganization in their public transportation system. However, since the para-transit system was almost viewed as an afterthought, a "handout" of sorts for the elderly and the disabled—in other words, the weak and the often voiceless—and hence, the system thought it could get away with it. Such injustice and insulting attitudes enraged me; I promised myself that, when I was more physically able and had less debilitating pain, I would seek "revenge" on behalf of all of us with physical disabilities who were treated as if we did not matter that we were somehow less than human.

In the meantime, and after almost two years of wasting far too much time waiting for my lift-van ride and suffering other indignities with Ann Arbor's para-transit system, I decided to look into getting myself a vehicle again. I learned that there were customized minivans for people in wheelchair. One very popular version was the "Braunability" minivans, designed and modified in conjunction with the minivan's manufacturer. It featured electric/power ramps, automatic kneeling/lowering of the vehicle for ease of ingress and egress for the wheelchair, docking for the wheelchair inside the vehicle, and special power driver's seat that rotated 180-degrees to facilitate transfer from a wheelchair. However, the cost was prohibitive; even a used one would sell for more than a brand new BMW sports sedan. Online videos showed how a disabled person could transfer into the driver's seat, dissemble his wheelchair and put the various parts on the front passenger seat, and then merrily drive away. I tried dissembling my wheelchair at one of my physical therapy sessions, but could not even get as far as taking the wheels off my wheelchair; I simply did not have the necessary upper-body strength. More online research had me considering outfitting a regular minivan with certain adaptive equipment. Finally, in late March 2010, I took the plunge and purchased a Volkswagen "Routan" minivan, and had it outfitted by an accessibility specialist shop with three pieces of adaptive equipment: a set of brake-and-throttle hand-controls; a small electric foldable platform-seat that would raise me up to the driver's seat level to transfer into the driver's seat, and lower me to the ground level for transfer back into my wheelchair; and a "robotic arm" in the cargo area behind the driver's seat that would lift my wheelchair into the minivan. The equipment still cost thousands of dollars, and took almost three months to install and troubleshoot for everything to work safely and reliably. That minivan served me well for a few years, but had its drawbacks. My wheelchair, which by then was a custom made-to-measure Quickie "GTX," had to be modified for grabbing and lifting by the robotic arm. As a result, its balance was off; once when I was trying to traverse a slightly uneven pavement, my wheelchair fell completely backwards and spilling me out of it. I was extremely fortunate that I was not hurt even as I fell onto the concrete parking lot head first, but it was too terrifying to even recount the incident. Then there were times when a parking lot was at an incline or in inclement weather, I would have a harrowing time fetching my wheelchair from or getting it hooked up with the robotic arm, and transferring back and forth between the platform-seat and my wheelchair. Chalk it all up to a day in the life of a paraplegic who was determined to live independently and remain as mobile as feasible.

Since my move to Ann Arbor, there was a sense of a new beginning, and as with any new beginning, new hopes and aspirations inevitably followed. While the previous four years had been a headlong and relentless search for my "miracle cure," by then I felt poised to savor the fruits of those years of healing, relish the opportunity for a brief repose, to regroup, to live life and simply coast for a while. In late July, I took Dad to the acclaimed and popular Ann Arbor Street Art Fair. For a change, instead of sweltering heat, we had a perfectly pleasant, cool and sunny day. We strolled from stall to stall, enjoying the art and crafts on display, and Dad even bought a trinket or two. We asked a bystander to take a photograph of us in front of a particularly interesting stall, and that turned out to be one of my favorite photographs of Dad. It has been displayed in an Italian-made parquetry wood frame, reminding me daily of our happy days together.

As I had reacted so favorably to Karen's craniosacral therapy, I located another Upledger-trained craniosacral therapist in Ann Arbor, Judy Liu Ramsey. Beginning in June, I had weekly sessions with her, and occasionally with her business partner, Rachel Egherman. Just as I put away the last items in my apartment in August, and told myself to exhale and look around to see what Ann Arbor had to offer me, I noticed another abrupt and marked decline in my overall stamina and especially leg strength and coordination. That was a most unwelcome realization and development. Judy highly recommended that I heal with one of her teachers, Dr. Bruno Chikly, who was a practitioner of an alternative healing modality called "Lymph Drainage Therapy." I had thought that my days of chasing a miracle cure were over, but the sudden and unexpected decline in leg function prompted me to seriously consider her suggestion. Hence, in October, I embarked on yet another costly trip in the hope of improving my health condition, or at least stemming further declines in whatever little leg function I had.

Dr. Chikly was located in Scottsdale, Arizona. It was interesting how I seemed to keep returning to Oregon and Arizona for my spinal condition. In retrospect, I was very brave to be traveling on my own. I had by then learned a few tricks to ensure that my travels would be as safe as possible. I stayed at a hotel that provided an in-room kitchenette as well as limited grocery shopping service. Of course, I stayed in an accessible room with wider doors and grab bars in the bathroom. I rented a car with hand-controls, because Dr. Chikly's home office was located outside of the public transportation service area. I still required help with getting my luggage and wheelchair in and out of the car, but most of the time, people were helpful. Of course, life as a paraplegic in a wheelchair was not easy even at home, and it was infinitely more so in a new environment. Even getting my clothes out of my suitcase was not without drama; it depended on whether I had carefully considered the placement of my suitcase.

I believe I had three sessions with Dr. Chikly. He was very optimistic from the first moment we met, repeatedly remarking that I would not even need my new custom wheelchair by the time we were done with our healing. From past experience, I had learned not to have unrealistic or high hopes about the outcome of my healing with Dr. Chikly. Indeed, after the course of treatment, while he claimed that I was able to walk much more steadily, I honestly did not see any improvement.

By December of 2008, my walking, even with my walker, had become very unreliable again. The little sensation that I had of my legs became infinitesimal, and I had even less control and coordination of my legs. More alarming was that my legs started cramping up so much that I was not able to straighten out my left leg when lying down. Dr. Chiodo ordered another round of physical therapy for me, and for a change, it was with a physical therapist at the University of Michigan Hospital, Priya Mehta. By then, I had halted my craniosacral therapy with Judy. In addition to craniosacral therapy, Priya gave me another form of alternative healing called Integrative Manual Therapy. In the course of two to three months of receiving IMT, I seemed to have been revived and come alive yet again.

In July of 2009, Carol-Ann surprised me by paying me a visit. She had emigrated to Melbourne, Australia, about two years earlier, having fallen in love with an Australian woman she met on a trip to Italy. They married in Australia, and Carol-Ann was carrying on her practice in Down Under. I remembered our days at Barnard decades ago when she was not sure of or had not declared her sexual orientation. Since her days in London in the 1980's, she had proven to be an intrepid standard-bearer in the progressive movements. She was back in the States to visit her mother in Florida, and decided to swing by to visit me and one of her high school friends in Troy. Her friend drove her to my apartment in Ann Arbor, and we both rode the lift-van to enjoy a leisurely lunch outdoors on the patio at the renowned Zingerman's Deli. Carol-Ann was a cancer survivor; she had lost much weight since I last saw her in March of 2004, but she looked radiant. I was obviously in my wheelchair, looking not so robust. She was at her humorous best when she remarked that we both were in our respective "new bodies." We spent the afternoon talking about everything, and as we did in her home in North Berkeley five years earlier, we listened to music for a while in my apartment. When it was time for her to leave, I had a slight sense of misgivings; I had no idea when I would see her again; we were akin to two ships passing in the night.

I felt as if I were in a time warp; days, weeks, months, years flew by while I floundered, stumbling, shuffling, in search of the unattainable, of regaining my ability to ambulate. It was in the fall of 2009 when I decided to pursue IMT with the founder of that healing modality, Dr. Sharon Weiselfish Giammatteo in Bloomfield, Connecticut. The very positive results of several months of IMT healing with Priya convinced me that it would be the most promising therapy yet for my paraplegia. I made an appointment for five consecutive days of IMT healing with Dr. Giammatteo and her trained therapists in early November. It was yet another substantial investment in my healing, but I was quite desperate by then as my legs seemed to be weakening by the day. I flew to Hartford, Connecticut, and their excellent para-transit system transported me from the airport to my hotel, as well as the clinic in the ensuing days. The therapy was very intensive—and very expensive. I was at the clinic for the entire day, and had continuous multiple sessions of healing, each with a slightly different focus and techniques, with trained therapists. Toward the end of the week, I had several sessions personally with Dr. Giammatteo. When the week was over, again, I could not honestly report that I had any observable improvement with respect to my paraplegia. Hence, I felt I had exhausted even my alternative healing options at the end of that week. It had reached a point where I felt exploited, financially and psychologically, by some of these hallowed healers, however well-intentioned they might have been. All was not lost, though, as there was a delightful surprise waiting for me at the airport when I was about to embark on my return flight. I ran into my former colleague, Henry Grix. He, along with the client's banker and accountant, had just finished a one-day visit to one of his clients in Bloomfield. We chatted merrily throughout our flight home; that was infinitely more healing than the entire week of IMT.

About a month before I left for Bloomfield, I was actually dealt a very cruel and atrocious blow. Out of the blue, Bev e-mailed me and informed me that her tenant had trashed and abandoned our former home, and without expressly stating it, she expected me to once again put the pieces back together and pick up the tab. What "tenant?" I asked no one in particular. In short order, I would learn that Bev had apparently moved out of the home in about October of 2008, and rented it out to a tenant. She had apparently moved to somewhere outside of Chicago, to be close to her daughter and granddaughter. Her tenant had not paid rent for a few months by the time she notified me of the chaos and shambles, had not paid water and sewer charges for the entire year, and had vandalized the home before he left. The coup de grâce was that he had notified the City to conduct an inspection, whereupon the City had promptly "tagged" the home with a long list of "deficiencies" that had to be rectified before it could be lawfully reoccupied.

I had never thought that Bev would ever leave that home; I was clearly mistaken. If I were not in a wheelchair, it might not have been as much a challenge to take over and inspect the home, fix it up, and rent it out again. However, as it was, I did not even have an affordable means of transportation to get there for an inspection. It would not have helped even if I could get there, as I would not have been able to enter the home in my wheelchair, what with the narrow doorways, and steps and stairs everywhere. Certainly, I was not in any position to do the repairs myself, as I used to do. My sense of helplessness, anxiety and bitterness was paralyzing, until I collected my wits to chart a plan of action. My first order of business was to hire a property manager to secure the property. As the property manager was extremely slow and uncertain about getting estimates for necessary repairs, I engaged the very capable and trusted—but not inexpensive—contractor that we had relied upon in years past to give me a comprehensive repairs proposal and estimate. That was accomplished promptly, and I was shocked yet again by the estimate. Bev had not maintained the property while she lived there for the five or so years, and her tenant had ravaged whatever was left. Major repairs included a new furnace, hot water heater, new carpeting and flooring throughout, interior painting, new window treatments, new appliances including refrigerator, dishwasher, washer and dryer, new garage door and opener, back wooden deck repairs, and yard clearing. The total cost, not unexpectedly, came to a hefty five-figure sum. I had no choice but to proceed with and pay for the repairs and renovations. The home could not even be sold otherwise. The most shocking of all, however, was what my contractor told me after he had a chance to thoroughly inspect the home. Other than heaps of garbage that the tenant left behind, there was not a trace of my belongings. When I e-mailed to ask Bev, she nonchalantly told me that she had supposedly given everything away to friends and pitched the remainder. I could hardly believe it; I could hardly accept it. My *zheng*, the guitar from my teenage years, my senior thesis, my master's degree thesis, my books (including *The Female Eunuch* that was part of my English achievement prize from SSGC), my diaries, my CD collection, the Chinese carvings, paintings, porcelain items and rosewood furniture from my parents, my Royal Copenhagen Christmas plate collection, even the thousands of copies of her book in the basement, and so on and so forth—all gone without a trace. It baffled me that she did not even have the decency of giving me a chance to retrieve my possessions before "tossing" them; she had no right to dispose of my possessions stored in my home without my consent. I suspected that she had sold many of my items for money to live on. Yet, there I was, and what could I do? It was *fait accompli*. It would take more than a month for the repairs to be completed, and more than eight months before a suitable tenant moved in; the fact that we were in the depth of the Great Recession might explain the difficulty in locating a responsible tenant. The saga of our former home would continue to include the fireplace catching fire and destroying the chimney during the first winter I had it rented out, and unsuccessful sale efforts, making it probably one of the very few parcels in Troy that did not sell. Nonetheless, I patted myself on the back for being able to muddle through, via "remote control," and in due time, rectify that convoluted and costly mess that Bev had wantonly tossed my way.

As my legs continued to weaken and the muscles continued to contract, seemingly for no ostensible reason, Dr. Chiodo ordered another spine MRI. When the MRI did not reveal any significant change, he prescribed another round of in-home physical and occupational therapy at the beginning of 2010. In the meantime, I had located another craniosacral therapist, Ann Zalek and then her business partner, Kathryn Hannan, to resume weekly sessions. After all those years, I had no illusions or unrealistic expectations about those weekly sessions. My wild goose chase for *the* healer who would restore my health or *the* healing that would enable me to regain leg function was over. As a case in point, Kathryn highly recommended my healing with her teacher and master healer, Dennis Adams, who came to Michigan from Mt. Shasta, California, several times a year. I did, twice, and even had Dad work with him for a session to heal his knees and legs. However, neither Dad nor I saw any quantifiable improvement. Nonetheless, Dennis was a most charming person, and we enjoyed healing with him. Besides, after our sessions with Dennis, as we were in Chelsea, about fifteen miles west of Ann Arbor, Dad and I enjoyed an excellent lunch at my favorite restaurant there.

By the time my "Routan" minivan was outfitted with adaptive equipment for me to drive in July of 2010, I noticed just how weak my core muscles had become as I transferred to the platform seat and as it lifted me up to the driver's seat level. I was not as steady as I was before with my balance and control of my trunk. Still, I enjoyed being able to drive myself again, not only to attend medical appointments, but occasionally to browse at the bookstore or for lunch at a nearby restaurant. I also relished being able to drive with Eric to do my own grocery shopping, with his carrying and shelving my groceries. In July, I and my SSGC classmates mourned the passing of Isabella who had fought a mighty battle with cancer but succumbed while she was still far too young. She had survived it in early 2003, but the cancer returned in 2009, and proved too ravaging even for our indomitable Isabella. She had been such a staunch supporter, an enthusiastic cheerleader and empathetic companion to me, during the two years I was in Hong Kong receiving alternative healing. I wrote a remembrance in her honor, and here are excerpts from that heartfelt July 20, 2010, musings:

> "It seemed only yesterday when we were racing each other for the ping-pong table during a recess, fretting over an upcoming Chinese History test, or making a royal mess of our cheese scones in our Domestic Science class. That popular, friendly, cheerful, and somewhat demure young lady had blossomed into a shining superstar. She had amassed more accomplishments and accolades, trophies and awards, diplomas and certificates in her 55 years than most people can only aspire to garner in 155 years. Not content with merely relying on her outstanding academic credentials and demonstrated management savvy to fast-track up the corporate ladder as a multinational banking executive, she dazzled us with her entrepreneurial brilliance in a diverse range of successful business ventures.

> "It's almost a cliché for an accomplished woman of the Boomers generation, but Isa was the quintessential multi-tasker who managed to excel in her own professional advancement, all the while bringing up two equally over-achieving children, relocating across cultural, ethnic and geo-political boundaries as her husband's job assignments required, and holding the

family together literally through flying bullets and life's myriad of trials and tribulations.

"But her message is far more compelling than just a laundry list of achievements, impressive as that was. Isabella is the very personification of a life lived to the fullest with zest, integrity, and authenticity. She followed her heart and dared to be unconventional. She followed her dreams and reached for the stars. She followed her passions, and had the rest of us following her in her unique vision of beauty, style and excellence.

"I was in Hong Kong for much of 2006 and 2007 to pursue alternative healing for my paraplegia. I still remember how Isa veritably bounded into the room where a bunch of us classmates were having a lunch get-together, bursting with vim and vigor even after several rounds of singles tennis on a bright summer day, and instantaneously lit up the venue with her infectious smiles and radiant energy. And who else but Isa would have had the chutzpah to admonish me ("straight up, no chaser") not to slouch in my wheelchair. Isabella was a caring, dedicated and loyal friend, a fiercely independent soul, and a fearless champion of causes just and righteous, defying all odds, and oh, how we were in awe as she stared down mortality itself.

"Just the other day, I was chatting with another one of our classmates, Anita Liu Chow, who reckoned that 'We've got may be only about 20% of our lifespan left.' A sobering thought indeed. However, if we are really hearing and not just tuning in, if we are really seeing and not just looking, if we are really tasting and not just masticating, if we are really present in the moment and not just being present, if we are really savoring life's infinite possibilities and not just going through the motions, in other words, if we live life as Isabella had so mindfully and fervently lived hers, then it makes no difference whether we have 20% or 20 seconds remaining in our lifetime.

"The greatest legacy Isabella left behind, though, is a much more subtle one, profoundly resonating through eternity. I visualize our sweet and fair Isabella cooing "A Song For You" by Karen Carpenter—another drummer in a family band:

> *I love you in a place where there's no space or time*
> *I love you for in my life you are a friend of mine*
> *And when my life is over remember when we were together*
> *We were alone and I was singing this song for you*

"May her loving husband, Rollie, daughter, Fay, and son, Julian, and may her mother and her siblings, find solace in the abundance of love Isabella reserved just for each of you. The rest of us who are privileged to have been her friends are counting our blessings."

We would learn the unbearable news that Rollie also died unexpectedly, and far too soon, in January of 2015, probably of a broken heart. On the other hand, over the years as I bided my time in my wheelchair, I watched and applauded as a number of my classmates attained professional recognition and achievements. A law school classmate, Paula L. Cole, who had been working as

Assistant Corporate Counsel for the City of Detroit, received the "Respected Advocate" award from the Michigan Defense Trial Counsel in November of 2005. Another law school classmate a couple of years my senior, Nancy J. Diehl, became the 70th–and the third woman—President of the State Bar of Michigan in 2004. In March, 2009, Roz was elevated to Associate Justice of the New York Appellate Division of the Supreme Court, First Judicial Department, only the fourth openly gay/lesbian jurist to be on that Court. Roz had been a rising star up the judicial ladder since her serving as an Administrative Law Judge in the New York City Office of Administrative Trials & Hearings in 1987. A Barnard classmate, Helene N. White, was one of the youngest, if not the youngest, judges on the Wayne County Circuit Court in Michigan, a trial court of general jurisdiction, in the early 1980's. She was elected to the Michigan Court of Appeals 1992, and after much political wrangling, was appointed to the Sixth Circuit Court of Appeals in 2008. While Pearl returned to academia and received her graduate degree in divinity in 2013 and became an ordained minister in the Anglican Church, Sylvia also returned to school and finished her Bachelor's degree in nursing and became certified as a Registered Nurse in 2014. There were countless more reports of accomplishments by my overachieving classmates as I read the "Alumnae Notes" in *Barnard Magazine* over the years. In the early years of my paraplegia, I felt somewhat left out, even a tad envious, when I learned about my peers' crowning moments. After almost six years in the wheelchair, however, I was pleasantly surprised to find my reaction to be one of gratitude. I was grateful for my life, as it was, in a wheelchair. My life could have been snuffed out so many times in those interim years, yet it was graciously spared, time and again. My "work" clearly was not yet done. I no longer felt "confined." I did not consciously notice precisely when that shift occurred, but I felt instead blissfully liberated. My burning desire to walk across the parking lot to deposit my trash in the dumpster, and certainly my yearning to travel the world again to take photographs, had given way to a gratifying knowledge that I had finally learned many of my life lessons that had eluded me in all the previous decades of my superficially full life. It was precisely because I failed to learn my life lessons time and again as I was busy rushing through life and hurtling down the wrong path that I was stopped "dead" in my tracks with paraplegia, going absolutely nowhere until I learned those necessary lessons. Besides, my mind and my soul could travel so much wider, farther and faster than my legs. It was not resignation, it was not a case of sour grapes; it was, finally, acceptance, and peace.

Dad returned from another three-month Hong Kong stay in May of 2010. Even though he was vibrant and looking hale and healthy, his walking was more labored. I had him examined by one of the orthopedic surgeons at the University of Michigan Health System for a second opinion, and the diagnosis was the same: age-related osteoarthritis in his knees, and surgery was out of the question due to his advanced age. The surgeon urged him to exercise on a stationary bike. Dad then bought a bike, but I believed he worked with it for just a few times. At his age of 87 years, he would rather have another gourmet meal with his friends than ride that stationary bike. I could hardly blame him. Dad was my buddy. We talked for hours on the telephone, and we discussed just about everything. We enjoyed our respective collections of cameras, pens, coins, stamps, books, and what not, and hunting for additions to our collections. I particularly enjoyed his monthly visits. He would often bring me my favorite chicken wings that he cooked up just for me. We would enjoy lunch together, which usually was carryout fare from a local restaurant. I would sometimes play music for him, and show him my latest fountain pen or camera or camera bag acquisitions. He would often bring me gifts of trinkets and knickknacks that he had stumbled upon, and I would likewise reciprocate, whether it was a new found favorite food item, or a new, ultra-luxe 900-gram Egyptian cotton bath towel. And we would talk and talk till it was time for him to return to Windsor. If I had not become a paraplegic in 2004, I would have spent much more time being physically with him, especially taking him traveling with me, all those years. That was one regret that was not within my power to overcome, even as I kept promising him, sincerely, that I would be ambulatory again, "soon." At least that was my honest intention.

It was otherwise an ordinary Saturday, just like any other, on September 25, 2010. In the late morning, as I tried to transfer in the bathroom, even though I was hanging on to the grab bar as usual, I fell down just as soon as I stood up momentarily for the transfer. In all the years since I had been a paraplegic, I had fallen down or out of my wheelchair only a handful of times, not more times than what I could count on one hand. I could get back into my wheelchair, but that was a tremendously difficult, and exhaustingly time and energy consuming maneuver. I had to crawl and align my body with my back against the foot of my chair. Sitting on the floor, with my lifeless legs more a hindrance than support, I would grab the rails above and on both sides of the footrest of my wheelchair, and try to push myself up, using just my arms, and drag my body back onto the seat. It would take many determined tries before I would succeed. Hence, I had always been extremely careful so as to avoid falling at any cost.

I steeled myself and tried to transfer again after half an hour or so, but again, I fell down just as soon as I stood up. That was when I realized something was terribly wrong: I had *no* legs; my legs could no longer bear weight whatsoever.

If I had thought that being a paraplegic the previous six years was undue suffering, I had no idea what real suffering was in store for me when I could not stand up at all, not even for a split second. The first few days of that seismic change were unreasonably challenging and frustrating, as I tried to adapt my transfer techniques, learned new means and methods, and attempted to cope as best I could with my "new body." I somehow was smart enough to order online a couple of additional adaptive equipment: a toilet seat riser to raise the height of the toilet seat to my wheelchair level to facilitate my transfers, and toilet seat safety rails so that I could grab onto them in transferring to the commode solely with my arms since I could no longer stand up and pivot over. Fortunately, I still had my much maligned but then necessary transfer board around, and I started practicing transferring to my bed using the board. I had also purchased several "reachers" of different length, design and construction to enable me to pick up a wide range of items. Basically, I had to learn to do everything all over again now that I could not stand up at all.

We take so many things for granted that we do not even realize that we are taking them for granted. For instance, have you ever considered how you would take your pants off or put them on if you could not stand up to do so? Hence, I even had to change my wardrobe to garments that I could put on and take off easily such as mostly polyester-type clothing with elastic bands, and loose-fitting button-less garb; in other words, the type of clothing that I would not have been caught dead in prior to my paraplegia. I reported my latest dysfunction to Dr. Chiodo who again ordered a spine MRI. Incredibly, the MRI was still not showing any significant change, even as I obviously had suffered a drastic functional decline. He again prescribed another course of in-home physical and occupational therapy. My therapists were experienced and well-meaning, but even they could not solve all of my problems with daily living activities. My occupational therapist suggested that I transfer to my bed to change, pull down or put on my pants. I had learned that "trick" when I was in inpatient rehab in Eugene, but it was not a practical solution, as I would have been exhausted by the numerous transfers needed to and from my bed throughout the day. Alas, there was one situation that clearly had no satisfactory solution or work-around: I could no longer use the public facilities as they would not have the safety rails which I needed to transfer safely. As such, I could only be out of my apartment for a maximum of a few hours at a time. Thus, there could be no more traveling for me, long distance or even local. My "world view," too, had become always about three-and-one-half feet off the ground.

I most certainly did not expect that my paraplegia could possibly get worse, but there it was, it did, after six years. It was a flagrant case of adding insult to injury, or adding injury to insult. All my hopes and dreams of walking on my own two feet again had to be put on hold while I tried to regroup and sort things out. My wheelchair had to be modified yet again to give my back more support. In the meantime, my hamstrings were getting ever tighter, my legs were cramping and suffering more painful spasms, and I was losing core and trunk strength. Worse, the involuntary sedentary life was a slippery slope, as I would learn the hard way. Opportunistic diseases, secondary and collateral dysfunctions, and decline in overall health all conspired in lockstep to further diminish the shadow of my former self. Not only was I beginning to experience much more pain in my legs as they atrophied, I was becoming weaker overall. My appetite waned, my digestion suffered, I became anemic, I lost weight, and the downward spiral threatened to spin out of control.

Life, however challenging and inconvenient, however humiliating and humbling for me, had to limp along somehow, though in reality I could no longer even limp with my legs. I remembered during the first couple of years of my paraplegia, I felt completely "naked;" it was brutal. The adage that you do not know what you have until have lost it is almost too glib. I had always prided myself as being a very "authentic" person; for instance, I did not wear much makeup, and even then, only when I was at work. Yet, my "persona" had indeed been a calculated presentation and a polished production. My "accoutrements" preceded me in my pre-paraplegia days, starting with my "armor": the designer pantsuit, the designer socks and shoes, the alligator belt with sterling silver buckle, the vermeil cufflinks, the famous maker watch, and even the designer gold-rimmed eyeglasses. My name brand leather briefcase announced my arrival, and my collectible fountain pen punctuated my pronouncements. It was a "package" necessary for success and advancement in the corporate legal world. However, once I became a paraplegic, I could not avail myself of any of those accoutrements. It was not practical for me to put on my former "uniform," and I could not very well carry a briefcase in my wheelchair. Even though I was, of course, wearing clean clothes and was otherwise presentable, the "props" were not there anymore. There was nothing to announce my special station in life or my entitled status or my assumed authority. On the contrary, I was piteously vulnerable, half-slumped in my wheelchair; I was "stripped naked" of my protective shell and the cultivated outer appearance. It would be years before I became "comfortable in my own skin," quite literally. That came when I had finally re-learned and realigned my priorities, and with that, fully accepted myself as a paraplegic. I was no longer in denial, nor did I have to make excuses for my physical disability. I was a good person, a worthy person, a valid person just as I had always been, *sans* props and accoutrements. I had lived the charmed, privileged, entitled and jaded life, even if mostly on credit. While I was not exactly super-rich or *nouveau riche*, I had glimpses of and had skirted at the edges of that socioeconomic stratum. Spiritually, morally and karmically speaking, it is not authentic or sustainable a lifestyle.

Hence, when Pearl asked to visit me in December of 2011, I did not hesitate and said, "Sure," even though I was in a much more vulnerable and "naked" condition than when she last saw me in October of 2007. She had been invited by Yale Divinity School to study for a semester in the fall of 2011. When she completed that semester, and before returning to Hong Kong, she wanted to swing by for a weekend visit. Two other classmates, Anita and Selina, immediately chimed in and joined Pearl for that weekend visit to frigid Ann Arbor. I was still able to drive my "Routan," and thus picked them up at the Detroit Metro Airport. We started our weekend properly with a lunch featuring live Maine lobsters brought by Anita from New Hampshire. We talked happily and incessantly, with our "talkathon" interrupted only by most satisfying meals, such as a most decent lunch at Zingerman's Roadhouse, and a most delectable homemade dinner that they whipped up after shopping at Whole Foods. We enjoyed a TV show and a couple of concert videos on my home theater. I believe Pearl could easily discern that I was much weaker physically than the last time she saw me, but she was polite and did not belabor the point. By then, it was a struggle for me to transfer onto the platform-seat that raised me up to the driver's seat of my "Routan," as I had lost much trunk stability and upper-body strength. Still, it was a much needed and welcomed gathering as I soaked up the goodwill, love and Sisterhood of my longtime close friends.

Since the start of 2012, my sisters and I, along with Juliana, were busy preparing Dad's 90th birthday celebrations. We had planned an elaborate Chinese feast for the evening of September 16th in Windsor, inviting more than sixty of his friends. The highlights, however, were the specially designed invitation card and a special souvenir for our guests. Dad was a perfectionist when it came to artistic and sentimental items. Hence, the design of the invitation card and the souvenir had taken months of intense collective efforts. The concept sounded straightforward enough, but the devil was in the details, and in the execution. The invitation card was in formal Chinese, with three panels of decorations. With his vast collection of beautiful Chinese traditional folk-art paper-cuttings, it took much time and effort for us to select three: a stylized Chinese character for "Longevity" for the front cover;

a crane and pine tree circular composition, symbols of long life in Chinese; and a dragon, fish and lotus themed paper-cutting for the back cover, all symbols of auspiciousness and abundance. Juliana saved the day as she deftly set those paper-cuttings in attractive settings and backgrounds for the card; she was educated and trained and had worked for years as a graphic designer. Still, it took quite a few drafts before Dad was finally satisfied with the design of the invitation card. The special souvenir was a personalized coffee mug that Vivian sourced in Hong Kong, onto which was imprinted a photograph of Dad standing next to an oversized calligraphy piece hanging on the wall with the character "Longevity" written by Dad with a huge Chinese ink brush the size of a broom. That was one of his masterpieces when he was taking calligraphy classes with a master in Hong Kong in 2008. He also took my advice to have Juliana inscribe with a gold-color Sharpie' on the bottom of each mug "1 of 90," denoting the "limited edition" status of the very special personalized mug. Last but not least, I was able to source an appropriate and sturdy carton to hold and present each mug. Dad was so delighted with the perfect-fit cartons that he embellished each with an additional red "sticker" with the Chinese character for "Good Fortune." Vivian was Dad's wardrobe department, making sure that he had new and ornate Chinese silk robes and gowns, complete with gold accessories, for the special occasion.

While we were fussing over the invitation card and souvenir, there was another substantial project that Dad had us buzzing about. At our Chan Family Estate, the headstone had only Mom's information engraved. That was quite an undertaking, because it took several years after Mom's passing before Dad fortuitously met the famed calligrapher, a retired physician Dr. Kai Yan Li, who was kind enough to write in glorious stylized Chinese all of our names, dates of birth and all the other characters necessary to form our future dates of death. For about six years since Mom's inscriptions were completed, Dad did not want his or our names and dates of birth engraved on the headstones even though we had the calligraphy penned by Dr. Li. I suppose that was because he felt a bit superstitious and queasy about inscribing on the headstone while he was still alive. Then, all of a sudden in 2012, he changed his mind and wanted to have all of our names and dates of birth engraved. He reasoned that he wanted to see his name and date of birth, in Dr. Li's beautiful calligraphy, engraved while he was still alive. We were, of course, delighted with Dad's change of heart to have that project accomplished while he was still very much alive. The gorgeous granite headstone that was sold with our Chan Family Estate plot had a tall center panel and two shorter, smaller panels on either side. Mom and Dad's information, in Chinese and English, would be engraved on the large center panel. However, it became clear to us that the two side panels would not be large enough to accommodate the inscriptions for us, the four sisters, as well as Juliana (and her future spouse and children), in both English and Chinese. Chris Kavanaugh, our "family counselor" at Heavenly Rest, proposed installing expansion panels, and promptly came up with sketches and drawings. Dad liked the new additional panels, but then, once again, the question of design, decorating and layout for the new panels was crucial. For us Chinese, an appropriate, pleasing, presentable and good *feng-shui* headstone was even more important than untold other things in life. Finally, after much deliberation and hand-wringing, we came up with the design of having our surname "Chan" in Chinese character, from a highly stylized chop/ stamp that Dad had, centered on the top of each of the two expansion panels. That Chinese character was then embellished on both sides with "Chinese clouds"—absolutely stunning rendition of "clouds" in the traditional Chinese style designed by Juliana. Of course, the multi-step layout, proofing and engraving process took many more months and much angst. It was finally completed before Dad's 90th birthday, truly a special birthday present for him. It was worth the "blood, sweat and tears" to see the unrestrained, satisfied smile on Dad's face when he viewed for the first time the newly inscribed panels at Chan Family Estate. As I could not be there physically with him, I vicariously shared his obvious and immense satisfaction through the many photographs taken that day.

Our collective family plate was thus quite full, along with much jubilation, during the first three quarters of 2012. Lina, Vivian and Juliana were all flying in for Dad's milestone birthday festivities. While I could not participate in the birthday feast in Windsor, I had planned the Michigan portion of the celebration by taking them all out for at least one if not several fancy dinners. We had all worked very hard in the preceding months, racking our brains at times and flowing with divine inspiration at other times, and constantly racing against self-imposed deadlines, in designing the invitation card, the birthday souvenir and the expansion headstones, and planning for the birthday celebrations. I did not realize how the almost year-long flurry of activities had taken a significant toll on my health. It was early afternoon on Sunday, September 2nd, and Dad's big birthday bash was just around the corner. I was transferring from the commode back to my wheelchair, a transfer that I had performed thousands of times and which was not a particularly difficult transfer. Just before I was able to sit down in my wheelchair, my left arm suddenly gave way, and I heard or felt a "crack." I had never broken any bones previously in my life, but instantaneously, I intuitively knew I had broken a bone in my left arm. There was immediate sharp pain in my left forearm, and I could not use it at all. Fortunately, I was practically in my wheelchair already. I managed to dial "911" for an ambulance. Pushing my wheelchair with only my right arm, I very slowly made my way to the apartment door to open the door for the arriving medics.

X-rays were taken while I was treated in the emergency room, and the orthopedic surgeon confirmed to me that I had indeed broken my left ulna. My left forearm was put in a plaster cast, and I was transferred from the emergency room and admitted to my room on a hospital floor that evening. Of my four limbs, I then only had one left. As this was unprecedented, I had no idea what recovery would entail other than being told that if all went well, the cast would be removed in a month. After a couple of days in the hospital, I was asked by the doctors whether I had anyone to care for me at home, to which I answered in the negative. I was told that Medicare would not pay for my stay in a sub-acute rehabilitation facility if I had been hospitalized for few than three days. Three days of my hospitalization had lapsed, but I was still asked by the doctors whether I had home care, to which my answer was, of course, still negative. By the fifth or sixth day, the doctors were still telling me that Medicare, for some reason, would not pay for my sub-acute rehabilitation facility stay. I was puzzled, but figured that if the "almighty" University of Michigan Health System could not convince Medicare to cover my sub-acute rehabilitation stay, I did not stand a chance of securing Medicare coverage in a hurry. I might sue Medicare later, but that would be a fight for another, later day, after I had recovered from my injuries. I could not afford to pay for the sub-acute rehabilitation stay myself. However, the doctors kept pushing and pressuring me on the issue of my somehow getting care at home upon my discharge from the hospital, I had no choice but started figuring out how and when and where I could get care and assistance at home.

I consulted with Eric and Reme, and Reme was available to care for me a few hours a day on weekdays, and a few more hours on weekends. She recommended that I contact a highly regarded home caregiver agency for additional caregiver coverage; I did so immediately. After I was informed of their hourly rate for a caregiver, I started tabulating in my mind the number of hours daily that I could afford to pay. I was in totally uncharted waters; I had no idea how my life would be as a paraplegic who could not transfer on my own. I worked out a schedule to have a caregiver from 8 o'clock in the morning to after lunch at about 1 p.m., then another shift from 4 p.m. to 6 p.m. for a bathroom break, and Reme would come in the evening from about 8 p.m. to 11 p.m. to help me with dinner and get me into the shower. The rest of the time, I would remain in bed. It was still expensive, but that was the best I could do financially. I was discharged home on September 9th.

Obviously, I could not join my family for Dad's birthday feast in Windsor, and I could not even take them out for fancy dinners in Ann Arbor; all we had was nondescript take-out food again. I also could not dress up and go with them to the Sears studio to take family portraits to commemorate Dad's milestone birthday. Instead, I had many photographs of me sitting haplessly in my wheelchair with my left arm in a cast, and flanked by Dad, my sisters and Juliana.

I was not used to the immobility and inconvenience, but with difficulty, I managed to survive one full month. At a return office visit to my orthopedic surgeon, the plaster cast was removed, and in its place was a soft, removable cast. I was told to return in another month when my fracture was expected to have fully healed. Patiently, I bided my time, until one day in late October when Reme noticed a small opening in my back near my sacral area. It became dime-size in just a couple of days. Alarmed, I immediately made an appointment to see my Rehab Physician Assistant, April. At the clinic on October 26th, she gave me the bad news that it was a stage 3 pressure sore. I had never had a pressure sore, even if I had vaguely heard of bed sores previously. All those additional hours daily of my lying in bed since I broke my left ulna must have been the culprit for this sore. April spent more than an hour debriding it. She also ordered daily visit by a visiting nurse to change my dressing, and a certified nursing assistant to assist me with showers every other day. I was given a return clinic appointment in two weeks. In the meantime, at the end of October, I returned to see my orthopedic surgeon and was given the welcomed news that my left ulna had indeed healed perfectly and completely, and the soft cast was taken off as well. I was to undergo physical therapy to strength my arms. My left arm had by then atrophied greatly; it looked boney thin and weak and simply pitiful. I wondered how I was going to re-learn my transfers, but for the moment, I was overjoyed with my full recovery from the fracture.

On November 9th I returned to the clinic for April to follow-up on my pressure sore. She had a most concerned look on her face, and she spent another hour debriding the pressure sore. While my left ulna had healed, the pressure sore was clearly still serious and menacing. Over that weekend, I started having increasingly severe chills. On Monday morning November 12th, the certified nursing assistant came to help me with my shower, followed by the visiting nurse who would change my dressing. I was by then shaking uncontrollably. I thought I was just feeling the cold as the temperature outdoors plunged in typical mid-November Michigan. The visiting nurse gently persuaded me to check into the emergency room, and I finally agreed only very reluctantly as I was by then sick and tired of hospitalization. She called the ambulance and packed my "hospital bag" for me; I would never forget her kindness.

It did not take long for the doctors in the emergency room to figure out that, most probably because of the open wound that was my pressure sore, I had contracted the dreaded Methicillin-resistant Staphylococcus aureus (MRSA) infection. I was immediately put on intravenous antibiotics and admitted to the hospital. I was told I needed intravenous antibiotics for at least six consecutive weeks. "Could matters possibly get worse?" I wonder out loud. Speaking of slippery slope, of snowball effect, of vicious circle, there I lay in my hospital bed, yet again, struggling to stay ahead of the game but was thwarted time and again. Instead of raging for a fight, I found myself calm and composed. I was not resigned, and I was not subdued; I simply felt secure in my knowledge and conviction that I would ultimately overcome this latest setback. I had no idea that a truly treacherous and trying journey awaited me.

After a week's hospitalization, I was transferred to a sub-acute rehabilitation facility. That was the first time I was an inpatient at such a facility. Because of my MRSA infection, I was in a private room, and doctors, nurses and nursing assistants, even my visitors, had to don disposable paper gowns when they came into my room. The course of intravenous antibiotics was very fatiguing and energy draining. I was given physical therapy but my legs were practically useless and my arms had lost much of their strength from the previous two months of immobility. I could not transfer myself but had to rely on the nursing staff. My pressure sore was still an open wound and required dressing change at least twice daily. I did not have much of an appetite, and the food was not all that appetizing. Hence, my weight was down to a dangerous 80 lbs.; I was far too underweight for my height and frame. I was plainly barely languishing. Toward the end of December, I was finally taken off the intravenous antibiotics; my MRSA infection had, alas, been abated. That was no mean feat; I patted myself on the back. However, before I could even celebrate the accomplishment, I was told that my transplanted kidney suddenly showed signs of an acute rejection. All the stress and strain of the lengthy course of antibiotics, hospitalization and inpatient stay at the sub-acute rehabilitation facility, must have adversely affected my kidney graft. Even as my MRSA infection had been quashed, the downward spiral continued its relentless assault. I opted to return to the hospital for appropriate treatment by specialists; it was New Year's Eve of 2012.

After three days of hospitalization, my kidney graft recovered and the acute kidney rejection episode subsided without further drama. However, I could not be discharged home as the doctors decided that I needed inpatient rehabilitation for intensive physical therapy to rebuild my physical strength and to bolster my transfer skills. I ended up spending a full month in inpatient rehabilitation at the University of Michigan Hospital. I underwent at least four hours daily of physical therapy, occupational therapy and what was billed as therapeutic recreation. Each room on the inpatient rehabilitation floor had a build-in lift which I very much appreciated. Without being so equipped, I would otherwise had to wait for two nursing assistants to come lift and transfer me, or wait for the nursing assistant to come with a rather scarce and cumbersome Hoyer lift to transfer me. The built-in lift was very simple and handy. The lift looked like a "handlebar" dangling from the ceiling; it was electrically powered and traveled along built-in tracks on the ceiling of the room, and within the area defined by the outer limits of those tracks. The nursing staff would "wrap" me in a sturdy sling which was then hooked onto the handlebar. The handlebar was operated by remote control; it would gently lift me in the sling from my bed and over to my wheelchair or a shower chair, at which point the nursing staff would "unwrap" me from the sling. The food was also more palatable. There were a clothes washer and dryer on the floor, and as part of my occupational therapy, I did my own laundry. One day around lunchtime, I heard live music emanating from a room two doors down. It was a woman with a guitar, and she was performing from room to room. She was one of several professional musicians hired by the hospital to sing and provide musical entertainment for the hospital's patients. I immediately invited her to my room, and she obliged me by singing whatever songs I requested, accompanied by her exquisite guitar playing; I happily sang my lungs out along with her. That was my most delightful and welcomed "therapeutic recreation." Four weeks of intense physical therapy were barely enough to retrain me to transfer on my own again. Since breaking my ulna five months prior, my health had taken a steep dive along with whatever little trunk stability, core muscles and upper-body strength that I had. When I was at long last discharged home in early February, 2013, I found each transfer an immense challenge and a risky maneuver. Once again, the adage that we do not know what we had until we have lost it was sneering in my face. It had been a very costly, financially and health-wise, five months.

Even though my broken left ulna had completely mended months ago, my pressure sore remained as unhealed as ever. Back at home, nurses resumed their twice daily visits to change my dressing, and the certified nursing assistant also returned to help with my showers. At least I no longer needed to pay for daily home caregivers as I resumed transferring myself, however dicey an exercise that had become. I was followed by a plastic surgeon, Dr. Jeffrey Kozlow, because of the sacral location of my pressure sore. If it would not close by itself, he advised surgery to close it "with a flap," using skin and tissue from another part of my body. That operation, he cautioned, had a very poor success rate of not more than fifty-fifty. Moreover, after the surgery, I would have to remain in bed, on my sides, for at least six continuous weeks for the wound to properly heal. That was a tall order. I thus consulted with another plastic surgeon at Beaumont Hospital in Royal Oak for a second opinion. In May, I was actually hospitalized at Beaumont Hospital, thinking I was going to have the surgery there. Instead, I had another debridement of the pressure sore, while the surgeon declined to surgically close it because he believed it was supposedly still infected. I thus returned to Dr. Kozlow, and surgery was scheduled for August 14th, almost a full year since this protracted nightmare began with my broken left ulna.

As I was tackling my tangled medical issues, Dad was having health challenges of his own. He kept complaining about his knees and his legs weakening progressively, yet he seemed to have exhausted medical options, both Western and traditional Chinese. He was a good trouper, though, and was still living by himself, and taking care of himself and the house well enough. He had a good friend who was about my age who helped him whenever he needed assistance, and visited Dad at least weekly for errands and odds and ends around the home. It was very frustrating and saddening for me not to be able to take care of him on a daily or even weekly basis. All I could do was to facilitate and assist from afar, and there was quite a lot that I could and had to do. Even though he could still walk slowly on his own two feet, he requested a wheelchair, and a custom chair was ordered by his family doctor before his 90th birthday. Over time, as his knees further weakened, in-home physical therapy was prescribed, along with more assistive devices. He had occasionally used a single straight cane to assist his walking since about 2010; by 2013, a walker with built-in seat was prescribed. In fact, he bought himself four walkers, one for each level in his home and one for outdoors. In early 2013, we came up with a solution to avoid fall risks and his unduly exerting himself in climbing up and down the stairs inside his quad-level home. We had "stair-lifts" installed at all the stairs inside the house. These were electric-powered chairs that glided along rail-tracks mounted on the wall to ascend and descend a stairway. Dad was thrilled with his new "toys," and we sisters collectively exhaled, at least for a while. Vivian returned to spend time with Dad at least twice a year, and they would often take a vacation trip together. I was so gratified that Vivian was willing to take time off work and to incur the expense for those trips which meant so very much to Dad. In addition to many trips to various destinations in China when Dad returned to Hong Kong numerous times between 2003 and 2010, Vivian had taken Dad to Vancouver and enjoyed an Alaskan cruise with Dad's best friend from his childhood. They had also taken a Caribbean cruise on the then newest and largest cruise ship. They had spent time shopping, sightseeing, and eating their way through Seattle, Charleston and Las Vegas, and had had many driving trips to Toronto. I supposed Vivian had plenty of practice pushing my clunky wheelchair when I was in Hong Kong; she was thus expert at pushing Dad in his wheelchair everywhere while they vacationed. Dad remained active socially, joining his friends for lunch at least weekly, and participating in the occasional house party, summer patio barbeque, and feasts and dinners on special occasions and Chinese festivals.

I wish I could have joined Dad, and I am sure he, too, had wished I could have been part of his social life. In fact, I would have loved to be able to go out and enjoy a meal occasionally, socialize, meet new friends, join an affinity group of one kind or another, attend a concert or lecture, or take in a movie. However, my not being able to use the public facilities and my escalating neuralgia, put a definite damper on my social agenda. It suffices to note that my hoped-for reversal, or even just lessening, of my paraplegia was nowhere near materializing. If anything, along with increasingly excruciating and debilitating pain, my legs were progressively worsening as they suffered frequent fits of uncontrollable cramping and spasms. I had to accept reality, however unfair, unjust, and savage it was. Even just a few short years earlier, I would not have been able to accept that cruel reality even reluctantly, let alone as calmly and sanguinely. Perhaps meditation indeed did the "trick;" by then, I had been a daily meditator and reciting the Heart Sutra for almost ten years. In the early years of my paraplegia, I would have jumped out of my skin, consumed by cabin fever, being not only confined in my wheelchair but in effect imprisoned in my own home. Yet, I found myself completely at peace and feeling enormously grateful for every breathing moment. Not only did I not feel deprived, I felt inspired to count my blessings which actually had become too numerous to enumerate. For instance, my not having to put on my "armor" everyday not only saved time and energy, but money. I had also stopped "collecting" cameras, camera bags, and pens, and in general, my not needing much of anything also saved money. Thus, unintentionally, I had overcome my life-long propensity for over-spending and spending frivolously; I actually and finally learned to save up money. Over time, I discovered that I could in fact indulge and afford items that I had previously considered a financial overreach and which items meant the most to me in the present: a decent home theater, upgrading my audio system with better and high-end components, and buying music recordings as I reasonably pleased. I had spent many wondrous afternoons and enchanted evenings enjoying music through the audio and video systems that I had gradually assembled over the years. Music listening and appreciation in turn lifted my spirits, soothed my soul, dulled my pain, and empowered me to carry on my life with purpose, conviction and gratitude. Just as photography saved my life the in the last few years before I attained clarity of mind and corralled enough strength and courage to leave my doomed relationship, music listening fed and sustained my soul, especially in the darkest hours of constant, unrelenting physical pain and seemingly endless hopelessness as I struggled with my paraplegia.

When the U.S. Supreme Court upheld marriage equality for gay and lesbian couples on June 26, 2015, it marked a milestone victory for the LGBTQ community. Yet I would not be directly or personally benefiting from that historic ruling. Marriage equality would have helped enormously thirty-some years ago when I was straining under the threat of running out of immigration status and being deprived of employment authorization, and even being deported. Ironically, now that same-sex relationships are recognized legally as marriage, yet for the first time in my life, I had been single for more than ten years. For most of my life before then, I was the hopeless romantic falling in love with love itself. Not only did I not have the knack for picking the "right" partner, I felt as if I was compelled to have a mate—even if a "wrong" one—lest I would somehow be incomplete or unfulfilled. Hence, I was rarely single for more than, say, three months. Fast forward to the here and now, clearly, I had been changed by my many well fought battles. My life had been transformed in adversity, and my priorities had been realigned in sync with a different calling altogether. My paraplegia had unwittingly morphed and tempered me over those very trying years. Instead of passionately charging with sabre rattling and guns blazing, slashing and burning, I no longer viewed life necessarily as a series of battles to be won or lost, from one extreme to its polar opposite. Rather stunningly, I found myself living life with balance, serenity, compassion and openness, not only with respect to others but more crucially, for myself. I had become a peaceful warrior.

August 14th rolled around soon enough and it was time again for surgery. I was thankful that the operation proceeded uneventfully, and I was resting comfortably, on my side, in a hospital bed. The nursing staff came in every other hour or so to rotate me so that I would be lying on my alternate sides. One of the benefits of being a paraplegic was that I had no sensation from my waist down; hence, I did not feel any pain from the surgical site in my sacral area. On the other hand, I had to learn to drink, eat and even brush my teeth on my side in bed. After a few days in the hospital, I was discharged to a very fine sub-acute rehabilitation facility. Lying on one side then another in bed for a few days was one thing, but I was then confronting strict bedrest on my sides for six consecutive weeks. I honestly do not remember how I managed to maintain my sanity and wherewithal through those torturous days. Meditation and reciting the Heart Sutra were practically life-saving during those weeks, along with talking to Dad on the telephone daily. I was not allowed to get out of bed other than for showers. There was nothing to do, or nothing that I could really do, other than to watch mindless television programs. I stuck with the news channels, mostly. Unfortunately for me, my wound was not healing as well or as fast as it was hoped, and by the end of the six weeks, Dr. Kozlow ordered another four weeks of strict bed-rest. I suppose I managed to stay alive for those four additional weeks because it was akin to a contest of will by then: I would not let Dr. Kozlow have the satisfaction of seeing me fail, that is, my wound failing to close even after the surgery. Hence, by sheer determination and chutzpah, I bided my time, one hour at a time. I was down in weight again, to about 90 lbs. and anemic, I was bored to tears, but I was alive and breathing, even if barely.

It was during this agonizing period of glacially slow recuperation in the sub-acute rehabilitation facility when, out of the blue, the ideas for this book crystalized. The event that was the catalyst for writing my memoir occurred a long time ago, in November of 2005—the interview of Joan Didion on National Public Radio. Nothing came of that idea for several *years* until August of 2009 when I tentatively wrote a page or two of preliminary thoughts and random musings. After those furtive attempts, my "book"— all of two or three pages—stalled and did not come to be. I had not a clue how to write it so that the end product would be of interest, if not of import, and not just a self-indulgent and egotistical exercise on paper. As I was lying in bed nursing my surgical wound in the sub-acute rehabilitation facility one day, the inspiration came from nowhere and with no forewarning; it simply suddenly surged into my consciousness when I was not even consciously thinking about my "book." "It" became very clear in my mind— crystalline clear—what and how my first chapter would be. I was startled, but then let my mind wander and savor the cascades of ideas for that first chapter. I was pleased with the concept; I also felt encouraged and supported by an unknown benevolent force. Sometime after that day, while I was still at the sub-acute rehabilitation facility, the ideas for the second chapter also came just as mysteriously. I then realized and acknowledged to myself that my book had at long last "crystallized." Even though I had absolutely no idea what would come after the second chapter, I knew I had to commit myself to the project. My tentative plan then was to get caught up with my life after my eventual discharge, presumably when my surgical wound had completely healed. Since I broke my left ulna in September of 2012, everything else in my life had been put on hold while I tended to my broken forearm, and then to the MRSA infected pressure sore, and then to surviving in hospitals and the surgery and rehabilitation. I had also promised Pearl that I would read her powerful manifesto of a graduation thesis and share with her my appreciation and praises. All told, it would be October of 2014 when I began composing the first sentence of the first chapter. Progress was even more glacial and halting than the healing of my pressure sore. Because of the increasingly severe and constant painful cramps in my legs, the debilitating nerve pain round the clock, I could barely sit still for an hour a day to focus on writing, and even then, depending on my pain and energy levels, not everyday could be a writing day. Painstakingly and resolutely, I persevered and trudged on, one word, one sentence, and one paragraph at a time.

By late October, 2013, I won. Dr. Kozlow's residents came to examine my wound, and pronounced it completely healed. Dr. Kozlow then came to personally inspect the wound, and he could hardly believe that I had indeed beaten the odds. It was a triumph of willpower and for that, I was thankful for the unseen forces that assisted me. However, the aftermath of three months of strict bedrest included loss of all muscle mass, loss of strength and my ability to transfer; I was in dire straits if I wanted to continue my independent living. I opted to return to the inpatient rehabilitation facility at the University of Michigan Hospital. Mathew J. Baltz was the best physical therapist I had ever had the privilege of working with. In just one short month, he managed to transform me so that I could confidently transfer myself again. It would take time for me to further rebuild my strength, and much more practice to have my transfers executed more elegantly, but at least everything was serviceable enough for me to go home.

No sooner than when I was discharged home on December 3, 2013, did the upsetting though not unexpected news come that Lilian was hospitalized. She had been losing weight over the years, and had been hospitalized a couple of years prior for a supposed bout of tuberculosis. I had the uneasy gut feeling that her breast cancer had returned and metastasized. This time around, she was put on oxygen. Although I did not learn of any definitive diagnosis, it seemed that her lungs were implicated, which was consistent with the spread of breast cancer. Vivian was frantic, and visited her every night after work, even though it was quite a distance for her to travel to the hospital. Vivian would bring Lilian her favorite foods and varied the menu every night, which greatly delighted Lilian. From the photographs Vivian took of Lilian in the hospital, I could well see that Lilian was suffering, languishing. My heart ached for her. Lilian was transferred from one hospital to another then another, given one test or scan or another, but it was quite clear that she was not faring well at all. Vivian would regularly put Lilian on the telephone with me and with Dad; sometimes she Skyped Dad so that Dad and Lilian could see each other while they talked. We were all still hoping against hope that Lilian would, like many times since her breast cancer diagnosis, rally and beat the odds. If I could, I would have rushed back to Hong Kong to be with her during those very difficult months. However, it was physically impossible for me to do so; I could only try to make her understand my love and to cheer her up when I talked to her on the phone. When I last left Hong Kong in October of 2007, I had dreaded this precise scenario. Lilian hung on for almost three months; she had always been very stout since she was a baby. She finally breathed her last in the hospital, with Vivian by her side, at 11:15 p.m. local time on Friday, March 14, 2014. Lina had in fact visited her and performed the Buddhist last rites more than a month earlier. Vivian telephoned Dad, Lina and me right away. I could not imagine Dad's grief, nor Vivian's. Vivian had loved and cared for Lilian all her life even better than she cared for herself. The void that Lilian's passing had left in Vivian's life had to be immeasurable and irreparable.

As for me, I could only count my blessings in at least three ways. Lilian's passing was not unexpected and thus did not come as a shock to my system. She had valiantly fought her cancer battle for more than a decade, and I could not have been prouder of her. Because Vivian was indulgent all those years in making sure that Lilian had just about everything and anything she wanted (mostly Lilian's favorite foods and preferred clothing), Lilian's quality of life had been unsurpassed through her last moments. Vivian had brought Lilian her favorite Shanghainese cuisine for dinner which Lilian "inhaled," according to Vivian, the night she passed away. Second, because of my paraplegia, I had the unexpected bonanza of an opportunity to spend almost two years with Lilian when I was seeking alternative healing in Hong Kong in 2006 and 2007. It was a pure and divine gift. I would otherwise not have been able to make up for lost time when I unintentionally "neglected" to visit her for twenty-five years from 1978 to 2003. Third, when Mom passed away in 2003, I was shaken down to my core. I had never been able to deal with death, or even the concept of death, ever since I was a young child with my first awareness of life and death. I internalized Mom's death, and carried on with life and work, outwardly, as if nothing significant had happened. In truth, her death motivated me to return to Hong Kong at once to see Lilian, and the rest, as they say, was history. In the eleven years since, it was not just the lapse of a decade's time, my paraplegia intervened as a great teacher of life lessons. During those interim years, I had waged my own mighty health battles, and resolutely railed against crippling bodily dysfunctions. I had even come close a few times to staring at my own demise, hanging on to life by a thread. Through it all, I finally comprehended the finiteness of life on the one hand, and on the other, the multiple incarnations that we had experienced and the many more yet to come. A decade of daily meditations and reflection allowed me to understand the futility of waging war against what cannot be changed or controlled. Mortality is not the end, but a new beginning, and certainly not something to fear. Misfortune and adversity are in the eyes of the beholder. With my new understanding, I was relieved and gratified that Lilian had moved on to her fresh start. In other words, life is truly more a cycle than we realize. That was an essential and priceless lesson in my metamorphosis to becoming a peaceful warrior: at peace with my own frailties and mortality, and thus becoming an even stronger—and invincible, if you would—warrior.

Vivian came in June with Lilian's ashes for interment at our Chan Family Estate. I could not attend that ceremony, but many of Dad's friends were in attendance to pay their last respects and lend moral support. Dad had been predeceased by Mom and now, one of his children; it had to be heart wrenching for him. We were grateful that he could oversee the process of having Lilian's date of death in Chinese and English inscribed on the headstone. We observed and learned the process so that we could carry on when he was no longer around.

Half a year had lapsed since the long-drawn-out episode of my MRSA-infected pressure sore concluded. It had become clear that I could not regain all of my core muscles or trunk stability or upper-body strength. While I managed to perform all the necessary transfers, they had become much more difficult than in years past. To my dismay, transferring to and from the small platform-seat, which lifted me to the driver's seat, became especially risky as I had lost too much upper-body strength and control of my trunk and legs. Hence, by late summer, I came to the reluctant conclusion that it was no longer safe for me to use the adaptive equipment to drive; I was simply too weak and unsteady to perform those transfers and maneuvers safely. If I really wanted to drive, I would have to buy one of those Braunability minivans, if I could afford one. I thus made the decision to have the adaptive equipment removed from my "Routan" so that I could sell it. I would again rely on the Ann Arbor para-transit system's lift-vans for transportation. That also meant I could no longer drive with Eric for grocery shopping. Instead, I had learned to anticipate my provisions needs, and prepare a detailed shopping list for him to execute.

I was very fortunate to have been physically disabled in this day and age, thanks to the "Internet of things," pervading or serving our daily lives depending on your point of view. I would be proud to proclaim that I was a confirmed "old fogey," preferring analog to digital, and had to be dragged kicking and screaming into the 21st century. I had, however, come to rely increasingly on advanced technology to maintain and even enhance my quality of life as a paraplegic with limited mobility. In the early years of my disability, I fretted about not being able to shop and purchase items that I needed. Then gradually, I learned to purchase just about everything online, starting with basic necessities such as clothes and shoes. Paying close attention to the description of the item, reading the fine prints and even trying to read between the lines, perusing peer reviews, assessing the reputation, reliability and the return policy of the seller, I was able to make satisfactory purchases online, needing to return merchandise only once in a blue moon. As the years went by, larger items also had to be replaced. If I had thought it difficult if not impossible to shop online for items such as furniture, I had apparently underestimated my imagination and abilities and the advancements in the virtual marketplace. I thus had proceeded to purchase online, "sight unseen," bookshelves, coffee table, chairs, audio and video racks, mattresses, bed frame, and even my large wooden pedestal desk. Eric was always available to expertly assemble furniture pieces for me, a task that I used to enjoy tackling by myself. In more recent years, I was overjoyed when home delivery service came online for my local restaurant orders, so that once in a while or whenever I had visitors, I could enjoy a carryout meal other than pizzas. Moreover, the menu choices had been broadening over the years as more restaurants signed on with the home delivery service. Then, there was the brave new world of online grocery shopping. Amazon started offering non-perishable food items, and in 2008, AmazonFresh started offering grocery home delivery service in selected cities, though not in Ann Arbor. There was a nearby supermarket that offered online shopping, but not home delivery, quite a few years back, but the selections were somewhat limited and the website was a chore to navigate. Other supermarkets joined in the fray, but they were also not offering home delivery. Then in 2015, at long last, an online grocery home delivery service debuted in Ann Arbor. That proved to be my lifesaver as they provided next-day service; hence, if I unexpectedly ran out of an item or two, that would be my backup service instead of troubling Eric. The delivery fee they charged, the premium price placed on each item, and again the understandably limited selections, all amounted to minor inconveniences; I was simply thankful that finally there was home delivery service for groceries. Apparently, online grocery shopping must have been popular in general and not just for the elderly or the disabled, as a major supermarket chain in my community in 2016 started putting all of its regularly stocked items online. That was a major advancement, because the online selections were as comprehensive as if I were personally in the supermarket, and no premium was added to the price of the items available online. Even though Eric would still have to go pick up the order for me, it had become almost as satisfactory as if I were shopping in person. The world had thankfully come to me, just as I was unable to venture out. The latest news, trends, information and data of all stripes, and research tools, were all available at my fingertips via the Internet.

On the other hand, life as a paraplegic in a wheelchair did have untold limitations and even humiliations. I used to tell my friends that I would not wish my condition on even my worst enemy, not that I believed I had any enemy. The daily challenges were legend and pervasive, popping up everywhere I was not looking or anticipating. People who were not in a wheelchair could not possibly understand the constraints we lived with. Someone could have shelved an item for me without considering that it would be impossible for me to safely fetch even with a reacher. Getting anything out of the freezer, which was at least two feet above my head, was mostly an exercise in dodging avalanching foodstuff, until I got enough practice over time to avoid getting bombarded. Objects were sometimes placed without regard to passage for my wheelchair. For instance, one day the workers were replacing the carpeting in the apartment above me, and had pitched rolls and bundles of the old carpeting helter-skelter across the pathway, thus completely blocking my wheelchair from the only access to my apartment door. Even getting a haircut became an issue after I was unable to stand up momentarily for transfers.

It was not practical to use the transfer board in all places and situations. Having to push my own wheelchair also made carrying a transfer board impractical in the first place. Thus, I had to find a hairdresser who was willing to make house calls for a reasonable charge. Going to the dentist was another hurdle; it took me quite a few tries to find a dental clinic with staff members who were willing and able to lift and carry me to and from the dentist's chair. If my mobile phone malfunctioned and the Internet was down, I could not very well "hop into my car" to get help right away or to get the phone repaired; I would not even be able to dial "911." That frightening scenario had me rushing to get a land-line telephone. Likewise with just about any repairs or service that I needed, whether it was my laptop or my prescription eyeglasses— getting things repaired was no longer straightforward and simple. I had to wait for Eric, or arrange for a lift-van ride, and in the meantime, I had to have a backup plan in place until the malfunctioning item could be repaired or replaced. I recalled when Hurricane Katrina devastated the Lower Ninth Ward and flooded much of New Orleans in 2005, the first year of my paraplegia, I had nightmarish visions of my drowning in my wheelchair should a similar catastrophe occur in my neck of the woods. I was not at all accustomed to the fact that I could no longer run or flee to safety on my own.

While many were considerate of disabled fellowmen and women, and even opened doors for me when I was struggling with one that was not automatic or powered, life as a paraplegic was definitely an eye-opener for me. I had discovered that when one was in a wheelchair, one was treated differently—mostly for worse, and mostly for ill—by others, other "able-bodied" people. Suddenly, there was a presumption that I was somehow an "imbecile," an "invalid," or "handicapped," simply because I was in a wheelchair. Some people were startled because I could actually speak and utter a complete and grammatical sentence.

From my perspective, however, of course I had not changed. I was still the same properly educated, well-trained, and experienced professional that I was before being confined in the wheelchair. The wheelchair had not affected my intelligence or my humanity. Yet, I had encountered many instances of disrespect, rudeness and even contempt, that would not have surfaced were I not in a wheelchair. In 2009, for instance, I had to battle the life insurance company which refused to waive my premiums even though total disability was a basis for such waiver. As I thought I had to seek injunctive relief to compel the insurance company to grant the waiver, I sought legal representation because I was not physically capable of handling the repeated court appearances that such a lawsuit would require. An attorney agreed to review my potential case for a courtesy half an hour without charge, for which I was grateful. Eric drove me to the attorney's office, and waited outside in the parking lot. I rolled myself in the wheelchair into the law offices, with my slim leather portfolio of documents on my lap. I was greeted by the receptionist and then the attorney with barely lukewarm and very superficial politeness. Toward the end of my consultation with the attorney, we exchanged business cards. I was and still am affiliated with my firm, as I was not required to resign but was on an extended and indefinite disability leave. The attorney's attitude suddenly underwent a 180-degree above-turn when he realized that I was a Dickinson Wright attorney. As I departed, he rushed to open the door for me and even pushed my wheelchair, with a smile, out to the parking lot where Eric had been waiting. No matter, I was grateful for the legal advice he gave me, and I did proceed to prevail in a lawsuit that I filed against the insurance company. I thus detest the label "invalid," as a noun and as an adjective, to describe people with physical disabilities. I was as "valid" as ever, if not more than ever, as I aged splendidly in my wheelchair.

Speaking of my wheelchair, there was the constant indignity whenever I needed it serviced or adjusted. My first so-called custom wheelchair, the Quickie "GTX," was a disaster after repeated piecemeal modifications to supposedly accommodate my weakening trunk and the adaptive equipment for me to drive the "Routan." Five years later in December 2014, the "GTX" was replaced by my second custom wheelchair, a Ti-Lite "Aero-Z." Essentially, the physical therapist, technician, and the designated Physical Medicine & Rehabilitation doctor decided all the parameters for my wheelchair, from the brand to the model to the seat cushion, even though in theory I was allowed input and to state my preferences. The only preference that ended up being mine was the color of the frame. The "Aero-Z" was much more unwieldly than even the "GTX," and required constant brake adjustments. I would learn very soon that the wheelchair vendor was basically a monopoly in town, as with many providers of other assistive and adaptive equipment for the physically challenged. As such, we were at their mercy in terms of scheduling service calls, reordering supplies, and just about each time we had to interface with them. Response time was unreasonably tardy, service was spotty depending on the technician assigned, and I could even suspect "waste and abuse" when an entire component or assembly was ordered when just a small part needed replacement. Not only was that wasteful, but I would usually have to wait an inordinate amount of time for the component to be ordered, processed, and shipped—with delays built in at every stage—and then a service call scheduled for some time in the "distant" future. That was just another insignificant example of how life could be maddening for a paraplegic. I also recalled when I started craniosacral therapy with Judy in June of 2008, her clinic was in an office building which did not have any curb cuts. That was in clear violation of the ADA. I made my voice heard, and the owner of the building was wise enough to promptly implement modifications to the sidewalk to provide for a curb cut and a ramp up to the entrance door. That and other similar experiences galvanized me to consider providing pro bono legal services and advocacy, if and when I was physically able, to ensure compliance with the spirit and the letters of the ADA on behalf of the physically challenged and other disadvantaged individuals.

As we mourned Lilian's passing, and as I regretted my not being able to spend her last days with her, it struck me that I had been a paraplegic for almost ten *years*. My hopes and dreams of walking on my own two feet had obviously taken much, much longer than I had ever anticipated. I kept promising Dad that I would be ambulating "soon;" over ten years' time, it was beginning to sound like a pipe dream, a broken record, wishful thinking, or all of the above. Nonetheless, I remained determinedly, steadfastly and sincerely convinced that I would heal, in due time. I had stopped craniosacral therapy with Kathryn when I broke my left ulna in September of 2012, and did not resume the healing when my pressure sore closed and I returned home in December of 2013. That decision came about as, after much trial and error through those years, I reached the understanding that true healing *came from within*; there was no miracle healer or magical cure "out there." I had expended more than enough money, time and energy in chasing after the miracle healer or the magical cure, one after another all over the globe. While each healer contributed to varying degrees to my well-being, my pursuit for *the* cure had largely been a disappointment. Henceforth, I decided to rely solely on my daily self-healing with Reiki, and on my abiding willpower and unwavering belief in ultimate full recovery.

My day-to-day life then was still monumentally challenging. By 2014, the level of pain in my legs, especially my hamstrings, had for some unknown reason been ratcheted up immeasurably. My legs had also become increasingly stiff, crampy and spasming. The pain was round the clock and unrelenting, even waking me up several times during the night. It was very fatiguing, and interfered with my carrying out even the simplest tasks such as replying to casual e-mails, let alone any chore that required concentration and focus. I was aware that my mind could not and did not function optimally when I was under such undue physical pain. The constant severe pain was distracting, and adversely affecting my quality of life; I could not even enjoy listening to music. I also needed to take a nap in the late afternoon, as the pain became unbearable, just to have a change of pace and position. I consulted with my neurologist Dr. Wade M. Cooper, who had been successfully following my migraine headaches since mid-2012, for pain relief medications. Unfortunately, I was indeed almost impossible to medicate. He had prescribed no fewer than five or six medications for my pain, but I had intolerable adverse reactions to each and every one of them. Hence, I had no choice but continued to suffer in relative silence.

Dad also seemed to be suffering from a gradual decline in health as well since 2014. While his mind remained sharp as a tack, his legs had become really unreliable. Since sometime in 2014, he used his wheelchair more regularly when going out, using his walker only for ambulation indoors. We had done everything we could think of to alleviate his discomforts and facilitate his mobility, but there was nothing we could do to strengthen his legs. He continued to visit me monthly, even though it was getting to be quite physically draining for him to make the trip. Both of us enjoyed our monthly get-togethers and frequent telephone calls, in spite of our physical aches and pain; nothing could disrupt our time spent with each other. In January of 2015, Vivian returned for a visit. I suggested that they visit Las Vegas to take in a show or two, and to enjoy a relaxing few days in a luxury hotel and indulge in gourmet dining. They had a fabulous time, so much so that I then suggested that Dad join the special Caribbean cruise that his friends were planning for September to celebrate the anniversary of the formation of their social group. Dad was very enthusiastic about it, and Vivian agreed to return to accompany him on the cruise.

In the meantime, it was another frigid winter in Michigan and Windsor. Dad complained about neck stiffness, and his family doctor ordered x-rays, and then pronounced that arthritis was the culprit. There supposedly was not much the doctor could do other than for Dad to take Tylenol for pain and discomforts. We encouraged Dad to resume massages with the therapist making house calls weekly. However, that was not proceeding smoothly as the therapist was too lazy to bring her massage table, while Dad was not comfortable having massages in his bed. We finally insisted on the therapist's bringing her massage table. I still did not realize anything was amiss with Dad. We continued our regular lengthy telephone conversations, and Dad continued to visit me monthly even though it was getting more difficult for him to make the trip in his wheelchair.

In early April, Vivian returned again to spend time with Dad, and they came over to visit me. That was when I noticed for the first time that Dad could not even use his hands well. He had been complaining to me about how his hands were feeling somewhat numb, and he had been examined by his family doctor many times, but the doctor did not come up with any diagnosis or treatment. In the visits he made in April, I could see that he could hardly hold his chopsticks or utensils to eat with; Vivian was more or less feeding him. His family doctor had finally ordered a CT-scan of his neck for late April, shortly after Vivian had returned to Hong Kong. The results of the CT-scan came almost immediately, as I was urgently notified by his family doctor: Dad had a C-2 fracture. He was immediately fitted with a full cervical collar and given an appointment to consult with a neurosurgeon the following week. The doctor added that Dad's was what was commonly known as "hangman's fracture," a serious condition indeed. That sent me conducting research online right away, and I almost passed out when I realized the full extent and the implications of Dad's injuries. The neurosurgeon fitted him with a less restrictive cervical collar after examining him and reviewing the CT-scans, and telephoned to advise me that the C2 fracture was sustained "a long time ago," that it was an "old" injury. Moreover, surgery was completely out of the question for Dad, given his advanced age, but he was of the opinion that Dad "should do just fine." Everything suddenly made sense to me; all the pieces suddenly came together, except that it might be too late to do anything constructive for him. As far back as early 2006 when Dad accompanied me to Hong Kong for alternative healing, he complained of weakness in his knees. Since then, he had been constantly complaining about his knees, not so much that he experienced pain in his knees, but increasing weakness. That condition degenerated over the years, with an incorrect diagnosis of osteoarthritis in his knees, while the true cause—the C2 fracture—was not discovered, let alone treated properly and in a timely manner. I further surmised that he must have fallen down around mid-2005 and sustained that cervical fracture, but he did not tell us about the fall. Previous to that time, he was as vital and robust as a 40-year-old. Then by 2010, and certainly by his 90th birthday in 2012, his legs were quite weak, and by 2014, even his arms were adversely affected as he lost sensation and control over them. I of all people, as a decade-long paraplegic, should really have figured out long ago that he was suffering from a spinal cord injury. He had all the classic symptoms—progressive loss sensation in and control of his limbs—all so familiar to me once I was told his C2 fracture diagnosis. Because the fracture was so high up in his spine, when that fracture was somehow aggravated around 2014, perhaps by his further falls, that was why even his arms were becoming nonfunctional. I did blame myself for not catching on much, much sooner, not that anything necessarily could have been done to rectify the breach.

Upon hearing the C2 diagnosis, I quickly swung into action as I was beyond flabbergasted and worried about Dad's safety and well-being. He definitely could no longer be living by himself. I wish I could rush over there to be with him and help him around the clock, but that was purely wishful thinking. Instead, I called a home caregiver agency in Windsor, and had a caregiver rush over to Dad's home right away that same afternoon. At that time, Dad was still able to walk with his walker a few steps to the bathroom and to bed, and so forth. I worked out with him a schedule for a caregiver to be with him twelve hours a day, helping him with meals and daily activities. The doctor had referred him to the social services agency in Windsor, which in turn provided him with health aides to assist with his daily shower. Lina and Vivian were alarmed, and everyone pitched in; we were basically circling our wagons and coming to Dad's aid from afar. I alternately worried about Dad, and was caring for him, via "remote control": making phone calls, making sure caregivers arrived on time, coordinating medical appointments, following up with doctors, and kept talking with him to keep him company. Vivian was considering an immediate return to Windsor, but since Dad was still managing daily life with the home caregivers, we did not want her to unnecessarily take leave from her job just yet. Sadly, we did have to cancel the September cruise, barely one month after we made the reservations for him and Vivian.

Life went on well enough for Dad for a few weeks, when his friends located a Chinese-speaking woman who could serve as caregiver except on weekends. That was much preferred as Dad could readily communicate with her, and she could cook Chinese food which Dad also preferred. Those initial weeks after his C2 fracture diagnosis were extremely stressful for me. As a fellow spinal cord injury sufferer, I fully comprehended the seriously of his injuries, and the increasing difficulties he faced in his daily living activities. I had many years to get used to my limitations, and I had had some physical and occupational therapy support in getting around some of those restrictions. On the other hand, Dad was older and less agile to begin with, and I could only imagine how overwhelmed he must have felt. The irony was that he was actually trying even harder than I was. He saw that I was brave enough to live, and even thrived in a sense in living my life all those years as a paraplegic, and thus, he, too, could drum up enough courage and endurance to live on. Oh, my Dad, my very intrepid, optimistic, invincible Dad, my fellow peaceful warrior!

Dad bravely soldiered on for another two months until the evening of June 22nd when I was expecting his telephone call that did not come on time, which was extremely unlike him. I, of course, telephoned him at his home repeatedly, but there was no answer, which was also extremely unusual, as he would have informed me in advance if he were going out with friends. Almost half an hour had lapsed since the appointed time for our telephone call. I started panicking; something did not feel right at all to me. I then telephoned the next door neighbor, begging her to go over to Dad's house to take a look and to knock on the door. She was reluctant at first, mumbling something about its being very dark outside. It was about nine o'clock at night. I finally coaxed and convinced her to walk over there as she kept being on the telephone with me. There were block-glass panels by one side of Dad's front door, which allowed her to see somewhat into the dining room area. Suddenly, she exclaimed over the telephone that Dad was lying on the floor. That was exactly what I had feared. I told her to call for an ambulance, while I called the alarm company about the emergency. Within minutes, the medics called me to ask for the passcode to the key in the lockbox outside the front door. I was so thankful that we had installed that lockbox about two years prior, precisely to facilitate emergency personnel to get into his house.

Dad was also wearing a medical alert pendant that he could press the button for emergency help. However, I supposed he had either passed out or his hands and fingers were so numb that he could no longer push the button to call for help.

I then e-mailed and called Lina and Vivian who in turned called Dad's friends and everyone started mobilizing to his aid. I felt somewhat relieved that he was rescued in time, and was hospitalized for observation. Obviously, he fell down from his chair while perhaps trying to stand up or to transfer to his wheelchair or to reach his walker. He did not tell me that he was practically not able to stand up or walk anymore. If we had known, we would have arranged for 24-hour caregivers to watch over and assist him. Vivian immediately requested no-pay leave for three months from her employer, which was humanely granted. She was due to arrive on July 9th. In the meantime, Dad languished in the hospital, somewhat bored, with no definitive diagnosis or meaningful treatment. Dad's friends were wonderful; some visited often, others even cooked delicious Chinese food for his enjoyment while in the hospital, and I was kept updated by his frequent visitors by telephone and e-mail. Of course, I talked to him by phone several times a day. It was a very worrying time for me until Vivian arrived when he was finally discharged home.

I would not know until later that by then, Dad had lost all use of his legs and hands. Vivian took it upon herself to take care of his every need, from cooking, to feeding, to cleaning, to changing him, to practically carrying him for transfers. We talked daily by telephone, but even then, I did not know the full extent of his worsening disabilities, and the increasingly onerous burden Vivian was carrying day after day. During the first month Vivian was with Dad, she had taken him back to the emergency room at least once, because he apparently lost consciousness momentarily after awaking in the morning. However, he was discharged the same day without any treatment after the doctors could not find the cause of his black-outs. Still, with Vivian being there caring for him around the clock, I could exhale for a while. We started a discussion on the feasibility of moving Dad to an accessible home, a ranch, a one-level home, so that he did not have to take the stair-lifts to negotiate the several levels at his home. We had actually engaged a real estate agent to scout for suitable homes, and Vivian had even gone to view several prospects. Moving Dad into a nursing home was not an option for two reasons. First, there was a lengthy waiting list for admission, much more than a year's wait. Second, we did not think Dad would fare well at all if he had to part with or live without or apart from his worldly possessions, his life-long collections of all stripes. Renting storage space—a warehouse, really—for his items would also be cost prohibitive. Meanwhile, a couple of his very handy friends had built a wooden ramp in the garage so that Dad in his wheelchair could be wheeled from the main level of the house to the garage for his friend to carry and transfer him into his minivan.

It would be almost a month after Vivian arrived before she could bring Dad over to visit me. I waited patiently as I understood Dad had to properly and sufficiently recover from the almost 3-week hospitalization in late June. It was on Thursday, August 6th, when they finally made the trip. One of Dad's friends drove them, and helped with carrying and transferring Dad. Dad looked splendid; he even seemed to have gained a bit of weight. Vivian had purchased carryout fried chicken for our lunch, and we merrily enjoyed that hearty meal. Dad could not use his hands anymore; Vivian lovingly fed him, bite by bite. As usual, we talked about everything, carrying on a very lively conversation. It was a picture perfect, beautiful, sunny summer day; I turned on my audio system and played some music for everyone while we ate. I was actually in a great deal of pain at the time, which had become my "new normal" by then. Since the beginning of 2015, my neuralgia and painful leg cramps had become devastatingly debilitating and intolerable, even for me who generally could endure a very high level of pain. I used to be able to get some respite with a nap or when I slept at night. However, the pain had become so unrelenting and punishing that it would wake me up several times each night as a matter of course. In March of 2015, I had actually broken down and asked Dr. Chiodo for pain medications, even as I was close to impossible to medicate. Dr. Chiodo stared at the computer for the longest time, checking my past medications and adverse reactions to various prescriptions. In the end, he shook his head and shook my hand, and mumbled something about seeing me in another six months; there was nothing he could come up with to prescribe for my pain. There I was, with Dad and Vivian and Dad's friend, able to overlook and endure my pain for an afternoon, as it was so exciting to see and spend time with Dad again. I recalled the many, many days that we spent together during his past visits, when we would talk, and look at cameras and bags and fountain pens that I had purchased, and he in turn would bring along "treasures" and "discoveries" from his flea market prowls for me to appreciate and comment on. The afternoon soon came to an end. The last item on the agenda was for me to demonstrate to Dad how I used my transfer board to transfer. I did a transfer from my wheelchair to my bed and back to the wheelchair. Vivian was taking photographs of my moves. She aptly noted that it would be quite impossible for Dad to use a transfer board as his arms were not very functional at that point. We took more photographs before they departed. The friend carried Dad into his minivan. I waved goodbye, and Dad waved back with a big smile as they drove off into the sunset.

Another week or so went by rather uneventfully. We were still looking for alternative housing and additional Chinese-speaking home caregivers for Dad who could care for him after Vivian left at the end of September. Sunday morning, August 16th, Vivian e-mailed us that she had taken Dad to the emergency room again, because he was passing out in the bathroom early that morning. By the afternoon, the doctors sent him home because, once again, they could not detect anything untoward in Dad. We were glad that it was just another false alarm. The next morning, I received another e-mail from Vivian about getting donuts for Dad. I had apparently missed reading her earlier e-mail about her having, once again, taken Dad to the emergency room because he had blacked out again early that morning; Vivian was apparently buying donuts at the hospital cafeteria while Dad was undergoing tests. Lina e-mailed her reply with a rather foreboding message for us to be mindful of taking Dad to the hospital, as the more often he was taken to the hospital, the more likely that he might not be able to come out from there. Sure enough, the doctors admitted Dad that day, because they had supposedly found a blood clot near his lungs, and he was placed on blood thinners in an effort to dissolve that blood clot. He was also put on oxygen to help with his breathing. By the following day, Tuesday, the doctors started telephoning me regularly with horrible news of Dad's rapidly declining condition. The blood thinners had apparently caused internal bleeding, and they had to give Dad blood transfusions. However, by Wednesday, the doctors were unable to stem the internal bleeds, and even the blood transfusions were not sustaining Dad as he continued the downward spiral. Vivian had been by Dad's side around the clock. By Wednesday night, Vivian had the clarity of mind to call Dad's friends to come visit him; many of them did. At the same time, the doctors were asking me if I wanted Dad to be taken to the intensive care unit for extraordinary life-saving measures. We sisters all agreed that we should try those measures. I was totally blindsided, utterly unprepared for how everything went downhill so quickly. Just three days earlier, Vivian was still fetching donuts for Dad. Around 9 p.m., Dad was on the telephone just before he was to be taken to intensive care. He was completely lucid and his voice was strong. I did not know what to say to him; in a hurry, I told him to be brave, and that everything would be fine. He acknowledged, and said goodbye to me. Minutes later, the intensive care doctor was on the phone with me, telling me that he would not advise reviving or resuscitating Dad in intensive care because several of his systems were failing badly already: his heart, his kidney and his lungs. He advised that all family members should come and be with him as soon as possible. There was no way I could make it there in time. I had stood vigilance for Mom twelve years earlier, but I could not do so for my dear Dad. I felt speechless, stunned and severely wounded.

Dad passed away at 6 a.m. the next morning, Thursday, August 20th, exactly two weeks after what turned out to be his last visit at my apartment. How could that have happened? I was expecting him to live till at least 105 years of age; he most certainly expected that himself. No more phone calls from Dad, no more lengthy discussions on every topic under the sun, no more sharing and admiring at our respective "collections," no more sage advice from him, no more happy times sharing meals, traveling and taking photographs; I had lost my mentor, my idol, my best friend. He did not wait to see my walking on my own two feet; but then again, he was all-knowing and all-seeing now, and would continue to see me heal—and walk—in due time. It was now up to the three of us sisters; we have to carry on the mantle, and pay homage to and honor the treasure trove of life's wisdoms that he had passed on to us.

We contacted the same funeral home, Families First Funeral Home, which took excellent and compassionate care of Mom's cremation and burial twelve years earlier. Dad preferred burial, and Chan Family Estate had been ready for him to come home for some years. He had over the previous twelve years made it a dignified, beautiful and peaceful final resting place for all of us, with the two Peking lion statues standing guard, marble benches for visitors, and tall and lush trees for shade and superb *feng shui*.

I have many photographs of him at our Chan Family Estate, looking pensive and gratified. I wrote his obituary in English for printing and posting online, while Vivian worked with one of Dad's friends on the Chinese version. Dad's funeral service was set for August 28th; Lina and Juliana flew in from Hong Kong on August 27th. As difficult as it was for me, of course I had to attend his funeral. Eric was the one who made it possible for me to see Dad for the last time. Eric not only drove, but practically carried me as I transferred into and out of his car numerous times. I arrived at Families First around 10:45 a.m. Lina, Vivian and Juliana were there already, as were a number of friends. Vivian and Lina had tended to Dad's garments and other items to be buried with him, floral blanket for the casket, and the many other details for the funeral service. I brought a camera as my final gift to Dad so that he would remember me as he rested forever, not that he would forget anyway. I also brought a CD, Imee Ooi's *The Chant of Metta*, to be played before the funeral service. I sat in my wheelchair in front of Dad's casket for a long time, taking long, final looks at him, talking to him silently, thanking him, and saying my pained final farewell. I had no more tears to cry; he went away all too soon, too unexpectedly, too abruptly. The service commenced at noon, with many of Dad's friends paying tribute with their tearful eulogies. The funeral was well attended by about a hundred friends, including some of his lifelong friends from as far as Toronto. Several of his friends had composed condolences written in Chinese ink brush calligraphy and displayed for the funeral service. The hall was filled with countless floral arrangements which were transported to Chan Family Estate after the service. I was not prepared to address the attendees, and Lina stood up to speak on behalf of the family. I then felt moved to say a few words from my wheelchair. I babbled something, but I distinctly remembered reiterating my promise to Dad that I would one day walk again on my own two feet. Shortly after 1 p.m., Lina, Vivian, Julian and I said our very last goodbye to our Dad who had loved us so much and so selflessly for all of our lives and whom we loved so dearly in return. That was an extremely sad and emotional moment. The funeral party then proceeded by cars to Heavenly Rest. Eric and I followed the hearse, followed by Lina, Vivian and Juliana in a limousine. The funeral director had planned a route that included a drive-by Dad's home; I particularly appreciate that as I had not been able to see Dad's house for eleven years. Chris, our family counselor at Heavenly Rest, was very considerate in laying down wood planks over the lawn to make a pathway for my wheelchair to access Chan Family Estate from where Eric's car was parked. The pallbearers brought Dad's casket from the hearse to the Chan Family Estate. Each of us bowed, burned and offered a stick of incense. Lina, Vivian, Julian and I bowed one last time to bid Dad farewell. I recited the Heart Sutra quietly for him just before the burial, while Lina burned written copies as an offering. I knew he would love the Heart Sutra offering, because ever since Mom's passing, he had burned and offered the Heart Sutra, which he personally wrote in Chinese ink brush calligraphy, each time he visited Mom at the Chan Family Estate. I felt solace to see that Dad was at long last resting in peace in this special place that he was clearly so dear to him while he was alive, and that he was finally reuniting with Mom. We had invited all the attendees to a Chinese restaurant for dinner after the burial, but I could not attend that last ritual because it had been a very long day for me already.

A couple of days after the funeral, Lina, Vivian and Juliana came over for a visit. I wish it were under more cheerful circumstances, but it was rare enough that we could all get together, and thus, the gathering was treasured all the same. We had a very filling lunch consisted of a combination of take-out food. We talked a great deal, including plans for various items to be taken care of for Dad, and we enjoyed watching a music video on my home theater. They stayed until quite late, almost dinnertime. I had the feeling that perhaps it was because Lina could see that I was certainly not in great shape, health-wise; she thus made a point of spending more time with me, as we had just learned the hard lesson: the future was unpredictable and uncertain, and life could be very fragile.

In the immediate post-Dad era, I was grateful that Vivian could stay in Windsor until the end of September as originally planned, so that she could take care of the odds and ends around Dad's house. Dad's departure was so unexpected that we were all just fumbling and improvising as we went along. In the first few weeks after Dad's passing, I very much felt his presence, or rather, his trying to contact me and to get my attention. It was palpable; I felt "agitated" in a positive way. Shortly after Lilian passed away in March of 2014, both Dad and I suffered unexplained minor nosebleeds, which was very unusual for both of us. We compared notes, and as we could not otherwise explain our nosebleeds, and we thus concluded that it was Lilian's trying to contact us. That went on for a few weeks, and we felt consoled and delighted that Lilian was reaching out to us. During the first few weeks after Dad passed away, sure enough, I again suffered nosebleeds. I rejoiced that he was obviously trying to communicate with me. He was not only reaching out to me, but there was a sense of excitement, of urgency even. I had to tell him that I was able to "hear" him, to assure him that his message for me had been received. He did calm down after my assurances. The nosebleeds would recur more than a year later, and by then, I felt more certain of my interpretation of his "message." Such was the special bond between Dad and me. When I reflected on our seemingly parallel lives, it was most uncanny. He lost a kidney to cancer in 1977; I suffered end-stage renal failure and lost both kidneys in 1994. Thanks to Vivian, I was saved from that life threatening health crisis. I suffered a surgically induced spinal cord injury and became a paraplegic in 2004; Dad also suffered spinal cord injury, probably from a fall or falls around mid-2005, and which injury ultimately claimed his life, while my life had been spared thus far. I do not believe our happenstance was coincidental. As a matter of fact, I also had a very strong bond with Mom but my experiences with her since her passing in 2003 had taken on a somewhat different tack. She had regularly come into my dreams over those years. Those were very vivid dreams that made me feel as if she was still alive and was talking to me, fixing me dinner, and spending time shopping and traveling with me. I felt very privileged to be guided by my parents even in their afterlife. Ten or twelve years earlier, I would have never admitted such ethereal happenings in my life, that is, if I had even been able to become aware of any such supernatural phenomena. I prided myself then on being perfectly rational, left-brained, analytical, evidence-based and sane, in the ordinary sense of that term. Time heals, and time can also change much, sometimes in the most unorthodox ways; and this newly knighted peaceful warrior continued to transform with the mysterious, the mystical, and the unfathomable.

XII.

Deliverance

Since Dad's passing, I did not fare well at all physically. As is often said of the putative "mind-body connection," my mournful heart must have cast its weighty, lamenting load on my already feeble body, pushing it to the verge of crumpling. I was under an insane amount of around-the-clock searing pain in my legs. The severe, unrelenting pain was extremely fatiguing, distracting, debilitating and ultimately unbearable. Not only was I unable to devote any meaningful time to writing my book, I could not do much more than trying to simply endure the pain and survive from hour to hour, from day to day. Basically, I woke up every morning only to look forward to enduring the intolerable pain for as long as I could bear for the rest of the day. I did not have much of an appetite because of the horrendous pain; it was thus difficult for me to maintain my "fighting weight." My legs would spasm with painful cramps without advance warning, making each transfer extremely difficult and risky. There was no respite at nighttime either, as painful leg cramps regularly woke me up several times throughout the night. By the end of 2015, even I was feeling challenged and desperate; I was literally at wit's end. It was

599

difficult for me to accept that, while I had survived many darkest hours in the previous eleven years, I seemed to be tumbling toward the abyss with wild abandon. It was the epitome of adding insult to injury: while I had no sensation to speak of from waist down that would enable me to control or use my legs, yet I could feel every molecule of pain in my legs. I began to understand how, at a certain point in one's life, there would simply be no more meaning, let alone quality, for one to carry on. There was such a thing, I was then learning, as simply too much pain and suffering. I was not quite ready to go gentle into that good night just yet, but I was as close to knocking on that door as I had ever come.

My cheerleading friends were kind enough to be calling or e-mailing me regularly to check on my latest. Rebecca, Sylvia, Anita, Ann and Linda, Mary, Pearl, Flora, and others telephoned me on a regular basis. My struggles would have been so much more vicious without their having my back. Sometimes I wondered, though, whether I in turn cheered them up, because my sorry physical state had to make just about anyone else feel not as decrepit by comparison.

I did rack my brains trying to come up with plausible healing modality or means of pain relief that I might have overlooked. Not only had I pursued and even exhausted alternative healing over the years, I had gone the extra mile in search of remedies or relief in mainstream Western medicine. My local neurosurgeons, at the University of Michigan Health System, had long declined to further operate on my spinal cord. In November 2007, the neurosurgeons at the Mayo Clinic also declined to surgically intervene. Even after the four operations by Dr. Halliday in Eugene, I had further consulted with a renowned neurosurgeon specializing in syringomyelia, Dr. Ulrich Batzdorf, of University of California in Los Angeles in late 2008. After reviewing my MRIs and pertinent medical records, he declined to see me, concluding that I did not have any surgical option. In December of 2015, I was desperate as the pain was literally consuming me. Even though I did not really want another operation, I sought out Dr. Batzdorf's esteemed colleague, Dr. Langston Tyler Holly; but he, too, was of the opinion that I did not have any viable surgical option. Then, there was the wisdom I had gleaned from hard earned personal experience over the decade, that healing came "from within," that there was no miracle cure or healer "out there." However, at that point in my life, I did not much care where or how relief would manifest, just as long as I could get some form of pain relief soon. So, I continued to hold out hope that pain alleviation, if not a cure for my paraplegia, would somehow manifest if only I could hang on in the interim. So I hung on, and on and on.

It was Christmas of 2015, and Dad's birthday without Dad for the first time. There was not much joy or rejoicing for me; I was doubling over in pain most of the time, cooped up in my apartment all by myself, and worse, I could not even enjoy music listening as I was simply in too much pain to sit still for long. Nevertheless, I managed to send out Christmas cards as I relished the once-a-year opportunity to reconnect with friends. Laura was one of many to whom I had been sending my annual "hello" since our Tong Ren distant healing days in 2005. Every year she would reply with an exquisite card designed by her talented, professional graphic designer husband. It was unusual, however, that that particular December she followed up with an e-mail with a detailed update on her growing family (she had three lovely young grandchildren by then) as well as her own very active and busy life. I was thoroughly impressed with her continuing devotion to alternative healing, both as a dedicated student and as an experienced healer. Ten years hence, she was still very involved with teaching and dispensing Tong Ren healing, serving as a volunteer leader for the free Tong Ren group healing sessions, as well as practicing and teaching tai-chi. Interestingly, she also mentioned that for the past few years she had been learning "Twelve Level Code" healing from another master healer, Sheilagh Durkin of Kittery, Maine. It seemed only yesterday, and not ten long years ago, when we enjoyed our conversations on the telephone while she gave me distant Tong Ren healing twice weekly. I was eager to share with her all that had transpired in my rather eventful decade. We thus arranged to have a telephone conversation after the Holidays.

The Holidays came and went and I was very much looking forward to starting 2016 afresh, and hoping for some ways of ameliorating my pain; to be able to walk again would be icing on the cake, a luxury that I knew well not to dwell on then. It suddenly occurred to me that I had overlooked something very obvious—too obvious: since I was scheduled to talk by telephone with Laura on January 5th anyway, why did I not ask her for a distant healing session? Granted, healing came "from within," but I could certainly use a boost from a trusted healer such as Laura. Ten years prior when she gave me Tong Ren distant healing, even though that energy healing did not "cure" my paraplegia, it did bring about certain health benefits as I felt stronger and more energetic. I was in so much excruciating pain that if Tong Ren healing could give me even a small degree of pain relief for a brief moment, I would have considered it a miracle and been very grateful for it. I e-mailed Laura accordingly to ask if she would consider giving me a distant healing session when we talked on the telephone, and she readily agreed to do so. I did not know then it was an enormously generous gesture and accommodation on her part, as Laura was apparently fully booked all the time. In a decade's time, she had become a very seasoned and highly sought after energy healer.

On January 5th and at the appointed hour, Laura and I were on the telephone for more than an hour, chatting enthusiastically and happily. Even so, we still could not finish our respective updates, and surely, there was not any time left for a healing session. Healing had to wait till the next day when she gave me another appointment. As she dispensed Tong Ren distant healing over the telephone, it was all coming back to me, the familiar recitations, and alas, also my very positive reaction to that energy healing. I felt a great deal of warmth, relaxation, and my pain subsided appreciably for a few hours, and thus, "miracles" did indeed manifest. I had not planned on continuing distant healing with Laura on a regular basis, but given the positive results from just one session, I reluctantly had to admit that sometimes, "healing from within" could be favorably complemented by empathetic healing from "out there." I had always felt a special karmic bond with Laura, and at that time, that bond felt particularly in sync. She was as excited to give me healing as I was eager to receive the healing; the empathy and kindness in her heart were palpable. In February, she mailed me a number of "gadgets" invented by Master Tam to supplement Tong Ren healing. I found one of those devices especially effective for me, and had been using it to alleviate pain ever since. Laura called it a lens, but to me it resembled an external viewfinder that one would attach to a vintage rangefinder. It was not connected to any electrical charge or outlet or battery; it was a simple, inanimate object. Laura advised me to point that "viewfinder" at a photograph of me when I was able-bodied. I had many photographs of me standing up before I became a paraplegic, and so, I pointed the "viewfinder" at one that I selected. Within minutes, the pain in my hamstrings would "dissolve" significantly. In fact, I had to be careful not to overdo it, as I would feel "burned" if I had allowed the "viewfinder" to stay on my photograph for, say, longer than twenty minutes. It was as if the "viewfinder" generated some sort of energy or warmth, which in turn was somehow transmitted to the parts of my body that needed healing or soothing. I asked Laura for additional distant healing appointments, and she generously gave me a session every ten days or biweekly. Significantly, starting with the second distant healing session, she spent most of the session using Durkin's "Twelve Level Code" healing on me. My receptiveness to that healing was off the charts; I instantly felt less pain and a much greater sense of wellness for more than just a few hours. I reported that to Laura, and she was thrilled for me. By February of 2016, after just two or three sessions, I was heartened to see and feel that I was beginning to be salvaged from the abyss that had held me for much of 2015.

As if that was not "miraculous" enough, I had another encounter with the esoteric in those first months of 2016. Since about 2006, I had subscribed to "Daily Om," a website that dispensed daily inspirational messages by Madisyn Taylor. On January 13th, the message was entitled "Working with a Shaman: A Soulful Cure." Shamans, I would learn, were "men and women [who] have felt called to heal the sick, to safeguard knowledge, to guide the lost, and to commune with the spirit world. These unique individuals…were mystics and seers, repositories of wisdom, and keepers of herbal lore." The word shaman "literally means 'he or she who knows.'" The article continued to note that "today… shamanism has reemerged….[A]s more individuals explore the notion that healing necessarily involves the soul as well as the physical self, people are consulting shamans in their search for wellness, wisdom, and guidance." I was captivated by the article; it definitely resonated with me. It went on to delineate that shamans heals not only the body, but the emotional and spiritual:

> *Shamans, in addition to acting as fonts of wisdom, are dedicated to diagnosing and curing human suffering—whether emotional, physical, or spiritual. To treat an illness, a shaman may communicate with the spirit world in order to connect more directly with the soul of their patient or with the force causing ill health…. Shamans, as intermediaries between the physical and*

spiritual realms, recognize that all objects are in man-
ner alive and retain information that can be utilized
to heal.

Shamanism is power in part because its practitioners
tailor healing to the individual needs of those who seek
them out. A shaman manipulates energy, giving you
power where you have lost it and removing misplaced
energy lurking within you.

Every word and sentence in that article seemed to be tai-
lored to addressing what I felt had been missing from my healing regime in all those preceding years. I had indeed tried a wide
range of traditional and alternative healing, but I had never
encountered healing that placed the emotional and spiritual front
and center. I immediately felt compelled to seek out a shaman, as
I felt strongly that "healing on a spiritual plane" might be what I
had been missing all along. Even if nothing came of my search or
healing by a shaman, I had hardly anything to lose at that point in
my protracted and convoluted healing journey.

Ann Arbor being the progressive city that it was, I had imagined that it should harbor a shaman or two within easy travel distance from my abode. My Internet search indicated otherwise;
there was no shaman located or based in Ann Arbor. However,
there was one in Southfield who intrigued me. Her name was
Connie Eiland, and her website indicated that she had studied with Sandra Ingerman, Herb Stevenson, Betsy Bergstrom,
and Ana Larramendi, and she had been practicing as a shaman
since 2000. Not that I knew any of her teachers, but that sounded
impressive enough for her "shaman credentials." The most fascinating qualification about her, as far as I was concerned, was that
she had been practicing as a licensed physical therapist for more
than forty years. That signaled to me that she should understand

both the physical and spiritual aspects of diseases and disabilities, and accordingly, offer truly holistic healing. How unique—a left-brained and right-brained thinker and practitioner. Besides, with that medical background and training, she could easily under-stand my complicated medical history and rare medical condi-tion, which should in turn be helpful in formulating whatever healing she had in store for me.

On a lurch, I picked up my telephone and dialed the number indicated on her website, fully expecting to leave a voice mail and multiple rounds of phone tags before ever talking with her. Surprise of all surprises, she picked up the telephone right away, and I had to gather my thoughts post haste. Obviously, I had no idea how she would go about her healing, but she was expecting me to come for an in-person appointment. When I told her I could not very well do that, because I was a paraplegic in a wheelchair, she imme-diately replied, "Say no more, I understand." Apparently, she had dispensed healing over great distance, to patients in a Southeast Asian country. I gave her a summary of my medical history; it was clear that she heard and understood me perfectly. She gave me a telephone appointment on February 2nd, at two o'clock in the afternoon. She then gave me instructions to prepare for our tele-phone appointment. First, I was to be in a "receptive state" during the appointed date and time. When I queried what "receptive state" meant, and she gave me the analogy of a tea bag steeping, which I thought was visually and creatively instructive. Second, she informed me that "the healing starts now." I was nonplussed, because I thought my appointment was not until the afternoon of February 2nd. She explained that the healing started right there and then because I had already "made the commitment." At that point, I could tell this was going to be healing like no other. Third, she told me to "ask for a dream." Excuse me?! I was totally lost as to this last command. She only added "healing" when I inquired, that I should ask for a "healing dream." I had no idea how to "ask" for a dream, healing or otherwise, as I thought dreaming was an involuntary occurrence.

I cannot explain or excuse how this occurred, except that it happened. Since that telephone conversation with Connie, and without my really trying on a conscious level, I started having dreams, very vivid dreams. In some of those dreams, I was "told" or was given revelations relating to situations or circumstances with which I was familiar but which had not been in my conscious mind for many years, even decades. Some of those revelations were very striking, others very upsetting, and still others instructive. Mom, even my beloved cat Smokey who passed away in March of 1999, came into my dreams often. Above all, the vividness of the dreams was stunning. For instance, in one of the dreams, I was telling a friend that I was low on cigarettes and that I had to stop to buy some, and the dream went on from there with my search for cigarettes. I awoke momentarily and wondered, as I was honestly confused, whether I was still a smoker, and if I was, I was even breaking out in cold sweat cussing at myself for somehow having resumed the nasty habit. The "real-ness" of the dreams was uncanny and alarming. One could say that those dreams were "healing" as they were so unreservedly revealing and honest, as if they were selected scenes from an insightful life review.

Around four o'clock in the early morning of February 2nd, the appointed date for my distant healing with Connie, I was awakened from my sleep abruptly and momentarily. In my grogginess I heard a "voice" saying to me very distinctly: "You are not a paraplegic." I was, of course, startled; I immediately muttered, "Wait; don't go away. Come back. Who are you?" I heard unmistakably what was said to me, but I could not tell whether it was a male or female voice, or whether it was a voice of someone I knew. I instinctively checked my legs to see if I could move them. They were as lame and lifeless as ever; I still could not move them. Hence, how was I "not a paraplegic?" I had heard only too many times from friends, healthcare providers and strangers alike, how I would supposedly walk again, but I had never heard being told my not being a paraplegic. If I were not a paraplegic, what was I, and why was I still not able to use my legs? I fell back asleep in short order. It would certainly take me more than a few minutes to appreciate the significance and cogitate on the implications of that otherworldly voice message.

At two o'clock, I sat quietly by my telephone, trying to be in a "receptive state," and waited for Connie's call. It was almost an hour before she finally rang. Apparently, "spirit" revealed much to her, and she in turn passed on what she learned to me. I took notes as best I could, but it was not easy to keep up with her as the terminology she used was unfamiliar to me. I was glad I wrote down verbatim her words in most instances, so that I could try to decipher what was told to me weeks and months later. She gave me many interesting and unique "pointers" for "reclaiming"—pointedly, not regaining—my health and mobility. In fact, as more time lapsed, the more her revelations and instructions became relevant and illuminating. Case in point were her comments about the "blockage" in my solar plexus area resulting from abandonment issues from Past Lives, and how she had cleared the scar tissue in my spinal canal for me to get the cerebral-spinal fluid flowing again and reconnecting my spinal cord to my feet. Of course, I had no idea that I even had any sort of blockage in my solar plexus area, nor would I dream that anyone could clear the scar tissue in my spinal canal, something that even the neurosurgeons could not accomplish. Moreover, she informed me that scar tissue would not show up on MRI scans; that would explain why I might have been experiencing blockages and impairment from scar tissue, but my doctors kept telling me that they did not discern any change from MRI scans. Months later, however, I would begin to observe and experience how prophetic her statements were when I started regaining more sensations around my mid-section. That

oon as I arrived in Ann Arbor
multiple myeloma I was in
June 2016, Dr. Bockenstedt
y was I no longer anemic, my
ald make a believer of anyone
r at least the type with which
ver given any medication or
half a year of energy healing
e-cancer condition vanished
th any other "rational" expla-
I had been receiving, healing

ing to have regular massages,
and certified massage thera-
few months in the summer of
e calls then, and brought her
ed the massages in September
t on her massage table. I was
s a massage therapist and still
reasoning was that having tac-
rlooked and underrated as an
pined that regular massages
ould promote circulation and
ut and understood that; as a
ntary, and as such, just about
d or circulated. That was cer-
or healing. Amy still remem-
via her website, and she was
ccommodate me. Seeing each
g years, was exciting. I started
s," with Amy working on my
y arms and shoulders, which
mits from transfers, began to

in turn triggered a cascade of progression: greater trunk control and stability, steadier and safer transfers, freeing the flow of *chi* or life force, which in turn helped to revitalize the long dormant parts of my body. That dovetailed perfectly with another stunning piece of advice she gave me on February 2nd: that my job was to take in the "parts" that had come back to me so that they would stay; she noted that I was "sitting on" all those parts, and I ought to "welcome them home." Moreover, sometimes some body parts needed to be retrieved more than once. In other words, I should exercise again, communicate to my body parts in order to become strong again, and most significantly, remember what my body parts and legs used to do. That last bit of reminder was especially prescient. Eleven years and counting was a long time, and I did not realize how I might have indeed forgotten how to stand up or walk, just as the converse was true for an able-bodied person who would not ordinarily, consciously think about standing up and walking. Hence, as my body parts "returned" to me, I had to pay attention to notice their return, and to integrate them back into my body and to utilize them again. In the months that followed, mostly I did notice that different small muscle groups were beginning to be "reawakened," thus "returning" to me.

Connie, unlike the many alternative healers I had worked with in Hong Kong, did not require me to commit to a course of healing of however many weeks or months. In fact, she thought the February 2nd session was sufficient for my purposes. I appreciated her honesty and sincerity; obviously, she was not conducting the healing for pecuniary objectives. At most, she intoned that I could ask for one more session about six weeks hence. I thought that was a good idea and did ask for a follow-up session on March 16th. The second session was even more esoteric, with concepts and revelations that were decidedly not anything that I had encountered previously. Even she noted that I could not have done that day's work without having learned the lessons from my last session in

February. During the second session, she informed me that she had conducted further healing on me: she had restored my craniosacral rhythm, which blockage had impaired my lower right abdomen as well as my right leg—my "stepping out" leg; she had healed my tethered spinal cord; and she had resolved scar tissue interfering with the flow of spinal fluid. She made the fascinating claim that I had a curse/spell when I was born as a girl instead of as a boy, but she had removed that curse, and as I had gotten back my "soul essence," I could then do my best and it did not have to be difficult. There were many other "nuggets" from her, including "homework" for me in the ensuing two weeks.

For many, it would take a great leap of faith to undergo "healing" with Connie, and many others yet might dismiss it outright as sheer hocus-pocus. My view is much more accepting. I believe in healing on many levels, including the soul or the spiritual level, and not only the physical or corporeal level. Healing our bodies, something tangible that we can see, touch and examine, is often difficult enough; healing our spirit or soul is reserved strictly for those brave or wise enough. Any healer who attempted to heal on the soul level had my profound admiration and respect. I arrived at this understanding from more than twelve years of great pain and suffering, and after a relentless pursuit for a cure or relief from my affliction and torment. It was after I had exhausted healing, surgery, treatment and therapy on the physical level when I began to consider what I could be missing—healing on a different and far higher level. That concept could sound nebulous and ethereal, and I certainly do not mean to be pompous or presumptive that healing on the soul level is the be all and end all. Perhaps to bring it back down to earth somewhat, it is as plain and simple as the concept of mind-body connection which is finally gaining widespread acceptance nowadays, even among the so-called mainstream medical practitioners.

consulting with Dr. Bockenstedt as in 2008. I had no idea how close all those years, but there and then smiled and pronounced that not on MGUS had "disappeared." That sho who should doubt energy healing, one would find resonance. I was n treatment for MGUS, yet after just with Laura, even that menacing p into thin air. I could not come up w nation than the energy healing that on the soul level.

In late June and at Laura's urg I contacted Amy Prior, a licensed pist with whom I had worked for a 2010. She was willing to make hous massage table with her. I discontinu after I was unable to stand up to g hoping that Amy was still working willing to make house calls. Laura's tile-touch therapy was too often ove essential part of any healing. She by a competent massage therapist w healing. I should have thought ab paraplegic, my life had become sed nothing in or about my body move tainly not conducive to good health bered me well when I contacted he willing to make house calls just to other again on June 21st, after six lo having weekly "wheelchair massag arms, neck, shoulders, and legs. M were often sore and stressed to the in turn triggered a cascade of progression: greater trunk control and stability, steadier and safer transfers, freeing the flow of *chi* or life force, which in turn helped to revitalize the long dormant parts of my body. That dovetailed perfectly with another stunning piece of advice she gave me on February 2nd: that my job was to take in the "parts" that had come back to me so that they would stay; she noted that I was "sitting on" all those parts, and I ought to "welcome them home." Moreover, sometimes some body parts needed to be retrieved more than once. In other words, I should exercise again, communicate to my body parts in order to become strong again, and most significantly, remember what my body parts and legs used to do. That last bit of reminder was especially prescient. Eleven years and counting was a long time, and I did not realize how I might have indeed forgotten how to stand up or walk, just as the converse was true for an able-bodied person who would not ordinarily, consciously think about standing up and walking. Hence, as my body parts "returned" to me, I had to pay attention to notice their return, and to integrate them back into my body and to utilize them again. In the months that followed, mostly I did notice that different small muscle groups were beginning to be "reawakened," thus "returning" to me.

Connie, unlike the many alternative healers I had worked with in Hong Kong, did not require me to commit to a course of healing of however many weeks or months. In fact, she thought the February 2nd session was sufficient for my purposes. I appreciated her honesty and sincerity; obviously, she was not conducting the healing for pecuniary objectives. At most, she intoned that I could ask for one more session about six weeks hence. I thought that was a good idea and did ask for a follow-up session on March 16th. The second session was even more esoteric, with concepts and revelations that were decidedly not anything that I had encountered previously. Even she noted that I could not have done that day's work without having learned the lessons from my last session in

February. During the second session, she informed me that she had conducted further healing on me: she had restored my craniosacral rhythm, which blockage had impaired my lower right abdomen as well as my right leg—my "stepping out" leg; she had healed my tethered spinal cord; and she had resolved scar tissue interfering with the flow of spinal fluid. She made the fascinating claim that I had a curse/spell when I was born as a girl instead of as a boy, but she had removed that curse, and as I had gotten back my "soul essence," I could then do my best and it did not have to be difficult. There were many other "nuggets" from her, including "homework" for me in the ensuing two weeks.

For many, it would take a great leap of faith to undergo "healing" with Connie, and many others yet might dismiss it outright as sheer hocus-pocus. My view is much more accepting. I believe in healing on many levels, including the soul or the spiritual level, and not only the physical or corporeal level. Healing our bodies, something tangible that we can see, touch and examine, is often difficult enough; healing our spirit or soul is reserved strictly for those brave or wise enough. Any healer who attempted to heal on the soul level had my profound admiration and respect. I arrived at this understanding from more than twelve years of great pain and suffering, and after a relentless pursuit for a cure or relief from my affliction and torment. It was after I had exhausted healing, surgery, treatment and therapy on the physical level when I began to consider what I could be missing—healing on a different and far higher level. That concept could sound nebulous and ethereal, and I certainly do not mean to be pompous or presumptive that healing on the soul level is the be all and end all. Perhaps to bring it back down to earth somewhat, it is as plain and simple as the concept of mind-body connection which is finally gaining widespread acceptance nowadays, even among the so-called mainstream medical practitioners.

A day after my first session with Connie, I had my second distant healing session with Laura. At that session, Laura used Durkin's "Twelve Level Code" healing on me, and not Tong Ren healing. The results were immediate and remarkable. Some sensations returned in my mid-sections and parts of my legs, and I could even feel my legs and use them for a fraction of a second during some of my transfers. Laura was very encouraged for me when I told her about my incredibly favorable reaction to Durkin's healing regime; of course, I also shared with her my healing experience with the shaman Connie. Laura quipped with delight that we had a healing "team." February was thus a pivotal month when hope returned for me in terms of pain relief, if not exactly functional improvement. In fact, with the appreciable improvement in the pain department, I felt more energetic and inspiration flowed freely as I continued writing this book.

Even as I continued "Twelve Level Code" distant healing with Laura every two weeks or so, my healing curve unfortunately was not a smooth trend upwards. Around April, I started experiencing a barrage of seemingly unrelated symptoms, ranging from swollen eyelids, to broken teeth, from simple cut wounds that would not heal to increased headaches, and from loss of appetite to adverse reactions to medications. I was practically blindsided; in good humor and jest, I called it my "Plagues of Egypt." Still, as I also felt more core muscles "returning" to me, the everlasting optimist in me thus again considered my glass "practically full." Bravely I soldiered on and on June 6th, I was rewarded with the best news yet in a long time when I attended a routine annual return visit with my hematologist, Dr. Paula Bockenstedt. When I was at the Mayo Clinic in November of 2007, the battery of tests revealed that I had a pre-cancer condition named Monoclonal Gammopathy of Undetermined Significance (MGUS); it was a precursor of multiple myeloma. I was instructed to follow-up annually with a hematologist and keep watch. I thus started consulting with Dr. Bockenstedt as soon as I arrived in Ann Arbor in 2008. I had no idea how close to multiple myeloma I was in all those years, but there and then in June 2016, Dr. Bockenstedt smiled and pronounced that not only was I no longer anemic, my MGUS had "disappeared." That should make a believer of anyone who should doubt energy healing, or at least the type with which one would find resonance. I was never given any medication or treatment for MGUS, yet after just half a year of energy healing with Laura, even that menacing pre-cancer condition vanished into thin air. I could not come up with any other "rational" explanation than the energy healing that I had been receiving, healing on the soul level.

In late June and at Laura's urging to have regular massages, I contacted Amy Prior, a licensed and certified massage therapist with whom I had worked for a few months in the summer of 2010. She was willing to make house calls then, and brought her massage table with her. I discontinued the massages in September after I was unable to stand up to get on her massage table. I was hoping that Amy was still working as a massage therapist and still willing to make house calls. Laura's reasoning was that having tactile-touch therapy was too often overlooked and underrated as an essential part of any healing. She opined that regular massages by a competent massage therapist would promote circulation and healing. I should have thought about and understood that; as a paraplegic, my life had become sedentary, and as such, just about nothing in or about my body moved or circulated. That was certainly not conducive to good health or healing. Amy still remembered me well when I contacted her via her website, and she was willing to make house calls just to accommodate me. Seeing each other again on June 21st, after six long years, was exciting. I started having weekly "wheelchair massages," with Amy working on my arms, neck, shoulders, and legs. My arms and shoulders, which were often sore and stressed to the limits from transfers, began to heal and suffer less pain and strains. Even my legs and feet became less spastic. Circulation was definitely improving when a small open wound on my left ankle, which had refused to close even though I had been under doctor's care all along, came alive and bled slightly as it started to heal. Besides, I enjoyed my wide-ranging conversations with Amy during our weekly sessions. Her companionship, in a way, was thus a bonus healing for my mind. After just the first few sessions, my pain level had decreased another noticeable notch. It was another milestone, then, in my healing journey, totally unexpected but most certainly welcomed. I at once recalled my dream in February of 2006 of Maxine and Mom strolling through the park, and Mary's mysterious comment of "And Maxine will heal you, too." Maxine was a lymphatic massage therapist, and Amy is a massage therapist; could it be that Amy would indeed heal me? There are no coincidences in life.

It seemed that I was on a roll all at once: in late July, I stumbled upon another discovery that would have far-reaching beneficial implications for my healing. In a regular clinic visit with my Rehab Physician Assistant Chelsea Burton in late July, I mentioned my painful leg cramps, even though by then they had let up appreciably by Laura's healing and the massages with Amy. Chelsea suggested that I increase my daily dosage of Baclofen from 30 mg. to 40 mg. I had been placed on Baclofen since I was in inpatient rehabilitation in Medford, Oregon, in December of 2004, with a very small dose of 5 mg. daily. In the past few years, my Rehab doctor kept raising my daily dosage as I experienced increasing leg cramps, spasticity, stiffness and pain in my legs. On the second or third day after I had increased the dosage to 40 mg. per day, I woke up in the morning almost unable to move my legs. My legs were extremely stiff and rigid, and they were wracked with painful cramps and spasms. An insight instantly came to me as a query: since the increase in Baclofen dosage had apparently caused such an increase in spasticity, could the inverse be true?

There was only one way to find out, and that was to reduce and gradually wean myself off Baclofen. I had visited that possibility about a year earlier with Dr. Chiodo, and he had no objection and in fact did even not think I needed any lengthy withdrawal period. For whatever reason, I did not follow through then. I was, however, finally ready and determined to wean myself off Baclofen to ascertain if my hunch hypothesis was correct.

I started reducing my dosage by 5 mg. weekly, and it took almost two months to be completely weaned of that medication. It was a gamble; at times, I even questioned my sanity. There were indeed times when my spasticity acted up wildly, and I would almost question the advisability of my decision; nonetheless, I persevered, and was ultimately rewarded. The biggest surprise was, by mid-September, the gradual and subtle lessening of the insanely severe round-the-clock blinding pain in my hamstrings. As if that was not enough cause for celebration, I was able to sleep through the night on September 21st. That was a first—for many years since my paraplegia, painful spasms woke me up every other hour or so throughout the night, and I would get up in the morning oftentimes even more fatigued than the night before. At first, of course, I thought that was a freak accident, a one-off lucky strike. However, when I slept through the next night as well, I stopped discounting reality. When I slept through the third consecutive night, I rejoiced that a significant milestone had been reached. And so it was.

Being able to sleep through the night had brought about a seismic change, a quantum leap in my overall well-being. Once I started getting quality and quantity sleep, the snowball effect in reverse kicked in. For the first time in years, I felt rested and energized; I could actually feel my life force come rushing back to me. It was a truly invigorating and revitalizing experience. There were even brief moments in late September when I felt my legs becoming sturdier and stronger as if they could bear weight again; I called those moments "sneak previews" of wonders to come. There was yet another surprise to throw in the mix. I do not recall specifically what it was that kept me so fully occupied on October 11th that I missed my afternoon nap time. It seemed ridiculous to take a nap at 7 p.m., and so I reasoned I would go to bed much earlier that evening to make up for lost rest. The next day came, and I reasoned that since I apparently survived the day before without my usual afternoon nap, I should try again to see if I could do without the nap. Indeed I could, as a matter of fact and without much fanfare. I successfully repeated that feat the ensuing day, and that confirmed that I had reached yet another milestone on my healing journey. Without needing to take a nap in the middle of the day, and with the appreciable lowering of pain level, I was able to devote much more time to writing. It was not just a matter of quantity, that is, the amount of time devoted to writing my book, but also quality of the writing, that is, the ability to focus so as to write to the best of my abilities. It was a very pleasant surprise, then, when I could clip along with my writing since around September of 2016. In comparison, the first few chapters had taken me *years* to grind out. If I only had a vague notion of the mind-body connection in years past, I am now a witness and a believer: healing not only comes from "within," but within one's soul; healing on the soul level is profound, mysterious and most potent.

If I were a cat with nine lives, I am—gratefully—already on my eighteenth life. After twelve years and counting, whether I will walk on my own two feet again has become an irrelevant, if not moot, question. Of course, I want to freely roam the earth again, but when you have been touched by divine (with a small "d") grace as much as I had been in the past twelve years, ambulation *per se* paled by comparison. Hence, when I finally depart this world, the lyrics to the song, "When I Go," by Dave Carter and as performed by Judy Collins and Willie Nelson, express my sentiments compellingly and eloquently:

I will climb the rise at daybreak, I will kiss the sky
at noon
Raise my yearning voice at midnight to my mother in
the moon
I will make the lay of long defeat and draw the cho-
rus slow
I'll send the message down the wire and hope that
someone wise is listening when I go . . .

Sigh, mournful sister, whisper and turn
I will rattle like dry leaves when I go
Stand in the mist where my fire used to burn
I will camp on the night breeze when I go.

And should you glimpse my wandering form out on
the borderline
Between death and resurrection and the council of
the pines
Do not worry for my comfort, do not sorrow for me so
All your diamond tears will rise up and adorn the sky
beside me when I go.

In retrospect, a clear pattern emerged; there were conspicuous signs that I had nevertheless overlooked at the time. I was at the zenith of vitality and good health when I returned from Hong Kong in December of 2003. Yet shortly after I moved out of my former home to start my new life, my health, especially my leg function, started declining at a scale and speed never seen before. Why? Since that fateful surgery in December of 2004 that rendered me a paraplegic, I had been raging a mighty campaign to regain mobility. Especially in the first few years, I had defiantly dared the odds, and put my body through all manner and gyration of treatment, surgery and therapy. In spite of my best intentions and efforts, one healing therapy after another failed, my health declined precipitously, and my pain and suffering increased exponentially with no end in sight. Each time a therapy or a healing regime yielded any tantalizing promise, worse pain and further dysfunction would intercept and dash all hopes for once and for all. The harder I fought, the harder I fell. It was a classic case of one step forward two steps back. By the end of the eleventh year of my paraplegia, the relentless descent to the abyss had reduced me to less than a mere shadow of my former self, physically and mentally, barely hanging on by the skin of my teeth. It was all as if there was an invisible force, an invisible hand—and a very sinister and demonic one at that—that had been body-checking me at every turn, blocking me at every healing opportunity, and indeed, gunning for my untimely demise.

Indeed there was. It was only after I had been healing with Laura for several months, and had the benefit of the refreshingly unorthodox guidance from shaman Connie, that I began to discern and comprehend those vicious and wicked dynamics at work. The pre-paraplegia me would have never considered the existence of malevolent forces or the pain, suffering, havoc and destruction they could wrought. However, as Master Yoda in the *Star Wars* saga instructed us, "Luke...Luke...do not...do not...underestimate the power of the Emperor or suffer your father's fate you will." The "dark side," for lack of a better term, exists and can be very lethal if it is allowed to be. As Master Yoda further observed: "Once you start down the dark path, forever will it dominate your destiny. Consume you it will." Yoda is only a fictional character and the *Star Wars* series are only movies, and many may thus offhandedly dismiss such far-fetched, nebulous notions of evil and the dark side. I, on the other hand, having unwittingly been on the receiving end of those nefarious supernatural forces for years, would no longer disregard, discount or even take lightly the very real mayhem and plunder they inflict.

Accordingly, I had been taking extreme precautions and mindful countermeasures; and as if by magic, my health started turning around. What I had learned was that in order to strive and thrive, I needed to tend to my wounds spiritually and physically, and heal as well on the metaphysical and soul level. I have now finally come full circle. I remember that when I was a very young child, I had a sense of being supported by an extraordinary knowingness that was not of this world. Of course, I was too young to verbalize it at the time; besides, I thought everyone felt the same way and had the same vibrations. As I grew up, I had strayed far and wide from that special connectedness. Decades later now, and having lived many lifetimes in one, I have rediscovered my sacred bond with that inner divinity that portends all things righteous and virtuous, and which in turn would overcome darkness and evilness. With that reawakening, not only healing and full recovery, but even the impossible is possible.

Epilogue: Parting Thoughts

Having lived through my 80's and 90's in my 50's and 60's, having endured enough pain and suffering for multiple lifetimes, more than once or twice, I felt as if I had reached the end of my life but was graciously pulled back from the brink. Of course then, *the End* hardly intimidates as such or even as much now. I have lived, honorably and gratefully, to the brim; I have dreamed, impossibly, sweetly, and ambitiously; and I have loved boldly, purely, and passionately. Yet the point remains that, in the here and now, there are places to go, things to do, people to see, photographs to take, music to get lost in, meditations to practice, life lessons to assimilate, wrongs to right, injustices to quell, dreams to realize, stars to chase, expectations to exceed, promises to keep, destinies to fulfill . . . and life, however impossible, to live.